Policing in Hong Kong

History and Reform

Advances in Police Theory and Practice Series

Series Editor: Dilip K. Das

Policing in Hong Kong: History and Reform
Kam C. Wong

Police Investigative Interviews and Interpreting: Context, Challenges, and Strategies
Sedat Mulayim, Miranda Lai, and Caroline Norma

Cold Cases: Evaluation Models with Follow-up Strategies for Investigators, Second Edition
James M. Adcock and Sarah L. Stein

Crime Linkage: Theory, Research, and Practice
Jessica Woodhams and Craig Bennell

Policing White Collar Crime: Characteristics of White Collar Criminals
Petter Gottschalk

Honor-Based Violence: Policing and Prevention
Karl Anton Roberts, Gerry Campbell, and Glen Lloyd

Policing and the Mentally Ill: International Perspectives
Duncan Chappell

Security Governance, Policing, and Local Capacity
Jan Froestad with Clifford D. Shearing

Policing in Hong Kong: History and Reform
Kam C. Wong

Police Performance Appraisals: A Comparative Perspective
Serdar Kenan Gul and Paul O'Connell

Los Angeles Police Department Meltdown: The Fall of the Professional-Reform Model of Policing
James Lasley

Financial Crimes: A Global Threat
Maximillian Edelbacher, Peter Kratcoski, and Michael Theil

Police Integrity Management in Australia: Global Lessons for Combating Police Misconduct
Louise Porter and Tim Prenzler

The Crime Numbers Game: Management by Manipulation
John A. Eterno and Eli B. Silverman

The International Trafficking of Human Organs: A Multidisciplinary Perspective
Leonard Territo and Rande Matteson

Police Reform in China
Kam C. Wong

Mission-Based Policing
John P. Crank, Dawn M. Irlbeck, Rebecca K. Murray, and Mark Sundermeier

The New Khaki: The Evolving Nature of Policing in India
Arvind Verma

Cold Cases: An Evaluation Model with Follow-up Strategies for Investigators
James M. Adcock and Sarah L. Stein

Policing Organized Crime: Intelligence Strategy Implementation
Petter Gottschalk

Security in Post-Conflict Africa: The Role of Nonstate Policing
Bruce Baker

Community Policing and Peacekeeping
Peter Grabosky

Community Policing: International Patterns and Comparative Perspectives
Dominique Wisler and Ihekwoaba D. Onwudiwe

Police Corruption: Preventing Misconduct and Maintaining Integrity
Tim Prenzler

FORTHCOMING

Democratic Policing
Darren Palmer

Corruption, Fraud, Organized Crime, and the Shadow Economy
Maximilian Edelbacher, Peter C. Kratcoski, and Bojan Dobovsek

Policing Terrorism: Research Studies into Police Counter-terrorism Investigations
David Lowe

Collaborative Policing: Police, Academics, Professionals, and Communities Working Together for Education, Training, and Program Implementation
Peter C. Kratcoski and Maximilian Edelbacher

Islamic Women in Policing: A Contradiction in Terms?
Tonita Murray

Female Criminals: An Examination and Interpretation of Female Offending
Venessa Garcia

Policing in Hong Kong

History and Reform

Kam C. Wong
Xavier University
Department of Criminal Justice
Cincinnati, Ohio, USA

Faculty Fellow
School of Criminal Justice
State University of New York (Albany), USA

CRC Press
Taylor & Francis Group
Boca Raton London New York

CRC Press is an imprint of the
Taylor & Francis Group, an **informa** business

CRC Press
Taylor & Francis Group
6000 Broken Sound Parkway NW, Suite 300
Boca Raton, FL 33487-2742

First issued in paperback 2019

ISBN-13: 978-0-4398-9643-3 (hbk)
ISBN-13: 978-0-367-86695-2 (pbk)

Visit the Taylor & Francis Web site at
http://www.taylorandfrancis.com

and the CRC Press Web site at
http://www.crcpress.com

Contents

Part II

POLICE REFORM IN 1950S

For my sister, Po Po

The joy of my life

Foreword

Kam Wong and I joined the Royal Hong Kong Police (RHKP) in the 1960s. This was a decade that witnessed major social and political upheavals. We witnessed firsthand the Star Ferry riots in 1966, sparked by an increase in ferry fares and the 1967–1968 confrontations prompted by China's Cultural Revolution which saw large-scale rioting, civil disturbances and a wave of bomb attacks directed at the government.

Kam Wong's book, *Policing in Hong Kong: History and Reform*, traces the origin of the Hong Kong Police from its beginning in 1841 and chronicles its various developmental phases which lead to its present form—a strong, closely knit police force fully equipped for its modern duties. I am delighted that my old colleague and friend has invited me to write a foreword to this book. This is a subject area that has fascinated me, not only as a former RHKP officer but also as a scholar at both Hong Kong University and later, at Cambridge University.

My academic interest in the subject of policing can be said to have begun while I was on attachment to London's Metropolitan Police Force in 1974. Having already witnessed, firsthand, the large-scale riots in Hong Kong in 1967, I was given the opportunity to watch the Metropolitan Police's anti-riot training. What amazed me was the total lack of suitable anti-riot equipment and tactics: the officers were dressed in conventional police uniforms with their traditional 'bobby' helmets and, although armed with transparent shields, appeared reluctant to raise them for protection when confronting the make-believe rioters. This highlighted a desire on the part of the British police to maintain their traditional image as 'civilian in uniform' despite the evidence from Hong Kong and elsewhere that a more military-style posture was needed to deal effectively with such public order situations. The subsequent Brixton Riots in 1981 which saw 280 police officers injured and another 45 civilian casualties, the growing threat from, first, Irish-inspired, and then, Islamic terrorism and more recently, the scenes of rioting and looting in inner London, have led to the gradual militarisation of the British police forces. There are now more specialist armed police units and more aggressive and better equipped anti-riot formations, signalling an albeit reluctant departure from the traditional 'civilian in uniform' model of British policing.

In contrast, the Hong Kong police have been gradually moving away from their colonial police antecedent as a wholly para-military force to a more conventional civilian establishment. As an ex-British colony, Hong Kong's police developed on a similar manner to other British colonial police forces. This development process has been commented on by Sir Charles Jeffries, a noted police historian, who, in a study of the colonial policing system in 1952, noted that colonial policing evolved through three distinct phases: the first phase being one of 'improvisation' where policing activities were directed towards securing the basic essentials of law and order. The second phase brought about the establishment of semi-military constabulary forces modelled upon the Royal Irish Constabulary, a force which combined civilian policing duties with an armed response capability that could be used in support of the military. The final phase resulted in the conversion of a semi-military constabulary into a civilian police structure similar to the British 'civilian in uniform' tradition. According to Sir Charles Jefferies, this transition resulted from the need to cope with changes in society brought about by modernisation, Westernisation and decolonisation. However, Jefferies did not touch upon the likely problems confronting a para-military police organisation during its period of transition to a civilian constabulary. This is an issue, which both Kam Wong and I had hoped to study and write about in respect of the Hong Kong police, but time and other commitments meant that I could not join him in this endeavour. So, it was with a great deal of pleasure and not a little guilt that I learned that Kam Wong had decided to forge ahead and complete a book—*Policing in Hong Kong: History and Reform*—which, while not wholly focused on the issue of transition, deals with aspects that have impacted on the Hong Kong Police Force's development against a background of political, social and economic change. Although, there have been a number of publications on the Hong Kong Police, and Kam Wong's book is by no means a definite study of the Force, it is one of a very few scholarly books combining an academic as well as a professional perspective on a Police Force still in transition.

I highly recommend this book to those who are as interested as I am in the history, development and transformation of the Hong Kong Police.

Douglas Tsui Yiu Kwong
Chief Superintendent (Retired)
RHKP

Series Editor's Preface

While the literature on police and allied subjects is growing exponentially, its impact upon day-to-day policing remains small. The two worlds of research and practice of policing remain disconnected even though cooperation between the two is growing. A major reason is that the two groups speak in different languages. The research work is published in hard-to-access journals and presented in a manner that is difficult to comprehend for a lay person. However, the police practitioners tend not to mix with researchers and remain secretive about their work. Consequently, there is little dialogue between the two and almost no attempt to learn from one another. Dialogues across the globe, among researchers and practitioners situated in different continents, are of course even more limited.

I attempted to address this problem by starting the IPES, www.ipes.info, where a common platform has brought the two together. IPES is now in its 17th year. The annual meetings that constitute most major annual event of the organisation have been hosted in all parts of the world. Several publications have come out of these deliberations and a new collaborative community of scholars and police officers has been created whose membership runs into several hundreds.

Another attempt was to begin a new journal, aptly called *Police Practice and Research: An International Journal*, PPR that has opened the gate to practitioners to share their work and experiences. The journal has attempted to focus upon issues that help bring the two on a single platform. PPR is completing its 12 years in 2011. It is certainly an evidence of growing collaboration between police research and practice that PPR, which began with four issues a year, expanded into five issues in its fourth year and, now, it is issued six times a year.

Clearly, these attempts, despite their success, remain limited. Conferences and journal publications do help create a body of knowledge and an association of police activists but cannot address substantial issues in depth. The limitations of time and space preclude larger discussions and more authoritative expositions that can provide stronger and broader linkages between the two worlds.

It is this realisation of the increasing dialogue between police research and practice that has encouraged many of us—my close colleagues and I connected closely with IPES and PPR across the world—to conceive and implement a new attempt in this direction. I am now embarking on a book series, Advances in Police Theory and Practice, that seeks to attract writers from all parts of the world. Further, the attempt is to find practitioner contributors. The objective is to make the series a serious contribution to our knowledge of the police as well as to improve police practices. The focus is not only in work that describes the best and successful police practices but also one that challenges current paradigms and breaks new ground to prepare a police for the twenty-first century. The series seeks for comparative analysis that highlights achievements in distant parts of the world as well as one that encourages an in-depth examination of specific problems confronting a particular police force.

Dr. Kam Wong's *Policing in Hong Kong: History and Reform* exemplifies what this Series seeks to offer. This author, a former Inspector of Hong Kong Police (HKP) and an attorney from the U.S., has provided us with a critical study of the Hong Kong Police in the colonial (1850s) era as well as during the decolonization periods (1950s). The book makes two claims. First, British colonial policing in Hong Kong must come to terms with local conditions and indigenous culture, best understood as "policing with Chinese characteristics." Second, fundamental Hong Kong Police reform began in 1950s as a post-WWII modernization initiative, and not in 1997 as a result of reversion of political sovereignty to China. The book challenges our conventional understanding of HKP. In so doing, it is hoped that it invites robust debate and further inquiry.

It is hoped that through this series it will be possible to accelerate the process of building knowledge about policing and help bridge the gap between the two worlds—the world of police research and police practice. This is an invitation to police scholars and practitioners across the world to come and join in this venture.

Dilip K. Das, PhD
Founding President, International Police Executive Symposium
http://www.ipes.info
Series Editor, Advances in Police Theory and Practice
(CRC Press/Taylor & Francis Group)
Series Editor, Interviews with Global Leaders in Police, Courts, and Prisons
(CRC Press/Taylor & Francis Group)
Series Editor, PPR Special Issues as Books
(Routledge/Taylor & Francis Group)
Founding Editor-in-Chief, Police Practice and Research:
An International Journal (Routledge/Taylor & Francis Group)
http://www.tandfonline.com/GPPR

Prologue

I write *Policing in Hong Kong: History and Reform* as much for myself as for others. It is a project of the heart, more so than that of the head. For me, *Policing in Hong Kong: History and Reform* is a journey of discovery, not a destiny. The journey began with me joining the HKP. Below I will share with you what this journey of discovery entails, reveals and forebodes, finishing with a section on 'How to do scholarship.'

An Intellectual Journey to Nowhere and Everywhere

In the 1960s, I joined the Royal Hong Kong Police. With my colleagues, locals and expatriates, we kept ourselves busy fighting crime, keeping order, and serving the community; living the dream of our lives.

As Chinese officers from Hong Kong, our dreams knew no bounds. Like young people everywhere, we were idealistic and energetic. We were in love with the HKP. We challenged each other to do better as a person, officer and citizen. To that end, we asked 10,000 questions, about the HKP, about Hong Kong, and most importantly, about ourselves:

Is the HKP a colonial force? Is colonialism a blessing or a curse for Hong Kong? Is there a need for a para-military force in a civil society? Is it fair to promote expatriate officers ahead of Chinese ones? How does one improve communication between British and Chinese, within and without the HKP? How does one eradicate institutionalised corruption within the HKP and in the society? How does one make the HKP more accountable to community? How can British police officers function effectively in a Chinese society, without coming to terms with its culture and custom? How can a Chinese in good conscience serve as a British colonial police officer, without severing his ethnic link and diluting the community bond?

In time and after the 1967 riots, HKP officers were called 'yellow running dog' (Chinese officers) or 'white skin pig' (British officers). We were also honoured as the 'Royal' Hong Kong Police, afterward. The year 1967 was a defining moment with the HKP. The 1967 riot pulled us together, giving the HKP a shared identity, and newfound respectability.

With 1967 on our backs, we discovered that as HKP officers we had more in common as humans than differences as nationals. That is not to say there was no discrimination, on both sides (British vs. Chinese) and at either ends (HKP and Hong Kong people). It just means that we did not allow racial animus to come between us, in doing what was right for Hong Kong and by the HKP. This rather obscure but important observation informs most of my thinking about colonial policing in Hong Kong, the central focus of this book.

In my unrelenting quest for understanding, I found more questions than answers, and answers beget more questions. Soon, I found that my curiosity out ran my experience, knowledge and capacity. I also found that, however hard I tried to understand my work, the public were not as appreciative of my effort and certainly did not share in my understanding. I was frustrated.

Frustration ('strain') is the mother of all adaptations. Some of my colleagues became bitter. Others became stoic. Still others reached out for innovations (education). Many of my colleagues stayed with the HKP to pursue professional development overseas and higher learning in Hong Kong. I left HKP to study forensics and became a lawyer in the United States. The self-enrichment process opened my eyes and broadened my vision. In time it changed my thinking and outlook. I was ready to rejoin the HKP, but the HKP was not ready for me. I promised to return one day; now I have, with this book. Time has changed. HKP has changed. I am welcomed as a valuable resource instead of being dismissed as an ill-fitting specimen.

After practising law for a number of years in the United States and overseas, I decided to pursue a PhD at Albany. Due to my professional experience and scholarly interest, I focused on cross-cultural policing. That was in the late 1980s.

Thirty odd years later I become an expert in comparative policing, with China and Hong Kong as the home base. My agenda is to bridge the gap between East and West. Intellectually, I see the need to dampen the scorched earth approach of aggressive cultural imperialism, in favour of a more critical but balanced and nuanced post-modernist style of inquiry. Multiculturalism is in my blood. Personally, my interest is pricked by my failed cross-cultural marriage. I need to bring some closure to that part of my life. This part of my intellectual journey tells me what, how and why we think about issues depends less on logic and facts, but experience and appreciation; that is, cultural awareness, not scientific analysis, holds the key to the understanding of colonial policing and HKP reform. Here I say nothing more than what Justice Holmes has imparted: 'The life of law has not been logic, but experience.'

The goal that I set for myself is a difficult one, bordering on being impossible. For anti-cultural warriors of all persuasions, the challenges are in fighting ethnocentrism and mediating 'clash of civilisations'. The lessons I learned from my lifelong engagement with cross-cultural affairs fill the pages of this book. The most important one being: in conducting cross-cultural research, such as depicting, characterising, debating and assessing colonial policing, we should withhold judgment and get away from generalisations. We should let the facts speak for themselves, preferably by listening to the people who are involved or afflicted by inter-cultural exchanges, with empathy, identification, immersion and sublimation.

In terms of methods: induction and not deduction; bottom up and not top down; up close and not afar, and involved not detached. In terms of perspective: insiders and not outsiders, practitioners and not theoreticians, and commoners and not experts. In terms of observations: particularisation over generalisation, details over abstractions, and pragmatics over utopia. In sum, understanding human affairs starts with what everyday life can teach us, and not what a few scientific inquiries have instilled in us (evidence-based this or that notwithstanding).

In the early 1980s, I returned to Hong Kong to conduct research at the Chinese University of Hong Kong. The Sino-British negotiation over the future of Hong Kong beyond 1997 had just started. Driven by such a watershed political event in the making, my research interest in the HKP naturally turned to how the HKP as a colonial force under British rule could be transformed into a civil community service agency under Chinese administration. Together with other Hong Kong criminal justice professionals we started the Hong Kong Society of Criminology (1983), as a platform to share information and exchange ideas. The seed for Hong Kong criminology study was planted.

In the 1990s, I returned to Hong Kong a second time, teaching public law at Chinese University of Hong Kong. By this time, the political future of Hong Kong had been settled under the Basic Law. My research interest shifted to how the transfer of political sovereignty under 'one country two systems' might affect HKP organisation, control and operations? To address such and other issues, I organised the first international policing conference in Hong Kong as President of the Asian Association of Police Studies (AAPS). The AAPS conference officially launched the study of policing in Hong Kong, as an academic discipline.

As 1997 got closer, the HKP leadership was much concerned with 'brain drain' from the HKP, due to political and economic reasons. As a policing scholar, I was more optimistic about the future prospect of HKP under Chinese rule. Many of my ex-colleagues, however, were worried; for example, one-time Special Branch officers or long-time career officers. When asked, I observed that the HKP would change after 1997 for the better, on its own terms and in its own way. I was proven right. As I make clear in this book, the HKP is a battle-tested professional organisation, with strong leadership, competent staff and deep culture. Coming to change and reform, the HKP is a continuously learning and reforming agency in pursuit of organisational excellence, after the Second World War (1950s). Viewed in this light, the 1997 HKP reform was an extension of 1950s reform, not a brand new adventure into uncharted territories.

Now (2014), some 45 years later, I am back at it again, asking questions about the HKP. This time with hindsight, I try to prospect what the HKP will be like in the future, in concrete terms.

What is the role of the HKP in protecting China's security interests in Hong Kong; for example, protecting the Chinese Prime Minister inside HKU? How should frontline HKP officers face up to radicalised youth or empowered public, such as in reacting to disrespectful citizens, insulting protestors and intimating Triads? How should the HKP be prepared to deal with a new form of public disorder, that is, 'colored revolution' by students? How prepared is the HKP in dealing with Western-incited violence; for example, 'non-violent revolution' (a la Dr. Gene Sharp)? More fundamentally, how can the HKP steer clear of the infectious storm of politicisation and the accompanying waves of volative social movement(s), now in full force?

This time, I am more prepared to reflect on such weighty issues. But the issues are also getting more complex and difficult. It is at this juncture that I start to pen the *Policing in Hong Kong: History and Reform* book.

Focus, Thesis, Findings

Policing in Hong Kong: History and Reform asks two kinds of questions: In what ways was the HKP a colonial police force? When did the HKP shed its colonial colour, and how?

As a thesis, from my vantage point as a HKP officer and now a policing scholar, I do not share in the conventional wisdom that colonial policing was brutal and abusive, in every way imaginable. Rather I am of the opinion that Hong Kong residents, British and Chinese alike, of necessity or due to utility, worked together to co-produce law and order in Hong Kong. With that supposition, I argue that in order to understand the HKP and policing in Hong Kong we must first engage in people-watching: studying their history and culture, ways and means, feeling and thinking. More to the point, we must understand how the British worked with the Chinese in policing Hong Kong. By seeking to understand this relationship, I discovered the first principle of colonial policing in Hong Kong: British colonial officers (who were in the minority) had no hope of ruling over the colonised majority (i.e. the Hong Kong people) without coming to terms with their history, culture and customs. Successful administration of a people is best negotiated, never imposed. In the words of my high school teacher at St. Paul's Boys College (Hong Kong): 'Happy people do not revolt. Unhappy people always do.'

With the above insight I started to research the book. What I found does not surprise me. The Hong Kong people accepted British rule not because it was politically legitimate but because the HKP delivered what the people wanted, especially after 1950, that is: law and order, safety and security, stability and prosperity. This allowed the Hong Kong people to make money, enjoy life and raise their families in a carefree manner. As for corruption and Triads, they were necessary evils of an alien rule and transient society. This was regrettable but not dysfunctional, given the historical circumstances that colonised Hong Kong. In essence, the HKP achieved performance legitimacy, though not political legitimacy. Pragmatism, not ideology, ruled the day.

As to historical development of colonial policing, from inception and at ground zero, the HKP did not behave like a colonial police force. Indeed, for much of the time, the HKP practised 'dual' administration and 'collaborative' rule. An integrated—unified and uniform—the HKP administration and operation did not exist before the Second World War.

As I point out in the book, policing has never been a one-size-fits-all operation. With the colonial HKP, policing the Peak ('little England') was not the same as policing Kowloon Walled City ('three lawless zone' 三不管) and far cry from policing Kwun Tong ('barbaric place' 紅番區). This suggests that the HKP adjusted their operations based on local conditions, a far-fetched idea for ideologues and colonialism basher.

As to the HKP reform, the rebuilding of HKP after the Second World War was a defining moment in the HKP's developmental history. By the time I joined the police in the mid-1960s, the HKP has transformed itself into a modern, professional, communal force, with very little vestiges of colonialism left, except perhaps paramilitary organisational style and corruption practice. There was even a Chinese police force run by the CID staff sergeants. It is here that the current book makes the most contribution to the study of the HKP. The Chinese in Hong Kong have always found ways to police themselves, under Colonial administration, if the British looked the other way.

Contributions

Altogether, the book makes the following observations about the HKP:

First, the HKP's reform in the 1950s gave Hong Kong a fully integrated police force across all areas (Hong Kong, Kowloon, New Territories, Water) and functions (UB, CID, SB, PTS, PTU, EU), with central administration in PHQ (Commissioner of Police), decentralised command at District level (District Superintendent) and delegated control at Sub-Division level (SDI).

Second, the decolonisation of the HKP started in 1950s, which gave us a fully integrated police force with British and Chinese working side by side ('localisation').

Third, the decolonisation and modernisation of the HKP started in 1950s with the introduction of CSI, evidence-based policing, problem-oriented policing and community-oriented policing.

Fourth, Chinese policing Chinese in colonial Hong Kong started with the District Watch Force in 1860s and blossomed into the Four CID Staff Sergeants era between 1950 and 1974.

Finally, the uniqueness of this book is in providing the readers with an external as well as internal views of HKP, as supported by indigenous theories and informed with local data; a first in Hong Kong policing research.

How Does One Do Scholarship?

I am often asked how I do scholarship: what subject matters I study; how I engage in research; in essence, what the tricks of the trade are; the prestige of research if you like.

The subject matter: Before I close, I think it is best to share with you how I pick my intellectual journeys, including this one. If you are like me who is drawn to serendipitious discoveries, it is best to consult Robert Frost's (1874–1963) poem: 'The Road Not Taken':

> Two roads diverged in a yellow wood,
> And sorry I could not travel both
> And be one traveler, long I stood
> And looked down one as far as I could
> To where it bent in the undergrowth;
>
> Then took the other, as just as fair,
> And having perhaps the better claim,
> Because it was grassy and wanted wear;
> Though as for that the passing there
> Had worn them really about the same,
>
> And both that morning equally lay
> In leaves no step had trodden black.
> Oh, I kept the first for another day!
> Yet knowing how way leads on to way,
> I doubted if I should ever come back.
>
> I shall be telling this with a sigh
> Somewhere ages and ages hence:
> Two roads diverged in a wood, and I—
> I took the one less traveled by,
> And that has made all the difference.

My research agenda has prompted me to find out all that I do not know, that is, what is 'unknown-unknown', instead of seeking to elaborate on what is 'known-known' or discover what is 'known-unknown'.

How I do research? The ultimate measure of good scholarship, you ask? To me, scholarship is a private love affair conducted behind closed doors, as a life course and life style. The process consists of a prolonged period of passionate liaisons mixed with cool discernment, away from the temperamental and tempestuous crowd. In the finest tradition of Chinese cooking: 'Soup (ideas) is to be simmered, never boiled.'

There you have it: passion, discernment, and patience makes for good scholarship.

Acknowledgements

Research and writing is a lonely job. But that is not to say that I do this book all by myself. Quite to the contrary, this book is very much a joint venture. Many ex-colleagues and former students helped me with data. More than a few scholars acted as sounding board for my ideas. A few police experts, from Hong Kong and around the world, read the manuscript and provided for valuable feedbacks. Then, there are hundreds of authors whose published work I consulted, interrogated and debated as I went about putting the treatise together. I cannot recognise them all, because the list is really that long. All that I can offer is a big thank you. This project could not have seen the light of day without their kind and selfless support. If I have my way, all their names would appear as co-authors. All the same, their contributions are detailed in the corpus and detail footnotes, which is the next best thing I can do.

I would be remiss if I do not name four individuals, who played an active part in compiling this book. First, I want to thank CSP Douglas Tsui of HKP (retired) for gracing this book with a Foreword. CSP Tsui was one of my closest colleagues at HKP, now a lifelong friend. Second, I want to thank my son, Mr Wong Chi-on for proofreading the manuscript, making it more error free. Third, I want to thank my wife, Rainbow Wong for putting up with my erratic writing schedule, and supporting me in every turn, from meeting publisher deadlines to softening writer's blue.

Last but not least, I want to thank my sister Po Po Wong who kept me company, by Skype or at heart, in those long sleepless nights, when I was short of ideas, and ran out of patience. Her ever present, pleasant smiles always saved my nights. She is a joy of our family. This book is dedicated to her and her family.

Part of the content, issues and ideas of this book have been presented at the Department of Sociology (Criminology), Hong Kong University,

School of Law, Chinese University of Hong Kong, School of Criminal Justice, University of Cincinnati, School of Law, University of Chicago, School of Law, University of Washington. I thank the participants of the above seminars and talks for their valuable feedbacks.

Last, I would like to thank Xavier University for providing me with a most pleasant and supportive environment to conduct my research and write this book. I would also like to thank Jennifer Stair at Taylor & Francis, Karthick Parthasarathy and editorial staff from Techset Composition for help in publication and editing the manuscript.

Kam C. Wong
CLC Library, XU

Author

Professor Kam C. Wong teaches at the Department of Criminal Justice, Xavier University, Cincinnati, Ohio; where he once was a chairperson. Concurrently, he is a faculty fellow at the School of Criminal Justice, SUNY–Albany, New York. Dr. Wong earned his bachelor of arts with honors, J.D. from Indiana University, Bloomington, Indiana; as well as a PhD in criminal justice from SUNY–Albany, where he received the Remington Award for Distinguished Work in Law and Social Science.

An Inspector of Police with the Hong Kong Police, Dr. Wong was awarded the Commissioner's High Commendation, and for 20 years, was a black belt karate instructor.

Professor Wong was a former Managing Attorney of the Legal Service Corporation in Michigan and Corporate Counsel for Everex, a public listed company. He was the director of the Chinese Law Program at the Chinese University of Hong Kong. He also served as the vice president (1999–2000) at the Center for Criminology, Hong Kong University and vice chair (2000–2002) at the Hong Kong Society of Criminology. Currently, he is a Honorary Fellow at the Center for Criminology at Hong Kong University.

Professor Wong published over 100 articles and 10 books, in 10 countries, which appeared in *Police Quarterly*; *Columbia Journal of Asian Law*; *Georgetown Journal of Law and Public Policy*; *Australian and New Zealand Journal of Criminology*; *British Journal of Criminology*; *Asian Journal of Criminology*; *Australian Journal of Law and Society*; *China Perspective* (French); *Crime Review* (Korea); *China Review*; *Herald of Law* (Yugoslavia); *International Journal of the Sociology of Law*; *Criminal Law Bulletin*; *Journal of Information Law & Technology*; *Pacific Rim Law & Policy Journal*; *John Marshall Journal of Computer and Information Law*, *Education and Law Journal*, *Asia-Pacific Journal on Human Rights and the Law*, *Michigan Journal of Race & Law*, among others.

Professor Wong was the managing editor for *Police Practice and Research: An International Journal*. He was the editor-in-chief for *Working Paper Series*, *International Police Executive Symposium*; editor, *Journal of Crime and Delinquency*; editor, Zhejiang *Police College Journal* (International Division, PR China). He is currently on the editorial board of the *Beijing Law Review*, *International Journal of Comparative Criminology*, *Open Journal of Law*, as well as *Open Journal of Sociology and Asian Policing*.

Professor Wong was an organiser and founding member of the Asian Association of Police Studies, of which he was also the vice president (2001–2002) and president (2002–2003). He is the founding board member of the Asia Criminological Society; Pakistan Society of Criminology; Asian School of Management and Technology (India); and the South Asian Society of Criminology and Victimology.

Professor Wong's latest books include: *USA PATRIOT ACT: The Impact of USA Patriot Act on American Society: An Evidence Based Assessment* (Hauppauge, New York: Nova Science Publishers, 2007); *The Making of USA Patriot Act: Legislation, Implementation, Impact* (Beijing: China Law Press, 2008); *Chinese Policing: History and Reform* (New York: Peter Lang, 2009); *Police Reform in China* (Boca Raton, FL: CRC Press, 2012); *Cyberspace Governance in China* (New York: Nova Science Publications, 2012); *Policing in Hong Kong* (Farnham, Surrey, UK: Ashgate, 2012), *Policing in China* (Pakistan: Pakistan Society of Criminology, 2012), *Policing in Hong Kong: History and Reform* (Boca Raton, FL: CRC Press, 2012) and *The Study of Policing in Hong Kong* (London and New York: Palgrave, 2016) (under review). His current project is 'Public Order Policing in China: The Case of Umbrella Resistant in Hong Kong' (2013–2017).

Professor Wong is a legal consultant to the Immigration and Refugee Board of Canada on Chinese law issues. He is an expert consultant to U.K. Beirut Police Integrity Workshop, the United Nations Office on Drugs and Crime on illicit financial flows resulting from transnational organised crime and an expert observer at the United Nations Congress on the Prevention of Crime and the Treatment of Offenders. He is a foreign expert to the Ministry of Public Security, People's Republic of China and trainer/consultant to the Hong Kong Police.

Professor Wong was on the advisory board of the Yale in China—Law program. He was a visiting scholar/fellow at Scarman Centre, University of Leicester, United Kingdom as well as a visiting scholar at the Institute of Criminology, Cambridge University, United Kingdom; Cyberspace Institute, George Washington University, Washington, DC, USA; Chinese People's Public Security University, Beijing, China; Zhejiang Provincial Police College, Hangzhou Zhejiang, China; Hubei Provincial Police College, Hubei Province, PR China; and the Hunan Police Officer College and Chinese Armed Police Force College, PR China.

Professor Wong has been a regular columnist on law and order issues with the *Hong Kong Standard* (1998), *South China Morning Post* (1999), *Hong Kong Economic Journal* (2000) and *Apple Daily* (2001). He also contributed to the *Far Eastern Economic Review*, *Apple Daily* and other major newspapers in Hong Kong. He is a media consultant on Chinese and Hong Kong law with RTHK, Commercial Radio, Radio Free Asia, CCTV, TVB, ATV, CNN, NPR, AP, Reuters, Australian National Radio, *Financial Times*, *Washington Post* and *Guardian*. In 2002, he was an editor/columnist for *Crime Review*, a web-based crime and justice journal organised by the faculty of the Korea National Police University.

Introduction

> The future of Hong Kong cannot but be built on its past. It is our belief that as Hong Kong looks forward, it must also make a dispassionate assessment of its experience under British rule.
>
> **David Faure (ed.), A Documentary History of Hong Kong Society (1997)**

Introduction

The Hong Kong Police (HKP) is 172 years old (1842–2014). It is a highly regarded professional force with a storied history, worldwide renown and domestic following. The HKP has evolved from a nearly all-white colonial police establishment in 1842 to a mostly Hong Kong—Chinese police organisation in 2014.

On the eve of taking possession of Hong Kong by British forces in 1841, the British Foreign Secretary dismissively observed Hong Kong to be a 'barren island'.[1] This statement registered British officials' displeasure in taking Hong Kong after a costly war.[2] It also reflected British public opinion of the times. The nation was tired of war and weary of burdensome colonial possessions. It is only later in Hong Kong's history that the 'barren rock' takes on a more upbeat note, along with her economic success: 'This barren rock legend, as one critic observed, has been reiterated in one way or the other by every British official implying that, since Britain created Hong Kong out of wilderness, it has contributed more to the development of Hong Kong than anyone else.'[3]

But Hong Kong before the British was fairly well settled by indigenous population with a vibrant external opium trade[4] and thriving internal economy: 'Do not decry Hong Kong too quickly. There are fine granite quarries worked by industrious stone masons who will benefit if we fortify the island. There is a thriving fishing village whose business will improve if we move in.'[5] In fact, according to an India Company's Select Committee charged with mapping out the safest passages up the China, it found Hong Kong to be an ideal place to conduct business: 'These observations lead us to conclude that if England is to occupy any part of South China it should be Hong Kong. If it was a free port it will be the most considerable mart east of the Cape. The Portuguese got it wrong—they accepted shallow water and exclusive rules. Hong Kong has deep water and should be a free port forever.'[6] The people were also well regulated living in segregated communities.[7]

As to who lived in Hong Kong at the time, we find that

> The inhabitants were of four Chinese races: The Punti or Cantonese, the Hoklos, the Hakkas or 'stranger families', and the outcast called Tankas or 'egg people' (perhaps because their boats had egg shaped canopies). They lived for the most part in segregated communities, speaking their own languages and generally behaving apathetically towards one another. The powerful land-owning families of the region, however were all Cantonese's and they were grouped into the Five Great Clans, Tang, Hau, Pan, Liu and Man, each dominating its own villages and possessing its inherited lands in common.[8]

Before the British, Hong Kong was governed by a Chinese imperial district magistrate working out of Nam Tau, on the shores of Deep Bay to the northwest with a fortified headquarter in Kowloon City. The magistrate reported to the Viceroy of Guangdong with troops and warships under his command.[9] For example, on 10 January 1839 Captain Ho Ko Chung, commander of the Chinese squadron at Kowloon Bay, Hong Kong, petitioned the Viceroy as follows:

> A small foreign ship with an awning over her aft deck (a schooner—likely one of the ferries banned from the river) is cruising off western Hong Kong between Apleichau and Green Island. I have sent boats to constantly observe her and prevent native fishermen, etc., from contacting with her.[10]

In the beginning, the British preferred 'indirect rule' with a strategy that came to be known as 'dual track' rule, with British 'steering' and Chinese 'rowing'; that is, rule by proxy was the norm.[11]

> The British crowd liked to extol the unique characteristics of British colonial rule, its beliefs in racial difference, its use of indigenous rulers and traditional institutions, and its creation of what (and some of their foreign emulators) believed was the most effective instrument of colonial power—the system of indirect rule.[12]

The system worked well for the most part, with British and Chinese performing their respective roles in unison. To be expected, there were many differences between the British and Chinese in culture and habits, which gave rise to perennial low intensity conflicts, occasional vocal protestations, and, in rare instances violent confrontations.[13] By the 1860s, the colonists preferred to integrate Chinese elites in the government structure and they were allowed to manage their own affairs (Nan Bei Hong) (1868) in providing for their own welfare at Tung Wah Hospital (1870, 1872) and partaking in policing and protection of the Chinese community with the District Watch Force (1866).

In order to study the governance and policing of Hong Kong, we need to dispel three myths on Hong Kong before British rule: First, Hong Kong was a 'barren rock' devoid of enterprising people and economic activities. Second, Hong Kong people were disorganised, uncivilised, disorderly and evil. Third, Hong Kong people enjoyed no government, administration or supervision before 1841.

This book is on the 'history and reform' of (colonial) policing in Hong Kong. Specifically, it is about policing in Hong Kong during the colonial years, historically, before and after the Second World War. Its basic approach is to question accepted colonial history. Is HKP a colonial force in theory and practice before 1945? Has the HKP been transformed from a colonial police establishment into a modern policing agency, after 1945? In both instances the organisation and operations of HKP is at issue.

Thematically, this book is divided into two parts. In Part I, it argues that 'colonial policing' in Hong Kong (as in elsewhere) takes on local colour and hue in practice: 'colonial policing with Hong Kong—Chinese characteristics.' In Part II, the book observes that the HKP has gone through four distinctive reform periods, namely, the 'formation period' (1845), 'reorganisation period' (1872), the 'modernisation period' (1950s) and finally the 'decolonisation period' (1990s). It argues that HKP reform in the 1950s was the pivotal point in transforming the HKP from a colonial force into a civil one, by way of localisation, legalisation, modernisation, communalisation and organisation.

This chapter provides some historical and theoretical background to this study, especially on how to re-conceptualise the relationship between colonial master and subjects with a 'more or less governmental control' model.[14] It first discusses the possession of Hong Kong by the British in 'Colonial Hong Kong' (Section I) and development of policing in Hong Kong, from colonial to SAR policing (Section II: 'The Origin of Hong Kong Police'). This chapter then turns to explore and explicate one aspect of colonial policing in Hong Kong, that is, how to conceptualise top-down British colonial policing of Hong Kong vs. bottom-up Chinese policing in Hong Kong as a colony, in a more functional term (Sections III and IV). This chapter ends with an outline of each chapter (Section V).

I: Colonial Hong Kong

The story of Hong Kong Police (HKP) and colonial policing of Hong Kong started long before the British ever set foot in Hong Kong. It started with the then-prospering British Far East trade, requiring a place for foothold and shelter.

British interest in Far East trade and commerce began in the seventeenth century with the establishment of the East India Company under Royal Charter: 'The Governor and Merchants of London Trading into the

East Indies.' Said Charter granted the East India Company a monopoly of all British trade east of Cape of Good Hope.[15]

In 1699, the East India Company set up its first British factory in China. Since then, and for the next two decades, Britain was in fierce competition with the France and the Dutch to monopolise trade in China.[16] This resulted in chronic violence.[17] In the end, the East India Company beat its rivals through monopolistic legal protection (British subjects could not work for competitors), sound trade practices (quality goods, favourable finances, reliable contracts), guaranteed home market (for tea and silk), superior trading organisation (a regional trading system extending to India), quiet diplomacy, and at times, crude corruptive practices and dominating military presence.[18] Trading in China thousands of miles away from home required logistic support and safe ports as back up. As early as February 1789, an exploratory party was dispatched to Lantau to scout out a good harbor:

> Secondly that the great extent of our commercial concerns in China requires a place of security as a depot for such of our goods as cannot be sold off or shipped during the short season that is allowed for our shipping to arrive and depart; and that for this purpose we wish to obtain a grant of a small tract of ground or detached Island, but in a more convenient situation than Canton, where our present warehouses are at a great distance from our ships, and where we are not able to restrain the irregularities which are occasionally committed by the Seamen of the Company's ships, and those of private traders… Or with as little trouble and with more advantage we might make a settlement in Lantao or Cow-hee (Ma Wan), and then Macao would of itself crumble to nothing in a short time.[19]

Until the Opium Wars (1842), the British merchants were not able to open up other Chinese trade ports, beyond Canton. Canton became the de facto British trade headquarters in China, with Macau as a wait station.[20] Hong Kong, while not being the first or best choice of the British imperial government, by default became the leading free trade port the British had hoped for in the region after 1841. With its strategic location and unsurpassed seaport, it ended up being one of Britain's most successful and prosperous dependents ever, allowing the British to claim victory by spreading her civilisation and economy abroad.[21]

British possession of Hong Kong began in earnest with the signing of the Treaty of Chuenpi on 20 January 1841, without the blessing of the Crown of England or concession from the Emperor of China. On that day, Captain Elliot issued a circular from Macao claiming Hong Kong as a British Crown colony for the benefit of all merchants, traders and sailors, worldwide. A free trade port with no duties and little restrictions[22] under British Administration in the heart of Asia (China) was born, and would remain under rule until 1997. The circular also made clear that the Chinese empire was welcome to levy import/export duties for goods outside Hong Kong territorial waters and within the confine of Wall City in Kowloon as she deemed fit and proper.

During that time, Hong Kong played a similar role as Macao had been playing since 1557. There were some differences between the two, however. First, during the Ming Dynasty, China welcomed foreign traders. As a result, Macao played a less strategic role for China-bound traders. This meant that Macao functioned as a support station for wayward travellers more so than a protective shelter for restricted traders. Second, Macao was not a free port. The use of Macao had to be negotiated with the Portuguese. In 1627, the East India Company wanted to trade with China (Canton) via Macao, but the Portuguese refused due to trade competition. Finally, in 1634, Court of Directors of East India Company was able to negotiate a treaty for the use of Macao with the Governor of Portuguese.[23]

With the cessation of Hong Kong accomplished, Her Majesty Queen Victoria appointed Captain Elliot on 26 January 1841 as the Chief Superintendent of Trade of British Subjects in China.[24] As such, Elliot was vested with the plenary power under the Great Seal of the United Kingdom on 29 January 1841 to execute the office of Her Majesty's Commissioner, Procurator, and Plenipotentiary in China.[25]

On 29 January 1841, as the first act of government of Hong Kong, in his capacity as the Chief Superintendent of Trade of British Subjects in China, and effectively the governor of Hong Kong, Captain Elliot issued his first proclamation, declaring: First, subject to the pleasure of Her Majesty the Queen of England, the Government of Hong Kong, was in the Office of Chief Superintendent of Trade of British Subjects in China. Second, Hong Kong natives and Chinese nationals were to be governed by Chinese law and customs, torture accepted. Third, all other persons in Hong Kong were subjected to British rule and Hong Kong laws.[26]

The aforementioned bifurcation of law and dual justice administration was introduced to accommodate two distinctively different kinds of people (Chinese and British) and cultures (East vs. West) as a stop gap measure, until such a time where the Chinese and British communities completely merged into one, that of Hong Kong.[27]

The dual legal system was also introduced for other philosophical, political and social reasons:

1. During the negotiation of the peace treaty, the British Government maintained that she was only interested in possession of Hong Kong as a trading post, not a British settlement.
2. Likewise the Chinese Government maintained that the right of possession of Hong Kong did not rise to the level of control over her people, that is, possession of land, not control of people.

3. Traditionally, Chinese ethnic identity and political nationality rights could not be divested, that is, 'born a Chinese person, die a Chinese ghost' concept.[28]
4. It would be unjust to impose British law on the local residents and Chinese nationals. The Chinese did not know English, and more importantly were not used to and were not comfortable with British justice.
5. It would be impractical to enforce British law on the Chinese. British officials had limited facilities and experiences with Chinese custom, culture and language.
6. It would be unfair to impose British law on the Chinese people when foreign powers, including the British, have insisted on dual legal and justice administration for foreign nations in China's trade ports in the form of extra-territoriality. Arguably, this was the first formulation of the 'one country two principle' doctrine.[29]

The first Hong Kong Government administration was formed in 27 February 1842 with the removal of the Superintendent of Trade office from Macao to Hong Kong. The organisation and staff of this department included: Mr. A. R. Johnson, Deputy Superintendent; E. Elmslie, Secretary of Treasury; J.R. Morrison, Chinese Secretary and Interpreter; L. d' Almada e Castro, A. W. Elmslie, and J.M. d'Almada e Castro, Clerks; Rev. Ch. Glitzlaff and R. Thom (Joint Interpreters), J.B. Redriguez, W. H. Medhurst, and Kazigachi Kiukitchi, Clerks.

The clearest signal yet of the Hong Kong Government intending to stay permanently came from 22 March 1842 'Notification of Sir H. Pottinger' appearing in Hong Kong's first local newspapers: the *Friend of China* and *Hong Kong Gazette* to the effect that a Land Committee was established to investigate claims, to mark off boundaries, to fix the direction and breadth of the roads, to order the removal of encroachments, and to assign new locations of Chinese and European dwellings.[30] Pottinger followed this 'Notification' with more domestication actions. Through enforcing monetary policy, establishing a post office, and precluding native Chinese from owning prime property, he stabilised the currency, created a communication facility and enforced land administration.[31]

The Hong Kong Government also showed a commitment to stay in Hong Kong for the long haul by making substantial infrastructural investment, including purchasing of Commissariat Building, and the building of roads, barracks,[32] hospitals, naval facilities and stores.[33] While the British Government had decided to stay, most the people of Hong Kong were sojourns treating Hong Kong as a wait station, on borrowed time in a borrowed place.[34]

The first order of business of the new Hong Kong colonial government, indeed any government to a new land, was to attend to order within and security without. But what kind of policing was envisioned for Hong Kong? Specifically, how was colonial policing performed in Hong Kong? To this subject we now turn.

II: The Origin of Hong Kong Police

Law and Order 1839–1844

How Hong Kong was controlled, governed and policed depended on British imperial mindset, local conditions and relationship with China; most pressing at the time—state of war, and later as evolved—haven for refugees. Well into the 1900s, Hong Kong was the Casablanca of the East, where personal loyalty mattered more so than obedience to law, and situational expediency dictated more so than moral principles.

In 1839, five years before the British colonists landed in Hong Kong on 25 January 1841, the East India Company's Select Committee has commissioned a study to discover safe passages in the South China Sea for trading with China. The survey was conceived and done without disturbing the relationship with the imperial officials at home who had few interests and little knowledge of the Orient. At that time, there was no intent to exploit Hong Kong as an opium centre, still less thinking about how to manage Hong Kong or administer Chinese indigenous residents. Hong Kong was sought only as a port of convenience, namely as a transit point and resupply centre, not as a permanent settlement. As the editor of *Canton Register*,[35] a mouth piece of British commercial interests in China, attested in 1839:

> The survey of the estuary was called by the India Company's Select Committee to discover the safest passages up the China Sea. It was not then intended to promote an extensive smuggling trade outside the river so not every bay was examined. Indeed a close inspection of the coast would have unsettled the local officials whom the Company was at pains to keep friendly...Now the situation has changed but what does England want with Hong Kong and its wretched village of poor fishermen (Chek Chu, later called Stanley). If 'A Passenger' is suggesting we possess the islet and oust its inhabitants that would be a thievish, cunning and cowardly deed, unbecoming to our country.[36]

The above editorial was written in response to 'A Passenger' letter to the *Canton Register* on 3 May 1839 reporting on its survey finding of Hong Kong earlier. A careful reading of the letter makes clear that 'A Passenger' (possibly working for the Company) was only concerned about the strategic location (within reach of Canton) and the natural attributes (ease of access, water hole, protected and deep harbors) of Hong Kong as a free trade port, as compared to other ports in the area (South China), such as Macau:

> I recently made a survey of the Pearl River Estuary. We started at Kap Shui Mun (the passage between Ma Wan and Lantau Islands) at the end of which was a perfect harbour. We then went to Lamma which had looked good but turned out to be unprotected from the weather—the best bay (Sok Kwu Wan) was too landlocked. We found a small but good harbour at the waterfall on Hong Kong opposite Lamma (Waterfall Bay, Pokfulam). This had good depth by two entrances. We then looked at Lyemun and, of all the harbours in this vicinity, this is the best. The entrance from Tai Tam is as safe as the Bogue and gives access to deep water passages both north and south of Lintin. Kowloon Bay is an excellent anchorage of 5-7 fathoms over a clay bottom, plenty of fresh water ashore and easy approaches east and west…These observations lead us to conclude that if England is to occupy any part of South China it should be Hong Kong. If it was a free port it will be the most considerable mart east of the Cape. The Portuguese got it wrong—they accepted shallow water and exclusive rules. Hong Kong has deep water and should be a free port for ever.[37]

During this time, Hong Kong and surrounding water was patrolled by the Chinese war junks against Chinese privates, smugglers and opium traders. The imperial officers were also tasked by an emperors' edict to prevent foreigners from buying provisions, causing mischiefs, committing crime and dealing with opium in Hong Kong. The law and order situation in Hong Kong deteriorated precipitously with the onslaught of rootless migrants from China, ill-disciplined soldiers from Britain, drunken sailors from many countries, and in huge numbers:

> A census of Queen's Town (the informally adopted name of the foreign settlement on Hong Kong Island) revealed the native population is primarily made-up of carpenters, bricklayers & masons (3000 of them) who are involved in the construction of our homes and warehouses. Apart from them we have 600 hawkers, 500 chandlers, 440 prostitutes, 300 unemployed people, 130 opium sellers and some others in food retail, services and the like to a total of 8200 residents. …The major village of Hong Kong at Chek Chu is believed to contain about 3000 people. There are a few hundred in each of the villages of Wong Nai Chung, Little Hong Kong, Shek Pai Wan and some other smaller hamlets making a total of over 12,000.[38]

On 24 August 1841, Elliot and Bremer visited Hong Kong from Macau. They were knocked down by the villagers and Bremer was stripped of all his possessions. As luck would have it, an ex-comprador came to the rescue and saved the day.[39]

On 2 June 1842, it was reported that '3 privates of the 49th regiment have been caught robbing a Chinese family in Hong Kong. Many Chinese inhabitants report there have been numerous similar events before but as the criminals are soldiers they have kept quiet.'[40]

Origin of the HKP

On 30 April 1841, British Plenipotentiary Charles Elliot appointed Captain William Caine of the 26th Infantry Regiment as Chief Police Magistrate to maintain law and order in Hong Kong.[41] Cain was charged with organising an orderly social life in the Colony 'according to the laws, customs and usages of China, as nearly as may be (every description of torture accepted) or the preservation of peace, and the protection of life and property, over all the inhabitants of the said Island,'[42] that is, in charge of land policing. Cain was given a herculean task, with little guidance and near *carte blanche* authority. The only limitation perhaps is that he could not impose imprisonment of over three months, fines of over $400 or corporal punishment of 100 lashes. William Pedder, Lieutenant of the Royal Navy, had the authority and responsibility of water policing, i.e., to secure peace, law and order in the harbor.[43]

Cain was in charge of the well-being of 7500 people; 4350 being in 20 odd villages, mostly fishermen. Of these, 2000 people were living on boats, 800 people were at the bazaar providing food and services to foreigners and 350 labourers were plying for hire. At that time, there were few houses, permanent residents, and very little commercial activities in Victoria, the capital town of Hong Kong. All this changed with the arrival of the British. By June 1842, Victoria was enlivened with construction and commercial activities of all kinds, with soldiers, traders, labourers of all colour and persuasion converging in Hong Kong, mostly Victoria. The population of Hong Kong grew exponentially. Policing in Hong Kong during this unsettled period was about maintaining order in Victoria and providing for security in the Hong Kong harbour.

The law and order situation Cain was confronted with is best retold by a contemporary account of a British traveller to Hong Kong at the time:

> The native population in Victoria, consists of shopkeepers, tradesmen, servants, boat-people, and coolies, and altogether form a most motley group. Unfortunately there is no inducement for the respectable Chinese merchant to take up his quarters there, and until that takes place, we shall always have the worst set of people in the country. The town swarms with thieves and robbers, who are only kept under by the strong armed police lately established. Previous to this, scarcely a dark night passed without some one having his

house broken into by an armed band, and all that was valuable being carried off or destroyed. The audacious rascals did not except the Governor even, for one night Government House was robbed; and another time they actually stole the arms of the sentries. These armed bands, sometimes a hundred strong, disappeared, as they came, in a most marvelous manner, and no one seemed to know whence they came or whither they went. Such attacks are fortunately now of rare occurrence. In all my wanderings on the island, and also on the mainland hereabouts, I found the inhabitants harmless and civil. I have visited their glens and their mountains, their villages and small towns, and from all the intercourse I have had with them, I am bound to give them this character.[44]

Report of crime in local papers was a daily routine from burglaries, to robberies, to theft, to piracy:

Burglaries: On 9 June 1842, the *Friend of China* reported:

Hong Kong burglaries: Mr Pybus' godown, Captain Duus' godown, Mr Kinsley's godown, the French consul's godown, the Victoria Hotel, and the naval commissariat stores have all been burgled by gangs from Kowloon who come across the harbour in boats at night. They scratch out the mortar and remove bricks from the walls to gain entry. This might happen less if our municipal police force had not been summarily disbanded.[45]

On 16 June 1842, the *Friend of China* reported:

Hong Kong burglaries: Mr Almack's China house, Townsend and Co's godown, D. Wilson and Co (of Calcutta)'s premises have all been burgled this week. Some stolen property was found at the waterside which suggests it might be the same Kowloon gang as last week. There are reports of similar burglaries in Macau as well. Carpenters living at and employed on buildings near Townsend and Co's godown knew of that crime but kept quiet as they said they themselves would have been attacked if they raised the alarm. One thief was caught and sentenced to 60 strokes of the bamboo (the revised punishment instead of the lash). Fortunately the attacks are only on property and not on the person. A few weeks ago the burglars forced open the treasury of "an eminent firm" in Macau and stole silver but the firm is keeping it quiet.[46]

Theft: On 23 June 1842, the *Friend of China* reported:

Crime report: Two thieves were caught stealing a cow worth $10 from Pokfulam village on Hong Kong Island. They were sentenced to caning and their queues were cut off…. John Northgate, a sailor of HMS *Druid*, bought two bottles of *Sam Shoo* from Ah Tuk for a rupee. At that time he had $8 in his pocket as well. He then got drunk and when he regained consciousness his pocket was empty. A friend, who was less drunk, swore he saw the theft committed by Ah Tuk. Ah Tuk got 4 months goal with hard labour and was ordered to remain in prison until he repaid the $8.[47]

Robberies: On 28 June 1842, the *Canton Register* reported:

> Robberies continue unabated at Hong Kong. Gangs sail across from Kowloon at night and burgle at will. More or less everyone has been affected. From Macau we hear it is the same group that robbed all the foreigners there, one by one, recently.[48]

Piracy: On 21 July 1842 *Friend of China* reported:

> Hong Kong crime report. Tuk Kwai has been charged with piracy: Ah Chu says he was sailing his laden boat to Hong Kong and at Kap Shui Mun (north of Lantau) was attacked by pirates. He made no resistance and he was dropped on shore and the boat and cargo was sailed away by the pirates. He now accuses Tuk Kwai of being one of the pirates and proves his evidence is true by cutting off a cock's head.[49]

To build a police force, Cain needed money and support. On May 1841, the Rate Ordinance was passed to fund the police.[50] Captain Cain established a rudimentary police unit with 32 Indian and British military officers, all of them misfits with dubious characters. The pay was low. The working conditions were poor. The climate was demanding. The job was dangerous. The discipline was slacked. The turnover was rapid. All said, Hong Kong was a hazardous duty station for most Europeans. *Friend of China* reported in 1843:

> Almost all who can leave this island have since departed. The best medical minds have ascribed the cause of sickness not to the climate or some other environmental factor but to the absence of suitable housing for Europeans living in the tropical climate of Hong Kong….What with the insecurity of life and property due to robberies and piracy, this present epidemic of sickness, the low tariff in China and particularly the attack on our 'free port' status over opium, it is not surprising that some of the earliest colonists have now departed.[51]

Cain's police contingent worked out of Central HQ and two distant outposts at Aberdeen and Stanley. None of the officers there spoke the language, much less knew or cared about local culture. Policing then had more to do with pacification of a foreign land and controlling an alien people—suppressing piracy, controlling locals, fighting crime, and imposing order—rather than civil policing. 'In those years the most pressing problem was the creation of an ordered society in which law should be respected by a largely lawless vagabond population, both European and Chinese… (with the)… lack of an efficient force.'[52]

Judging by crime rates, public opinion and self-help initiatives, the police were not effective, and may have even been counterproductive. And, to most of the local residents and more than a few foreigners, the police were more trouble than they were worth, being corrupt, abusive and protective of vices and illegals. Without recourse to any meaningful control of police character, conduct and performance (which would be made possible by better recruitment, training, supervision and accountability), the colonial administration was left adopting draconian countermeasures, from stiff military discipline to mass dismissals. On 31 May 1842, the *Canton Register* Editorial reported:

> The unprofessional conduct of the police at Hong Kong has caused Pottinger to discharge the entire force and replace it with soldiers. These men have also proved inadequate to the task and robberies are out of control. Hong Kong still lacks its own legislature and is fundamentally a garrison town.[53]

Three years after British took possession of Hong Kong, and in spite of the gallant effort of Cain, law and order in the colony had not improved, and to some has deteriorated, as evident by this Letter to the Editor of *Friend of China* on 3 August 1843:

> Robbery is a serious problem. Some say the population is divided into two classes—those who have been robbed and those who are about to be robbed. As soon as the moon is in its 1st or 3rd quarters the robberies commence in spite of 44 JP's and 28 constables. The constables are insufficient and the magistrates have mostly already been robbed. How can they look after the thieves when they cannot look after themselves? Pottinger has been robbed, Caine has been robbed, the assistant magistrate (Hillier) has been robbed. Mr Bruce has been robbed. Mr Farncomb has been robbed. I don't have enough paper to list them all. Sgd Old Stager.[54]

On 21 May 1844 the first Police Force Ordinance was passed (Ordinance No. 12). Captain Charles May (1844–1862) started to organise the HKP along British lines. Funding was limited. The governor dropped his plan to staff the HKP with Chinese officers. On instruction from Sir Henry Pottinger, Lieutenant Colonel J.S. Malcolm provided the following overall assessment and strategic plan for organising the first HKP force:[55]

> Previous to my leaving China, I received instructions from Sir Henry Pottinger, to lay before your Lordship, the necessity of some arrangement being made for the establishment of an effective Police, in the Colony of Hong Kong. At present that duty is carried on, by Soldiers, chosen from the Regiments quartered in the Island, but Sir Henry only looked on this, as a temporary arrangement, and considered that the best plan would be to raise a body of men in England, expressly for this service, the expense of which would be met, in part, by a rate levied on the residents on the Island. As however he was not aware of either the expense, or practicability of this plan, he left it to me to explain to your Lordship the circumstances of the case and the necessity of some persons being sent from England, owing to the impossibility of trusting entirely to Chinese Policemen and the great difficulty of obtaining Europeans

> for that duty. Since the personal communication I had with your Lordship on this subject, I have made every enquiry as to the expense of carrying out Sir Henry's wishes and find, that to send out and maintain a force of 50 men and four Inspectors would cost at least six thousand pounds a year. From a rough calculation I have made I do not think that at present more than £3000 a year could be raised by a rate of a shilling in the pound on the houses now built on the Island, but this of course would increase yearly, without any corresponding necessity for increase in the Police force.

It was then agreed between the Hong Kong Governor and the British White Hall that Commissioner of London Metropolitan Police would dispatch three officers to lead the construction of the HKP, namely, Inspector Charles May and Sergeants Thomas Smithers and Hugh McGregor. They arrived on the 15th of March 1845, and were duly advanced to the ranks of superintendent and inspector.[56]

The first HKP had three London Metropolitan officers and 168 men (71 Europeans, 46 Indians, 51 Chinese).[57] The Chinese officers were not trusted. They were relegated to playing mostly insignificant roles and supportive duties, for example, guarding and translating.

In 1867, Walter Meredith Deane (1867–1892), a Cadet Officer who spoke fluent Chinese (Cantonese), was appointed Captain Superintendent of the HKP. The longest serving HKP head, he led the first HKP reform with a Commission of Inquiry. He also started the first policing training establishment—a language school. Notwithstanding his fluency with the Chinese language and familiarity with Hong Kong culture, he managed to stir up a first of its kind anti-imperialist protest in Hong Kong with the removal of 500 to 895 rickshaws from the streets of Hong Kong, out of concern for traffic control (Government Gazette, Nov. 2, 1883: 843). In this, Captain Deane was more responsive to foreign public opinion in high places than the solicitations of local pullers' grievances in the street[58]:

> Is there a 'rule of the road' for jinrickshas or is there not? If there is—as I understand to be the case—what means, if any, age taken to enforce its observance? I may safely answer—judging by results—no means whatever beyond perhaps the immediate neigh hood of [Hongkong] Club, and even this is very doubtful. There is practical chaos as regards any knowledge or observance of 'the rule of the road,' and jinrickshas run on the left or right side of the road just as their inclination prompts and drawers. The result is, confusion worse confounded, collisions and general loss of temper, and abominably bad language all around (Hong Kong Daily Press, November 10, 1883).

In October 1943, interim Commissioner John Pennefather-Evans (1940–1941, 1945) penned the 'Interim Report on the Hong Kong Police.' In it he called for the complete reorganisation of the HKP, following the example of the Water Police, making it a more integrated and egalitarian work force, with the enlistment of 'more educated type of Chinese' serving alongside with 'a few Eurasian lads of good standing.'

> The European contingent who monopolized the rank of inspector should be phased out, in the meantime they should be given more strenuous instruction in the Cantonese language, and in general 'every effort should be made to enlarge the outlook and contacts of European members of the Force'.[59]

This marked the beginning of an era of localisation for the HKP.[60] It would take many false starts and another 54 years to eventually complete the project in 1997.

Over time, with the arduous process of building and rebuilding, the HKP was able to transform itself in philosophy, mission, role, organisation, and style: from an instrument of political control to an agency of public order maintenance, from functioning as crime fighters to taking up the role of social services, from being organised as a para-military unit to being run as civil establishment, from authoritarian command and control to consultative management, from corrupt to clean culture, and from abusive to professional conduct.

Over the years, the HKP have been called many 'colorful' names: 'licensed thugs' (before 1970s) by the locals, 'yellow running dog' or 'white skin pig' by the rioters (1967 riots), 'Royal Hong Kong Police' (since 1968) by the British Royals, 'Asia's Finest' by the world (after 1968), and 'shrinking neck tortoise' by post-eighties generation. Each of the iconic names tells us something about the image of the HKP in the eyes of the public, as they served as cultural markers in the HKP's growth from one era to another.

The proudest achievement yet of the HKP perhaps is that it is the only colonial police force in the world that has been decolonised successfully and re-invented itself seamlessly, in better form and style; out shining its colonial mentor, the London Metropolitan Police and admiringly copied by its administrative master, the Chinese Ministry of Public Security:[61]

> With statistics showing unusually high rates of assent for characterizations of the current police as honorable, hardworking, and dedicated to the public, the Hong Kong Police are known worldwide as a historical and theoretical impossibility that effected massive growth with the full support of the public. Moreover, such peculiar and unique success of the Hong Kong Police confirms that long-standing history of hybridity and exceptional ability by illustrating how the police's ascendancy was predicated on shift from a colonial to a local to a colonial-as-local identity.[62]

To earn its keep, the HKP had to face up to continuous challenges and crises: In the early colonial years, the HKP fought against lawlessness in

Hong Kong, disorderly migrants from Kowloon, prevalence of privacy in the Pearl estuary and hapless drifters and unruly sojourns from everywhere in the early colonial years (1841). In 1958, it met the challenge of settling corruption charges in high places by Attorney General Antsey in 1958[63] (The Caldwell Inquiry).[64] Or consider its competition for control of the Chinese with the District Watch Force in the 1870s. More instances range from its dealing with police abuses and corruption in the 1890s, to containing the bubonic plague in 1891, to battling rickshaw anti-imperial protests in 1893, to doing running battle with Canton—Hong Kong strikers in 1925, to stamping out gun running in 1926–1927, to rebuilding of the HKP in the 1940s, to controlling of Chinese refugee in 1950s, to quelling of riots in 1859 and 1967, to purging of corruption in 1970s, to weathering pre-1997 transition pains in 1980s, to the reinventing of the HKP in 1990s and finally to the discovery of politics in policing in 2000 and beyond.

After 34 years of service and on the eve of his retirement, Hong Kong Island Regional Commander, ACP Eric Leung Chi-bun has this parting comment on the latest chapter of HKP continuity and change, that is, transformation of law enforcement environment in Hong Kong from imposing (colonial) to negotiated order (democratic):[65]

> As an officer, we must always be politically neutral, but we should not be politically ignorant. Knowing what is happening in society and understanding the cause and effect of every incident is the key to an effective and fruitful negotiation with the public. It is so important when handling public processions and demonstrations.[66]

Transition from Colonial to Administrative Policing

Hong Kong is divided into three parts: Hong Kong Island, Kowloon Peninsula and the New Territories. The island of Hong Kong and peninsular of Kowloon were acquired by the British Crown in perpetuity from the Chinese Government by treaties (Treaty of Nanking, 29 August 1842 and Convention of Peking, October, 1860) after the Opium War. The New Territories were leased to the Crown for a term of 99 years by a second Convention of Peking entered on 9 June 1898. The term expired in 1997.[67]

In 1979, the soon-to-expire New Territories lease term caused uncertainties to Hong Kong trade and investment.

> The deadline for Sir Murray was not 1997 but sometime in the mid-1980s because of a practical issue: all individual land leases in the New Territories expired in June 1997. And since mortgages tended to be for 15 years, from 1982 on those mortgages would get shorter and shorter and there would be an inevitable impact on investment and on confidence in general.[68]

This precipitated an extended negotiation between the two governments (Governor Maclehose in 1979; Prime Minister Thatcher and Deng Xiaoping in 1982) on the future sovereignty and governance of Hong Kong. The British wanted to maintain the status quo; failing that to trade sovereignty for administration rights to Hong Kong. China wanted nothing short of reuniting with Hong Kong. China prevailed.

> The Government of the People's Republic of China declares that to recover the Hong Kong area (including Hong Kong Island, Kowloon and the New Territories, hereinafter referred to as Hong Kong) is the common aspiration of the entire Chinese people, and that it has decided to resume the exercise of sovereignty over Hong Kong with effect from 1 July 1997.[69]

On 27 May 1985, the British and Chinese governments signed a Joint Declaration providing for the return of Hong Kong sovereignty to China on 1 July 1997, as a Special Administrative Region (HKSAR). Under the Declaration, the HKSAR would be self-governing and enjoy a 'high degree of autonomy' under the 'one country two system' concept, with Hong Kong's prevailing lifestyle and all major institutions unchanged for a period of 50 years.[70]

In 1997, Hong Kong was decolonised, with sovereignty reverted to China. The HKP weathered the transition with determination and poise, keeping HK secure and safe, contrary to the expectations of pundits and admirers.[71] Since then, the HKP has secured the confidence of a vast majority of Hong Kong people and earned the praise of many foreign observers for its quiet efficiency and sure-footed effectiveness in enforcing law,[72] fighting crime, maintaining order, controlling crowds[73] and performing internal security functions. For all that it has achieved, administratively and operationally, it is known around the world as the 'Asian's Finest'.

III: Police and Policing

In this study, 'police' is referenced as an institution of political control in organisational form.

Conceptually, 'policing' approximates Foucault's idea of 'governability'.[74] It refers to the totality of what government[75] does in achieving control through discipline of self.[76] In practice and everyday life, 'policing' is the actualisation of 'government social control',[77] formally or informally, structurally or situationally, directly or indirectly, coercively or persuasively, physically and mentally. The ultimate objective of 'policing' is to achieve predictability[78] of conduct or conformity with government norms. The former is a 'governmentality'[79] project which Freud envisioned as 'governance rationality'[80] and the later a 'government' project which Austin called 'habit of obedience' to law enterprise.[81]

Historically speaking, long before there is a specialised, bureaucratised and legalised police agency by the state, there are policing functions performed by the people.[82]

In pre-state kinship society, there is no organised, specialised and institutionalised police. Policing as a social control function is diffused throughout the community. It is being performed by everyone, some more so than others. It is naturally conceived, historically developed, traditionally assigned and culturally enacted role sets, for example, parents over kids or teachers over students. In practice, policing is informal in nature and ubiquitous in kind. It is integrated with and embedded into everyday life. It is manifested as disapproval here and gossip there. Ostracism and expulsion, or social death, are the most serious sanctions.

Norm violations are treated as a denial of expectations—a challenge to good order and discipline—to be managed, not punished, with the deployment of applicable resources.[83] As such disorderly conducts are considered as inter-personal disputes, corresponding to one-to-one, one-to-many, many-to-many disputations. In face-to-face, intimate society, disputes between people signal violation of trust and breach of relationship. Dispute resolution requires mutually agreed upon settlement arrived at through negotiation, restitution and reintegration (what we now called reintegration shame process). The capacity to manage expectations and settle disputes by the group internally is called 'collective efficacy'.[84] When no mutuality of relationship between people exists, dispute settlement is not possible, and violence ensues.

With the emergence of a state comes a class-based and economically-determined formal social control system that is institutionalised, organised, specialised, bureaucratised and legalised, to be enforced by coercive agents sanctioned by the state, such as parents at home, teacher in school and police in the street.[85]

Policing in the old days and before the 'new police' is the internal administration of a state or states such that people are secured, have enough to eat and a healthy environment to live. In the past, people were policed (regulated) by various agencies, from tax authorities to health departments to educational organisation. In time, police have taken on more specialised functions, that of maintaining law and order.

With the discovery of the state, 'state police' and 'people's policing' co-existed uncomfortably, with the state police performing formal law enforcement (by physical force) and people's policing conducting social control (with moral persuasion or social pressure).[86] The theory and practice of 'dual track' policing appeared. In imperial China 'state' policing was conducted by the magistrate with the help of the local intelligentsia[87] and 'people' policing was performed with family control and clan rule, supported by the state.[88]

With the advent of late stage class-based capitalistic society, the ascension of state coercive control in the form of centralised and organised police, for example, London Metropolitan Police Act 1829 has come at the expense of communal social control in the hands of dispersed and natural policing agents such as village heads.

Philosophically[89] and theoretically,[90] the relationship between formal state 'policing' and informal people 'policing' is a competitive and contentious, not corroborative and harmonious, one, with both speaking the language of mutuality and each hiding the intent of exclusivity.[91] Communist police doctrine[92] and colonial policing paradigm[93] have made the dominance of state policing over people's policing explicit, unimpeachable and non-negotiable.

In the context of colonial Hong Kong, the challenge was in fusing of state—colonial policing with indigenous policing, disguised as a rule of law vs. sanction by custom project.[94] The solution is 'dual track' justice. 'Dual track' justice conjures up image of two systems of control. This runs counter to Karl Marx's police as instrumentality of state theory[95] or Max Weber's sovereignty as monopoly of coercive power thesis.[96] 'A theory of more or less government control' seeks to integrate state—colonial rule vs. people—indigenous control.

IV: Integrating State vs. People Policing

A Theory of More or Less Government Control

The 'theory of more or less governmental control'[97] provides a framework to delineate and elucidate the relative relationship and respective role between state and people policing. The theory postulates that in any society there can only be one duly constituted governmental authority with right to use force to control the people.[98] The theory also postulates that such right to control with force can be delegated, making such delegated social control agents, one or more, an integral part of 'governmental social control', in more or less way.

The theory explains under what circumstances and contingent on what conditions would a private social control agent become a state policing authority. Under this theory, 'dual track' justice (here policing) does not mean two separate and distinct control systems, working at cross purpose with each other, as is commonly assumed. 'Dual track' justice really means two complementary control systems serving one political master, that is, the political sovereign,[99] otherwise known as collaborative policing.

The difference between pure colonial policing and hybrid colonial—collaborative policing is that the former speaks to the dominating aspect of theoretical colonial rule and the later reveals the mutuality of colonial policing in real term.

The Myth of Unitary Government

People have long associated state and government with omnipotent, omnipresent, undivided, perpetual and absolute political control over an area (country) or people (association) or conditions (status).[100] This image of government is so entrenched that it is deemed self-evident and uncontroversial, such that even now, when we speak of government, we immediately identify any government, as 'the government' (much like 'the nature')—a superorganic body with a life force of its own.

Deconstructing the Myth of Unitary Government

Conceptually, the recognition of the political reality of fungible government *authority* (more or less) and divisible government *jurisdiction* (bigger or smaller) is necessary to ply open the conceptual black box of unitary governmental social control.[101] The debunking of the myth of government makes way for the proper construction of a sociological definition of law enforcement which recognises the *relativity* of governmental social control, that is, more or less governmental social control with multiplex law.

The deconstruction of the myth of government as a holistic and integrated unit can be achieved in two ways: internal deconstruction and external deconstruction.

Internal deconstruction. There is substantial division of labour within the government, particularly when government services are bureaucratised (Weber), horizontally and vertically. Thus, while the political sovereign makes policies at the top, it is up to the professional administrators to carry them out at the bottom. For example, a zero tolerance drug policy from the President of the United States has to be executed by the Department of Justice and implemented by the FBI. This is a vertical division of political vs. administrative labour, policy making vs. policy execution role. Even in medieval Europe, the sovereign in the body of the King could not be everywhere at the same time; there was substantial delegations of governing powers and responsibility to appointed officials, for example feudalism. The political sovereign then as now could also expand his span of control or fine tune his administration by creating coordinated horizontal specialised departments, for example establishing judicial vs. legislative, vs. executive branches of government. This is a horizontal division of labour.

External deconstruction. There may be competing sovereign powers (legal pluralism) in a state, each commanding the loyalty, allegiance, and obedience of a group of the citizen of the state in a point of time and over a geographic bottom. For example, a citizen of the United States is subjected to multiple jurisdictions at any point in time: county, state and federal law applies, depending on the time, place, matters, issues involved and a citizen of imperial China is subjected to overlapping social control as a son to his parents, as a member to his family, and as an associate to his professional guile.

The idea of *relative* government is not new in theory or practice, nor is the functional *distribution* of government powers to private parties a recent invention. Sovereign governments since antiquity have been willing to part with some or all of their powers to others (private parties included) to facilitate domestic rule, further their own interests or allow for foreign conquests. Let us now turn to examine the theoretical construct of relative—more or less—governmental social control.

The Theory of Relative Government or Governance

The idea of more or less governmental social control can be adequately captured by two concepts, that is, *delegation* of government social control rights to non-state parties (alternatively private or civil society) and government *sponsorship* of non-state social control measures.

More or Less Government by Delegation of Social Control Rights

More or less government in social control can result from the affirmative delegation of social control rights and responsibilities. Delegation of social control rights (and responsibilities)[102] is a re-redistribution of constitutional rights.[103] They are rights conferred upon or acknowledged to exist in a private party by the state to take part in governmental social control, for example family discipline or clan rule in traditional China, sheriff deputies in the wild West, and private policing in modern America.[104] Depending on the scope of delegated control, extent of delegated authority and degree of supervision over delegation, that is social control responsibilities (jurisdiction), powers, and accountability, the delegated party acts more or less like an autonomous government. The broader the delegation—more responsibilities, bigger power and lesser accountability—the more a private party behaves like an autonomous government. The more restricted the responsibilities, the lesser the powers, and the closer the supervision, the less a private party behaves like an autonomous government.

Social control authority is of three kinds. In decreasing order of authority, they are authority to define social norms, authority to establish social norms and authority to enforce social norms; corresponding to our Western notions of legal policy setting, law making and law execution (which encompasses in broad terms law enforcement, prosecution, adjudication and punishment).

More rights of social control means more power *sharing* with the dominant *political* authority and in turn power *domination* over subordinate

Table I.1 Governmental Delegation of Public Social Control (Policing) Authority[a]: An Analytical Framework

Theoretical Concepts	Operational Definition	Example (Ideal Type)
Government delegation of police powers	*Delegation of social control authority*[b]—the redistribution of government's constitutional power to use force to enforce the law and maintain (political or social) order	Constitution provisions enabling legislation
	Delegation of norm-defining authority—the extent to which the government delegates the authority to define normative expectation	Government social control philosophy Jurisprudential thought Law enforcement policy
	Delegation of norm-setting authority—the extent to which the government delegates the authority to set normative expectations	Police legislation Police adm. rules
	Delegation of norm-enforcing authority—the extent to which the government delegates the authority to seek compliance with the normative expectations	Policing

[a] The delegation of state authority thus can be analysed along three critical dimensions: scope of authority delegated (i.e., jurisdiction), nature of authority delegated (i.e., norm defining vs. norm setting vs. norm enforcing) and coercive authority delegated (fine vs. imprisonment vs. deadly force)

[b] The delegation of state authority necessarily implies the delegation of power to use force to secure the delegated authority. Thus *Black's Law Dictionary* defines authority as: 'Right to exercise powers; to implement and enforce laws; to exact obedience; to command; to judge… Often synonymous with power.' (Abridged Sixth Edition) (St. Paul, MN: West Publishing Co., 1991), p. 89.

social subjects. Power sharing is manifested in negotiation for control as give and take. Lesser power allows for negotiation over outcome. More power allows for negotiation over substantive law. Power parity allows for negotiation over procedure law. Power domination (from more to less) is manifested in the imposition of decision making norms, process rules as well as results.[105]

More or Less Government through Sponsorship of Private Social Control?[106]

More or less government in social control due to state sponsorship of private social control activities is state participation in private social control. State sponsorship means state countenance, approval, endorsement, promotion, sanction and/or enforcement.

Table I.2 Governmental Sponsorship of Private Social Control Measures: An Analytical Framework

Theoretical Concepts	Operational Definitions	Example (Ideal Type)
Government endorsement (passive—sponsorship)	*Endorsement*—the extent to which the government accepts and approves of the existence of private social control or self help	Neighbourhood watch[a]
	Countenance—the extent to which the government tolerates the existence of private social control	Vigilante, self-help[b]
	Approval—the extent to which the government tacitly acknowledges the existence of private social control	Guardian Angel[c]
	Endorsement—the extent to which the government affirmatively approves of the existence of private social control	Community watch
Government involvement (active—sponsorship)	Involvement—the extent to which the government actively participates in bringing about the private social control scheme	Family disciple over juvenile
	Promotion—the extent to which to which the governments takes steps to establish, maintain, expand or improve the private social control scheme	'Crime Stoppers'[d]
	Sanction—the degree to which the government made available legal sanctions and resources for private social control	Non-intervention in domestic abuse[e]
	Enforcement—the degree to which the government actively corroborates with private social control agency in enforcing private social control regiment	Family discipline over Juvenile[f]

[a] J. Garofalo and M. McLeod, The structure and operations of neighborhood watch programs in the United States, *Crime and Delinquency* 35: 326–344, 1989. (The police works closely with the residents by providing training, speakers and liaison.)

[b] J. B. Perry, Jr. and M.D. Pugh, Public support of guardian angels: Vigilante protection against crime, Toledo, Ohio, 1984, *Sociology and Social Research* 73: 129–131, 1989.

[c] See S. Pennell, C. Curtis, and J. Henderson, *Guardian Angels: An Assessment of Citizens Responses to Crime*, vol. 2, technical report to the NIJ (San Diego, CA: San Diego Association of Governments, 1985).

[d] D. P. Rosenbaum, A. Lurigio, and P. J. Lavrakas, Enhancing citizen participation and solving serious crime: A national evaluation of crime stoppers programs, *Crime and Delinquency* 35: 401–420, 1989.

[e] J. D. Hirschel, I. W. Hutchison, C. W. Dean, and A-M. Mills, Review essay on the Lae enforcement responses of spouse abuse: Past, present, and future, *Justice Quarterly* 9: 247–283, 1992. S. F. Berk and D. R. Loseke, 'Handling' family violence: Situational determinants of Police Arrest in Domestic Disturbances, *Law and Society Review* 317–348, 1981. (Traditionally, police often refused to make an arrest even when the victim appeared to be in danger and requested that the assailant be arrested.)

State sponsorship can be in the form of passive endorsement or active involvement corresponding to the two extremes of sponsorship, that is, from minimal endorsement to maximum involvement.

Passive endorsement includes countenance, approval or endorsement. Countenance is implied acceptance. It is demonstrated by knowledge of private social control and failure to act. Approval is expressed acceptance. It is demonstrated by formal acknowledgment of private social control. Endorsement is positive acceptance. It is acceptance plus quality assurance. It is demonstrated by certification or recommendation.

Active involvement includes promotion, sanction or enforcement. Promotion is active development. It is a step taken to facilitate the establishment, maintenance, growth, expansion and improvement of social control, including enabling legislation but short of making available legal sanctions for private control enforcement. It is measured by efforts contributing to development, for example making available material resources or lending needed advices. Sanctions are making available legal punishment for private social control. Enforcement is directly participating in social control activities through the exercise of state social control powers and institutional authorities.

State sponsorship can attach to various aspects of the control activities: origination, conceptualisation, construction, organisation, implementation, supervision, monitoring and control.

Discussion

According to the above-proposed 'more or less government' social control model, we can now begin to explicate and delineate how indigenous Chinese can exercise government social control powers, by delegation and with sponsorship from the British, over the Chinese people in the colony. In this way we can say, indigenous self-policing is an integral part and extension of colonial policing, with colonial police being more engaged in control policy and indigenous policing more involved with control operations. This makes the colonial policing vs. indigenous policing relationship more

[f] R. J. Lundman, R. E. Sykes, and J. P. Clark, Police control of juveniles: A replication, In: ed. R. J. Lundman, *Police Behavior: A Sociological Perspective* (N.Y.: Oxford University Press, 1980), pp. 130–151. State juvenile law allows the police to take into custody a child who is unruly, unmanageable or ungovernable. Georgia statue defines an unruly child as 'habitually disobedience, and ungovernable' and 'deserts his home or place of abode', *Ga. Code Ann.*, S 15-11-2(12) (1990). See also R. K. Schutt and D. Dannefer, *Detention Decisions in Juvenile Cases, JIN, JDs, and Gender, Law and Society Review* 22: 509–520, 1988. (A study of 2489 cases from N.J. found that six juvenile courts' detention decisions are very much influenced by family configuration and parents, cooperation.) Evidence suggests that where family discipline fails, the criminal justice system begins.

functionally distributed than heirarchically organised; that is, British colonial police holds the balance of control power (high policing) and indigenous social control agents part taking in peripheral control functions (low policing).[107]

V: Book Organisation

Overview

This is about 'Policing in Hong Kong: History and Reform'. Thematically, it is divided into two separate but mutually reinforcing parts, i.e., colonial policing (Chapters 1 to 4) and HKP reform (Chapters 5 to 9).

Chapter Outlines

'Introduction' states the focus of the study and briefly discusses the law and order situation in 1840s and origin of the HKP before proposing a framework to analyse and explicate the relationship between state police (top down) vs. people's policing (bottom up). It argues that in the end, policing in Hong Kong, before and after 1997, can best be understood as a (re)distribution of government powers and functions, along more or less government control lines. In doing so, it allows us, for the first time, to look at colonial vs. decolonised policing not as two distinct and discrete adversarial concept, institutional form and organisational practice, in opposite extremes, but as fungible and changeable practices, each accommodating the other as in the case of colonial Hong Kong, befitting the political, social and cultural circumstances of the day (1840s vs. 1950s vs. 1970s), or during critical moments of the time (1957, 1961 riots).

Chapter 1 'The Studying of Policing in Hong Kong' provides an overview of the development of police studies in Hong Kong, as an emerging field, since the 1990s. The chapter variously describes the state of the field and its key data sources, methodology and literature, before attending to its problems and prospect. This chapter is organised into four sections. First, 'Police Study in Hong Kong: A Brief History' traces the development of studying policing in Hong Kong. Second, it reviews some noteworthy Hong Kong police research and publications (Section II). Third, it discusses some of the difficulties, problems and issues in conducting research on policing in Hong Kong and into the HKP (Section III). The main problems are a lack of scholarly interest, data and capacity. Section IV is a 'Conclusion' to the chapter.

Chapter 2 is on 'Debating Colonial Policing'. The chapter defines as it deconstructs the 'colonial policing' as a construct and practice, first analytically than empirically. It observes that long before its demise in 1997, colonial policing in Hong Kong was not what it is made out to be; it has its own existential characteristics and behaviour. This chapter has four sections. Section I defines as it discusses the 'Concept of Colonial Policing' before raising the issue, stating the premises and defending the thesis that conventional idea of colonial policing ill fits grounded observation of policing in colonial Hong Kong. Section II 'Deconstructing Colonial Policing' problematises colonial policing as applied to Hong Kong. It adopts four premises in unpacking colonial policing in Hong Kong, that is, colonial policing takes many forms; colonial policing is a pluralistic enterprise; colonial policing is a collaborative effort, and finally, colonial policing is an existentially relative, not essentially absolute, phenomenon. It offers up the idea of 'people's policing' and 'collaborative policing' to debunk the myth that colonial policing is a one-sided (British) and unidirectional (top down) affairs. The contention here is 'it takes two to Tango'. Section III reveals the 'The True Nature of Colonial Policing' summaries as it discusses the implications of the findings while Section IV is a 'Conclusion' that takes stock of lessons learned.

Chapter 3 'Assessing Colonial Policing' provides an assessment of colonial policing, theoretically and empirically. The chapter proposes adopting a multifaceted cultural model instead of a dualistic conflict framework in analysing and assessing the HKP as a colonial force. It further observed that the use of Western legitimacy test to gauge citizen approval or acceptance of HKP is ill advised. Specifically, it argued that, in the context of Hong Kong and with the Chinese people, a process-based political legitimacy test is not as appropriate as a performance-based social acceptance test. In Chinese terms people's livelihood is more important than people's democratic rights in evaluating the sufficiency and acceptability of government. The chapter then discusses a first-of-its-kind assessment of the HKP by serving Chinese officers in 1960s. The chapter concludes with the call for more study of how Chinese culture impacts on colonial policing and vice versa.

Chapter 4 is on 'Policing with Hong Kong Characteristics'. This chapter explored the defining features of colonial policing in Hong Kong; addressing the question of what makes colonial policing in Hong Kong unique. The supposition is that policing of whatever persuasions—colonial, communist or democratic—takes on local colour when applied[108] and must be customised to be effective.[109]

This chapter is organised into six sections. Section I 'Colonial Policing as Policing Chinese' discusses how the Hong Kong colonial officials faced up to difficulties in policing the Chinese communities. Section II is on 'Colonial Policing as "Chinese" Policing'. It investigates into how Chinese policing Chinese works in philosophical, theoretical and practical terms. Section III 'Colonial Policing as "Self-Help" Policing' advances a 'Theory of Chinese Policing' (formally, 'State Police Powers as a Social Resource Theory' (STR) that looks at policing with the people and not the state's perspective. Section IV 'Colonial Policing as Policing Migrants' looks into the effect of residency status of control subject on policing strategy and tactics. This gives rise to the issue of relationship policing, from intimate to stranger. (Section V: 'Colonial Policing as Relationship Policing.') Recounting Mao Tse-tung's theory of contradiction, Section V postulates that the more intimate the relationship, the less the need for coercive policing. Section VI is a 'Conclusion'.

The beginning of the second part of the book is marked by Chapter 5: 'Police Reform Literature', which variously investigates into the nature, topologies, conduct, impact and assessment of police reform. Section II 'HKP Reform Inquiries' reports on a number of high-profile 'HKP Reform Inquires', from The Caldwell Commission (1858) to the Sir Alastair Blair-Kerr Commission (1973) to The Coopers & Lybrand Consultant Report (1993) to Hong Kong Audit Commission (1999) to Lan Kwai Fong Disaster Report (1993) to Hong Kong Audit Commission (1999). Section III is a brief 'Conclusion'.

Chapter 6 'Colonial Policing in Hong Kong' has five sections. 'Policing with Colonial Characteristics' (Section I) provides us with a list of defining characteristics of colonial policing: a macro picture. It allows us to look at (colonial) policing in Hong Kong in snap shots: historically, locally, culturally and politically. Section II 'Historical Developments of the HKP' provides an official view of how the HKP develops over time. This allows one to see how HKP sees its own development. 'Colonial Policing: Continuity and Change' (Section III) informs us on how it is like to police Hong Kong in different era, 1880s and 1920s, with three case studies of police careers, two in officer's voice. This allows us to see 'up close and personal' how the HKP and policing in Hong Kong have changed, over time. Section IV 'Police Reformers' discusses selected HKP senior officers who have contributed to HKP reform or leave a mark. It makes the point that police reform is as much about personality as it is about leadership. Section IV is a brief 'Conclusion'. All told, this chapter allows readers to see HKP reform in different light, making this an enrichment project.

Chapter 7 describes the 'Formation of Hong Kong Police in 1840s', to be compared with HKP reform in the 1950s, later. This chapter has seven sections. Section I is on 'Crimes in Hong Kong', which discusses crime and disorder problems in Hong Kong before and after British took possession in 1849. Section II is a discussion on 'Crime Control Measures' being deployed to fight crime, addressing the issue of why such discriminatory and harsh measures—'brute suppression and divisive seclusion'—were necessary. Section III 'Policing in Hong Kong' is about how Chief Magistrate, Captain William Caine, Hong Kong's first police chief fought crime and maintained order. Section IV 'The Legal Framework' describes and discusses the provisions, merits and impact of various police laws, from Police Force Ordinance to Gambling Ordinance to Native Chinese Peace Officer Ordinance, and others ('The legal framework') on policing and Chinese community. Coming to the last two sections, 'V. The Police Laws and Role of HKP' and 'VI. Police Leadership and Policing in Hong Kong', the chapter turns to discussing the role of HKP in enforcing the law (V) and the impact of police leadership on policing Hong Kong (VI). The chapter concludes (VII) with two major observations, namely, first, from its inception HKP as a colonial force functioned less as a legal agent than a moral and culture one. Second, in its formative years, the HKP was led by powerful men, strong characters and colourful personalities, as in the case of Cain, May and Deane. This observation allows us to conclude that personal leadership, not rules or system, drives and defines policing in Hong Kong, until well into the 1960s and 1969s.

Chapters 8 and 9 are devoted to 'Police Reform in 1950s' and should be read together, with the Chapter 8 explaining on data and method, and Chapter 9 devoted to presenting on major findings and conclusion.

Chapter 8 informs us of the data, context and framework of the research into 'Police Reform in 1950s'. In the main, it provides a foundation for Chapter 9 to build upon. Section I 'Research Data' describes data consulted and analysis framework adopted. Section II 'Context of Reform' is devoted to discussing a number of contexts helpful in understanding HKP reform in the 1950s, such as social, political, cultural and law and order context. Section III 'Direction of Reform' informs us as to where the HKP is heading with the reform, gathered from official pronouncements, for example Commissioner of Police or Governor of Hong Kong, or private opinion, for example, experts. After being informed of the 'Context' and 'Direction' of reform, we are ready to discuss 'Process and Methods of Reform' in 'Decolonisation' (Section IV) and 'Localisation' (Section V).

The final chapter, Chapter 9 'Hong Kong Police Reform in 1950s' building upon Chapter 8, investigates into HKP reform and development in the 1950s–1960s, as compared with HKP reform in 1840s and after 1990s. As a whole, this chapter makes three claims.

First, HKP modernisation reform began in 1950s. It was substantially completed by 1960s. There were two objectives to the reform, that is, making the HKP less colonial (a liberation process) and making it more modern (a professionalisation exercise).

Second, of all the HKP reforms, past and present, the 1950 HKP reform counts as one of the most ambitious and transformative. It created the HKP in its modern form, with brand new structure, different process and progressive ethos to match. It gave birth to the HKP as we know it today, as a legalised, modernised and communalised force, all be it in an embryotic state. The 1950 reform also laid the foundation and provided the platform for future police reform in Hong Kong, such as 1997 reform.

Third, the much-hyped 1997 HKP reform[110] was neither new nor innovative, in conception, process or outcome. It was built upon an old (though not worn) reform platform, with much continuity amidst gradual changes, from the past (1950).

This chapter is organised as follows. Section I is on 'Localisation'. It is followed by 'Legalisation' (Section II), 'Modernisation' (Section III), 'Communalisation' (Section IV), and 'Organisation' (Part V). Section VI is a 'Conclusion' summarising the lessons learned and contribution made by this book.

Endnotes

1. J. Carroll, *Edge of Empires: Chinese Elites and British Colonials in Hong Kong* (Cambridge, MA: Harvard University Press, 2005), p. 21. British Foreign Secretary Lord Palmerston; 'a barren island with hardly a house upon it.'
2. C. Elliot, Hong Kong's first administrator British Superintendent of Trade in China, as with Pottinger, first governor of Hong Kong, felt otherwise. He felt that Hong Kong was best fit to serve British interest in replacing Macau as the centre for economic, political, military and diplomatic activities in China. J. Carroll, *A Concise History of Hong Kong* (Lanham, MD: Rowman & Littlefield, 2007), p. 5.
3. T-W. Ngo, *Hong Kong's History: State and Society under Colonial Rule* (New York: Psychology Press, 1999), p. 1.
4. *Canton Register*, Vol. 12, No. 11–12th March 1839. http://www.houghton.idv.hk/?p=22
5. *Canton Register*, Vol. 9, No. 18–3rd May 1836. http://www.houghton.idv.hk/?p=22
6. Ibid.
7. J. Morris, *Hong Kong* (New York: Random House Digital, 1987).
8. Ibid.
9. Ibid.
10. *Canton Register*, Vol. 12, No. 3—15th January 1839. http://www.houghton.idv.hk/?p=22
11. I. Loader, Plural policing and democratic governance, *Social Legal Studies*, 9 (3): 323–345, 2000.
12. J. Osterhammel, *Colonialism: A Theoretical Overview* (Princeton, NJ: Markus Wiener Pub, 1997), p. viii.
13. J.-f. Tsai, *Hong Kong in Chinese History: Community and Social Unrest in the British Colony, 1842–1913* (New York: Columbia University Press, 1955).
14. K. C. Wong, Black's theory on the behavior of law revisited III: Law as more or less governmental social control, *International Journal of the Sociology of Law*, 26 (3): 365–392, 1998.
15. G. B. Endacott, *Government and People in Hong Kong, 1841–1962: A Constitutional History* (Hong Kong: Hong Kong University Press, 1964), p. 6.
16. E. H. Pritchard, The struggle for control of the China Trade during the eighteenth century, *Pacific Historical Review*, 3 (3): 280–285, 281, 1934.
17. Ibid.
18. Ibid.
19. J. L. Cranmer-Byng and A. Shepherd, A reconnaissance of Ma Wan and Lantao Islands in 1794, *Journal of the Royal Asiatic Society Hong Kong Branch*, 4: 105–125, 107, 1964.

20. E. H. Pritchard, The struggle for control of the China Trade during the eighteenth century, *Pacific Historical Review*, 3(3): 280–285, 281, 1934.
21. A. Robins, *Almost Liberal: The British Government of Hong Kong in the Middle Nineteenth Century*, 2003 ('Hong Kong serves as an interesting test case for the universalistic aspirations of British liberalism in the mid-1800s'). http://www.stanford.edu/group/journal/cgi-bin/wordpress/wp-content/uploads/2012/09/Robbins_Hum_2003.pdf
22. The pledge of free trade was repeated by Sir Pottinger, second governor of Hong Kong (10 August 1841 to 8 May 1844). E. J. Eitel. *Europe in China: The History of Hong Kong from the Beginning to the Year 1882* (London: Luzac & Co., 1895), p. 282 ('Eitel').
23. Eitel, pp. 1–2.
24. Captain Elliot tenure ended on 10 August 1841 and was replaced by Sir H. Pottinger as Plenipotentiary. He departed the Colony on 24 August 1841. Eitel, p. 177. He was later appointed the Counsel General of Texas on 1 June 1842 by Sir Robert Peel. Ibid. 265.
25. Eitel, p. 164.
26. Eitel, p. 164.
27. Much like the political settlement in returning Hong Kong to China, with 'One Country Two Systems' of governance. K.C. Wong, *One Country Two Systems: Cross-Border Crime between Hong Kong and China* (New Brunswick, NJ; London: Transaction Publishers, 2012), 'Chapter 7: Policy Analysis', pp. 165–193.
28. In 1987, the author was doing business—setting up a fish farm—in China. The author was arrested and detained for Chinese Public Security Officers (police) for not registering at a hotel. The author asked for intervention of the U.S. government on account of his U.S. citizenship. The lead Pubic Security officer used the above to describe the author's national status.
29. K. C. Wong, *One Country Two Systems: Cross-Border Crime between Hong Kong and China* (New Brunswick, NJ: Transaction Publishers, 2012).
30. Eitel, p. 183.
31. Eitel, p. 185.
32. Ibid. Barracks were erected on Cantonment Hill, Stanley and Aberdeen.
33. Eitel, p. 182.
34. R. Hughes, *Borrowed Place, Borrowed Time: Hong Kong and Its Many Faces* (London: Andre Deutsch Ltd, 1976).
35. See *Chinese Repository*, Vol., V.–August, 1936–No. 4: European periodicals beyond Ganges—*Canton Register*. First published in Canton on 8 November 1827 and printed every two weeks, it was one of China's first English-language newspapers. 'The free traders appear to cherish high hopes of their claims and privileges. Under their auspices, a free press is already maintained at Canton. They will regard themselves as the depositories of the true principles of British commerce', Charles Grant *Canton Register*, 8, 1835.
36. *Canton Register*, Vol. 9, No. 18—3rd May 1836.
37. Ibid.
38. *Canton Register*, Vol. 15, No. 13—29th March 1842.
39. *Canton Register*, Vol. 14, No. 34—24th August 1841.
40. *Friend of China* 2.6.42 edition.

41. Chapter 8: W. Cain, In: pp. 60–88. G. B. Endacott, *A Biographical Sketch-Book of Early Hong Kong* (Hong Kong: Hong Kong University Press, 2005). William Caine was born in 1798. He lived his life with the army since being a child. He aspired to be an officer when young. He was commissioned in 1841 and was known for his efficiency and devotion to duty. He came to China as part of an expeditionary force. He landed the job as Chief Magistrate, in part because he was a member of the Military Commission of Control at Chusan island and Chief Magistrate there (p. 60).
42. Ibid., p. 61.
43. *Friend of China* 5.5.42 edition.
44. R. Fortune, *Three Years' Wanderings in the Northern Provinces of China, Including a Visit to the Tea, Silk, and Cotton Countries* (London: John Murray, 1847), pp. 27–29.
45. *Friend of China,* 9.6.42 edition.
46. *Friend of China,* 16.6.42 edition.
47. *Friend of China,* 23.6.42 edition.
48. *Canton Register,* Vol. 15, No. 26, 28th June 1842.
49. *Friend of China,* 21.7.42 edition.
50. Hence, the Chinese name for rates 'Chai. Heung' (差餉) which literally mean 'official rate'. HKP was known as 香港差役 (Hong Kong officials). https://zh.wikipedia.org/wiki/%E5%B7%AE%E9%A4%89
51. *Friend of China,* 31.8.43 edition.
52. Chapter 12: C. B. Hiller, In: pp. 84–88. G. B. Endacott, *A Biographical Sketch-Book of Early Hong Kong* (Hong Kong: Hong Kong University Press, 2005).
53. *Canton Register,* Vol. 15, No. 22, 31st May 1842.
54. *Friend of China,* 3.8.43 edition.
55. Lieutenant-Colonel J.S. Malcolm to Secretary Lord Stanley, letter of 22 December 1843 (Source: C0129/4).
56. 'The British Bobby' Hong Kong Police Ancestor September 2, 2012. http://hongkongpoliceancestors.blogspot.com/2012/09/the-bristol-bobbies.html
57. Chapter 15: 'Charles May', In: pp. 100—104, G. B. Endacott with new introduction by John M. Carroll, *Biographical Sketch-Book of Early Hong Kong* (Hong Kong: Hong Kong University Press, 2005).
58. F. C. Ming, *Reluctant Heroes: Rickshaw Pullers in Hong Kong and Canton, 1874–1954* (Hong Kong: Hong Kong University Press, 2005).
59. P. Snow, *The Fall of Hong Kong: Britain, China and the Japanese Occupation* (New Haven, CT: Yale University Press, 2005).
60. N. Miller, The localization of the Hong Kong police force, 1842–1947, *The Journal of Imperial and Commonwealth History,* 13 (3): 1990.
61. S. H. Lo, *Policing and Policy Transfer: Is Mainland China Learning from Hong Kong? Hong Kong Institute of Education.* Center for Government and Citizenship, 2011.
62. K. Fang, Britain's finest: The Royal Hong Kong police. In: *Antoinette Burton, After the Imperial Turn: Thinking with and through the Nation* (Durham, NC: Duke University Press, 2003), pp. 293–307.
63. Parliamentary Papers, House of Commons and Command, Vol. 48 (London: Her Majesty's Stationery Office, 1860). http://books.google.com/books?id

=cvkSAAAAYAAJ&dq=Hong+Kong+Police,+Caldwell+Inquiry&source=gbs_navlinks_s

64. Chapter 13: T. C. Anstey, In: pp. 89–99. G. B. Endacott with new introduction by J. M. Carroll, *Biographical Sketch-Book of Early Hong Kong* (Hong Kong: Hong Kong University Press, 2005), pp. 93–m94. See a Vindication of the Character of the Undersigned from the Aspersions of Mr. T. Chisholm Anstey, Ex-attorney General of Hong Kong as Contained in His Charges, His Pamphlet, and His Letter to the Secretary of State for the Colonies (1860).
65. 'Eric's words of wisdom,' *OffBeat* Issue 705, 20 June to 3 July 2001.
66. Ibid.
67. K. Hopkins (ed.), *Hong Kong: The Industrial Colony* (Hong Kong: Oxford University Press, 1971), p. 339.
68. F. Ching, Looking back: How London and Beijing decided the fact of Hong Kong, *Hong Kong Journal Online*. 10 April 2010. http://www.hkjournal.org/archive/2010_summer/2.htm
69. Article 1, Joint Declaration of the Government of the United Kingdom of Great Britain and Northern Ireland and the Government of the People's Republic of China on the Question of Hong Kong (Beijing, 19 December 1984).
70. 'Paragraph 3(12) of the Joint Declaration provides that the basic policies of the People Republic of China (PRC) regarding Hong Kong will be stipulated in a Basic Law of the Hong Kong Special Administrative Region promulgated by the National People's Congress (NPC) of the PRC, and will remain unchanged for 50 years'. See generally 'Constitution and Administration', in *Hong Kong 1989: A Review of 1988* (Hong Kong: Government Printing Office, 1989), especially p. 52.
71. E. Gargan, 'Hong Kong fears unraveling of rule of law,' *New York Times*, 7 May 1997.
72. 'Sorry out of question as Ho lauds enforcing rule of law', *The Standard*, 1 April 2011. (Seventy percent of people support Hong Kong's police to enforce the law. Only 20% like hurling bananas and occupying the street. The street belongs to Hong Kong people'.)
73. 'How the Hong Kong Police Created the Conditions for the People to Criticize the Government'. (Yang Hengjun's blog), 14 March 2010. http://www.zonaeuropa.com/20100315_1.htm
74. M. Foucault, *Naissance de la biopolitique. Cours au Collège de France. 1978–1979* (Paris: Gallimard/Seuil, 2004). Victor Tadros, 'Between Governance and Discipline: The Law and Michel Foucault', *Oxford Journal of Legal Studies*, 18 (1): 75–103, 1998.
75. Foucault defines government as conduct, more precisely as 'conduct of conduct'.
76. In Imperial China, 'governmentality' is actualised through 'self-cultivation'. Fabian Heubel (July 30–6 August 2008). 'Foucault in Chinese: Methodological Reflections on a Transcultural Philosophy of Cultivation', presented at the World Congress of Philosophy (Seoul, Korea), as reinforced by 'Confucianization of Law'. See K. C. Wong, 'Confucianization of Law: A Study of Speech Crime Prosecution in China', *Murdoch University Electronic Journal of Law*, 2004. http://www.austlii.edu.au/au/journals/MurUEJL/2004/24.html
77. D. Black, *Behavior of Law*, 1976.

78. As used here 'predictability of conduct' recalls 'predictive policing' but they are not the same idea. While both speak to predicting criminality, the former is about reducing probability of victimisation, making society orderly, and the later is about preventing the potentiality of offending, holding criminal responsible. The former is present oriented, the later is future focused, that is, 'Minority Report' revisited. Z. Friend, 'Predictive policing: Using technology to reduce crime', *FBI Law Enforcement Bulletin* (April 2013). http://www.fbi.gov/stats-services/publications/law-enforcement-bulletin/2013/April/predictive-policing-using-technology-to-reduce-crime
79. C. Lemert, Foucault, Govern mentality, and critique, 2002. http://www.andosciasociology.net/resources/Foucault$2C+Governmentality$2C+and+Critique+IV-2.pdf
80. M. R. Dutton, *Policing and Punishment in China: From Patriarchy to the People* (London and New York: Cambridge University Press, 1992).
81. J. Austin (1790–1859), *The Province of Jurisprudence Determined*, (London: John Murray, 1832).
82. P. Rawlings, Policing before the police, In: T. Newburn (ed.), *Handbook of Policing*, 2nd edition (Cullompton, Devon: Willan Publishing, 2008).
83. K. C. Wong, State police power as a social resource theory. See Chapter 10 to D. Wisler, I. D. Onwudiwe, *Community Policing: International Patterns and Comparative Perspectives* (Boca Raton, FL: CRC Press, 2013), pp. 215–257.
84. S. Ansari, Social capital and collective efficacy: Resource and operating tools of community social control, *Journal of Theoretical and Philosophical Criminology*, 5 (2): 75–94, 2013.
85. C. D. Robinson and R. Scaglion, The origin and evolution of the police function in society: Notes towards a theory, *Law & Society Review*, 21 (1): 1987, 109–154.
86. E. A. Ross, *Social Control: Control A Survey of the Foundations of Order* (Piscataway, NJ: Transaction Publishers, 2009) (1901).
87. Byron Brenan, The office of district magistrate in China, Shanghai Mercury Office, 1899.
88. H-C. W. Liu, *The Traditional Chinese Clan Rules* (June 1959).
89. 'Kant's Social and Political Philosophy' *Stanford Encyclopedia of Philosophy* (SEP). http://plato.stanford.edu/about.html
90. J. C. Turner, Explaining the nature of power: A three-process theory, *European Journal of Social Psychology*, 35: 1–22, 2006.
91. D. H. Bayley and C. D. Shearing, The future of policing, *Law & Society Review*, 30 (3): 585–606, 1996. (The monopoly of public police has been broken effectively since 1980 (p. 586), in favour of plurality of control and commodification in risk management, led by private policing and self-help policing (587). For a rejoinder, see T. Jones and T. Newburn, The transformation of policing? Understanding current trends *in policing* systems, *British Journal of Criminology*, 42 (1): 129–146, 2002 (Acknowledging the trend but disputing the magnitude and extent of global transformation. The 'transformation thesis' (Cohen and Shearing) based in large part on North American experience is not replicated in other parts of the world where tradition policing still dominates.
92. Chapter 2, K. C. Wong, *Policing in China: History and Reform* (New York: Peter Lang, 2009). (Doctrinally, Communist China conceived police as an instrumentality of the state: 'Police is a historical phenomenon. It originates with the state

and disappears with the state. The basic characteristic (*benzhi teshi*) of police is an important instrumentality of the state to effectuate dictatorship (*guojia zhuanzheng gongju*)' Definition of 'Jingcha' *Chinese Public Security Encyclopedia* (1989).

93. See 'Policing in Hong Kong as colonial policing', *infra*.
94. T-W. Ngo (ed.), *Hong Kong's History: State and Society under Colonial Rule* (New York: Routledge, 11 September 2002), p. 55.
95. Ernest Mandel, Marxist theory of the state (October 1969).
96. *Politics as a Vocation* (1919).
97. K. C. Wong, 'Black's theory on the behavior of law revisited III: Law as more or less governmental social control, *International Journal of the Sociology of Law*, 26 (3): 365–392, 1998.
98. P. Dan, 'Sovereignty', *The Stanford Encyclopedia of Philosophy* (Summer 2010 Edition), Edward N. Zalta (ed.). http://plato.stanford.edu/archives/sum2010/entries/sovereignty/.
99. 'A theory of more or less government control' is anticipated by Weber to the extent that Weber makes allowance for delegation of state sovereign authority to use violence.
100. D'Entreves observes that the 'intrinsic logic of sovereignty' speaks to its perpetuity, absoluteness, unity, indivisibility and the highest or ultimate power of law making. See D'Entreves, A. Passerin, *The Nation of the State* (Oxford: Clarendon Press, 1967), Ch. 5. See also J. Bodin: 'Majesty or sovereignty is the most high, absolute, and perpetual power over the citizens and subjects in a commonweal.' Quotes by Alexander Passerin D'Entreves from Richard Knolles English translation of Bodin's *Les Six Livres de la Republique* (1st ed., 1956): McRae, K. D. (ed.), *The Six Books of a Commonweale* (1606), (facsimile reprint, Harvard University Press, 1962). See also *Daniel J. Elazar Exploring Federalism* (Tuscalossa & London: University of Alabama Press, 1987) (In the Old World and traditional Europe, the state as a sovereign is undividable and holds all authority.), p. 11.
101. Not surprisingly, it takes the pragmatic and resourceful politicians to penetrate the 'black hole' that is the state. In 1983, the People's Republic of China (PRC), in order to achieve the political integration of Taiwan, is willing to give Taiwan a high degree of autonomy as a special administrative region (ASR) of the PRC, including the powers to make domestic law and the command of its army. See the policy of 'one country, two system' as advocated by Deng in his speeches of 26 June 1983, 22 October 1984, 31 October 1984, 2 September 1986, 16 May 1989, 15 September 1990 in *The Selected Works of Deng Xiaoping* (Beijing: Foreign Language Press, 1993). See also discussion in Lo Chi Kin, 'Relations across the Taiwan Straits in *China Review*' (Hong Kong: Chinese University Press, 1993), Ch. 4.
102. It is often assumed that the delegation of social control rights comes with them social control responsibilities or vice versa. This need not be the case. The delegation of social control rights and imposition of social control responsibilities are two entirely different governmental delegations. Take the case of children's discipline and control as an example. Until very recently and under the common law, the parents were given the rights and responsibilities to discipline and otherwise control the children. Lately, the parental rights to discipline has been interfered with, for example, law against physical punishment, and the

opportunity to control has been diminished, for example, law restricting (defining) parents' rights on abortion consent. However, increasingly the parents are being held civilly and criminally responsible for their children's misconduct or illegal acts. The theoretical question which needs to be addressed at some point is how the delegation of social control rights and delegation of social control responsibilities, separately or together, affects the behaviour of law. For example, what is the sociological significance on the behaviour of law (exercising of parental discipline and control) of imposing on the parents a set of children's disciplinary responsibilities without giving the parents the right to discipline? Can we expect more or less discipline? How might such discipline be distributed in the social space?

103. Constitutional rights are also called fundamental, basic and organic rights. As used here, they are rights pertaining to the structure of government, particularly the distribution of powers of government with respect to the people. If we conceived of the government being vested with the rights and responsibilities to enforce law, that is, secure governmental social control, to start with, then any delegation of those rights and responsibilities, for example, to make (legislative), enforce (executive) and interpret law (judicial) amounts to a redistribution.
104. Private social control is converted into governmental social control in two ways, that is, through government sponsorship of private social control or government delegation of public social control rights. In the first case, the government lends its support to what essentially is a private activity. In the later case, the government allows the private party to be deputised as state social control agent. Where government participation ends, government delegation begins.
105. In political and practical terms, the debate is between a rival (horizontal) relationship or dominant (vertical–central vs. local) relationship. In the rival case, the terms of engagement is negotiated. In the dominant case, the terms of engagement are dictated. My insight is drawn in part from recent political settlement talks over the return of Hong Kong to China, the absentee sovereign, after 1997 and the re-integration of Taiwan with China the motherland, in the distant (near?) future. A 'One country—two system' model is proposed for Hong Kong. A 'One county—two region' is proposed for Taiwan. Terms for the return of Hong Kong to the PRC are dictated. Terms for the reintegration of Taiwan with the PRC are negotiated. See Byron Weng, 'Sovereign Split—Towards a Theory of Divided Nation', in *Professorial Inaugural Lecture Series 20* (Chinese University of Hong Kong, 1995), pp. 21–37, especially 23–33.
106. The development of this concept is necessary for studying the Confucianisation of Qing law.
107. J.-P. Brodeur, 'High policing and low policing: Remarks about the policing of political activities', *Social Problems*, 30 (5): 507–20, 1983.
108. C. M. Christensen & Raynor, Why hard-nosed executives should care about management theory, *Harvard Business Review*, 81 (9): 66–74, 2003.
109. D. Jianzhong, On several problems in legal transplantation, *Journal of Politics and Law*, 2 (3): 107–109, September, 2009.

110. P. Tam, *From Enforcement to Service Delivery: A Study of Strategic Change in the Hong Kong Police Force*. MPA dissertation, Hong Kong University, 2012. As a HKP officer, Tam observed the successful transformation of HKP from a law enforcement agency to a service organisation with the arrival of New Public Management against the backdrop of 1997. The author did not place HKP reform in a historical context. He used limited contemporary sources, such as Lo and Cheuk on community policing to make his case.

I

Colonial Policing with Chinese Characteristics

Study of Policing in Hong Kong

1

Introduction

The scholarly study and research of policing has been an uphill battle[1] worldwide. Hong Kong is no exception. To many police officers, policing is a vocation,[2] better learned from peers, on the job and in the street rather than through scholars, from books and at the library.[3] From the police perspective, the study and teaching of policing is best left to 'insiders' and 'experts'. Here is a case in point:

At one of the author's presentations at the University of Hong Kong (HKU) 'Police Forum' (3 September 2011), a young Ph.D. student related his experience with teaching police officers. A number of HKP officers challenged the Ph.D. student's understanding of the HKP. They claimed the young teacher lacked personal experience and access to implicit knowledge of how policing works in practice.

On another occasion, when this author was making an invited presentation at a professional development seminar in the HKP Police College on 16 October 2009, a police commissioner in the audience openly and pointedly raised issues with the relevancy and practicality of 'academic' approach to community policing in Hong Kong, without knowing that much of the presentation was drawn from personal street experience and feedback from police officers across the world.

Both encounters point to the same problem: there is a wide gap between academic and professional policing within the HKP. Some note that the gap is shortening (personal discussion with Deputy Director, Hong Kong Police College, 3 September 2011), many others observe that it is not getting narrower (many discussions with the author's HKP students), and more than a few think that it is widening (retired CSP, former head Police Cadet School, 1–2 September 2011). All agree that the best hope for narrowing the gap is for police scholars and policing practitioners to meet and discuss more,[4] with scholars accepting practitioners' experience-based implicit knowledge and practitioners deferring to scholars' research based on scientific process. The best is, of course, an integration of both by way of practitioner-scholar or scholar-practitioner approach to knowledge generation and distribution.[5]

Focus and Organisation

This chapter investigates into police study and research as an emerging discipline in Hong Kong. This study has two objectives, that is, to provide a brief account of police study and research development in Hong Kong on the way to proposing a new way of studying of the HKP, that is, 'inside out–bottom up' approach.[6]

This chapter comprises four sections. The first section 'Police Study in Hong Kong: A Brief History' traces the development of studying policing in Hong Kong. The second section reviews some noteworthy research and publications about the HKP. The third section discusses some of the difficulties, problems and issues in conducting research on policing in Hong Kong and into the HKP. The main problems are a lack of scholarly interest, data and capacity. The fourth section is a 'Conclusion' to the chapter. It observes that the HKP practised 'dual track' policing in the colonial days (1841 to the 1950s). Thus, there are two realities to policing in Hong Kong, that is, top down—colonial and professional—policing world versus bottom up—Chinese policing and street policing—world, where more is known about the former than the latter. It is argued in this book that for the purpose of understanding colonial policing in Hong Kong, it is the latter that is more important. Such a knowledge gap can be narrowed with 'inside out and bottom up research'.

I: Police Study in Hong Kong: A Brief History

Introduction

In Hong Kong, policing research and study still lags far behind other traditional academic disciplines, such as law, political science, sociology or criminology.[7] The first-ever independent study of the HKP was the official investigation[8] into the Attorney General Anstey[9] versus Registrar General Caldwell affair,[10] in 1858, with the former charging the latter with corruption in office.[11]

The second self-study of the HKP was mounted in 1877, this time over the need for HKP reform.

In August 1992, and in anticipation of 1997 reversion of political sovereignty, the Law Reform Commission (LRC) investigated into police powers of stop, search, arrest and detention in Hong Kong leading to the publication of 'Report on Arrest'. The report recommended the adoption of the U.K. Police and Criminal Evidence Act 1984 (PACE) to rein in abuse of police powers. The implementation of the LRC report was left to an interdepartmental working group chaired by the Security Branch (SB) consisting of all the disciplinary forces, ICAC and Legal Department that finally recommended for the implementation of 30 of the 60 LRC recommendations, and another 21 accepted in principle. The working group report was first entertained by the Hong Kong Legislative Council in November 2006 to act on.[12]

The latest independent review of the HKP was conducted by the consulting firm Coopers & Lybrand on the eve of 1997 over the restructuring of the HKP (October 1992–March 1993). The purpose of the study was to conduct a systematic and comprehensive review of the HKP management structure and make necessary preparation for the transfer of power on 1 July 1997.[13] The report was completed in March 1993. It made 116 recommendations. It concluded that 'The Force already has a powerful culture[14] and the question is whether this culture is appropriate to support and under pin the changes that are needed in order to continue to provide a high quality service to the public'.[15] In 1 April 1994, the HKP Quality Service Wing was established to reform the HKP. After that the investigation of the HKP started to blossom, all in fits and starts.

As illustrated, a representative sample of scientific studies of the HKP and policing in Hong Kong from 1990 to 2012 includes the following:

1990: W. K. Che, The Triad Societies in Hong Kong in the 1990's, *13 Police Studies: The International Review of Police Development* 13: 151–154, 1990. This article, in four sections, describes the origin and policy implications of triad societies in Hong Kong. The research is based on observations, interviews and case data by the author as an 'investigator' (of ICAC). Its basic premise is that triad societies are losing all of its original purpose (anti-foreignism, first against Qing, then British), values (blood brotherhood, mutual aid), structure (centralised leadership, strict discipline) and process (ceremonies), and morphed in two directions. The more powerful groups became organised crime syndicates. The lesser street gangs claimed the allegiances of the disaffected youths. As to policy, the author observed that the Hong Kong government was moving towards dealing with transformed triads as organised criminals and emerging youth gangs with education (by former reformed triad members) and rehabilitations (p. 153).

1991: M. S. Gaylord and J. F. Galliher, Riding the underground dragon—Crime control and public order on Hong Kong's mass transit railway, *British Journal of Criminology*, 31 (1): 15–26, 1991. 'This study examines the causes of the MTR's remarkable success in providing to its patrons a nearly crime-free transportation system' (p. 17). The authors conducted research through 5 months of field research, that is, riding on MTR and talking to people. The ability of the HKP to effectively patrol the long MTR lines and control massive MTR passengers depends less on the HKP as on environmental engineering, technology support, shared responsibilities with the MTR staff and law-abiding culture and collective discipline of the HK people.

1993: I. Dobinson, Pinning a tail on the dragon: The Chinese and the international heroin trade, *Crime & Delinquency* 39 (3): 373–385, 1993. The author investigated the organisation, power, reach and influence of Hong Kong organised criminals and triad societies in international (South East Asia) heroin trade mainly through interviews with police officials—HKP, ICAC, HKAG, DEA (p. 373) and two case studies (378–381), with few original data and limited secondary literature sources, and found that such claims of connection, dominance and influences are much inflated. The observation here is not that the HKP do not know what they are doing, it is just that their professional capacity and self-confidence (on matters as important as organised crime and drug trades) are subject to second guessing by foreign experts, such as FBI. One would expect more from the 'Asia's Finest'.

1994: M. S. Gaylord and H. Traver, *Introduction to the Hong Kong Criminal Justice System* (Hong Kong: Hong Kong University Press, 1994).[16] Chapter 3 focusses on 'The Royal Hong Kong Police'. It offers a descriptive account of the RHKP based on working knowledge rather than on extensive research. It is meant to be an informational and instructional piece for novices and students, rather than an analytical and critical piece for researchers and scholars. The chapter can still be considered a rare find of that period.

1998–1999: B. Tully, Applied and forensic psychological contributions to policing and expert witness work: Collaboration and conflict. *International Journal of Police Science Management*, 1: 192, 1998–1999. Bryan Tully was the head of the RHKP psychology unit when it was first set up in the 1980s. In the article, he related many instances where a psychologist was able to help the HKP, including the use of cognitive interviews to solve crime (p. 192). His services ranged from diffusing police complaints by understanding complainants' true motives, such as paranoia (p. 192) to offering counselling for distressed officers (p. 198). The article shows that the HKP is a progressive force. It has long relied on scientists and expertise to investigate crimes and counsel staff.

2006: S. L. Shiu-hing, The politics of policing the anti-WTO protests in Hong Kong, *Asian Journal of Political Science*, 14(2): 140–162, 2006. The 2005 anti-World Trade Organization (WTO) protestors versus HKP was explained with David Waddington's flashpoint model. This article shows that other factors at the structural, political/ideological, cultural, contextual and situational levels were at play, creating an environment conducive to violence. Waddington's model provides a useful framework for us to comprehend the interactional dynamics of the anti-WTO protests in Hong Kong. However, it has neglected the possibility of an interactive bond between protestors and the public. The contextual uniqueness of forging a dynamic relationship between protestors and the public can enrich Waddington's analytical framework.

2012: M. Chiu, Development and impacts of a new performance management system in the Hong Kong police force, *Policing: An International Journal of Police Strategies & Management* 35 (3): 468–490, 2012. 'The purpose of this paper is to outline the development and implementation of the "values-driven competency-based performance management system" (VDCBPMS) and report the findings of a study that aims to examine the effect of the new PMS on officers of the Hong Kong Police Force. …The research focuses on the officers' perceptions and attitudes resulting from the intervention and hypothesises that the new system will increase their organisational [sic] commitment and job satisfaction, job-effort and value alignment with the Force, as well as overall performance of the Force through enhanced performance of individual officers. The study employs a staff survey and interviews with a cross section of officers in different ranks to examine the impact on them of VDCBPMS'.

Until very recently, no tertiary institution in Hong Kong offered police studies as a recognised degree subject. There was no demand for it. Few Hong Kong people, especially the university-bound ones, are attracted to policing as a career. Nor does the HKP require a university degree for being a police officer and promotion to high ranks.[17] There is also little interest in studying policing because it is felt that there is little to study, and still less utility to studying. Simply, police studies' degree is not a 'real' degree. Those who want to study policing have to go abroad.[18]

In 1980, the HKP started a far-sighted programme of sending promising officers to study at local universities, for example, Department of Sociology or School of Law at University of Hong Kong, and Department of Government and Public Administration at Chinese University of Hong Kong,[19] to groom future police managers and as an incentive for good performance. The programme was discontinued because many officers, especially those in law, resigned soon after they finished their university studies or were professionally qualified.

In the early 1980s, a group of criminal justice professionals, including police officers, gathered together informally at HKU to discuss criminal justice issues, including policing.[20] The group later evolved into the Hong Kong Society of Criminology in 1982 and lasts to this day.[21] The objectives of the society include the following:

- To promote the discussion and dissemination of the latest international and local research on topics related to crime, law enforcement and criminal justice
- To promote awareness of the issues and problems involved in the control of crime and the administration of justice
- To encourage the discussion of ideas and practices that will assist in crime prevention, improve services to victims and the treatment of offenders

- To promote the role of criminology and develop the use of scientific approaches to the study of crime, victims, offenders and crime suppression in Hong Kong and neighbouring jurisdictions[22]

In the mid-1980s, a British university started to offer a distant learning undergraduate degree in policing, mainly for police officers. It was very popular, but was discontinued for lack of qualified local tutors.[23] The teaching materials were all based on the U.K. modules. No local instructional materials were developed or made available.

In 1996, the Open University of Hong Kong took the leadership to aggressively develop an undergraduate programme in police studies, with infusion of ample funds and resources, since the university catered to non-traditional students and working professionals, like the police and other disciplinary forces.[24] At the time, there was also a growing demand for more professional education in the HKP, as part of a lifelong learning initiative. It was the first and only police studies programme at a local university, albeit a non-traditional one, at that time. It has since been very well received, especially as a career-building step.[25] One of the problems then was with the mixing of police officers of all ranks, inhibiting free exchanges in class and project collaboration outside school.

At about the same time, the School of Continuing Education of the Chinese University of Hong Kong also started to develop its own diploma courses in policing and security studies, with a view of offering undergraduate degrees in the not too distant future.[26]

In September 2000, Hong Kong University offered the first undergraduate criminal justice degree programme in Hong Kong. It attracted mostly in-service disciplinary officers from all fields—prison, customs, immigration and police.[27]

Later, the City University of Hong Kong developed an undergraduate criminology programme that dedicated itself to applied research, within the Department of Applied Social Science. 'Graduates may further their study in the more specialised fields by applying to PGD in Psychology, MSSc in Counseling, MSSc in Applied Sociology, MPhil or PhD in Criminology, offered by the department'.

For graduate education in policing, today, the Department of Sociology (Criminology) at University of Hong Kong offers one of the first graduate programmes in criminology at the masters and Ph.D. level. Many police graduate students also choose to study at the Department of Politics and Government Administration for an MPA, because of its administrative and policy orientation best fitting police managers' needs.[28]

The Masters' Program in Criminology at the University of Hong Kong was started in 1986:

> The programme consists of four core courses—Criminal Justice: Process and Politics; Methods of Research for Criminology; Social Theory and Criminology; and Theoretical Criminology—which aim to equip students with a strong practical and theoretical foundation in sociological criminology. In addition, students choose four elective subjects, which encompass the range of expertise in the Department. Courses currently offered include Crime and Deviance in PR China; White Collar and Corporate Crime; Cultural Criminology; Youth and Delinquency; Drugs and Crime; Policing: An International Perspective; Crime and Media; Gender and Crime. Full-time students will also be required to complete a dissertation, in which student learning will be consolidated and developed in an original field project.[29]

The Master in Criminology programme is geared towards police officers and other disciplinary services, for example, ICAC, custom and immigration. When it was first launched, it was oversubscribed with a ratio of 10 to 1, most of them police officers. HKP officers also pursue police-related studies in the MPA stream, offered by HKU.

HKU offered a newly minted Bachelor in Criminal Justice in September 2000 with 67 students enrolling; nearly all of them were police officers.

At a sub-degree level, the Police Study Diploma offered by the School of Continuing Education, Chinese University of Hong Kong is specifically designed to cater to the needs of HKP officers at a lower rank, for example, some courses in the curriculum teach very rudimentary police skills, for example, English and first aid. It is also in heavy demand and oversubscribed, given the transformation of the HKP, in expectation, lifestyle and culture, for example, lifelong learning. The teachers are mostly retired or serving police officers.

Until recently, instructional materials on criminal justice and policing were imported. These materials were taken from Portsmouth University, Leicester University and Hull University, England, which were active in criminal justice and security studies since the 1980s and produced content from experiences within the United Kingdom. Substantively, there are thus few research-based instructional materials with local content and local context.[30] More significantly, there is little attempt to conduct research or develop theory of policing based on Chinese society.[31]

In 2002, this author organised the first international police conference in Hong Kong, the third Asian Association Police Studies (AAPS) as the president of the AAPS. The thematic title of the 2002 AAPS conference—'Asian Policing in the 21st Century'—focussed attention on the following Asian police studies needs:

1. There is a need to study police problems and issues that are of local concern, with local content and in local context. As Professor Brogden

observed at this AAPS conference: 'Policing has to be tailored to social context and to the local history of police–society relationships—whether it is in downtown Chicago, "new" territories such as Papua New Guinea, or transitional societies faced with major crime problems'.[32] The reason is a simple one. Social problems are local in origin and so must the (police) response, and associated studies.[33]

2. There is a need to study police problems and issues from an Asian indigenous (theoretical) perspective and with local (empirical) data. In Wong and Wong's research into policing computer crime in China, they conducted 'a comprehensive and exhaustive review of the English language legal literature and find that research in the area is limited in scope, lacking in theoretical orientation, inadequate in empirical support, superficial in analysis, and above all not giving necessary and adequate attention to indigenous perspective and local empirical data'.[34]
3. There is a need to investigate the cause, process and effect of changes—evolution or revolution, positive or natural—to Asian police and policing at the dawn of a new century.

In the author's inauguration speech, he championed for the establishment of a Hong Kong police studies discipline and research field that is informed by indigenous theory and supported by local empirical data, with an 'inside-out, bottom-up' approach.

The 2002 AAPS conference was a milestone in Hong Kong police study and research. It served to launch the study of the HKP and policing in Hong Kong with Chinese characteristic. It charted the course for future study in Asia policing, including Hong Kong.

Looking into the future, there are two approaches, in opposite directions, that the Asian police study and research can move towards. The first is to focus on the uniqueness of historical traditions, local context and indigenous perspective, or the 'local context' approach. The other is to focus on the universality and generality of policing all over the world by comparing police experiences across borders, between people and cross-culturally, or the 'comparative study' approach.

How can the 'local context' approach be effectively implemented and actualised? One strategy is to promote collaborative and cooperative research efforts between police scholars and practitioners.[35] Collaboration and cooperation can be achieved in many ways. One way is to allow or invite police 'outsiders' (scholars) to study police.[36] The other is to encourage police 'insider'[37] (serving police officers) to study police.[38]

Commissioner Lee of the HKP presentation at the AAPS conference exemplified the insider's approach. The paper is written from an 'insider's' perspective. It is also based on local knowledge and practical experience.

This contributes to the development of police scholarship with local content and in local context. This is most important if police study and research in Hong Kong is to move ahead.

Yet another alternative is to have police 'insider' (former police officers) turned academic 'outsider' (scholars) to study police.[39]

The comparative study approach was exemplified by the field works of Dr. Krishnamurthy, a senior police practitioner–scholar from India ('Trends in Community Policing and the Option to Innovate as Well as Internalize New Ideas in People's Participation in Building Safe Societies') and Professor Brogden, an eminent police scholar from Ireland ('The Export of Community Policing—Buyer Beware').

In his presentation, Krishnamurthy reported upon his field observation of community policing in six jurisdictions worldwide: Singapore, San Francisco, San Diego, Dallas, New York and Manchester, and five cities in India, namely, Bombay, New Delhi, Hyderabad, Chennai and Bangalore. He came to the conclusion that community policing is the answer to effective democratic policing.

This is the direction in which Hong Kong police study and research should be heading. As yet, the comparative police studies discipline, unlike other more established fields, for example, political science and anthropology, has not made any fruitful attempt, much less achieved any demonstrable results, in this most critical area of systematic comparative research.[40]

In hindsight, 15 years later, Hong Kong police study and research has blossomed and borne fruits, but there is still a lot more work to be done in infusing it with local content and context[41] and engaging in more cross-cultural comparison.[42]

II: Research Output[43]

Thesis/Dissertations/Articles

Apart from a few doctoral[44] and a master's thesis,[45,46] mostly by serving police officers, and a handful of published articles, an occasional paper and book chapters (many of questionable quality), there were very few scientific studies of the HKP or policing in Hong Kong, until well into the 1990s.

A careful and critical examination of HKP officers' academic output provides readers with a ground-zero view of the HKP and policing in Hong Kong by serving officers at the grassroots and in the frontline. They also provide lots of insider information, which would otherwise not be easily accessible. A case in point is the MPA dissertation by Lo Yam, Wai-chun, Yvonne (盧任惠珍) on 'A Balanced Approach to Training: Another Step Forward in Improving Retention of Junior Police Constables'[47] (1994). Lo's work was built upon another officer's work, namely, Ip, Choi-ching, Amfium; 葉賽清's An

Evaluation of Training Programmes for Constables in the Royal Hong Kong Police Force, Master of Social Science, Dissertation, Department of Political Science Faculty of Social Science, University of Hong Kong (1984).

Ip's dissertation is a description and evaluation of the Royal Hong Kong Police over 10 years (1974–1984). It professes three research objectives. First, it documents policy and regiment of RHKP constable training between 1974 and 1984, noting its changes and impact. Second, it evaluates RHKP constable training, noting its effectiveness and limitations, problems and issues. Third, it provides recommendations for future improvements (Aims of the Study, p. 15).

From Lo one learns about the history, philosophy, policy and more importantly programme implementation and impact of the HKP training regimen.

One learns about the importance of training to the HKP. Training prepares employees for the job, socialises employees into the organisation and helps the employees to reach their fullest potentials. With the HKP, good training also helps in attracting recruits and securing retention. Here, one finds that at the beginning of April 1989, the HKP rank-and-file officers were steadily declining; there was a retention and recruitment problem. In 1991–1992, for political (uncertainties) and economic (boom) reasons, the HKP failed to reach its recruitment targets by 2310. A study group was formed to study the problem with recruitment and retention of JPO. In 1992–1993, the recruitment fell still shorter of targets by 9%, that is, 1785 (recruits)/1890 (target). In May 1992, the study group made 42 recommendations, including more civilian staff, higher female ratio, better staff relations and better pay and benefits (p. 4, n. 1).

Training contributes to retention because (1) Training shows that the employer is committed to doing the job right and in delivering the best services possible. This helps build organisational identity, culture and morale. (2) Training shows that that employer cares about the well-being of the employees and inspires loyalty. (3) Training helps the employees to be prepared for work and fit into the organisation. It reduces a sense of frustration due to incompetence and alienation due to lack of belonging. This reduces incentives to leave. (4) Training reduces distance and differences between individual employees and groups, unifying and integrating them as a collective whole, starting with a shared training experience and common language. This creates bonding in officers to stay. (5) Training makes for more competent, proficient and professional workers. This creates more satisfied and prideful employees. (6) Training helps deliver better services. This reduces complaints and attracts compliments. (7) Training enhances commitments in two ways. First, training fosters personal commitment to corporate identity, values and missions. Second, training acts as a sunk cost for officers (p. 15).

Traditionally, HKP recruit training focusses on foot drill, law, procedure, weapons and physical development. There was little focus on human relations. In 1982, social studies was introduced. But the utility and impact of recruit training have neither been studied nor empirically validated.

Finally, the study group report informs about the need for and impact of HKP training reform, the main focus of the dissertation. The dissertation addressed two issues principally[48]: What are the needs for social studies training with the HKP recruits? What are the benefits with social studies training at Police Training School? The authors addressed two research questions with two surveys—one with new recruits at PTS (RPC) (80/248 or 30%) and the other with in-service trainees at Regional Continuation Training (RCT) (340/2200 or 10%). The surveys were conducted in May 1994 with 100% response rates (p. 5). The surveys show that both RPC and RCT found social studies relevant and useful with their work. RPC considered social studies training to be 'good' while the RCT considered it to be 'satisfactory'. Both groups thought that such courses should be taught by social workers and with the use of current issue cases of the police (p. 7).

A cursory review of the HKP literature before 2000 shows that there were fewer than 30 journal articles and book chapters on HKP and policing in Hong Kong. There does not appear to be any major focus, well-developed theme or building on each other's work. There is also little attempt to develop theory or to use empirical evidence to support findings, most of which are based on secondary materials. A careful reading of the entire research output shows that few references were made to the Chinese literature, except perhaps Chinese *guanxi* management in corruption and integrative function of *Guan Di* worship in policing.[49]

Academic Books and Monographs

The few academic books that were available before 2000 were very much historical in nature and descriptive in kind (e.g., I. Ward, *The Hong Kong Marine Police: 1841–1950* (Hong Kong: Hong Kong University Press, 1991). A few of them were written for lay readers, for example, R. Wacks, *Police Powers in Hong Kong: Problems and Prospect* (Hong Kong: University of Hong Kong Faculty of Law, 1989).

The Hong Kong Law Reform Commission published a number of well-researched, systematic, comprehensive, comparative, authoritative reports, including *Report on Confession and Their Admissibility in Criminal Proceedings*, Topic 8 (14 December 1984); *Report on Bail in Criminal Proceeding*, Topic 16 (December 1988); *Report on Loitering*, Topic 23 (May 1990); and *Report on Arrest*, Topic 25 (1992). But they all suffered from being too focussed and unduly legalistic. They were not informed by social science research. None of the Law Reform Commission studies draw upon Chinese ideas and local culture.

There are a few scholarly investigations into police corruption, organised crime and triads (e.g., R. Lee, *Corruption and Its Control in Hong Kong* (Hong Kong: The Chinese University Press, 1981)). There are also a few law books on police powers and criminal procedures in Hong Kong, for example,

G. Heilbronn, Police powers: Arrest, detention, and seizure, *Criminal Procedure in Hong Kong*, 3rd Edition (1998).

Textbooks

Currently, there is no police textbook in Hong Kong. The closest ones are the following: K. C. Wong's *Policing in Hong Kong* (Aldershot, UK: Ashgate Publishing Ltd., 2012); *One Country Two Systems: A Case Study of Cross-Border Crime between Hong Kong Special Administrative Region and People's Republic of China* (Brunswick, NJ: Transactions Publications, 2012) (a case study of how the 'Big Boss' case was handled by the HKP); *Cyberspace Governance in China* (New York: Nova Scientific Publication, 2012) (including 'Cyberspace Governance in China in Hong Kong') and Jiao's *The Police in Hong Kong* (University Press of America, 2007).

Starting in the 2000s, instruction materials on criminal justice policing started to appear. Before 2000, the first comprehensive text on Hong Kong criminal justice was an edited volume (*Introduction to the Hong Kong Criminal Justice System* [Hong Kong: HKU Press, 1994]) by Mark S. Gaylord and Harold Traver, two leading Hong Kong criminal justice scholars of the time.

It is a short book (180 pages) with an extensive coverage but average treatment of the subject. It reviews 13 aspects of the Hong Kong criminal justice system, including the HKP, with an appendix on 'Hong Kong's Principal Criminal Ordinances and Common Law Offences' (184–192).

The foreword is written by Louise I. Shelley ('it provides a useful framework for subsequent comparative analysis', the authors provide an overview of the Hong Kong criminal justice system anchor within a historical context.). The book contains 13 chapters: Chapters 1 to 13 are titled 'The Hong Kong Criminal Justice System', 'The Measurement of Crime', 'The Royal Hong Kong Police', 'The Customs and Excise Department', 'The Independent Commission against Corruption', 'Criminal Law', 'The Prosecutions Division of the Legal Department', 'Legal Assistance', 'The Judiciary', 'The Court Interpreters' Office', 'The Correctional Services Department', 'The Social Welfare Department' and 'The Basic Law', respectively. As a first venture in the field, the book was an invaluable contribution to fill a void. While the book serves its essential function in providing the readers a brief overview of the Hong Kong criminal justice system, it does little else. Like many academic books on Hong Kong criminal justice and policing at the time, it is not a scholarly research book if scholarly research means that it is based on systematic literature review, clearly articulated research question, precisely postulated thesis, specific scientific method of inquiry, well-grounded theories, valid and reliable data, with critical analysis and portable findings. Additionally, it raised more questions than answers.

To be more specific, the major shortcomings and limitations of the book are three. First, it takes for granted the relevancy and applicability of foreign

(Western) criminological materials to Hong Kong,[50] an issue that is still very much alive today. Second, it is not based on empirical research, as there were few available data at that time. Since the situation has improved much, since then, a lot more needs to be done. Third, it is more about how Hong Kong criminal justice system functions in the book, rather than whether or not and how things work in the street. This critique still holds true today. As observed in a critical review by Janice Brabyn:

> The truth is we know almost nothing about what actually goes on in the minds of Hong Kong police officers or in Hong Kong police stations or police vehicles, or during street-comer encounters between Hong Kong police and civilians, or indeed about most aspects of police practice. The other uniformed services have also largely escaped public scrutiny let alone detailed research. Surely we need to know a great deal about these things so that we can design our own Police and Criminal Evidence Ordinance (PACO), one which at least has a fighting chance of actually achieving some of the due process goals they are intended to serve....[51]

In short, the book is intended for novices and students. It can best be used as a barometer of the state of collective knowledge of Hong Kong criminal justice, including policing as an emerging study field. Read reflectively and discerningly, it also provides ideas, raises issues and suggests a road map for future inquiry. For a pioneering book, this is no small achievement.

Introduction to the Hong Kong Criminal Justice blazed the way for others to come. It was followed by C. Jones, *Criminal Justice in Hong Kong* (Routledge–Cavendish, 2007), M. S. Gaylord, D. Gittings and H. Traver (eds.), *Introduction to Crime, Law and Justice in Hong Kong* (Hong Kong: Hong Kong University Press, 2007) and W. H. Chiu and T. W. Lo, *Understanding Criminal Justice in Hong Kong* (UK: Willan Publishing, 2008).[52] Other than Professor Jones' book, these books are more instructional than investigative.[53]

Finally, if one is interested in researching into the HKP, one should begin by consulting the comprehensive list of the Hong Kong police literature compiled in L. Siu-Kai, W. Po-san and S. Kwok-cheung, *Hong Kong Politics: A Bibliography* (Hong Kong: Hong Kong Institute of Asia Pacific Studies, Chinese University of Hong Kong, 1999). Though a bit dated, it remains an important bibliography.

The other compilation of source materials is: *Policing in the Turbulent Hong Kong: 1940—1960s: Witnessed by Frontline Police Officers.*[54]

Popular Readings[55]

There are also a number of popular books written by retired police officers. They are locker-room chats and personal anecdotal accounts of how police work is done. They are about police officers' daily encounters and life-long experiences. Together, they tell us about HKP organisational practices, police personality and culture. Some noteworthy works include CIP Kenneth Andrew's *Hong Kong Detective* (London: John Long Ltd., 1962); Anthony Annieson's *The One-Eyed Dragon: The Inside Story of a Hong Kong Policeman* (Moffat, Scotland: Lochar Publishing, 1989); Lau Kai Fat's (劉啟法) (1932–2007) 警界幕後 [Inside Police Stations] (博益, 1991); 總督察手記, [Footprints of Chief Inspector of Police] (博益, 1990); 總督察獨家檔案 [Personal Files from Chief Inspector of Police] (博益, 1991); and 總督察回憶錄 [Memoirs of Chief Inspector of Police] 5 Vol. (年聚贤馆出版, 1991/93).

Of these gems, Lau Kai Fat's series of 'police story' books stands out as the most representative. Lau Kai Fat served with HKP for 35 years, from 1952 to the 1990s, in various postings, branches and districts, and on a variety of assignments. He retired as a CIP.

Kelvin Wong (黃奇仁) published 警官手記—六十年代香港警隊的日子 [Footprints of a Police Officer—Hong Kong Police Force in the 60's] (香港三聯書店, 2008). The book is about the experiences of the author, who worked as an Inspector of Police in HKP from 1963 to 1971, after having worked as an accountant for five years.

Lui Kei's (呂奇) 我的警察生涯 [My Life as a Policeman] (博學出版社, 2008) documents the journey of the author, starting as a juvenile delinquent and overcoming the odds to become a police officer, from police training in PCS/PTS to a life-long police career until 2008.

Mike Smith's In the Shadow of the Noonday Gun (Windsor, 24 January 2013) is a collection of 16 police stories. The stories tell us how policing is done in Hong Kong, behind the scenes, from an expatriate's perspective. Smith worked for the HKP for five years and intended to tell all: 'The Noonday Gun is really a play on the "shadow" part…To me the gun represents Hong Kong's establishment. I'm trying to tell human stories in the shadows of the establishment—the other side, as it were'.[56]

With the advent of the Internet and the World Wide Web, people can gain free access to the HKP's official newspaper, the *OffBeat*,[57] police blogs, for example, SIP Ling,[58] websites, for example, Hong Kong Police Club,[59] Gwulo; Old Hong Kong–Royal Hong Kong Police,[60] and HKP officers' blog entries; for example, on 8 August 2009, a former HKP officer (1995–2009), pen named Water, posted an article on the web titled 'Are You Suitable to Be a Police Officer?'[61] The lengthy article related his short career as a PC with the HKP. His message to young people who aspire to join the HKP is not to join the HKP if they have other choices. The article related his experience working in the HKP for 10 plus years. It was meant to be an *exposé* of sorts; to inform the public of what it is like to work for the HKP in the hope that young people will think twice before joining the HKP. As intended, the carry-away lesson is that the HKP is not what it appears and working for the HKP is not what it is made out to be:

> HKP is most certainly not a career for everyone. While the pay and benefits are fairly good to start with, it is also a demanding job—physically, emotionally and morally, and dead-end job. More importantly, in order to negotiate, survive and/or prosper in the HKP system, police constables must be prepared to sacrifice ones integrity, ethics and dignity. This includes kissing up to the boss and dressing down by the public, and subjecting to criminal prosecution and civil liability when things go wrong.[62]

Newspapers, English and Chinese, are also printing police columns, for example, Senior Superintendent (Retired) Lam's column, relating his 32 years of experience working in the HKP.[63] Investigative reporting in Hong Kong also provides lurid details of police misconducts, for example:

- Former PC Wong Chi-ho (36)[64] was charged with 9 counts of indecent assault on female students, aged 10–11, in a Wong Po primary school where he worked as an audio technician, in between October 2005 and January 2006. According to prosecution at the Kowloon City Magistrate, the defendant approached the students at recess from the back and grabbed the kid's hand to touch his penis. The kids reported this to their parents. The defendant was arrested. He was convicted and sentenced to imprisonment for 20 months (DCCC 665/2006).[65]
- On 4 September 2004, Wong was working at the Police Training School, recruitment section. He was found hiding in one of the female toilet cubicles. When confronted, Wong told the female officer that he entered the toilet by mistake in an urgent call of nature. He was placed on probation (ESCC 4648/04).
- The records show that the defendant had two prior sex-related criminal records. In 2004, Wong was found coming out of Wanchai Police Quarter, after having locked himself in a cubicle. He was put on probation for loitering (KCCC 4281/06).[66]

The more substantial and research-based popular reading on the HKP are: K. Sinclair, *Asia's Finest: An Illustrated Account of the Royal Hong Kong Police* (Hong Kong: Unicorn, 1983), which is an illustrated story of 150 years of the HKP. It was followed by L. Sinclair and N. K. Ng, *Asia's Finest Marches On: Policing Hong Kong from 1841 into the 21st Century* (Hong Kong: Kevin Sinclair Associates, 2009), which brings the original 'Asia's Finest' up to date.

An official version of HKP history recently appeared on the HKP website: *HKP Staff (2012). Police History: History—The First Century* (警队历史：历史-第壹个壹百年'． 香港警务处) (in Chinese [simplified and traditional Han] and English), Government of the Hong Kong Special Administrative Region.[67] It was also accompanied by other interesting topics: 'The Modern

Era: 1945–67', 'Creating a Legend: 1967–94', 'Changes to the Policing Model and the Return of Sovereignty 1994–94', 'The New Century', 'Women—An Equal Force', 'Ballistics & Sciences' and 'Down Memory Lane'. Besides being an easily accessible source of information on the HKP, past and present, such an institutional history tells a lot about how the HKP looks at itself, from periodisation to issues of note to trial and tribulation. In this regard, as a discerning HKP observer, it matters less what the HKP said of itself, true or false. It matters why and how it presented itself the way it did.

The latest entry of this kind of writing is that of L. Ho and Y. K. Chu, *Policing Hong Kong, 1842–1969: Insiders' Stories* (Hong Kong: City University of Hong Kong Press, 2011), which contains a lot of facts about the HKP, from history to police jargons, with substantial contributions from old timers. One of the distinguished features of this book is that it uses a lot of Chinese sources, of varying degrees of validity and reliability, as the authors readily concede, and in some cases make allowance for.[68] The other interesting feature is that the book takes time to explain the origin of some of the police jargons that have a long history and are culturally rich, for example, 'cha ren' (official runner) or 'green coat' (police officer).[69]

Another source of popular readings is those written by people, local or foreign, who have lived under, experienced with or have had exposure to the HKP. These include the following:

Patrick Shuk-siu Yu (余叔韶), a famous Crown Counsel from Hong Kong who specialised in criminal cases from Hong Kong,[70] shared with us his experience of working as a Police Reserve in Hong Kong in his memoir *Tales from No. 9 Ice House Street* (2002).[71] In January 1953, Yu joined the HKP as a Police Reserve constable at Cai Wan. He was mentored by a sub-inspector from his old high school Wah Yan College. On their rounds of patrol duties, they ran into open drug markets, gambling establishments and prostitution brothels.

> The sub-inspector was naturally more than embarrassed, … 'Barrister Yu,' he said 'you will have to get used to certain unpleasant facts which individual officers like me can do nothing to change. To save our skin, we have to learn to hear no evil, see no evil, and speak no evil. As a member of the Police Reserve and a lawyer, you may be able to do something about it, but we regulars are less fortunate'…[72]

This frank exchange between a serving HKP inspector and a part-time Police Reserve allows one to understand how the HKP works in practice and in real terms, away from self-promotion and subjective bias.

Elsie Tu,[73] a long-time Hong Kong resident and social activist, revealed how the HKP behave against the less fortunate. She shares her run-in with the HKP as part of her client advocacy and public service in her book *Colonial Hong Kong in the Eyes of Elsie Tu*:

> I dealt with numerous complaints from the public, and it was cleared that most unwarranted arrests were made near the end of the month, confirming the belief that officers had to show a good detection rate in their monthly report… unwarranted arrest were often teenagers, or men rather poorly dressed or poorly education, and, worst of all, mentally handicapped persons.[74]

There are books about people who encounter the HKP on a daily basis as part of their life course, that is, lower class or marginalised people. Such literature is best exemplified by G. Mathews, *Ghetto at the Center of the World: Chungking Mansions, Hong Kong* (2012).[75] This book informs that the HKP exercise their legal authority sparingly and judiciously, lest they disturb the settled expectations of the people dependent on the police for survival, for example, illegal immigrants and suppliers of illicit service or products.

The literature also includes those people who were arrested by the HKP officers. Andrew Bailey was an American. He was arrested by the HKP for money laundering at the Hong Kong International Airport. He writes about his experience in *Hell in Hong Kong: 134 Days of Torture* (2012) in vivid detail that only people who have first-hand experience can offer.[76]

People who grow up and live in a police family household offer us an inside look at HKP officers away from the office and speaking from their hearts. P. Craggs's *When Harry Met Vicky—A Fatal Attraction: Growing Up with My Parents* (2012)[77] tells us how it is like growing up in a British HKP officer's household. This book tells a story of a cross-cultural marriage between a Chinese refugee and a famous HKP inspector (1959–1971) that ended in a tragic in-family murder.

The book describes how it is like, from the son's perspective, to live a family life, on the edge of the cultural boundary. With raw emotion and biting gossips fully on display for all to see, Craggs presents a behind-closed-doors account of a tightknit police community. Craggs offers a personal glimpse and intimate look at Inspector Craggs on and off the job from negotiating promotion and coming to terms with corruption, to family happenings and social gatherings 'Family Life and the 1960s Era' (p. 79). For example, Inspector Craggs once regretted accepting pocket changes as a traffic officer. His wife felt differently, however, telling her son: 'Your father was a stupid fool. Everyone was doing it and even for more money' (p. 80). Even worse, Craggs intimated that he was denied promotion and shifted from station to station (four times) because he was not on the take. He took to binge drinking and became an alcoholic. Inspector 'Happy Harry' no more:

> From the moment that I was born in 1959 up until his death in 1971…he had been moved from each division and area of his police work four times. Whether it was his request or that he was ordered to move is unclear, but the effect on my mother and us as children was quite establishing…By 1967, he had been an inspector now for fifteen years, and to see other colleagues getting

> to at least senior inspector or chief inspector must've demoralized him. His drinking now had made him into an alcoholic…He told my mother that the local constables were muke tau (wooden-headed), meaning that they were basically useless and had no guts or initiative in dealing with that situation. Of course he was seeing through his British eyes and did not understand that Chinese were not on the whole confrontational people, or that they believe confrontation can offer a solution. It was indicative that my father's impression of the Chinese in general was similar to that of the old colonialists of the earlier period of the British Empire, seeing and treating them in a rather patronizing and dismissive way, labeling them as 'yellow', meaning that they lacked a certain amount of chivalry and courage.

The book ends with a lengthy discussion of the murder of Inspector Craggs by Vicky, his wife. The trial ended with an acquittal.[78]

There are still those pieces of literature that look at the HKP[79] through the eyes of people who work for the organisation, not in the capacity of a police officer but as that of migrants, such as C. Knowles and D. Harper, *Hong Kong: Migrant Lives, Landscapes, and Journeys* (University of Chicago Press, 15 December 2009).[80] This line of scholarship informs what these individuals feel and think as a working foreigner in Hong Kong.

All of the above-mentioned popular books and e-sources make for informative and interesting reading on the HKP. While all of them claim to be accurate accounts of the HKP, none of them pretend to be scholarly work, in theory, method or findings. But from the perspective of the target audience, the general public who are interested in the lores and adventures of HKP, the series promises to be both enlightening and entertaining. As intended, they are successful in projecting a larger-than-life image of the HKP, making it an integral part of Hong Kong's collective memory and popular culture.

The more scholarly but still easily accessible *The Other Hong Kong Reports* (now defunct) has chapters on the HKP that offer the general public a different and critical view of the HKP from the 'public' perspective.[81]

NGO Reports

Finally, Hong Kong NGOs, from human rights groups (Hong Kong Human Rights Monitor[82] and Hong Kong Human Rights Watch[83]) to lawyers' associations (Hong Kong Bar Association[84] and Hong Kong Law Society), often compile extensive accountability reports and timely press releases on police activities and issues,[85] with clear political stances, for example, Hong Kong Bar Association on the left and Hong Kong Law Society on the right. The Hong Kong Human Rights Monitor is more indigenous[86] and the Hong Kong Human Rights Watch is more foreign. Both promote universal rights over collective welfare and individual freedom over police powers. Individual

LegCo members' press releases or issue reports also make for good reading on policing[87] (e.g., those from Margaret Ng for liberal accounts and those from Raymond Wong for a more radical spin.

III: Studying Policing in Hong Kong: Problems and Issues

There are a number of reasons accounting for this lack of scholarly interest in the investigation of policing in Hong Kong:

First, there is a pecking order within the Hong Kong academic world. Police studies have been marginalised, both as a subject matter of study and focus area of research. There is a common perception among the scholars in Hong Kong that police institution and the practice is not worth studying. This means two things. First, the studying of police work is considered not intellectually as stimulating, that is, it is theoretically not interesting and empirically mundane. Second, there is not much to study about the police, that is, rhetorically, what is there to study but how to detect crime and arrest people? In support of the above observation and as an example, in the late 1990s, this author was asked by one senior academic at a leading Hong Kong university in a most paternalistic and patronising way (all well intended) as to why this author, as a lawyer by profession and with a social science background, did not put his 'talent' and 'energy' to work to pursue more mainstream research, for example, law or politics. The subject the senior scholar had in mind is the study of law in China historically and sociologically, a matter of great interest to him. The senior scholar concluded by saying: 'You should be teaching lawyers, not police officers'. On another occasion when this author talked to another senior scholar-administrator about his plan to help in developing course materials for a Hong Kong police studies programme in another higher education unit, the administrator informed the author that such activities are not counted as 'academic' research for the purpose of assessment and evaluation and it might not be time well spent. The message is as clear as it is frustrating: scholars should be directing their research effort in conducting 'real' research, not police studies.

The author mentions both stories not because he thinks ill of his colleagues or they are necessarily wrong, but because they tell of a discriminatory mindset. The fact that these scholars are speaking from the bottom of their heart and not the top of the head made their comments all the more revealing and disconcerting, as they reflected and reinforced the intellectual climate in Hong Kong. It does not bode well for Hong Kong police studies development. The lesson one can draw from both of these respected scholars and powerful administrators is that scholars in Hong Kong hold a dim view of police studies and low regard for police scholars.

Together, these two persons have 60 years of experience in Hong Kong academia. Their views and opinions, though they may not be representative of or shared by all others in Hong Kong (particularly the new comers), are authoritative in shaping the academic environment in Hong Kong, and thus deserve attention. This is a problem scholars have to deal with in mounting police research in Hong Kong.

For some, the above put-down of a rising discipline by another can be dismissed as 'trash talk' in the politics of higher education. Still, talk has consequences, to put down others in promoting self is evidence of close-mindedness.[88] In order to elevate one's importance, as administrator ('I know more than you do in this business') or scholar ('I am more distinguished than you ever can'), one needs to stand on the bodies of others. The pollution of academic environment through denigration needs to be reckoned with, lest the local police scholars suffered from discrimination, affecting their sense of self-identity and progress of professional advancement.

Second, before 2000, from the HKP's perspective, policing is a vocation.[89] It is a craft, not a science. Thus, to learn about the police, it is best to join the police. Police work can best be learnt through practice, not scientifically-based research.[90] While there is a shift of emphasis within the HKP to promote continuous education and a lifelong learning culture, as reflected by many senior officers having or pursuing graduate degrees, for example, in 2011, there were two assistant commissioners of police (ACP) with Ph.D. and one ACP pursuing Ph.D. (graduate), education does not assure promotion, and may even be a liability.[91]

Third, the HKP resists any attempt to study their organisation and operations, especially by outsiders. The HKP is afraid that this might penetrate their mystique. If the public knew more about how policing really worked, this might compromise their operational effectiveness, professional autonomy and political legitimacy.[92] This view still holds, in spite of a more liberal stance towards scientific study of the HKP. This is to say, there is a need to be careful about the competing demands of good intent to open up the HKP and zealous effort in protecting HKP secrets.

Gathering data for Hong Kong police research is also difficult for the following reasons:

First, the HKP is fearful of sharing information with outsiders for a number of reasons. As an organisation, the HKP is subjected to political accountability and, increasingly, exposed to public scrutiny. The HKP is genuinely fearful of how information will be interpreted (when taken out of context) and used (when being exploited). Thus, it follows that the less the public knows the better. In this regard, a very senior HKP officer has confided in this author that, in his opinion, one of the problems with police–citizen relationship today is that the people know too much and the police are sharing too much information.[93]

Second, the HKP as a result of its mission (as defender of law and order) and because of its ideology (as promoter of ethics and morality) is a conservative organisation. Consequently, the HKP does not accept alien ideas instantaneously. Researchers asking novel questions and introducing new perspectives are immediately suspected. In and around the HKP, they are considered as 'juveniles' (young kids having problems), a derogatory reference that speaks to a deeply held attitude towards outsiders and academics.

Third, as required by the job, the police officers need to be in control of a situation and not allow it to get out of hand. The police have learnt that once information is released to the public they lose all control over how information is being used. Releasing information is a risky business.

Fourth, the HKP is concerned with possibly compromising operational secrecy. There is a need to keep organisational and operational secrets from the public, for example, information source, law enforcement priorities and police tactics.[94]

Fifth, the HKP is much concerned with protecting individual privacy. In as much as information the police acquired are dedicated for law enforcement purposes, others using the information could potentially create a breach of confidence scenario.

In practice, serving police officers must apply for permission from the commissioner of police on a case-by-case basis when conducting research into the HKP. The application must cover the purpose, scope, method and use of research. Finally, a copy of the research report and findings must be cleared by the HKP headquarter of all objectionable materials before final distribution or publication. Sometimes, restricted circulation is mandated. It goes without saying that both as a researcher and as a research subject, a police officer is required to abide by the official secrecy pledge at all times.

As the change of police culture within the HKP takes root, the HKP top leadership's attitude and organisation culture towards research is slowly changing. Increasingly, the HKP is opening its doors for researchers.[95] Even then, the opening is not total. As recent as 2006, SIP Chan had problems getting data from the HKP:

> Although data, figures and previous analysis in relation to the concerned recruitment system are rather adequate and readily available, there is information being withheld by Personnel Wing of the Police Force that the author considers as relevant to this research. Personnel Wing has clearly indicated those information is within the ambit of confidentiality and relates to the Police Force's internal policy, which should not be disclosed to assist an academic research.[96]

This author has also personally experienced denial of information requests, in his research into police handling of the 'Big Boss' case in 2000.[97]

IV: Conclusion

This chapter investigates the historical development of police studies in Hong Kong, as an education and research field. Investigation into the HKP suffers from the usual problems of lack of source materials, scholarly interests and intellectual capacity. As a result, not much has been written on the HKP,[98] still less on policing in Hong Kong.[99] Given the storied history of Hong Kong as a colony and importance of the HKP on colonial administration (1941–1997), it is surprising that there is such little interest and effort to explore the HKP's political role in colonial administration and document its social impact on Hong Kong development. It is doubly strange that policing in Hong Kong has never been studied from a Hong Kong–Chinese and cultural perspective, for example, in what way and how can it be said that policing in Hong Kong is Hong Kong–Chinese policing? What does policing with Hong Kong characteristic mean? In what way and to what extent is the HKP affected by Hong Kong[100] versus Chinese[101] versus Western culture[102]?

As to a perspective, historiography is about discovering and interpretation of obscured and scattered facts, not the rendering of a monolithic ethnocentric reality, still less Eurocentric one. Thus far, the history of the HKP can be described as story-telling by colonialists (the privileged), elites (the rich) and learned (intellectuals), with a legal focus, a political analysis framework and top-down perspective. More specifically, the study of HKP history has been focussed on the HKP as a law and order institution. The framework is one of colonialisms. The perspective is from the top down (HK government), outside (scholars) and afar (England). Seldom are the voices of the people of Hong Kong on policing taken into account;[103] nor are there any HKP history built upon the testimonials[104] on frontline (Chinese) officers.[105] An institutional history of the HKP written from the above by the administration, and afar by Western elites and aloof with 'pure' scientism has little hope of capturing the 'Spirit of the Age' or Zeitgeist. Viewed in this way, HKP history is a biased, distorted and constructed/interpretative narrative about rulers and the ruled and corruption and progress rather than what the Hong Kong people experienced, perceived and received of their police, as lived.

Finally, in investigating into the HKP, there is a need to draw a clear distinction between studying the HKP as a political instrument of control or suppression versus social institution to provide order or deliver service. For the first 160 years (1844–2004), the HKP knew the first, not the second, from the Hong Kong government's, British Parliament's or Hong Kong people's perspective. It is high time to see the HKP and policing in Hong Kong in its natural light.

In concluding this review, it is observed that, since the earliest time, there are two realities to policing in Hong Kong, with British colonialists at the top and Chinese subjects at the bottom, resulting in a 'dual track' colonial policing versus people's policing system. After 1997, the duality in policing still persists, this time with professional policing up top and street policing at the bottom. The observation to be noted is that on all sides there is ample knowledge about colonial policing and professional policing but little about people's policing and street policing.[106] Such a knowledge gap can be narrowed with 'inside out and bottom up research'. One of the contributions of this book is to demystify colonial policing and current professional HKP reform, making it clear that the duality of policing, from colonial versus local, to professional versus street policing, is here to stay.

Endnotes

1. F. Morn, *Academic Politics and the History of Criminal Justice Education* (Wesport, Connecticut: Greenwood Press, 1995).
2. The problem is not unique to policing education. As a practising lawyer once, the author has engaged in many professional discussions over whether the knowledge of law and skills of lawyering can be best taught in school or at work. The same can be said of all street-level bureaucrats, for example, social workers, or service agents, for example, nurses. To do justice to this observation, we need to delineate the issues on hand. What is the nature and characteristics of the problem on hand and focus and scope of the issues being debated? Very few people would argue that the philosophy of law or theory of policing could (feasibility issue) and should (desirability) be researched and taught only in school (formal education) without input from the street. However, many readily accept the idea that the practice of law or art of policing can be learned in school, by way of clinical education (with legal internship or from police war stories) or simulation (mock trial for lawyer, table top exercise on terrorism). The current approach is a hybrid one: having experienced lawyers using case study to get law students to think like a lawyer; or, for a police instructor, using experiences to train police through role playing and tactical rehearsals.
3. J.-P. Brodeur, Police studies past and present: A reaction to the articles presented by T. Feltes, L. T. Hoover, P. K. Manning, and K. Wong, *Police Quarterly*, 8: 44–56, 2005.
4. The author, K. C. Wong, is a founding member of IPES (International Police Executive Symposium), which tries to bring police practitioners and policing scholars together, in sharing knowledge, advancing understanding and facilitating collaboration.
5. Practitioner scholar refers to practitioner-turned scholar or practitioner who engages in scholarly research. Scholar practitioner refers to scholars becoming cops.
6. Kam C. Wong, *The Study of Policing in Hong Kong (2005)*, in progress. Chapter Three: Inside Out–Bottom Up. (Draft manuscript on file with author).
7. Academic study of sociology was introduced in Hong Kong in the 1950s and approached 'take-off' stage in the 1960s, with the establishment of Hong Kong Sociological Society (1966), Department of Sociology at Hong Kong University (1967) and integration of sociology programmes at Chung Chi College (1951),

United College (1956) and New Asia College (1959) at Chinese University of Hong Kong under one roof as the new Department of Sociology (1963). R. P.L. Lee and S.K. Lau, *The Birth and Growth of Academic Sociology in Hong Kong*. Occasional Paper Series. Hong Kong Studies, Hong Kong Institute of Asia-Pacific Studies, CUHK (1993). http://www.cuhk.edu.hk/hkiaps/publications/op/OP28-text.pdf. See also T. L. Lui, 'From being the other to becoming the local: Hong Kong's sociological exploration'. The Workshop on Asian Sociology, Seoul, South Korea, 18 December 2010. http://hub.hku.hk/bitstream/10722/138324/1/Content.pdf?accept=1

8. On 20 May 1858, Governor John Bowring appointed a Commission of Inquiry to investigate into Attorney General Anstey's charges, sent directly to the Secretary of Colony. See 'Warrant of Commission'. J. W. Norton-Kyshe, *The History of the Laws and Courts of Hongkong, Tracing Consular Jurisdiction in China and Japan and Including Parliamentary Debates, and the Rise, Progress and Successive Changes in the Various Public Institutions of the Colony from the Earliest Period to the Present Time, Vol. 1* (London: T. Fischer Unwin, 1898), p. 508.
9. T. C. Anstey, *Crime and Government at Hong Kong, A Letter to the 'Times'* (1859) RareBooksClub.com (4 July 2012).
10. D. R. Caldwell, *A Vindication of the Character of the Undersigned from the Aspersions of Mr. T. Chisholm Anstey, Ex-Attorney General of Hongkong as Contained in His Charges, His Pamphlet, and His Letter to the Secretary of State for the Colonies to the Secretary of State for the Colonies* (Hong Kong, Noronha's office, 1860).
11. See Chapter 6 Police Reform Literature, *infra* for details.
12. Minutes of meeting of the Panel on Security on 11 November 1996 (LC Paper No. CB(2) 1545/96-97). http://www.legco.gov.hk/yr96-97/english/panels/se/minutes/se111196.htm
13. Coopers and Lybrand, *The Review of the Top Management Structure of the Royal Hong Kong Police: Final Report* (London: Coopers & Lybrand, 1993).
14. Emphasis on discipline with a 'can do spirit' and problem-oriented approach; life-time commitment with a strong sense of loyalty and 'esprit de corps', strong rank consciousness, and formalized internal communication and control system.
15. Coopers and Lybrand, *The Review of the Top Management Structure of the Royal Hong Kong Police: Final Report* (London: Coopers & Lybrand, 1993), p. 71.
16. 'Less welcome are restatements by some authors of comparatively commonplace Western criminological material with the implicit assumption that such material is relevant to the discussion of the Hong Kong criminal justice system'. 25 *Hong Kong L.J.*, 429, 1995, 430. See information at Note 49.
17. Commission Lee Ming-kui (2003–2007) was the first Chinese Commission with an undergraduate degree, though many senior officers were sent for higher professional education overseas.
18. The author, Kam C. Wong, resigned from the HKP to pursue policing studies, at the Department of Forensics, Indiana University (Bloomington) in 1972.
19. The author, Kam C. Wong, was a lecturer with the Department of Government and Public Administration, Chinese University of Hong Kong, and Acting Secretary of Chinese Law Program (1983–1985).
20. The author, Kam C. Wong, was a steering member of the group. He was the then Acting Secretary of the Chinese Law Program at Chinese University of Hong Kong, and was intimately involved with the HKP scholars' program.

21. The author, Kam C. Wong, was elected the vice chair in 1998 and served until 2001.
22. Hong Kong Society of Criminology. http://www.crime.hku.hk/hksoccrim.htm.
23. The author, Kam C. Wong, was one of its lead tutors.
24. The author, Kam C. Wong, acted as consultant, course developer and external examiner to Open University, Police and Society Program (October 2000–2002); external examiner, Department of Sociology (Criminology), Hong Kong University (2001–2004); adviser and reviewer to Chinese University of Hong Kong, Police Studies Project Proposal (June 1997).
25. K. Fang. Royal Hong Kong police, In: Antoinetter Burton (ed.), *After the Imperial Turn: Thinking with the Through the Nation* (Durham, NC: Duke University Press, 8 May 2003), pp. 293–307, 200.
26. The author served as an internal faculty adviser and consultant to this initiative.
27. Discussion with numerous HKP students at CUHK and HKU.
28. http://www.ppaweb.hku.hk/programmes/tpg/mpa Its graduates include Ms Lau Chi Wai, Edwina, Deputy Regional Command, HKP, 2001; Mr To Chun Wai, Clarence; Mr Au Chi Kwong, Sonny, ACPs, HKP, MPA 2006.
29. Opinion Survey: Full Time Masters in Criminology. Survey https://docs.google.com/spreadsheet/embeddedform?formkey=dDFwNzhmWS1wRy0yMmcxc2JzN2J1Umc6MQ
30. Numerous discussions with Andrew Willis, Deputy Director of Scarman Center, University of Leicester, major provider of criminal justice distance learning instruction in Hong Kong, from 1998 to 1999.
31. K. C. Wong, *Chinese Policing: History and Reform* (New York: Peter Lang, 2009).
32. M. Brogden, The export of community policing—Buyer beware, *Proceeding Papers, Third AAPS Annual Conference* (Hong Kong: AAPS, 29 July 2002), p. 20.
33. It is now commonly accepted as truism that economic condition, social structure, family integrity and school education have more to do with the cause and prevention of deviance than any police intervention methods.
34. See K. C. Wong and G. Wong, Law and order in cyberspace: A case study of cyberspace governance and Internet regulation in PRC, *Proceeding Papers, Third AAPS Annual Conference* (Hong Kong: AAPS, 29 July 2002). For an example of one such approach, see K. C. Wong, The philosophy of community policing in China, *Police Quarterly*, 4 (2): 186–214, 2001. ('It finds that the Chinese philosophy on community policing differs substantially from that of the U.S.'.)
35. M. L. Birzer, Writing partnership between police practitioners and researchers, *Police Practice and Research: An International Journal*, 3 (2): 149–156, 2003.
36. This gem of a scholarship is exemplified by the pioneer work of M. Ng-Quinn, Bureaucratic Response to Political Change: Theoretical Use of Atypical Case of the Hong Kong Police (Hong Kong: Occasional Paper No. 2, Hong Kong Institute of Asia Pacific Studies, Chinese University of Hong Kong). More recently, A. Y. Jiao, Organizational behaviors and political sensitivities: Policing Hong Kong after 1997, *Public Administration and Policy*, 11 (1): 41–60, 2002.
37. There is a continuous debate over the relative contribution to police scholarship between 'insider' versus 'outsider' research. (The 'insider' vs. 'outsider' dichotomy does not do justice to the many other possibilities, e.g., 'insider-outside', e.g., police officers turned police researchers, and 'outsider-insider', e.g., scholars,

turned police officers.) The contributions and limitations of 'insider' to police research, particularly in the Hong Kong context, must be acknowledged. This is a 'forum issue' for another day. In passing, while an 'insider' brings with him/her original data, first-hand experience, indigenous perspective, and inside-out perspective, he/she suffers from (charges of) a lack of objectivity resulting from institutional bias, from conflict of interests to a lack of vision.

38. This gem of scholarship is exemplified by the pioneering work of D. Y. K. Tsui, *Problems of a Para-Military Police Force in a Changing Society—A Case Study of the Royal Hong Kong Police Force* (CUHK, 1979) and *The Promotion System in the Officer Cadre of the Royal Hong Kong Police* (HKU, 1982); More recently, C. Y. Cheuk, *Community Policing in Hong Kong: An Institutional Analysis.* DBA Thesis. Hong Kong Polytechnic University, 1999.
39. This gem of scholarship is exemplified by the pioneering works of K. C. Wong, Beat patrol deployment in Hong Kong, *International Journal of Comparative & Applied Criminal Justice*, 25(2): 111–138, 2001.
40. A review of comparative CJS text old and new does not reveal any sophisticated comparative methodology. See G. F. Cole, S. J. Frankowski, and M. G. Gertz. *Major Criminal Justice Systems: A Comparative Survey* (Beverly Hills, CA: Sage, Sage Focus Editions, No 32, 1981); E. Fairchild, *Comparative Criminal Justice Systems* (Belmont, CA: Wadsworth Publishing Company, 1993).
41. Numerous discussions with Andrew Willis, Deputy Director of Scarman Center, major provider of criminal justice distance learning instruction in Hong Kong, 1998–1999; Rod Broadhurst, Associate Professor, Center for Criminology, Hong Kong University, 1999–2002; Dr. Garland Liu, Program Coordinator, Police Studies Program, Open University of Hong Kong, 1999–2000. Professor Raymond Lau, Police Studies Program, Open University of Hong Kong, 2002. More recently, discussion with Deputy Commandant, HKP College, 2012. This is supported by my extensive experience in reviewing HKP manuscripts as Managing Editor of Police Practice and Research: An International Journal and other scholarly outlets.
42. K. C. Wong, *Policing in Hong Kong* (Farmham, UK: Ashgate, 2012), Chapter Seven: One Country Two Systems of Policing; A. Jiao, Y. Allan and E. B. Silverman, Police practice in Hong Kong and New York: A comparative analysis, *The International Journal of Police Science & Management*, 8 (2): 104–118, 2006. CRJU4010/7010: Comparative Justice Systems Criminal Justice Study in Taiwan and Hong Kong, 5 June–19 June 2012. Department of Sociology, Anthropology, and Criminal Justice, College of Arts and Sciences Valdosta State University.
43. See details in Section IV Literature Review, *infra*.
44. C. Y. Cheuk, *Community Policing in Hong Kong: An Institutional Analysis.* DBA Thesis. Hong Kong Polytechnic University, 1999; A. Kerrigan, *Policing a Colony: The Case of Hong Kong 1844–1899.* Ph.D. Dissertation. University of Wales, 2001; G. Mitchelmore, *How Do Extrinsic Performance Incentives Affect the Alignment Between Frontline Police Performance and Police Strategy?* DBA Thesis. Heriot-Watt University, August 2010.
45. See HKU Scholarly Hub – HKU Theses Online (HKUTO). Search date 1941 to 2014. Search term: 'policing' and 'Hong Kong'. There are 90 plus HKP thesis, a majority by HKP.

46. A review of HKU HKP-related theses and dissertations shows that little references were made to Chinese literature, except perhaps Chinese guanxi management in corruption and integrative function of Guan Di worship in policing.
47. W. C. Lo Yam (盧任惠珍), *A Balanced Approach to Training: Another Step Forward in Improving Retention of Junior Police Constables*, Master Thesis, Master of Public Administration, Department of Public Administration, 1994.
48. The dissertation consisted of seven chapters. Chapter 1 states the context, focus, contribution, method, and findings of the dissertation in brief. Chapter 2 begins with a brief review of public administration literature on the importance of training to human resource development. It then discusses the HKP—Civil Service Branch's policy towards human resource development, particularly as provided for in the 1989 Public Service Reform Report. The chapter concludes with a discussion of retention and training and development with the HKP. Chapter 3 addresses two HKP human resource development issues. First, it reports on human resource—career development in the HKP, with reference to changing roles and relations of police in Hong Kong society. Second, it reports on the changing role and responsibilities of police constables and PTS training. Chapter 4 is a historical account of development of PTS and PC training. Chapter 5 documents the introduction of social studies at PTS, its rational, process and impact. Chapter 6 is the heart of the research. It reports on the research: methods, data, analysis and findings. Chapter 7 is a conclusion summarising the research findings, with recommendation rendered on how best to conduct social studies at PTS.
49. D. W. Pope and J. Hui, The Royal Hong Kong Police, preventive policing and young people, *Police Journal*, 57: 26–31, 1984; J. C. Alderson, Hong Kong, Tokyo, Peking: Three police systems observed, *Police Studies*, 3 (4): 3–12, 1981; M. S. Gaylord and J. F. Galliher, Riding the underground dragon: Crime control and public order on Hong Kong's mass transit railway, *British Journal of Criminology*, 31 (1): 15–26, 1991; J. Vagg, The borders of crime: Hong Kong–China cross border criminal activity, *British Journal of Criminology*, 32 (3): 310–329, 1992; Chapter 6: Hong Kong: Colonial Capitalism, In: R. I. Mawby (ed.), *Comparative Police Issues* (London: Unwin Hyman Ltd., 1990), pp. 86–101; G. Benton, *The Hong Kong Crisis* (London: Pluto, 1983); J. Vagg, The legitimations of policing in Hong Kong: A non-democratic perspective, In: O. Marenin (ed.), *Police Change, Changing Police* (New York and London: Garlan, 1996); J. Vagg, Policing in Hong Kong, *Policing and Society*, 1: 235–247, 1991; H. Traver and M. S. Gaylord, The Royal Hong Kong Police, In: H. Traver and J. Vagg (eds.), *Crime and Justice in Hong Kong* (Hong Kong: Oxford University Press, 1991); R. Mushkat, *Freedom of Association and Assembly* (pp. 153–186); P. Morrow, Police powers and individual liberty, In: R. Wacks (ed.), *Civil Liberties in Hong Kong* (Hong Kong: Oxford University Press, 1988), pp. 243–278; G. Edwards and A. C. Byrnes, David Hodson, Criminal Investigation, In: *Hong Kong's Bill of Rights: The First Year* (Hong Kong: Faculty of Law, University of Hong Kong, 1993), pp. 9–17; M. Ng-Quinn, *Bureaucratic Response to Political Change: Theoretical Use of Atypical Case of the Hong Kong Police* (Hong Kong: Occasional Paper No. 2, Hong Kong Institute of Asia Pacific Studies, Chinese University of Hong Kong); there is no serious empirical research into Hong Kong policing, not to mention any original indigenous police theory building effort.

50. Book review by J. Barbyn: M. S. Gaylord and H. Traver, *Introduction to the Hong Kong Criminal Justice System* (Hong Kong: Hong Kong University Press, 1994), xvi + 200 pp, paperback, HK110. *Hong Kong L.J.* 25, 429–430, 1995.
51. *Ibid.*, 432.
52. W H Chiu and T. W. Lo, *Understanding Criminal Justice in Hong Kong* (UK: Willan Publishing, 2008). Reviewed by L. A. Jacobs. Canadian Criminal Justice Association. http://www.ccja-acjp.ca/en/cjcr300/cjcr335.html
53. M. Lee, Criminal justice in Hong Kong, *Asian Journal of Criminology*, 4 (2): 187–188, 2009; D. Bindzus, Criminal justice in Hong Kong, *Hong Kong L.J.* 21, 181, 1991.
54. http://lib.hku.hk/general/research/guides/Hong%20Kong%20Police_bib.pdf
55. Not to be ignored are popular media stories or investigative reporting on HKPF, such as the acclaimed 1978 BBC series on 'Hong Kong Beat'. 'Hong Kong Beat' 1978 BBC TV Theme by Richard Denton & Martin Cook. 1. Detective, 2. Chasing The Dragon, 3. The Bamboo Curtain, 4. The Streets of Hong Kong, 5. The Great Payroll Robbery, 6. The Big Swoop, 7. Country Coppers, 8. Buns, Boats and Bombs, 9. The Uneasy Summer. https://www.youtube.com/watch?v=YNiR0LHXa30
56. *In the Shadow of the Noonday Gun* (Hong Kong: Time Out, 2 January 2013). http://www.timeout.com.hk/books/features/55130/in-the-shadow-of-the-noonday-gun.html. See also K. C. Wong, *Policing in Hong Kong: Voices*, 2016, Manuscript under preparation.
57. OffBeat. http://www.police.gov.hk/offbeat/996/eng/index.html
58. Ling Sir's website. http://lingsir.org. See also K. C. Wong, *Policing in Hong Kong: Voices*, 2016, Manuscript under preparation.
59. http://www.pcchk.com/forum-28-1.html
60. http://gwulo.com/royal-hong-kong-police-force-history
61. '你適合做警員嗎' Water (pen name) 2009-8-21. 08:38. http://www.discuss.com.hk/viewthread.php?tid=104211751240
62. K. C. Wong, *Policing in Hong Kong: Voices*, 2016, Manuscript under preparation.
63. Laws are made to be upheld by all, *The Standard*, Tuesday, 24 April 2012. http://pda.cellinnet.com/free/hk_standard/stdarticle.php?we_cat=5&art_id=121770&sid=36148161&con_type=1&d_str=20120424&fc=8
64. PC Wong Chi-hon (Ah Ho) joined the HKP in 1988. Wong made a name for himself. He worked with Marco Tam Siu-ming and Chief Inspector Tse Yiu-tak, then the Western District Training and Staff Relations Officer, District Bulletin and training materials with real-life police officers in mind. They were fondly called 'Filming Trio' (拍戲三人組). The Force is with you….on the silver screen, *Police Beat*, 712: 26 September–9 October 2001. http://www.police.gov.hk/offbeat/712/022_c.htm
65. Former police officer involved with indecent assault of female students, *Sun News*, 19 July 2006. http://the-sun.on.cc/channels/news/20060719/20060719030232_0000.html
66. Former police officer loitering in female toilet preliminary proven, *Sun News*, 6 July 2005. http://the-sun.on.cc/channels/news/20050607/20050607021707_0001.html
67. http://www.police.gov.hk/ppp_en/01_about_us/ph_02.html

68. L. Ho, and Y. K. Chu, *Policing Hong Kong, 1842–1969: Insiders' Stories* (Hong Kong: City University of Hong Kong Press, 2011). For example, Chapter 2, notes 1, 2, 5, 6.
69. *Ibid.*, Big head in green coat whistle, p. 17.
70. http://en.wikipedia.org/wiki/Patrick_Yu
71. P. S. Yu (Chinese: 余叔韶), *Tales from No. 9 Ice House Street* (Hong Kong: Hong Kong University Press, 2002), pp. 42–46.
72. *Ibid.*, p. 44.
73. E. Tu, a self-styled social activist, tirelessly championed for Hong Kong people against police corruption and government wrongdoing. 'A tribute to centenarian E. Tu', Lau Nai-keung, *China Daily*, 6 June 2013. ('During the 1960s and 1970s, Elsie was a fierce opponent of the corruption, then endemic in many areas of Hong Kong life, and the influence of the Triads. She also campaigned for better working and housing conditions for the poor. Though many in ruling circles disliked Elsie "rocking the boat", her efforts led to the establishment of the Independent Commission against Corruption in 1974'.) http://www.chinadaily.com.cn/hkedition/2013-06/04/content_16562675.htm (Elsie Tu, GBM, CBE (née Hume; Chinese: born 2 June 1913) is a social activist, former elected member of the Urban Council of Hong Kong, and former member of the Legislative Council of Hong Kong. She moved to Hong Kong in 1951 following a period as a missionary in China.) http://en.wikipedia.org/wiki/Elsie_Tu
74. E. Elliot, *Colonial Hong Kong in the Eyes of Elsie Tu* (Hong Kong: Hong Kong University Press, 2013), p. 86.
75. G. Mathews, *Ghetto at the Center of the World: Chungking Mansions, Hong Kong* (Chicago: University of Chicago Press, 2012).
76. A. Ajukwu, *Hell in Hong Kong: 134 Days of Torture* (Denver, Colorado: Outskirts Press, 2012).
77. P. Craggs, *When Harry Met Vicky—A Fatal Attraction: Growing Up with My Parents* (Bloomington, Indiana: Xlibris Corporation, 2012), 2012, 95, 97.
78. Wife cries for joy as she is cleared of murder, *The Standard*, Hong Kong, 28 March 1972.
79. K. C. Wong, *The Study of Policing in Hong Kong*, 2016, Manuscript under review.
80. *Ibid.*, 218–224. 'On Patrol'.
81. T. L. Tsim and B. H. Y. Chen (eds.), *The Other Hong Kong Report* (Hong Kong: The Chinese University Press, Hong Kong Series, 1989), Chapter 3: People and Chapter 4: Laws—Role of Police (p. 157).
82. Hong Kong Human Rights Monitor. http://www.hkhrm.org.hk/
83. Human Rights Watch, Human Rights Watch World Report 1997—Hong Kong, 1 January 1997. http://www.refworld.org/docid/3ae6a8b10.html
84. Hong Kong Bar Association—Press Releases. http://www.hkba.org/whatsnew/press-release/
85. 'Statement of Hong Kong Bar Association on the Security Arrangements of the Hong Kong Police Force during the Visit of Vice Premier Li Keqiang', Hong Kong Bar Association (24 August 2011). P. Siu, Human rights head blasts police action at protest, *SCMP* 14 August 2012; Hong Kong: Investigate Police Actions at July 1 Rally, *Human Rights Watch*, 11 July 2011. http://www.hrw.org/news/2011/07/11/hong-kong-investigate-police-actions-july-1-rally

86. Hong Kong Human Rights Monitor. http://www.hkhrm.org.hk/
87. 'Police Power and Civil Liberties' (p. 11) Magaret Ng. Final Submission, LegCo Report 2011—12. http://www.margaretng.com/download/Annual%20Report/MNG_REPORT_2012.pdf
88. A. Broom, *The Closing of the American Mind* (New York: Simon and Schuster, 30 June 2008, original 1987).
89. J. H. Scholnick, A sketch of the policeman's working personality, In: *Justice without Trial*, 3rd edition (New York: Wiley, 1994), pp. 41–68.
90. G. L. Kirkham, From professor to patrolman: A fresh perspective on the police, *Journal of Police Science and Administration*, 2: 127–137, June 1974.
91. Police-informant, CIP. BA, MA, 42, SIP Marine HQ./CID/Adm., prior assignment CID HKI, 18 years of service, married, two children.
92. P. Manning, Researcher: An alien in the police world, In: A. Niederhoffer and A. S. Blumberg (eds.), *The Ambivalent Force* (Hinsdale, IL: The Dryden Press, 1976), pp. 103–121.
93. The officer might not be completely incorrect in his way and style of reasoning, objectionable though it might first appear. The lack of total information and full understanding of what, how and why HKP police works make for erroneous judgment and distorted views about HKP's relative effectiveness and degree of accountability. Since the people can never be totally informed (police have legitimate reasons not to share all information, e.g., cost, privacy, secrecy) and do not have the motivation, time or expertise to fully understand how police work, this is one of the evils of popular government, Sir Henry Sumner Maine, Popular Government (Indianapolis: Liberty Class, 1976) (First published 1885), they are likely to form a distorted view about the police or on issues relating to the police. If this should be the case (just as with imperfect market condition calling for state intervention to prevent the market from being abused, e.g., monopoly), the HKP might be tempted to control and manipulate what information should be made available to the public in order to 'protect' or 'correct' the people from structural ignorance of an unintended kind. This mindset towards information control, though appearing reasonable, is fraught with danger. Chief among which is the inclination on the part of the police to withhold information not favourable to the police, and further manipulate, if not even manufacture information putting the police in a more favourable light. It is the opinion of the author that, proceeding this way, the situation could reach a *1984* Ministry of Truth scenario.
94. 'Although data, figures and previous analysis in relation to the concerned recruitment system are rather adequate and readily available, there is information being withheld by Personnel Wing of the Police Force that the author considers as relevant to this research. Personnel Wing has clearly indicated those information is within the ambit of confidentiality and relates to the Police Force's internal policy, which should not be disclosed to assist an academic research. Thus, the author concentrates on open materials only' (p. 6). H. Chan, *An Analysis of the Dual Police Inspector Recruitment System of the Hong Kong Police Force.* A dissertation submitted in partial fulfillment for the degree of MPA, Hong Kong University, 2006.
95. A. Y. Jiao, *The Police in Hong Kong: A Contemporary View* (Maryland: University Press of America, 2007).

96. H. Chan (陳霞), *An Analysis of the Dual Police Inspector Recruitment System of the Hong Kong Police Force*. Dissertation, MPA, Hong Kong University, Department of Politics and Public Administration, 2006.
97. K. C. Wong, *One Country Two Systems Cross Border Crime between Hong Kong and China* (New Brunswick, NJ; London: Transaction Publishers, 2012).
98. K. C. Wong, *Policing in Hong Kong* (Farnham, Surrey, UK: Ashgate, 2012); A. Jiao, *Police In Hong Kong: A Contemporary View* (Lanham, Maryland: University Press of America, 2007); and I. Ward, *Sui Geng: The Hong Kong Marine Police 1841–1950* (Hong Kong University Press, 1991).
99. S. E. Hamilton, *Watching Over Hong Kong: Private Policing 1841–1941* (Hong Kong: Hong Kong University, 2008).
100. See SIP Ling case study.
101. See corruption and its control with HKP. S. Jing, *Corruption by Design? A Comparative Study of Singapore, Hong Kong and Mainland China*, Crawford School of Economics and Government, 2007. https://crawford.anu.edu.au/degrees/pogo/discussion_papers/PDP07-01.pdf
102. See CIP Andrews case study, Chapter Three, *supra*. See also M. Hampton, British legal culture and colonial governance: The attack on corruption in Hong Kong, 1968–1974, *Britain and the World*, 5: 223–239, DOI 10.3366/brw.2012.0055, ISSN 2043-8567. Available online September 2012.
103. Beyond public opinion survey.
104. Such as oral history.
105. K. K. Ho and Y. K. Chu, *Policing Hong Kong, 1842–1969: Insiders' Stories* (Hong Kong: City University of Hong Kong Press, 2012).
106. S. F. Gu, *A Study of Ethical Policing in Public Order Events*, MPA, Department of Government and Public Administration, University of Hong Kong, 2012.

Debating Colonial Policing

2

> The Study of colonial policing was, for many years, the neglected stepchild of colonial and imperial history, preserving and perpetuating untested generalisations and myths as undifferentiated assumptions were reiterated and reified. In an academic process that resembled nothing so much as the colonialism it described, the multiple roles of colonial police forces went unexplored, their positions in colonial power structures for the most part went unexamined, and their status as key apparatuses of the state was underplayed.[1]
>
> **Melvin Eugene Page and Penny M. Sonnenburg (2003)**

> Legally there was no such thing as a British Empire. Physically, too, it was a kind of fiction, or bluff, in that it implied a far stronger power at the centre than really exist. (p. 197)
>
> **Jan Morris (2010)**[2]

> Hong Kong did not posses the conventional attributes of a colony and that late twentieth century Hong Kong showed little sign of a colonial presence, and even less of a past.[3]
>
> **Tak-Wing Ngo (2002)**

Introduction

Colonisation resulted from the globalisation of trade, in tandem with 'humanising' and 'civilising' the world. Western nations lacked cheap labour to make their goods and open market to ply their wares. They looked for slave hands and free markets overseas. Progressive imperialists and spiritual leaders, in order to salvage the world, looked overseas in search of backward race and lost souls.

Colonial conquests started with European settlements in Latin America in the fifteenth century (Spain and Portugal in Central and South America), followed by British domination of the rest of the world in the twentieth century (British and French settlements in North America, New Zealand, Australia and China). At its height, 50% of the world's population were labouring under colonial rule of one form or another. In terms of reception, colonialism has been more maligned than understood, so said Frederick Madden:

> Journalists and min-historians dismiss careful analysis and repeat their ready-make conclusions; and public opinion always prefers the folklore of sensational Sound Bits to historical truth. The obsession, politically correct of course is to denigrate empire, to pillory the conspiratorial machinations of empire builders, and to blackwash the whole British experience of overseas rule.[4]

Until very recently (1990), colonial policing was an understudied field (Mawby, 1990). Since then, Anderson (1992) and others have tried to catch up. The reason for the lapse is not clear. The impact of the neglect is evident: people's understanding of colonial policing is simplistic and impressionistic; driven more by ideology than reality, conviction than evidence, and emotion than rationality.

To date, what little is known about colonial policing requires drawing a distinction between colonial policing in settlements versus pacification in protectorates. Additionally, there is much more known about 'colonial' policing[5] in settlements over white people than 'pacification' policing in protectorates over coloured subjects.[6] The image of high-handed, militaristic, suppressive colonial policing, for example, Royal Irish Constabulary (RIC),[7] is associated with the second, not the first. Still there are many variations in form and much difference in functions to pacification policing in various parts of the colonial empires that resist uniform treatment and tidy summation:

> Generally, policing in these areas developed in an ad hoc fashion, in reaction to particular needs but more importantly in reaction to the nature of the local acceptance or resistance to colonial rule. Pacifying the 'natives', protecting colonial economic interests, uphold the legitimacy of colonial political authorities and maintaining basic essentials of law and order in order to open up trading routs, were some of the factors that promoted the establishment of police forces in the protectorates.[8]

Finally, evidence shows that colonial policing in Hong Kong is not unique. There is much cross-over of personnel, experience and practices throughout the British Empire:

> Colonial policing in Hong Kong is not entirely unique. Ideas and practices from one colony were borrowed and applied in another; this was especially true both for administrative practice and of legislation. Police administration in Hong Kong is also not far from Metropolitan policing, to the extent British police are seconded for a short time to be in Hong Kong, with an expectation of returning to London. The pool of experience that senior officers in the colonial police were able to draw upon was likely to have been a significant

> element in defining the character and development of policing. By examining these imperial linkages and by comparing experience of the colonies we may yet learn a great deal more about policing the empire.[9]

The intellectual challenge is set: What is the best way to describe colonial policing? To what extent is colonial policing different in Hong Kong and in what way is it the same with other colonies? Ultimately, what are the defining characteristics of the HKP, as a colonial force? The thesis of this book is that the HKP is neither British nor colonial. It is unique unto itself, more appropriately called 'colonial policing with Hong Kong characteristics'.

This chapter has one purpose. It tries to debunk the myths of 'colonial' policing in Hong Kong. It allows people—researchers and the public alike—to see the HKP in its naked light, unencumbered by historical baggage and tinted by ideological blinders. It observes that long before its demise in 1997, colonial policing in Hong Kong is not what it has been made out to be. It has its own existential properties and associated defining characteristics. This observation should give pause to ideological zealots, political junkies and cultural warriors, who, for self-serving reasons or due to cultural ignorance, insist that 'colonial policing' inherits a certain immutable form and essential functions, such as that of RIC—militaristic and suppressive, thereby making it *ipso facto* illegitimate and dysfunctional in serving the Hong Kong people's best interests and basic needs.

As an intellectual project, the ultimate challenge with this chapter is to ascertain what colonial policing is all about, conceptually and in practice, as applied to Hong Kong, over the course of 170 years.

This chapter has four sections. Section I defines as it discusses the 'Concept of Colonial Policing' before raising the issue, stating the premises and defending the thesis that conventional idea of colonial policing ill fits grounded observation of policing in colonial Hong Kong. Section II 'Deconstructing Colonial Policing' problematises colonial policing as applied to Hong Kong. It adopts four premises in unpacking colonial policing in Hong Kong, that is, colonial policing takes many forms; colonial policing is a pluralistic enterprise; colonial policing is a collaborative effort; and finally, colonial policing is an existentially relative, not essentially absolute, phenomenon. It offers the idea of 'people's policing', 'collaborative policing' and 'discretionary policing' to debunk the myth that colonial policing is a one-sided (British) and unidirectional (top down) affair. This framework of understanding colonial policing as people-collaborative-discretionary policing is nothing new. Personal experience informs and empirical research instructs; all policing is about people working together in a give-and-take manner. The contention here is 'it takes two to tango'. Section III 'The True Nature of Colonial Policing' summarises as it discusses the implications of the findings while Section IV 'Conclusion' takes stock of the lessons learned.

I: Concept of Colonial Policing

Defining Colonialism

Colonial policing escapes definition when one cannot agree on what constitutes colonial policing, in form, style and conduct. Colonial policing defies assessment when people cannot agree on its basic purpose, functions and utilities. Nevertheless, definition and assessment of colonial policing is necessary to study HKP reform during the course of colonisation and decolonisation.

To define colonial policing, one must first define colonialism, since colonial policing exists to secure colonialism. Commonly understood, colonisation is the subjugation or domination of one people over another, economically, socially, culturally, legally and militarily.[10] Colonisation can be achieved without force, for example, with cultural imperialism, or secured by economics, for example, multi-national corporatisations, but force is always implied and reserved as the ultimate sanction.[11] This makes the colonial police handmaiden of economic masters.

There are many kinds of colonial rules, with different characteristics (Table 2.1). The typologies and characteristics of colonial rule necessarily affect government policy and policing strategy. Hong Kong belongs to the indirect rule group, in political, economic and social policy. From the very beginning, the British colonial office wanted to spend as little as possible in Hong Kong in developing its infrastructure or improving social conditions, thus the notion of laissez-faire economics and indirect rule in governance. As a result, much of the colonial policing was left to private funding and stewardship.

As to the justification, the formation and characteristics of colonial police Charles Jeffries describes as follows:

> The fact is that the really effective influence upon the development of colonial police forces during the nineteenth century was not that of the police of Great Britain, but that of the Royal Irish Constabulary...Into the merits or demerits of this system, as applied to Ireland, it is not for me to enter, but it is clear enough that from the point of view of the colonies there was much attraction in an arrangement which provided what we now call a 'paramilitary' organization or gendarmerie armed and trained to operate as an agent of the... government in a country where the population was predominately rural, communications poor, social conditions were largely primitive, and the recourse to violence by members of the public who were 'against the government' was not infrequent. It was natural that such a force, rather than one organized on the lines of purely civilian or localized forces of Great Britain, should have been taken as a suitable model for adaption to colonial conditions.[12]

The colonial policing model of policing, as exemplified by the RIC, is distinguished from the civilian model, made famous by Sir Robert Peel and

Table 2.1 Varieties and Characteristics of Colonial Rule

Type of Colonial Rule	Political Characteristics	Economic Characteristics	Social Characteristics
Company rule	Minimum government since primary interest is profit. Little government support for education, health care, and other services. Primary emphasis on 'law and order'-keeping peace.	Exploitation of natural resources. Profits for company most important economic goal. Alienation (taking away) of land from African peoples. Forced labour policies necessary for profits.	No money spent on social services such as education and health care. Social/cultural dislocation brought about by forced movement of people for labour.
Direct rule	Practised primarily by French, Belgian, and Portuguese colonialists. Minimal government lack of revenue. Laws created and enforced by European colonial officials, even at the local/rural levels. Emphasis on law and order. Traditional political authorities such as chiefs removed from power. Used 'divide and rule' tactics.	Exploitation of natural resources for export. Minimal taxes on exports so as to maximise profits for European companies. Revenues used to support law and order. Harsh labour policy to insure ready supply of inexpensive labour. Limited development of economic infrastructure.	Little revenue spent on developing social services schooling, health care, social security. Social and cultural dislocation due to economic and labour policies. Urbanisation. Spread of Christianity in non-Islamic areas.
Indirect rule	Practised primarily by the British in West Africa (Ghana, Nigeria, Sierra Leone) and parts of East Africa (Uganda, Tanganyika). Minimal government lack of revenue. Laws made by European colonialists, but used traditional African leaders (chiefs, headmen) as intermediaries in local government. Emphasis on law and order. Used 'divide and rule' tactics.	Exploitation of natural resources for export. Minimal taxes on exports so as to maximise profits for European companies. Revenues used to support law and order. Harsh labour policy to insure ready supply of inexpensive labour. Limited development of economic infrastructure.	Little revenue spent on developing social services schooling, health care, social security. Social and cultural dislocation due to economic and labour policies. Urbanisation. Spread of Christianity in non-Islamic areas.

(*Continued*)

Table 2.1 (*Continued*) Varieties and Characteristics of Colonial Rule

Type of Colonial Rule	Political Characteristics	Economic Characteristics	Social Characteristics
Settler rule	Stronger government system to protect political rights of settlers. Government policy oriented to protect and support settler population. African populations denied political participation or rights. Harsh repression of African political movements. African populations ruled directly by European (often settler) officials. Strong emphasis on law and order.	Infrastructural support for settler-owned businesses. Heavier taxes to support the development of the settler population. Harsh labour policies used to guarantee an inexpensive labour force.	Little revenue spent on developing social services schooling, health care, social security. Social and cultural dislocation due to economic and labour policies. Urbanisation. Spread of Christianity in non-Islamic areas.

Source: Unit Two: Studying Africa through the Social Studies. Module 7B: African History, the Era of Global Encroachment. http://exploringafrica.matrix.msu.edu/students/curriculum/m7b/activity3.php.

spread around the world in the form of community policing, by the following structural, functional and stylistic characteristics:

First, structurally, the colonial police establishment is organised in such a way so that it is not part of the people, but part of the colonial government. As such the police officers do not mix with the people. This works in two directions. The police are insulated from the public, that is, it is not accountable to the public. The people are isolated from the police, that is, they have little to no relationship with the police. To this end, police live physically apart from the public.

Second, functionally, the colonial police officers, by mandate, are there to serve the imperial government's interests, not that of the people, that is, they are there to secure the empire and control the people, not to serve and protect. To this end, the police rarely perform any civilian policing duties.

Third, stylistically, the colonial police are militaristically disposed. Force of arms is used to resolve political disputes and suppress social dissents. To this end, the police are organised in paramilitary ways.

Colonial HKP: Context Matters

A colonial police force was established in Hong Kong with the passage of 'an ordinance for the Establishment and Regulation of a Police Force in the Colony of Hong Kong' (Ordinance No. 12 of 1844) on 1 May 1844, otherwise known as the Police Force Regulations (PFR).[13]

The PFR laid down the legal framework,[14] specifying the necessary conditions of service[15] and associated powers of an officer for the formation of the first-ever police agency in Hong Kong, under British rule.

The preamble of the ordinance reads, in a pertinent part:

> [I]t is considered expedient that provision should be made for the establishment of an effective System of Police within the Colony of Hong Kong.... His Excellency the Governor of Hongkong, to nominate, and appoint a proper person to be Chief Magistrate of Police, throughout the Colony of Hongkong, who shall reside in the town of Victoria, and shall be charged, and invested, with the general direction, and superintendence of the Force to be established under this Ordinance, and to appoint from time to time, fit and proper persons to be respectively marine, and assistant Magistrates, and Superintendents of Police, under the said Chief Magistrate.

The preamble is telling of a colony under siege. After 3 years of British occupation, Hong Kong was still infested with vice (opium,[16] prostitution,[17] gambling[18]) and afflicted with crimes of all sorts[19] perpetrated by evil Chinese,[20] listless sojourns,[21] ill-disciplined soldiers, drunken sailors,[22] marauding criminals,[23] organised gangsters[24] and roaming pirates, which defies treatment and requires an 'effective System of Police' to control and a harsh punishment regime to deter.[25]

Since the HKP's inception, there has been a continuous debate about whether or not the HKP is a colonial police force. As an analytical framework, scholars have used Charles Jeffries' RIC model to explain HKP's origin and development. In his classical treatment of 'The Colonial Police',[26] Jeffries observed that colonial policing required the adoption of an RIC type of paramilitary force to maintain control, suppress dissent, impose governance and ultimately achieve dominance.

However, Jeffries also made clear that 'colonial police' is not a static concept, still less a one-size-fits-all practice. It is capable of adjustment, mutation and change, in context, and most certainly over time. In time, when law and order in the colony is achieved and a habit of obedience of the people is obtained, the colonial police revert or advance to[27] a more civil kind of policing, with paramilitary policing held in reserve. Since then, Jeffries' classical model of 'colonial police' has been questioned and revised in some quarters.[28] In the case of Hong Kong, the constant question being asked is whether and to what extent the HKP was a 'colonial police' force, in mission, organisation and means.

In 1999[29] and 2001,[30] two Ph.D. dissertations disputed Charles Jeffries' crude treatment of HKP colonial policing. Ng, a historian, argued that the HKP adopted paramilitary policing, less to suppress the indigenous Chinese, but to bring law and order to Hong Kong, and as a defence against nationalist rebels from China. Kerrigan, an (ex) HKP commissioner, argued that the HKP, while organised in a paramilitary fashion, in actuality functioned much like London Metropolitan Police, in using coercive force to tame outlaws and secure order in Hong Kong. In essence, coercive policing, a defining feature of sovereignty, is everywhere to be had, with consensual policing in London as in colonial policing of Hong Kong.

Both authors saw the need to revisit the issue of what counts as colonial police and what stands for colonial policing. Their work invites more analysis of the true nature and defining characteristics of colonial 'policing' in Hong Kong more so than just describing 'colonial police' in military terms and documenting 'colonial policing' practice with an oppressive overtone. As a research project and field of discourse, the former analytical approach seeks to understand what 'colonial policing' is like in Hong Kong and the latter tries to understand how policing works in colonial Hong Kong. The difference between the two approaches is more than academic. It holds the key to the proper grounding of an emerging discipline of Hong Kong policing studies.

This chapter takes another stab at the colonial policing debate in Hong Kong. It argues that the HKP did not copy the RIC paramilitary tradition, but adopted military organisation (discipline) and measures (punishment)[31] entirely due to the influence of one person, William Caine, the putative father of the HKP who tried to bring law and order to a place and people he hardly knew. Since then and until the 1890s, there was no influence of the RIC to be found.[32] In so doing, the author subscribes to the idea that a strong personality, limiting conditions and prevailing circumstances make historical theses.[33]

First, Hong Kong was acquired through conquest. The administrators of Hong Kong were nearly all military officers at the time. Second, Hong Kong was very much at war with China, until well into the 1900s. Although British troops landed in Possession Point in 1841, the treaty of Nanking was not signed until 1842. From that point onwards, disaffected Hong Kong residents, nationalistic Chinese people, anti-foreign Triads and disgruntled economic migrants never stopped causing problems for the Hong Kong Government, from invading Victoria from Kowloon, to poisoning foreigners, to rioting in the streets to mass blockading of Hong Kong. Third, Hong Kong was a dangerous place, with a restless, mostly male population. Stern control and draconian punishment were necessary; military discipline thus came to the rescue.[34] To Major Cain, under the Command of Major General Pottinger, waging a war on crime was a type of *military* campaign[35] and did not represent a clash of civilisations[36] (though for the Chinese who bore the brunt of the crime campaign, and suffered disparate impact,[37] the difference hardly mattered). Fourth, there was no plan for governing Hong Kong. For example, Pottinger was asked to

> [E]stablish the Colony without being supplied with the usual model guide in the shape of printed instructions from the Colonial Office containing orders clearly defined as to almost every particular matter which would be required of him, and his establishment was at a disadvantage in many other respects, and his establishment was formed with such rough material as first came to hand.[38]

The British had never commanded a Chinese colony. As a spear for the British Empire, the military had a tradition in bringing order to untested land and alien people, with force of arms if need be. Fifth, Caine was a competent and zealous military officer. He had earned the trust of the British Government, in Hong Kong or at the Colonial Offices, with a can-do spirit and take-no-prisoners approach to fighting crime and disorder. But Major Caine who dispensed justice as Magistrate of Police was no lawyer, and had few inclinations to follow the law.[39] Seventh, the colonial administration in general and Caine in particular were given a lot of (unbound) authority to pacify Hong Kong, the way Caine deemed fit and proper.

Until 1844, Caine was the personification of the HKP and embodiment of justice in Hong Kong.[40] Hong Kong then looked like a penal colony more so than a civil society; one big military depot, in an epic war against British civilised rule.

Study of Colonial Police

The study of colonial police is the study of how the HKP functioned and was structured, in theory and practice. More specifically, the study of colonial policing is the study of how the HKP, as a colonial political institution, conducted its business of colonial rule, by law (legal ordering) and with coercion (militant control). Additionally, it is the study of the negotiations over power (norms and process), substance (values and interest) and style (coercive vs. persuasive) as they existed between British law enforcement and Chinese customary social control, at the sufferance of the sovereign state (here the British colonial government). In 'more and less government' theoretical terms, this conflict was a negotiation over the relative delegation of public control authority and relative sponsorship of private social control measures.

The ultimate question to be discussed in colonial policing is to what extent the two radically different control systems—colonial versus indigenous—were in conflict and in what way they were complementary. More significantly, how did such observed conflicting and complementary elements of control manifest themselves in daily life as routines, and how were they resolved when in conflict, such as in crisis?

A cursory review of extant literature shows that with rare exceptions,[41] the investigation into policing in Hong Kong has been exclusively focussed on the HKP, its origin, development, role and functions, organisation, powers and mode of operations. Specifically, the coverage is mainly on HKP's 'imperialistic' role and 'colonial' legacy,[42] and less on its 'localised' functions and 'indigenous' makeover.[43] There are few investigations into policing in Hong Kong, its philosophy, functions, style and impact.[44] Worse, scholars and students have confounded the two, creating unnecessary confusion, causing inevitable distortion and precipitating perennial contentious debates.

In the study of colonial policing in Hong Kong, the question that is most often asked is how was Hong Kong policed, before and after 1997,[45] that is pre- and post-colonisation, as an internal[46] and international[47] comparative project. By this line of questioning, what people really want to know is whether or not the HKP changed.[48] An even more practical question on everyone's mind is that which most coincides with post-colonial study[49]: how might Hong Kong's colonial past affect post-1997 policing in Hong Kong?[50]

Such kinds of inquiry require investigation into the nature and characteristics of the HKP and the conduct and performance of colonial policing[51] in Hong Kong as distinctive colonial policing practices,[52] including charter and mission, ideology and philosophy, role and functions, organisation and operations, strategy and tactics,[53] and problems and issues.[54] Subsequently, three inter-related questions present themselves:

First was the HKP a colonial police force in philosophy, organisation and function? What did the HKP as a 'colonial police' look like? This focus on seeking answers to how the HKP, as a colonial force, originated, developed and operated in Hong Kong, top down. The assumption here is that if the HKP is determined to be a colonial police force in the form of organisation and style of operations—paramilitarily organised and trained, isolated from the public in barracks, heavily armed during operations, devoted to public order policing and routinised secret political surveillance—one is entitled to assume that the HKP was conducting colonial policing. More colloquially, if it smells and looks like a rat, it must be a rat.

Second, what did colonial policing in Hong Kong look like in the street and with the people? The issues raised here include (1) How did the HKP act when conducting social policing, for example, maintaining public order or providing social services? More generally, how did the HKP conduct 'high' versus 'low' policing? (2) How did local and indigenised expatriate officers behave in doing colonial policing? If the HKP did not act in colonial ways all the time and colonial officers did not behave in colonial manner uniformly, what then was the nature of colonial policing in Hong Kong?

Finally, how can two divergent policing patterns—colonial HKP (top down) policing versus people policing in Hong Kong (bottom up)—be reconciled?

In pursing these queries into colonial policing, this investigation takes up Ngo's invitation:

> In the words of Bloch, when the passions of the past blend with the prejudices of the present, human reality is reduced to a picture of black and white. It is the danger of gross simplification of the nature of colonialism in Hong Kong that the present volume needs to address. Our aim is to present new empirical evidence that can lead to a more balanced understanding of the multifaceted nature of Hong Kong's colonial past.[55]

II: Deconstructing Colonial Policing

Introduction

A (re)newed understanding of colonial police requires breaking ranks with the past usage of the term, a deconstruction project.

The deconstruction project starts with an understanding of how British colonial rule over Hong Kong was actualised, with law (Letters Patent, Royal Instructions), through delegation (Governor) and by way of bureaucracies (Secretary of State and Colonial Office). Alternatively, there is a need to ascertain the relative powers of British versus Hong Kong Government officials in influencing, setting and implementing colonial policies. Ultimately, whether, in what manner and to what extent Hong Kong Government was allowed to work autonomously, and if needed, at cross-purposes from the sovereign in the best interests of Hong Kong, is the puzzle.

Conventional wisdom has it that legally the Governor in Hong Kong worked at the pleasure and behest of the Crown. Historically, this is not how Hong Kong was governed. The colonial governance in Hong Kong, as a political act, was the joint product of a collective enterprise involving the Crown, colonial officials, Governor, Cadets and Chinese community members, each playing their assigned role separately and collaboratively:

> The interaction of these different component parts had an important bearing on the power relationship between them. Governors appointed by Britain, often with no prior experience of Hong Kong, to govern for a term of five years through senior civil servants who has spent a whole career there. Unofficials were leaders in their own communities, who may have been new to Governors but were well known to senior civil servants. Some Secretary of State were influential and strong-minded such a Churchill, Passfield and Lyttelton, Some has a clear idea of what they wanted to achieve…Some Colonial Office officials, through the force of personality and intellect exercised considerable influence on Hong Kong's policies, in particular Gerald Gent and Sidney Cain. Parliament could also be a conduit for the expression of British public opinion on Hong Kong's affairs. Its influence…was more often indirect.[56]

If one were to ask who spoke for Hong Kong and promote her interests in the colonial bureaucracy, one need not venture too far outfield to find this representation in the Hong Kong governors. Most Hong Kong governors knew and cared about Hong Kong, for example, Governors Davis (8 May 1844 to 21 March 1848), and more than a few were in love with Chinese culture and Hong Kong people, for example, Governors Hennessy (22 April 1877 to 30 March 1883), to the point of challenging the Colonial Office's assumptions on and prejudices against Hong Kong, as a place, people and culture. The contentious relationship and conflict of interests between the role of Colonial Office and Hong Kong Government is best attested to by Alexander Grantham, upon assuming the Hong Kong Governorship after WWII:

> But in a crown colony, where does the allegiance of the governor lie: to the Colonial Office or to the colony? Normally, no conflict arises, but occasionally it does, and the situation is not improved by a tendency on the part of the

> Colonial Office to treat a crown colony as though it were a sub-department of the Colonial Office. I know that the Colonial Office officials do a conscientious and honest job at which they work hard, but it is just a job. They have no attachment or loyalty to the colony with which they are at the moment concerned. They do their best, but their loyalty, naturally, is to Britain and, in the last resort if a clash of interests occurs, the colony is scarified. Nor do I think that people in Britain fully appreciate the fact that Britain acquired, and remains in, Hong Kong for her own purposes—principally trade. She therefore became, and is, responsible for the welfare and protection of the people. Undeniably, the residents should play their part, but there is too much an assumption in Britain that the people of Hong Kong are fortunate to be there—which is true enough—and that therefore it is they who owe a duty to Britain, which is also true up to a point. *Fundamentally, though, it is Britain that owes the duty to the Colony.*[57] (Italic supplied)

Through the years and with many people, colonial policing has taken on ideological meanings, far away from its historical context, factual content and empirical anchor, to the point of being distortive, and in more than a few cases inflammatory. Six assumptions inform the current inquiry:

First, colonial policing took many forms, explored in '(A): Colonial Policing in Multiple Forms'.
Second, colonial policing was 'people' policing explored in '(B): Colonial Policing as "People" Policing'.
Third, colonial policing was 'pluralistic' policing, explored in '(C): Colonial Policing as "Pluralistic" Policing'.
Fourth, colonial policing was 'collaborative' policing, explored in '(D): Colonial Policing as "Collaborative" Policing'.
Fifth, colonial policing was 'discretionary' policing, explored in (E): Colonial Policing as "Discretionary" Policing'.
Sixth, colonial policing was 'more or less government control' policing, explored in '(F): Colonial Policing as 'More or Less Governmental Control'.

Breaking down 'colonial policing' this way allows one to see that the term 'colonial policing' has little essential communicative content, and must derive meaning from application and context.

A: Colonial Police in Multiple Forms

One Crown Colony—Many Colonial Policing

From a critical reading of colonial policing history, one learns that colonial policing was not all alike everywhere, nor did it remain unchanged over time. Even the putative father of colonial police, Sir Charles Joseph Jeffries, recognised that colonial policing evolves over time and would get to be more civil in late-stage colonial policing.[58] However, there are exceptions in WWII decolonization process,[58] whereby informal de facto decolonization come before official decolonialisation[59] as with HKP.[60] That is a clear and indisputable evidence pointing to the fact that colonial policing in Hong Kong after the 1950s was more civil than colonial, except for ongoing political surveillance, for example, strengthening SB functions with British Palestinian Police transferred, and exceptional public order management, for example, the 1967 riots.

Simply, colonial policing improvised, adjusted, mutated and morphed to suit colonial missions and/or soothe liberal conscience. For example, by the late 1960s (if not earlier), Hong Kong was a colony only in name. In 1968, a copy of Governor Sir David Trend's press release was published in Hong Kong Police Magazine—Chinese edition, arguing that the HKP was an institution subject to law and held accountable to the people, that is, was democratic. Sir Trend started off by making clear that the Hong Kong government cannot do whatever it wants, and most certainly cannot do anything without legal authority, public approval and people's best interest. If Sir David Trend were taken at his words, by 1968, the HKP was more a democratic institution than a colonial force. Thirty years later (1996), another Hong Kong Governor took the initiative to democratise Hong Kong, this time formally, contrary to the spirit of the Joint Declaration. This angered the People's Republic of China leadership, who wanted the HKP to be run very much the same way as in the colonial days.

The thesis that colonial administration and colonial policing had to adapt to social circumstances of the moment and change with the political tempo of the time in complex, delicate and dynamic ways is best captured by the last Governor of Hong Kong, Chris Patten, in his farewell to Hong Kong book:

> Naturally, there were always reasons why the time was not quite right for democracy (in Hong Kong). The postwar Governor, Sir Mark Young (1941–47), had unveiled ambitious plans for beginning the same process of democratization that was being triggered at the time in other British colonies. After his departure, and for three decades to come, the development of representative government was buried in a permafrost of official disapproval. Some of the reasons for this made passing sense. The flood of refugees into Hong Kong, and the social and economic demands they made, created administrative priorities other than political reform. There were worries that free elections would see the community polarized between supporters of the principal mainland political identities, the Communists and the Kuomintang. And there was the brooding and military presence of China. Treat Hong Kong like other British colonies, senior Chinese officials including Premier Zhou Enlai warned, and the territory may be deluded into thinking that it will one day share their destiny and achieve independence. Not for the last time, the Chinese Communist party's shadow was allowed to blot out the sun.[61]

B: Colonial Policing as 'People' Policing

One Crown Colony—Many Kinds of Colonial Officials[62]

This section begins with a necessary clarification. 'People' policing alludes to the fact that all policing is a people's business. This does not mean the conventional notion of policing for and by the people, as in Peel's policing by consent.[63] What 'people's' policing refers to is the fact that it takes colonial officials (British and Chinese) to act as human beings, not agents of the state, in order to police the people of Hong Kong. If colonial policing is to be understood, the HKP must be unmasked. The living, breathing people behind the badge, uniform and gun must be revealed. The impact of personal attributes and collective mentality of the colonial officials must be reckoned with. By the same token, learning more about the colonised people, their history and culture, hopes and dreams, fears and apprehension is a vital part of reconstructing their perception and reception of the HKP and colonial policing.

The starting assumption underscoring this line of inquiry is that people are not the same in what they think (cognition), feel (emotion) and act (behaviour). British and Chinese, within and between groups, do not share the same values and interests, personality or culture.

Take the case of HKP expatriate officers. They are not a homogeneous group, in background and outlook. Their character and personality were formed long before they arrived in Hong Kong. Many of them worked as police officers before in England or other colonies.

According to anti-colonialism critiques, the HKP was commanded by these expatriate officers, zealously devoted to colonial cause and loyal only to the Crown. They were pre-disposed by character and ingrained in training to be abusive to the Hong Kong people as lower-class subjects. However, in real life, Hong Kong-bound expatriate officers, like all young people of their time, had their own personal agenda, for example, adventurism or to realise a dream, and life course to follow, for example, economic security, professional achievements and personal actualisation, and in that order.[64]

Many Colonial Personalities

If there is anything that is evident to students of Hong Kong political development, especially with those who study the HKP, it is that for most of the time Hong Kong and the HKP were not run by rule of law, but were far more driven by distinct personality, from Governor to Chief Magistrates to Police Superintendent. As a result law and order of Hong Kong under Governor Davis was not the same as under Governor Hennessy all for good reasons and with huge impacts. The same can be said about policing philosophy and style between Walter Deane (1866–1892) and Francis May (1893–1902),[65] both cadet officers turned Captain Superintendents.[66]

More pointedly,[67] Governor Lockhart believed that the Hong Kong people should have a dominant voice in the running of Hong Kong, since they were in the majority, educated, and capable and were responsible for financially supporting in Hong Kong, whereas British and Europeans were sojourns, having no intention to stay and improve Hong Kong, beyond ways that would help them get rich.

As an aggregate, expatriate colonial officers might share commonalities in demographics, personal disposition, work experience and life stages, to sufficiently distinguish them from their cohorts in England or Europe, but they were certainly not predictable to the point of sharing the exact outlook of life or conduct at their job.[68]

Like many of their Chinese counterparts coming to Hong Kong at the time, the expatriate officers came for an adventure and ended up calling Hong Kong a home (away from home); making friends, getting married, building career, amassing fortunes, and yes, getting drunk with the locals. Their personal values, interests and fortune were inevitably and irrevocably tied to Hong Kong, where they now work, live and play. For all intents and purpose, for better or worse, Hong Kong is their home,[69] if only temporarily and transitionally, as Professor Gold's research into the mindset and lifestyle of British migrants revealed[70]:

> Hong Kong is a place of opportunity (and high rewards)...Aside from work, leisure, travel opportunities and general 'lifestyle', augmented by low rates of income tax (15 per cent), are key motivators among British migrants. In the taxonomies of migration they operate at the intersections of 'economic' and 'lifestyle' migration, categories that need to be understood as capturing a lose collage of individually negotiated motivations...Transience and transition lie at the centre of migrant lives and landscapes. *Transience captures the substance of the lives of British migrants who live permanently temporary lives in Hong Kong*...Temporariness surfaces in mundane decisions about storing furniture in the UK and in deferring decisions to buy curtains and sofas sometimes for up to twenty years. Temporariness also avoids confronting conflicting futures within families and between couples who may disagree on its geographical location. Temporariness and its subverted conflicts thus structure the configuration of intimacy in migrant families. Transition captures the shifting global and local social and political landscape on which they operate. All social landscapes are in transition in the sense that they are always in process, always being made, but transition in Hong Kong has additional and particular elements of transition set out above. (italic supplied)[71]

Colonial policing research also needs to take into account the domestication of colonial officers, some by choice, for example, marriage, and others by force of circumstances, for example, economic needs. Still the result is the same. Hong Kong was not only a place to live but was part and parcel of their life, and in time personality. Hong Kong has caught up with them.[72] For example, Sir David Akers-Jones, 86, served the Hong Kong Government for 30 years, ending as Chief Secretary and Acting Governor. He has lived in Hong Kong for 67 years, that is all his life. He is no more an expatriate than any other Hong Kong person, born and bred locally, with a Hong Kong heart, mind and soul.[73] As Ackers-Jones said in his memoir: 'We stayed on after retirement because we scarcely knew anywhere else and because in Hong Kong we have so many friends and so much involvement'.[74] So did Elsie Tu, British social activists turned legislative councillor.[75]

Finally, there are those who have left, but still want to return, and retire in Hong Kong, as a permanent foreigner:

> I first arrived in Hong Kong as an 18 year old in 1976, recruited in the UK to join the as was then, Royal Hong Kong Police Force. I spent until 1982 there until I finally left. I regret that decision to this day and regularly go back for short trips. As my current UK career draws to an end I would love to retire back to where I spent my formative years.[76]

Independent Colonial Officials

The British Empire was run by people, not rules. People are moved by ideas and ideals, seldom by charters and mandates. Realising this, it is best to investigate into imperial and colonial officers, how they think and what they do, in context and with issues, in order to fully understand how colonial policing worked in Hong Kong. As applied, this means policing policy and practice in Hong Kong ultimately depended on who was in charge of what; here, people's demographics, background, training and experience matter. Thus, one can be fairly sure of the following, when it came to colonial policy formulation and execution—British imposed, Hong Kong disposed, and people matters:

> [T]he secretary of state for the colonies was ultimately responsible to the British government, and thence to the UK Parliament, for the peace, order and good government of the colonies, day-to-day responsibility for administration was effectively devolved to the governors and the colonial governments. There were occasions when London made demands on the colonial authorities—which might be accepted or vigorously resisted—*but in most respects British colonies were governed internally rather than by the imperial centre.*[77] (Italic supplied)

That said, it is a well-known fact that the form and content of 'colonial policing' as with direction and course of 'colonialism' are driven by personalities (both coloniser and colonised) and less so by British Colonial office. In this regard, Gavin Ure observed:[78]

> There was no clear linear progression in the development of the Hong Kong government' autonomy... The exercise of autonomy was as much the result of changing political pressures as it was of the personalities and the belief of the principle actors involved, in Britain as well as Hong Kong, and their willingness and determination to act upon.

The HKP is a disciplinary paramilitary force. Within the HKP, officers, from Commissioner to Constable, are trained to obey legitimate order. Thus, it is rare for HKP officers disobeying orders from above. But that does not mean that the HKP, particularly those at the senior levels, are robots in accepting instructions they find in their professional opinion not to be appropriate, feasible, or more simply not for the good of Hong Kong.

One such case is that of the sudden resignation of Commissioner of Police Edward Tyrer (December 1966 to July 1967) for health reasons during the May 1966 to December 1967 communist riots. The 'resignation' was shrouded in secrecy.[79] On 4 July 1966, five HKP officers were killed at the Sha Tau Kowk border police post by communist militias. On 14 July 1966, Commissioner Tyler flew to the United Kingdom for consultation of HKP organisation matters with senior members of the Commonwealth Office. On 21 July 1966, the Commonwealth Office announced that Commissioner Tyler's resignation for health reasons was approved by the Secretary of State for Commonwealth Affairs, with Deputy Commissioner Yates taking over the HKP with immediate effect. It was later revealed by a journalist Gary Ka-wai Cheung that Commissioner Tyler had not resigned but was relieved of command because of a disagreement with the then acting Governor Gass, who wanted the riot to be suppressed. This is the first and last time within public knowledge that an HKP Commissioner was relieved of command for failure to obey a legal order.[80] Whatever the true reasons may have been for the relieving of command, the sudden dismissal of a Commissioner of Police due to disagreement of policy indicates that behind closed doors colonial officials did disagree.

Middle-Class British Cadets

In discussing the influence of British cadet officers on Hong Kong administration, Lethbridge, an old Hong Kong hand and esteemed professor at Hong Kong University, observed:

> At that time it was a small territory with a population squeezed into a few urban enclaves, where everyone lived cheek by jowl and officials were highly visible and often met in the street. In such a constricted society the quirks of an official, given the system of government, often influenced important administrative decisions, over which the general public could exercise little control.[81]

Beginning in the 1860s, OxBridge 'cadet officers' had tremendous influence in the administration of the colony. These 'cadets' resembled each other in family background, education training, social connection, political philosophy and personal sentiments.[82] They were also proficient with the Chinese language, knowledgeable about Chinese culture, subscribed to Confucian teachings and adopted a paternalistic attitude towards the Chinese. Eventually, these 'Cadet Officers' made Hong Kong what it is today, by their personality, conviction and drive. Professor Lethbridge again observed that in the early colonial years for the most part, Hong Kong Government was run by well-established cliques and personalities (with the HKP, it is the 'horse stable' system):

> Between 1862 and 1941 the top ranks of the British colonial civil service were chosen from a small group of Oxford and Cambridge trained English 'cadet officers'. Most served in several colonial ports during their careers, and spoke multiple languages. They were often assigned to lead government departments in service of commercial trade. According to a historian, three future cadets became Hong Kong governors, five others were high commissioners, and four more were chosen Colonial Secretary. The successors to Grand Pre', Hyndman, Cavalho, and d'Almada all came from the cadet list.[83]

Who then are these people who came to govern Hong Kong?

They were middle-class Britons with a mission to serve and protect the Hong Kong people from their own perils who, to them, were not unlike those of the underclass in England. It is true that cadets were not there to liberate Hong Kong, but it is also true that they are not there to domesticate and exploit the people either as an expression of racial superiority, as mainstream anti-colonialists would have it. Unlike the military officers, commercial traders or spiritual gurus, who came to Hong Kong for conquest, market or salvation, the cadets came to build a better society in British image, at the nadir of its world power. As observed by Faure: 'Even at its mightiest, Britain had no social policy on Hong Kong as such. It applied British justice and periodically enforced standards that had been tried in Britain, whether or not they had succeeded in Britain or were suited to Hong Kong'.[84]

What was good for the British people was good for the Hong Kong people, including a rigidly enforced paternalistic, class system. In this way, colonial rule by the cadets is meant to be a replication of British paternalistic society at home, more so than the creation of an oppressive dominion abroad; however, much of it is viewed to the contrary by the subservient locals at the roots and critical foreigners from afar.[85] Again in Professor Lethbridge's words:

> In sum, the typical cadet came from a solid, though not rich, upper middle-class family, went to a public school, but not to the most prestigious, and then went up to one of the older universities, where he read classics or history and

> was noted for his application to study and interest in healthy recreation. The bounder, the aesthete, the hearty and the rake were not represented in the ranks of the cadets. Given this common background, training, and the fraternity of class, cadets came to the field with many shared assumptions about, and attitudes towards, the people they governed in the colonial territories. Robert Huessler, for example, argues that the attitude of British Colonial officials 'was not unlike that which they maintained from childhood towards the lesser orders at home. One ruled the people and protected them from local and foreign injustice. Otherwise one lived apart'. Perhaps a better analogy would be the model prefect at an English public school. The model prefect is expected to be fair, just, upright, dignified, and withal concerned about his charges. However, he is not likely to support ideas of equality and permissiveness: he must exercise authority.[86]

In conclusion, it was Professor Tsang who observed that good governance does not require having the most intelligent people up top.[87] Good governance must have efficient, effective, productive and non-corrupt individuals at the frontline. In essence, good administration is more important than good policy in the provision of good government. In Hong Kong and since the 1870s, this is exactly what the cadet provided.[88] The Hong Kong cadet officers had to pass extremely difficult civil service examination and lengthy Chinese language and culture training before they were allowed to serve under the watchful eyes of senior cadet officers in high places. Once appointed, they were also expected to be familiar with local customs, ways and means, and functioned in 'paternalistic' ways much like the 'fuwu guan' in imperial China in solving Chinese citizens' problems, resolving people's disputes and promoting community interests, in line with Chinese traditions and community expectations.[89]

The institutionalisation of this cadet scheme, with a benevolent ethos and infectious *esprit de corps*, led to successful mediation and effective translation of what would have been ill fitting and offensive colonial policies in the service of the local people. In fact, Tsang is confident that the best protection against British colonialism was none other than its own colonial officers, first the governors, and then the cadets. While appointed by the Crown, these wayward and prideful officers had grown to love Hong Kong as much as the Britain they left behind. They were ready, willing and able to champion and shelter the Hong Kong people from the prejudices, errors, abuses and excess from the White Hall or Colonial Office, in making Hong Kong a better place to live, work and play. It was the dedication and sacrifice of these colonial officers that created the miracle that Hong Kong became. Again, in Professor Tsang's words:

> The most basic safeguard is, however, the nature of the Hong Kong government itself. The highly sophisticated modern bureaucratic structure of the

> government means that senior civil servants have tremendous scope for frustrating the wishes of a Governor, particularly a new arrival...Conservative, cautious, and with a worldview narrowly focused upon Hong Kong, their *esprit de corps* requires them to act as the guardians of what they believe to be Hong Kong's best interests, and to prevent anyone, even the British government, from rocking the boat.[90]

This is exactly what cadet Walter Deane (1840–1906) did when he served as the Captain Superintendent (1866–1892) at the age of 25. His tenure lasted 26 years, the longest ever. While in service, Deane was able to make the HKP more efficient, clean and responsible to the Chinese.[91]

Working-Class Europeans

Europeans in Hong Kong come in all sizes and shapes, having reached Hong Kong both with intentionality and by fortune. The British Cadet grade colonial police officers were hand-picked and grown for high places; a rare breed. Many of the European officers recruited from abroad were from the lower class, not to speak of those who dropped out, jumped ships and deserted.[92] Where people come from usually determine how they end up, in the social ladder, and these officers were no exception. The lower class ended up being a working class unto themselves, ostracised by the European middle and upper class, and isolated from the Chinese community. The street officers—constables and sergeants—before they made ranks belonged to the lower class. This group of expatriate officers were the ones who executed colonial policing policy in the street every day. How they interpreted their mandate and applied the law define what colonial policing was in practical terms. However, the European working class, like working class everywhere, cared more about making a living and making do, than upholding the lofty goal and high expectations of their occupation; they did not understand them in the first place. Their life experience and home culture might have disposed them towards thinking and acting like a Western, for example looking down on the locals, but they were definitely not only driven by colonial policy, whether the policy was exploitative or paternalistic.

More significantly, it is better to understand what the HKP frontline officers did in context of their situation in life; guided by self-interests and determined by utility calculus. In the end, the working class police did what was right by them and not that of the British Empire. In the context of Hong Kong, with a decadent lifestyle and much tempting opportunities, it was (and still is) most necessary not to rock the boat, and to get rich fast[93]:

> In 1845, Charles May, a London police officer, was brought out to organize the new police force. Most of the early police recruits were obtained locally from the army, navy, and merchant marine; but in time policemen were recruited

directly from Britain or from other colonial territories. The quality and morale of the force was never high....But to this class, unfortunately, the chief objection was the readiness with which they yield to the temptation offered by the many public houses, and many of the deaths among the European constabulary were ascribed to their excessive indulgences in ardent spirits, a great portion of which, sold by the low tavern-keepers, was of the most abominable and deleterious description.[94]

Adventurous Expatriate Souls

Hereunder are the background and aspirations of a few expatriate officers when they first came to Hong Kong, and joined up as HKP officers.

Claude and Reginald Earnshaw, who are brothers to each other, came to Hong Kong in 1918 in search of job and better opportunities. After a few years, they moved on to pursue other interests:

Claude and Reginald Earnshaw were born in Battersea at the turn of the 20th Century...After the war the brothers wanted to broaden their horizons and they joined the Hong Kong Police. Recruiting had ceased during the war but a large intake of 34 men arrived during 1919 and a further 21 in 1920. However, after a couple of years the brothers decided that there were better opportunities to be had outside of the Force. Reginald became the Manager of the Kai Tack Motor Bus Company and Claude became the Manager of the Palace Hotel.[95]

A British university graduate joined the HKP in 1978. He was unhappy with the social and economic conditions in the United Kingdom. He did not know what to do with his life, still less about Hong Kong:

When I left U.K. in 1978 to join the Hong Kong Police, this country was still in the grip of the 3-day week. Uncollected rubbish littered the streets. Unemployment was on the rise. Punk rock was a busted flush and disco was forging ahead powered by the hair and hips of Mr. Travolta. I had a so-so psychology degree and not much idea what the future held. My only mental images of Hong Kong were scenes from *Enter the Dragon* with Bruce Lee kicking ass—or the opening moments of *You Only Live Twice* which showed James Bond (as ever) shagging for England and suggested MI6 operated from a sunken liner in Hong Kong harbour. Well, I thought, if it's good enough for James Bond...[96]

Another British applicant for the HKP in the 1980s joined for the adventure, who never intended to make a career, still less calling Hong Kong home:

I applied as a RHKP Inspector way back in the late 80's. It looked like a great adventure, and I'd always had a mild fascination with that part of the world. Even at that time, the writing was on the wall for Hong Kong and they were taking very few Europeans into the Officer entry program each year. While I was in the application pipeline the whole Tiananmen Square massacre

> occurred and made me rethink the whole plan. I didn't ever see myself making a long term career over there but I could've fulfilled the first contract (5 years IIRC) and been out of there before the Chinese came in. I knew I could never stay on after the 'handover'…I just couldn't see myself working for one of the most brutal, murderous, totalitarian regimes ever known in history. But, maybe that was just me !!![97]

The above three testimonials from 1918, 1978 and 1980s point out that expatriates joined the HKP less for serving the Crown than to realise their own dreams.[98]

Ambivalent Local Officers

What about the locals who joined as colonial police officers? Why did they join? What did they want? Did they change overnight into colonial officers? Did they work for the British in the day, reverting to being indigenous self at night?

Take the case of the recruitment of local young men into Papua New Guinea Colonial Police (PNGCP)[99] as an example. Colonial (police) policy in Papua New Guinea requires local representation, facilitation and execution. Ultimately, it needed local people's acceptance, by way of personification and embodiment, failing that at least symbolic representation. This fell on the shoulder of local young men joining the PNGCP, swearing allegiance to the Crown.

Who were the young who joined up with PNDCP? What were their motivations? More importantly, were their motive and purpose to join PNGCP compatible with official colonial rhetoric, namely, for love of colonialism and loyalty to the Crown?

It turned out that the young people, like young people everywhere, did not join PNWCP to pacify the nation nor civilise the people. They joined for individual reasons and personal gains, which often had few things in common with the PNGCP's espoused goals and objectives, secular or moral. Most young people joined PNGCP because of money, power and respect, not aspiring to be a colonial police officer, still less to serve the noble cause of colonialism.

For example, Naguwean learned 'that policemen earned more money than mine workers. He was impressed with the power of the government and…deflected to those who worked for the government….the perceived respect that would be forthcoming from the villagers because of it…'[100]

Many did join for a higher cause, namely, to put an end to internal strife and civil war: 'Boino, Kambian, and Yegova, for instance, believed that the colonial government could put an end to internecine warfare and brought pace and "development" to the communities…they wished to contribute to the process…'[101]

A few joined with personal agenda, such as to settle scores, to protect the highland people and teach the coastal people a lesson:

> I joined the police force because the policemen from the coast came and made a mess of the life of the people from the highlands. I wanted to stop their arrogant behavior…make sure the policemen from the coast did not overstep the line. We very much wanted to take revenge… demonstrating to them that our own people were capable of looking after us.[102]

A minority joined PNGCP to follow the footsteps and achievements of their fathers; to become the big man and leader—head man—of their village. Since accumulating wealth, experience, and leadership capacity through traditional means took a long time (or in some cases would be impossible to achieve), joining the PNGCP was a much preferred if not the only viable alternative:

> At the time of his enrollment…he (Amero) was preparing himself to achieve the status of his father. However…becoming big-man…involved much toil and hardship…Achieving these leadership qualities and accumulating the required wealth promised to take a long time…he was not keen on working for the government…He wanted to work for the government for five or more years and then return to the village, with the symbolic 'power' the government had bestowed on him, and, through its influence, achieve the status of a big-man, quietly and cheaply.[103]

Finally, some people joined to take revenge on others who took their family's life:

> Kamuna's younger sister, Sobia…(was fetching water when)…enemy tribe pounced on Soba and killed her…When the opportunity came for him to join the police force, he did so gladly, because he hoped to get his revenge through the police…Kamuna in 1920 was still very much influenced by the beliefs and aspirations of his ancestors, payback killing for unwarranted deaths was the law that he and his people understood.[104]

To sum up, locals joined PNGCP for all sorts of reasons, none of which has anything to do with colonialism, for or against.

In the context of Hong Kong, young people also joined the HKP for various reasons. Most joined for security of employment and good welfare and benefits. More than a few joined for illegal and lucrative payoffs in fame and fortune. This is how five HKP officers described their reasons for joining.[105]

Kong Chi Yin[106] joined the HKP in 1967 as a PC and retired in 2011 as a sergeant. It was written as an oral history project. Since it is a non-directed biographic account of his career with the HKP, it is useful as a no-holds-barred first person account of his circumstances and reasons for joining the

HKP. Kong joined the HKP, against his parents' wishes, because he wanted a better career prospect than steel and iron work.

> After dropping out of junior secondary school, CY Kong was referred by his distant uncle to work as boy at a trading company, which would allow him to further his studies at an evening school after work. He was indecisive then, and at last he made up his mind to work at the iron and steel works. Later on CY Kong was influenced by his fellow countryman and was determined to enter himself for an exam for prospective policemen. That fellow countryman, who was one year older than Kong, lived in a squatter at Pei Bin Street in Nga Tsin Wai. When in Form 1, CY Kong was entrusted by that fellow countryman's mother to look for a school for her son, so he accompanied her son to apply for a place in a school at Boundary Street. As the squatters were cleared, that fellow countryman was resettled in Kwun Tong, and joined the Police Force at the age of 18. CY Kong, upon learning about it, was lifted and convinced that he was good enough for a try. In his opinion, the work at the iron and steel works was rough, and his poor qualifications would hinder him from competing with the many other job hunters and confine him to such occupations as ticketing officer, fireman and driver. A recruit police constable was paid about 300 dollars a month, which was quite good compared with those occupations. His father was in opposition to his becoming a policeman due to the deep-rooted belief that good boys never become cops. His mother never had much expectation of him and simply hoped that he would have a normal job. CY Kong's rank was Police Constable when entering the cadet school. He graduated in August 1965, and was posted in a police station report room in the beginning. He planned to study English after his employment, but it fell through in the end due to others' influence. Today he still regrets about this. In 1971, he became Detective Police Constable (DPC, commonly known as CID). He had been attached to Yau Ma Tei, Kwun Tong as other police stations. In 1976, he was promoted Sergeant. He had been married before the promotion. In 1977, his eldest daughter was born. In the same year, he applied for the police quarters, and moved out of Nga Tsin Wai right after that. The requirements of applying for quarters in those days depended largely on the no. of family members and length of service.[107]

Sergeant Mr. Leung Shiu-yuk joined the HKP in December 1966 and was subsequently promoted to Sergeant and Station Sergeant in 1978 and 1984, respectively. He joined the HKP to get rid of the Triad. His first encounter with the Triad came in the 1960s:

> At that time, I was only a 14 year old naughty boy. One day, one of my playmates came to my home with his father after I had a quarrel with him. The man kept on complaining to my father and even claimed he was a triad member. My father, who was a teacher, was so scared that he slapped my face to calm the man down.[108]

Leung was speaking on the record with *OffBeat*. One can only wonder what his true reasons were. Official or not, people have multiple reasons for joining, and many of them changes over time as with one's life circumstances. This was no different for Leung.

Another PC joined in 1974 because he thought it was a good-paying, secure and fun job:

> I joined HKP in 1974 and thought of making a living, and not have to use my brain to study hard....after 20 years, I am about to retire....I would choose to be a police officer again, because in policing, I can learn about knowledge, wisdom and courage.[109]

PC Ling joined HKP in 1977, the year the HKP officers staged its first-ever police rebellion against the ICAC, in order to clean up the HKP:

> A good person does not become police officers...My parents are from the grassroots. Mother was a hawker in the street. When I tended the stall, I witnessed police and gangster soliciting protection money from the hawkers. The police constables also wanted the hawkers to volunteer to be arrested for obstruction, to show they are doing their job. We lived then in subsidised government housing. People living in resettlement district witnessed many police conduct which is much like licensed thugs. In order to change the quality of the police, I sincerely believe that it cannot be done by public opinion, alone. There need to be more young people with idealism and competency to join the HKP. If everyone believes that good people cannot change the police. There will be no hope for the police. I make up my mind to be a good police, to serve the people and enforce the law, setting an example for others.[110]

Finally, there are those who joined because the HKP wanted them as a result of their past service, for example, defended Hong Kong in WWII, proven loyalty, supported British in controlling Hong Kong and needed their connections, communication with N.T. villagers.[111]

> After Cheung Koon Fu was trained in the East River Column's base, he worked as a liaison officer in Sha Lo Tung until the Japanese surrender in 1945. After the war, East River Column departed for Mainland China and the Hong Kong-Kowloon Independent Battalion was disbanded. Members of the Battalion could choose to go north to China or quit the force and stay in Hong Kong. Cheung Koon Fu had a wife and daughter, so it was not convenient for him to leave. In 1946, he was admitted into the police to become Hong Kong's first police officer from Sha Lo Tung. After the war, Hong Kong businesses were in a depression, and the young Hakka settlers faced unemployment because village agricultural land was short, causing

> a serious problem to public order. To reassure the public, the Hong Kong Government encouraged young Hakka people to apply to join the police, fire service, artillery and other disciplinary forces. Several villagers from Sha Lo Tung worked in the artillery and fire service at that time. The police made the exception to admit Hakka indigenous inhabitants. They sent a Hakka Inspector of Police to the New Territories to recruit police cadets. Candidates had to pass a language test by writing out a piece of newspaper clipping ready by the police's translator in the local dialect (Cantonese). Before the war, young Hakka people only received education in Hakka language, so most of them could not speak the local dialect well. Many people failed the test as a result and faced difficulties also in finding jobs in the urban area. Cheung Koon Fu used to study in Tsim Sha Tsui and took private tutoring from a primary school teacher, so he passed the test smoothly. For those Hakka people who failed test, the government encouraged them to move to Britain. The immigration application procedures then were simple. Cheung Koon Fu thought that encouraging enlistment and immigration was a political means by the British to solve security problems in Hakka villages in the New Territories.

In 1963, Inspector Wong joined because he was bored with his desk job as an accountant:

> After high school graduation, I was admitted to University of Hong Kong for architecture studies. My father felt that our family has doctors, accountant and financial related occupation. In order to get people to mentor me, I joined the historical and prestigious Peak, Marwick, Mitchell & Co. as an accountant under study. While I worked for 'Peal' I was engaged with numbers all day long. I did not have any interest. I am an action oriented person. How can I sit still in a chair and live with numbers? At that time, I am bored with commercial law. I failed the examination. I wasted five years without achieving anything….I then proposed to join the HKP.[112]

The above examples and discussion focus entirely on the individual motivation for joining the colonial police, here and overseas. But 'people policing' analysis goes beyond individual contributions to the shaping of the HKP; the culture of British officers and ethos of Chinese rank and files, collectively, also had much to do in how the HKP behave as an organisation.

With this introduction of cultural theory of colonisation, it is possible to map the contour and gradient of colonial policing in Hong Kong. Adopting this mode of analysis departs from the elite rendition of colonial policing as imagined, with a heavy dosage of ideological bent, and proceeds in favour of a grassroots understanding of colonial policing, as lived, with tantalising details of each individual case. Such cases defy typecasting, and all of them yearn to be heard.

Many Colonised People

Turning to the colonised people, they also had a decisive role to play in shaping colonial rule. Hezel observed the complexity of colonial rule in the Marshall Islands as follows:

> The conventional view of colonial rule is that, outgunned and over-awed by superior might, islanders simply submit to the inevitable and bowed before their conquerors. Truth is more complex. Certain factions in these island societies, even if they have no direct hand in the political takeover, welcomed the new colonial masters and saw to it that their own interests were served and their power enhanced under a foreign flag.[113]

Neither 'colonial policing' in IRC mode[114] or Chinese 'dual track—indirect rule approach' fairly and accurately portrait the complexity and dynamism of the 'colonial policing' in action.[115] 'Colonial policing' as practised by HKP was 'colonial policing' with Hong Kong–Chinese characteristics. As such, it could not be understood without thorough understanding of Chinese historical, cultural and social context.[116] It is of interest to note that thus far the issue of how Hong Kong Chinese society and culture affected HKP culture, conduct and performance has rarely been studied.[117]

C: 'Colonial Policing' as 'Pluralistic' Policing[118]

This section begins with reference Leo F. Goodstadt, first Head of the Central Policy Unit. In his recent book, he has this to say about British attitude towards collaboration with the Chinese: 'In dealing with internal challenges, the colonial administrations' instinct was to disengage itself from the Chinese world. From the earlier way of British rule, colonial officials preferred to minimise the scope for conflict with the Chinese population by using intermediaries'.[119]

'Pluralistic policing'[120] means that there are many social control agents doing policing duties working side by side at any moment than what meets the eye. Theoretically, there is only one central police agency; in fact there were many others who work with the central police agency to bring about effective control. For example, in the case of auxiliary policing, police functions were organised along regular versus reserve dimension, commodity policing along principle versus agent dimension, private policing along public versus private dimension, community policing along legal versus social dimension. In as much as many policing theories—rational choice theory,[121] routine activities theory,[122] nodal policing theory,[123] expectation theory[124]—call attention to the existence of multiplicity of social control—policing agencies/agents, there is a need to determine what counts for a gem or species of 'plural mode' sufficient to be integrated under the rubric of 'pluralistic policing' regime. Otherwise, the concept of 'pluralistic policing' is either too porous (everything goes) or ill defined (escape observation) to be of use.

In the current context, in order to illuminate and explicate, for purposes of deconstruction and reconstruction of colonial policing', 'pluralistic policing' describes the active cooperation and/or collaboration of other policing agents—agencies under HKP control for the purpose of advancing 'colonialism' purpose or interests.

In Hong Kong, 'people policing' developed alongside with 'colonial policing'.[125] However, they had few things in common. Still, the two did intersect spatially, for example, marine versus land division, Hong Kong versus Kowloon versus N.T., Peak versus Central, functionally, for example, Special Constable in time of war versus Police Reserve in times of emergencies, interact collaboratively,[126] for example, HKP versus District Watch Forces, for mutual benefits, due to convenience and/or out of necessity.

The rationale for 'pluralistic policing' is best supplied by the advocates in a different era, that is, in the twenty-first century, for a different cause—social integration:

> At the same time most western societies have become more and more heterogeneous. In major cities diverse ethnic and lifestyle groups lead separate lives. Rules for one group about acceptable conduct will seldom entirely agree with another's—Born Again Christians and gays are unlikely to agree, for example. Outside of a thin core of public morality—almost everyone will agree that murder, theft and fraud are crimes—groups would be better off setting and policing their own standards. Citizens would have to accept that different rules applied to different communities with informal self-regulation and arbitration.[127]

Theoretically speaking,[128] 'pluralistic policing' exists and existed because a single agency has limited resources to satisfy different expectations, due to inadequacy or mismatch of resource to a problem. 'Pluralistic policing' is also needed in tending to single problem with many expectations, for example, from multiple expectations to multiple constituents.

'Pluralistic policing' requires coordination and integration: such as whom to do what and how, given a problem set. Who is responsible for what jurisdictional domain, for example public disorder versus family deviance, with what method, for example, compensatory settlement versus punitive control,[129] and under what circumstances, for example, crisis intervention versus problem solving.

Similar 'pluralistic' challenges existed in other 'realms' of social control beyond policing, such as dispute resolution with 'rule of law versus customary social control':

> The international community largely remains unsure of how to approach customary justice and tends to design interventions that alternately ignore or replace customary systems. The best approach, we have found, lies more in the middle. Customary justice systems should not be seen as separate or parallel, but an integral, if often deeply flawed element of the wider justice sector.[130]

D: Colonial Policing as 'Collaborative' Policing

'Pluralistic policing' calls for multi-party involvement with crime control or problem solving. 'Collaborative policing' details the nature and kind of relationship and interaction between parties engaging in crime control and problem solving.

The premise that 'colonial' policing is 'collaborative' policing is based on the simple but compelling thesis that the 'dictatorship' (minority) cannot impose its will and secure its rule without the consent and compliance, cooperation and collaboration of the ruled (majority), however strong. That is to say 'colonial' powers could not have securely ruled by force alone. As political scientist Karl W. Deutsch observed in 1953:

> Totalitarian power is strong only if it does not have to be used too often. If totalitarian power must be used at all times against the entire population, it is unlikely to remain powerful for long. Since totalitarian regimes require more power for dealing with their subjects than do other types of government, such regimes stand in greater need of widespread and dependable compliance habits among their people; more than that they have to be able to count on the active support of at least significant parts of the population in case of need.[131]

Elaborating on that, Dr. Gene Sharpe, the grand master of non-violent struggle, informs us that all political powers, especially dictatorship, have an Achilles' heel and are vulnerable to attack.[132] The first of the flaws is the aforementioned non-cooperation of the people: 'The cooperation of a multitude of people, groups, and institutions needed to operate the system may be restricted or withdrawn'.[133] This is particularly the case with essential services, for example, knowledge workers or army/policy. Sharpe further suggests 198 ways of defying the will of the dictatorship through non-cooperation:

> Methods of nonviolent protest and persuasio.n are largely symbolic demonstrations, including parades, marches, and vigils (54 methods). Noncooperation is divided into three sub-categories: (a) social noncooperation (16 methods), (b) economic noncooperation, including boycotts (26 methods) and strikes

(23 methods), and (c) political noncooperation (38 methods). Nonviolent intervention, by psychological, physical, social, economic, or political means, such as the fast, nonviolent occupation, and parallel government (41 methods), is the final group.[134]

From the perspective of the British colonial ruler, the incentive to collaborate is that of necessity: Niccolo Machiavelli had much earlier argued that the prince '…who has the public as a whole for his enemy can never make himself secure; and the greater his cruelty, the weaker does his regime become'.[135]

As applied to Hong Kong, and in the heyday of colonial rule in the 1860s, Sharp's observation that a colonial master depends on the colonised for effective rule and survival makes a lot of sense:

> The challenge for the colonial government in the 1860s was how best to re-established its credibility and how to organise, and communicate with, the large and increasingly permanent Chinese population in the colony without having to reply so exclusively on the narrow points of contact provided by middlemen such as Caldwell…At the same time, the colony could not survive without its Chinese population: not only did its economy and revenue depend on the network of Chinese trade that now embraced Hong Kong; the daily functioning of European society was paralyzed without the supplies, labor, and connections they provided, as the mass boycott in 1858 demonstrated.[136]

Advanced here, 'collaborative policing' is not a new discovery. In the annals of colonial Hong Kong history, 'collaborative policing' has been intimated many times. Several of these intimations are henceforth discussed.

First, in 2005, Cindy Yik-Yi Chu wrote about 'Foreign Communities in Hong Kong, 1840s–1950s' which provide the social and cultural context for pluralistic and collaborative ordering.[137] Professor Chu's book *Foreign Communities in Hong Kong, 1840s–1950s* is an edited volume documenting the experiences of various foreign communities—British (Chapters 2 and 3), German (Chapter 4), Catholic (Chapter 5), Japanese (Chapter 6), Interment (Chapter 7), Indian (Chapter 8) and China Hand (Chapter 9) in adjusting to Hong Kong during their time, chronologically from 1840 to 1950.[138] In so doing, the book captures the change of circumstances in Hong Kong and how people relate to the changes, in making history, at the individual, community and society levels.[139]

One key lesson learned from the book is captured by the following paragraph: 'Foreign communities are far from being monolithic entities….Hong Kong was made of different ethnic and professional groups, with different background and experiences, minding their own business, with their own dreams'.[140] The study of policing in Hong Kong is the study of how these people come to terms with securing their life (in dealing with crime) and ordering their relationship (in resolving disputes), in a conciliatory way, if not collaboratively.

Understood this way, the study of policing in Hong King is actually the study of cultural exchange and group interface, in meeting different individual expectations and collective desire, in the midst of conflicting personality and custom, attitude and tradition.[141]

Second, at around the same time (2005), John M. Carroll in *Edge of Empires: Chinese Elites and British Colonials in Hong Kong*[142] made out a case for collaboration between British and Chinese. In Chapter 3, 'Strategic Balance: Status and Respect in the Colonial Context', Carroll explores the fissures in British colonial rule that left room for local Chinese elites to cultivate their power and influence. In early Hong Kong, a wide gulf separated the colonial government and its Chinese subjects:

> Colonial ignorance, indifference, and incompetence created a demand for services that these merchants were in a special position to offer. Through charitable and voluntary organizations, they resolved civil and commercial disputes, provided medical facilities, and created a voice for the Chinese community. By offering such services, local Chinese merchants were able to take advantage of Hong Kong's position at the edge of the Chinese and British empires to enhance their own power and prestige.[143]

To emphasise this point, Carroll repeated the now-familiar stories of the founding and operation of the Man Mo Temple (1847), the Tung Wah Hospital (1872), the District Watch Force (1866), the reorganised District Watch Committee (1891), the Nam Pak Hong Kung So Merchant Association (1868), and the Po Leung Kwok charitable organisation (1880).

Since collaboration is working together to achieve a common objective—peaceful coexistence, 'collaborative policing' presupposes a mutuality of goal(s), shared interests amidst divergence in values; an assumption that while values can never be compromised, interests are always negotiable. In contested relationship and situations of conflict, finding mutuality amidst differences (求存同異) or finding common grounds amidst differences) is the goal of all goals.

From here, the first observation is that the mutuality of goal(s) underscoring 'collaborative policing' in colonised Hong Kong means that the perspectives of the coloniser (British) and colonised (Chinese) did not need to be identical. For example, order and stability was a desired goal for the British and Chinese, albeit for different reasons, purposes, and to a different degree. British colonists wanted order to promote trade; to them, order was an instrumental good. The Chinese wanted order for the sake of harmony and out of a loathing for chaos, both ideological goods.

To the British colonialists of the time, the 'indirect rule' governance model as 'collaborative policing' was justified as follows:

> Indirect rule reduced the costs of colonial administration, gradually incorporated indigenous authorities into the colonial bureaucracy and enlisted them as agents to implement two essential aspects of colonial rule: the collection of revenue and the maintenance of law and order…the gradualist polices of running Empire at minimal cost and with minimal force was a cause of self-congratulation by many colonial powers, who saw their systems of trusteeship as fulfilling the main criteria of good, if somewhat authoritarian governance…[144]

Second, mutuality of interests in 'colonial policing' leading to 'collaborative policing' is likely to happen when both parties viewed coercive or imposed control as a non-zero sum game, where collaboration yields more benefits to coloniser and colonised alike. In collaborative policing, that is, 'dual track justice' or 'indirect rule', the British defined the rule and the colonised part take in self-governance. Here, the British traded concrete administrative control for symbolic sovereign control. Such an arrangement brings to mind the principal versus agent relationship in common law, wherein the principal appoints and empowers agents to act on his behalf, with contractually defined scope, duty and authority, negotiated beforehand:

> Inherent in the Principal–Agent (P–A) relationship is the understanding that the agent will act for and on behalf of the principal. The agent assumes an obligation of loyalty to the principal that she will follow the principal's instructions and will neither intentionally nor negligently act improperly in the performance of the act. An agent cannot take personal advantage of the business opportunities the agency position uncovers. A principal, in turn, reposes trust and confidence in the agent. These obligations bring forth a fiduciary relationship of trust and confidence between P and A….An agent must obey reasonable instructions given by the P. The A must not do acts that have not been expressly or impliedly authorised by the P. The A must use reasonable care and skill in performing the duties. Most importantly, the A must be loyal to the P. The A must refrain from putting herself in a position that would ordinarily encourage a conflict between the agent's own interests and those of the principal (note: one might reflect on the role of certain Enron executives on 'outside' limited partnerships that did business with Enron in the early 2000s). The A must keep the P informed as to all facts that materially affect the agency relationship.[145]

Finally, mutuality of (separate) interests might collapse into one 'colonial policing' when the British and Chinese used each other to achieve their respective goals, now merged. This is what is called in Chinese 同床異梦, 互相利用 (same bed, different dreams, using each other to achieve individual goals).[146] For example, in colonial Hong Kong, the British colonialists

(Caldwell) used Chinese middlemen to gain control (information, influence) over the Chinese.[147] The Chinese middlemen use their association—access to British authority (through Caldwell) to consolidate their power, secure their leadership and advance their interests.[148] Another example is the Tanka:

> For more than a thousand years, the Tanka had been treated as uncivilized people or sea pirates and had been discriminated against by the land people....they were prohibited from taking the civil service examination... owning property and marrying inland inhabitant... Collaboration with the Westerners brought to them not only economic gain but also advancement in political and social status. In return for their help, the British granted them land, and they were able to speculate on property and became rich. To reverse their fate of political exclusion, some of those successful under the British rule assumed the functions of leaders of the local gentry, equivalent to traditional literati... (without)...take the civil service examination...[149]

The mutually beneficial 'collaborative policing' regime survived the early colonial days, and eventually turned into institutionalised corruption rackets with detective staff sergeants acting as go-between for the British expatriate officers and Chinese crime syndicates in the 1950s–1970s. The British enjoyed a semblance of effective crime control and the detective staff sergeants got rich and powerful: a deal made in heaven. The ICAC described it in 'The rise of the detective sergeant' thus:

> The territory was then divided into three main police regions: Hong Kong Island, Kowloon and the New Territories. Each region had its own chief detective sergeant, and under him were detective sergeants responsible for criminal investigations and were invariably Chinese. This was largely because many high ranking expatriate officers could not speak Chinese. They therefore had to rely on their Chinese detective sergeants when carrying out investigations. This core group of detective sergeants also served as a bridge between non-English speaking citizens and expatriate police officers. Despite their lowly rank, they wielded enormous influence.[150]

It was an open secret in those days that the detective staff sergeants were in control of the HKP, not the CP.[151]

> In (Detective Staff Sergeant) Lui Lok most powerful moment, if a new Commissioner of Police did not give him face, such as not visiting him when coming on duty, he would react by not taking serious criminal investigation, until the Commission visited him personally. As to dealing with the gangsters' world. Lui Lok insisted that the four big gang families all give him face. 'I do not need to make arrest personally. If there are cases to be solved. I will go to the head of the gangs and demand delivery of criminals'. It can be said that he cover up the sky with one hand.[152]

From ICAC records, it is now understood that before the 1970s, 'collaborative policing' in Hong Kong involved three parties, namely, the expatriate officers, the Chinese CID officers and the underworld, through their respective leadership.

In as much as 'collaborative policing' was an inter-dependent relationship, with collaborating parties relying on each other to achieve goals of policing, it promised to turn 'colonial policing' on its head, with the tail (Chinese CID officers) wagging the dog (British colonial officers), instead of the other way round.[153]

E: Colonial Policing as 'Discretionary' Policing

The image of a crisp uniform and stern discipline, often associated with colonial policing, suggests a well-oiled paramilitary machine, in service of the Crown. But appearances are deceptive. Police everywhere have power to selectively (not) enforce the law as they deem fit and proper, on policy ground, due to factual circumstances, or for self-interest, individual or institutional. In the annals of police research, police powers have often been used against the marginal and powerless, making for discrimination charges. The same charge has been levelled against the HKP, as not keeping faith with the rule of law, in early colonial days: 'Caldwell was in a position to pervert course of justice at the expense of the Chinese community. This was achieved "by influencing proceedings in the Magistrate's Court, and to have used his powers to silence his enemies" or by selective enforcement of the law'.[154]

Selective enforcement of law (discretionary policing) is a defining characteristic of colonial power, employed in order to soften opposition or consolidate power. In the former case, full force of law only applies to the most radical and intransigent political elements, lest it inflame the populace.[155] In the latter case, colonial policing is held in reserve in support of indirect rule.

A careful examination of history of colonial policing in Hong Kong finds that 'discretionary' exercise of power was often used to shield native Chinese from the brunt of culturally disagreeable Hong Kong law, for example, use of opium by Chinese elites and opera singers was tolerated,[156] such as in the case of the fame opera singer Sun Ma Sze Tang.[157] Discretionary policing was even conducted in such a way by frontline HKP officers to subvert British colonial law in favour of local justice, for example, use of law to harass disagreeable or immoral conduct. Otherwise, not enforcing colonial law was used to compel cooperation with 'Chinese' policing scheme. Under the Four HKP CID Staff Sergeants era in the 1950s, CID Sergeants were able to use selective (non) enforcement of law as inducement for gangs to police themselves:

> Many police officers, knowingly or unknowingly, had informers who were Triad members and through them the societies obtain a certain degree of official protection, either directly through bribed or indirectly by obtaining advance informant of Police action contemplated against them.[158]

F: Colonial Policing as 'More or Less' Governmental Control

'Colonial policing' can accommodate and incorporate 'colonised policing' under the rubrics of 'more or less government' social control theoretical framework.

As a final analysis, the key to understanding colonial policing in Hong Kong is to investigate in what manner, to what extent and under what circumstances was the HKP organised (mission, role, function) and operated (method and style) in colonial versus indigenous ways. This requires answering two separate but related questions. First, could policing in Hong Kong, at a given point in time,[159] be characterised as (non) 'colonial' in nature, form or style? Second, was the HKP organised like and did it function as a colonial police force in theory or practice? Both of these questions require one to first address the overall question of: What is colonial policing and how does a colonial police force look like? More simply put: What is the true nature of colonial police? To this final subject matter, the last section of this chapter turns.

III: True Nature of Colonial Policing

Colonial HKP Is Not Monolithic, Omnipresent and Omnipotent

The colonial HKP, like all other agencies of control, was not monolithic, omnipresent and omnipotent. As an organisation and bureaucracy, it had many ill-fitting parts, pursuing multiple goals, with different strategies and level of resources, engaging in multiple tasks in variegated context. As such, the HKP cannot be distilled into this or that, much less colonial or dictatorial.

The takeaway from the study of policing is that police work is never done. Simply put, available police resources are limited, and the demands for services are unlimited. Thus, priorities were set, opportunity costs were considered, cost effectiveness and marginal utility calculation were the cornerstone of police resource deployment, zero tolerance was the exception, not the rule, and discretion was the norm.

The other observation is that policing is more about surveillance and monitoring than policing and controlling. The colonial HKP were not exempt from this observation. In as much as that is true, the HKP could not be expected to be present in all time and space due to the aforementioned limited resources. Without knowing all, the police cannot be all things to all people at all times. In this way, the colonial HKP could not afford to or otherwise be made to be omnipresent.

Finally, the colonial HKP is not and could not hope to be omnipotent. This is so because the HKP had at its disposal only limited resources, that is, law, gun, and legitimacy in solving people's variegated problems, changing needs and dynamic expectations.

Colonial Policing Is Not Anti-Local

First, colonial policing should not be considered *ipso facto* as anti-local, confrontational or adversarial, in form or substance. This is not to deny that colonial police had an indispensable and important role to play in defining the relationship between the coloniser and the colonised, either as a ready reserve or emergency force, when the coloniser or colonised people's values or interests were in a collision course, or when they could not come to terms with each other. Still, both parties realised, from experience and with foresight, that they needed to go along and get along, in reducing their differences and managing their distances sufficiently so as not to cross each other's path to thereby require intervention of colonial policing. In this regard, Cole observed, 'A major misconception about colonial policing is the assertion that it was mainly public order policing—a viewpoint that over-emphasises the confrontations with "natives" and creates an impression of colonisation as dealing mainly with anarchy and 'barbarism'.[160]

Second, colonial policing, whatever its agenda or method, did not preclude, and in fact necessitated the performance of routine law, order and service functions, in a responsible, efficient and effective manner. That is to say colonial policing and civilian policing did intersect and converge, requiring long- and short-term coordination and integration, whether this cooperation occurred for the public good or out of self-interest. At the end of the day, law and order and crime and punishment are everybody's business. Cole observed:

> But the colonial society was not, itself, crime free. Crime in the colonial society could be liked, although not entirely, to new socio-economic problems created by colonial political economy. Hence, some of the colonial police forces were established specifically to control crime...[161]

Good political policing entails good social policing, for example, social policing can be used as a way to achieve socialisation or surveillance functions, such as household registration in China. Social policing buttresses political policing, for example, in a stable society with a happy people, it is much more easy to reproduce colonial order. In fact, in order to govern well, a coloniser needed to conduct effective social policing and to avoid partaking in dysfunctional political policing, in order to earn the trust of the ruled, that is, gain legitimacy, allegiance, obedience, and failing that induce instinctual compliance with the law. More succinctly, superlative (colonial) policing—fighting crime, providing order and delivering service—was the most effective way to connect and unite the coloniser and the colonised. Beyond that, the colonial police's capacity to fight crime effectively, ability to maintain order efficiently and readiness to provide service satisfactorily sent a clear message that colonial police was an institution or force to be reckoned with. The colonised people needed to be told by repeated iteration and consistent reinforcement that colonial policing could be tough and rough or soft and measured, in tending to the needs of the people or quelling discontent. The colonised people have a real choice: follow the law and they will be protected; challenge the system, they will be sanctioned as criminals.

Third, colonial policing did not prelude, and indeed welcomed, civilian policing. A negotiated peace between the coloniser and the colonised, even with sub-optimal terms and conditions for both, was better off than constant skirmishes between the two, as they tried to maximise each other's goods. This was Hobbes' central message, in calling for social contract in the midst of a dog-eat-dog world.[162] In stating this, the argument is that Hobbes' social contract has application to all sorts of governance arrived at between (un) equals, not just democratic government. The assumption is that a coloniser's power to rule is never total or perpetual. In relationship building, with friend or foe, co-existence is the rule and conflict is the exception. Justice principles aside, functionally speaking, induced consent to colonial rule was as good in effect as consent freely arrived at. That is the lesson of 'free' market. Economic agents are never free. They all laboured under limited choices, as constrained by their own economic circumstances. Like economic market, there is no perfect democracy between equals, everyone's choice is constrained and limited.

'Indirect rule' was just one such kind of negotiated settlement. It was much less risky and costly for a coloniser to negotiate a settlement with the colonised people to govern themselves with their own rules, by their own leaders, within their own community, than for the colonisers to supervise and punish them, from outside in, top down and high-handed fashion. Cole observed:

> Generally, civilian policing appeared to prevail during the latter years of colonization....after the pacification process was completed and the colonial states were well established. The most conspicuous features of civil policing during the colonial era, however, were the various forms of local police systems that were set up at territorial, village or district level...often referred to as 'native' or 'tribal' administration...[163]

True Nature of Colonial Policing in Hong Kong

As observed and discussed, there is no denial that colonial policing, as a political instrumentality, spoke the voice of the colonial master, at the expense of the colonised. But it is also observed that seasoned, prudent and judicious colonial masters, for political or personal reasons, were inclined to reconfigure or align colonial policy with local values and interests, catering to the colonised's hopes and dreams, meeting their needs and wants, and finding common ground with colonisers if possible (and trading favours if they could not), to make colonial rule a win-win situation. This is to observe that pragmatism not ideology, reality not theory, was the guiding principle of colonial administration.[164] In this way, colonial policing took on a Janus-faced, hybrid personality: customised in response to the complexities of the situation, adapted to the vagaries of the time and adjusted to take account of the dynamic change in the moment.

Colonial policing took shape on the fly and mutated over time, with the colonial police knowing what not to do, than what ought to be done. Necessity, expediency, exigency are the motherhood of colonial policing; speaking in ideological terms and justifying with higher principle only as an afterthought, and most likely in passing.

IV: Conclusion

This chapter problematises the idea, ideal and practice of colonial policing in search of a more grounded understanding of the true nature and nuanced reality of colonial policing.

First to notice is that in the beginning (1841–1844), there was no colonial police or policing to speak of. For one thing, there was no (coherent and stable) colonial policy over the governance of Hong Kong. For another, there was no idea on how to pacify—bringing about law and order to—Hong Kong. Without policy on governance and idea of policing, personalities, events and situations rule the day. That being the case, policing in Hong Kong is not central and uniform, that is, colonial policing, with one (British) or limited (in-direct) rule fits all, as much as it is, decentralised and diversified, that is, 'pluralistic', where each to his/their own.

'Pluralistic' policing should not be understood as unbounded, unprincipled, unstructured or undisciplined, worse dysfunction. 'Pluralistic' just means the obverse of 'monopolistic', with many social control agents, centres or organisations, competing for dominance, as in the case of family versus church, and collaborated or coordinated for effect, as in the cases of District Watch Force.

Looking from the perspective of colonial history, 'pluralistic' policing makes sense in describing law, order and control in early colonial Hong

Kong. Policing in colonial Hong Kong was to be filled by 'colonial police', failing that the void was filled by default with ready and willing policing agents or institutions of all colour and shape, from family discipline to private guards, and even Triads.

However, from a Hong Kong-centric perspective, looking at Hong Kong history, especially from bottom up, one finds that neither 'colonial policing' nor 'pluralistic policing' quite describes the situation. Hong Kong and its residents were fairly well ordered and sufficiently protected, before the arrival of the British. The crime and disorder brought on by colonisation—commercialisation, urbanisation and seafaring—while beyond the control of the locals, were not impacting their life, as much. Personal/family self-help and commercial private policing were ready to resolve disputes, fight crime and maintain disorder in Hong Kong. At the end of the day, before 1945, the British colonial HKP had little motivation or capacity to interfere in Chinese ways of life.

During those years, pirates prowled the water outside Hong Kong and thugs roamed the city at night. Public police existed in name only. To secure their own safety, the European elites retained personal guards. To protect their property, commercial establishments hired private security. The safety and security of local residences and sojourn Chinese labourers were left to their own accord, to the charge of village pack (*baojia*) or mutual aid organisations (Man Wu Temple). In time, the indigenous and informal Chinese social control was found wanting, and the Chinese elites took the initiative to start the District Watch Force to fight crime and Tung Wah detectives to protect women and children. This initiative was kidnapped by the colonial police to pacify and regulate a resentful indigenous crowd:

> As years passed and the Chinese community grew numerically and in sophistication, the need for indigenous private security was felt by this Chinese elite....Chinese merchants in their attempt to initiate the District Watch Force... control by...the Government exerted from the outset.[165]

Investigating into colonial policing of Hong Kong requires perspective and discernment to avoid being sidetracked by ideology and misled by conventional wisdom. Here, Professor Carroll has much to offer with his book *Edge of Empires* (2005). The book seeks to 'explore the fissures in British colonial rule that left room for local Chinese elites' to exert control, specifically, in early British rule in Hong Kong. In the book, Carroll cautioned:

> We need more than theoretical criticisms or defenses of Orientalism, subaltern studies, and post-colonialism; we need more local histories that both engage and challenge these approaches...Colonies were not just about exploitation; they were also about how people learned to work within cracks (pp. 9–10).[166]

In the case of colonial Hong Kong:

> The gulf between government and governed, the government's failure to provide adequate medical facilities for its Chinese subjects, and its inability to provide a secure business environment all helped Chinese merchants obtain recognition by providing services to the local Chinese population and the government (p. 10).[167]

Finally, in Chapter 3, 'Strategic Balance: Status and Respect in the Colonial Context', Carroll explores the fissures in British colonial rule that left room for local Chinese elites to cultivate their power and influence. In early Hong Kong, a wide gulf separated the colonial government and its Chinese subjects:

> Colonial ignorance, indifference, and incompetence created a demand for services that these merchants were in a special position to offer. Through charitable and voluntary organizations, they resolved civil and commercial disputes, provided medical facilities, and created a voice for the Chinese community. By offering such services, local Chinese merchants were able to take advantage of Hong Kong's position at the edge of the Chinese and British empires to enhance their own power and prestige.[168]

At the end of the day, colonial policing had more to do with Chinese policing Chinese, than total British rule.

One more important issue needs to be raised. Throughout this chapter, there has been a focus on debunking 'colonial policing' as a concept and practice. There is little attention paid to the idea that Chinese are not alike, in ethnic origin (Hakka vs. Punti), cultural sentiments (Hong Kongese vs. Chinese), and regional identity (Shanghai refugees vs. Hong Kong locals), which suggests many degree of separateness between and among Chinese groups. Given this sensitivity to and understanding of the Chinese diaspora, it is necessary to revisit the issue of what counts for 'colonial policing' and what counts for 'Chinese policing'. As applied and in more concrete terms, how did different 'Chinese' policing organisation and style, individually or in collaboration with the HKP, affect understanding of 'Chinese policing' as 'colonial policing', free of essentialist tendency and chauvinistic pretensions? At this juncture, it bears to recall the admonition of Wing Shing Law:

> Criticizing the essentializing tendencies manifested in those Chinese nationalistic discourses, diaspora cultural studies passionately argue for a kind of post-colonial politics which can engage battles on two fronts: that is to say, they try to safeguard Hong Kong as a space for identification where both British colonialism and chauvinistic Chinese nationalisms can be held in check. (p. 4)[169]

Otherwise there is a risk of jumping from the fire-pan of anti-colonialism into the fire of politically correct nationalism, both of which are myth bearing and factually distortive in the effort to unravel the mystery behind 'colonial policing' with Chinese characteristics. The fact of the matter is, if colonial policing with Chinese characteristics means anything, it is the fact that Chinese characteristics come through in numerous ways, and change over time and space. The only thing that is certain in the study of colonial policing with Chinese characteristics is that such policing takes up unique forms and styles within indigenous political economy.[170] That being the case, it is imperative to investigate how the Chinese elites and powers-to-be used colonial policing to their own personal advantages (political) and for the benefit of the group. For them, to be successful in improving Hong Kong–Chinese interests, it was best to embrace and deploy British colonial policing, in the image and to the liking of the Chinese, rather than to resent and dismiss it outright.[171] Viewed in this manner, Hong Kong colonial policing was neither British nor Chinese, but a hybrid, with concepts from the British, such as legal justice, and practices from the Chinese, such as street justice.[172]

Endnotes

1. M. E. Page and P. M. Sonnenburg, Police and policing, *Colonialism: An International, Social, Cultural, and Political Encyclopedia.* A-M. Vol. 1 (ABC-CLIO, 2003), p. 475.
2. J. Morris, *Pax Britannica* (London: Faber and Faber, 25 November 2010), p. 197. It is ironic that while the people usually enjoyed the grandiose of British imperialism in far-fetched places, there was no serious thought about what to do with British settlement and possession, later dependency and association. In fact, to the public and politicians: 'the issues of Empire were mostly glamorous irrelevances, whose effect on domestic politics was normally peripheral…' (p. 202). There was never a Minister of Empire (p. 204). The Parliament left the colonies to the executive branch. The Colonial Office was established in 1854. Before that, colonies were administered by Secretary of State for War and the Colonies, and some (like India) with the Foreign Office. The office was run by 23 'clerks' who while experienced as foreign experts had little research support. They knew very little about the ins and outs of colonies, and perhaps cared less. In the end, the colonies were trusted to be run themselves, baring extraordinary circumstances, for example, insurgency in Malaysia or riots in Hong Kong (p. 205). Cultural ignorance aside and political disinterest notwithstanding, this does not stop Britain, as the titular head of a vast empire, to claim moral superiority and assert social distance from the colonised people. (See Chapter 8: 'Caste'.)
3. It is argued that Hong Kong has thrived under a kind of indirect rule, resulting in the people enjoying increased autonomy T.-W. Ngo, *Hong Kong's History: State and Society under Colonial Rule* (London and New York: Routledge, 2002).

4. F. Madden, *The End of Empire: Dependencies Since 1948, Part 1: The West Indies, British Honduras, Hong Kong, Fiji, Cyprus, Gibraltar, and the Falklands*, Vol. 1 (Westport, CT: Greenwood Publishing Group, 2009), p. xiii.
5. 'German European townships of Windhoek and Swakopments in Southwest Africa; the French "communes" and European settlements in Algeria, Cochin-China (South Vietnam), Senegal, French Equatorial Africa, New Caledonia and the New Hebrides; the Spanish colonial township of Santiago in Chile; the Portuguese colonial settlements in East and West Africa'. (B. A. Cole, Post colonial policing, In: R. I. Mawby (ed.), *Policing across The World: Issues for the Twenty-First Century* (New York: Psychology Press, 1 February 1999), pp. 88–95. (Cole discusses the characteristics and impact of colonial policing.)
6. *Ibid.*
7. This note moves the RIC discussion and debate in two directions. First, it is said that a picture is worth a thousand words, and seeing is believing (literally and figuratively); both hinted at the impact of visual presentation on our sense, affecting our understanding, which is cognitively based but emotionally laden, if not driven. Second, meaning of things is cultural in nature. Culture as ideas and beliefs are people based. To get to the roots of what RIC is or is not, we need to know how people think, and more importantly, feel. For these reasons, some RIC pictures and discussion on the web is helpful with our analysis. http://www.boards.ie/vbulletin/showthread.php?t = 2056739068
8. R. I. Mawby, *Policing across the World: Issues for the Twenty-First Century* (London: Psychology Press, 1 February 1999), p. 88.
9. *Ibid.*, p. 13.
10. 'Colonialism' in *Stanford Encyclopedia of Philosophy* ('Colonialism is a practice of domination, which involves the subjugation of one people to another'.) First published Tuesday, 9 May 2006; substantive revision Tuesday, 10 April 2012. http://plato.stanford.edu/entries/colonialism/
11. R. J. Horvath, A definition of colonialism, *Current Anthropology*, 13 (1): 45–57, 1972.
12. C. Jeffries, *The Colonial Police* (London: Max Parrish, 1952), p. 30.
13. L. A. Leach, *The Ordinances of the Legislative Council of the Colony of Hongkong Commencing with the Year 1844* (Hong Kong: Norton and Government Printer, 1890), p. 45.
14. The language of the PFR (preamble) reads in pertinent part: 'it is expedient that provisions should be made "it is considered expedient that provision should be made for the establishment of an effective System of Police within the Colony of Hong Kong…under a Police Ordinance…"'
15. Section III: '3. And in order to provide for one uniform system of rules and regulations, throughout the whole establishment of police in Hongkong: Be it enacted, that the said Chief Magistrate may from time to time, subject to the approbation of the Governor for the time being, frame such orders and regulations, as he shall deem expedient for the general government of the men, to be appointed members of the Police Force under this Ordinance…'
16. Hong Kong was the by-product of opium trade, and the spoil of the Opium War (1839–1844). C. Munn, Four: The Hong Kong opium revenue, 1845–1885, In: B. Timothy and B. Wakabayashi, *Opium Regimes: Britain, China and Japan – 1839–1952* (CA: California University Press, 2000), pp. 105–125. As expected, opium

was a big business for the British as exports and a steady revenue in Hong Kong on retail consumption. The value of opium imported from India between 1903 and 1915 amounted to the following: 1903–1904 3,576,431 pounds sterling; 1904–1905 4,036,436, 1905–1906 3,775,82.6; 1906–1907 3,771,409; 1907–1908 3,145,403; 1908–1909 2,230,755; 1909–1910 3,377,222; 1910–1911 3,963,264; 1911–1912 3,018,858; 1912–1913 2,406,084; 1913–1914 1,084,093; 1914–1915 110,712 'Statistical Abstract Relating to British India, 1905–1906 to 1915,' and 'Statistical Abstract Relating to British India, 1903–1904 to 1912–1913'. E. L. Monte, *The Opium Monopoly* (New York: Macmillan, 1920), p. 37. Opium retail and monopoly generated a sizable and steady income for the Hong Kong government, which was strapped for cash with limited Home Office assistant, especially in the early years. The role of the police was in enforcing the opium regulations, formulated to protect monopoly of opium farm and integrity of the export opium trade. Munn, p. 110.

17. P. Howell, Race, space and the regulation of prostitution in colonial Hong Kong, *Urban History*, 31 (2): 229–248, 2004. (As a subject of sexual politics, the prevalence of prostitution in a new-found colony challenges the colonist's sense of self, purity of race, and vision for the world, civilisation of others (Chinese), denominated in moral, scientific and cultural terms. Prostitution as practised in China (spilled over to Hong Kong), as distinguished from European varieties, does not bespeak passion of (men) run amok or commercialisation (of sex) gone astray but reflects fundamental flaws of a degenerated nation, bent on contaminating all those who cross its path (European colonists) and promise to destroy the civilized world as we know it (in the West.)
18. Ordinance 14 of 1844, An Ordinance for the Suppression of Public Gaming in the Colony of Hongkong. [10th June, 1844.] The preamble reads: 'Whereas, it is expedient to suppress the pernicious Practice of Public Gaming in the Colony of Hongkong…' Notwithstanding Ordinance 14 of 1844, gambling in Hong Kong spread like wildfire: 'Gambling on the part of the navies had reached such a climax at this period (1860s) that neither the law regulating the subject nor the steps taken by the Government to endeavor to eradicate the evil had been of any avail'. The fact that the police was on the payroll of illicit gamblers did not help. J. W. Norton-Kyshe, The *H*istory of the *L*aws and Courts of Hongkong (Hong Kong: T.F. Unwin, 1898), p. 109.
19. From the Editorial: 'The report of the Acting Captain Superintendent of Police for the last year is of special interest…The figures… show that… both serious crimes and minor offences have increased to…an alarming extent. So far as statistics are concerned, there was more crime in the Colony last year than in any similar period for at least a decade'. *China Mail*, 8 April 1898.
20. According to the first Registrar General of Hong Kong, Samuel Fearon: 'Chinese people whose habits, character and language mark them as a distinct race. Careless of the ties of home and those moral obligations, the observance of which is deemed absolutely necessary to the preservation of the national integrity; uneasy under the restraint of law and unscrupulous of the means by which they live, they abandon without hesitation their hearths and household gods, their birthright and their fathers' tombs to wander, unrespected, whither gain many fall. The unsettled state of the Colony, and the vast amount of crime during its infancy afford abundant proof of the demoralizing effects of their

presence'. C. Munn, *Anglo-China: Chinese People and British Rule in Hong Kong, 1841–1880* (Hong Kong: Hong Kong University Press, 2008), p. 68.
21. C. Yik-Yi Chu (ed.), *Foreign Communities in Hong Kong, 1840s–1950s* (New York: Palgrave Macmillan, 2005).
22. 'Letter to the Editor: Sir, the disgraceful scenes of which our streets are the arena, call loudly for magisterial interference; each day they become worse and worse…I can only allude to the drunken delinquencies of our soldiers and sailors; for the conduct of our native population, by contrast, is truly admirable'. *Friends of China*, 25 April 1842.
23. 'From the Editorial: Robberies, and attempts at robbery, have been very frequent…we are aware of two instances in which gentleman had their silk umbrellas snatched out of their hands, and the rogues disappeared in the gloom of night and eluded pursuit…'. *Friends of China*, 23 December 1843.
24. K. Chin, Triad societies in Hong Kong, *Transnational Organized Crime*, 1 (1): 47–64, 1995. (Abstract: Triad societies, which originated between 1842 and 1930 when secret society members from China emigrated to Hong Kong and formed mutual aid organisations, can be categorized into four major groups: the Chiu Chao, the Wo, the 14 K and the Big Four. There is a conflict of opinion on how tightly structured these groups are. Triads appear to be involved in criminal activities ranging from drug trafficking and prostitution to gambling and extortion.)
25. F. Dikötter. A paradise for rascals: Colonialism, punishment and the prison in Hong Kong (1841–1898), *Crime, History and Society*, 8 (1): 49–63, 2004. http://chs.revues.org/515
26. C. Jeffries, *The Colonial Police* (London: Max Parrish, 1952) (Colonial policing requires the imposition of order against populist resistance calling forth the adoption of Royal Irish Constabulary (RIC) model of policing in organisation, operations and style, as distinguished from Peele's London's Metropolitan Police (LMP), that is, civil order maintenance with law and consent. Jefferies also postulates that militaristic RIC policing would in time be replaced by civil LMP policing when habitual obedience to British rule is obtained.)
27. Whether colonial policing in the body of RIC 'revert back' or 'advance to' civil mode is more than a semantic difference. 'Revert back' suggests that policing is always civil in nature, thus it is abnormal and exceptional for it to take up arms. Advance to suggests that the policing has always been militaristic in form and militant in operations, and gets to be civil when historical or social conditions allows.
28. D. M. Anderson and D. Killingray, *Policing the Empire: Government, Authority and Control, 1830–1940 (Studies in Imperialism)* (Manchester: Manchester University Press, 1991), pp. 2–4.
29. C. W. Ng, The Establishment and Early Development of Police System in Hong Kong. Ph.D. Thesis, Department of History, Chinese University of Hong Kong.
30. A. Kerrigan, Policing a colony: The case of Hong Kong 1844–1899, Ph.D. dissertation with Cardiff Graduate Law School, University of Wales, under the supervision of Dr. Carole Jones.
31. P. Burroughs, Crime and punishment in the British Army, 1815–1870, *The English Historical Review*, 100 (396): 545–571, 1985.
32. There is evidence to suggest that HKP was not influenced by the RIC, in its formative year. Captain Superintendent of HKP Henry May (1893–1902) was an

Irish who arrived in Hong Kong in 1897. The first batch of Irish officers did not arrive until 1898. Attempts to recruit from the RIC were made in 1871, 1880, 1881 and 1893, but to no avail. See Public Record Office (CO): CO 129/154, 31-59; CO 129/191, 69; CO 129/196, 51-7, CO 129/259, 393.

33. R. E. Neustadt and E. R. May, *Thinking in Time: The Uses of History for Decision-Makers* (New York: Free Press, 1986), Chapter 9: Placing Strangers, pp. 156–180.
34. P. Burroughs, Crime and Punishment in the British Army, 1815–1870, *The English Historical Review*, 100 (396): 545–571, 1985.
35. President's special message to the Congress on crime and law enforcement, dated 9 March 1966.
36. S. Huntington, The clash of civilizations? *Foreign Affairs*, 72 (3): 27–47, 1993.
37. While disparate impact might suggest discriminate intent, and has been taken as such in U.S. Constitutional jurisprudence, it is not necessary so. For example, Chinese were treated to harsher punishment, such as flogging, because the British adopted Chinese punitive law and because the British did not know how to reform the Chinese. F. Dikötter, A paradise for rascals: Colonialism, punishment and the prison in Hong Kong (1841–1898), *Crime, History and Society*, 8 (1): 49–63, 2004.
38. J. W. Norton-Kyshe, *The History of the Laws and Courts of Hongkong* (Hong Kong: T.F. Unwin, 1898), p. 51.
39. *Ibid*., p. 57.
40. I do not say 'law and order' because Chinese do not know law, and Caine put order about law. Thus, Caine obtained some measure of respect from the Hong Kong people.
41. S. E. Hamilton, *Watching over Hong Kong: Private Policing 1841–1941* (Hong Kong: Hong Kong University Press, 2009/12), especially Chapter 3: District Watch Force, pp. 39–58.
42. Institutionally, the HKP is haunted by its colonial past, authoritarianism and paramilitarism. A. Jiao, *The Police in Hong Kong: A Contemporary View* (Lanham, MD: United Press of America, 2007), Chapter 3.
43. H. Y. F. Choy, Schizophrenic Hong Kong: Postcolonial Identity Crisis in the *Infernal Affairs Trilogy*, *Transtext(e)s Transcultures 跨文本跨文化* [En ligne], 3 | 2007, mis en ligne le 15 octobre 2009, consulté le 21 mai 2013. http://transtexts.revues.org/138.
44. K. C. Wong, *Policing in Hong Kong* (Farnham, Surrey, England: Ashgage, 2012), Chapter Five: Policing Computer Crime in Hong Kong.
45. M. Farley, Colony's expatriate police see '97 as incentive to hand in badges, *S.F. Times*, 6 December 1996. D. Greenless, Hong Kong's police force is a handover bright spot, *New York Times*, 24 June 2007.
46. K. C. Wong, *Policing in Hong Kong* (Farnham, Surrey, England: Ashgage, 2012). Chapter Seven.
47. B. Cole, Post-colonial systems In: R. I. Mawby (ed.), *Policing across the World* (London: UCL Press, 1999), pp. 88–108.
48. A. Jiao, *The Police in Hong Kong: A Contemporary View* (Lantham, Maryland: University Press, 2007), Chapter 2.
49. P. Childs and R. P. Williams. *An Introduction to Post-Colonial Theory* (London, New York, Toronto, Sydney, Tokyo: Harvester Wheatsheaf/Prentice Hall, 1997).
50. K. T. So (蘇錦棠) The Hong Kong police as a new paradigm of policing in a post colonial city. MPA Thesis, Department of Politics and Public Administration,

University of Hong Kong (1999), Workshop on British Colonial Policing in Historical Perspective, University of Hong Kong, Hong Kong, 22 June 2010.

51. Policing in versus policing of Hong Kong draws the distinction between general policing by all people/institutions versus specific policing by the government.
52. M. Brogen, Emergence of the police—The colonial dimension, *British Journal of Criminology*, 27 (1): 4–14, 1987.
53. In determining the nature of policing, colonial or others, strategy and tactics matters. For example, the trademark of imperial–colonial policing is to impose order. With indigenous–democratic policing is to facilitate self-governance. Yet the strategic goal of imposed order could be achieved through induced compliance or indirect rule. In the case of New Zealand, this was achieved through minimal policing and tribal rule. In the case of Hong Kong, it was achieved through 'dual track' justice and indirect rule. R. Hill, Chapter Four: The policing of colonial New Zealand: From informal to formal control, 1840–1907, In: D. M. Anderson and D. Killingray (eds.), *Policing the Empire: Government, Authority, and Control*, 1830–1940 (Manchester, UK: Manchester University Press, 1991), pp. 52–68, 52–53. J. Gallagher and R. Robinson, The imperialism of free trade, In: A. Seal (ed.), *The Decline and Fall of the British Empire* (Cambridge: Cambridge University Press, 1982), pp. 1–18.
54. Chapter 1: Governance in a Colonial Society, In: S. Tsang (ed.), *Governing Hong Kong: Administrative Officers from the 19th Century to the Handover to China, 1862–1997* (London and New York: L.B. Tauris, 2007).
55. T.-W. Ngo, *Hong Kong's History: State and Society under Colonial Rule* (London: Routledge, 2002), p. 2.
56. G. Ure, *Governors, Politics and the Colonial Office: Public Policy in Hong Kong, 1918–58* (Hong Kong: Hong Kong University Press, 2012).
57. A. Grantham, *Via Ports: From Hong Kong to Hong Kong* (Hong Kong: Hong Kong University Press, 1 January 2012), p. 108.
58. *The Colonial Police* (London: M. Parrish, 1952).
59. R. Hawkins, Chapter Two: The 'Irish model' and the empire: A case for reassessment, In: D. M. Anderson and D. Killingray (eds.), *Policing the Empire: Government, Authority and Control, 1830–1940* (Manchester: Manchester University Press, 1991), pp. 14–30.
60. With HKP reform, the HKP has gone through decolonisation without being decolonised.
61. Chapter 1 to C. Patten, *East and West: China, Power, and the Future of Asia* (New York: Times Book, 1998). http://www.nytimes.com/books/first/p/patten-east.html
62. S. Tsang, *Governing Hong Kong: Administrative Officers from the 19th Century to the Handover to China, 1862–1997* (London: I.B. Tauris, 15 December 2007).
63. Sir Robert Peel Principles of Policing #7: 'To maintain at all times a relationship with the public that gives reality to the historic tradition that the police are the public and that the public are the police, the police being only members of the public who are paid to give full-time attention to duties which are incumbent on every citizen in the interests of community welfare and existence'.
64. G. Schloss, Expat cops on the outside, *SCMP*, 3 July 2001. http://www.scmp.com/article/351387/expat-cops-outside (There was a time when expatriate police in the then Royal Hong Kong Police Force were treated like royalty. Recruited from overseas, mostly Britain, they were given spacious flats, a job for

life—or at least until 1997—on pensionable terms with promises of fast promotion and annual trips home.)

65. May was born in May in Dublin, Ireland on 14 March 1860 to a distinguished family. His father was Rt. Hon. George Augustus Chichester May, Lord Chief Justice of Ireland. He went to Harrow School and Trinity College, Dublin, graduating with 1st Honour in Classics and Modern Languages (B.A. in 1881). He was appointed to a Hong Kong Cadetship in 1881 and was the Assistant Protector of Chinese, private secretary to Governor Sir George William Des Vœux and later private secretary to Acting Administrator Digby Barker from 1889 to 1891. He went on to be Assistant Colonial Secretary in 1891 and Acting Colonial Treasurer in 1892 before ending up as a Legislative Councilor in 1895. From 1893 to 1902, May was the Captain Superintendent of the Hong Kong Police Force, and Superintendent Victoria Gaol and Fire Brigade for Hong Kong between 1896 and 1902. After that he held the position of Colonial Secretary for Hong Kong in 1902–1910, and became an acting administrator of Hong Kong in 1903, 1904, 1906, 1907, and 1910. In 1910, May was appointed Governor of Fiji and High Commissioner Western Pacific, a position he would hold until 1912. http://www.absoluteastronomy.com/topics/Francis_Henry_May
66. Heads of the Force 1841–1945, *OffBeat* Issue 772. http://www.police.gov.hk/offbeat/772/eng/f04.htm
67. H. J. Lethbridge, Sir James Haldane Stewart Lockhart: Colonial civil servant and scholar, *Journal of the Hong Kong Branch of the Royal Asiatic Society*, 12: 56–86, 1972.
68. P. Leonard, *Expatriate Identities in Postcolonial Organizations* (Farnham, Surrey, UK: Ashgate Publishing, Ltd., 2010), pp. 84–87. Old colonial or new cosmopolitan? Changing white identities in the Hong Kong Police, *Social Politics*, 17 (4): 507–535, 2010.
69. A. Memmi, *The Colonizer and the Colonized* (Boston: Beacon press, [1957] 1996), 19–25
70. C. Knowles, 'It's not what it was': British migrants in postcolonial Hong Kong, *Sociology Working Papers*, 11: 1–25, 2007. http://eprints.gold.ac.uk/8376/
71. *Ibid.*
72. A set of photos: 'Hong Kong 70s & 80s' (1965–1990) posted by Tom Jackson who went to British school in 1960s elicited the follow remarks:

> Steve 14-Feb-2011 12:35
>
> Oh btw. I am always explaining to people here in mainland China that many English/Europeans were also often born in HK and that these people are in fact also Hong Kong people. Here they seem to think that ONLY Chinese people can be called Hong Kong people in mainland China & that is very racist thinking in anybodies book! When they ask where do I come from I say Hong Kong, they often look at me confused as if I am joking and then ask where my family is from
>
> …. Steve 14-Feb-2011 12:19
>
> I live near Nanjing, Jiangsu in mainland China now. Hong Kong was and is a very important childhood memory and made me feel part Chinese (I am 100% Anglo), but my wife is Chinese and I love so many Chinese

things. Living in Hong Kong introduced me to a different culture than my own and led to a love for & respect for Chinese things that has stayed with me my whole life. I am 41 now! I still feel betrayed by the UK government about the handing back of the whole of Hong Kong and not just the NT as was agreed in the 99 year lease! http://www.pbase.com/anubis_photo/hong_kong_70s__80s

73. Sir D. Akers-Jones, *Time-Out Hong Kong*, 11 April 2012. http://www.timeout.com.hk/big-smog/features/50004/sir-david-akers-jones.html
74. D. Akers-Jones, *Feeling the Stones: Reminiscences by David Akers-Jones* (Hong Kong: Hong Kong University Press, 2004), p. xii.
75. E. Tu, *Colonial Hong Kong in the Eyes of Elsie Tu* (Hong Kong: Hong Kong University Press, 2003).
76. Homesick For Hong Kong, 11 November 2009. http://www.batgung.com/Twenty-years-in-Hong-Kong.
77. M. Banton, *Administrating the Empire, 1801–1968: A Guide to the Records of the Colonial Office in the National Archives of the UK* (London: Institute of Historical Research and the National Archives of the UK, 2008), p. 21.
78. G. Ure, Governors, *Politics and the Colonial Office: Public Policy in Hong Kong, 1918–58* (Hong Kong: Hong Kong University Press, 1 June 2012), p. 217.
79. S. Kevin, Ex-police chief takes secret of his departure to the grave, *South China Morning Post*. Hong Kong: SCMP, 5 September 2004.
80. 張家偉，《六七暴動：香港戰後歷史的分水嶺》。香港：香港大學出版社 [K. W. Cheung, *The 1967 Riots – The Watershed of Post-war Hong Kong History* (Hong Kong: Hong Kong University Press, 2012), pp. 121–122], 2012年
81. H. J. Lethbridge, Hong Kong cadets, 1962 to 1941, *Journal of the Royal Asiatic Society Hong Kong Branch,* 10: 37–56, 38, 1970.
82. *Ibid*. (Given this common background, training, and the fraternity of class, cadets came to the field with many shared assumptions about, and attitudes towards, the people they governed in the colonial territories.)
83. Over the Bamboo Ceiling, *Far East Culture*, 31 May 2013. http://www.macstudies.net/2013/05/31/over-the-bamboo-ceiling-early-macanese-enterprise-in-hong-kong/
84. D. Faure (ed.), *A Documentary History Hong Kong* (Hong Kong: Hong Kong University Press, 1997), p. 12.
85. G. Bickley, Chapter 3: British Attitudes toward Hong Kong in the nineteenth century, In: Y. Y. Chu (ed.), *Foreign Communities in Hong Kong, 1840s–1950s* (New York: Palgrave Macmillan, 2005), 39 pp.
86. *Ibid*., p. 44.
87. S. Tsang, *Governing Hong Kong: Administrative Officers from the Nineteenth Century to the Handover to China, 1862–1997* (London: I.B. Tauris, 2007), p. 1.
88. *Ibid*., Chapter 2: 'The cadet scheme'.
89. *Ibid*., Chapter 3: 'Benevolent paternalism'.
90. S. Tsang, *A Documentary History of Hong Kong: Government and Politics* (Hong Kong: Hong Kong University Press, 1995), p. 11.
91. S. Tsang, *Governing Hong Kong: Administrative Officers from the Nineteenth Century to the Handover to China, 1862–1997* (London: I.B. Tauris, 2007), *Ibid*., p. 25.

92. H. J. Lethbridge, Condition of the European working class in nineteenth century Hong Kong, *Journal of the Hong Kong Branch of the Royal Asiatic Society*, 15: 88–113, 1975.
93. This is the same individual mentality and organisational ethos that perpetuate the institutionalised corruption in Hong Kong. For the individual officer, the reasoning went something as follows: I am here to have a good time. Or, I do not know why I am here. (For that matter whatever opportunistic reason would do: 'I am to make money'.) I will do what I am told to do, but with minimal effort. As to enforcing the law, such as gambling, drugs or prostitution, it is useless. Gambling is the Chinese favourite past time. Drugs are condoned by the Chinese and promoted by the British. As to prostitution, there is nothing wrong with it. Besides, we are all lonely here. No one really cares: Not the British. Not the Chinese. Not the Europeans. Thus, they cannot be eradicated. If I do something about them myself, I am the one to get hurt by the Chinese operators and British who are on the take. It is thus best for me to go along and in order get along. No one is getting hurt, since all these elicit behaviour is mostly done by the Chinese. Why should I care? I might as well close my eyes and get paid for it.
94. H. J. Lethbridge, Condition of the European Working Class in nineteenth century Hong Kong, *Journal of the Hong Kong Branch of the Royal Asiatic Society*, 15: 88–113, 1975.
95. The Earnshaw Brothers, 25 August 2012, Hong Kong Cemetery. http://hongkongcemetery.blogspot.co.uk/. For a few of the life stories of how many expats from the United Kingdom came to join HKP, see Hong Kong Police Ancestors. http://hongkongpoliceancestors.blogspot.com/2012/09/the-bristol-bobbies.html
96. S. Griffins, What was it like as a Brit in the Royal Hong Kong Police? *The Crime Vault*, 19 April 2013. http://www.thecrimevault.com/exclusives/what-was-it-like-as-a-brit-in-the-royal-hong-kong-police/
97. http://www.policespecials.com/forum/index.php?/topic/99871-former-royal-hong-kong-police-officers/
98. For the dreams and aspirations, adventures and misadventures, fame and fortune, of those few British police officers who ended serving HKP in a bygone and long forgotten era (the 1880s and 1890s), see 'The British Boobies' Hong Kong Police Ancestry, Sunday, 2 September 2012. http://hongkongpoliceancestors.blogspot.com/2012/09/the-bristol-bobbies.html
99. A. I. K. Kituai, *My Gun, My Brother: The World of the Papua New Guinea Colonial Police, 1920–1960* (Honolulu, Hawaii: Hawaii University Press, 1998), Chapter 2: 'Recruitment of Police', pp. 42–85.
100. *Ibid.*, p. 52.
101. *Ibid.*, p. 52.
102. *Ibid.*, p. 52.
103. *Ibid.*, p. 53.
104. *Ibid.*, p. 54.
105. K. Y. Wong, *The Lighter Side of a Hong Kong Police Inspector's Career in the 1960s* (Hong Kong: Joint Publication, 2008).
106. Kong Chi Yin, Treasury, Nga Tsin Wai Village Committee. Male. DOB: 1946. 66 years old. 'Reason for and course of becoming a policeman through exams

after dropping out'. (09/06/12) Hong Kong Memory. http://www.hkmemory.hk/collections/oral_history/All_Items_OH/oha_86/records/index.html#p64820

107. *Ibid.*
108. Lifelong Battles against Triad, *OffBeat* Issue 662, 5 November–18 November 2003. ('The incident reinforced Mr Leung's determination to become a policeman. Despite disapproval from his parents, he did not give up his ambition'.) http://www.police.gov.hk/offbeat/763/eng/
109. kee14840 2010-5-13 21:54 Hong Kong Police Club. http://www.pcchk.com/thread-25729-1-1.html
110. 好仔當差 Last updated: 01/06/2012 07:25:24. http://lingsir.org/pol02.htm
111. Cheung Koon Fu. DOB: 1921. 90 'The Government encouraged young indigenous settlers in New Territories to enlist in the army or immigrate in the early post-war period (I)' (26/11/2011). Hong Kong Memory. http://www.hkmemory.hk/collections/oral_history/All_Items_OH/oha_112/records/index.html#p73018
112. 成長篇 Last updated: N/A. http://lingsir.org/grow.htm. I (author) joined for the same reason to reform and transform the HKP. My father was against me joining because to him it was corrupt beyond repair. I felt otherwise. I recall telling him: 'This is a Hong Kong dollar coin. It has two sides to it. You are right to observe that the HKP is corrupt and cannot be changed. I am also right to take up the challenge. If no one join the HKP. It will never be changed'. In spite of his objection, my father helped me to join, without me knowing it.
113. F. X. Hezel, SJ, *Strangers in Their Own Land: A Century of Colonial Rule in the Caroline and Marshall Islands* (Honolulu, HI: University of Hawaii Press, 2003), pp. xiii–xiv.
114. C. J. Jefferies, *Colonial Police* (London: M. Parrish, 1951). Colonial police in 'Irish Constabulary' mode is characterised by (1) organised along rigid military line; (2) police lived in barracks and away from the people; (3) centrally controlled, nationally.
115. D. M. Anderson and D. Killingray, Consent, coercion and colonial control: Policing the empire, 1830–1940, In: D. M. Anderson and D. Killingray (eds.), *Policing the Empire: Government, Authority and Control, 1830–1940* (Manchester: Manchester University Press, 1991), pp. 1–2. (Recent colonial policing research 'has raised serious questions about Jeffries's oft quoted assertion that Irish and Metropolitan models of policing determined developments in the colonies. The colonial reality was clearly much more complex'), p. 12.
116. *Ibid.* In the study of colonial police, historical and local context matters a great deal, p. 12.
117. J. T. Martin, *How Chinese Culture Might Inform a Distinctive Kind of Modern Policing. Paper presented at University of Sidney Forum at University of Hong Kong*, 2010.
118. Colonial 'dual track' policing bracket, as it anticipates 'pluralistic policing' in modern time with both conceding the inadequacy, inefficiency or ineffectiveness of a centralised policing authority in the state. J. Merritt, Pluralist models of policing: Legislating for police powers, a cautionary note from England and Wales, *Policing: An International Journal of Police Strategies & Management*, 32 (2): 377–394, 2009.

119. L. F. Goodstadt, *Uneasy Partners: The Conflict between Public Interest and Private Profit in Hong Kong* (Hong Kong: Hong Kong University Press, 2005), p. 10.
120. J. Merritt, Pluralist models of policing: Legislating for police powers, a cautionary note from England and Wales, *Policing: An International Journal of Police Strategies & Management*, 32 (2): 377–394, 2009.
121. R. V. Clarke and F. M. Marcus, Introduction: Criminology, routine activity, and rational choice, *Advances in Criminological Theory: Routine Activity and Rational Choice*, 5: 1–14, 1993.
122. L. Cohen and F. Marcus, Social change and crime rate trends: A routine activity approach, *American Sociological Review*, 44 (4): 588–608, 1979.
123. A. van Sluis, P. Marks, and V. Bekkers, Nodal policing in the Netherlands: Strategic and normative considerations on an evolving practice, *Policing*, 5 (4): 365–371, 2011.
124. Expectation theory of policing proposes: 'The person closest to a person, by impact or with request, is the person to solve the problem'. (Problem is defined as expectation denied. Expectation is met by suitable resources.) K. C. Wong, *Chinese Policing: History and Reform* (New York: Peter Lang, 2009), Chapter 8: Chinese Theory of Community Policing, pp. 185–227.
125. Most colonial police forces are supplemented by indigenous enforcers. *Ibid.*
126. The 'collaborative policing' thesis is part political critique and part revisionist historiography of 'colonial policing' paradigm. It challenges the long-held assumption that Hong Kong as a colony can be effectively policed, imperialistically, imposingly and coercively, without the active participation of the Chinese, in multifarious ways and in a variety of sites. J. Carroll, *Edge of Empires: Chinese Elites and British Colonials in Hong Kong* (Cambridge, MA: Harvard University Press, 2005), Chapter 1.
127. P. Hirsh, Statism, pluralism and social control, *British Journal of Criminology*, 40 (2): 279–295, 2000.
128. *Ibid.* See State Police Powers as a Social Resource Theory, pp. 195–198.
129. Chapter 1: Styles of Social Control, In: A. V. Horowitz (ed.), *The Logic of Social Control* (New York: Plenum Press, 1990), p. 22, Table 1; D. Black, *The Behavior of Law* (New York: Academic Press, 1976), p. 5.
130. Engaging Customary Justice Systems. Haki Legal Empowerment, White Paper. October 2011. http://www.lepnet.org/group/access-justice/file/haki-legal-empowerment-white-papers
131. K. W. Deutsch, Cracks in the monolith, In: C. J. Friedrich (ed.), *Totalitarianism* (Cambridge, MA: Harvard University Press, 1954), pp. 313–314.
132. G. Sharpe, 'Chapter Four: Dictatorship Have Weakness'. *From Dictatorship to Democracy*, 4th edition (Boston: Einstein Institute, 2010), pp. 25–28.
133. *Ibid.*, p. 26.
134. *Ibid.*, p. 31.
135. N. Machiavelli, The discourses on the first ten books of livy, In: *The Discourses of Niccolo Machiavelli* (London: Routledge and Kegan Paul, 1950), Vol. I, p. 254.
136. C. Munn, *Anglo-China: Chinese People and British Rule in Hong Kong, 1841–1880* (New York: Routledge, 16 December 2013), p. 323.
137. Y. Y. Chu, *Foreign Communities in Hong Kong, 1840s–1950s* (New York: Palgrave Macmillan, 2005).
138. *Ibid.*, pp. 3–4.

139. *Ibid.*, p. 4.
140. *Ibid.*, p. 5.
141. *Ibid.*, p. 6.
142. J. M. Carroll, *Edge of Empires: Chinese Elites and British Colonials in Hong Kong* (Cambridge, MA: Harvard University Press, 2005).
143. *Ibid.*, p. 60.
144. D. Killingray and D. Omissi (eds.), *Guardians of Empire: The Armed Forces of the Colonial Powers C. 1700–1964* (Manchester: Manchester University Press, 1999).
145. Principal–Agent Relationship. http://www.ruf.rice.edu/~schuler/principal-agent.html
146. J. M. Carrol, Chinese collaboration in the making of British Hong Kong, In: T. W. Ngo (ed.), *Hong Kong's History: State and Society under Colonial Rule by Tak* (New York: Psychology Press, 1999), pp. 13–30; W. S. Law, *Collaborative Colonial Power: The Making of the Hong Kong Chinese* (Hong Kong: Hong Kong University Press, 2009), Chapter One: 'Social Fabric of a Collaborative Colonialism', pp. 9–31.
147. C. Munn, *Anglo-China: Chinese People and British Rule in Hong Kong, 1841–1880* (Hong Kong: Hong Kong University Press, 2008).
148. Yen-p'ing Hao, A 'new class' in China's treaty ports: The rise of the comprador-merchants, *The Business History Review*, 44 (4): 446–459, 1970.
149. W. S. Law, *Collaborative Colonial Power: The Making of the Hong Kong Chinese* (Aberdeen: Hong Kong University Press, 2009).
150. A Police Detective Sergeant and the Mystery of His Wealth, ICAC, http://www.icac.org.hk/new_icac/eng/cases/detective/DETECTIVE%20SERGEANT_Eng.pdf
151. This author was told by CIDs boastfully, at dinner parties. See also R. Godson, *Menace to Society: Political-Criminal Collaboration around the World* (New Brunswick, New Jersey: Transaction Publishers, 2003), especially T. W. Lo, Chapter 8: Minimizing crime and corruption in Hong Kong, pp. 231–257, 241.
152. 'It is a myth that the son of Lui Lok worked for ICAC (呂樂個仔係做廉署只係虛構) 2010-5-21 09:42. http://www.pcchk.com/viewthread.php?tid = 28072&extra = &page = 1
153. J. Cheng. Police corruption control in Hong Kong and New York City: A dilemma of checks and balances in combating corruption, *BYU Journal of Public Law*, 23 (2): 185–220, 2009.
154. S. Tsang, *A Modern History of Hong Kong* (New York: I.B. Tauris, 15 August 2007), p. 52.
155. B. Bowling and J. Sheptycki, *Global Policing* (Sage, 16 December 2011), p. 21.
156. P. Lee, *Opium Culture: The Art and Ritual of the Chinese Tradition* (Rochester, Vermont: Inner Traditions/Bear & Co, 2006), p. 99.
157. N. Tosches, *The Last Opium Den* (New York, NY: Bloomsbury Publishing USA, 5 January 2002), p. 30 (Sun had a permit to use opium until he died in 21 April 1997).
158. Before 1900, Hong Kong was infested with Triads. This inhibited crime prevention, investigation and prosecution. In fact, many police officers were Triads. The use of Triads in aid of policing is real (p. 63). The use of Triad to control the lower class is nothing new, for example, Republican era (1897) (p. 64) or WWII Japan Occupation (p. 72). K. Bolton and C. Hutton (eds.), *Triad Societies: Triad Societies in Hong Kong* (London and New York: Taylor & Francis, 2000).

159. Policing in Hong Kong, colonial or indigenous, changes with time. With colonial police, there is much difference between early colonial (1841–1860s) versus middle (1950s) versus late (1970s–1990s) colonial periods. Royal Hong Kong Police Force taking on a less colonial look, *The Daily Gazette*, 17 September 1995.
160. *Ibid.*
161. *Ibid.*, p. 91.
162. 'In such a condition, there is no place for industry, because the fruit thereof is uncertain, and consequently, not culture of the earth, no navigation, nor the use of commodities that may be imported by sea, no commodious building, no instruments of moving and removing such things as require much force, no knowledge of the face of the earth, no account of time, no arts, no letters, no society, and which is worst of all, continual fear and danger of violent death, and the life of man, solitary, poor, nasty, brutish, and short'. Hobbes, *Leviathan* (1651), XIII.9.
163. *Ibid.*, p. 91.
164. J. S. E. Opolot, The resilience of the British colonial police legacies in East Africa, Southern Africa, and West Africa, *Police Studies*, 15 (2): 90–99, 1992. ('British tried to pursue a policy of pragmatism, caution and compromise for a number of reasons, e.g., lack of manpower and resource, to lack of understanding and facility. British then turn to use of local institutions and leadership or create new ones'.)
165. Abstract.
166. S. E. Hamilton, Private security and government: A Hong Kong perspective, 1841–1941, Ph.D. Dissertation, Hong Kong University (1999) (Abstract).
167. *Ibid.*
168. *Ibid.*, p. 60.
169. W. S. Law, *Collaborative Colonial Power: The Making of the Hong Kong Chinese* (Hong Kong: Hong Kong University Press, 2009), p. 4.
170. *Ibid.*, p. 200.
171. *Ibid.*, Chapter 4: Double identity of the colonial intelligentsia: Ho Kai, pp. 76. Hong Kong intelligentsia of the time, the likes of Wu Ting Fang and Ho Kai, was keenly aware of the weakness of China, and were thus less critical of colonial rule and method. This is quite apart from, and indeed is in spite of their vested interest. (Jia Yang Gui Zhi—'false or pretend foreign barbarian'.) For them, as public intellectuals and sage scholars in their preferred identity and call, they have adopted the maxim of the 'Yangwu Yundong' of borrowing from the West to strengthen the East.
172. S. C. Lau, Worshipping KuanTi: A study of subculture in Hong Kong police force and the triad. Hong Kong University Thesis, 2000.

Assessing Colonial Policing[1]

3

> British in Hong Kong often felt that they had to compromise their own cultural values and moral standards in order to deal with local circumstances and demands...strike a balance between morality and pragmatism.[2]
>
> **Cindy Yik-Yi Chu (2005)**

> This top-down view renders imperialism a phenomenon which is catalyzed by and viewed from the metropolis. In many instances, it is an emphasis that results in a one-way reading of empire, in which ideas and politics flow from the center to periphery. My reading is a more fluid one, which contends that changes in nations are as much the product of influences from empires as from internal and domestic pressure, dissent, and debate.[3]
>
> **Philippa Levine (2013)**

Introduction

This chapter is devoted to assessing colonial policing in Hong Kong.

The need for and the contribution of such a study is pressing and apparent. First, there are current few assessments of colonial policing in Hong Kong, in theory or practice. This study promises to do both, thereby filling an important literature gap. Second, so far, investigation into colonial policing has been mostly descriptive. Critical analysis and evidence-based assessment of colonial policing is in short supply. Third, whatever assessment there is, it is of a 'knee-jerk' kind, to the effect that colonial policing is *ipso facto* objectionable as an instrumentality of British imperialism.

The chapter is divided into five sections. Section I 'Framework of Analysis' discusses the importance of context and perspective in assessing policing work. It adopts conflict theory as a point of departure for analysis, but argues for a much more expansive and inclusive application. It suggests moving beyond passionate but narrow-minded political advocacy that is dressed up as critical analysis of the HKP's legitimacy, to a more dispassionate and multi-faceted social, moral and utility discussion on the HKP's performance. Section II 'A Cultural Model of Analysis' moves away from a more cynical conflict model to a more accommodating cultural process of sharing and understanding. Cultural analysis asks, what do the people on the street think and feel about colonial policing, rather than what the intellectual elites and political partisans do? Section III on 'Theoretical Assessment' argues that for the street people in Hong Kong, Western political legitimacy is not the only litmus test of acceptance for Hong Kong government and compliance with HKP. Hong Kong people, being pragmatic, can and do approve of HKP based on performance criteria, such as social utility tests, or for no reason at all, that is, they could not care less. Section IV is on 'Empirical Assessment'. In this section, the chapter discusses first-of-a-kind reaction to the HKP by Chinese rank-and-file officers through allegoric essays written in the official *Hong Kong Police Magazine*—Chinese edition (HKPM-CE) in the 1960s. The essays, individually and as a corpus, tell of how Chinese officers view HKP on a range of issues, from Western cultural imposition, to HKP discipline, to personal coping strategies. Section V is a 'Conclusion' calling for an increasingly in-depth and nuanced study of the impact of (Hong Kong, Chinese) culture on HKP and policing in Hong Kong, a subject matter that has escaped attention despite its obvious relevance and importance. The assumption is that colonial policing in Hong Kong is 'Policing with Hong Kong characteristics', the title of the Chapter 4 to follow and a take away from this chapter.

I: Framework of Analysis

In formulating an analytical framework, the following methodological questions are necessary: from whose perspective, in what context, with what assumption and for what purpose is the assessment being conducted? A perspective limits as much as it focusses our attention. Context informs as it distorts analysis. Assumptions (factual and value) anchor analysis but skew judgement. Purpose provides direction as it restricts investigations. Together, perspective, context, assumptions and purpose facilitate as it hinders our assessment process. The lesson here is not only whether perspective, context, assumption and purpose (generally 'perspective and context') be taken into account. Undoubtedly they should. The lesson is that we should be balanced and judicious in considering all these factors.

As to the necessity of perspective and importance of context, one is once again reminded by Waddington, a police officer who turned academic, that in assessing the role and performance of the police during public order policing, there is a need to take into account viewpoints of police (state) versus people (rioters), anchored within a larger social–political context (political marginality of rioters, legal impotency of police):

> The Police role is justified by the claim that they are not suppressing protest inconvenient to the government, but merely enforcing laws against violence

> and disorder. However, for politically marginal groups, expressing dissent through constitutional channels is a recipe for continued subordination.[4]

The message here is that there are always two (and more) sides to a story, competing for dominance, endlessly.

As to the significance and utility of context in helping to understand the nature of policing, Waddington has this to say:

> The main lesson is that the nature of policing, including the role that weapons play, cannot be divorced from the context in which policing takes place. Particularly influential are whether the civil population are considered 'citizens', the relationship of the police to the military, and the scale of resistance to state authority.[5]

This means that what the colonial police stood for—protector or oppressor, friend or foe—cannot be understood without first understanding the police and society relationship.

Waddington's invitation to look at public order policing (a defining colonial policing function) with perspective and in context is much welcomed. However, his mode of analysis does not go far enough. It should be expanded.

As a critique, Waddington's analysis appears unduly political and stereotypical. Still, taking Waddington's dualistic analysis of public order policing to heart, the perspective can be expanded to include all stakeholders' perspectives other than the police and rioters. For example, within the ranks of the police and rioters, there are infinitely more perspectives than political, and there are more roles people play than nemeses. Most certainly, there are more interests and values at stake.

In real life, when the HKP engages the public, especially in violent confrontations, there are more than two parties with vested interest. An untold number of people are affected, if only circumstantially and indirectly, incidentally and marginally and fleetingly and temporally.

Stakeholders to colonial policing (including participants and afflicted parties), depending on their role and involvement, disposition and perspective, values and interests and status and stature, are likely to hold a different opinion about colonial HKP performances. Furthermore, police–public encounters are infinitely more complex, dynamic and fluid to be painted with a broad brush and summarised in general terms.

People, especially those on the street, are rarely, if ever, disposed towards 'for this' or 'against that'. Drawn to grandstanding and given to exaggeration, the rallying cries of ideologues or utopians see no middle group. Likewise, police in the eyes of the public and at street level are more different and colourful than just black and white. This is especially the case when HKP officers and Hong Kong people come from diverse backgrounds, with unique experiences and dissimilar convictions. For example, to the Hong Kong people, HKP officers are as likely to behave as ruthless Police Tactical Unit (PTU) officers in suppressing civil disturbance (1956, 1967 riots) as they act as resourceful street officers or brave Emergency Unit (EU) officers tending to citizens' personal needs (999 calls) and the community's collective crisis (1962 Typhoon Wander). In essence, HKP officers, notwithstanding their colonial roots and steep PTU traditions, are men for all seasons, reasons, occasions and situations.

To most Hong Kong people on the street, the perception and reception of HKP is defined by the moment: a traffic ticket here and a 999 call there, or a young beat officer everywhere. It is always a routine and low-visibility encounter, but with huge personal consequences, for example, a tired officer acting out of role that leads to an otherwise resolvable domestic incident that turns sour. Such encounters do not allow for political considerations at the moment, and are still less fitted for ideological rendering in hindsight. Any generalisation of HKP and officers' performance is likely to be misinformed inadvertently or politicised intentionally.

PTU and EU officers are mentioned as examples to make a point. More often than not, these outfits are singled out by liberal elites and critical scholars for damnation for re-enacting their pre-1997 colonial para-militaristic role[6] and repressive colonial functions,[7] and in doing so, obstructing HKP reform and setting back Hong Kong's political development. In this regard, critical scholars and liberal elites might just as likely be overestimating HKP's para-military ethos of the past as they are underestimating the HKP's civil mentality of the present. In their headlong and heart-strong rush to demonstrate (demonise) that militaristic HKP is not compatible with democratic governance, they fail to understand what the HKP–PTU–EU is doing, and how they are acting in post-1997 Hong Kong.

To the liberals and critically inclined, both PTU and EU are cut out of the same cloth, before and after 1997. Both are organised in para-military ways, are controlled centrally, are isolated and insulated from the people, organisationally and culturally, have enhanced coercive capabilities, are mobile, first responders to emergencies and crisis and are symbols of force field extension, on a moment's notice. As a result, by association, the HKP is still considered as a para-military, repressive and coercive force, serving the colonial interests of the British master then (pre-1997) and acting as an instrumentality of the state (alternatively HKSAR or PRC) now (post-1997). In making such an observation, it rarely matters to the detractors (ideologue and political pundits) that the HKP can use its militaristic organisation and coercive skills in the service of people, in both colonial setting and community-policing era, for example, keeping violent criminals, the likes of 'Big Boss' at bay[8] or forestalling 'terrorists' on the edge.[9]

The Dr Jekyll and Mr Hyde persona of the HKP police officer defies easy and clear demarcation, and to some, definitive assessment. Furthermore, there is also a distinct possibility that the militaristic mentality and aggressive conduct of HKP officers might be a result of HKP culture or training, and more to do with the Hong Kong people's culture. Hong Kong–Chinese are given to rank consciousness, hierarchy and strict discipline in the pursuit of perfection. Thus, it is hardly co-incidental that Hong Kong people like uniform organisations of any kind—from Boy Scout, to Red Cross, to Civil Aid Service.

II: A Cultural Model of Analysis

Reflecting on Conflict Theory

The analytical model and assessment approach utilised by this work, while informed by conflict theory, is not confined by it.

As a political theory, Marx's conflict theory observes the existence of class conflicts and ideological dominance in a capitalistic world, manifested as class warfare ending in revolution[10]:

> The history of all hitherto existing society is the history of class struggles. Freeman and slave, patrician and plebeian, lord and serf, guild-master and journeyman, in a word, oppressor and oppressed, stood in constant opposition to one another, carried on an uninterrupted, now hidden, now open fight, a fight that each time ended, either in a revolutionary re-constitution of society at large, or in the common ruin of the contending classes.

The stage is set, according to the conflict theorists and post-1997 radical reformers: the HKP, the last and most iconic symbol of colonial power, needs to be destroyed, completely and resolutely, to free up cultural space for a new Hong Kong to grow and blossom.

Whatever the merit and contribution of conflict theory to political development in Hong Kong, it does not help with understanding the HKP's mission, vision, role and function, which requires an open-mind discourse and dispassionate analysis, far removed from the diatribes of the morally right or wrong, politically correct or incorrect and ideologically pure or corrupted.

In the face of death and destruction, pain and suffering, the options of HKP are to savage the moment. Nothing more. Nothing less.

Return of Human Agency

Cultural theory (of risk)[11] argues that people's disposition towards colonialism and colonial policing is contextual, constructed, relational and interactive in formation. In doing so, it rejects Marx's (pseudo) scientific worldview that the world is stratified along the pre-existing capitalistic versus proletarian lines. Instead, it advocates for the return of the human agency with autonomy, creativity, transcendence and indeterminacy of thought and action.

As a social agent, a human being is capable of configuring and transcending circumstances he finds himself in; in denying the past, transcending the present, forging the future and most importantly, in (re)defining of the self. Thus observed, there is not one super-ordinary, true or correct meaning to a social phenomenon, towards colonialism or otherwise. Colonialism and colonial policing are many things to many people; in time, place, situation and context. As Rayner[12] observed with defining risks:

> [A]n encompassing definition (of risk) is impossible. Instead he prefers a polythetic concept of risk which implies that there is a 'family' of definitions with many links but no single feature that is common to all of them. We shall see that this approach may lead to a community of deliberation rather than consensus over a single interpretation. It is this 'framed' flexibility that may provide cultural theory with its best opportunity for theoretical advance in the coming years.[13]

As such, the meaning of colonialism depends less on the 'objective' reality of what it is but rather on what people—all those who are in contact with or afflicted by colonialism—subjectively perceive, feel and understand of what colonialism is all about.

Before and after 1997, the impact and implications of colonisation and decolonisation, in process and outcome, hinge on the perception and reception, thinking and feelings of individuals caught up in the social milieu that is a new statehood—a lifestyle in the making.

Assessment Standards

After providing for a multi-faceted cultural frame of reference in deciphering colonialism, it is possible to set forth standards or criteria to evaluate colonial practices, such as policing. In most instances, frame determines standards and evidence. More simply, what is it that counts for successful reform in a decolonisation/democratisation project? Here again, the person, perspective and purpose matters.

Varieties of Perspectives: In the past, HKP expatriate officers would assess the HKP in more ideological terms, for example, has the HKP been efficient and effective in conducting colonial policing in Hong Kong? Chinese HKP frontline officers would assess colonial policing more pragmatically, that is, how colonial political mandate affects their delivery of social service, ethnic morality and street justice. With the public, they were only interested in how well the colonial police performed in maintaining order, stopping crime and doing justice. For example, suppressing triads, and keeping violent demonstrations at bay. Above everything else, the public asked 'how do the police, when called or encountered, meet with my expectations in solving my problem as a social resource'?[14] Viewed in this light, the acceptance of the HKP by the Hong Kong people was and is based on one simple and straightforward criterion, that is, in what way and to what extent the HKP, when mobilised or encountered, is meeting with my expectations, of all kinds. This is a performance, and not a process test.

III: Theoretical Assessment of the HKP: Colonial Policing and Political Legitimacy[15]

Introduction

People have been fascinated with the legitimacy of HKP, as a colonial force, since 1844.[16]

In the West, there are two ways of assessing the political legitimacy of a government and policing, that is, with process or by performance.[17] First, with legitimacy based on the process, one focusses on the process of HKP formation, for example, fair recruitment,[18] and performance, for example, being transparent ('process legitimacy' or PP1).[19] Second, with legitimacy based on performance, we focus on what and how well the HKP conducted policing ('performance legitimacy' or PP2).[20] In the traditional Chinese moral universe, this would be a debate between *minsheng* (民生—public welfare) versus *minzhu* (民主—democratic practices). Safe to assume, from a Chinese perspective, there is little necessary relationship between process and performance. For example, fairness of recruitment does not *ipso facto* bring about better police performance in result, for example, the integration of woman police constable (WPC) into HKP in the 1950s.

The conventional wisdom in Western democracies is that PP1 determines PP2, absolutely and completely.[21] There are two renditions to this thesis:

First, without PP1 in process (political accountability, e.g., check and balance) and/or practices (legal accountability, e.g., substantive or procedure due to process rights), PP2 (fight crime, maintain order, protect rights and provide service) is not possible, in theory. To the public this means that PP1 is a pre-requisite for PP2, a necessary but not a sufficient test for legitimacy. As applied, without PP1, the HKP as a colonial force could not earn the trust, respect and approval of the colonised people (PP1), however well it performed (PP2).

Second, without PP1 in process and practice, PP2 is not or less likely to be obtained, empirically. That is to say, undemocratic police (non-PP1) performs less well or not at all as compared to democratic policing, to the satisfaction of the public. In context, since the HKP was a colonial force and served the interests of the British government, it was not or less responsive to the needs and aspirations of the public. Thus, it was not a legitimate institution.

The Debate

Both of the above PP1 and PP2 assessment standards reference a political legitimacy test. Since the common (not elite) Chinese in Hong Kong do not participate in a Western moral universe, still less subscribe to the Eurocentric ideological imperative, Western political legitimacy tests have little relevance and at worst are inappropriate in assessing the merits or acceptance of colonial policing in Hong Kong. If that is the case, the continuous assault on the HKP during the post-1997 period, in particular, the accusations of the HKP perpetuating an illegitimate colonial policing mentality and practice are ill placed. It certainly is putting the cart before the horse.

In Hong Kong, the debate between an efficient–effective government and legitimacy of governance is a timeless one. In its heydays, the Hong Kong colonial government was known for its administrative efficiency and effectiveness, and not political accountability. Thus, even in the 1970s when the Hong Kong government tried to change from 'benevolent authoritarianism' to 'consensual government' and came up short, the government was still able to earn a high mark for keeping the public satisfied 'with an efficient administration which could meet the needs of the population'.[22]

Turning to post-1997 with the ascendance of political awareness, government efficiency is put to the test, and the people found it wanting. Professor Cheung observed: 'Since 1997, the Hong Kong SAR has been suffering from one legitimacy crisis after another. The infallibility of the administrative state, long held responsible for Hong Kong's success story in the final decades of British colonial rule, has by now been largely eroded'.[23]

The proposition advanced here is that the legitimacy of HKP should be judged by Hong Kong people in local context and with Chinese standards, and not based on imported Eurocentric standards, claimed to be universal. This is called cultural legitimacy test, which, broadly defined, includes the material, moral and social considerations, without accentuating one over another.

On top of the colonial-in-name versus non-colonial-in-fact discussion (Chapter 9: 'Hong Kong Police Reform in the 1950s'), this study aims to explore the issue of whether Western political legitimacy standards are compatible with Hong Kong–Chinese cultural (or social) acceptability test.

The thesis here is that HKP might be less politically legitimate (before 1997) and still be deemed culturally acceptable by a large number of 'sweat and labor' (劳苦大众) Hong Kong people. In essence, political legitimacy is not the only, nor is it the sole litmus test for public acceptance, especially for people on the street. People's acceptance of others in everyday life, including government institutions, hinges on a multitude of considerations, including economic, moral and social factors: ultimately, what people believe to matter, matters.

Conversely, the HKP might be able to be considered politically legitimate by the Western (or Westernised) Hong Kong elites but still fail the cultural legitimacy (social acceptance) test to a vast majority of Hong Kong people. This is the most likely scenario when Chinese cultural versus Western legitimacy litmus tests are mutually exclusive as Hobson's choice. The case in point, Hong Kong Democratic Party wanted 'Big Boss' to be tried in Hong Kong in the name of the rule of law and procedural justice (PJ), while most of the Hong Kong people were very happy for 'Big Boss' to be executed in China, expeditiously and summarily without a lengthy trial. Professor Vagg wrote:

> One can thus envisage a police force operating illegitimately in the narrow sense of the word but enjoying a popular legitimacy. In addition, it may be that certain illegitimate police activities are widely thought to be socially useful and to that extent legitimate.[24]

The point Vagg is trying to make, that is, narrow (elite) versus broad (popular) legitimacy or to some political legitimacy versus social utility, points to a larger debate that has thus far escaped well-deserved attention, that is, for what kind (educated vs. uneducated), segment (foreign vs. local) or number (majority vs. minority) of people and with which value frame (Western vs. Chinese vs. Westernised Chinese) should the HKP be assessed, historically and currently. Thus far, the discussion and debate over the approval of HKP performance has always been one sided, that is, dominated by Western values, without realising that Hong Kong–Chinese values and interests need to be taken into account, philosophically (what does legitimacy mean in policing of Hong Kong?) and empirically (how might Westernised policing affect the Chinese way of life?), in any legitimacy or acceptance test.

In a larger context and more fundamentally, debating legitimacy in Hong Kong is a debate over cultural hegemony and imperialism, conducted in the name of universal rights and natural law versus collective welfare and local custom.[25]

The legitimacy–acceptability of the HKP brings to the forefront the perennial and tenacious struggle for dominance between Eastern and

Western culture globally, which Huntington aptly labelled as 'clash of civilizations' and Fukuyama dismissively called it 'end of history' debate, presaging intermittent global war (Huntington) and permanent peace (Fukuyama):

> There is not only a profound difference between classical Eastern and Western thought at the metaphysical level (with many commonalities between Daoism and the postmodernist thought supported by Cohen), but much evidence to suggest also a correlation between East-West metaphysical divergences and other East-West differences in cognitive and behavioral patterns. These differences are not rooted in race or biology; indeed, they are not only socially constructed but highly malleable, with considerable variety within cultures, and exposure to a different culture eventually alters one's own mode of thinking and even one's understanding of selfhood. They also vary considerably within cultures. At the same time, these differences are reflected in many forms of East-West interpersonal interaction, from business negotiations, to dispute resolution mechanisms, to the development of international human rights standards, in ways in which those participating in such cross-cultural dialogue may not be fully or consciously aware.[26]

The differences between Huntington and Fukuyama are more than a matter of discourse on the divergence versus convergence on culture, susceptible to mediated, middle-ground settlement. At heart, it is a cultural identity and national character struggle, not given to the give-and-take compromise. So far, the HKP has been re-inventing itself (post-1997) with a Western playbook, unreflectively, without attending to the Chinese sense and sensitivity, mindfully. The same can be said of most of what HKP did. This is the pernicious effect of colonialism.

A Political Legitimacy Test Defined

What is a political legitimacy test? There is no simple answer to this question. One rendition of colonial policing is: 'Policing throughout the period was imposed on the people and never enjoyed their consent...colonial policing had little to do with serving the community and everything to do with upholding the authority of the colonial state'.[27]

This definition separates colonial policing from other kinds of policing, for example, civil and democratic policing, solely on the basis of political legitimacy, that is, imposition of authority versus the consent to rule. This definition makes two claims, one is philosophical (strong–absolute) (PP1) and the other empirical (soft–relative) (PP2).

The philosophical claim (PP1) asserts that undemocratic colonial police were *ipso facto* not entitled to rule and deserving of obedience because they violated personal autonomy and the social contract. In essence, lack of consent amounts to illegitimacy and denial of self-determination, and a vitiates authority. This is an ontological argument. The foundation of this claim is based on social contract, that is, an atomistic individualism claims.[28] It goes without saying that the philosophical foundation of Western polity is not only alien but obverses to Chinese thinking, such as individualism versus collectiveness.[29]

The empirical claim (PP2) postulates that colonial policing being unconsented to is *more likely to* work against public interests and thus *more likely* to be resented and rejected by the people. This is a teleological statement. The foundation of this claim is based on utility. This claim has two species. First, unconsented-to policing breeds discontent leading to disobedience. Second, unconsented policing leads to uninformed (bad) policing. Bad policing ill served the interests of the public. Both claims are based on one simple assumption—political legitimacy matters.[30] The question is, does political legitimacy matter, for what, to whom, in what way and under what circumstances?[31] It is on this front that the Western legitimacy test versus Chinese social acceptance test finds a common ground, based on utility auditing.

Why and What 'Legitimacy' Test for Colonial Policing?

There are three objections to judging the popular acceptability of 'colonial policing' on Eurocentric legitimacy grounds alone.

First, legitimacy is an open-ended search for a normative standard for acceptance of political authority. There are many normative legitimacy standards, other than European standards.

Second, political legitimacy is not the only test for the 'acceptance' of government. The Hong Kong people could reject colonial policing on political legitimacy grounds and still accept the HKP on other moral (street justice), social (order and security), utility (collective social welfare) or personal (harmonious relationship, reciprocity) grounds. In Professor Vagg's words:

> Formal legitimacy and popular legitimacy[32] are not necessarily related, and the latter is more likely to be influenced by popular views of police behavior than by the legitimating accounts and processes of legitimation… (118)[33]

In other words, even if the Hong Kong people accept a certain kind of legitimacy test, it might not be (predominately) political. Hong Kong people can adopt their own legitimacy benchmark in assessing the merit of colonial policing, for example, performance benchmarks, such as efficient and effective policing.

Finally, the act of respect for office and compliance with the police, especially in a cross-cultural context, might be beyond normative reasoning or above logical accounting. People might be 'motivated' or 'disposed' to do things for no 'good' reasons by following 'dao' or following what comes with nature;[34] or what amounts to 'go with the flow'. Or, in some instances for no reason at all: 'I have better things to do. This is not worth my time'.[35] In most instances, on most issues, for most of the time and with most of the people, government performance is accepted by the people just because they could not care less, that is, falling within a 'zone of indifference'.[36] That is also the reason why people do not vote. True autonomy knows no bound.

By saying so, there is of course no denying that reasoning as a way of making sense of the world and decision making is very much a cognitive process for rational people trained to think in a certain way. It is culturally bound, in style, process and content.[37] As such, 'reason' has been tied to logic ('logos'), allowing people to claim non-reason and reason, as illogical and unacceptable. But for most people, non-reasoning is the default mood—people couldn't care less, most of the time, with a 'live and lets live' attitude .[38] The mantra on the streets of Hong Kong is and was, 'Knowing you can change in life and living with those things you cannot'. It is the science of letting go, in colonial Hong Kong as of now.

Hong Kong People Can Define Legitimacy Differently

Conceptualising 'Legitimacy'

Gilley has defined legitimacy as follows: 'Legitimacy is an endorsement of the state by citizens at a moral or normative level. It is normative by conceptual definition. It is analytically distinct from that form of political support derived from personal views of goodness'.[39]

In the West, the most dominant school of thought on legitimacy is that of process or constitutive legitimacy. Consistent with Weber, Tyler defined legitimacy as a 'belief that legal authorities are entitled to be obeyed and that the individual ought to defer to their judgments'.[40] Conceptualising this way, 'legitimacy' is a concept that is content-neutral, and open-ended, but also context specific and culturally bound.

In theory and as applied to the United States, Tyler's legitimacy concept turns to procedural fairness rather than performance effectiveness, that is, legitimacy based on fair procedure (quality of decision-making process) rather than on legitimacy based on the pragmatic effect of police performance (in deterrence, performance and distributive justice).

Tyler's legitimacy definition is sufficiently vast to take on culturally relative, situationally contingent characteristics as a concept. It takes on values in context and embraces standard as applied. What is legitimate authority worthy of respect, as an inner personal compass, needs to be discovered in time, place and people.

Thus, the replication of Tyler's idea of legitimacy based on Western conception to colonial policing in Hong Kong without conceptualising legitimacy in a whole new cultural context might just be obeying Tyler in the breach.

How legitimacy looked and felt in colonised Hong Kong is the challenge that needs to be addressed. In what way did the concept of legitimacy differ in democratic policing in the United Kingdom versus colonial policing in Hong Kong is the issue. In essence, how does legitimacy of authority differ across cultures?

In studying legitimacy and obedience in imperial China, one finds that what makes for a legitimate authority worthy of respect and obedience depends on personal virtuosity of the ruler, social status of leaders and moral standing of people, and not PJ. For example, benevolence (virtuosity test) and parents (status test) deserve respect and obedience.

Traditional Chinese people are taught to defer to and comply with official personifying integrity, benevolence and fairness, that is, 'qing guan' (清官). A virtuous and benevolent official commands instant respect and lifelong obedience. The case in point is the folk hero and cultural icon gracing the annals of Chinese social control literature: 'Bao Gong' or Bao Zheng (包拯) (999–1062) of the Song dynasty was known for pursuing factual truth and substantive justice without fear or favour, and at all cost, with little concern for procedure nicety.

Furthermore, in contemporary Asian societies, in Hong Kong as in Taiwan, status and relationship matter. Legitimacy of authority hinges on a person's status (seniority, rank), the relationship between parties (intimacy, guanxi) and reciprocity (*bao*). For example, officials are supposed to behave like parents, earning trust and demanding respect by providing protection, care, support and guidance to his/her charges; within a mentor versus protégé reciprocal relationship of trust and loyalty for life.

The lesson here is that legitimacy is socially constructed and culturally bound. Finding of legitimacy and obedience in Hong Kong ought to start with a cultural audit, and not the transplanting of a sterile political–moral imperative.

Finally, in attributing legitimacy and commanding obedience, situation matters. After 9/11, President George W. Bush violated every rule in the constitution, procedural ('Terrorists Surveillance Program') and substantive ('enhanced interrogation'), but his extra-legal order was followed by the public, with enthusiasm and without fail.[41]

Measuring 'Fairness'

It is now common to measure Tyler's concept of 'legitimacy' as 'procedural justice'. This is measured by questions such as 'How often do the police … solve problems in a fair manner' or 'treat people with dignity, respect, equality and human rights'. This way of measuring 'procedural justice' raises a number of issues that need attending to lest we run into difficulties interpreting the findings. For example, what if HKP violates the rights of the criminal to save innocent life (i.e., the 'ticking bomb' issue in fighting the terrorism context)?

First, PJ is not a one-size-fits-all construct. PJ takes on many forms and consists of many dimensions that differentiate one kind of PJ from another. For example, the U.S. due process and the U.K. natural justice are both procedural in nature (procedural due process), that is, rule following, and substantive in kind (substantive due process), that is, fundamental fairness doctrine (an outcome test) trumps procedural rules (a process test). Thus conceptualised, procedural fairness is a product of the process and substance combined; each of them intersecting and inter-penetrating, with one implying the other. The two kinds of due process justice—procedure and substantive—are symbiotic twins, with each living the life of the others. That is to say, procedural process makes for a (more) right outcome (a kind of substantive justice) and substantive justice (including the right outcome) trumps procedure rule in exceptional cases, for example, to avoid unfair rule to an unjust outcome. PJ thus favours the accused at the expense of victims and society, whereas substantive justice favours the victim and society against the offender. Both are subject to claims of wrongful decisions: violations of the former case mean many guilty people would be free to do more harm (violating more rights) and in violation of the latter, a few innocent persons would be convicted (to vindicate more victims' rights and offer more protection).

Given this understanding of the procedural and substantive justice interface, there needs to be a renewed effort to ascertain what is measured in PJ—what does being treated in a 'fair manner' mean? One thing is for sure, whatever it means, it cannot mean 'procedural justice' as a rule-bound process alone, without being mindful of substantive justice considerations. If that should be the case, Tyler's theory fails and for a good reason: the Emperor has no clothes on. PJ is not the end-all-be-all of legitimacy.

Second, the legitimacy survey asks respondents whether the police have performed their duties in a 'fair manner' as indicators of procedural fairness. But what does 'fair manner' mean?—Does 'fair manner' policing mean full enforcement of all laws or only zero tolerance for some laws/cases? If so, how can 'fair manner' assessment get away from a distributive justice debate over selective enforcement at a policy level and street justice at an operational level? More significantly, how can zero-tolerance policing with an eye towards substantive merits (who and what deserves zero tolerance) be termed procedurally fair at a policy, strategic and operational level?

—Does 'fair manner' policing apply to enforcement of 'unfair law' in origin (H.L.A. Hart), content (segregation law) and impact (disparate impact law)? If not, how can it be said that 'fair manner' policing is a valid measure of police legitimacy, and is not being contaminated by other social, political and economic corruptive forces at work? 'Fair manner' enforcement of unfair law has the potential of making for more unfairness. This is the claim of Marx. Capitalistic rule is never fair because elections favour the rich and the powerful.[42]

Additionally, in measuring 'fair manner' policing, it is important to identify whether or not respondents are capable of disassociating police performance (activities-based legitimacy), from what the police do (role-based legitimacy), who they are (identity-based legitimacy) and how they perform policing (style-based legitimacy). Beyond that still, can respondents separate 'fair manner' policing from what other political authorities, for example, executive and legislative branches of government, do or do not do in instructing and confining the police? If there are no means to separate and validly identify 'fair manner' policing from 'fair' legislation and/or 'fair' police role, how can it be said that police legitimacy alone in procedural matter brings about law compliance? In essence, there is more to legal compliance than (narrow) procedural fairness.

Third, 'fair manner' policing, if it ever matters, has little to do with fairness in substance (fair rule) or process (fair application of rule), but everything to do with the attitude of officers and style of enforcement. How law is applied in a manner and style turns people on and off, to the extent that it affects the citizens view of the law, in fairness and utility. This is the lesson with alienating versus integrative shame (Braithway, Sherman). Tyler's 'procedural fairness' measures respect and politeness which has nothing to do with fairness of procedure, but everything to do with mannerism in the process of rule enforcement.

Hong Kong People Can Accept 'Colonial Policing' without Legitimacy

It is time to move away from judging colonial policing with a sterile, ethnocentric and elitist conception of 'legitimacy' in search of other dynamic, pluralistic, populist 'acceptance' or 'tolerant' yardsticks that allow the input of the colonised Chinese people. The suggestion here is that legitimacy test is but one of the many tests for qualifying acceptance (degree of embracement) or tolerance (degree of dissention) of political authority. Alternatively, government authority need not be legitimate and still is accepted. In real terms, to the Chinese people on the street of Hong Kong, and arguably with people everywhere, people's livelihood (民生) and well-being is much more important than people's (abstract) rights (民權), as a litmus test for government acceptance.

Survey data from China show that most people are extremely satisfied with the central government performance to the tune of 80% on an average (rising each year between 2003 and 2009) (Figure 3.1) (notwithstanding the fact that China is rejected by many as a non-democratic, one-party state).

In the early days of Hong Kong, merchants came to Hong Kong to make money and sojourners came to Hong Kong to escape persecution. They were not concerned with colonialism and its administration. In the post-World War II years, Chinese immigrants came to Hong Kong to find a fortune and build a new home. They were not interested in politics. After 1997, a whole new generation of Hong Kong people, born and bred, were and are more in tune with politics. But still, they are more fond of making money and desirous of stability, than pursuing political reform. Public opinion surveys are fairly clear and consistent—Hong Kong is more of a free, equal and rule-bound commercial centre, and is most certainly not a political town.[43] Hong Kong people know it; they vote with their feet to come and stay. This shows that process legitimacy is not the only game in town.

To corroborate this argument, an account is presented of what an imagined HKP PC with an American education[44] would say about the acceptability of 'colonial policing' which has failed the Western-liberal legitimacy test. Interviewer question: What do you think legitimacy means in the context of Hong Kong?

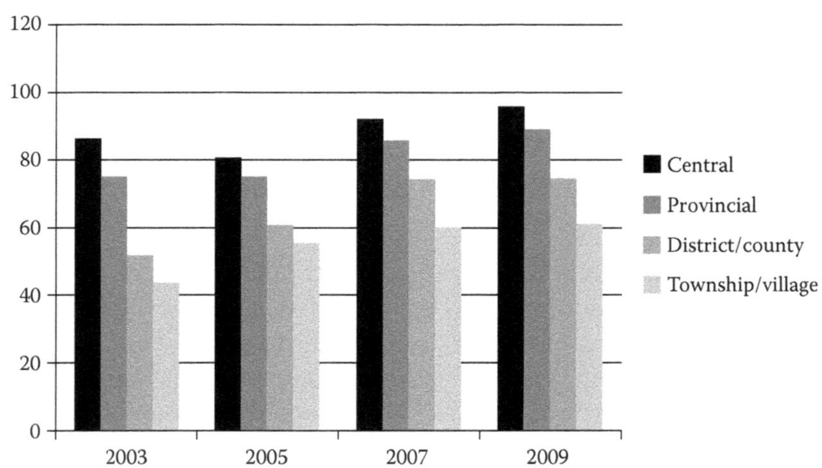

Figure 3.1 Percentage of citizens relatively satisfied or extremely satisfied with government. (Professor Saich Surveys: 2003–2009. Tony Saich is the professor and director of the Ash Center for Democratic Governance and Innovation at the Kennedy School of Government, Harvard University. This article also appeared in the most recent edition of East Asia Forum Quarterly, 'Governing China'.[43])

Respondent—HKP PC:

In the beginning, due to necessity, people all around the world naturally pursue survival, security, order and happiness as end goals. These are substantive goods or end goals of life.

With the advent of industrialisation, many people around the world set up a machine-like process to achieve, secure or maintain survival and happiness. These are called process goods, that is, instrumentalities for living and survival.

It is my understanding that people all around the world prefer substantive goods over process goods intuitively, that is, felt, not cognitively,[45] and instinctively, that is, not mediated by mental processing. For example, when in conflict, substantive goods will trump process goals, instinctively.[46]

The strongest claim for preferring substantive goods over the process is that the process does not necessarily guarantee substantive goods. It might have a contrary effect: witness India, the biggest democracy with a dismal record of economic equality. Process goods benefit others, and substantive goods benefit the self. No individual or country can survive for long if they allow process goods to come before substantive goods. The case in point is the U.S. 'exigency rule' allowing for doing away with Fourth Amendment warrant requirement for search and seizure when in pursuit of a dangerous suspect. Or, the suspension of the U.S. Constitutional check-and-balance regime in favour of the Presidential executive leadership in national emergencies, such as in fighting terror.

The Arab Spring is a case study of substance versus process goods. If Arab Spring stands for anything, it stands for the fact that rules are to be disobeyed, at times violently, if the rules stop people from getting what they want, in survival and happiness.

On occasion of the Arab Spring, President Obama had this to say about process goods—democracy:

On December 17, a young vendor named Mohammed Bouazizi was devastated when a police officer confiscated his cart. This was not unique. It is the same kind of humiliation that takes place every day in many parts of the world—the relentless tyranny of governments that deny their citizens dignity. Only this time, something different happened. After local officials refused to hear his complaint, this young man who had never been particularly active in politics went to the headquarters of the provincial government, doused himself in fuel, and lit himself on fire. Sometimes, in the course of history, the actions of ordinary citizens spark movements for change because they speak to a longing for freedom that has built up for years. In America, think of the defiance of those patriots in Boston who refused to pay taxes to a King, or the dignity of Rosa Parks as she sat courageously in her seat. So it was in Tunisia, as that vendor's act of desperation tapped into the frustration felt throughout the country. Hundreds of protesters took to the streets, then thousands. And in the face of batons and sometimes bullets, they refused to go home—day after day, week after week, until a dictator of more than two decades finally left power.[47]

> As a consummate politician, President Obama used Bouazizi to make his case for a new dawn in democratising the Middle East, as he should. But what he failed to grasp is the fact that the only reason why Bouazizi, the street vendor, killed himself, is not that he yearned for freedom and democracy, it is that he was not allowed to make a living. Simply put, Bouazizi's death had nothing to do with civil rights or dignity, but still less freedom and democratic governance. It has everything to do with survival. In Chinese, it is called 'min-sheng', which literally means 'people's livelihood'.
>
> If Bouazizi lived in a more prosperous place, such as Hong Kong, there is considerable doubt that Bouazizi would need to burn himself. This is evidenced through Hong Kong's history: the city experienced a civil disturbance (riots) that led to many deaths and injuries, and 1800 people were arrested in 1966 over a 25 cents (50%) fare increase in Star Ferry harbour crossing, when Hong Kong was very poor and laboured under an 'enlightened' British colonial rule. Forty-five years later, Hong Kong, with few democratic institutions and processes has one of the highest Kennedy ratios (rich vs. poor index) in the world. Police arrest street hawkers daily, but there is no suicide, and no riots. This is not a result of democratic institutions, competent policing nor fair judiciary. This is because street vendors can always find other economic opportunities to 'put a roof over the head'.
>
> In essence, people on the street and people in the corridor of powers do not see eye to eye on the cause of and cure for public grievances. Street people talk about survival; in Hong Kong, it is colloquially termed 'find eat'. Elites talked about ideals, colloquially known as 'blowing water'. From the 'street' people's perspective, concrete—particular—material needs for economic survival, and not abstract—general—philosophical ideas such as democracy and justice, are the cause for discontent and rioting.
>
> The elites always do things in the name of the people on the street, to satisfy their sense of being. Their worldviews, such as globalisation, are beyond the reach of the commons. Street people are doers. Elites are thinkers. Street people are rewarded externally and in small dosages; the elites are rewarded internally, and dream big. In terms of values, street people are materialistic and pragmatic, and elites are idealistic and principle minded. In terms of interests, street people want immediate gratification and elites tend to defer gratification.

The above discussion is meant to show that governance is not (or less) about process goods (democracy) favoured by the rich people/country, but it is always (or more) about substantive goods (survival at the low end and happiness at the high end) for the working people.[48]

What the HKP PC shows is that any decision-making starts from an identification of all the relevant factors for consideration and an evaluation of such factors. The outcome of such an identification and evaluation process is entirely dependent on the decision makers' perception, perspective, values and interests.[49] The range of one's perception and mix of one's values can either be given at birth (nature) or acquired through social conditioning (nurture), and press into service in situations (pragmatic considerations). They can also be affected by outside constraints, for example, blind sided by one's social/institutional role or restricted by legal/customary norms. People's perception and values are influenced by factors as diverse as personal background, individual experience, cultural expectations, institutional loyalty and organisational structure.

The ultimate issue being raised by the HKP PC is why the minority intellectual elite's right-based process goods are allowed to trump the majority street people's utility-denominated substantive goods.[50]

The answer is with Darwinism, that is, survival of the fittest. The people with the brain are able to outsmart and out talk the people from the street, much like the weak but intelligent humans are able to put the strong but mindless animals behind the bar. The same goes for civilian control of the military. The military has arms. The civilians have the smart. What if, one day, the military has both smart and arms, would they not rise to the occasion and disband the civilian government, as in Egypt disposing of President Morsi, an elected official?

Returning to HKP and colonial policing, to the liberals, it matters not whether HKP is giving the people of Hong Kong what they want the most—order and security and with it stability and prosperity. The liberal elites want something different. They want to have their vision of the world vindicated, all in the name of the people and democracy.

The elites know too well without 'convincing' the people that it is in their best interest to struggle for individual rights and not materials goods; the elites' personal privileges (free speech) and lifestyle (air-conditioned library work) cannot be sustained. The magicians call this 'prestige' and the crooks call this slight of hands. Both are meant to deceive others for personal gain. Freedom of speech allows elites to speak their mind but make possible pornography that ruins family values.

This is the true story behind the legitimacy debate of colonial policing in Hong Kong: elite Eurocentric liberalism versus popular Hong Kong pragmatism.

Cross-Cultural Law Enforcement

The legitimacy debate over colonial policing presupposes the sharing of the universal moral universe, thick or thin.[51] But what if there is a separate and distinct moral universe dividing the Chinese and British? Then, the topic is not easily penetrable. Such was the case in the 1840s, and was arguable for each generation of migrants, in the 1950s, 1960s and 1990s. In such cases, both parties would have had their own reasons for enforcing and complying with rules. To the extent that the coloniser and colonised did not share in a unifying and integrated moral universe, talks of one-size-fits-all legitimacy have little relevancy. As a result, the decision to accept colonial policing or comply with colonial police hinged any number of other more pragmatic considerations, from fear of punishment to avoidance of trouble, or more simply adaptation and escape.

A Chinese Legitimacy Test

Legitimacy in China, defined as the morality authority to govern,[52] was based on Mandate in Heaven (天命).[53] The Mandate existed if the nation is prosperous and happy; the Mandate was denied when the country was afflicted with calamities—storm, flood and famine. An Emperor who was worthy of a Mandate from Heaven and the support of the people was one who was virtuous in character (moral legitimacy) and benevolent in deeds (performance legitimacy).

Given this rudimentary understanding of the traditional Chinese notion of legitimacy, the study proceeds to how the HKP Chinese police officers assessed British colonial rule.

IV: Empirical Assessment: HKP Chinese Officers on HKP

Introduction

The investigation into HKP has suffered from the usual problems of lack of source materials and scholarly interests. As intimated (Chapter 1), not much has been written on HKP,[54] still less on its history, especially from below and on the street.[55] Given the storied history of Hong Kong as a colony and the importance of HKP on colonial administration (1941–1997), it is surprising that there are very few efforts to explicate the HKP's political role in colonial administration and document its impact on social development. Of those few that are available, they are hardly accurate and complete. They fail to tell the readers the whole story of what HKP means to the Hong Kong people.

Historiography is about discovering and interpretation of obscured and scattered facts, and not rendering of a final reality. It is story telling by victors (gun), elites (rich) and intellectuals (pen), with a given focus, framework and perspective to match. Thus far, the study of HKP history has been focussed on HKP as a law-and-order institution, for good (British) or ill (Chinese). The framework is one of colonialism, masked as benevolent paternalism. The perspective is from the top down (HK government) and afar (England). The voices of the people of Hong Kong on policing are rarely, if ever taken into account,[56] nor are there any HKP historical records built upon the testimonials[57] on the frontline (Chinese) officers. In the 1950s, the HKP tried to decolonise without democracy, and voices from below started to surface (Chapter 9).

An institutional history of HKP written from above (administration), afar (political) and aloof (economics) has no hope of capturing the 'Spirit of the Age' or Zeitgeist. Viewed in this way, HKP history is both subjective and constructed: a narrative about the ruler and ruled, corruption and progress, and not about what and how Hong Kong people perceived and received their policy.

In investigating into HKP history, there is a need to draw a clear distinction between studying HKP as a political instrumentality of control or suppression versus social institution to maintain order or provide service. For the first 100 years (1844 –1944), HKP knew the first, not the second.

Finally, it must be realised that investigating into the HKP institutionally is not the same as studying policing in Hong Kong, functionally. The same goes with political analysis and social observations. In Chinese society from antiquity, a Weberian type of police existed. A formal, bureaucratic, legal, professional and coercive organisation of social control, did not exist. Policing (social control, order maintenance) was conducted informally and pervasively, with education, surveillance and sanction, by the family and community, with the endorsement and support of the state. Thus observed, studying the HKP as a political–social control institution historically, while a valuable and interesting intellectual exercise, would still be relatively uninformative about how policing—social control of Hong Kong people—was conducted or realised. The study of how Hong Kong policing works requires the studying of much more than how the HKP works as an institution.

After the Second World War, policing of Hong Kong was conducted by the Hong Kong–Chinese under British command and control, that is, CID under the head of Detective Sergeants (Chapter 9). At the end of the day, HKP rank-and-file officers applied the law, executed the policy and provided services to the public, as they see fit. To understand colonial policing at the time, the typical HKP Chinese police officer's disposition, attitude and sentimentality towards policing in Hong Kong matters.

Research in this area is handicapped by lack of sources. Thankfully, it is now possible to ascertain the views of the HKP rank and file on a range of issues in HKPM-CE that first appeared in the 1960s. An offspring of HKPM in English, HKPM-CE was edited mostly by HKP-serving officers. Both were HKP official publications to improve internal communication and external public relationship. HKPM-CE was under the stewardship of a Chinese

Inspector (Lee Fok Cheung)[58] working with a number of rank-and-file officers. It is supported by HKP Welfare Department.

Beyond the news of the day, for example, 'Remembrance day ceremony'[59] and informational materials, for example, 'Christmas custom',[60] provided by the editorial staff, many of the original contributions came from HKP-serving officers, occasionally outsiders and civilian staff, in the form of essays, for example, 'Men and Animal',[61] short stories, for example, 'Snow'[62] or personal reflection, such as 'The first time'.[63]

As a data source, the HKPM-CE is unique. The editorials and contributions allow the public, for the first time, to get into the mind of the HKP officers, who speak on aspects of their job or reflect generally about policing, on their own terms, with their own words and about their own feelings.[64] This is how one Chinese police columnist first described, then compared and contrasted HKPM and HKM-CE, lending credibility and validity to the publications:[65]

> At first the magazine is in English. Gradually, half of the content was in English. The English version is more humorous. Authors write about interesting stories in their divisions. Each sub-division (環頭) is allowed to write whatever they like. If there are more 'stories' then the 'column' (地盤) becomes bigger. Stories are all about police canteen culture, sport activities and officers mess and transfers/promotion. As to Chinese version, it tilts towards more culture and explanation and personal development. It is more practical. This is especially helpful to the rank and file.... It can be said that HKPM reflects the effective side of HKP. Since it is written by the police themselves, the writing may not be as professional, but it is well liked, because it is about the 'family' and thus more intimate.[66]

A number of factors, however, affect the utility and limitation of this set of HKP officer-generated materials.

First, HKPM-CE is an official HKP publication. The materials appearing were subjected to editorial censorship, in theme, content, style and tone. While purportedly: 'The magazine is a free forum', it is also subject to explicit screening criteria: 'Ideas must be pure'.[67] In the context of time (the 1950s) and place (HKP), this means that what was being published must have passed an internal litmus test. Only those information and opinion found not to be contrary or offensive to HKP policy and stance were allowed to be published. In essence, it was a politically correct, rather than totally free, publication.

Second, the editors and contributors were mostly serving officers, with seniors in the lead. As such, beyond official editorial policy, there were rules that set the outer limits of what is deemed to be fit and proper. There was also a subtle effect of explicit self-censorship, due to professional considerations. The HKP, then more so than now, is a strict disciplinary force. Officers are supposed to do as they are told, and not speak their mind, freely. Speaking one's mind is not against policy, but it is against organisational culture.

Third, HKP officers shared in a 'kiss up' mentality. They say things to 'please' (affecting what is said) or at least 'not to offend' (affecting how it is said). This raises the issue of whether what was (and is currently) said is truthful, reliable and valid.

Fourth, all the above, to a large extent, are exacerbated by a Chinese culture, which is rank and status consciousness, and is habituated to please.

Fifth, unlike HKPM, many of the pieces published in HKPM-CE are under a pen name. That means that there is little personal accountability. It is arguably good that lower-rank officers can speak with anonymity and thus more freely. But anonymity also means that there is no check on reliability and validity.

Sixth, the HKPM-CE is a first attempt to offer an open forum for the rank and file to offer their opinion and express their views. The novel nature and experimental status of the publication undoubtedly affected the editors and contributors, for example, editors and contributors were likely to be more cautious and conservative before they learn about the acceptance of the magazine by the powers to be.

The above conditions and caveat notwithstanding, it is clear that HKPM-CE is a valuable resource to researchers, that is, an opportunity to listen to voices from below. As to the cultural significance of Chinese officers speaking up, it offered a forum for the Chinese to comment on their work, for example, what Confucius thought about free speech.

Confucianism and HKP Free Speech

There is no right to free speech in China. In fact, open criticism of the Emperor and Imperial officers were dangerous encounters, courting death.[68] However, there was a duty to speak the truth to power, in circumspective ways.

> Inherent in Confucianism was the obligation for any degree holder to speak out when the government deviated from Confucian ideals. Unlike the West, Confucianism did not legally guarantee a loyal opposition, but it justified one ideologically. To criticize government misdeeds was not the literati's rights, as in the West, but their responsibility.[69]

In imperial China and now with the HKP, speaking up was done indirectly, and tactfully, but unmistakably and forthrightly, in allegorical ways:[70]

> Indirect methods reduced risks of criticism. Hence there is a tradition of allegorical political criticism. This indirect method, called 'pointing at the mulberry to revile the ash'[71] or 'killing the rooster to warn money', obliquely chided the regime under the guise of discussing another historical period or

> an abstract philosophical concept.... Their messages were more abstract than concrete, more general than specific. They, too, shrouded their ideas in erudite discussions of ideology, philosophy, literature, and history.[72]

The HKPM-CE, examined closely, allows readers to ascertain the views and opinions of the Chinese HKP officers on colonial administration and HKP management. Indeed, if one were to read and interpret the contributions of the Chinese officers in HKPM-CE beyond the plain text and literal construction, one soon finds that many of the writings have indirect and allegoric meanings critical of, at the very least divergent from, HKP colonial policy and practices. Viewed in this light, HKPM-CE is one of the very first HKP official internal staff survey, speaking of several issues of importance and concerns to the officers.

Research Data Overview

For the current research project, a convenient sample of six (6) issues of HKPM-CE has been selected for analysis.[73] As an illustration, HKPM-CE, Vol. 8 (4) (Winter, 1964) contains 24 published pieces including two cartoons in 25 items. Eighteen longer pieces are reported here so that readers can have a feel of how the HKPM-EC is organised.

1. 'Police Training Camp' (PTC) by 3311 is an introduction to PTC, Fanling—its purpose, mission, organisation, training process and experience at PTC (pp. 2–3).
2. 'Unique discussion on forensic skeleton examination' from an information archive educates HKP officers as to what skeleton examination as a species of forensic science is all about; from how it is conducted and what one can tell by examining the skeleton (pp. 4–5).
3. 'Police and politeness' by Cpl. 255 admonishes HKP officers to be polite in interacting with citizens lest they get into trouble from causing physical fights to attracting citizens' complaints (p. 5).
4. 'Bird of a feather' by Huang Yang (黃羊—pen name) is a personal-interest story. It describes in great detail bird rearing as a hobby in Hong Kong (p. 6).
5. 'Business and creativity' by PC7237 is an opinion piece about deteriorating work ethics with young officers in the HKP (新兵). They are afraid of working hard and try to avoid responsibility at every turn. In the HKP, the bad habit of leaving to others what one can do for oneself is called 大腳傳中, a soccer jargon describing how one passes one's ball to another (p. 7).
6. 'Black Pool' is an information piece by an editorial office in the city of Black Pool, where the annual conference of the International Police Association was held (pp. 8–9).

7. 'Money and the law' by PC3795 observes the corrosive effect of money on law. The essay uses a case study from China, statistical data from the United States and teaching of *Mengzhi* (Mencius: 孟子) to make the point that people who are preoccupied with money are likely to ignore the law. On its face, the author is just making a general observation about the corrosive and corrupting effect of money on the rule of law and justice administration. But the essay could also be interpreted as saying that HKP is very corrupt. Everyone is trying to get more and more money while on the take. During the time, HKP coined the term—'police businessman' (差商) to describe police officers who were on the take with the rank and office for sale. In modern economic terms, each post has a market value with return on investment (ROI) calculation. The real message is about HKP corruption because the author closes the essay with the following: *Mengzhi* (孟子) visited with the Emperor of Liang (梁惠王). When the Emperor asked how *Mengzhi* could benefit his country, *Mengzhi* said that people should not be talking about benefits or utility but should only be talking about benevolence and righteousness. If everyone from top to down is consumed with personal utility, the nation is doomed. This is because everyone is coveting others' wealth and treasure, with no end to the utility quest (p. 10).
8. 'Personal Radio' by HKPM is a correspondent's description of the personal radio carried by the U.K. police (p. 11).
9. 'Goodbye' by PC 6536 is a short poem (p. 11).
10. 'Thousand face monster' is a martial art story by Cheng Kong (pp. 12–13).
11. 'The Royal Canadian Mounted Police' is an essay by Cheng Kong describing RCMP CID and Identification Bureaus (pp. 14–15).
12. 'Around New Territories' by PC3793 takes the readers once around NT (pp. 16–17).
13. 'A story about photographing' by Sung Chai Gong is a story the author enjoys on taking photo (p. 19).
14. 'Editorial' invites readers to share what the HKPM-CE has to offer (p. 20).
15. 'Life responsibility' by PC2032 tells about the author's attitude towards life and work. It makes clear that life is there for working hard and discharging duties; not for being lazy and avoiding responsibilities. The opinion piece serves as an admonition for young people (p. 21).
16. 'Selected Hong Kong Law' is from the information archive. It provides an overview of HK criminal law for police officers (pp. 22–23).

17. 'Road safety campaign' is an information piece on the purpose and conduct of road safety in the Colony (p. 24).
18. 'Preliminary discussion on finger printing' by PC4720 is about the author's work experience with the fingerprint unit (p. 25).

After reading this volume of HKPM-CE, one gets the impression that there was a substantial difference between Chinese versus British in the choice of subject matter, perspective, reasoning process and writing style, more generally cultural variations.

In terms of subject matter, there were four main groups of publications, that is, experiential (day at work with the fingerprint unit), to personal (bird earing, fishing), to reflective (life as a duty) and to creative (poetry).

In terms of perspective, they all looked at the world differently and in nuanced ways. Their accounting of the shared universe was all very individualistic, subjective and particularistic, leaving one with a distinctive feeling that deep inside, each of them lived a different world of their own. This challenges the basic assumption that Chinese in general, because of culture, and HKP officers in particular, as a result of personal background, professional, training, peer socialisation and work experience, thought, felt and acted in a uniform manner.

In terms of reasoning, there were a shared moral universe and similar conduct norms (*Mengzhi*, Confucianism). All of them tried to reconcile the utopian world they had aspired towards, since birth, with the reality they observed and confronted, at work, again in their own ways.

In terms of writing style, they ran from classical to popular. Overall, two things are gleaned from the writings:

First, the Chinese were as good a thinker and writer as the British. Thus, one is hard pressed to dismiss the Chinese as lesser of an equal as the British, in intelligence, education and culture. In fact, in some cases, the Chinese demonstrated that they were much better thinkers than the British, in classical or modern terms. For example, in 'Money and the law', PC3795 was able to draw upon Chinese authority and the U.S. data to support his thesis that at a theoretical, empirical and practical level, that Hong Kong society (by extension of the HKP as an organisation) being financially dominated and utility driven, was a morally flawed (by traditional Chinese measures), dysfunctional and unsustainable order.

Second, it is clear that the Chinese officers shared a different value system and adopt alternate world views, than the British.

On Wisdom of Colonial Rule

The essay 'Everyone has some small smartness' from the archive retells a fable from Africa, with a message: listen to other people who have some creative ideas and wisdom to share, as an adage in Africa says: 'A single mind cannot be trusted to offer up good solution'.

As told, the fable is a simple but instructive one. There is an old spider. It is so smart that he knows everything there is to know. It knows how to build bridges, construct dams and weave cloth. It embarks on a journey around the world and collects the wisdom of the world to put it in a jar, without sharing it with any other. It then wants to place the jar on top of the world's tallest tree. As it climbs up the tree, it puts the jar in front of itself. A young spider tells the older spider that it can climb faster with the jar on its back. The old spider thinks for a while and realises that it does not have all the ideas, since ideas can grow. It drops the jar on the ground, and it breaks open. People come from all over to recover the knowledge.

The fable might very well have been included as a simple story with a kernel of wisdom from Africa. But it could also be interpreted as a vehicle to send a message to the colonial government and the HKP boss in particular. In the HKP then, as a colonial force and military organisation, orders were given above, to be followed below. The rank-and-file officers were not supposed to have any ideas because the colonial master and those in military commands know best. However, because the colonial master and police bosses did not know the local culture and ground condition/situation, their decisions were likely to be wrong, and in many cases failed in reality.

The allegory here is that the British colonial government might have gone around the world and collected all the knowledge and wisdom in the world in those matters that matter—'building houses, constructing dams, weaving cloth'—but they should not be so quick to dismiss the ideas from the 'small spider' who has an experience of its own. The second message here seems to be while the British are busy collecting and storing old ideas, other people are generating more and more new ideas. In that case, of what good are ideas when they are not put to good use, for example, sharing with others and in the process generating more and better ideas?[74]

On HKP Discipline

In 'Baber's authority'[75] the author (Stupid and Dumb) related his experience in having to face up to the police station barber four times a month, as a matter of HKP discipline; short hair and crisp turn out. The essay could be construed as reflecting rank-and-file opinion about HKP discipline at the time, in a light hearted, but truthful way. The observations are not flattering ones: HKP discipline is strict, intimidating, agonising and above all else, discretionary (discriminatory) and undemocratic.

The pen name of the author, title of the essay and the introductory two headlines tell us clearly that this is an allegorical piece. The pen name of the author is 'stupid and dumb'. It is a way to show how 'stupid and dumb' the HKP was, in maintaining tight discipline and strict rule.[76] The title 'Barber's

Authority' in Chinese ('髮官的權威') sounds exactly the same as 'judge's authority' ('法官的權威'). The essay is thus more about dispensation of discipline by police officials (法官) than the cutting of hair by a barber (髮官). The thematic headline is also a dead giveaway of the purpose of the essay. It tells us that in front of 髮官 or 法官, that is, colonial police authority, everyone has to bow their heads, from high to low ranks: 'You have conquered the world with both of your fists, who dare to fight back? With a small iron in hand, shaving of heroes and notables, who dare not to bow heads'? The HKP, just like the barber, imposed discipline on all who come before it, foreign and domestic.

There were a number of allegorical statements made with going to the barber, as working for the HKP:

First, the barber, as with the head of HKP, is all powerful. Within the HKP (and the colonial government), there is a central authority that controls all the heads, absolutely and unforgivingly (see below). No one is excused, or spared, in the hands of the barber or colonial authority. In the hair saloon, it is the barber who has ultimate control. In the HKP, it was the Commissioner of Police:

> From my own perspective and feeling, barber is the most authoritative person in the world. He not only controls the head of laminates and dignitaries, but all the heads in the world. The 'head' (頭) means 'first' (首), respectable people in high place are called 'leaders' (首領) ('head that leads'). Head is the most important part of the body. You can see under the hands of the barber, heads of leaders and VIP up above and common people and lackeys down below, are all controlled by the barber.

Second, colonial authority and HKP discipline were exercised at real (on whatever you do) and symbolic levels: 'Each police officer, must be subjected to barber authority four times a month'. The short hair-cut requirement reminded the HKP officer that he/she was in a disciplinary force. Failure of appearance was deemed as failure of the pledge of loyalty. The length of the hair is made a conclusive measure of one's commitment and competence.

Third, working for the HKP, as with visiting the barber, was an agonising and excruciating experience; like sitting on an electric chair. The only difference was that visiting the barber is a short-term engagement with an end, and working for the HKP was a 24/7, lifelong engagement.

> How unpleasant it is to have the hair cut (alternatively working for HKP) … first, one needs to report to the barber (HKP authority). Once sit in the honorable chair (working with HKP), people feel like they are sitting in an electric chair. While sitting on an electric chair would be over in a moment, sitting in a barber's chair is torturous. This barber chair promises at least one hour of

> enjoyment. Short time pain is better than long term. How about going to barber? There is at least three times a month? Who ask you to join the police. You have to cut your hair more.

Simply put, once you join the HKP, you can expect the discipline to last regularly and intermittently for the rest of the career, and for some, life.

The message here is that HKP owns and controls every rank-and-file officer 24/7, completely and totally, and for life. There is no escape. When you are not with your barber, you still have to think about the next barber visit. The failure of discipline is death by electrocution and with torture along the way.

Fourth, when you visit the barbershop (work for the HKP), you will be covered with a white cloth (HPK green uniform) with a white collar around your neck (HKP uniform with a blue tunic collar in winter and a starchy shirt collar in winter):

> From the mirror, one looks 100% like a clown, like a baby screaming for milk, with both hand under the white sheet (in HKP uniform or otherwise private life), and cannot move (your professional, personal self is under discipline). Even if you are the most troublesome person. You will be sitting there in a civilized and polite way. (You would conform, at least pretend to put up and put out) Peacefully and properly seating, awaiting the disposition of the barber. (You just sit back and relax, and take what is coming. The HKP owns your life.)

Once a person joined the HKP, he has to be well behaved, even for the worse kind of people. (In the 1950s, the HKP recruited a lot of people with unsavory background because the standards were low, or non-existent. Many of these came across the border. More than a few joined because they were not fit for jobs outside. Some of them were gangsters. Finally, decent people do not join the HKP.)

Sixth, once a person is on the barber chair, he is completely at the disposal of the barber, at will and with wimp. The hairs, dropped on your neck, are causing pain and itch. What can you do? Tolerate:

> Short hair falls on your neck … you cannot scratch, even though you cannot tolerate. Then the barber demonstrates his authority, and move your head left and right according to the need of his work…entirely according to his wish and wimp. Tiredness is yours, tolerance and self control is dependent on training and discipline…

The above passage is perhaps the best description of what it was like to be working for the HKP as a PC. One was completely at the disposal of the British officials, with intolerable and enduring pain of the body, itch of the heart and bruise of the soul, with no way out other than to tolerate and endure.

The conclusion tells all:

> The whole face becomes a battle ground for him. All you can do is to close your eyes and pray. But he does not allow you to take his work for granted. He specifically shaved around the corner of your eyelids 'unnecessarily', in order to make you shiver in cold sweat. But whatever the pain, you can only object and cannot complain.
>
> Notwithstanding advances in political system, going to barber shop it is traditionally dictatorial. Once you sit on the barber chair, there is no democracy, the barber is king.

In the 1960s, Hong Kong government might have been democratising but the HKP, steeped in tradition and stern in discipline, did not follow suit.

On Rule of Law

In 'Mass psychology and the law', [77] the author (with a pen name)[78] of 'Horse not going forward' (馬不前)[79] commented on the purpose, function and operation of the law. The focus is on how to make the 'mass' (群眾) follow (voluntarily) or conform (coercively) with the law, psychologically.

The thesis of the essay is that in order for the law to work, it must serve the needs of the Hong Kong people and be voluntarily obeyed. The wholesale cross-cultural transportation and imposition of British law on Hong Kong is not well conceived and ill advised. It is a doomed project, from the beginning to the end.

The essay starts with a preface statement from *Guanzi*:[80] 'If everyone from high to low officials, from the respectful to the base people, obeys the law, then we would have achieved perfect governance'. In a straightforward way, the statement just means that law should operate in such a way that everyone would see fit to obey. However, read allegorically, it might be suggesting that the current legal system is a huge failure in that perfect governance is not achieved, since it is not applicable to the high officials and is not effective against the privileged. Interpreted this way, it was a direct indictment against the Hong Kong government and British governance, with the HKP as a prime example. It would be doubly insulting since it was one of the avowed purposes and consistent justifications of colonisation to bring the rule of law to Hong Kong in an effort to tame the Chinese and develop trade with China. That is to say, as suggested by this allegory, the idea (law as an instrumentality of the government) and ideal (law as an ideology of governance) promoted by colonialism failed in Hong Kong, at both theoretical (ideological and not scientific) and operational (coercive and not psychological) levels.

The author starts the essay with the premise that 'law is not self executing', citing *Mengzhi*: '徒法不能自行'.[81] For the law to be truly effective, it must be designed in such a way as to optimise its 'stimulating' impact on people.

The author asked rhetorically: 'What is law? From a psychological point of view, law is a stimulus (刺激物) to stop or induce average people to engage in certain conduct'. Thus, it is imperative to study the psychology of the mass towards law, in cognition, emotion and disposition.

The author further opined that if one were to study the mass psychology of law, an effective legal regime (specific legal provisions) must fulfill three constitutive and operational conditions: (1) Having a stimulating—deterring or inducing—impact on average people; (2) the stimulating impact must be proportionate with conduct under control and (3) stimulating impact must not be counter-productive to the purpose of law.[82]

From a reading of the essay, the constitutive–operational conditions of law are very clear: (1) law has a deterring or inducing impact, and (2) law as a stimulus has a proportionate impact on conduct. If so, the question is why colonial rule-policing failed in Hong Kong.

The author's central thesis is that British colonial rule failed its essential purpose of re-enacting British rule of law in Hong Kong because, as a transported and imposed foreign control system, it failed to first understand and then meet Hong Kong–Chinese people's cultural orientation and psychological needs.[83] This is what the author said:

> Why is there a need for the third condition (adjusting to local conditions)? It is because if the law is not build upon mass psychology, then the stimulating effect of law on the people might be against the purpose of the legal stimulus, that is to say the punishment might be running counter to the purpose of the law.... To conclude, we cannot use laws from a psychologically different ethnic group to any other ethnic group.[84] A certain system of law cannot be made to apply to another ethnic group with different psychological make up. If the law is not fitting with the psychology of the ethnicity of the mass, this would inevitably and invariably lead to violating of law by all people. If few people violate the law, it is treated as criminal, if a majority of people violate the law, this is treated as a right. Violating the law becomes a necessity of living.[85]

The essays tell us how HKP Chinese rank and file officers thought about British law and HKP discipline:

First, law is not self-executing.

Second, law cannot be imposed coercively. It must be followed voluntarily and willingly, which is an inducement proposition.

Third, in order for law to work, it must be enforced or obeyed across the board, from senior British to junior PC. The law must be applicable to all and enforced without fear or favour.

Fourth, in order to make people follow the law, the law must cater to Hong Kong people's needs, culture and conditions.

Fifth, a legal regime cannot be transported from the United Kingdom to Hong Kong without being customised to fit local conditions and culture, and expect to work.

The pen name of the author was a dead giveaway of the intent and purpose of the piece. The name '馬不前' or 'a horse that does not move forward' tells us that the law could not work until it reflected the local culture, protected local interests and was applied evenhandedly. Alien colonial law imposed was no law—ineffective, dysfunctional—at all.

On Accommodating Alien Culture

In the short essay 'The meaning of Christmas', PC Li seeks an answer to the question: 'What is the real meaning of Christmas (in Hong Kong)'? Is it for the rest and relaxation of overworked HKP officers? Is it for wining and dining with friends and relatives? Is it for gifts giving? (Of course, these questions are posed for non-believers, including the author). The real question for the author was why HKP and the HK public have to celebrate a religious holiday and pay tribute to a God from another culture?

The answer given by the author, a non-believer, is that Jesus has proven by his act to be worthy of respect. Jesus died on the cross to save the world. He showed us that love conquers hate and mends conflicts. He also showed us that with self-sacrifice and unrelenting effort that we can bring peace and love back to the world.

> Between people, only love brings people together forever, creating a glorious history. Hate and conflict can never solve any problem. But I believe that Jesus is a heroic figure deserving of our respect. We have endured a lot of pain and suffering, and all kinds of misunderstanding requiring us to compromise our integrity and dignity to beg for survival (委曲求全).[86] But we should understand that the suffering endured by Jesus Christ was thousands of times more than ours. He loved all people, including the worse ones, the selfish ones. He loved them all universally. To love people, he is willing to sacrifice and suffer.[87]

The essay would not be worth attention and further examination for allegory, without the above gratuitous statement on: 'We have endured a lot of pain and suffering, and all kinds of misunderstanding requiring us to compromise our conscience, integrity and dignity to beg for survival (委曲求全)'. What did the HKP officers endure, that required surrendering of their dignity for survival? The author must have been alluding to the HKP officers' humiliating and agonising experience in having to work for a colonial government, as a second-rate citizen in a wholly-controlled place and organisation.

By joining HKP ranks, the author and his peers suffered from two kinds of indignities. First, the author and others had given up their nation for personal glory (賣國求榮)[88] instead of sacrificing their lives for righteousness (舍身取義).[89] Second, the author and others had now sided with the powerful to exploit the weak, that is, helping the British colonisers to control their own. Worse, the British could not effectively rule Hong Kong without the help of the Chinese officers.

The humiliation and suffering of Hong Kong people as colonised people and the Chinese HKP officers as colonising agents were brought on by the British grand colonial scheme. The British colonising acts need to be forgiven with God's love before any healing begins. (Here, the author is talking about God forgiving the British for coming from thousands of miles to make life difficult for the Hong Kong people generally and HKP officers specifically.)

By writing the essay, the author is also pleading for understanding and forgiveness from the HK people. HKP are also victims of historical circumstances. Hopefully, with love and compassion, their personal relationship with the HK people can move beyond the past to build a better future.

The last allegory is a profound one. According to the author, while Hong Kong people might not have believed in Jesus as a religious figure, what Jesus did was for real, and deserves respect. In essence, Hong Kong could still learn to love and follow Jesus's example without believing in him as a spiritual figure. By the same logic, Hong Kong people should judge British rule not by its colonial title, but by what the British performed in real terms. Should that be done, like in the case of Jesus, Hong Kong people would find that British rule is more civil than colonial.

Seeking Truth: Integrating Culture, Science and Experience

In an essay 'Discussion on autumn noises',[90] the author (PC9676 from N.T. Division—Da Mai Du Police Station) debated the epistemology of 'autumn noises' (秋聲). Does it come from cultural icons' imagination (speculation), people's experience or scientific evidence?

The essay begins with the author relating different Chinese poets' and philosophers' ('yin yang') understanding of where 'autumn sound' comes from: To the poets, it comes from birds. To *Ou Yangzhi,* it derives from the yin-yang and five elements. The author then offers up his own foot patrol experience at night in the wilderness. He experienced exactly what the poets talked about. Then, he discussed the contribution of science in helping to understand the natural principle of things and cause-and-effect relationships between matters. He closes with the following:

> With every phenomenon in the society, generally speaking, they all have causal relationship, if we observe these university rule, we can get proper understanding and draw logical conclusion…Of course, things are never that simple. From academic principle to practical use, there must be

> practical application, before one can grasp what is real. What Auyang wrote about origin and reason for 'autumn sound' is based on yin and yang cosmos relationship and five elements which I was briefly exposed to in passing. My true exposure to autumn sound: came after that (by experience and with science.)[91]

This essay tells us a lot about HKP Chinese officers at the lowest rank, that is, how PCs thought, discovered knowledge and sought truth.

Chinese PCs, given the opportunity, could think deeply, articulate clearly and engage others provocatively.[92] PC5447 might have been a minority, but HKP at the lowest rank was populated by deep thinkers and well-read Chinese philosophers, who were not properly recognised by the British, for the lack of (British) recognised credentials. For human resource management and research, it raises the issue of how to properly ascertain the qualification and capacity of police officers under the British rule.

The way PC5447 posed the question—how do we learn about 'autumn sound'?—is very creative and original. It shows that PCs were not only followers of orders, but were capable of asking independent questions, of the most complicated and discerning kind. To insist that PCs only obeyed, but not questioned, orders, the HKP might have been a valuable human capacity and resource.

The way PC5447 goes about analysing the puzzle shows that he is cross-disciplined and integrative in thinking: philosophy provides for untested ideas, scientific research provides evidence in support of theory building and clinical street experience perfects the scientific discovery. Speculation, observation and experience provide for a comprehensive approach to the understanding of a phenomenon, here 'autumn sound'.

Allegorically, PC5447 might be trying to show that colonial policing theory and policy on the book must take into account reality and conditions on the street of Hong Kong, and are supported by scientific research based on natural principles of things. More importantly, words of wisdom by philosophers or the imagination of poets while not substantiated by scientific evidence still merit attention if they comport with work experience on the job.

In essence, at the end of the day, implicit knowledge (experience) should be able to add to what we know through cultural assimilation as wisdom and scientific discovery. The other message might just be discovery of the truth—or to PC5447—what works on the job requires an integration of culture, science and application.[93]

On Dealing with Adversities (under British Rule)

'Turbulence vortex of life' by WPC Kwok Siu Fung (郭小鳳) deals with a recurring subject in HKPS-CE, that is, how to negotiate the recurring and unending adversities of life, within and without the HKP. It discusses, in personal terms and intimate ways, how a young WPC feels and acts in the face of life course challenges within the HKP, community and society. The WPC explains the impact and her response to distresses in life, though not the cause. We can only guess. The WPC was troubled because she had to deal with some of the wise aspects of policing: ridicule by the public as a colonial 'running dogs'; rejection by family/friends for joining an all less-than-honourable job; harassment from male officers and belittling from the public as a WPC, dismissive treatment by the Chinese superior and discrimination from British superiors. The problem as described as WPC Kwok:

> Ever since I was hit by a life course event due to unavoidable circumstances, I have to face up to meaningless and laughable situations. I begin to understand what fate has installed for me. I now understand what sadness means. Living in an ugly world and cruel reality makes me realize, that those senseless ridicules made me feel that I am being abandoned by the society. I have now a person without self-confidence. I have no desire, with life as tasteless (meaningless). Life and living is old, too old. I know that a weak person cannot beat the strong in being achieved. What good are consoling words (from others)? Swirling in my heart is a vortex of turbulence and sorrow. I go round and round in the vortex, finding no way out. Should I be swimming upstream against the current or drift down stream with the flow? But I do neither. I just go round and round in the vortex, until my brain swirls and heart sinks. But I am still living, and force to live those brand and meaningless life, one day at a time.

On first look, the essay suggests a troubled mind, needing help. The solution the WPC offers for her mental anguish is to put things in perspective, realising what she has to encounter in life is the same for everyone, since antiquity: 'The world and human have billions years of history. Our life is just a small part of this larger whole'.

> If we realize our plight is not unique, but a common cause for sorrow and despair of the whole humankind, then we should not blame ourselves or anyone for what is happening. Instead we should find meaning of life in our living space…we should not be hiding in a corner in a sullen manner blaming self and others…We should stand up and defeat the vortex of turbulence, clarify our life goal, and dash forward with all our might.

While written up as an individual account of personal problem solving—what to do when one is down and out, having turned unto a laughing stock of others—Kwok's piece is anchored within a larger social context and cultural milieu. To that extent, it is revealing of common sentiments, for example, frustration, and universal tendencies, for example, avoidance, within the Chinese diaspora and HKP ranks. Extrapolating from the observations made and applying lessons learned to a colonial policing context, one can begin to understand how a WPC at the time dealt with self-doubts and public ridicule working as an Imperial police officer and colonial 'running dog' in a Chinese society. The choices were few, consequences stark and the prospects dim. The take away lesson is a simple one, and very Chinese: look inside, not outside for one's problems—be confident, be resilient, be resourceful and be hopeful. A resilient person has to be able to create meaning to and purpose of life, and act upon it in a resolute way. Fight and do not relent in the face of adversities is a life challenge for everyone.

The WPC story of the self is a poignant account of how Chinese, in general, deal with life problems (here in facing up to colonialism). Unlike the Western culture, Chinese people are taught to accept, to fit in, not change or challenge the reality; at least not radically. The personal challenge for the Chinese officer was in how to make an intolerable situation marginally better when it cannot be optimally changed. This requires tolerance and sufferance in equal measures.

When Occidentals think of rebellion, the Orientals talk about acceptance. For the Chinese, adopting a non-confrontation to colonial rule was to rationalise things out like the WPC, that is, being strong and resilient, creating meaning of survival and for survival, one day at a time.

The WPC's attitude finds resonance with another author (Lo Su's) in a poem titled 'Be Strong'.[94] The context there is that Lo was responding to a police friend's essay on 'Imaginative song in a traffic kiosk' which was too pessimistic in content: 'People have sadness and happiness, togetherness and separation. The sky above has full as well as half moon. Why do you have to be down and out all the time, with sullen face'.[95] He pointed to successful people from the past (Han Shun) and present (Sun Yat Shan). Europe (Beethoven) and America (Edison) to suggest all successful people have confronted insurmountable difficulties, Beethoven was blind and Edison was dumb. Why not take lessons from them in living adversities and creating the meaning of life with your own hand: 'Difficulties and despair is not rope that ties people…Why not throw away worries, and take out the knife, to cut the mountain in half…Life is struggle. Loving with every "moment", "minute", "hours" has its own high purpose'.[96]

Concluding Thoughts

There is a substantial difference between Chinese versus Western culture (Table 3.1). In a close study of HKPM, one finds that the Chinese look inside for satisfaction. The British look outside for excitement. The Chinese are engaged in more soul searching, for example, writing poetry, while the British take part in more sensation seeking, for example, going around the world. The Chinese wanted to find internal order in an inherently disorderly world, for example, adapting to British values without compromising the Chinese core. The British tried to reshape order in making new ones, for example, imposing British values on a Chinese population, at least on the surface.

Table 3.1 Some General Differences between Chinese and Western (American) Cultures[99]

	Chinese	Americans
Conception of the self	*Collectivist:* Higher value placed on group cooperation and individual modesty.	*Individualist*: Higher value placed on self-reliance. Self-promotion is more accepted. High value placed on '*freedom*' from externally imposed constraints.
Social relationships	*Formal, hierarchical:* People are most comfortable in the presence of a hierarchy in which they know their position and the customs/rules for behaviour in the situation.	*Informal, egalitarian*: People are most comfortable with their social equals; importance of social rankings is minimised.
Friendship	*Small number of close, lifelong friends* who feel deeply obligated to give each other whatever help might seem required.	*Large collection of 'friends' and acquaintances which changes* over time and involves only limited mutual obligations.
Obligation	*Relationships* with other people involve *reciprocal obligations.*	*People avoid interdependent relationships* and situations that might entail long-term obligations.
Task versus relationship orientation	*Relationship oriented:* Maintaining a harmonious relationship has priority over accomplishing tasks.	*Task oriented:* Relationships are less important than getting the work done.
Harmony versus 'Truth'	*Avoid direct confrontation,* open criticism and controversial topics. Concern maintaining harmony and with '*face*'.	*Willing to confront directly,* criticise, discuss controversial topics and press personal opinions about what they consider the truth. Little concern with '*face*'.
Role of laws, rules and regulations	*More faith in personal relationships* than in written rules and procedures for structuring interactions.	*Written rules presumably apply* to everyone and are assumed to produce fair, reasonable procedures and decisions.
Time consciousness	*Relatively more attention to the past* and to the longer-term future.	*Less interested in the past*; an eye on the near-term future.
Ascribed versus achieved status	*Traditionally, a person's status in the society was based importantly on inherited characteristics* such as age, gender and family. This is changing.	*People's status is based mainly on their own achievements*, including education obtained and level of success realised in their line of work.

How the Chinese HKP officers dealt with cultural imposition at a personal level is an issue. The above brief venture into HKPM-CE affords a rare opportunity to investigate the sentiment, disposition and attitude of the HKP rank-and-file officers towards work and life, and more importantly, how to deal with issues and problems on and off the job.

From the evidence, Chinese officers harboured a lot of resentment and pent-up frustration against British colonial rule, from how colonial rule was administrated to how HKP discipline was fashioned. As reluctant colonial citizens and dutiful HKP officers, they found ways of speaking back to the colonial master and HKP superiors with allegorical stories and essays, while at the end of the day obeying and complying with British rule.

Finally, what was the effect of placing one set of values—culture—order (British) over another set of values—culture—order (Chinese)?[97] How did the British (coloniser) and Chinese (colonised) co-exist under one roof—organisationally (formally), professionally (interactively), socially (informally) and personally (intimately)? Specifically, how did the Chinese officers adjust to the British aspiration, feeling and thinking, ways and means and vice versa?

Here, Robert Merton might be of help with his anomie—strain theory. According to Robert Merton, criminality and deviance in America resulted from a disjuncture between cultural goals—what it means to be successful, and structural means—how best to go about to achieve success.[98] By this, he means when society tells us to chase after the American Dream to be successful, for example, get rich and money talk, but does not provide people with the legitimate structural means to do so, for example, having no education or given no opportunity, we now have an adjustment problem, that is, an anomie condition. People do not know what to do: should they work hard, still hoping to be successful? Or fight back, by breaking rules to attain goals? Merton identifies five modes of adaptation: conformity, innovation, retreatism, ritualism and rebellion. Each adaptation mode corresponds to a person's understanding of his own situation. For example, a law-abiding person who has a deep faith in the American Dream would work harder to be successful, against all odds. These are the 'conformist'. However, there are people who yearn for success, but are jilted by the system, which offers an unequal opportunity or no means to be successful. This group of people will do whatever it takes to get rich without necessarily following rules. These are the 'innovators', some ending up as deviants (Table 3.3).

One way for the HKP to live the British dream with few opportunities (lack of promotion opportunities) and little skills (language) was for them to adjust, as Merton suggested. A Chinese police officer could act as a conformist in conduct but still remains dissentered at heart. In Chinese terms, being one heart (with) two utilities (一心二用). This 一心二用 strategy allowed the Chinese to reconcile the two distinctive different systems of values and culture. As a strategy, 一心二用 was realised in two ways.

Table 3.2 Merton Modes of Adaption when Strained

Typology of Modes of Individual Adaptation			
Modes of Adaptation	Culturally Defined Goals (Values)	Structurally Defined Means	Explanation
Conformity	+	+	Conformity occurs when individuals accept the culturally defined goals and the socially legitimate means of achieving them. Merton suggests that most individuals, even those who do not have easy access to the means and goals, remain conformists.
Innovation	+	–	Innovation occurs when an individual accepts the goals of society, but rejects or lacks the socially legitimate means of achieving them. Innovation, the mode of adaptation most associated with criminal behaviour, explains the high rate of crime committed by uneducated and poor individuals who do not have access to legitimate means of achieving the social goals of wealth and power.
Ritualism	–	+	The ritualist accepts a lifestyle of hard work, but rejects the cultural goal of monetary rewards. This individual goes through the motions of getting an education and working hard, yet is not committed to the goal of accumulating wealth or power.
Retreatism	–	–	Retreatism involves rejecting both the cultural goal of success and the socially legitimate means of achieving it. The retreatist withdraws or retreats from society and may become an alcoholic, drug addict or vagrant.
Rebellion	+/–	+/–	Rebellion occurs when an individual rejects both culturally defined goals and means and substitutes new goals and means. For example, rebels may use social or political activism to replace the goal of personal wealth with the goal of social justice and equality.

Source: Robert K. Merton, *Social Theory and Social Structure* (New York: The Free Press, 1968).

Note: Key + = acceptance of/access to, – = rejection of/lack of access to and –/+ = rejection of culturally defined goals and structurally defined means and replacement with new goals and means.

The 'conformist' way was to act as a British colonial officer at work (public) and behave as a Chinese person at heart (private); a Dr Jekyll and Mr Hyde kind of approach.

The more 'rebellious' option was not to adjust but play 'obey in public but' to disobey in private (陽奉陰為), that is, conforming in words but disagreeing in action.

Still, a third alternative was to conform ritualistically. Again, there were two renditions to this strategy, that is, 假戲真做 versus 遊戲 人間。

假戲真做 is acting to conform in such a realistic manner that for all intent and purpose, it is real, both to the actor and to the audience. This strategy was most often deployed by undercover cops who had to live the life of another person, and be completely submerged in gang culture before they could do the job effectively. With this kind of strategy, there is a real risk of going native with play acting, and may in time lead to conversion of values after long submersion in an alien culture.

The utility of 假戲真做 is that it reduces cognitive dissonance.

遊戲人間 is to not to take things seriously, translated into doing things as told, in a mindless and non-chalant, and playful way. 遊戲人間 attitude and conduct is personified and made famous by 济公 ('Jigong'). The common expression for people who engage in this strategy or work ethic is: 'It is just a job' or more blatantly: 'It is all a game'. The suggestion here is that if you play the game well, you will be rewarded and promoted, the same as those who worked hard, and has nothing to show for it.

In the end, there were those officers who refuse to go along and get along. These were officers who challenged the British at every turn. In Hong Kong, these were people who resist, rebel and stir up trouble for the British. These were the people who engage in confrontation (搞對抗) and make trouble 搞麻煩. In time, such officers would leave as protesters or be driven out as a result of disloyalty.

V: Conclusion

This chapter examines and assesses colonial policing in theoretical as well as empirical terms. In the process, it argues for a pluralistic and cultural analytical framework, taking into account the perspective, context and purpose of the assessor. Theoretically, it argues that Western legitimacy test for colonialism based on the process is not compatible with the Chinese basis of acceptance of rule based on performance. Empirically, the chapter offers up, for the first time, Chinese officers' opinions towards colonial HKP in the form of essays in HKPM, with allegorical meaning. The result is a revealing bared-for-all account of how it was like to work for the British in the 1950s, with different officers adopting different coping strategies to accommodate the alien rule, all with a Chinese cultural orientation.

This preliminary and exploratory study points to the need for further study of how Chinese officers engaged British colonial policing, and how Chinese culture impacted on HKP and policing in Hong Kong. Further research direction or issues include:

What kind of Chinese people joined the HKP? Why did they join?

How did demographics and the background of Chinese police officers affect their performance as a colonial official?

What kinds of identity and image, strategy and tactics, method and style, did Chinese officers adopt in doing colonial policing? How did they compare with the British or Indians?

How did Chinese culture impact upon HKP, organisationally and operationally? How was policing colonial Hong Kong similar to or different with policing other colonies?

Ultimately, in what way can it be said that there was a specific kind of policing called: policing with Hong Kong characteristics? As intimated by another author, speaking about researching into police in Hong Kong[99]:

> But, again, projects may need to be tailor-made for Hong Kong's very different conditions, e.g., police officers within the same force who cannot communicate in each other's languages let alone the languages of the civilians they encounter, very limited involvement of legal advisors during police interrogations, local attitudes towards official use of force, local attitudes towards the benefits of obtaining confessions, and the colonial and paramilitary history of the police force.[100]

To answer this most important question, it becomes necessary to the pursuit of a new line of inquiry, that is, 'Policing with Hong Kong Characteristics'?

Endnotes

1. M. Brogden, The emergence of the police: The colonial dimension, *British Journal of Criminology*, 27.1: 4–14, 1987.
2. Y. Y. Chu (ed.), *Foreign Communities in Hong Kong, 1840s–1950s* (New York: Palgrave Macmillan, 2005). ('The close and frequent contact with Chinese has significant impact as they went through the process of adaptation and adjustment. And just as the various members of the disparate British community had different opinions on various issues, so they came to create and embrace quite diverse images of the Chinese and other foreign communities.') (p. 40).
3. Chapter 1: Comparing colonial sites, In: P. Levine, *Prostitution, Race and Politics: Policing Venereal Disease in the British Empire* (New York: Routledge, 11 Jan., 2013).

4. P. A. J. Waddington, Towards paramilitarism? Dilemmas in policing civil disorder, *British Journal of Criminology*, 25 (1): 37–47, 37, 1987.
5. Chapter 9: Armed and unarmed police, In: R. I. Mawby (ed.), *Policing across the World: Issues for the Twenty-First Century* (Psychology Press, 1 February 1999), pp. 151–165. Mao has considered counterrevolutionaries as a class enemy, thus deserving harsh treatment, with no recourse. 4. The correct handling of contradictions among the people Mao Tse Tung, Quotations from Mao Tse Tung. http://www.marxists.org/reference/archive/mao/works/red-book/ch04.htm
6. A. Jiao, *The Police in Hong Kong* (Latham, MD: University Press of America, 2007).
7. In 2004, Raymond W. K. Lau, Community policing in Hong Kong: Transplanting a questionable model, *Criminal Justice*, 4(1): 61–80, 2004, in which he argued that CP failed in Hong Kong for a number of reasons, from a lack of cohesive community (new immigrants without roots, mainlanders in conflict with locals and the rich and poor divide) to institutionalisation of para-militarism in HKP to threats of instability pre- and post-1997. This has led Lau to the conclusion, intimated in the title, that imported (Western) community-policing model is questionable when applied to Hong Kong.
8. K. C. Wong, *One Country, Two Systems: Cross-Border Crime between Hong Kong and China* (New Brunswick, NJ; London: Transaction Publishers, 2012).
9. K. C. Wong, *The Impact of USA Patriot Act on American Society: An Evidence Based Assessment* (Nova, 2007).
10. K. Marx, *A Contribution to the Critique of Political Economy*, 1859. https://www.marxists.org/archive/marx/works/1848/communist-manifesto/ch01.htm or in the common ruin of the contending classes.
11. J. Tansey and T. O'riordan, Cultural theory and risk: A review, *Health, Risk and Society*, 1 (1): 71–92, 1999.
12. S. Rayner, Risk perception, technology acceptance, and institutional culture: Case studies of some new definitions, In: B. Ruck (ed.), *Risk Is a Construct* (Munich: Knesebeck, 1993), 93.
13. J. Tansey and T. O'riordan, Cultural theory and risk: A review, *Health, Risk and Society*, 1 (1): 71–92, 1999, p. 72.
14. K. C. Wong, *State Police Power as a Social Resource Theory*, 2000. Citizens below as distinguished from the police above do not look at crime as legal violation, but as a problem, personally.
15. Bradford, Ben, Jackson, Jonathan and Hough Mike, Police legitimacy in action: Lessons for theory and practice (21 March 2013). (Forthcoming, 2013). B. Bradford, J. Jackson and M. Hough, Police legitimacy in action: Lessons from theory and practice, In: M. Reisig and R. Kane (eds.), *The Oxford Handbook of Police and Policing*. Oxford: Oxford University Press. Available at SSRN. http://ssrn.com/abstract=2236691
16. J. Vagg, The legitimation of policing in Hong Kong: A non-democratic perspective, In: O. Marenin (ed.), *Policing Change, Changing Police: International Perspectives* (London: Taylor & Francis, 1996), p. 107.
17. 'In 1947 a former commissioner of the prewar Hong Kong Police responded to the crisis in local policing by composing the Pennefather-Evans Report, an analysis and recommendations for problems with the HKP. The chief weakness the report identifies was the failure of the Hong Kong Police to inspire identification

among the public it governed (294). Among the strategies for police reform, the report advised an increase in local hires, an expansion in operational duties, and an enhancement of professional training'. A. Burton (ed.), *After the Imperial Turn: Thinking with and through the Nation* (Durham, NC: Duke University Press, 2003), p. 293.

18. H. L. A. Hart, *Concept of Law* (London: Oxford University Press, 25 October 2012).
19. D. Beetham, *The Legitimation of Power* (Basingstoke, Hants: Macmillan, 1991) (Political legitimacy is realised through following established rules, providing justifiability of the law and consent of the people.)
20. 'The requirements of performance legitimacy commonly agreed upon by scholars, with varied emphases notwithstanding, include maintaining stability and economic progress, government efficiency, an incorrupt government, the rule of law, provision of basic social services, and protection of civil liberties'. W.-man Lam, Revisiting political legitimacy in Hong Kong, *Paper Presented at the 61st Political Studies Association Annual Conference* (Transforming politics: New Synergies). Department of Politics & Public Administration, The University of Hong Kong (Email: lamwm@hku.hk), p. 7.
21. I. Scott, *Political Change and the Crisis of Legitimacy in Hong Kong* (Hong Kong: Oxford University Press, 1989).
22. T.-Wing Ngo, *Hong Kong's History: State and Society under Colonial Rule* (New York: Routledge, 2002).
23. A. Cheung, Governance in Hong Kong: In search of identity, legitimacy and trust. This paper was first presented in a lecture of the Chair Professors Public Lecture Series of The Hong Kong Institute of Education on 23 October 2009.
24. J. Vagg, *The Legitimation of Policing in Hong Kong: A Non-Democratic Perspective*, p. 107, O. Marenin (ed.), *Policing Change, Changing Police: International Perspectives* (New York: Taylor & Francis, 1996), p. 119.
25. K. C. Wong, *Policing in Hong Kong* (Farnham, Surrey, UK: Ashgage, 2011), Chapter 5.
26. L. A. Ballard. The Dao of privacy, *Express,* 2011. Available at: http://works.bepress.com/lara_ballard/1
27. B. Cole, Post-colonial systems, In: R. I. Mawby, (ed.), *Policing across the World.* (London: UCL Press, 1999), pp. 88–108, 89 citing Killingray, 1991, p. 123.
28. R. Ashcraft, *John Locke: Critical Assessment* (London: Routledge, 1991), p. 524. ('The argument of the [*Second*] *Treatise* is that the government is not legitimate unless it is carried on with the consent of the governed'.)
29. C. Biddle, Individualism vs. collectivism: Our future, our choice, *Terms of Service,* 7(1): 2012. http://www.theobjectivestandard.com/issues/2012-spring/individualism-collectivism/
30. Legitimacy is the basis of government authority. ('Legitimitätsglaube') is: 'the basis of every system of authority, and correspondingly of every kind of willingness to obey, is a belief, a belief by virtue of which persons exercising authority are lent prestige' M. Weber, In: T. Parsons (ed.), *The Theory of Social and Economic Organization* (New York: Free Press, 1964), p. 382. R. Bendix, *Max Weber: An Intellectual Portrait* (CA: University of California Press, 1977), pp. 294–297. (According to Weber, there are three kinds of legitimate authorities, being legal, traditional and charismatic.)

31. G. LaFree and N. A. Morris, Does legitimacy matter? Attitudes toward anti-American violence in Egypt, Morocco, and Indonesia, *Crime and Delinquency*, 58 (5): 689–719, 2012.
32. I take Vagg to mean popular reasons.
33. See note 16, surpa.
34. '道德經 - Dao De Jing'. http://ctext.org/dao-de-jing
35. As a young traffic cop in Hong Kong (1970), I have been told many times that time is money. Violators just take the traffic ticket as a cost of doing business. They treat police enforcement just as one of their employee missing work or kids getting sick; happenings that need to be dealt with as a matter of course. When asked by HKU surveyor: 'Hong Kong is currently facing various problems. What kind of problems are you most concerned with? (per poll), a majority of HK people are more much concerned with 'livelihood problem' then 'economic problems' and last 'political problems'. Last survey return (16–19 June 2014) it was 55.9 vs. 18.3 vs. 21.8%. Eight years ago (19–21 June 2006) it was 53.1 vs. 41.7 vs. 3.7%, with the rest do not know. Hong Kong University, Public Opinion Poll. http://hkupop.hku.hk/chinese/popexpress/mostcon/mconq88/poll/datatables.html'
36. R. T. Golembiewski and K. W. Kuhnert, Barnard on authority and zone of indifference: Toward perspectives on the decline of managerialism, *International Journal of Public Administration*, 17 (6): 1195–1238, 1994.
37. N. Kompridis, So we need something else for reason to mean, *International Journal of Philosophical Studies* 8 (3): 271–295, 2009.
38. 'Live and let live' have nothing to do with moral relativism, and everything to do with following the 'dao' (way) or what matters to a person. By implication, there are many things in life and with the world all of us care about, but we have one life to lead and 24 h to spend. We are managing our time judiciously. In practice, this means hold fast and let go at the same time. R. A. Epstein, Live and let live, *Wall Street Journal*, 13 July 2004, http://online.wsj.com/articles/SB108967435840661816. ('The path to social peace lies in the willingness on all sides to follow a principle of live-and-let-live on deep moral dispute'.)
39. B. Gilley, The meaning and measure of state legitimacy: Results for 72 countries, *European Journal of Political Research*, 45 (3): 499–525, 2006, 499.
40. T. Tyler and Y. Huo, *Trust in the Law: Encouraging Public Cooperation with the Police and Courts* (New York: Russell Sage Foundation, 2002), p. 16.
41. K. C. Wong, *USA Patriot Act on American Society: An Evidence Based Assessment* (Hauppauge, New York: Nova Science Publishing, 2007), Chapter 1.
42. The rich get richer, and the poor get a prison.
43. HKU: 'Trend of core social indicators (1-6/1997 to 1-6/2014)' shows that degree of democracy (D) bears no relationship to compliance with the rule of law (F), degree of freedom (F), degree of prosperity (P) and degree of stability (S). For example, in **1-6/97**: D is 6.76, L is 7.25, S is 7.45, F is 7.75 and P is 8.1. **In 1-6/07**: D is 6.1, L and P are 6.8, S is 7.3 and F is 7.6. **In 1-6/14**: D is 6.35. S is 6.85, L is 6.9, P is 7 and F is 7.35.
44. This fictitious account of the HKP officer is driven by the research method in this book, that is, listening to the voices of HKP officers at ground zero (rank) and at frontline (duties).
45. This does not mean that there is no reason, or in the ultimate analysis, it is unreasonable for preferring end goods over process goods.

46. This means that it is a matter of reaction, as a matter of disposition and out of habits; commonly called the survival instinct.
47. Remarks by the president on the Middle East and North Africa. White House, Press Release, 18 May 2011. http://www.whitehouse.gov/the-press-office/2011/05/19/remarks-president-middle-east-and-north-africa
48. Mengzhi made clear that people must be well fed before they can enjoy other things in life.
49. See generally D. Needham, *The Economics and Politics of Regulation* (Boston: Little Brown, 1983), Chapters 3 and 4.
50. The same observation applies to China. Tony Saich at Harvard's Kennedy School of Government finds that between 80% and 95% of Chinese people were either relatively or extremely satisfied with the central government.
51. A. A. An-Na'im, Problems of universal cultural legitimacy for human rights, In: A. A. An-Na'im and F. Deng (eds.), *Human Rights in Africa: Cross-Cultural Perspectives*. (Washington, DC: Brookings Institution Press, 1990).
52. Professor D. Bell, *Political Legitimacy in China: A Confucian Perspective The Inaugural Confucius Lecture*, co-presented with the Confucius Institute at the University of Sydney (5 October 2011).
53. Mandate from heaven was first used in Zhou Dynasty to overthrow Shang Dynasty.
54. A. Jiao, *Police in Hong Kong: A Contemporary View* (Latham, NJ: University Press of America, 2007).
55. I. Ward and S. Geng, *The Hong Kong Marine Police 1841–1950* (Hong Kong University Press, 1991); S. E. Hamilton, *Watching over Hong Kong: Private Policing 1841–1941* (Hong Kong University, 2008).
56. Such as opinion survey.
57. Such as oral history.
58. HKP Chinese Inspector (1940–1960) (香港華籍督察(一九四〇—六〇年代)). http://www.police.gov.hk/offbeat/851/chi/h14.htm
59. *Hong Kong Police Magazine—Chinese Edition,* 11 (4): 5, Winter, 1966.
60. Ibid., p. 24.
61. Ibid., p. 16.
62. Ibid., p. 10.
63. *Hong Kong Police Magazine—Chinese Edition,* 11 (4): Winter, 1966.
64. The 'insider's view' of HKP is a fast-growing literary gem in Hong Kong, post-1997. See Devil besieged police station—Experience with HKP for 10 years. (猛鬼差館 ~ 香港警察十年經歷). http://cforum.cari.com.my/forum.php?mod = viewthread&tid = 2650053 W. Wadsworth, Book: *In the Shadow of the Noonday Gun, South China Morning Post,* 23 December 2012. ('His anthology's finest yarn, *Inside Job*, about an attempt to apprehend a cat burglar at the force's living quarters, hints at life in a colonial-era "chummery". But nostalgia buffs might feel that the author could have opened up more on the day-to-day aspects of colonial police life via conversations over beer and curries at The Hermitage, the banter after rugby training at Boundary Street, and hushed asides on careers and cases on the bowling green. Policemen are people too.'); 'Grandfather class retirees of retiree association discussed police history'. '元老級退役會會員談警察歷史'. http://www.police.gov.hk/offbeat/826/chi/h14.htm
65. 占 Sir on Duty—— 《警察雜誌》 17 April 2013.

66. Ibid.
67. *Hong Kong Police Magazine—Chinese Edition,* 11 (4): 18, Winter, 1966.
68. K. C. Wong, A comparative study of laws of assembly in China: Historical continuity or political departure? *Asian-Pacific Law and Policy Journal*, 7 (1): 184–241, 182–199, 2006.
69. M. Goldman, *China's Intellectuals: Advise and Dissent*. (Cambridge, MA: Harvard University Press, 1981).
70. Ibid.
71. 指桑罵槐 / 指桑骂槐 (Zhǐ sāng mà huái) is one of the 36 Startagems (三十六计) @26. http://www.cob.sjsu.edu/jiang_w/winter2012/ClassMaterials/36stratagems.pdf
72. Ibid., p. 7.
73. *Hong Kong Police Magazine—Chinese Edition*, 10 (4): 6, Winter, 1996.
74. *Hong Kong Police Magazine—Chinese Edition,* 11 (2): 11, Summer, 1967.
75. 髮官的權威 *Hong Kong Police Magazine—Chinese Edition,* 11 (4): 6, Winter, 1967.
76. K. Mading, Research on family values and culture change in Hong Kong's modern Chinese novels, *Journal of the Royal Asiatic Society Hong Kong Branch*, 8: 156, 1968. (The author, Dr Mading who is a vice-consul in the German Consulate General in Hong Kong, observed in his doctoral research that HK people, particularly lower class and juveniles, reject British rule of law.)
77. 群眾心裡與法律 *Hong Kong Police Magazine—Chinese Edition,* 11 (4): 8, Winter, 1967.
78. Chinese authors sometimes use 'pen name' to make a statement about self and/or others. J. Sterling and S. Jiang, Prolific Nobel winner's pen name? Not talking, *Cable News Network*, 11 October 2012. http://www.cnn.com/2012/10/11/world/sweden-nobel-prize-literature/ ('Mo told local media in 2003 that his pen name is a word play on his original middle name, but also a reminder to himself that he should talk less and write more'.)
79. The name, read in context of the time, might suggest that he/she is fast with ideas/action but is staying behind, by choice (humility in Chinese culture) or due to force (British policy of restricting Chinese or PC or both as a colonial policy).
80. 《管子·任法》 (*Guanzi*. Deploying law): 君臣上下贵贱皆从法, 此谓为大治。 (If everyone from high to low officials, respectful and base people, obeys the law, then we have perfect governance). http://tieba.baidu.com/p/1659540104
81. 《孟子·离娄（上）》徒善不足以为政，徒法不能以自行 *Menzhi*: Li Lou: 'Benevolence itself is not sufficient for administration, having law is not self executing'. http://www.confucius2000.com/confucian/tfabnyzxzdjjhy.htm
82. The author did not cite any source. But what the author's suggestions recall is the classical criminological stance as to the purpose and effect of punishment. See T. Draper, An introduction to Jeremy Bentham's theory of punishment, *Journal of Bentham Studies*, 5: 1–17, 2002.
83. Post, Robert, Law and cultural conflict. UC Berkeley, Public Law Research Paper No. 120. Available at SSRN: http://ssrn.com/abstract = 396860 or http://dx.doi.org/10.2139/ssrn.396860
84. J. Da, On several problems in legal transplantation, *Journal of Politics and* Law, 2(3): 107–109 (September, 2009). (Internally, China has experienced with multiple transplantation of law, e.g., from Tang and Qing dynasties. Law must reflect

history and culture. Transplanted law must be customised and localised before it is accepted and operative.)

85. L. Benton, *Law and Colonial Cultures: Legal Regimes in World History* (New York: Cambridge University Press, 2002), pp. 7–12.
86. Online dictionary. http://cy.5156edu.com/html4/11089.html
87. *Hong Kong Police Magazine—Chinese Edition,* 10 (4): 6, Winter, 1966, second to last paragraph.
88. http://baike.baidu.com/view/262636.htm
89. Mengzi said: I desire to live, I also desire being righteousness. If I cannot have both, I will sacrifice life for righteousness. http://baike.baidu.com/view/27507.htm?fromId = 658767
90. *Hong Kong Police Magazine—Chinese Edition,* 10 (4): 6, Winter, 1966.
91. Ibid. Last two paragraphs.
92. That the HKP was filled with talented people at the lowest ranks might be surprising to some who assumed that lower rank necessarily means low education achievement, or laziness of mind. This was certainly not the case in the 1950s and 1960s. During the time, many refugees came from the mainland because of the civil war in China (1945), establishment of PRC (1949), cultural revolution (1966) and famine. These new immigrants were of a different kind, some with very good educational background, professional achievements and personal experience. Many of them were rich and from the middle class.
93. In this regard, Sherman's evidence-based policing, dismissive of police practical experience and implicit knowledge is ill advised.
94. 堅強起來 *Hong Kong Police Magazine—Chinese Edition,* 11 (2): 13, Summer, 1967.
95. Ibid. First stanza, last four lines.
96. Ibid. Last stanza.
97. M. C. Davis (ed.), *Human Rights and Chinese Values* (Hong Kong: Oxford University Press, 1995).
98. R. K. Merton, *Social Theory and Social Structure* (New York: The Free Press, 1968).
99. Book review by Janice Barbyn: *Introduction to the Hong Kong Criminal Justice System*, In: M. S. Gaylord and H. Traver (eds.) (Hong Kong: Hong Kong University Press, 1994. xvi + 200pp., paperback, HK110).
100. Ibid.

Policing with Hong Kong Characteristics

4

Existence precedes essence.

Jean-Paul Sartre (1905–1980)[1]

A superimposed government was the mark of the colonial status. But there must have been a society on which it was superimposed.[2]

D. Faure (1997)

Introduction

This chapter explores the defining features of colonial policing in Hong Kong: addressing the question of what made colonial policing in Hong Kong unique. The supposition is that policing of whatever persuasions—colonial, communist or democratic—took on local colour when applied[3] and was customised to be effective.[4] That is to say, in doing and understanding colonial policing, local context mattered.[5] People might differ on the relative contribution of specific contextual factors—social, political, economics, cultural—in shaping policing, but few can deny that they were all important in their own way.[6]

It is argued in this chapter that colonial policing in Hong Kong exhibited a number of characteristics, otherwise not shared by other colonial police forces as a result of geography, history and culture. These characteristics defined the HKP in the 1840s as it is now, albeit in different mix and shifting significance. For example, over the years, Hong Kong people's core identity has changed from more China oriented to now Hong Kong disposed[7]:

> A June 2013 poll, the latest in a series released every six months, shows that identification with Hong Kong has even increased since the handover: today, 62 percent of the population identify primarily with Hong Kong and 38 percent exclusively. More surprisingly, the proportion is 84.3 percent among the 18 to 29 group (of which 55.8 percent identify exclusively with Hong Kong).[8]

Hong Kong people, starting with the young, are more in love with Hong Kong[9] than being patriotic towards China. This shift in allegiance has caught the HKP in-between, when called upon to secure Hong Kong's democratic rights versus defend China's national interests.[10]

Looking further back, in the 1840s, Hong Kong people were predominantly Chinese in culture, with nationalism and anti-foreignism orientation on display. In the 1950s, while the basic character of Hong Kong people—patriotism and anti-foreignism—has not changed, the basic constitution of Hong Kong people has changed, as a result of WWII. With the change in Hong Kong demographics and political orientation—KMT versus PRC—the HKP has to stand ready to deal with political unrests, like the 1956 Double Ten Riots.

The above brief discussion is to highlight the fact that there is much continuity amidst drastic changes with the HKP and policing in Hong Kong, before and after 1997. It follows that the conventional wisdom that policing in Hong Kong has fundamentally and completely changed after 1997 is a myth. In fact, as observed, there is more continuity than change with the HKP throughout the years, for example, HKP reform in the 1990s is built upon the foundation of HKP reform in the 1950s, which radically transformed the HKP under colonial rule.[11] This is so because conditions in Hong Kong that inform upon or set conditions for policing, such as social structure, communal culture, organisational ethos, collective identity and racial disposition rarely change. Long before 1997, Hong Kong people were integrated with mainland China, in culture, custom and habits. Otherwise, British policing culture and style has become embedded in and is part of the HKP's genetic code.

This chapter is organised into six sections. Section I, 'Colonial Policing as Policing the Chinese', discusses how the Hong Kong colonial officials faced difficulties in policing Chinese communities, who were long established and well disciplined before the British, making colonial rule superfluous, as applied to them. Section II, 'Colonial Policing as "Chinese" Policing', investigates how Chinese policing works in philosophical, theoretical and practical terms. It observes that in policing and social control, the Chinese adopt an internal cultivation—discipline model, and the West pursues an external—punitive strategy. The challenge to the British was in reconciling these two kinds of control system under one roof, which they did with moderate success with dual track justice and indirect rule. Section III, 'Colonial Policing as "Self-Help" Policing' advances a 'theory of Chinese policing' (formally, 'State Police Powers as a Social Resource Theory' [STR]) that looks at policing from the people and not the state's perspective. It argues that from the Hong Kong–Chinese people's perspective, crime is less a legal violation than it is a personal problem (with expectations denied), requiring appropriate resources to address or redress. One of the fundamental propositions to STR is that: 'The person who is closest to the problem, by impact and with resource, is the person to take care of the problem'. The mismatch of Chinese expectations and resources offered by the HKP precludes Hong Kong people from resorting to the HKP for help in solving their problems. Section IV, 'Colonial Policing as Policing Migrants', looks into the effect of residency status on control by policing strategy and tactics. This gives rise to the issue of relationship policing, from intimate to stranger. Recounting Mao Tse-tung's theory of contradiction, Section V, 'Colonial Policing as Relationship Policing', postulates that the more intimate the relationship between individuals, the less necessary coercive policing is. Section VI is a 'Conclusion' to this chapter and an overview to 'Part I' of the book in theories proposed, methods suggested, findings discovered, lessons learned and contributions made.

I: Colonial Policing as Policing Chinese[12]

The Hong Kong population, then (1841) and now (2014), is predominantly Chinese,[13] and Cantonese at that (Table 4.1). Before the British arrived to take over Hong Kong as a 'barren rock', Chinese people of different ethnicities and clans had lived there for centuries.[14] When Commodore James Bremer, Commander-in-Chief of the British Forces in China took possession of Hong Kong on 26 January 1841, the population in Hong Kong Island was: 'In the Villages and hamlets: 4,360; In the Bazaar: 800; In the Boats: 2,000; Labourers from Kowloong: 300'.[15] In April 1843, there were about 19,000 people (12,561 people in March 1842) of which no more than 500 were foreigners. By 1862, there were 123,511 residents in Hong Kong and Kowloon, of which about 1640 were European and American. The distribution of Hong

Table 4.1 Population of Hong Kong According to Ethnic Group: 2001–2011

	Census 2001		Census 2006		Census 2011	
Ethnic Group	Number	%	Number	%	Number	%
Chinese	6,364,439	94.9	6,522,148	95.0	6,620,393	93.6
Indonesian	50,494	0.8	87,840	1.3	133,377	1.9
Filipino	142,556	2.1	112,453	1.6	133,018	1.9
White	46,585	0.7	36,384	0.5	17,342	0.2
Indian	18,543	0.3	20,444	0.3	28,616	0.4
Pakistani	11,017	0.2	11,111	0.2	18,042	0.3
Nepalese	12,564	0.2	15,950	0.2	16,518	0.2
Japanese	14,180	0.2	13,189	0.2	12,580	0.2
Thai	14,342	0.2	11,900	0.2	11,213	0.2
Other Asian	12,835	0.2	12,663	0.2	12,247	0.2
Others	20,835	0.3	20,264	0.3	30,336	0.4
Total	6,708,389		6,864,346		7,071,576	

Kong population has not changed much (c. 2011), while it has become more diverse, Chinese still dominate (93.6%). How alien (British) colonial officials in the minority came to rule an indigenous people (Chinese) in the majority effectively is the challenge of study and analysis.

The challenge in policing the Chinese was prominently on the mind of the colonists. In 1858, *China Mail* has this to say about HK governance:

> With about 50 officials to govern five hundred merchants and not to govern 60,000 Chinese, who can wonder at disputes, which all our English, American, French, Germans, motormen, parsers, merchants, storekeepers, opium-sellers, gamblers and pirates, each under the supervision and control of his own control or commander, Secretary or Protector, who in their term and are under the control of a Governor, who is under the control of a Secretary of a State? All these are crowded together in a place about half as big as Hyde Park, and people at home wonder that they fall out and fight, slander, and go to law perpetually.[16]

The above *China Mail* is reported here to put into perspective the challenge faced by a British minority (500) in ruling over a Chinese majority (60,000), of different ethnicities, stations in life and intentions.

In understanding the British philosophy of governance towards Hong Kong, it is best to understand Britain's perception of China–Hong Kong. For this, it is best to consult James William Norton-Kyshe's seminal work *History of the Laws and Courts of Hongkong* (1898) (HKLXHK).[17] The preface of HKLCHK refers to Hong Kong as the last frontier ('Ultima Thule'), literally and figuratively beyond the boundary and reach of human civilisation, to which the British empire courageously, tenaciously and determinatively reach out 'for the benefit of all mankind':

> Placed on the borders of an Empire so full of contradictions and prejudiced is China, with its uncontrolled millions, conservative and prejudiced to the backbone, a people totally ignorant and indifferent as to Western idea or modes of government, it seems as if Hongkong by its position had been destined to become the starting point from whence a civilizing power by its beneficent rule and humane laws was to endeavor to effect those reform which an uncivilized power China was ever in need of.[18]

As described, Hong Kong was a desolate and uncivilised place from nowhere, waiting for the British people to dominate, domesticate and civilise. Naturally, this would not turn out to be an easy task.

That said, policing in Hong Kong, then as now, is the policing of the Chinese, as distasteful a thought it was in the eyes of the coloniser. The only difference between then and now is that under British colonial rule, Hong Kong was to be governed by 'indirect rule' coupled with 'social isolation' and 'dual track' justice.[19] Nevertheless, whether it was 'indirect rule', 'social isolation' or 'dual track', the task on hand was to tame the Chinese, failing that, to put them in their rightful place with draconian punishment.[20]

The 'indirect rule' governance model is justified as follows:

> Indirect rule reduced the costs of colonial administration, gradually incorporated indigenous authorities into the colonial bureaucracy and enlisted them as agents to implement two essential aspects of colonial rule: the collection of revenue and the maintenance of law and order… the gradualist polices of running Empire at minimal costs and with minimal force was a cause of self-congratulation by many colonial powers, who saw their systems of trusteeship as fulfilling the main criteria of good, if somewhat authoritarian governance…[21]

According to G.B. Endecott, during the first two 100 years of colonial rule (up until 1960s), the colony practised indirect rule. (He further opined that after the 1960s, there was equal administration under the law). Thus, Chinese communities co-existed with European communities in an autonomous and self-sustaining way. (This was the same with other Western communities at the same time.)[22] In fact 'the colonial authorities did indeed leave much of the work of government to the Chinese communities and made little effort to assimilate the Chinese to British rule'.[23] In 1844, Governor David, himself an achieved sinologist, has this to say about regulating Chinese:

> The attempt to regulate and restrain the Chinese population by European police is attended with difficulties. The ignorant of their language, their customs and their persons give an insuperable advantage to the vicious part of the population and it becomes moreover a sort of patriotic combination against the rule of the foreigner. I was accordingly led to the conclusion that the Chinese in towns and villages would be best locally governed by their own system… self government will be most efficient in its results and at the same time entails no charge on the colonial funds…[24]

As to 'social isolation' (*de facto*) in time 'legal separation' (*de jure*), in 1858, the fourth governor of Hong Kong, Sir John Bowring made this forthright observation:

> The separation of the native population from the European is nearly absolute. Social intercourse between the races is wholly unknown.[25] A few Chinese speak a strange 'jargon' by which they are enabled to convey their ideas to foreigners. I do not believe there is a single merchant or Tradesman in Hong Kong who speaks or understands the naive dialect, who has seen a Chinaman at his table, or admitted him to the slightest confidential intimacy. The influence of the European settler upon the native mind may be said to be nil… There is an absolute abyss between the governors and the governed. We rule them in ignorance, and they submit in blindness.[26]

As to 'dual track' justice, according to Munn, for the most part during the early colonial period (1841–1880), the relationship between the rulers, political (British) and commercial (European), and the ruled (local Hong Kong–Chinese, migrant Chinese), was a rocky and contentious one. There was no love lost between the two. The relationship was made more difficult by the separation of race, class, language and culture made apparent by habits, custom and lifestyle, often reified in good versus evil terms. This led to suspicion and discrimination from the coloniser and misunderstanding and resistance from the colonised. Still, the differences between the British and Chinese—social, cultural, economic and political—had to be reconciled.

The colonists were afflicted by this sense. In the end, instead of leaving the Chinese alone, as envisioned by 'indirect' rule, the British sought to regulate and control the Chinese in multifarious ways.

> Rather than simply dismiss the 'maintenance of law and order' as the simple and unremarkable qualification to a general policy of non-intervention, as many historians do, it focuses on the issues of criminal justice by a government that sought legitimacy in 'equal law' an 'impartial justice' yet believed that the solutions to the colony's many problems lay in special forms of policing and punishment for the Chinese population.[27]

Thus, racial isolation and political submission had to be secured by separate legal regimes, with the barrel of the gun if needed.

Still, the British government hung on to their belief that it was their professed destiny as a superior race and advanced culture to pacify and, in time, civilise the Chinese population through British high ideology, magnanimous rule, benevolent governance and effective administration. In this regard, Hong Kong was not only to be a free trading port par excellence, but also a shining example of the best colonial rule the British had to offer in China.

However, many Hong Kong residents, including the foreign communities, resented direct British rule from the White Hall. They considered it a bad idea to apply English law to Hong Kong. They wanted to be left alone. Failing that, they wanted to have a say over what and how British law was applied to Hong Kong[28]:

> We are far from London where government is uncertain of local conditions. It should welcome information from Hong Kong officials and local residents about our needs. The Plenipotentiary is active and zealous but he is only one man and may not be able to think of everything. The administration of justice in cases of serious crime must be considered. *We need laws adapted for enforcement here rather than a precise copy of English law.* We do not need the whole English statute book—just those laws that relate to our specific problems like property crime ashore and afloat. (Letter to the Editor from *Observer* dated 2.5.43) (*Italics supplied*)

The major problem with policing Chinese then was how to adapt British law to Chinese culture and Hong Kong conditions. When in doubt and frustration, the British colonial high officials and HKP street officers often turned a blind eye and took a could-not-care-less attitude, unless something happened that required their attention or where the community sought help.[29] This was the case with street hawking in the 1950s at Yau-ma-tei, one of Hong Kong's principal urban areas. The HKP refused to do anything, so the responsibility of regulating the hawkers fell on the shoulders of the Chinese community leaders[30]:

> In the pre-war period there used to be fewer hawkers on Temple Street than today. The street was deserted. Ng Kong lived in Mau Lam Street and Nathan Road. He seldom strolled around Public Square Street and Yung Shu Tau. As soon as the war was over, many outdoor singing stands were erected on Market Street (present site of the Public Library). Performances were staged every night and $10 was charged. Now the stands have moved into shopping premises and there are performances throughout the day. When Ng Kong joined the Yaumatei Kai Fong Welfare Advancement Association, he started to patrol around Temple Street and Yung Shu Tau frequently in order to fulfill his responsibility in the Association. When Tang Kai took the post of chief director, Temple Street became prosperous. Hawkers sometimes fought and quarreled with one another, fighting for more booth space. The police took a blind eye on this. The Association worked on reconciliation and delineated booths of 3″ × 6″ all along Temple Street. Hawkers were invited to register in the Association. Hawker numbers were allocated by lucky draw. Everyone was satisfied at this arrangement. Yet, the cooked food stalls on Temple Street were not managed by the Association. Now the task of booth delineation is done by the police. The area under control is similar to the one managed by the Association in the past. Yung Shu Tau was close to Yau Ma Tei Police Station. The police handle all the vice there. In the past, Tau Hau Temple was not enclosed by walls. People did not care about public order when worshipping. When Guan Yin opened the repository, worshippers crowded the Temple. Some of them worshipped and burned incense outside the Temple. Now the Temple was enclosed by shorter walls. And the police will set up barrack to maintain order at various festivals.

This is community policing at its best—community self-regulation, with the HKP in the wing. To this age-old theory and practice of Chinese community policing, this chapter turns.

II: Colonial Policing as Chinese Policing

From the earliest time, the Hong Kong Chinese residents were left to their own accord, in fighting crime and policing community. This was especially the case in the Kowloon, New Territories and water region.

Thus, colonial policing was also Chinese policing, that is, Chinese policing Chinese, such as the District Watch Force. One of the least explored subject in HKP research is how Chinese police the Chinese, then (in different colonial era: before 1900, before 1945, before 1997) and now (SAR era), comparatively. In the following, the principles and practices of Chinese policing are explored.

Social Control Organisation and Philosophy

Historically, social control in China is decentralised and organised around natural communal and intimate groups, for example, family and clan,[31] with governmental endorsement and support.[32] Local social control is institutionalisation. The emperor rules the state by and through his officials who in turn govern the people by and through the family head and community leaders.[33] Such decentralised, grassroot, social control practice was informed by Confucian teachings[34]:

> Wishing to govern well in their states, they would first regulate their families. Wishing to regulate their families, they would first cultivate their persons. Wishing to cultivate their persons, they would first rectify their minds. Wishing to rectify their minds, they would first seek sincerity in their knowledge. Wishing for sincerity in their thoughts, they would first extend their knowledge.[35]

When asked, 'What is meant by "in order rightly to govern the state, it is necessary first to regulate the family"', Confucius answered:

> It is not possible for one to teach others, while he cannot teach his own family. Therefore, the ruler, without going beyond his family, completes the lessons for the state. There is filial piety:—therewith the sovereign should be served. There is fraternal submission:—therewith elders and superiors should be served. There is kindness—therewith the multitude should be safe. [36]

Thus, functional social control in China was supplied informally and extra-judicially. This resulted from deliberate state policy,[37] building upon existing natural communal structure,[38] established cultural habits[39] and entrenched customary practices.[40] Hence, while in theory, the local magistrates ('yamen') were supposed to be in total control on all matters in rural China, in practice, broad police powers were conceded to the local community and exercised by the family.[41]

> The authority of the Chinese pater familias was much stronger than intra-familial leadership required; and he owed his extraordinary power essentially

> to the backing of the despotic state. Disobedience to his orders was punished by the government. On the other hand, the local officials could have him beaten and imprisoned, if he was unable to keep the members of his family from violating the law. Acting as a liturgical (semi-official) policeman of his kin group, he can scarcely be considered the autonomous leader of an autonomous unit.[42]

James Hayes described in detail how customary law and informal social control in China worked in China at the turn of the century, which was maintained in New Territories until it was eroded due to industrialisation and urbanisation after WWII and with the creation of new towns:

> Overall, the customary law catered for most situations arising in the family, the village and the market. It provided a highly effective means of carrying out local administration without the presence of imperial officers in the village, or even in the sub-districts. Up to a point, one could even say that communities ran themselves. So long as they kept the peace and paid the land-tax, enabling the District Magistrate and his superiors in the provincial administration to fulfil their prime obligations to the central government in Beijing, they were generally left alone. Application of the customary law rested upon public opinion. The consensus view was a powerful force in each place. People were usually acquainted with each other, and everyone was presumed to know the rules. Deviations from accepted practice were soon known and usually condemned. Social and economic sanctions of different degree were applied to offenders, including the ultimate deterrent of expulsion from the lineage or village, or even execution. They were administered by the elders and local gentry, with public consent and official support, and carried much weight within what was virtually a closed society. Behind the elders stood the more fearful figure of the county magistrate, to whom serious offenders could be referred, or in some cases even conveyed bodily.[43]

James Hayes' observations as a Hong Kong district officer working in New Territories echoed those of Professor Mark Anton Allee, a sinologist conducting research on state and society relationship in Taiwan:

> A significant dynamic in late imperial Chinese history is the escalating tension between private and public at the local level. The proliferation of guilds, temple associations, and sectarian assemblies, and poetry and literary societies, secret societies, militia and self-defense organizations and the like were manifestations of a trend toward the creation of interest groups whose operation was largely outside local government. … In response, during the nineteenth century some local governments made strenuous efforts to increase the articulation and sophistication of their administrative control by utilizing town and village leaders a step below the gentry elite in status.[44]

What then are the philosophical principles, theoretical postulates, and cultural parameters informing such practices. More significantly, how do they justify and explain colonial policing in Hong Kong, from inception to 1997.

Social Control Principles

Chinese traditional thoughts on social regulation and crime control were informed by the following premises (Table 4.2):

1. Crime control is a local, indigenous and above all a family affair.[45]
2. Crime control starts with prevention. Prevention addresses early symptoms.[46]
3. To be effective, crime prevention must be a multi-faceted, comprehensive and integrated enterprise, involving the individual, family, clan, neighbour, community and the state.[47]
4. To be effective in controlling people and fighting crime, a variety of measures have to be used. Thus it was said by a Confucians that the best way to regulate people was to 'inspire them with justice, correct them with administration, guide them with rites, keep them straight with honesty, appeal to them with benevolence, reward them with

Table 4.2 Traditional Social Control Philosophy Compared: East (China) versus West (United States)

	China	West
Justifications of control	Reformation (offender)[53] Restoration (social relationship)[54] Reintegration (communal harmony)[55]	Retribution (victim/society)[56] Deterrence (individual/ society)[57] Rehabilitation (individual)[58]
Subject of control	Personal character[59]—internal thought	Social conduct[60]—external behaviour
Basis of control	Moral wrong[61]	Legal wrong[62]
Method of control	Education—to reform[63]	Punishment—to deter[64]
Strategy of control	Root of the problem	Manifestation of the problem
Site of control	Collective	Individual
Sources of control	Multiple layers: Individual-family-neighbour-clan-state Multiple focus: Psychological-physical-social-economical-legal-political-cultural	Unitary system- Judicial-legal-penal
Nature of control	Informal-social[65]	Formal-legal[66]
Time of control	Preventive-proactive	Remedial-reactive[67]
Assumption of the controlled	Affective-social[68]	Rational-autonomous[69]

benefits, persuade them to follow'.[48] More specifically, crime control can be best achieved through moral education and supplemented by fast, severe and speedy punishment.[49]

5. Crime control will not be successful without also addressing the root causes of crime, such as the moral degeneration of the individual[50] and criminogenic conditions of the environment.[51]

Consistent with the above Confucius ideas and ideals, crime prevention and social control in traditional China was realised through indigenous groups—starting with the family that provided the education and discipline for character building, the neighbours who provided the supervision and sanction against deviance, and the community that set the moral tone and customary norms to guide conduct. Finally, the state acted as the social control agency of a last resort in providing punishment against crimes, and economic maintenance and social welfare to anticipate civil disorder.[52]

Chinese Jurisprudential Ideas and Ideal: 'Qing Li Fa'

The British rule of law and concept of justice was not accepted by the Hong Kong people because they laboured under different jurisprudential principles and ideas of justice. To the Chinese, rule of law (*fa*) is not a supreme conduct norm, but the particularity of human circumstances (*qing*) is.

The legal concepts and jurisprudential principles of 'Qing' 'Li' 'Fa' (<<情理法>>) (hereinafter *QLF*) or 'ren qing' ('human nature/relation/compassion')[70] versus 'tian li' ('heavenly principles')[71] or 'qing li' ('accepted code of conduct')[72] or 'lun li' (ethical principles)[73] versus 'guo fa' ('state law') dominated ideals and ideas behind Chinese legal qua general culture.[74]

QLF are embedded and inter-related[75] cultural tenets, espoused and dynamic[76] ethical percepts in imperial China.[77] Together, they informed social practices and guided personal conduct. As jurisprudential principles, *QLF* considered independently and as a whole is central to the formulation of legislation, implementation of law and dispensation of justice, and indeed all life choices, in imperial China.

The importance and impact of *QLF* in Chinese culture and social intercourse can be gauged by looking at popular culture practices.[78] Chinese people then as now make and evaluate social, economic, political or legal judgement of all kinds as 'he qing he li' (compatible with human nature and reason)[79] or 'bu he qing li fa' (not being compatible with 'QLF').[80]

The ultimate objective of lawmakers and judicial officials was to actualise *QLF* as a way of life, that is, to establish a harmonious[81] and peaceful world wherein the ideas and ideals of Confucius hold sway.[82] Everything should be found in its proper place and intercourse with each other should be conducted in a harmonious and well-balanced[83] manner without conflicts or disputes.[84]

However, notwithstanding the importance of *QLF*, there are very few Occidental legal or jurisprudential publications on this subject matter. This lack of Western literature hampers existing understanding and scholarship of Chinese (Hong Kong) law in theory and practice.

Supremacy of 'Qing' over 'Li'

In imperial China, human conduct was judged by and regulated with 'li' (rites), which were inculcated through 'jiao' (education) and not with 'fa' (law) enforced by means of 'xing' (punishment). Law is established to *supplement* the rites, and brought into play *as a last resort*. Doctrinally, this is called the Confucianisation of the law.[85]

Confucianisation preached that rites provide the law with content and spirit. Law is used to promote Confucian ideas and ideals. In judicial practice, law is based on Confucius teachings and Confucius teachings are resorted to in interpreting and applying the law. This is called 'jing yi jue yu' (deciding cases based on Confucius teachings).[86]

How Judges Apply 'Qing-Li-Fa'[87]

What was being called for in order to be a *QLF* judge in imperial China?

When resolving disputes or rendering judgement,[88] Chinese imperial officials started with a search for the truth before exercising discretion, as guided by law. Song Emperor Gao Zhong called for 'yuan qing ding zui' (determining guilt based on true facts): 'Once a law is promulgated, it will never change. However, facts and circumstances are always different. Since law is to forestall evil, (judges need to) ascertain all the facts before positing guilty. They need to get to the truth of the matter'.[89]

'Yuan qing ding zui' (deciding guilt based on true facts) required the officials to discover the cause of the incident and motive of people, before passing judgement.

First, by understanding others (motives), there comes an understanding of their action, and with that, naturally, more identification with and compassion for their plight. This is the doctrine of 'yuan qing shi you ke men'. In essence, the more one knows, the more one understands, and the more one understands, the more one can identify—empathise and sympathise—with the offender.

Second, the more knowledge there is, the more one can see the person's act as normal than abnormal. People have their own reasons, inaccessible to others and incomprehensible to society, in doing things the way they do. Epistemologically, understanding requires knowing more, judging less.

Third, a person's liability and punishment should be determined with reference to motive or what comes from the heart ('xin').[90] Well-intended action should not be punished, or at least punished less. Evil intentions are punished with or without being manifested in action.

Fourth, in passing judgement, the yardstick is 'ren qing' and 'tienli'. The issue here is did the defendant do something a normal person would do in a similar situation,[91] or what comes naturally to a person of similar status and under similar circumstances?

Fifth, officials were required to apply law on the books to facts in the street, finding concrete individual justice with abstract general justice principles. This required the fitting of sterile, monolithic and inflexible laws to divergent contexts, moving events and dynamic situations. This required officials to differentiate between people and determine the existence of mitigating and aggravating circumstances that ultimately bore upon moral culpability, social accountability and criminal liability. Specifically, officials should treat offenders lightly when circumstance dictated, that is, 'qing qing fa zhong' (literally 'facts light and law serious'). In 'qing zhong fa qing' cases (literally 'facts serious and law light'), the officials were supposed to levy more punishment.[92]

Finally, officials followed the principle of compassion, that is, 'zui yi cong qing' (treat doubtful cases lightly). In essence, if in doubt, offenders should be spared heavy punishment.[93]

Given different social control philosophies, structures and practices and divergent jurisprudence principles and justice percepts detailed herein, it should come as no surprise that the Chinese resented colonial rule. They avoided British justice, rather seeking out self-help to solve their problems. Lest people misconstrued Chinese resentment and avoidance as signs of challenge to colonial government's political legitimacy and acts of defiance, it is straightforward to show they were not. Chinese resentment and avoidance were acts of (negative) self-help. Why pile up more problems (expectation denied) by wasting time and getting frustrated in teaching old British dogs new tricks? Visiting with British officials on their best of days was an identity-denying and culture-bruising experience. Interfacing with the British at any level and in all occasions disturbed one's authenticity, sense and sensitivity.[94]

III: Colonial Policing as Self-Help Policing[95]

Self-Help Policing in Chinese Philosophy

What is meant by 'self-help policing' in a Chinese context? Historically, the Chinese sage scholars adopted a governing philosophy and offered a system of moral principles that aimed at creating an orderly world by developing a wholesome person and promoting harmonious relationship, not by imposing rules, sanctioning conduct and punishing people. More specifically, people are to be internally driven, not externally regulated, starting with self-cultivation[96]:

> The ancients who wished to illuminate 'illuminating virtue' all under Heaven first governed their states. Wishing to govern their states, they first regulated their families. Wishing to regulate their families, they first cultivated their personal lives. Wishing to cultivate their personal lives, they first rectified their hearts and minds. Wishing to rectify their hearts and minds, they first authenticated their intentions. Wishing to authenticate their intentions, they first refined their knowledge. The refinement of knowledge lay in the study of things. For only when things are studied is knowledge refined; only when knowledge is refined are intentions authentic; only when intentions are authentic are hearts and minds rectified; only when hearts and minds are rectified are personal lives cultivated; only when personal lives are cultivated are families regulated; only when families are regulated are states governed; only when states are governed is there peace all under Heaven. Therefore, from the Son of Heaven to the common people, all, without exception, must take self-cultivation as the root.[97]

Thus observed, self-cultivation (self-policing) holds the key to the betterment of mankind and personal discipline leads to an orderly society.[98] The most famous of all of Confucius' admonitions in this regard is perhaps the following: 'Direct the people with moral force and regulate them with ritual, and they will possess shame, and moreover, they will be righteous' (Analect: 2.3). As a result, Confucian ideas of 'self-cultivation, discipline the family, govern the country and pacify the world' (*xiushen qijia zhiguo pingtianxia*) are well integrated into China's cultural beliefs, social practices[99] and political programme.[100]

There were five reasons why the people in China shunned the involvement with the 'police', socially and intellectually.

First, the police were considered as not necessary in an intimately related, tightly bonded and closely watched community that was China's past.[101] Self-discipline, family surveillance and social pressure were considered sufficient to induce conformity and regulate conduct.

Second, officials/police were considered to be outside the community one is born into. Community disputes and personal problems are to be resolved within the tight-knitt in-group.[102]

Third, culturally, the Chinese were taught to avoid confrontation and absorb affronts.[103] They were expected to seek accommodation through tolerance and resolve disputes through mediation,[104] at all costs.[105]

Fourth, involvement with the officials and association with the police spelled trouble for all concerned, that is, punishment and loss of 'face' or 'reputation'.[106] The saying 'not entering officials' doorstep while alive, not going to hell when dead' ('shen buru guan men, si buru diyu') was widely shared and strictly abided; hell and government were considered similarly horrendous, unfathomable experiences!

Fifth, petty law enforcement agents (*xuli*) enjoyed low socioeconomic status in Chinese society. They were uneducated and came from usually the underclass, if not the underworld. They were mostly corrupt,[107] exploitative and oppressive.[108] Their work was considered as dirty or profane, that is, associated with law breakers and involved with disputes.[109] Thus, policing was best left to the police, not to be heard from.[110] There was no need to record their activities much less study them. This attitude still prevails today, for example, young people are discouraged from joining the police.[111]

Self-Help Policing as Imperial Rule

Long before the police came to China, the emperor relegated social control responsibility to the locals, namely, family and clans. When the Chinese are away from home, as sojourns or migrants, they look towards multi-aid organisation for support and security, and are bonded therewith. This was done in deference to ideology (Confucianism) and out of necessity (small government). Groves observed:

> Even at times of optimal efficiency, the ability of the imperial government was limited only because officials and military forces were thinly spread over China's large land mass. Routine police functions were largely rested in mutual responsibility systems, the heads of which were answerable to the district magistrate.[112]

The Chinese self-help approach to local policing–social control anticipated the Western mode by thousands of years. This is what is said of the need for and the advantage of 'self-policing society' in the 1990s; basically, institutionalised and professionalised policing, however efficient and effective, is not able to deal with crime and disorder problems, living among the people 24/7 and with every social transaction and human encounter. Conversely, as the Chinese Emperor realised, he was not omnipotent and omnipresent and thus was likely not to be of much help when things happened tens of thousands of miles away:

> The principles that lie behind this self-policing approach are simple. Society needs to change its relationship with the police. Rather than relying on the police to solve our crime problems society must take more responsibility itself. But that means creating effective intermediate institutions within civil society as well as links with the police which would allow more effective self-policing. One of the police's main roles should be to strengthen sources of authority within society, to strengthen society's ability to police itself.[113]

Self-Help Policing before the British

Long before the arrival of the Chinese magistrate and British colonialists to Hong Kong, the indigenous Chinese population learned to look after themselves, that is, self-help.[114] Traditional Chinese society yearned for harmony (安寧) and abhorred chaos (亂).[115] They relished personal relationships (關係) and loathed disputes.

The family held disorderly conducts in check and disputes were resolved through mediation, self-help in action.

In colonial Hong Kong, the operative unit of self-help was not the individual or community, but the family.[116]

> The elemental organization unit of the Chinese society in Hong Kong is the familial group, which constitutes the primary focus of identification of the Chinese people. It is also the core of a primary resource network within which resources and services are exchanged, and through which many of the salient needs of the Hong Kong Chinese are met.[117]

Indeed, it is said, every person (household) tends to his own snow, and not worry about the frost on other's roof (各人自掃門前雪, 莫管他家瓦上霜). More to the point, each family had its own rule, just as the country had its own law (家有家規, 國有國法).

The repair of broken relationships brought about by disputes rested with insiders (the head of household), not the outsiders (magistrate).[118] The justifications were threefold. First, the family head has the interest, knowledge, status, capacity and authority to intervene. Second, the family is closest to the manifestation (impact test) and roots (solution test) of a family problem. Third, the magistrate, as an outsider (家醜不宜外傳[119]), has little legitimacy or competency to meddle with family affairs, a small kingdom unto itself.[120] The conventional wisdom was that even a good judge cannot resolve a family dispute (清官難審家庭事). In theoretical terms, the magistrate is furthest from the problem to be resolved. The rationale was that the father being the head of the family (一家之主) is responsible for the well-being of the family because he knows best, cares more and has the personal capacity and moral obligation to keep the house in order; failing that, the father is held personally responsible. The saying here is 'harmonious families are prosperous families' (家和萬事興). Lastly, visiting the magistrate was the last and worst option. Visiting the magistrate brings shame on the family and punishment to the individual. The conventional refrain is never enter official door when alive, nor hell after death (生不入官門[121] 死不入地獄). Visiting the 'yamen' would end up being punished, as the Chinese saying goes: 'One is spanked before ever seeing an official' (未见官先打八十大板).

When the head of the family intervened in a dispute, he assumed an all-purpose problem-solving role (family-oriented problem solving [FOPS][122]:

determining facts, pacifying parties, articulating rules, finding responsibility, settling grievances, anticipating future, imposing discipline, resolving differences, mediating arguments, rehabilitating relationship, or generally mending expectation gaps of all kinds and shape wherever it can be found. FOPS is *Q–L–F* in action.

FOPS is a restorative and integrative project, what we now call 'restorative justice'[123] and 'reintegration shame'.[124] Much like problem-oriented policing (POP) (Goldstein), in modern-day community policing, problem solving in a Chinese family is directed at finding a solution to a multifaceted problem, in a comprehensive and integrated manner. Unlike POP, it is not about solving other's problem (community oriented), but only one of self (family anchored). Whatever it is, family problem solving is not about rule enforcement or punishment. It is about restoring order, starting with rebuilding relationships.

The head of the household is the best person to solve problem because he has all the resources—personal, intellectual, moral, social, economic and legal—at his disposal to solve the problem on hand (see 'State Police Power as a Social Resource Theory' below). If the head of the family cannot solve the problem, for example, lack of legal resource, the magistrate (in the modern day, a police officer) can be called upon to help as a last resort, and reluctantly so. This is what is meant by self-help policing.[125]

Chinese Theory of Self-Help

Self-help policing is also called expectation policing. It is so called because at the end of the day, what everyone wants is to solve his or her problem by having his or her expectations met. The theory behind self-help policing is 'State Police Power as a Social Resource Theory' (SRT).

SRT is a people's theory of policing. It looks at disputes, crime and problem solving of all kinds from the people's, not the state's perspective. The central thesis of SRT is that people are given to self-help problem solving, naturally and instinctively, since birth. When people fall, they instinctively try to break their fall. Collaterally, the person who is closest to a problem is the best person to solve the problem. We are the first and only one who know our own problem best. When we fall, we and only we know where it hurts and how to alleviate the pain.

SRT addresses three main questions: What is the role and function of the police? What is the relationship of the police with the people? Why do people call the police? SRT (re)conceptualises crime and police from the perspective of the people, not that of the state. From the people's perspective crimes are personal problems. Problems are unmet expectations resulting from resource deficiencies. Police are a social resource made available to the people by the state in solving their own problems. In terms of foundation,

SRT is a theory of the people, a theory of democratic governance, a theory of empowerment and a theory of self-help.

SRT Theoretical Statements

Proposition #1: Police are born with and tend to problems.[126] People confront problems routinely; some of them are called crime.

Proposition #2: To the people, problems of everyday life are unmet expectations, resulting from the existence of expectations and a lack of resources to fulfill them.

Proposition #3: All problems can be solved by redefining expect actions and/or acquiring necessary resources.

Proposition #4: When people have unmet expectations, they will take affirmative action to solve problems; this is called self-help.

Proposition #5: People experience crime as a personal problem not as a legal violation.

Proposition #6: People call the police because they do not have (or unwilling to spare) the necessary resources to deal with their problems, crime and non-crime.

Proposition #7: People call the police because they are resources of legitimacy and coercion.

Proposition #8: Police power is a kind of emergency (social) resources made available to the people to solve their problems.

Proposition # 9: The more the resources at the disposal of the people, the less the problems the people will be confronted with.

Proposition#10: The more the resources at the disposal of the people, the less they have to call on the police when the problem (crime) happened.

Proposition #11: The more (adequate and appropriate) the resources at the disposal of the police, the more effective they are in solving people's problem.

Proposition #12: The less (adequate and appropriate) the resources at the disposal of the police, the more likely they will resort to illegal or extra-legal means in solving people's problem.

Proposition #13: The person who is closest (impact, information, knowledge) to a problem is and should be the person to solve the problem.

Definitions

'Police' is defined as follows: 'Police is a depository and coordinator of social resources. Police is an all-purpose emergency problem solver who is authorised to use "legitimacy" and "coercive" resources to solve people's problems in a domestic situation and during peaceful time'.

'Expectation' is defined as 'human wants and needs, materially, mentally or psychologically'.

'Problem' is defined as 'Unrealised expectation(s) of wants or needs due to resource deprivation'.

'Resource' is defined as 'things of all kinds, including power, time, materials, skills, culture, ideas, and knowledge that can satisfy ones expectations of want and needs'.

'Legitimacy' is defined as 'that which is endorsed, supported and promoted by duly constituted political authority, which illicit intuitive respect and demand habitual obedience'.

'Self-help' is defined as 'action taken by individual or groups to solve a problem, that is, meeting expectations with resources'.

Radical Theory of Policing

SRT starts with a basic observation that in a state run by the people we must understand how the people conceive of the nature of crime (as expectations) and role of the police (as a resource).[127]

From the perspective of the state, crime is a legal violation. From the perspective of the people, crime is a set of life experience, and a multifaceted personal problem.

From the perspective of the state, police power is a political resource to secure control, maintain order[128] and command obedience.[129] It is defined coercively, structured legally, organised bureaucratically and imposed unilaterally.

From the people's perspective, police power is a social resource made available by the state and drawn upon by the citizens to handle personal emergencies or crisis situations. More significantly, in the eyes of the people, police power is not reconstructed in political image, structured by law, organised with reference to police needs[130] but dictated by the people and negotiated to fit the personal circumstances and situational needs the problem calls to mind.

Policing from People's Perspective

Looking at the police's role and functions from the public's perspective, they can be justified on a number of grounds.

First, SRT calls for looking at life course problems from the people's perspective, as a matter of birthright and process of maturation. In Kant's words, 'Enlightenment is man's emergence from his self-imposed immaturity. Immaturity is the inability to use one's understanding without guidance from another'.[131]

This means empowering the people to meet their own personal needs, supplying them with the necessary resources, on demand and as required.

Second, SRT corrects the lopsided relationship between police and the people by returning the people to the centre stage, and putting them in control, thus achieving the communalisation, socialisation or personalisation of crime.

Third, SRT marks a shift of focus from a state-centred community-oriented policing to a people-driven policing.[132]

Fourth, SRT gives 'social' meaning and lends 'emotional' content to police–people activities, which is what policing is all about, that is, dealing with personal issues, human problems and relationship difficulties of one form or another.[133] In so doing, it socialises and humanises the police–people interface, making police business a truly peoples' business.[134]

Fifth, SRT liberates the police from the sterile confinement of the law and stifling restrains of the bureaucracy. It gets away from the one-size-fits-all 'McDonaldisation' of police (burger, cheese burger and double cheeseburger are still a burger) strategy and practices.

Sixth, SRT recognises that police work should be as diverse and complex as people's problems, that is, policing changes with time, place, people, context, circumstances and situations.

Seventh, and most importantly, SRT allows the people to be heard. For all too long, the public is an object of policing when in fact they are, and should be, the subject of policing. Instead of being policed, police and people are engaging in problem solving.

The legal anthropologist has contributed much, through the study of 'trouble cases', to our understanding of how indigenous people of other cultures settle disputes and deal with problems. Such research informs that the problems of everyday life look and feel very differently from the inside rather than the outside point of view.[135]

SRT as proposed—people solving their own problem with state resource—is consistent with the civil society movement,[136] privatisation of police trend[137] and alternative dispute resolution initiative.[138] The theory, if ever fully realised, allows people to be masters of their own affair. They have the right to dictate and control the extent and manner of the state's involvement in their life choices.

Legalisation of People's Problems

When police powers are exercised by state officials to enforce the law, for example, criminal arrest, or invoked by the public to deal with a problem, for example, call for police assistance, it automatically transforms the nature and handling of the 'situation'[139] on hand.

When the public calls the police, it gives the state the opportunity to transform a private/personal matter into a public/legal one. This amounts to the bureaucratisation/legalisation/professionalisation of a private or personal problem, transforming/converting it into one that is recognisable by the police and actionable in court.

In being captured by law, a personal problem loses much of its attributes and meaning derived from the social milieu, communal setting, interpersonal relationship, historical context and situational dynamics of which it is an integral part, or what the 'situation' *in situ* is all about.

The process and effect of transformation of a private affair into a public matter on the event and people involved is best described by Manning:

> As the message moves the system, it loses the implicit, connotative meanings associated with the polysemic nature of what was reported to have happened and becomes more denotative, represented in police classification, and is treated by the organization more as something to sort out and deal with and less as a reflection of a complex, emotional, sensate event. I shall refer to this as bureaucratization of social and personal problems. (Manning 1983:176)

Legalisation of a problem also shifted the ownership and arena of dealing with the problem from the public to the state.

Discussion

In scientific theory, building conceptual building blocks that are existentially authentic and beyond dispute are necessary. The concept for theory of self-help is personal and individual expectation. People all over have expectations and unmet expectations give rise to problems requiring resource supplement.

What the SRT describes, at a theoretical level, is that people are born with expectations of all kinds, for example, Maslow hierarchy of needs, from security needs to actualisation needs.[140] Expectation is the motivator and driver for personal action. People react to expectations in different and unique ways. This is 'self-help' in action. When we are hungry, we seek food. When we are exposed to cold, we seek shelter. Each life encounter and personal experience, reducible to stimulus, generates multiple unmet expectations. Each unmet expectation results in untold number of self-help action to fulfill. Expectations dissipate when met by appropriate and adequate resources. Since a problem is constituted of multiple expectations denied, no one person has all the appropriate or adequate resource to meet with all the expectations.

Self-help entails gathering of resources. Self-help resource gathering process moves in three directions for different reasons.

First, it moves from the most impacted to the least—from victims, to family to society. Impact gives rise to self-help. People are differentially motivated, depending on impact factor, more or less.

Second, it moves from the most intimate to the least intimate—family, clan, community and strangers. Intimacy predicts impact, and with it motivation to act. Intimacy is itself a valuable resource.

Third, it moves from one with most, and most appropriate resource to the least—from expert to novice.

The most versatile and powerful resources, in ascending order, are information, knowledge and wisdom. A wise person as a resourceful person can define problems through reflection and understanding. To the wise, all problem as expectations denied is a figment of imagination.[141] On the other extreme, the person who lacks information or knowledge can also avoid problem through ignorance (ignorance is bliss thesis).

Finally, a person can remove expectation at its source, that is, cognition, by suicide. Suicide is ultimate self-help.

SRT is a scientific theory of policing. It postulates that, when people are confronted with crime, they will conduct self-help policing. The first step is an expectation versus resource audit. After the audit, people will seek resources, wherever they can be found, to reduce expectation deficits, starting with the closet to the furthest, for example, putting hands over a wound to stop bleeding, calling family for emotional support and summoning police for legal remedy.

Application

In the early years of Hong Kong, that is, before 1900, the expectations of the Chinese, indigenous and migrants, were many, and resources were few. They had to rely on self-help or resourcefulness in tending to their expectations and needs. This was so for a number of reasons.

First, the Chinese (locals—residents [Hong Kong—Chinese]; transient workers [Chinese—Hong Kong]; economic migrants [Chinese—Chinese]) lived in a different—social, cultural, economic, geographic—world than the British. For analysis purposes, expectations are real in consequences, however derived. The Chinese had different expectations in life and about life than the British. The Chinese also differed among themselves, depending on where they came from, what they did and with whom they were associated. These are commonly called cultural differences, but they might have been due to any number of causes and conditions, such as ethnic rivalry or economic competitions, that had little to do with culture. The differences of Chinese within Chinese and British were real, and did not go unnoticed in overseas Chinese community and scholarship: 'Rather, it is to foreground the fact that, in the insistent invocation of a Chinese tradition—and with it Chinese readers with Chinese habits, sensibilities, perspectives, points of views, and so forth—seldom, if ever, has the question been asked; what exactly is meant by Chinese?'[142] The above hints at the fact that Chinese were not all alike in their sense and sensitivity, perspective and points of view. Of necessity, their expectations of matters are different in kind and degree. This creates expectation problems that cannot be easily solved, adequately by self or family.

For example, in real life, a migrant working in Victoria and away from home in Stanley, without taking care of his parent violated a number of self-imposed expectations, requiring corrective action, of which four comes to mind: (1) A disrespectful son is a son without filial piety (不孝). This brought disrepute to the family name and loss of 'face' for the father.[143] (2) A son who was without filial piety was a disloyal person (不忠). A disloyal person was an unreliable and untrustworthy person at home or in society. (3) A son without filial piety was a person who also failed to reciprocate (報答) (or reciprocity) what the parents had done; a failure of foundational ethical obligation in China. (4) A son without filial piety was not a virtuous person. This shows that there was either a failure in discipline or a lapse of leadership. In both cases, it reflected poorly on the parents' own character and conduct. In common terms, the migrant was guilt ridden.

In most instances, whatever the source, such expectations, when denied, could not be easily resolved, internally within Chinese diaspora and externally under colonial rule. The impacted person thus had to find self-help personally or by and through other sources. If he was an overseas Chinese, he needed to form or find mutual aid organisations, such as clan association, and failing that, seek help from outlawed brotherhood, such as mutual aid organisations[144] or Triad society[145] or Tong.[146]

Second, an examination of police history in Hong Kong observed that the colonial HKP failed to provide police coverage for the Chinese, leaving them to their own accord, due to policy (indirect rule), economic (funding) and capacity (language) reasons. The aggrieved Chinese were then required to resort to self-help measures.

Coming to self-help, in urban Hong Kong, the Chinese could depend on the District Watch Force for protection or the Tung Wah Hospital in providing welfare support. In rural Kowloon (1871), they had to rely on family discipline and communal mediation:

> Two of my informants recall that stealing crops in their villages was a matter for the village elders. If the offender were an outsider the elders would take him back to his own village and expect his own leaders to deal with him. Failing an agreeable settlement the offender would be taken to the nearest police station. For a long time, it seems, the realities of local power lay with the elders .... The same degree of local autonomy existed above the village level where the village organisation was augmented by small regional groupings which were usually based on a temple.[147]

This rendition of colonial policing in Hong Kong in its formative years fails to note the real reason for self-help policing under colonial rule. The real reason for the Chinese to seek self-help was because their expectations (*guanxi* and harmony) were not met with the right kind of resources made available by the HKP (law and gun). Specifically, the British philosophy and style of policing did not address the needs and expectations of the Chinese, who were not interested in rule of law or independent judiciary or blind justice.

The strength of resentment against British policing style is best illustrated by Chinese prostitutes refusing to expose their body to European doctors for health-related inspections in 1878:

> Chinese prostitutes catering for Chinese clients objected vigorously to being examined internally by a European doctor, and would prefer to suffer any punishment rather than submit to such an indignity .... The Registrar General has the legal power to compel other prostitutes to be medically examined, but if they became deceased they normally made their own arrangements with Chinese doctors or herbalists or were sent back to Canton by the brothel keepers.[148]

The Chinese wanted their grievances resolved in Chinese ways; with restorative justice as the goal, QLF as the adjudicating principles, and the head of family and clan as mediator. Chinese dispute–crime resolution needed an apology by the offender, compensation for the victims and repair of social relationship. Closer to home, the Hong Kong Triad dispute resolution process, notwithstanding its illegality, best exemplified and approximated what victim-driven problem-solving process would look like.[149] In observing the Triad society dispensing justice, one would notice the following: it was fast, resolute, retributive, restorative and compensatory. For example, a violating gang member was expected to kneel before 'Guandi' and fess up their wrongdoing, in a personally remorseful and publicly humiliating way. The offender was also required to apologise to the injured, begging for their forgiveness, and promise not to do it again. Then, and only then, would the offender be re-integrated within the gang.

In colonial Hong Kong and currently, when Hong Kong people have a (crime) problem with various expectations denied, they will turn to self-help, first from the family, and then clan and communal groups. Failing that, they still would not call the HKP because the resource the HKP possesses—legitimacy, gun and law—is not effective in meeting their expectations, in restoring justice and repairing relationship. The Chinese under British colonial rule preferred to consult the Triad than go to the HKP to solve their problem because the Triad, unhindered by law and unencumbered by bureaucracy, was better able to meet the expectations of the Chinese,[150] who yearned for brotherhood and the honorable way of doing things.[151] The Triad society in China, with Hung Mun, Tien Tei Wei or San Hwo Hui in the lead, was a patriotic and mutual aid organisation in the twentieth century, committed to overturning the Qing (anti-foreign) and coming to the assistance of their brothers in arms (mutual).[152] In time, it mutated, transformed and to some degree degenerated into hired guns, offering protection for a fee and illegitimate services as a business.[153]

The Triads were appealing to the Hong Kong—Chinese under colonial rule because they espoused traditional Chinese moral principles, for example, reject alien rule and uphold integrity, and embrace contemporary customary practices, for example, respect to parents and loyalty to friends, under colonial rule. The Charter—Oath of Heaven and Earth Society included[154]

1. After having entered the Hung gates I must treat the parents and relatives of my sworn brothers as my own kin. I shall suffer death by five thunderbolts if I do not keep this oath.
2. I shall assist my sworn brothers to bury their parents and brothers by offering financial or physical assistance. I shall be killed by five thunderbolts if I pretend to have no knowledge of their troubles.
3. When Hung brothers visit my house, I shall provide them with boarding and lodging. I shall be killed by myriads of knives if I treat them as strangers.
4. I will always acknowledge my Hung brothers when they identify themselves. If I ignore them I will be killed by myriads of swords.
5. I shall not disclose the secrets of the Hung family, not even to my parents, brothers, or wife. I shall never disclose the secrets for money. I will be killed by myriads of swords if I do so.
6. I shall never betray my sworn brothers. If, through a misunderstanding, I have caused the arrest of one of my brothers I must release him immediately. If I break this oath I will be killed by five thunderbolts.
7. I will offer financial assistance to sworn brothers who are in trouble in order that they may pay their passage fee, etc. If I break this oath I will be killed by five thunderbolts.
8. I must never cause harm or bring trouble to my sworn brothers or Incense Master. If I do so I will be killed by myriads of swords.
9. I must never commit any indecent assaults on the wives, sisters, or daughters, of my sworn brothers. I shall be killed by five thunderbolts if I break this oath.

10. I shall never embezzle cash or property from my sworn brothers. If I break this oath I will be killed by myriads of swords.
11. I will take good care of the wives or children of sworn brothers entrusted to my keeping. If I do not I will be killed by five thunderbolts.
12. If I have supplied false particulars about myself for the purpose of joining the Hung family I shall be killed by five thunderbolts.
13. If I should change my mind and deny my membership of the Hung family I will be killed by myriads of swords.
14. If I rob a sworn brother or assist an outsider to do so I will be killed by five thunderbolts.
15. If I should take advantage of a sworn brother or force unfair business deals upon him I will be killed by myriads of swords.
16. If I knowingly convert my sworn brother's cash or property to my own use I shall be killed by five thunderbolts.
17. If I have wrongly taken a sworn brother's cash or property during a robbery I must return them to him. If I do not I will be killed by five thunderbolts.
18. If I am arrested after committing an offence I must accept my punishment and not try to place blame on my sworn brothers. If I do so I will be killed by five thunderbolts.
19. If any of my sworn brothers are killed, or arrested, or have departed to some other place, I will assist their wives and children who may be in need. If I pretend to have no knowledge of their difficulties I will be killed by five thunderbolts.
20. When any of my sworn brothers have been assaulted or blamed by others, I must come forward and help him if he is in the right or advise him to desist if he is wrong. If he has been repeatedly insulted by others I shall inform our other brothers and arrange to help him physically or financially. If I do not keep this oath I will be killed by five thunderbolts.
21. If it comes to my knowledge that the Government is seeking any of my sworn brothers who has come from other provinces or from overseas, I shall immediately inform him in order that he may make his escape. If I break this oath I will be killed by five thunderbolts.
22. I must not conspire with outsiders to cheat my sworn brothers at gambling. If I do so I will be killed by myriads of swords.
23. I shall not cause discord among my sworn brothers by spreading false reports about any of them. If I do so I will be killed by myriads of swords.
24. I shall not appoint myself as Incense Master without authority. After entering the Hung gates for three years the loyal and faithful ones may be promoted by the Incense Master with the support of his sworn brothers. I shall be killed by five thunderbolts if I make any unauthorised promotions myself.

25. If my natural brothers are involved in a dispute or lawsuit with my sworn brothers I must not help either party against the other but must attempt to have the matter settled amicably. If I break this oath I will be killed by five thunderbolts.
26. After entering the Hung gates I must forget any previous grudges I may have borne against my sworn brothers. If I do not do so I will be killed by five thunderbolts.
27. I must not trespass upon the territory occupied by my sworn brothers. I shall be killed by five thunderbolts if I pretend to have no knowledge of my brothers' rights in such matters.
28. I must not covet or seek to share any property or cash obtained by my sworn brothers. If I have such ideas I will be killed.
29. I must not disclose any address where my sworn brothers keep their wealth nor must I conspire to make wrong use of such knowledge. If I do so I will be killed by myriads of swords.
30. I must not give support to outsiders if so doing is against the interests of any of my sworn brothers. If I do not keep this oath I will be killed by myriads of swords.
31. I must not take advantage of the Hung brotherhood in order to oppress or take violent or unreasonable advantage of others. I must be content and honest. If I break this oath I will be killed by five thunderbolts.
32. I shall be killed by five thunderbolts if I behave indecently towards small children of my sworn brothers' families.
33. If any of my sworn brothers have committed a big offence I must not inform upon them to the Government for the purposes of obtaining a reward. I shall be killed by five thunderbolts if I break this oath.
34. I must not take to myself the wives and concubines of my sworn brothers nor commit adultery with them. If I do so I will be killed by myriads of swords.
35. I must never reveal Hung secrets or signs when speaking to outsiders. If I do so I will be killed by myriads of swords.
36. After entering the Hung gates I shall be loyal and faithful and shall endeavour to overthrow Ch'ing and restore Ming by co-ordinating my efforts with those of my sworn brethren even though my brethren and I may not be in the same professions. Our common aim is to avenge our Five Ancestors'.[155]

In short, the Triads offered unavailable cultural goods for a colonised people and inaccessible legal services for illegal immigrants.

Theoretically speaking, in the first situation, when legal supply does not meet natural cultural demands, there is a black market for desired goods, for example, illegal gambling, prostitutes, drugs, debt collection and revenge. This falls under 'illegal market' study in the field of economic sociology, which observed that when market supply does not meet natural demand for goods, a private sector black market emerges and public sector rent-seeking activities in the form of corruption appears, creating market distortions affecting valuation and distribution.[156] The disjuncture between goals and means is otherwise studied by criminologists, such as Merton's anomie–strain theory.[157] Here Merton postulated that when culturally promoted goals (American dream) cannot be achieved with institutional approved means (hard work), anomie and strains set in, leading people to adjust in five ways: conformity (+goal, −mean), innovation (+goal, −mean), ritualism (−goal, +mean), retreatism (−goal, −mean) and rebellion (new goal, new means). To Merton, when a person buys into strong cultural goals but with little respect for institutional means, innovation or deviance results. This theory was applied in 1934 to explain outburst of crimes in America after the Great Depression of 1932. But it can be equally explored to explain colonial Hong Kong when sex, gambling and drugs (cultural goods), which were not otherwise deemed illegal in Chinese society, were prohibited by colonial laws (institutional means). In Merton's articulation, there was a disjuncture between culturally desired goals and institutional normative means, resulting in anomie and causing strain. This new rendition of Merton strain theory can now be reconfigured as 'colonial criminology theory', which postulates that when cultural desired goods are not met with colonial normative means, deviance would occur, for example, indentured maids and foster children.

When the supply of legal services, such as legal protection and police services, was not meeting the legitimate needs of illegal immigrants, people sought illegitimate supply.

The above theoretical treatment is best demonstrated with a study of corruption in Hong Kong in the 1960s. Before the ICAC came into being in the 1970s, the Triad offered up their services for the people, from illegal enterprises, for example, gambling, to protective services, for example, blackmailers.

In those days, triads lived with the people. The public found it more convenient and effective to befriend Triad members, and seek the help of Triad in settling disputes and offering protection, rather than seeking the HKP. The triad was doing no more, no less than what another family or community member would do for them; for these services, they would exact a fee, and at times extort payment. Still it was better to engage the triad than the HKP who were as demanding, coercive, costly, but less effective.

Yuen Gor, a lifelong Hong Kong resident, was born in 1950. He grew up in Yaumati. This is how he remembered the community's relationship with police and triads in the 1950s:

> Bullying from the police was inevitable, but Yuen Gor never yielded to the triad elements who extorted money from the stall. The triad gangs in Yau Ma Tei ran illegal business such as loan sharking, drug trafficking, territorial fights, brothels and gambling parlours. Yuen Gor believed that the triad gangs run profitable business. Sometimes, the residents might even ask the triad elements to settle their disputes. It was common that the triad elements would make troubles on a pretext, evade bill or extort money. Having lived in Yau Ma Tei since childhood, Yuen Gor grew up with many of the triad elements and became their good friend. The Yeung family's stalls were thus free from triad disturbance and exempted from regular payment of protection fees. But, Yuen Gor was glad to offer free meals to his triad friends and occasionally gave them a small payment. Sometimes, when drug addicts visited Lai Heung Yuen for a free meal, Yuen Gor would entertain them, although he emphasized that it shall be a one-off offer only.[158]

IV: Colonial Policing as Policing Migrant[159]

Hong Kong and China share a long and porous border. Through the years, people and materials have crossed the border routinely for economic, social, political and cultural reasons. The policing of Chinese migrants has been a major concern of the HKP, in the past as well as the present.

Policing is subject-sensitive, for example, policing the intimate[160] is not the same as policing strangers, which is different kind of policing. Until very recently, Hong Kong people were rootless and restless people.[161] There were very few Hong Kong permanent residents, still less with a homegrown identity.[162] Migrants, Chinese and Europeans were quick to come to Hong Kong for fame and fortune, leaving just as quickly to seek opportunities and avoid trouble. They had no intention of remaining; everyone harboured a desire to return home, to live, to retire, or just to die (落叶归根, leaves fall to roots).

Hong Kong is a prototypical transient community. For example, in the 1840s, most migrants to Hong Kong were young and single. There were few families. Males outnumbered females by 6–7 to 1. In 1841, thousands of labourers and craftsmen came to the colony to serve the British colonists. In 1948, on the eve of Communist takeover, two million people left China for Hong Kong.[163] Since then, Hong Kong has adopted an open-door policy to refugees from other places, such as China and Vietnam. Many have entered illegally, and more than a few stay beyond their period and have to be deported. This means that Hong Kong has a difficult time in setting boundary and imposing control on who is coming and going.

In the early days of the colony, the Chinese from Kowloon would make a trip across the harbour with ease. Many of them who were dutiful and diligent workers in the day, turned ruthless and violent ruffians at night. It also means that except for the European elites there were few cohesive communities. In time, Hong Kong earned the right to be called 'Borrowed Time, Borrowed Place'.[164]

Social structure, organisation and relationship affected policing, purpose, method and style. Loosely knitted groups have little community spirit,[165] incentives and capacity to police itself. [166] Intimate groups are cohesive, with common values, mutual interest and collective capacity to self-regulate. In policing an alien or migrant society, that is the Chinese, Hong Kong policing was more about maintaining security, averting (natural) crisis, keeping order and controlling people, and less so about enforcing law, promoting justice and delivering service. Self-help was the norm. Private security was the rule.[167] In-group sanctions,[168] informal social ordering[169] and extra-legal strong-arm control[170] was accepted as a way of life.

V: Colonial Policing as Relationship (Guanxi) Policing[171]

Policing of migrants and dealing with cross-border crimes raises a whole host of issues, from appropriateness of norm applied to effectiveness of means deployed. The former recalls the juvenile versus adult justice debate. The later implicates terrorist versus criminal controversy. In theoretical terms, both the treatment of juvenile and terrorist raise issues with policing of relationship, from strangers to intimates, best played out in rural (family—intimate policing) vs. urban (bureaucracy—stranger policing) policing context and setting. Intimate policing calls for socialization and persuasion. Stranger policing requires rewards and punishment, failing that excommunication (intimates—juveniles) and extermination (strangers—terrorists).

Juvenile versus Adult Debate

Juveniles have long been treated differently than adults in common law in England and at family court in Chicago, because of their mental capacity. In common law, children under seven cannot be charged with a crime because they are considered to be mentally incompetent. In 1899, in Chicago, a family court was introduced to protect the best interests of the child because they are considered to be less developed, cognitively, emotionally and behaviourally. The rationality of both common law and Chicago family practice is that a juvenile does not belong in adult courts, which presupposes a logical mind and mature personality. If the same reasoning was applied to Chinese migrants, it is not difficult to see that Chinese migrants had little understanding of British culture and identification with British rule. To that extent, and from the perspective of the British colonialists, Chinese behaved very much like juveniles. Measured against British civilisation, the Chinese were developmentally retarded, an atavistic throwback of a kind. They lived in a world of their own. As a result, they were treated differently, if paternalistically. They were to be lectured at and spoken down to, not treated as equals. Much like the juvenile law in Chicago or extra-territoriality in Shanghai, British law had little application to the foreign-born. They have a tenuous relationship with the British. To do otherwise would not be fair or effective.

Terrorist versus Criminal Controversy

The terrorist versus criminal controversy centres on the entitlement and effectiveness of state sanctions on terrorist and community control of criminals. President Bush drew a clear distinction between terrorist, an enemy of the state, and criminal, a deviance of community norm. Enemy has no rights, offenders do. Thus, it is acceptable, indeed necessary, to torture ('enhanced interrogation') terrorists for information and not put pressure on criminals to confess.

Half way around the world, Mao anticipated Bush by 44 years.[172] On 18 June 1957, Mao delivered 'On the Correct Handling of Contradictions among the People' before the Supreme State Conference. In the speech, he made the case that contradictions (conflicts) between people should be treated differently than contradictions between people and the enemies. Contradictions among the people should be treated to persuasion, education by the mass (criticism, self-criticism) and, if need be, remedial sanctions (criminal law). Contradictions between the people and the enemy should be treated with coercive means, including death (elimination) if need be:

> Since they are different in nature, the contradictions between ourselves and the enemy and the contradictions among the people must be resolved by different methods. .... Our state is a people's democratic dictatorship led by the working class ...What is this dictatorship for? Its first function is internal, namely, to suppress the reactionary classes and elements and those exploiters who resist the socialist revolution...Dictatorship does not apply within the ranks of the people. The people cannot exercise dictatorship over themselves, nor must one section of the people oppress another. ...The people's democratic dictatorship uses two methods. Towards the enemy, it uses the method of dictatorship, that is, for as long a period of time as is necessary it does not permit them to take part in political activity and compels them to obey the law of the People's Government, to engage in labour and, through such labour, be transformed into new men. Towards the people; on the contrary, it uses the method of democracy and not of compulsion, that is, it must necessarily let them take part in political activity and does not compel them to do this or that but uses the method of democracy to educate and persuade. Such education is self-education for the people, and its basic method is criticism and self-criticism.[173]

Driven by 'moral panic', the imagery of Chinese migrants as 'terrorists' was fair game. They were very much beyond the cultural boundary of society and effective range of existing law and process. They were both inaccessible by moral reasoning and not amenable to rational law. Laws were for the civilised, not the barbarians. As in the case of an animal in a different universe, when moral discourse and rational reasoning failed, violence would be the only common language of behavioural modification.

Policing Relationship: Strangers versus Intimates

The above discussion on debate (juvenile versus adult) and controversy (terrorists versus criminals) points to the need to develop a theory of policing based on the nature and strength of relationship between the police and the policed. Such a relationship moves from the more intimate (blood) to no relationship (stranger), with the supposition that if there is no relationship, there is no crime or control. Viewed this way, crime is the alternation of relationship expectations for personal gain.

To the Chinese, the starting premise is that policing (more appropriately, social control) is not about punishing offensive person or harmful conduct. It is about maintaining predictable relationships. Crime happens when relationships ruptures. The second premise is that without a relationship between the police and the policed, there are few ways to control, except by force. To investigate a crime is to presuppose a prior existing relationship between offender and victims, individual and society, with information freely available. Without a relationship between the police and the policed, there is little meaning to norms and sanction for the policed.

Thus far, in policing studies, there has been more interest in policing of strangers (urban policing, professional policing) and not policing of intimates (rural policing, community policing); thus the focus on coercion and not persuasion.

Relationship Policing: Rural versus Urban

Rural policing is the policing of relationship. In a rural (close, or close-knitted) community (submarine, Seal Team, PTU), there is little mobility and high solidarity. Everyone is related to everyone; everyone knows each other. Everyone depends on each other for materials and social and emotional support. The decisions and actions of each affect the other. Control is customary (moral), easy (by surveillance), effortless (social pressure), total (omnipresent), cheap (opinion) and democratic (everyone has a say). People's action is judged less (only) on the quality of the act, and more on the character of the person and nature of the relationship (in its totality).

The stranger, a tourist or a gang member, is judged by his actions. A stranger who acts as an offender would be discriminated against (insider vs. outsider). As a result outsider–strangers would be dealt with formally and harshly because outsider–strangers share nothing in common with the locals, and can only be punished according to the law, retributively and as a deterrent. (Strangers have no prior or after relationship with the rural area, and cannot be properly supervised.)

If we were to develop a 'criminology' of 'guaxi', we can start with the following testable principles applicable to social relationship policing:

1. Crime is a function of social relationship distance (intimacy) between people and society, from stranger to family. The more intimate the relationship, quantitatively and qualitatively, the lesser the crime (more supervision, guardianship, bonding).
2. Crime detection is a function of relationship distance (intimacy) between people and society. The more intimate the relationship, the more easier it is to detect a crime, as in time and resources.
3. Response to crime is a function of the relationship between people and society.
   a. The more intimate the relationship, the less formal the response.
   b. The more intimate the relationship, the more compensatory and less punitive the response.
   c. The more intimate the relationship, the more integrative and less retributive the remedial measures.
   d. The more intimate the relationship, the more future oriented and less past oriented the evaluation of harm.
   e. The more intimate the relationship, the more the focus on repairing of relationship than punishment of act.
   f. The more intimate the relationship, the more the focus on personality than act-based assignment of liability.
   g. The more intimate the relationship, the more the particularistic justice than rule-based justice.

VI: Conclusion

The single most important lesson offered by this book (Part I) is that the investigation into the HKP and policing in Hong Kong should be based on theory, informed by evidence, and anchored within Chinese history, culture and society.

Applying the above lesson, this study theorised that in practice, colonial policing in Hong Kong, as with policing generally, is not a one-size-fits-all proposition. It takes on different strategic goals and tactical means, organisational form and operational style, in different countries, at different times and with different tasks.[174]

In order to maximise its utilities, increase its efficiency or promote its effectiveness, colonial policing as an instrumentality of the state (colonial empire) must be able to adjust its goals and means to fit with local conditions. Specifically, as deployed, colonial policing, if it is to work, must be made dependent on the vision and mission, conviction and commitment, and capacity and resource of the coloniser, while tending to the idiosyncratic nature of an alien population, separated by distances of space and culture. For example, Cole made it clear that colonial policing changes the purpose of settlement (pacified vs. settlement) and area of control (rural vs. urban):

> A clear distinction eventually emerged between the development of policing in colonies that were annexed for purpose of settlement and the development of policing in the 'pacified' colonies annexed mainly for trade. Generally, civilian policing structures were pre-dominant in 'settlement' colonies of North America, Canada and Australia whilst para-military policing was common in 'pacified' colonies located mainly in Africa, Asia, Central and South America. In the latter, two-tier policing systems were operated whereby urban areas where European settlers, administrators and traders lived (usually designated 'colonies') were policed differently compared with rural areas where the bulk of 'natives' lived (usually designed 'protectorates').[175]

Beyond the purpose of the ruler and the character of the ruled, historical conditions and contemporary circumstances bearing upon law, order and security situations of the colony come into play. Generally, maintaining an orderly society calls for civilian policing, pacifying conflict-ridden states requires military rule and securing disturbance-prone communities needs para-military policing. For example, colonial policing of crime and disorder in Hong Kong (1841–1844) differs substantially from colonial policing of political unrests (civil disturbances) (1923–1924, 1954, 1967) or social protests (civil disobedience [the 1990s]) in Hong Kong.

Even under the rubric of colonial policing, different strategies and tactics are used to deal with different governance issues and control problems in a colony. In the 1950s, Hong Kong Communists sympathisers (political risks) were treated to secret surveillance policing and social activists (disorderly crowd) were exposed to public order management policing.

Colonial policing manifested itself in all of the above social control methods and styles. If colonial policing means different things in different places, at different times, with different people, under different circumstances, then the central meaning of colonial police can only be particularised in use and contextualised when discussed. The traditional understanding of colonial policing as imposed and coercive serves only to obfuscate the multifaceted nature of colonial policing.

Endnotes

1. See generally J. P. Sartre, *Existentialism Is a Humanism*. Tr. C. Macomber. (New Haven: Yale University Press, 2007).
2. D. Faure (ed.), *A Documentary History Hong Kong*. (Hong Kong: Hong Kong University Press, 1997), p. 12.
3. C. M. Christensen and M. Raynor, Why hard-nosed executives should care about management theory, *Harvard Business Review*, 81 (9): 66–74, 2003.
4. J. Z. Dai, On several problems in legal transplantation, *Journal of Politics and Law*, 2(3): 107–109, September 2009.
5. G. Bickley, *A Magistrate's Court in 19th Century Hong Kong: Court in Time* (Hong Kong: Proverse Hong Kong, 2005).
6. W. S. Law, *Collaborative Colonial Power: The Making of the Hong Kong Chinese* (Hong Kong: Hong Kong University Press, 2009).
7. Categorical Ethnic Identity—Half-Yearly Average (23/12/2013) (市民的身份認同感) People's Ethnic Identity, HKU, Public Opinion Program. http://hkupop.hku.hk/english/popexpress/ethnic/index.html
8. S. Veg, Hong Kong's enduring identity crisis, *The Atlantic*, 16 October 2013. http://www.theatlantic.com/china/archive/2013/10/hong-kongs-enduring-identity-crisis/280622/
9. The HKAM movement, started by Professor Chan Wan, called for more administrative autonomy for Hong Kong and less political integration with China. Hong Kong City-State Autonomy Movement (HKAM) (香港城邦自治運動). http://hkam2011.blogspot.com/
10. Hong Kong fears 'mainlandization', *The China Post*, Taiwan (ROC), 9 September 2011. Retrieved 30 October 2011.
11. See Chapter 9: 'Hong Kong Police Reform in 1950s', infra.
12. S. Georgina (ed.), *Globalising British Policing* (Farnham, Surrey, UK: Ashgate Publishing Limited, 2011).
13. 'Chinese society is to be envied by much of the so-called developed world, in that not only is much of the old traditional way of life, still visible in people's behavior but is also so deeply instilled from parent to child and it is difficult to see it totally disappearing' (p. xi). M. Topley and J. DeBernardi, *Cantonese Society in Hong Kong* (Hong Kong: Hong Kong University Press, 2000).
14. R. T. Sigler and D. J. King, Colonial policing and control of movements for independence, *Policing and Society: An International Journal of Research and Policy*, 3(1): 13–22, 1992.
15. W. F. Mayers and C. King, *The Treaty Ports of China and Japan: A Complete Guide to the Open Ports of Those Countries, Together with Peking, Yedo, Hongkong and Macao. Forming a Guide Book & Vade Mecum for Travellers, Merchants, and Residents in General* (London: Trübner and Co., 1867), pp. vi, 17.
16. Ibid., Note 5.

17. J. W. Norton-Kyshe, *History of the Laws and Courts of Hongkong, Vol. I* (London: Noronha and Company, 1898). (HKLCHK). http://www.archive.org/details/historylawsandc00nortgoog
18. Ibid., VII.
19. C. Munn, *Anglo-China: Chinese People and British Rule in* Hong Kong, *1841–1880* (Richmond, Surrey, UK: Curzon Press, 2001), Chapter One; K. C. Wong, *Policing in Hong Kong* (Farnham, Surrey, UK: Ashgate, 2012), Chapter One.
20. E. Marcks, English law in early Hong Kong: Colonial law as a means for control and liberation, *Texas International Law Journal,* 35: 265, 2000.
21. D. Killingray and D. Omissi (eds.), *Guardians of Empire: The Armed Forces of the Colonial Powers c. 1700–1964* (Manchester: Manchester University Press, 1999).
22. G. B. Endacott, *Government and People in Hong Kong* (Hong Kong: Hong Kong University Press, 1964), note 3, p. 3, p. 4.
23. Ibid., p. 3.
24. Davis to Stanley, 27 February 1844. CO 129/6, p. 131.
25. D. E. Evans, Chinatown in Hong Kong: The beginnings of Tai Ping Shan, *Journal of the Royal Asiatic Society Hong Kong Branch*, 10: 70–77, 1970. ('But for a very long time, there was indeed an area thought of by the Europeans as a part of the city into which they would not normally go. This area has, right from its inception, been known as "Tai Ping Shan" or Mountain of Peace, after the Chinese name for the mountain the Europeans called Victoria Peak'.)
26. C. Munn, *Anglo-China: Chinese People and British Rule in Hong Kong, 1841–1880* (Richmond, Surrey, UK: Curzon Press, 2001), p. 1.
27. Ibid., p. 4.
28. *Friend of China*, 18.5.43 edition.
29. 'The police never intervened the distribution of free food and money. However, in the last two years of his office as chief director, an old lady stumbled accidentally when she was collecting rice. The police then stepped up their actions in maintaining the order on the occasion'. Memories of being Chief Executive of Yau Ma Tei Kaifong Welfare Advancement Association. 11/03/2011. http://www.hkmemory.hk/collections/oral_history/All_Items_OH/oha_50/records/index.html#p46053
30. Ng Kong. Chairman, Yaumatei Kai Fong Welfare Association. Male. DOB. 1919. 'The role of Yau Ma Tei Kaifong Welfare Advancement Association in the regulation of hawkers along Temple Street and Public Square Street'. (11/03/2011). Hong Kong Memory. http://www.hkmemory.hk/collections/oral_history/All_Items_OH/oha_50/records/index.html#p46056
31. R. J. Troyer, Chinese social organization, In: R. J. Troyer, J. P. Clark, and D. G. Rojek (eds.), *Social Control in the PRC* (New York: Praeger, 1989), pp. 26–24. For a more comprehensive treatment, see K. C. Hsiao, *Rural China: Imperial Control in the Nineteenth Century* (Seattle and London: University of Washington Press, 1960), pp. 261–370.
32. Dutton observed that the state sponsored and supported the exercise of control by natural and indigenous communal groups, for example, family, clan, as an extension of state power. Dutton, *Policing and Punishment in China* (Cambridge, New York, Melbourne: Cambridge University Press, 1992), Chapter Three. Kam C. Wong, building upon the conceptual scheme of Black's definition of law as 'governmental social control' (Black, 1976), has argued that sponsorship and support of government transformed informal/private social control into

formal/governmental ones. K. C. Wong, Black's theory on the behavior of law revisited II: A restatement of Black's concept of law, *International Journal of the Sociology of Law*, 26: 75–119, 1998.

33. See the organisation and functions of 'baojia' as a formal social control institution in imperial China. J. T. Wen, *Zhongguo baojia zhidu* (Chinese Baiojia System) (Taibei: Shangwu Yinshuguan, 1971). For the role played by community leaders, see C. Chung-li, *The Chinese Gentry: Studies on Their Role in Nineteenth Century Chinese Society* (Washington: University of Washington Press, 1955).
34. 'The ideology of the really successful Chinese merchant in the harsh competitiveness of Hong Kong went beyond self-help; there was also a strong sense of comradeship and responsibility to his fellow men. Mr Fung Ping-shan, himself an exemplar of this tradition, described it as lipin (laap-ban in Cantonese), which may be loosely translated as "establishing one's character". Mr Fung was a philanthropist, not only in Hong Kong, which he made his home, but also to his home village and county in China where he was born. The character pin in Mr Fung's term incorporates a hidden agenda which can be understood in the light of the Confucian classics: The Chinese gentleman subscribes to the principle that social harmony can be achieved only by putting one's character and then one's household in order, and putting them in order means behaving in propriety to one's social station'. D. Faure, *A Documentary History of Hong Kong Society* (Hong Kong: Hong Kong University Press, 1997), p. 17.
35. *Sources of Chinese Tradition*, p. 115.
36. The Great Learning, Chapter IX: 4, James Legge (trans.) *The Four Books* (Hong Kong: Culture Book, 1981), p. 23.
37. H. Befu, The political relation of the village to the State, *World Politics*, 19(4): 601–620, 1967.
38. For example, *baojia* was build upon the mutuality of economic and social dependency of families and clans. Dutton, 1992, pp. 84–85.
39. S. W. Williams, *The Middle Kingdom, Vol. 1* (New York: Scribner, 1883), p. 507. (In nineteenth century China, as was earlier, people did not want to come before the court.) The courts were observed to be oppressive, corrupt and unresponsive. Generally, the legal and judicial systems were deemed non-approachable by the people; to use a more modern jargon—not 'user friendly'. They were thus not utilised by the people to address their needs and concerns, for example, crime and disputes. J. Cohen, Chinese mediation on the eve of modernization, *California Law Review*, 54(2), 1222–1223, 1966. T. T. Chu, *Local Government Under the C'hing* (Cambridge: Harvard University Press, 1962). (Yamen was corrupted and inefficient. To the people, the officials were described as 'tigers or wolves' or 'rats under the altar'. 'Customary fees' and bribes were 'as numerous as the hairs on an ox'.) The centrally dispatched local officials (e.g., magistrates) were not only socially and emotionally removed from the people, but they were also physically isolated. D. C. Buxbaum, Some aspects of civil procedure and practice at trial level in Tansui and Hsinchu from 1789–1895, *Journal of Asian Studies*, 30(2):255–279, 1971.
40. H. C. Wang Liu, *The Traditional Chinese Clan Rules* (Locust Valley, New York: J.J. Augustin Incorporated Publisher, 1959). (Clan rules admonished against settling disputes through court.), p. 56.
41. Chapter II: 'General Analyses of the Clan Rules', In: H. C. Wang Liu, *The Traditional Chinese Clan Rules* (Locust Valley, New York: J.J. Augustin

Incorporated Publisher, 1959). (State recognised that the clan had quasi-autonomous authority to deal with minor cases and among its members.)

42. K. Wittfogel, *Oriental Despotism: A Comparative Study of Total Power* (New Haven: Yale University Press, 1957), p. 50.
43. J. W. Hayes and E. Sin, *Colonial Administration in British Hong Kong and Chinese Customary Law* (Hong Kong: Centre of Asian Studies, University of Hong Kong, 2001), pp. 66–67. https://archive.org/stream/colonialadminist00jame/colonialadminist00jame_djvu.txt
44. M. A. Allee, *Late Imperial China: Northern Taiwan in the Nineteenth Century* (Stanford, CA: Stanford University Press, 1994), p. 254.
45. *Sources of Chinese Tradition*, p. 115. ('Only when families are regulated are states regulated'. The family and to a lesser extent the clan were made the primary mechanism of social control. The family social control system was sanctioned by law.) T. Z. Qu, *Zhongguo falu yu zhongguo shehui* (Beijing: Zhonghua shuju, 1981), Chapter One: 'Family'. For an English translation, see T. T. Chu, *Law and Society in Traditional China* (Ecole Pratique des Hautes Etudes-Sorbonne, Sixieme Section: Sciences Economiques et Sociales, Le Monde d'outre-Mer, Passe et Present, Premiere Serie, Etudes IV, Mouton, Paris and The Hague, 1961). See also S. H. Wu, *Zhongguo Zhuantong Wenhua* (Traditional Chinese Legal Culture) (Beijing: Beijing Daixue Chubanshe, 1995), pp. 437–510. The theoretical foundation for using the family as the basic unit of social control is supplied by Sutherland's differential association theory and Hirschi's bonding theory. As to empirical evidence, it has been demonstrated that the family is an important social control site for imparting values and establishing bonds. See J. Q. Wilson and R. J. Herrnstein, *Crime & Human Nature* (New York: Touchstone Book, 1985.), Chapter 8: 'Families', pp. 213–244. (Constitutional factors and family factors are most important in explaining the behaviour of the most serious offenders.)
46. S. L. Feng, *Zhongguo Yufang Fanzui Fanglue* (Chinese Crime Prevention Strategy) (Beijing: Falu chubanshe, 1994), pp. 67–76.
47. *Sources of Chinese Tradition*, p. 115. At its heart, POP is a divide-and-conquer strategy. After an analysis is done on a 'crime problem' government agencies and community groups have to be engaged, either as guardian or as controller, to keep control of the multitude of factors contributing to problems. Collaboration, coordination and integration of community social control agents and forces is at the heart of a successful community crime control program. K. J. Peak and R. W. Glensor, *Community Policing and Problem Solving* (New Jersey: Prentice Hall, 1996), pp. 88–92.
48. J. F. Lee, *Zhongguo Fazhi Shi* (History of Chinese Legal System) (Liang-jin chubanshiwu gongsi, 1988), p. 61. POP, as a crime problem-solving strategy, calls for early intervention in the crime causation chain of event by dealing with the root causes of the crime problem through multiple means. Take the case of 'drug trafficking among juveniles in low-income housing, Tulsa, Oklahoma'. K. J. Peak and R. W. Glensor, *Community Policing and Problem Solving* (New Jersey: Prentice Hall, 1996), pp. 411–414. (Upon analysis of the problem, the officers took the following steps to remove the drug problem: by improving the youths' self-esteem, by teaching them values, by imparting with decision-making skills, by providing with positive role model (Boy Scout), by sponsoring youth activities, by teaching them job skills, by improving their manners, by teaching them driving.) The

Tulsa POP has components of modelling, education, character building, norm setting—all thought to be important by Confucius to control people.

49. The best way to control people is to use benevolence and punishment at the same time. The idea is captured by the phrase: 'Dezhu xingfu' (Primarily use benevolence as supplemented by punishment). See 'Kongyou de Falu Shixiang' (The legal thoughts of Kongyou), H. N. Liu and Y. F. Yang, *Zhongguo Gudai Falu-shi Zhishi* (Knowledge in Chinese legal history) (Helungjian renmin chubanshe, 1984), pp. 56–64. This is similar to the philosophy and approach adopted by the juvenile authorities during the 'child-savers' era when the juvenile justice system was socialised. T. Platt, *The Child Savers: The Invention of Delinquency* (Chicago: Chicago University Press, 1969), pp. 54–55. (Platt articulated a nine-points statement of the ideal reformatory scheme for juvenile delinquent. The fifth point being, 'resort to punishment where it became necessary means to reform'.) More significantly, the delinquent child should be viewed individually. His criminal acts should be assessed comprehensively and within the totality of circumstances he finds himself in. A comprehensive treatment program is then tailored to address the needs of the juvenile: personally and environmentally, emotionally, physically as well as spiritually, educationally as well as vocationally. Family, schools, social agencies, churches, courts and police are all involved in saving the troubled child.
50. Confucius said: 'From the emperor down to the common people, all without exception, must consider cultivation of the individual character as the root. If the root is disorder, it is impossible for the branches to be in order…' *Sources of Chinese Tradition*, p. 115.
51. Guanzhi observed: 'When people are rich, they will be contended at home and treasure their families. If they are contended at home and treasure their families, they will respect their superior and avoid crime. If they respect their superior and avoid crime they will be easy to rule'. See S. L. Feng, *Zhongguo Yufang Fanzui Fanglue* (Chinese Crime Prevention Strategy) (Beijing: Falu chubanshe, 1994), p. 72.
52. In this regard, the Chinese have taken a broad notion of control that includes the internalisation of norms (by the individual) (Durkheim 1933; Freud; Mill 1953; Piaget 1949), socialisation and disciplinary regime (by the family) (Sutherland 1949), setting up custom and accountability system (in the community) (Folkways 1906; Etzioni), removal of criminogenic conditions (by the administration) and defining the moral and social boundary (by the state) (Merton). See Notion of control, In: J. P. Gibbs (ed.), *Social Control* (Beverly Hills, CA: Sage, 1982), pp. 9–11. (Control can be used at any level—macro, micro or intermediate.) The Chinese approach comes close to Edward A. Ross' definition of social control—'the molding of the individual's feelings and desires to suit the needs of the group'—including supernatural, ceremonies, public opinion, morals, art, and education which formed the normative structure of a society. *Id.*, 13. In a very real sense, Chinese social control is of a totalitarian gem (Owen 1984; Wittogel 1957).
53. Confucians believe in the malleability of man. The Communists subscribed to the idea that 'All history is nothing but continuous transformation of human nature' and 'central function of government will be treated as the transformation of the social natures of the citizen'. See D. J. Munroe, *The Concept of Man in Contemporary China* (Ann Arbor, MI: University of Michigan Press,

1977), pp. 9–13. Reformation started by admission of guilt and assumption of responsibility. The PRC police preached: 'Leniency to those who confess; severity to those who resist'. When Bao Ruo-Wang, a political prisoner of Mao, met with his captor, he was told: 'In front of you are two paths: the one of confessing everything and obeying the government, which will lead you to a new life…' R. W. Bao and R. Chelminski, *Prisoner of Mao* (New York: Coward, McCann and Geoghegan, Inc., 1973), p. 73. See also D. Bayley, *Forces of Order: Police Behavior in Japan and the United States* (Berkeley, California: University of California Press, 1976). (Japanese believe that apology is the first step towards personal reform, repairing of relationship, and re-integration to communal life), p. 134, 140.

54. D. Bayley, *Forces of Order* (California: University of California Press, 1976). (Police promotes the mending of relations.) K. C. Wong, 'Legal Opinion' *China Trade Report* (December 1984) (In dispute resolution, Chinese are more concerned about a reasonable solution which would keep the parties in a workable relationship.)
55. Erving Goffman provided a useful framework for the analysis of this 'reformative–restorative–reintegration' justice model. Goffman observed that when expectations and norms were broken in the public place, the rule breaker and victim engages in a series of highly ritualistic 'remedial exchanges' for the purpose of reestablishing social relationship between the offender and victim. The process involves the offender providing an innocent excuse or sincere apology for the transgression to show personal remorse (reformation) in order to reestablish the broken relationship. E. Goffman, *Relations in Public* (New York: Harpers, 1971), Chapter 4, pp. 95–187.
56. A. von Hirsch, *Doing Justice* (New York: Hill and Wang, 1976) ('We take seriously Kant's view that a person should be punished because he deserves it'.), p. 6.
57. T. Honderich, *Punishment* (Middlesex, England: Penguin Books, 1984). (General prevention [citing Bentham] ought to be the end of punishment.)
58. N. Morris, *The Future of Imprisonment* (Chicago: University of Chicago Press, 1974) (Rehabilitative programs in prison must be expanded and improved.), p. xi.
59. 'The determined scholars and the man of virtue will not seek to live at the expense of injuring their virtue. They will even sacrifice their lives to preserve their virtue completely'. *The Analects*, Book XV, Chapter 7.
60. H. L. A. Hart, Positivism and the separation of law and moral, In: R. M. Dworkin (ed.), *The Philosophy of Law* (London: Oxford University Press, 1977), pp. 1–17.
61. Confucianisation of the law calls for the penal sanction of Confucius ethics. See Zhonghua faxi tedian tanyuan (The research into the origin of the characteristics of the Chinese legal system) In: J. F. Zhang (ed.), *Zhongguo falu shi lun* (Discourse on Chinese legal history) (Beijing: Falu chubanshe, 1983), pp. 11–25.
62. Devlins, *The Enforcement of Morals* (London: Oxford University Press, 1965). (Law should be used to enforce moral.); J. S. Mills, *On Liberty*, first published in 1859 (Chicago: Gateway Edition, 1955), p. 13 ('The only purpose for which power can be rightfully exercised … is to prevent harm to others…' Morality is not part of law's regiment.)
63. D. J. Munroe, *The Concept of Man in Contemporary China* (Ann Arbor, MI: University of Michigan Press, 1977), pp. 9–13.
64. T. Honderich, *Punishment* (Middlesex, England: Penguin Books, 1984). (General prevention [citing Bentham] ought to be the end of punishment.)

65. H. E. Pepinsky, The people v. the principle of legality in the People's Republic of China, *Journal of Criminal Justice*, 4: 51–60, 1973; Reliance on formal written law, and freedom and social control in the United States and the People's Republic of China, *British Journal of Sociology*, 26(3): 330–342, 1975. (U.S. relies upon formal legal control because of weak community structure occasioned by social, geographical, and occupational mobility. China uses informal communal social control because of relatively stable community structure.)
66. *Id.*
67. *United States* vs. *Salerno*, 481 U.S. 789, 107 S. Ct. 2095, 95 L. Ed. 2d 697 (1987). (The U.S. Supreme Court upheld the constitutionality of the Bail Reform Act of 1984, 18 U.S.C. Section 3142 (e): 'the judicial officer finds that no condition or combination of conditions will reasonably assure the appearance of the person as required and the safety of any other person and the community, he shall order the detention of the person prior to trial…' against the challenge that it impermissibly detained a criminal defendant based on anticipated future actions. William v. United States, 95 L. Ed. 1379, 1382 (1950). ('Imprisonment to protect society from predicted but unconsummated offenses is … unprecedented in this county…').
68. See K. C. Wong, Confucianization of Qing Law II, In: *The Selected Works of K. C. Wong*, 2004. Available at: http://works.bepress.com/kam_wong/33
69. J. Bentham, An introduction to the principles of morals and legislation (1789), In: *The Utilitarians* (New York: Anchor Books, 1973). (Mankind governed by utilitarian calculus.)
70. One of the major difficulties in comprehending, interpreting and applying *QLF*, as jurisprudential concepts is that 'qing' and 'li', like justice and fairness, means different things to different people. Furthermore, the weighting, prioritising and balancing of *QLF* in arriving at an optimal *QLF* decision is not something that everyone can agree upon. In fact, different mixes of *QLF* in various decisions can satisfy most people. Conversely, any imbalance of *QLF*, no matter how slight, might attract detractors and dissenters. It goes without saying that any change in findings or interpretation of facts might affect outcome.
71. What is deemed reasonable. *Pinyin Chinese English Dictionary* (Hong Kong: Commercial Press, 1990) (*PYCED*), p. 676R.
72. What is deemed reasonable. *PYCED*, p. 556L.
73. *PYCED*, p. 449L.
74. In the popular culture, *QLF* has often been routinely borrowed to justify one's action; oftentimes contrary to or deviation from what *QLF* truly entails or actually requires. In other circumstances, people have failed to grasp the true meaning of *QLF*. For example, *QLF* has been equated with human emotion—reasoning—law.
75. LF is inter-related in the following senses: (1) 'qing' versus 'li' versus 'fa' are not independent of each other, conceptually, theoretically and operationally. For example, conceptually 'qing' or 'renqing' (human nature) while born to human is shaped by law of nature (tian li) and conditioned by rules of culture (li). (2) The formulation and content of 'li' is less an arm chair contemplative product as it is a grounded intuitive, experiential and empirical exercise. In this regard, 'li' must cater to natural forces, social conditions, human nature, life circumstances and situational factors. (3) In terms of application, what is proper 'li' is

never a stand alone ethical-principle derivative (as with categorical imperative of Kant) but very much a factual ethical product (much like determination of negligence).

76. *QLF* is dynamic in many ways. (1) *QLF* are not static concepts. The content and contour, meaning and feelings of *QLF*, individually and collectively, changes with time, people, place and issues. (2) *QLF* interacts with each others dialectically and continuously in shaping content and defining practice. (3) Outcome of *QLF* is contingent on the totality of material context and all aspects of prevailing circumstances. (4) Process of *QLF* is as important as standard of *QLF* in shaping outcome. Change in process leads to change in outcome. (5) There is no one correct or best *QLF* disposition, but many acceptable *QLF* outcome.
77. A legitimate question is raised as to the content and viability, priority and mix, identification and subscription of *QLF* in modernised China, Westernised Hong Kong or globalised Taiwan. Like questions can, and should, be raised about how *QLF* fare within diverse population in Hong Kong, for example, Hong Kong belongers versus new immigrants, Western educated versus domestic breed, professionals versus blue collars.
78. A keyword search with '情理法' on yahoo.com turned up 23,600 items. A search on Google Scholar turned up 240 items.
79. 'Qing li fa in management' ('Guanli zhong de "qing li fa" '管理中的 "情理法') (Modern business management can improve with 'qing' 'li' 'fa'. Q is human sentiment and individual feelings. Li is reasoning. Fa is fundamental principles adopted by the company. http://admin.asiaec.com/wenzhang/11023763/20050513/130035.html; E. W. Yun, 'Qing li fa conflicts in maintenance disputes') (赡养纠纷的情理法冲突), *Law in Oriental Eyes*, 26 April 2007. (In China there is a venerable tradition: 'old people are to be supported' ('老有所养'). This is changing with time and with the breaking of old social and moral order. This sea change of culture, custom and attitude affects how old people should be taken care of. The law has to provide for the old people when they were not maintained by their child out of *qing* and *li* in the process. This raised a whole host of QLF issues the law has yet to satisfactorily resolve. For example, maintenance issues arose because one or more children do not want to assume responsibility due to lack of education, lack of ability, feeling being unfairly treated by parents over estate dispersal, unequal burden because only male has to pay maintenance, parents versus children discord.) http://www.dffy.com/fayanguancha/sh/200704/20070426194557.htm
80. Q. D. Wu, Revelation about traditional Chinese law which accommodates qing li fa ('Qing lif fa jian ron de zhonguo gudai falu ji qishi' 'Accommodating *QLF*, revelation of Chinese imperial law'. http://www.legalhistory.com.cn/ (A newly wed couple refused to move into a house they bought in Shanghai because their painter committed suicide in the house.)
81. Y. M. Huang, Hexie shehui yujing xia de 'zhifa ru shui' linian ji qi shijian (The concept and practice of 'implementation of law like water' within the language of harmonious society) *Jiangcha Fengyun* (检察风云) 2007-03-05 12:04:15 (The vision of a socialist legal system is to achieve harmony. This lofty goal is made unattainable by litigation explosion. People are taught to fight for their legal rights at all costs. They also resort to court to resolve interpersonal problems as a first instead of last resort.). http://www.cnjccn.com/article/2007/0305/article_329.html

82. Gu Yuan (顾元), Conflict and reconciliation between following and not following the law: Balancing qing and fa 'Xun fa yu beifa de maodun you tuoxie, zhuo yu fail zi ping'. http://www.legalhistory.com.cn/ 2007-2-16.
83. The Chinese character for 'law' ('fa') consists of two radicals. The radical to the left represents water and the radical to the right represents wash way. The function of law is thus to wash away bad things with water and return to normality, tranquil and peaceful. Thus, justice to Chinese is levelling of upheaval to a prior state of tranquility, much like the natural tendency of water. Water will return to flatness in due course. Y. M. Huang, Hexie shehui yujing xia de 'zhifa ru shui' linian ji qi shijian'. The concept and practice of 'implementation of law like water' within the language of harmonious society, *Jiangcha Fengyun* (检察风云) 2007-03-05 12:04:15 X. Zhongming, *Precedents, Stories and Judicial Culture of Ming Qing Dynasties* (Anli, Gushi yu Ming Qing shiqi de shifa wenhua) (Beijing: Falu Chubanshe, 2006), pp. 336–339.
84. Z. P. Liang, *Seeking Harmony in Natural Order* ('Xuzhao zhiran zhixu zhing de hexie') (Zhongguo zhengfa daxue chubanshe, 1997).
85. K. C. Wong, Confucianization of the law: A study of speech crime prosecution in China, *Murdoch University Electronic Journal of Law*, 11(3): September 2004. See text to notes 6, 7.
86. 'Ling yi jue yu' is also referred to as 'Chunqiu jue yu'. 'Chunqui' (*Autumn and Spring Annals*) of course is one of the five classics (wujing) authored by Confucius to teach his followers. 'Chunqiu jue yu' as with complete Confucianisation of law was achieved in the Han dynasty (206 BC–24 AD). The basic principles of 'Chunqiu jue yu' cases are decided upon with reference to the Confucius doctrine, starting with determining the 'heart' and 'motive' of people, not just intent, act or harm. Z. W. Ma, *Chinese Traditional Legal Culture* (Zhongguo gudai falu wenhua) (Jinan daixu chubanshje, 1998), pp. 136–142.
87. X. J. Liu (劉馨珺), A discussion on the use of 'qing li fa' in 'prison litigations' (Lun Songdai 'yusong' zhong 'qing li fa' de yuyong) ('論宋代「獄訟」中「情理法」的運用'). Professor Liu studied judicial opinions from Song dynasty to understand the principles and application of *QLF*, inductively.
88. Imperial Chinese officials closest to the people are likely to be the local magistrates. The magistrates were called 'fu wu guan' (father and mother official). Like parents they take care of all the needs, wants and problems for the people. In deciding cases, the magistrate do not only apply the law and decide right or wrong. Instead they try to resolve the disputes between the parties with an eye towards solving the problems once and for all. They are responsible for educating the people, making them better with higher moral standing, and also the society a better one in the process.
89. http://web.ncyu.edu.tw/~hsinchun/word/study/3.pdf, see text at note 22, at p. 5.
90. *Id.*, 6.
91. There is an issue as to whether 'ren qing' as a reasonable person standard is to be set empirically (custom) or prescriptively (Confucius). *Id.*, p. 7.
92. *Id.*, 9.
93. *Id.*, p. 12.
94. To make Chinese pliable to collective demands, Chinese people are trained to be thin skinned, that is, face matter, and always mindful of others opinion about oneself. This together with a high cultural expectation of self to be perfect, in

Confucius image, makes Chinese uncomfortable with alien culture. A. Bartz, Sense and sensitivity, *Psychology Today*, 5 July 2011, last reviewed on 20 May 2013. http://www.psychologytoday.com/articles/201107/sense-and-sensitivity

95. C. Leadbeater, *The Self-Policing Society* (Demos, 1996); B. Godfrey, Law, factory discipline and theft, *British Journal of Criminology*, 38(1): 59–71, 1999. The article examines textile factory organisation on workplace 'theft' or 'appropriation' in mid-Victoria (c. 1800–1850) in Yorkshire; particularly the deterrent effect of criminal law on such illegalities. The articles made clear that (1) The factory owners would take steps to deal with run-away misappropriation problems themselves without resorting to the police, for example, by building factory to centralised workforce in order to better facilitate the monitoring and disciplining of workers.
96. There are to be differences between schools of thoughts, for example, *Fa jia* or the legalists certainly believe that punishment is necessary to deter people. Y. P. Liu, *Origin of Chinese Law* (Hong Kong: Oxford University Press, 1998), pp. 173–201.
97. 'The Great Learning', see W. T. Chang, trans., *A Source Book of Chinese Philosophy*, p. 86, as translated and cited in footnote 11 to *Tu Weiming*, The Ecological Turn in New Confucian Humanism: Implication for China and the World, In: *Daedalus (Journal of the American Academy of Arts and Sciences* (Fall, 2001).
98. P. J. Ivanhoe, *Confucian Moral Self Cultivation* (Hackett Pub Co; 2nd edition, 1 March 2000).
99. G. Fang, F. X. Fang, M. Keller, W. Edelstein, T. J. Kehle and M. A. Bray, Social moral reasoning in Chinese children: A developmental study, *Psychology in School*, 40(1): 125–138, 2003.
100. F. Zakaria, Culture is destiny; A conversation with Lee Kuan Yew, *Foreign Affairs*, 73(2): 109–126, March/April 1994.
101. J. H. Liu, L. Zhang and S. F. Messner, *Crime and Social Control in a Changing China* (Greenwood Press, 2001).
102. This tendency to keep problems at home and away from officials is best captured by the saying: 'family shame should not be spread outside'. It is also appropriate to have elders in the family to resolve any dispute. They are considered wiser and more knowledgeable, than any outside officials, to find out the truth and decide the punishment. C. K. Fei, *The Family and Clan Rules in China* (Zhongguo de jiafa zhugui) (Shanghai: Shanghai shehui kexue chubanshe, 1998), Chapter 4: 'Adjudication and Punishment' ('Cheng Chu'), pp. 106–129.
103. C. Chan, The cultural dilemmas in dispute resolution: The Chinese experience, Conference of Enforcing Equal Opportunity in Hong Kong, Hong Kong University, 14 June 2003. http://www.hku.hk/ccpl/pub/conferences/documents/14062003a-CeciliaChan.pdf
104. D. C. Clarke, Dispute resolution in China, *Journal of Chinese Law*, 5(2): 245–296, 1991. See also; B. K. Y. Wong. Traditional Chinese philosophy and dispute resolution, *Hong Kong Law Journal*, 30(Part 2): 304–319, 2000.
105. When dealing with external relationships, that is, clan and society, family rules (*jia gui*) incorporated seven admonitions: (1) having good relationship with neighbours; (2) avoid litigation; (3) avoid hurting others; (4) avoid conflict; (5) defend the clan; (6) punish thieves and robbers; (7) protect the environment. Four of the seven, that is, (1) to (4), consisted of avoiding conflicts. C. K. Fei,

The Family and Clan Rules in China (Zhongguo de jiafa zhugui) (Shanghai: Shanghai shehui kexue chubanshe, 1998).

106. J. R. Watt, *The District Magistrate in Late Imperial China* (New York: Columbia University Press, 1972).
107. B. W. Reed, Money and justice: Clerks, runners, and the magistrate's court in late imperial sichuan, *Modern China*, 21:3: 345–83, 1995.
108. C. Yu and M. Wei, The three social stratum and legal practice in Chinese characters, ('<<Ruulin waishi>> zhong de sange jieceng yu falu shijian') *Journal of Jiangsu Police Officer College*, 17(2): 109–119, 116R, 2000. (Petty officials were all corrupt. They were hated by the people and avoided by the public.) [Author note: The title of the article in the original was wrongly translated. It should be 'The three classes in the <> and legal practices'.]
109. M. Macauley, *Social Power and Legal Culture: Litigation Masters in Late Imperial China* (Stanford, CA: Stanford University Press, 1999). Chapter 1: 'The Evolution of a Crime and Its Punishment' describes how songshi or litigation masters were being considered as 'habitual litigation hooligan' in stirring up disputes, pp. 19–46, at 19.
110. This is not unlike policing in America when we leave the dirty work of policing to the police, only holding them accountable when we are forced to be exposed to them, for example, scandal. P. K. Manning, *Police Work: The Social Organization of Policing* (Cambridge, MA: MIT Press, 1997).
111. The common admonition in Hong Kong is 'Good boy does not become a police'. While such an attitude is fast disappearing because of increased salary, opportunity, professionalism, and status a police career, it still strong felt and articulated in some quarters of the community, for example, well-to-do families. K. C. Wong, Police Power: Misconduct and Accountability, In: *Unit 4 to Police and Society* (Hong Kong: Open University, 2000), p. 120.
112. R. G. Gove, Militia, market and lineage: Chinese militia, market and lineage: Chinese resistance to the occupation of HK's new territories in 1899, *Journal of the Royal Asiatic Society Hong Kong Branch*, 9: 31–65, 32, 1969.
113. C. Leadbeater, *The Self-Policing Society* (London: Demos, 1996), p. 28. http://charlesleadbeater.net/wp-content/uploads/1996/01/theselfpolicingsociety1.pdf
114. J. Hayes, *Hong Kong Region 1850–1911, The: Institutions and Leadership in Town and Countryside* (New York: Columbia University Press, 2012) (Neither China imperial bureaucracy nor the British colonial administration reached into the running of local village affairs.)
115. A traditional Chinese idiom states '宁为太平犬，不做乱世人 (traditional, Pinyin níng wéi tàipíng quǎn, bù zuò luànshì rén') as: 'It's better to be a dog in a peaceful time than be a man in a chaotic period'.
116. J. Salaff, *Working Daughters of Hong Kong: Filial Piety or Power in the Family* (Cambridge: Cambridge University Press, 1981).
117. S. K. Lau and Z. J. Liu, *Society and Politics in Hong Kong* (Hong Kong: Chinese University of Hong Kong, 1984), '5: Linkages between the Bureaucratic Polity and the Chinese Society'. p. 121.
118. G. M. Chen and W. J. Starosta, Chinese conflict management and resolution: Overview and implications, *Intercultural Communication Studies*, 7(1): 1–17, 1997–1998. http://www.trinity.edu/org/ics/ics%20issues/ics%20vii/ics-vii-1-chen.pdf

119. Shameful things stay at home. Saving 'face' is important in Chinese family, K. K. Hwang, *Guanxi and Mientze:* Conflict resolution in Chinese society, *Intercultural Communication Studies*, 7(1): 17–38, 1997–1998. http://www.uri.edu/iaics/content/1997v7n1/02%20Kwang-Kuo%20Hwang.pdf
120. Jurisprudentially speaking, positive law has little authority and still less legitimacy in the home front, best left to family or community to order, naturally and customarily. Theoretically, law is to proscribe conduct with 'thou shall not', social regulation is there to solve problem in line with expectations with 'thou shall'. Law is a closed-end command to cease and decease.. Social regulation is an open-ended invitation to participate. T. V. Svogun, *The Jurisprudence of Police: Toward a General Unified Theory of Law* (Palgrave Macmillan, 10 October 2013), p. 7.
121. Not entering official gate during one's life time.
122. Not being legalised and bureaucratised, FOPS is an order maintenance task. The objective is to solve problem with a view to promote the best interest of the family. Policing (as in Problem Oriented Policing [POP] in the West) is act based (adult) or status oriented (juvenile), and rule specific. The question is how can we respond to or deal with people who violate rules? FOPS in China is family based and order specific. The issue is how to secure order that would contribute to the smooth functioning of the family as a whole. Rule enforcement is a negative activity. Order promotion is a positive venture. The former is punitive and backward looking. The later is remedial and forward looking.
123. Restorative Justice Online. http://www.restorativejustice.org/
124. J. Braithwaite, *Crime, Shame and Reintegration* (Cambridge: Cambridge. University Press, 1989).
125. There is an age-old Chinese saying: 'Not entering government door alive, and not entering hell in death'. There was also another saying: 'Receiving 300 lashes even before seeing the officials'. The later saying has some validity. In Imperial China, those who sought the Magistrate's help in resolving disputes would be penalised whether their claim is legitimate or not. Thus, to the Hong People before the 1980s, visiting with government officials, especially police, is an unpleasant experience. 'In Hong Kong… to avoid having contacts with bureaucrats as far as possible, either through "self-help" activities or to make do with shortage of services is the only way to relate oneself to the bureaucratic polity' (p. 112). S. K. Lau and Z. Liu, *Society and Politics in Hong Kong* (Hong Kong: Chinese University of Hong Kong, 1984).
126. People are 'born with' problems because they have expectations. People are 'born to' problem because resources, personal or social, are always limited. When expectations are unlimited and material resources are limited, there are always problems. The only way out is to reduce expectations, that is, be contented.
127. Conflict theorists have long observed that it is impossible to have all the people agreed upon a uniform understanding of the social order. The radical theorists have challenged consensus theorists' understanding of law and order from the perspective of the dominant class, while totally ignoring the contribution of the dominated class. This is a major oversight; people's mentality and sensitivity matters. The nature and distribution of police power take a different shape viewed from above, as it is from below.

128. C. D. Robinson and R. Scaglion, The origin and evolution of the police function in society: Notes toward a theory. *Law & Society*, 21(1): 109–154, 1987.
129. J. Austin, *Lectures on Jurisprudence; or, The Philosophy of Positive Law* (London, J. Murray Year: 1885), pp. 226–230 (habit of obedience).
130. P. K. Manning, Organizational constrains and semiotics. In: M. Punch (ed.), *Control in the Police Organization* (Cambridge, MA: MIT Press, 1983), pp. 169–194.
131. I. Kant, An Answer to the Question: What is Enlightenment? (1784). https://web.cn.edu/kwheeler/documents/What_is_Enlightenment.pdf
132. There is an urgent need to draw a clear distinction between the 'community' and the 'people'. They are conceptually different categories for analytical and operational purposes. Analytically, a community is a collectivity (group of people) sharing certain identifiable characteristics and relationship, that is, 'a group of people who share certain demographic and socio-economic traits and fellowship'. (Fessler, 1976). The people are an unbounded group of individuals sharing few things in common other than a universal social nature (humanity) and particularistic political character (nationality). Operationally, COP means that 'The police designate a community in which they will engage in problem solving, develop relationships (that hopefully become partnerships) with the population, collaborate with them to diagnose problems that have some generalised impact, prescribe and implement interventions to solve the problems, and continuously monitor the results' (Flynn, 1998). In the case of people's policing, it is the people's problem, individually or as a group that should be of dominant concern.
133. Crime is never more than a breach of human trust, destruction of social relationship and infringement of personal rights. Breach of trust as failed expectation of predictability generates fear (of crime). Destruction of relationship as failed expectation of intimacy results in alienation (from others). Infringement of personal rights as failed expectation of entitlement causes loss (of property) or injury (to body). A reintegration strategy is much better than punishment strategy in renewing faith-building relationship and repairing harm. In this way, my theory echoes the concerns of Braithwaite with traditional punishment (cf. Braithwaite, 1989).
134. At its heart, all policing is a policing of relationship.
135. L. Nader, *Law in Culture and Society* (CA: University of California Press, 1969), pp. 337–348.
136. R. Madsen, The public sphere, civil society and moral community: A research agenda for contemporary China studies, *Modern China*, 19 (2): 183–198, 1993.
137. E. E. Joh, The paradox of private policing, *Journal of Criminal Law and Criminology*, 95 (1): 49–134, 2004. Available at SSRN: http://ssrn.com/abstract=643184.
138. J. Gross, Introduction to alternative dispute resolution, *Alberta Law Review* 34 (1): 1–33, 1995.
139. P. K. Manning, Organizational constrains and semiotics. In: M. Punch (ed.), *Control in the Police Organization* (Cambridge, MA: MIT Press, 1983), pp. 169–194. [Alternative, See Manning, supra, note 130.]
140. A. H. Maslow, A theory of human motivation, *Psychological Review,* 50(4): 370–396, 194.
141. Letting go of expectation, Buddhist Blog, 23 December 2010. http://thebuddhistblog.blogspot.com/2010/12/letting-go-of-expectations.html.

J. Sherman, Ambigamy, *Psychology Today*, 5 October 2009. ('Expectation is what Buddha said is the source of suffering'.) http://www.psychologytoday.com/blog/ambigamy/200910/ups-downs-expectations-and-attachements-what-the-buddha-missed

142. H. Liu, *The Chinese Overseas, Vol 1.* (London: Routledge, 2005), p. 307.
143. A. Chan, The Chinese concepts of Guanxi, Mianzi, Renqing and Bao: Their interrelationships and implications for international business. Conference Paper, *Australian & New Zealand Marketing Academy (ANZMAC) Conference 2006*, Brisbane, Australia. (2006). http://smib.vuw.ac.nz:8081/WWW/ANZMAC2006/documents/Chan_Alvin.pdf
144. E. Sinn, *Power and Charity A Chinese Merchant Elite in Colonial Hong Kong* (Hong Kong: Hong Kong University Press, 2003).
145. Y. K. Chu, *The Triads as Business* (London: Routledge, 2000).
146. K. L. Chin. *Chinese Subculture and Criminality: Non-traditional Crime Groups in America* (New York: Greenwood Press, 1990), see 'Chinatowns and Tongs' at p. 53.
147. J. Hayes, Old British Kowloon, *Journal of the Royal Asiatic Society Hong Kong Branch*, 6: 121–137, 125, 1966.
148. R. J. Miners, State Regulation of Prostitution in Hong Kong, 1857–1941, *JRAS (HK)*, XXIV: 143–161, 143–144, 1984.
149. For political nature of mafia justice and order keeping, see L. M. McCartney, Democracy and the dangerous man: Mafia justice versus citizen virtue (January 1, 1997). *Electronic Doctoral Dissertations for UMass Amherst*. Paper AAI9809366. ('The study finds that the mafia variety of organised crime tends to substitute for the state as the recognized political authority when at least three basic conditions are met: (1) when the state fails to adequately protect its citizens, (2) when a climate of cultural mistrust of state authority exists, and (3) when there is an adequate supply of dangerous men who know how to employ force to obtain order in the manner described by Niccolo Machiavelli in The Prince'.) http://scholarworks.umass.edu/dissertations/AAI9809366
150. This rendition of Triad justice was captured in the first scene to *Godfather I* (15 March 1978), when people line up to see the Don Vito Corleone to ask for favour. http://en.wikipedia.org/wiki/The_Godfather_%28film_series%29
151. R. Catanzaro, *Men of Respect: A Social History of the Sicilian Mafia* (Free Press, 1988). ('Two well-known codes of Sicilian and Mafia culture are crucial: honor and instrumental friendship. These cultural codes and the modern forces that shaped them gave the Mafia its essential competitive character which, in turn, imbued the organisation with its criminal dynamism'.)
152. Y. K. Chu, *The Triads as Business* (London: Routledge, 2000).
153. Ibid.
154. W. Stanton, *Triad Society or Heaven and Erath Society* (Hong Kong: Kelly and Walsh, 1900).
155. K. Bolton and C. Hutton, *Triad Societies: Western Accounts of the History, Sociology and Linguistics of Chinese Secret Societies, Vol. 5* (London and New York: Taylor & Francis, 2000).
156. J. Beckert and F. Wehinger, In the shadow: Illegal markets and economic sociology, *Socio-Economic Review*, 1–26, 2012. http://ser.oxfordjournals.org/content/early/2012/09/26/ser.mws020.full.pdf?keytype = ref&ijkey = T5CNlKXvI3EBggc

157. R. K. Merton (1968-08-01). *Social Theory and Social Structure* (1968 enlarged ed.), (New York: Free Press, 1968); Robert K. Merton (October 1938). Social structure and anomie, *American Sociological Review*, 3(5): 672–682, 1938.
158. 'Street-side business faced bullying from the police and triad elements' (05/05/2011). ('Yeung Hon Yuen: Owner of Lai Heung Yuen Café, 61' Hong Kong Memory.) http://www.hkmemory.hk/collections/oral_history/All_Items_OH/oha_74/highlight/index.html#p56936
159. There are many migrants travelling to and living in Hong Kong, as sojourns, and in time temporary permanent. But in the mind of Hong Kong people, migrant conjures up images of mainland Chinese invading Hong Kong, economically and culturally. For the purpose of policing in Hong Kong, the focus is on mainland migrants, legal or otherwise. C. Knowles and D. Harper, *Hong Kong: Migrant Lives, Landscapes, and Journeys* (Chicago: University of Chicago Press, 2009).
160. J. A. Schafer and M. J. Giblin, *Policing Intimate Partner Violence in Rural Areas and Small Towns*, Women & Criminal Justice 20(4): 283–301, 2010.
161. Cindy Chu, *op. cit.*, Chapter One.
162. In 2010, only 17.3% identified themselves as Hong Kongese. The Identity and National Identification of Hong Kong People, Center for Communication Research, Chinese University of Hong Kong, 2010.
163. Annual Report, 1948, p. 9.
164. R. Hughes, *Borrowed Place Borrowed Time* (Singapore: Andre Deutach, 1968).
165. C. R. Shaw and H. D. McKay, *Juvenile Delinquency in Urban Areas* (Chicago: University of Chicago Press, 1942).
166. G. B. Endacott, *Government and People in Hong Kong* (HK: HKU, 1964), p. 4.
167. S. E. Hamilton, *Watching over Hong Kong: Private Policing 1841–1941* (Hong Kong: Hong Kong University Press, 2008).
168. H. C. Wang Liu, *The Traditional Chinese Clan Rules* (New York: J.J. Augustin, 1959).
169. S. K. Lau, *The Ethos of the Hong Kong Chinese* (Hong Kong: The Chinese University Press, 1988) with S.K. Lau.
170. W. P. Morgan, *Triad Societies in Hong Kong* (Hong Kong: Government Press, 1960). (Reprinted 1982, 1989).
171. Professor Black is the first to observe that the behaviour of law as government control is a function of social and cultural distance. D. Black, *The Behavior of Law* (1976), K. C. Wong, Black's theory on the behavior of law revisited III: Law as more or less governmental social control, *International Journal of the Sociology of Law*, 26(3): 365–392, 1998. Available at: http://works.bepress.com/kam_wong/18
172. On the correct handling of contradictions among the people, *Selected Works of Mao Tse-tung*, 27 February 1957. (Speech at the Eleventh Session [Enlarged] of the Supreme State Conference. Comrade Mao Tse-tung went over the verbatim record and made certain additions before its publication in the *People's Daily* on 19 June 1957.) http://www.marxists.org/reference/archive/mao/selected-works/volume-5/mswv5_58.htm
173. Ibid.
174. M. Deflem, R. Featherstone, S. Sutphin, and Y. Li. Policing the pearl: Historical transformations of law enforcement in Hong Kong, *International Journal of Police Science and Management*, 10: 349–356, 2008.
175. B. Cole, Post-colonial systems, In: R. I. Mawby (ed.), *Policing across the World.* (London: UCL Press, 1999), pp. 88–108, 89.

Police Reform in 1950s

II

Police Reform Literature[1]

5

Introduction

Police reform is ubiquitous.[2] It is all around us. Reform is necessary to keep up with change, political or social. Reform is inevitable to assure survival of the fittest, for example, with scandal comes reform. Reform is wholesome as it stands for improvement, for example, with President Lyndon Johnson's war on crime in the United States (1968) and Governor Murray MacLehose's war on corruption in Hong Kong (1974). Last but not the least, police reform is welcomed as it allays public concerns and promises future hope. In doing so, it serves the interests of some and fulfills the aspirations of many. Police reform is all of the above and more. According to Professor Savage, in concrete terms, police reform in the United Kingdom results from: 'public inquiries, miscarriages of justice, legal changes, political agendas and cultural shifts…'[3]

This chapter reviews literature on 'Police Reform'. It variously investigates into the nature, topologies, conduct, impact and assessment of police reform. Section II: 'HKP Reform Inquiries' reports on a number of high-profile HKP Reform Inquires, from The Caldwell Commission (1858) to the Sir Alastair Blair-Kerr Commission (1973) to The Coopers & Lybrand Consultant Report (1993) to Lan Kwai Fang (LKF) Disaster Report (1993) to Hong Kong Audit Commission (1999). Section III is a brief 'Conclusion'.

I: Police Reform

Why Police Reform?

Why police reform? As the public faces a faceless and removed government, police agencies stand for all that is wrong with government and governance. As an all-purpose, 24/7-service agency, the police offers the public ample opportunities and the only readily available forum to air their grievances, with the police, in the name of transparency and accountability, which is actively encouraging. As the premier social control agency empowered to use coercive force to enforce law, impose order and deal with problems of all kinds, it attracts criticism and demands for accountability.

Why, then, are there recurring and persisting calls for police reform? The reason is simple. The police are set up to fail. The public is dissatisfied because the police can never meet all their legitimate demands. The first to observe is that police labour under a limited resource in the face of unlimited demands. For example, police cannot answer all service calls. Police also cannot hope to arrest all prostitutes or drug users when the public has demands for such illicit service and illegal commodities. The public is disillusioned because the police cannot meet all their (unrealistic) expectations, that is, deter or suppress all crimes. The public expects customised and personalised service but is given bulk and routine services. The public expects final solutions to their problems but is only provided with partial and interim patch-up remedies, for example, when called police can drive rowdy juveniles away, only to have them return once the police are gone. The public is frustrated because the police are not able to resolve conflicting expectations, for example, domestic abuses. Frustrated citizens make good complaints. Police become the target of anger management.

To further complicate matters, different parts of the public have different expectations, which cannot be reasonably reconciled. For example, conservatives prefer substantive justice and liberals want procedural justice. For example, the public want full enforcement of the law, and protestors demand to be left alone. The public is jilted because the police over promise and under deliver. For example, the police claim to be able to suppress crime when many causes of crime are beyond the reach of the police, for example, family discipline, school education, peer influence, economic conditions and social discrimination. Viewed in this light, the call for and rendering of reform is natural and inevitable. For the misguided public, reform is a stopgap measure to deal with recurring police transgressions. For the pragmatic police, reform is a survival strategy, to meet increasing demands and rising expectations, of one reform at a time.

Typologies of Police Reform

The Police Reform Organizing Project (PROP) in its 'Mission' statement, is instructive on why people seek police reform:

> Through research and analysis, public education, policy advocacy, and coalition building, PROP aims: to stop the current wasteful, ineffective, unjust, illegal, bullying, homophobic, transphobic, and racially biased practices of the NYPD; to establish an outside independent agency that will investigate police priorities and punish abusive conduct; and to implement local problem solving measures that strengthen communities while reducing crime.[4]

According to the 'Mission' statement, PROP wants police to be less abusive, more accountable and totally responsive to the people.

The 'Mission' statement also tells us another reason for reform. Police reform is driven by the public's (or a part thereof) unhappiness with the status quo, from corruption to abuse of power to incompetence.

Depending on the context—purpose, issue and people—involved, there are many types of police reform.

Nostalgic Reform

Some people look back, asking why their police are not performing what they used to be, in role and functions, ways and means, appearance and style. They complained that the police are not doing what they had been doing. These are the 'nostalgic' reformers. Yesterday is always better than today, is the battle cry. To them, the best of policing lived in the past. Mark Doyle has this to say about Prime Minister Cameron as a 'romantic' reform par excellence:[5]

> Last month the Cameron government enacted perhaps the most sweeping police reform since the Second World War, a reform that is very much in line—on the surface, at least—with the Victorian idea of community policing… What British policing really needs, it seems, are more men like Inspector Field, even if the literary Inspector Field was himself, as I suspect, largely a product of Dickens' fecund imagination. The myth of the genial bobby-on-the-beat, feared but respected by criminals, fawned over by toothless hags, swimming like a fish through the criminal underworld, a veritable cocktail of honesty, integrity, and grit poured into a buttoned blue suit, may have been a Victorian fantasy, but it is a useful fantasy all the same. The Tories, not exactly immune to the odd fit of Victorian nostalgia, would do well to return to Robert Peel's original blueprint for the Met (but not for the Irish Constabulary) and the model of engaged, cooperative community policing they were meant to embody. …

Normative Reform

Others look at the present, lamenting why their police are not living up to their expectations, in ideology, morality, law or custom, more generally, expectations of all kinds: Can the police be more polite? Can the police be more efficient? Can the police be more competent? Ten thousands complain, one universal concern: the police are not doing what they should be doing. Why can't the police meet all my reasonable expectations, and beyond? These are the 'normative' reformers. To them, the best of policing is in keeping faith with the present, making police more accountable to the people and living up to the law.[6] The various human rights organisations and international police assistant programmes are best known for their effort in holding the police accountable.

> The United Nations Code of Conduct for Law Enforcement, adopted in 1997 General Assembly, recognizes the crucial role the police play in

> protecting human rights and ensuring equal treatment of citizens before the law. Subsequently UN documents, including Guidelines for the Effective Implementation of the Code, and the Basic Principles on the Use of Fore and Firearms by law Enforcement Officials, adopted in 1990, provide further guidance on the appropriate role of the law. Despite the existence and with formal endorsement of these international principles, police reform as an area of rule of law reform was largely ignored until the past 15 years and remains a sensitive topic.[7]

Take any expectations you might have with the police, the chances are the police would be most likely not be able to meet people's ever-regressing expectations. Expectation begets expectation. Perfection knows no bound.

Progressive Reform

Still others look to the future, questioning why their police are not performing as they could or should, in ideology,[8] philosophy[9] or theory terms. These are the 'idealistic' or 'progressive' reformers. To them, the best of policing rests with the future, not the past or the present. What they want to do is to change that status quo, by moving the performance bar. By far, the best known of all police 'progressive' reformers are those who champion for professionalism in policing:[10]

> The ideal of professionalism retains its allure in policing for some of the same reasons it retains its allure in other fields: it conjures up a body of practitioners who bring meaning and dignity to their work through dedication, collective self-improvement, and ethical commitment, aligning their own interests with the interests of those they serve. If anything, that ideal has even greater appeal in law enforcement than in medicine or law, probably the two most paradigmatic professions, because aligning the interests of police officers—the personification of state violence—with the interests of the public has for decades been thought a particularly pressing and particularly vexing problem throughout the Anglo-American world. …For police reformers, professionalism offers an antidote to corruption and underperformance, and a way of emphasizing that the police have, or should have, special skills and knowledge that can be written down, taught, and continually improved. It offers, too, an avenue of reform that promises to enlist the police themselves in the cause of reform, by offering them pride, respect, and status.

In the United States, progressive police reform[11] was born out of progressive movement of the late nineteenth century (1890–1920),[12] with Theodore Roosevelt (1858–1919), the Police Commissioner of New York City and later President of the United States, in the lead.[13] Progressivism championed the dealing of social problems (poverty, inequality, racism and violence) of industrialisation in America in an enlightened and scientific way, for example, through education and with scientific research. They called for regulating cooperation, purging corruption and controlling the police.

Progressive police reform calls for the professionalisation of police, by way of removal of political patronage and in the reduction of corruption.

Critical Reform

Finally, more than a few are not happy with the police—past, present or future, in whatever they do or do not do. They want change for change's sake. 'Police can be done differently' is made to stand for 'police can be done better'. These are the 'critical' reformers. To them, the best of policing is an ever-changing policing, in meeting expectations, in ratifying mistakes, in seeking improvement, in keeping up with time or just experimenting with new ideas. Radical reformers are also known for shifting the paradigm of policing, away from the historical and conventional.

In the face of racial challenges, the police are either unwilling or unable to changes proposed by radicals.

Political Reform

The above reasoning for police reform pre-supposes the existence of an entrenched, if not functional, police agency. The need for political reform might result from doing away with the old altogether, for example, regime change, post-conflict societies and revolutionary change in political governance. These kinds of police reform have one thing in common; police reform is required not as a growth process but as a change in governance.[14] This suggests an assertive change in political philosophy[15] or the governing paradigm, such as the Europeanisation of Bosnia[16] or commercialisation of China.[17] Post-conflict police reform (PCPR) (a/k/a transitional society reform) is one such political reform.[18]

As the name of such kinds of reform denote, 'post conflict police reform' or 'transitional society police reform' (TSPR) is a kind of reform engaged by security—police or police–security forces when the nation as a whole is moving; thus, it is 'transitional', from a conflict (war) stage to an order (peace) state, and is thus 'post-conflict'. The objective of the PCPR is in transforming the wartime military security forces ('demilitarization') into a peacetime civilian police agency ('civilianization') through re-defining the role and changing the relationship of the security versus police with respect to the society in transition. The other objective to be achieved is to 'democratize' the security forces and police agency, making them more accountable to the public and working within the 'rule of law'. As such, nearly all PCPRs, especially those that are sponsored, assisted and funded by external donors (United Nations, United States, Canada, Japan and Spain) are also 'democratization' and 'rule of law' reform programmes. The three major challenges to PCPR are:

First, how to 'demilitarize' the functions of the security forces or 'civilianize' the para-military role of the police. The former requires taking away powers of the security forces. The latter requires changing the culture of the police. In both cases, the values and interests of security forces versus civil police agency are at stake.

Second, how to maintain security of the nation and law and order of the society, when the war-torn nation is still in transition, with the real threat of war by political–military leaders and fear of crime by the people.

Third, how to provide law, order and security in a war-torn nation, without violation of the rule of law or human rights.[19]

As intimated above, there are many kinds of police reform. The challenge is in how to classify and characterise them, in a systematic, coherent and meaningful manner.

Forces of Change

The initiation and conduct of police reform is very much affected by the media:[20] The FBI has its own radio show—'This is *Your* FBI' on ABC from April 6, 1945 to January 30, 1953. LAPD was made famous by its own TV show—*Dragnet*.[21] Without the glitz and over-the-top drama, this show brings 'the story of *your* police force in action'—'just the facts'.[22] These shows and others 'make a rendering of what truly constitutes the good cop from the bad cop more difficult'.[23]

In the United Kingdom, it is not different. British press leads the call for police reform:

> IT IS the hot new idea: local services ought to be accountable to local people. And everyone seems to agree that the police are a public service ripe for reform. Combine the two, and you get the government and both main opposition parties all pushing the same way, for local oversight of the men in blue. The Liberal Democrats aim, vaguely, to put them under regional control; the Conservatives want neighbourhood sheriffs. Labour proposes elected 'police boards' and community advocates to keep chief constables on their toes.[24]

Most calls for police reforms, however, come from outside. The public and interest groups variously complain about police scandals of one kind or another: abuse, corruption or incompetency. Reform initiative from within the police agency is extremely rare[25] and from rank and files, is unheard of.

Globally, police reform moves along predictable and familiar lines: establishing legitimacy,[26] recovering public trust,[27] building integrity,[28] promoting democracy, [29] building the rule of law,[30] improving accountability,[31] increasing cost-effectiveness[32] and forging community engagement.[33]

They are often sold as 'best practice' or 'universal model' or 'progressive principles' or 'modernization method'.[34] In most cases, there is rarely any serious discussion over the need for utility of reform direction and method.

Traditionally, police reform is made synonymous with democratic policing of the West, justified on the grounds of globalisation and trans-nationalisation of policing[35] and achieved through conditionality, socialisation and the impositions with agreement, funding or incentives, from abroad. It is always Western-developed nations dictating to the other lesser-developed countries. Bayley observed 'we are in a period of unprecedented effort to expand democratic institutions around the world, with the explicit recognition that reform of the police, and of the larger criminal justice system, is a critical component'.[36]

Of late, police reform chases after crude improvements in managerial operations, made famous by the New Public Management with the transference of private sector productivity management techniques, management by objective (MBO), total quality management (TQM) to the public sector and police included.[37]

How to Conduct Police Reform?

There are many ways to conduct reform: administratively, legally, politically and socially.

Depending on history, nature, reason and issues for reform, how to conduct reform differs between countries, and communities. That is to say that the reform process is invariably contingent and contextual. No two reforms are alike, though some similarities can be observed, such as obstacles presented and lessons learned. Such obstacles and lessons have more to do with reform in general, than police reform in context.

Accountable to What, Whom and How?[38]

Reform is about changes to the organisation, people, process and action to enhance performance or achieve objectives. While there are many kinds of changes, reform is about meeting expectations, either reporting to a superior or giving an account of one's performance.[39] In both instances, things should not have happened, happened with a performer. To many and in real terms, reform is accountability in action.[40] As such, police reform cannot get far away from issues of what, whom and how police reform should be conducted. In this, Skogan's remark is most apt and pertinent: 'Police reform is risky and hard, and efforts to innovate in policing often fall short of expectations'.[41] This is to say that the police (especially in a democratic society) intersect with society at multiple points and are involved with people's life in every way. As such, police actions and reform are bound to have a material and substantial impact on people's value and interests; psychologically and physically, politically and socially, ideologically and materially. Simply put, police reform matters to people in multifarious and discernible ways, near or far, directly or indirectly, more or less, salient or obscured, dominant or marginal, real or imagined. The symbiotic relationship between police society recalls Hemingway's book *For Whom the Bell Tolls* which draws upon John Dunn's famous line: ***Devotions upon Emergent Occasions***, specifically 'Meditation XVII':

> Olde English Version No man is an Iland, intire of itselfe; every man is a peece of the Continent, a part of the maine; if a Clod bee washed away by the Sea, Europe is the lesse, as well as if a Promontorie were, as well as if a Manor of thy friends or of thine owne were; any mans death diminishes me, because I am involved in Mankinde; And therefore never send to know for whom the bell tolls; It tolls for thee.[42]

The study of and understanding about police reform regarding the origin, process and impact of reform, requires looking at police reform from a variety of stakeholders' perspectives, inside and outside of the police.

Impact of Police Reform

Without fundamental changes in the socio-political environment, police reform would only be superficial, local and temporal.[43] The impact of police reform must be understood in a historical and cultural context, lest we draw the wrong conclusion that democratic governance or community policing would be embraced with open arms by local people, without considering their values and interests towards reform.[44] Police reform is less like a lock step military march as it resembles a collaborative dance in Waltz.

How to Assess HKP Reform?

As previously implied, the assessment of HKP reform in a process and outcome is a long overdue. The question is how to get it done. Depending on the purpose and needs, accountability or debriefing, and parties calling for assessment, for example, internal versus external, there are many ways to conduct assessment audit.

In 2001, David Bayley published a defining study on the: 'Democratizing the Police Abroad: What to Do and How to Do It' (2001).[45] In it, Bayley provides a checklist by which to conduct reform. Some of the most important 'generic'[46] criteria of assessments are:

1. *Objective-linked action:* 'Any reform program must be based on a clearly articulated understanding of the connections between the objectives to be achieved and the actions proposed' (p. 19).
2. *Leadership commitment:* 'Sustained and committed leadership by top management, especially the most senior executive, is required to produce any important organizational change' (p. 20).
3. *Organisational members responding and responsive:* 'The key to changing any aspect of policing is management, that is, the way in which the members of a police organization are brought to do what policies call for' (p. 20).
4. *Changing the system–culture and not people:* 'Organisational change does not occur through changing personnel; it requires changing the system and culture of an organisation' (p. 21).
5. *Formal organisation change cannot change behaviour:* 'Police behavior cannot be changed by formal reorganization within the police or by restructuring on a national basis' (p. 21).
6. *Material resources are necessary but not sufficient for change:* 'Material resources may support desired changes, but they are rarely essential and never sufficient to bring them about' (p. 22).
7. *Significant reform requires 'buy-in':* 'Significant reform requires widespread acceptance across ranks and assignments in a police department. ...To obtain this necessary "buy-in" by all members of a police force, successful reform generally involves the following sequential activities: "brainstorming" by senior managers and carefully chosen colleagues about operational problems, creation of task forces from all ranks to devise concrete plans, discussion of proposed plans in seminars in all units and among all managerial ranks, development of pilot projects to test feasibility in the field on the clear understanding that the objective is to determine how to carry out the program and not whether to undertake it, and implementation of the new program throughout the department' (p. 22).
8. *Pilot projects required committed leadership and dedicated personnel*: 'When pilot projects are undertaken, they must have committed leadership and personnel who are not continually pulled away for other purposes' (p. 23).
9. *Police officers change due to self-interests:* 'Police officers will not change their behavior unless they perceive it to be in their personal interest to do so' (p. 23).
10. *Effective reform requires change performance criteria:* 'Reform will not occur unless the criteria for evaluating individual performance encourage the sort of behavior that reform requires' (p. 24).
11. *Reformers should not denigrate established people with old behaviour:* 'Reformers both inside and outside police organizations should be

careful not to denigrate the motivation, knowledge, or skill of the people whose behavior they are trying to change' (p. 24).

12. *Evaluation should be based on outcome, and not output:* 'Program evaluations that emphasize outputs rather than outcomes as a measure of success inhibit organizational creativity' (p. 24).
13. *Reform should be monitored for change, not too burdensome:* 'Reform requires that new programs be monitored so that midcourse changes can be made. At the same time, burdensome evaluation can discourage reform' (p. 25).
14. *Change results from new resources and not redistribution:* 'Change is more likely to occur when new resources are made available rather than when existing ones are redistributed' (p. 25).
15. *Reform sensitive to the rising crime*: 'If the incidence of crime and disorder is thought to be unacceptable or increasing, police reform will be inhibited' (p. 25).
16. *Service oriented accountable policing results from an increased contact with respectable citizens:* 'Increasing contacts between police personnel and respectable, noncriminal members of the public is an important way of encouraging the development of an accountable, service-oriented police organization' (p. 25).
17. *Changed behaviour depends on a clear policy and matched sanctions:* 'Issuing clear statements of organizational policy accompanied by appropriate positive and negative sanctions is a powerful way to change the behavior of police officers, even in situations of high stress and urgency' (p. 26).
18. *Reform is likely to occur if officers are connected to professional and progressive networks:* 'Reform is more likely to occur if police officials are connected to professional networks of progressive police leaders (regional, national, and international)' (p. 26).
19. *Labour organisation must be included in reform planning and development:* 'Labor organizations within the police must be included in the development and planning of any reform program' (p. 27).

Professor Bayley provides 19 items that police reform leadership or planners must be made aware of and insisted on when conducting a successful police reform.

Coming at the beginning of Section II on Hong Kong Reform, this is hardly the venue to go through each and every one of them in evaluating HKP reform. Reform assessment has to wait its turn. Sufficed to say, the list passes the most stringent facial validity test. The road ahead is for external police researchers or internal policy makers to operationalise the audit items in order to measure them objectively.

For example, with item one: In determining in what way and to what extent reform objectives, one and all, are linked with reform actions (programme, policy, strategy, tactics, measures and actions), it is necessary to look at the intent, purpose, objective and desired outcome of the reform, before we turned plan execution and impact, both formally and informally. We then need to find a way to determine the degree of closeness of fit between the objective and action, before we can come to a judgement whether the action in kind and degree is best designed to reach the objectives. The closeness-of-fit index must also be evaluated in the context, that is, an action that might work in one setting (people, places, functions and circumstances) might not be appropriate in any other setting. This raises the issue of the least-best choice, after comparing the positives and negatives through cost-benefit analysis of matching means and goals.

Turning our attention to HKP reform in the 1990s, consider the case of item seven. In tying HKP reform (in Knowledge Management [KM]) with employees 'buy in', evidence provided by the senior management suggests that KM has not been fully accepted by HKP members because of 'Resistance to change; Limited awareness of knowledge management leading to over expectation of its impact and results; A lack of ownership of the project; Misconception of "knowledge is power"; Rank consciousness; The absence of a change management mechanism; and A lack of incentive to motivate members to adopt the changes'. It is clear from the above that the 'resistance to change' resulted from 'a lack of ownership' (internal motivation) due to 'limited awareness' resulting in 'misconception'. A 'lack of incentive' (external motivation) also plays a role (item nine, 10).[47]

II: HKP Reform Inquiries[48]

The Caldwell Commission (1858)

The first independent study of HKP was Governor John Bowring's commissioned investigation[49] into the Attorney General Anstey[50] versus Registrar General Caldwell affair,[51] in 1858. The former Attorney General Anstey charged the Superintendent of Police Caldwell with corruption in office. Specifically, Caldwell was charged with speculating on brothel licences and dereliction of duties, including associating with Mr Chow Wong, a pirate and informant, while acting as the Superintendent of Police. As a historical backdrop, Caldwell was one of the very few British police officers who spoke fluent Chinese at the time and was well connected with the local communities, including the underground. He was very successful in keeping crime, vice and triads at bay through collaboration with unsavory Chinese, and infamous pirates included. As a result, Chinese middlemen enjoyed free rein of power to fight crime and maintain order in the Chinese community, with ways and means known but not sanctioned by their British handlers. In doing so, Caldwell's agents were able to deviate from normal criminal justice process, and compromised the purity of colonial rules, in search of self-serving ends of dubious legality and morality.[52] Viewed in this context, the charges of Caldwell Commission that Caldwell associated with characters of disrepute, the like of Ma-chow Wong and operating of brothel, while true is besides the point. What Caldwell was really charged with was not acting like a British in treating Chinamen, the way they should.[53] Mum observed:

> In openly marrying a Chinese woman according to Christian form, and by raising what by all accounts was a happy family, Caldwell, uniquely, has overstepped the tacitly agreed boundaries and provoked complex and unstable responses in the colonial community. …it was these questions abut racial barriers, as much as concerns about bribe-taking or piracy, that were at issue during the enquiry.[54]

In a more understanding language of the time: Conduct unbecoming of a British officer.

The Police Commission (1871)

The second was a self-study of HKP by 'The Police Commission' in 1871. The precipitating cause for concern about worsening the crime situation and deteriorating police performances observed by the community:

> The subject of the inefficiency of the Police continued to engross the attention of the authorizes. Secret societies and the elements composing them produced crimes a great deal faster than the Police could find the out; the Government seemed all engrossed with the gambling licenses; and the General administering of the Government, naturally reluctant to interfere in the annexed of Sir. Richard MacDonnell has enough to do so to keep things quite in his absence. Mr. Deane, the Captain Superintendent of Police, in his last report stated 'robberies with violence, burglaries, and assaults with intent to rob had increased nearly fourfold'. The Chief Justice instanced the demoralization of the police, due to the debasing influences of the gambling houses, and has suggested that the 'hope of obtaining government rewards led to conspiracy to convict innocent men of murder'.[55]

Chief Justice Smale complained of disorganisation of the HKP and lack of control over the policing observed by the Chief Justice:

> The Chief Justice expressed himself strongly on the organization, or rather disorganization, of the Police on the Legislative Council on the 18th August. He considered discipline could only be obtained by the whole Force being

> concentrated under one efficient head. At this period there were constables under the orders of ten Harbor Mater and others under the Registrar-General, and all, more or less interfered with by Mr. D. R. Caldwell, who either in connection with the gambling farm of otherwise, now kept 'runners' of his won, or a sort of private detective department employed occasionally by the Government no one knowing to what use these detectives may not be turned—this 'questionable element' in the local administration inducing the Chief Justice to state that Mr. Caldwell was ta this date 'virtually at the head of the Police'.[56]

There was also a disagreement over who—Chinese versus South or West India versus Sikhs—should be employed as officers.[57]

The Police Commission was called forth by the Justices of Peace backed by a petition of 400 Hong Kong foreign residents complaining. The Commission was empanelled by Governor MacDonnell on 22 December 1871 but implemented by Sir Richard McDonald, the next governor. The charter of the Commission was to make: 'to consider whether under the circumstances of the alarming increase of crimes in the Colony, some steps might not be taken on behalf of the community at large to ascertain the cause of the existing state of matters and inaugurate some reform for the future'.[58] Specifically, to conduct: 'inquiries into the efficiency and organization of the Police Force and the prevention of crime in the colony'.[59]

The Commission was one of the most extensive and comprehensive studies of HKP by external parties at that point of time. The Police Commission was composed of: the Acting Attorney General T.C. Hayllar, Council Member William Keswick; Representatives of Gibb and Co. Messers F. W. Michell and Henry Lowcock; Merchant William Lemann; with Hayllar as the Chair, Leister as the Interpreter and Coroner as the Secretary. The scope of the inquiry included:

a. Crime during the past 6 years;
b. Increase or decrease, cause of: How far due to individual execution;
c. Reports and suggestions of Messrs. Deane and Rice, especially the later;
d. 'Divided Authority';
e. Fusion of all classes of police;
f. Present organisation: Suggestion for reform;
g. Sikhs, East Indians and Negroes;
h. District watch;
i. Police force badge.[60]

In terms of process, the Police Commission was very professional and thorough. It interviewed witnesses, including Captain Superintendent of

Police Dean and Chief Judge of the Supreme Court Hornby. It inspected key official documents, including reports on the police (1968–1970), criminal statistics and parliamentary papers. It called for public participation (though not the Chinese).

Overall, the Report of the Police Commission (July 1872) came to the following observations:

First, crime in Hong Kong was exceedingly high, with a large amount of crime unreported, that is, according to the Superintendent of Police May, it was upward of 50% in 1862. More than 60% of crimes were not detected.[61]

Second, the British criminal justice system, as applied to Hong Kong, was unsuitable to the Hong Kong native population. For example, criminal punishment was not harsh enough. 'Except for the mere restrains of confinement, which to most Chinamen is not irksome, he finds himself surrounded with every comfort-roomy clean quarter, congenial society, the kindest of treatment, wholesome and plentiful food, work about sufficient to give him an appetite to enjoy it, medical attendance and comfort…'[62] In essence, British criminal justice has no deterrent effect on the Chinese, individually and as a group.

Third, branding had little effect on Chinese who knew no shame, except to arouse sympathy from compatriots due to anti-foreign sentiments.[63]

Fourth, the Chinese people were not cut out for British criminal justice system.

The British justice system required 'fair play' and 'honesty' in order to pursue 'justice' and attain 'truth'. Chinese people had no respect for oaths and were given to perjury, even in the face of punishment.[64] Without branding, there was no way of keeping track of the habitual offenders.

Fifth, the leadership of the police force should be promoted from within and not appointed from outside, that is, with Cadet officers, such as Deane, who were not trained to be or have experience with police officers.[65]

With respect to the Water Police, The Commission supported the recommendations of the Harbor Master, Captain H.H. Thomset, namely: Water Police should be commanded by an Assistant Superintendent whose 'duties being confined to Policing the Waters of Hong Kong'; that the areas covered by policing rowing boats should be better planned and that a 'fast steam launch' should be added.[66]

The Commission was not in agreement on most of the issues, such as registering the complexity of the issues and diversity of views, especially on the ethnic composition of HKP, for example, Mr Lowcock—mostly Europeans, a few Sikhs and Chinese and no native detectives; Mr Lemana—agrees with Lowcock, and uses native detectives cautiously; Mr Steward—uses Europeans and Negroes, no native detectives and Major General Whitfield—same as Steward. All Commissions unanimous: Minimum Europeans; command and control by Europeans; increase in pay and encourage studying the local dialect.[67]

The Commission did not achieve the purpose it was intended.

Sir Alastair Blair-Kerr Commission (1973)[68]

Since its inception (1844) and until recently (1974), the HKP has suffered corruption that is endemic, open, rampant, accepted, and institutionalised in a syndicated form.[69] According to the one-time ICAC chief:

> Every part of public service was infected, especially the disciplined services, namely the police, the customs, and exercise service, the immigration department, the fire and ambulance services and prison service. Certain other government departments shared the notoriety of the disciplined services: housing, public words, education and health.[70]

To say that corruption within HKP is syndicated is to say that it is systemised, organised and rule bound. 'Neil Maloney, a British expatriate who joined the Hong Kong police force in 1969 before becoming an ICAC investigator in 1974, recalled that each police station had a dedicated room for a "collector", whose sole job was to buy the bank drafts to send bribes to local and overseas accounts'.[71]

Officers who were on the take were protected and promoted,[72] and those who were not, were sanctioned.[73] Inspector Allen Ellis who served the HKP between the mid-1960s and mid-1970s and alleged his career was damaged because he refused to take bribes.[74] Corruption was so pervasive and engrained within HKP that young recruits or honest cops were told on their first day of duty:

1. 'Get on the bus', that is, if you wish to accept corruption, join us; or
2. 'Run alongside the bus'—If you do not wish to accept corruption, it does not matter, but do not interfere;
3. 'Never stand in front of the bus'—If you try to report corruption, the 'bus' will knock you down and you will be injured or even killed or your business will be ruined. We will get you, somehow.[75]

In the days before ICAC, the public did not get service without paying lucky money,[76] street hawkers could not ply their trade without paying a licence fee[77] and gambling establishments could not operate without paying protection money.[78]

HKP corruption finally came to light with the landmark Godber corruption case[79] that called out for radical reform of corruption in Hong Kong, starting with the HKP.[80]

In 1971, the Chief Superintendent Peter Godber was investigated by the HKP Anti-Corruption Office for corruption as a result of suspicious banking transmittals, in and out of Hong Kong. A bank audit of all 480 banks in Hong Kong showed that he amassed a fortune of $330,000. Further inquiry worldwide—United States, Canada, Singapore, England and Hong Kong found that the total bank deposits were to the tune of $4,377,248, six times his career earnings as a HKP officer, since 1952. During the investigation, he asked for early retirement. He was instead suspended from duty and was asked to explain his ill-gotten gain under Section 10 of Prevention of Bribery Ordinance, within 7 days, that is, before 11 June 1973. Sensing trouble, he escaped using his police authority (special airport security permit) to bypass airport security and immigration on 8 June, arriving in England on 8 June 1973.

Godber was finally arrested in England on 29 April 1974 and extradited back to face justice in Hong Kong on 7 January 1975, after 8 months of legal rankle for accepting a bribe of $25,000 from a Chinese Superintendent[81] to arrange for his appointment as the Division Superintendent of Wai Chai.[82]

Godber was tried in front of Judge Yang Ti-liang in Victoria District Court 7, Central, Hong Kong, for accepting a bribe of $20,000. He was convicted on 25 February 1975 and sentenced to 4 years in prison with HK$25,000 in restitution, in the presence of 100 plus press officers and cheering public.

The Godber case is considered as a landmark case because of a number of distinctive characteristics:

First, it was for the first time a high ranking and decorated expatriate HKP officer was investigated by the HKP—Anti-Corruption Office under the supervision of the Commissioner of Police, and later arrested by the ICAC after it was established.[83]

Second, it was for the first time Section 10 of Prevention of Bribery Ordinance was used to ask a senior HKP officer to explain his financial holdings, beyond his earnings.

Third, it was the first case that shows that Hong Kong Government is committed to clean up corruption in Hong Kong. No one, not even high-ranking British officials, was above the law.[84]

Fourth, it was the first case that was able to generate a public outcry against HKP corruption, fostering an anti-corruption ethos in Hong Kong.[85]

Fifth, it resulted in the establishment of the ICAC, a recommendation of the Sir Alastair Blair-Kerr Commission appointed by then Sir Murray MacLehose.[86]

A report by the Blair-Kerr Commission in 1973, on its investigations into corruption in Hong Kong contained an analysis of factors affecting public attitudes towards corruption in Hong Kong.

1. Refugees with experience of China before 1949 brought expectations that officials would be corrupt. 'This belief in itself breeds corruption because it leads to voluntary bribery by people who consider it normal practice …'

2. To such immigrants, the Hong Kong Government was alien and its language different, but while they would grumble among themselves they would not complain.
3. Overcrowding and fast development led to businesses not observing regulations, willing to pay 'black money' rather than lose their livelihood.
4. Time was valuable, bribes for faster service were found helpful.
5. Also, bribes were paid to jump the queue, for example for low cost housing.
6. Middlemen would make bribes appear as legal commission to the ignorant.
7. Junior civil servants claimed bribes had to be shared with senior officers.
8. People feared trouble, court appearance, etc., if they reported corruption.
9. Stringent controls and high standards were not accepted by the public, making them more willing to pay bribes.
10. Tea money was considered normal, tips for service not seen as bribes.
11. Public sympathised with needs of officials because their pay was too low.
12. Younger generation [then] were much more critical of government corruption and its links with crime.
13. Public concern was especially strong about police corruption.[87]

The Blair-Kerr Commission ushered in a new era of clean anti-corruption government movement. Between 1974 and 1993, 9000 people were prosecuted for corruption with a claimed 84% conviction rate.

The rate of complaints has fluctuated over the years, with a downward trend. For example, a total of 3189 cases were reported in 1974, the first year of the ICAC. This was dropped to a low of 1234 or a decline of 62% in 1980. Since then, it rises again and stabilised at the 2000 plus range between 1981 (2344) and 1992. Beginning in 1993, it hits a 3000-cases range (3276), until it hits the 4000-cases range in 2000-cases range (4390) and remained for 4 years, with 2003 at 4310 cases. From 2004 (3746), it was again on the downward trend until 2013 when, for the first time since 1995 (2987), it reported 2514 cases (see Table 5.1). It is clear that the ICAC has been successful in keeping corruption down in Hong Kong, after 1997, in spite of the change of political sovereignty, leadership and culture, and with mass influx of Chinese into China.

Turning to the most recent 2 years 2012 versus 2013 (Table 5.2), one sees that the government sector has seen a decrease in corruption complaints of minus 32%, with the HKP close behind at minus 27%. While the total number of corruption complaints might have been dropped by 33%, the people

Table 5.1 Number of Corruption Reports Received (Excluding Election-Related Reports)

Year	Total
1974	3189
1975	3179
1976	2433
1977	1700
1978	1234
1979	1665
1980	1772
1981	2344
1982	2286
1983	2516
1984	2365
1985	2474
1986	2545
1987	2299
1988	2162
1989	2388
1990	2390
1991	2186
1992	2257
1993	3276
1994	3312
1995	2987
1996	3086
1997	3057
1998	3555
1999	3561
2000	4390
2001	4476
2002	4371
2003	4310
2004	3746
2005	3685
2006	3339
2007	3600
2008	3377
2009	3450
2010	3427
2011	3868
2012	3731
2013	2514

Table 5.2 Breakdown of Complaints: 2012 versus 2013 (Excluding Election-Related Complaints)

	Jan.–Dec. 2012	Jan.–Dec. 2013	Percentage Change
Total	3932	2652	–33%
Government sector	1192	808	–32%
—Police	342	250	–27%
Other government departments	850	558	–34%
Private sector	2483	1649	–34%
Public bodies	257	195	–24%

Note: The breakdown is based on complaints against different departments/public bodies/industries. As a corruption report may have multiple complaints in respect of the above, the total number of complaints may be larger than the total number of corruption reports.

Table 5.3 Prosecutions[90]

	Jan.–Dec. 2012	Jan.–Dec. 2013	Percentage Change
Persons prosecuted	196	215	+10%
Completed prosecutions	227	198	–13%
Persons convicted	171	155	–9%
Persons cautioned	27	24	–11%
Government servants recommended for disciplinary/administrative action.			

prosecuted for prosecution have increased. This suggests that there has been more focussed investigation on successful cases (Tables 5.2 and 5.3).

The LRC: Report on Arrest (1992)[88]

In August 1992, and in anticipation of the 1997 reversion of political sovereignty, the LRC investigated into police powers of stop, search, arrest and detention in Hong Kong leading to the publication of: 'Report on Arrest'. The Report recommended to the adoption of the U.K. PACE to rein in abuse of police powers. The implementation of the LRC report was left to 'An Inter-departmental Working Group' chaired by SB consisting of all the disciplinary forces, ICAC and Legal Department which finally recommended for implementation of 30 of the 60 LRC's recommendations and another 21 were accepted in principle. The Working Group report was first entertained by the Hong Kong Legislative Council in November 2006 to act on.[89]

The Coopers & Lybrand Consultant Report (1993)

The reform of HKP started before 1997. It began in 1992. In that year, then CP Hui announced the vision, mission and values underscoring the incipient reform. In the same year, the HKP formed a Police Study Group and enlisted private consultants from Coopers & Lybrand to conduct a study of 'The Command Structure and Manning Level Review of the Royal Hong Kong Police Force' (a/k/a '*Police Management Review* (PMR)'. According to the Secretary for Security:

> The *Police Management Review*, begun in 1992 and completed in 1994, critically examined ways to improve the command structure, the use of modern technology and the manning levels of the entire Police Force so that it will be properly prepared and equipped to meet future challenges.[90]

The independent review of HKP was conducted by the consulting firm Coopers & Lybrand on the eve of 1997 over the restructuring of HKP (October 1992 to March 1993). The purpose of the study was to conduct a systematic and comprehensive review of the HKP management structure and make the necessary preparation for the transfer of power on 1 July 1997.[91] The Report was completed in March 1993. It made 116 recommendations. It concluded that: 'The Force already has a powerful culture[92] and the question is whether this culture is appropriate to support and under pin the changes that are needed in order to continue to provide a high quality service to the public'.[93] On 1 April 1994, the HKP Quality Service Wing was established to reform the HKP.

The Consultant Report and recommendations serve as the blueprint of and building block for HKP management reform, with an oversight of the Hong Kong Legislative Council Panel on Security.

In time, 42 reports[94] derived from PMR became the strategic plan.[95] The PMR is one of the most comprehensive, systematic, far ranging and deep-reaching review conducted on the command, management and operations of HKP, ever.

> The objective of the review is to determine the appropriate level of manning for the Police Force to carry out its functions efficiently. It also critically examines whether certain tasks should continue to be performed by the police; whether more modern technology can be used; and the maximum extent of civilianization. This is the most comprehensive study of the police establishment ever undertaken and obviously takes time to complete; we must get it right. Initial examination of the 42 reports has just recently been completed, and I am working at presenting the reports to the Security Panel of this Council for examination next month.[96]

The PMR was very much anticipated by the LegCo members.[97] In November of 1994, frustration, the senior member of the Democratic Party in charge of security and policing was heard demanding for the early release of the PMR:

> Mr President … (a) when the details of the Report will be disclosed, so that the public and Members of this Council can have specific and accurate information for analysis and discussion and will thus be able to reflect their views to the Government; and (b) whether the Government is of the view that the appropriate time to release details of the Report is when it applies to the Finance Committee for funds to implement the measures recommended in the Report; if so, what the reasons are and whether the Report will be released in full then?

The 42 PMR reports were finally shared with the LegCo Security Panel in May of 1995,[98] with one being withheld as against public interest because it dealt with the Security Wing.[99] With the release of the Reports, the LegCo Panel on Security formed a subcommittee to examine the Reports from May of 1995 to July of 1997.[100] With the participation of the LegCo, the structural and organisational reform to HKP then began in earnest.

On 9 July 2006, HKP requested funding from the LegCo-Establishment Subcommittee of finance committee for a major reorganisation of HKP management structure to cope with changes in population growth and work-related changes in Hong Kong, since 1983, and finally, the current command and control administration structure was put in place. Specifically:

> We need to streamline and update the management and control structure of the Police to take account of the changes in the demography and nature of crimes in Hong Kong that have taken place since the introduction of the existing directorate structure in 1983. The proposed re-organisation has taken into consideration the recommendations made by a management study on the Police command structure… The organisational changes …are as follows

a. Strengthening the operational support role of the Support Wing;
b. Strengthening the Crime Wing's capacity to combat organised crimes;
c. Following up on the consequential changes brought about by disbandment of the Special Branch;
d. Rationalising the command structure of police formation in the New Territories to take account of the population changes there;
e. Enhancing the human resource management capability of the Personnel Wing;
f. Replacing the Inspection Services Wing with a new Service Quality Wing to further promote the concept of accountability; and
g. Transforming and retitling the existing Management Services Wing to Information Systems Wing to take charge of the promotion of a wider use of information technology in the Force.[101]

The first to be observed is that the 1997 HKP reform involved real, substantive and substantial changes instead of cosmetic, nominal and minor changes, involving the destruction of the entire branch/post, for example, disbanding Special Branch and Bangkok counsellor post, or establishing a new bureau/functions, for example, Criminal Intelligence Bureau (CIB) and In-Service Training (IST) Branch.

Second, it involved fundamental reorganisation to HKP command and control structure, for example, removing the Traffic Wing (renamed as Traffic Branch command by an ACP) to a Support Wing (command by a CSP), territorial jurisdiction and operational functions, for example, splitting of N.T. into North and N.T. South Region in the face of added responsibilities and shifted priorities. The result was a more streamlined, efficient and cost-effective HKP.

Third, it involved changes to every aspects of HKP, from vision and mission, organisation and culture, structure and process, management and operations, staff and line.

Fourth, it involved facing up to new development, challenges and demands of the day.

Fifth, it involved doing more (productivity gain) and better (quality enhancement) policing with less resources, that is, achieving cost-effective policing, through re-defining of priority, integration of functions, alignment of services, leveraging of resources and introduction of technology.

Finally, it involved an expert-designed and evidence-based reform platform, process and outcome.

Lan Kwai Fong (LKF) Disaster Report (1993)[102]

In 1993, 20 people died and 71 odd were injured on New Year eve at LKF, one of Hong Kong's primer nightspots, as a result of a stampede by a frantic crowd.[103] An international crowd control scholar described the day's event thusly:

> 1993 (Jan 1st) LKF, Hong Kong. 21 died in crowd crush incident. The LKF disaster that took place in Hong Kong in the early hours of 1 January 1993. It was a crush crowd incident, catching thousands of party-goers off-guard and resulted in 21 persons dying. The location (narrow streets and a sloped gradient), poor police planning and bad weather all played their part in this disaster. The crowd. In January 1993 at LKF, not far from the Happy Valley Racecourse a disaster occurred. More than 20 people died in a crowd crush on a busy street. From Mr. Justice Bokary's Interim Report into that disaster. A number of persons, more or less in a row and more or less at the same time, lost or were deprived of their footing and fell. Because the press from behind was overwhelming, more and more people started falling. People piled upon those who had gone down before them. The pile grew until it reached such a height that the people immediately behind it were propped up by it and pinned against it by the press of people behind and upslope of them. Thus came about what some witnesses have called a 'human wall'. Tragically, men,

> women and children had the breath of life crushed out of them. 20 persons died very quickly, one more died in hospital some days later.[104]

The tragic incident, the first of its kind,[105] was thoroughly investigated by Mr Justice Bokhary.[106,107] Mr Justice Bokhary summarised the causes of the tragedy by isolating the main and contributing factors. He identified the main factor causing the incident as too many, densely packed, people in a small area. The other contributing factors were: gradient of the road, slippery road surface, pushing and jostling and drunkenness. The other unexpected factor was people from a cross road coming up against a downward crowd. The convergence of all these factors resulted in 'a massive, crushing human pile up'. The police officers on duty were not spared.[108]

The HKP was faulted for not doing its job in controlling the crowd, estimated to be 15–20,000 strong. The nature, complexity, mood and behaviour of the crowd was not explicitly considered, but implicitly suggested, for example, it distinguished LKF crowd from political crowd, and described them as 'milling' around, instead of behaving passively. In the final analysis, Justice Bokhary recommended that: 'an effort should be made by the police and other bodies having responsibility for crowd control in Hong Kong to expand their knowledge of the problem and how to deal with it'.[109]

The LKF tragedy spawned a number of studies, and many academic and professional, domestic[110] and foreign,[111] were undertaken by a variety of disciplines and with multiple perspectives.[112] As a tragic incident, the LKF stampede ranked high on Hong Kong people's awareness. According to a research conducted in March to September 2008,[113] people of Hong Kong rated LKF as one of the top three most likely 'disasters' to reoccur. LKF is a noteworthy event notwithstanding its low test rate (compared to the first two: severe acute respiratory syndrome [SARS]: 299/1775; Garley fire: 41/80) and avertable nature (namely crowd behaviour, not natural disaster (1) SARS or human error, (2) Garley Building fire). More significantly, it was one of the only three that makes the list before 1992 (landslide (1972), embankment collapse (1992)).

When the respondents were asked: 'Events in Hong Kong that are considered as disasters with likelihood of their occurrence according to parents with young children (*N*198)'.[114] The responses were (*N*: percentage):

1. SARS outbreak (299 deaths, 1755 infected) in 2003 (187/94.4%);
2. Garley Building fire (41 dead, 80 injured) in 1996 (143/72.2);
3. LKF tragedy (20 dead, 71 injured in stampede) in 1992 (130/65.7);
4. Building demolished in a landslide (67 dead) in 1972 (113/57.1);
5. Embankment collapse on Sau Mau Ping (71 dead) in 1972 (108/54.5);
6. Avian flu (18 infected, 6 dead) in 1997 (94/47.5);
7. Landslides in Baguio Villas (2 dead, 1500 evacuated) in 1992 (65/32.8);

8. China Airlines crash in 1999 (3 deaths, 209 injuries) (58/29.3);
9. Petrol bomb in Top One Karaoke (17 dead) in 1998 (55/27.3);
10. Far East jet-foil wreck (1 death, 119 injuries) in 1998 (51/25.8);
11. Explosion caused by oil leak from the transformer in West-rail Kowloon–Canton Railway Corporation (KCRC) (12 injuries) in 2007 (41/20.7);
12. Poisoning and food additives (frequently reported) imported from China (17/8.6);
13. Ministerial conference of World Trade Organization (5000 protesters, over 1000 arrested and nine injured) in 2005 (14/7.1).

Culturally, the iconic happenstance was seared into the (sub) consciousness[115] of foreigners[116] and the Hong Kong people alike:[117] 'The LKF Tragedy shocked many of us habitual patrons … is a mixed, hybrid space, a crowded and dangerous pace, carnival-like event in times of crisis, heavenly and not far from disasters…'.[118]

At an operational level, for the HKP, LKF instantly became ingrained in institutional memory, with external-perceived organisational ineptitude and internal professional frustration in the mix. Long known for its outstanding performance in crowd management and control in the face of crisis (1967) and challenges, against all odds, LKF stood as an enigma. Learning from the incident, the HKP proposed the use of closed-circuit television (CCTV)[119] as one of the many crowd control[120] and emergency relief measures, in all later mass public gatherings.[121] However, while most people, including more than a few tourism guides, warned people to stay away from LKF in holiday seasons and with festive occasions, the HKP–CCTV proposal was rejected on privacy and related (business) grounds.[122]

Law makers' objections notwithstanding, CCTV was widely used before the LKF incident, both in public (ICAC—interview, HKP—border and Transport Department—tunnel, housing—security) and in private (banks, retail shops, train, bus and MTR) and was taken for granted by the majority of the Hong Kong people, with placid acceptance to many, and openly embraced for more than a few.[123] It turned out that the HKP was the only agency that did not use CCTV aggressively or law enforcement purposes. In fact, the HKP had few administrative guidelines developed providing for their use. This is especially surprising given that the HK government had no law-regulating CCTV.

The HKP, as part of HKSAR post-1997 reform process, heavily leveraged technology, from a computer to CCTV, to keep Hong Kong safe and crime free. The latest bout over CCTV and privacy was fought over the installation of eight CCTVs without prior notice and conspicuous disclosure in and around the Legislative Council meeting as authorised by the Legislative Council Commission. The CCTV units were employed for security reasons.

'The installation of CCTV is aimed at proper management of public order activities outside Legco… The installation of CCTV is aimed at proper management of public order activities outside Legco, and police have notified related government departments and organisations'.

The employment of CCTVs was roundly criticised by a LegCo member from intrusions of privacy ('Public who join protests outside Legco will be under a threat that they are all under surveillance'. Pan-democrat unionist Lee Cheuk-yan) to lack of due notice (Privacy Commissioner's 'guidance note' requires: 'people should be explicitly informed that they are subject to CCTV surveillance') to being unnecessary. LegCo and Legislative Council Commission member, Cyd Ho Sau-lan observed: 'Police already have a video team to record protests and I do not see a need to install those permanent surveillance cameras'.[124]

Hong Kong Audit Commission Audit of HKP

The Audit Department (Audit Commission after 1997) is one of the oldest departments of the Hong Kong Government. It was first established in 1841.

The Audit Commission is charged with conducting oversight, operational (regulatory) or financial (value for money) audits. Its main mission being: 'To provide independent, professional and quality audit services to the Legislative Council and public sector organisations in order to help the Government enhance public sector performance and accountability in Hong Kong'. Its major objective is 'to enhancing the performance and accountability of the Government and other public sector organisations in Hong Kong'. The Audit Commission achieves its mission by:

1. Conducting regularity audits which provide the Legislative Council with an overall assurance that the government's financial and accounting transactions and those of funds of a public or quasi-public nature are proper and that they conform to accepted accounting standards; and
2. Conducting value-for-money audits which provide the Legislative Council with independent information, advice and assurance about the economy, efficiency and effectiveness with which any bureau/department of the government, agency, other public bodies, public office, or audited organisation has discharged its functions.[125]

The authority to audit was granted to the Director of Audit Commission.

According to the Audit Ordinance (Cap. 122), the Director of Audit 'has wide powers of access to the records of departments', 'can require any public officer to give an explanation and to furnish such information as he thinks fit to enable him to discharge his duties' and 'is not subject to the direction or control of any other person or authority in performing his duties and when exercising his powers under the Ordinance'.

The Audit Commission carries out two kinds of audits, namely regularity audit and value-for-money audit.

Regularity audit is conducted to assure the Legislative Council that the government finances, accounts and funds (of public and quasi-public) the agency.[126]

Value for audit examines the economy, efficiency and effectiveness of government organisations pursuant to established guidelines agreed between the Legislative Council—Public Accounts Committee and Director of Audit.[127]

In the year of February 2000 to October 2010, the Hong Kong Audition Commission completed a total of eight audits, with three of them in the first year, with a management of leave in the Hong Kong Police Force (October 2007, 2010); collection of fines imposed by Magistrate Courts (March 2006): road safety: accident investigation and law enforcement (March 2006); station improvement and amalgamation projects (March 2005); construction of the Government Flying Service Headquarters (March 2002); provision of staff recreation, catering and welfare services for the Hong Kong Police Force (October 2000); the provision of vehicle removal service and permanent vehicle pounds (February 2000).

Many of these audit reports were very critical to the HKP, especially when it came down to police administration in traffic law enforcement, planning of station upgrade, working with external partners and leave administration. In the history of the HKP, this was for the first time that any external agency called into questions of the HKP's operating capacity, efficiency and effectiveness, with the use of objective data obtained independently.

Station Improvement and Amalgamation Projects (April 2005)[128]

In 1999, the HKP started an ambitious station (physical and security) improvement, to appease the public, and amalgamation project, to facilitate effective deployment and save costs, for $649.2 million.[129] The audit showed that the project suffers from time delay (21 months),[130] space wastages (1686 square metres)[131] and failure of purpose (hardware not in use).[132] The problems as identified by the audit resulted from mal-administration, from failure of internal communication—consultation over needs[133] to lack of external coordination with contractors,[134] to delay in implementing feedbacks,[135] to inadequate needs assessment[136] and so on.

The audit uncovered the following (selected) shortcomings with the improvement and amalgamation project:

First, there was a substantial delay of station improvement project because there was inadequate internal communication between and within formations over the needs for and limitations to improvements to be made.[137] There was a lack of coordination between builder works contractors and security system contractor, resulting in duplication of work.[138]

Second, the audit identified a utilisation of spare space problem with three police stations under improvement.[139] Specifically, the audit noted that 1686 square metres of station space were not put to good use for 2 years, without the Government Property Agency (GPA) ever being consulted.[140] Similarly, when New Territories South Regional Headquarters moved out of Tsing Yi Police Station to Tsuen Wan, the extra space at Tsing Yi was not utilised.[141] Finally and more generally, the space savings—surplus accommodation, changing room and night-duty room—from the overall station improvement programme was not reported to GPA for alternate disposal.[142]

Third, with the 'remodeled report room',[143] the audit found that after visiting 16 report rooms (July to September 2004), that in six out of nine of the reception areas, there was no one on duty.[144] This reflected inadequate needs assessment and poor planning process.[145]

Fourth, the audit found that officers reported that the carpet at the 'back of house' area was not easy to clean and asked for replacement in 2001. But such feedback was not heeded until January 2003. By that time, nearly all police report rooms (49 of them) had been carpeted. The replacement costs with synthetic tiles were $1.7 million. This was a costly mistake.[146]

Fifth, the audit found that the information kiosks located in 16 different report rooms were underutilised,[147] in both hardware[148] and by citizens.[149] As a result, many of the information kiosks were used for different purposes, for example, officer briefing,[150] or found to be dysfunctional.[151]

Sixth, the audit found that resource centres for police officers that have little resource materials, were rarely used[152] and otherwise too close to each other.[153]

Seventh, the audit found that with the installation of 'automated station security system', the stakeholders were not fully briefed, consulted or involved beforehand resulting in confusion and misunderstanding.[154]

Eighth, with the station amalgamation project, the audit found it to be a success, saving the HKP of $44.3 million through the deletion of 117 posts in the first 5 years.[155] However, the amalgamation also caused temporary congestions in some merged stations, such as The Castle Peak Police Station and the Chai Wan Police Station.[156]

III: Conclusion

This review of police reform literature illustrates that police reform is natural, necessary and continuous, as a by-product of social, political and cultural changes. In the case of Hong Kong, police reform was driven by events (reactionary change to scandals, such as Caldwell and Godber incidents) as by institutions (pro-active change as a result of audits, HKLR).

It is now necessary to turn to the final chapters to see how HKP reform was conducted in the 1950s, as a case study.

Endnotes

1. R. K. Yin, *Case Study Research: Design and Method*, 4th edition (Thousand Oaks, CA: Sage, 2009). ('A case study is an empirical inquiry that investigates a contemporary phenomenon in depth and within the real life context, especially when the boundaries between phenomenon and context are most clearly evident'. p. 16).
2. S. Savage, *Police Reform: Forces for Change* (London: Oxford University Press, 2007). http://www.theguardian.com/books/2008/jan/12/crime.society
3. J. Grieve, A fair cop, *The Guardian*, Friday 11 January 2008. http://www.theguardian.com/books/2008/jan/12/crime.society
4. Mission Statement Police Reform Organizing Project. http://www.policereformorganizingproject.org/?page_id=2
5. M. Doyle, The police reform that wasn't, *The British Scholarly Society*, December 2012. http://britishscholar.org/publications/2012/12/02/the-police-reform-that-wasnt/.
6. M. J. Trebilcock and R. J. Daniels, *Rule of Law Reform and Development: Charting the Fragile Path of Progress* (Cheltenham, UK: Edward Elgar Publishing, 1 January 2009).
7. Ibid., 107–108. Normative Benchmarks. A re-conceptualizing the role of the police in developing countries.
8. M. Trivunovic, Police reform—Introduction 1, *Helsinki Monitor*, 15 (3): 171 (1 January 2004). ('Police reform is widely recognized as a key process of democratic transformation, particularly from the perspective of protecting human rights and democratic institutions. ...two experiences from Southeast Europe—Macedonia and Serbia—have seen police reform launched precisely with this objective'.)
9. M. Kempa and L. Johnston, Challenges and prospects for the development of inclusive plural policing in Britain: Overcoming political and conceptual obstacles, *Australian and New Zealand Journal of Criminology*, 38 (2): 181–191, 2005.
10. D. A. Sklansky, The promise and the peril of police professionalism, In: J. Brown (ed.), *The Future of Policing* (Oxon and New York: Routledge, 2013). http://www.law.berkeley.edu/php-programs/faculty/facultyPubsPDF.php?facID=4878&pubID=60
11. J. S. Berman, *Police Administration and Progressive Reform: Theodore Roosevelt as Police Commissioner of New York* (Westport, CT: Greenwood Press, 1987); H. Toch, The democratization of police in the United States: 1895–1974, *The Police Forum: Academy of Criminal Justice Sciences*, 7 (2): 1–8 (April 1997).
12. The progressive era (1890–1920). http://www.gwu.edu/~erpapers/teachinger/glossary/progressive-era.cfm.
13. T. Roosevelt (1858–1919). *An Autobiography* 1913 (New York: The Macmillan Company, 1913).

14. P. Albrecht and L. Buur, An uneasy marriage: Non-state actors and police reform, *Policing and Society*, 19 (4): 390, 2009.
15. Ibid.
16. A. E. Juncos, Europeanization by decree? The case of police reform in Bosnia, *Journal of Common Market Studies*, 49 (2): 367–389, 2011.
17. K. C. Wong, *Police Reform in China* (Boca Raton, FL: CRC Press, 2012).
18. W. O'Neill, Police reform in post conflict societies: What we know and what we still need to know, *International Peace Institute*, Policy Papers—14 April 2005. http://reliefweb.int/sites/reliefweb.int/files/resources/AB276AF8A1C3261E852570B20077F20C-police%20reform%20post-conflict.pdf; Rama Mani, Policing in post-conflict situations, *Concept Paper for Whitehall Policy Seminar*, London. http://www.ssrnetwork.net/document_library/detail/2978/policing-in-post-conflict-situations.
19. Ibid.
20. J. Sovell, *Good Cop/Bad Cop: Mass Media and the Cycle of Police Reform* (Monsey, NY: Willow Tree Press, 2003), p. 177 ('One of the central features of postmodernity . . . is the prominence of mediated experience in our daily lives. No longer do we encounter reality firsthand . . . worldly events are increasingly experienced only second-hand [which] has tremendous consequences' (p. 45).)
21. Ibid., p. 103.
22. Ibid., p. 93.
23. Ibid., pp. 158–160.
24. Britain: Hard to turn the coppers round; Police reform, *The Economist*, 369: 52 (15 November 2003). https://www.google.com/search?q=Britain%3A+Hard+to+turn+the+coppers+round%3B+Police+reform%2C%E2%80%9D+The+Economist+&ie=utf-8&oe=utf-8&aq=t&rls=org.mozilla:en-US:official&client=firefox-a
25. G. Dean, Police reform: Rethinking operational policing, *Journal of Criminal Justice*, 23(4): 337–247, 1995.
26. Reforming police: Legitimacy and effectiveness, *ECPR Joint Sessions of Workshops* 2014, Salamanca. European Consortium for Political Research. http://www.ecpr.eu/Events/PaperDetails.aspx?PaperID=15818&EventID=12.
27. A. Goldsmith, Police reform and the problem of trust, *Theoretical Criminology*, 9 (4): 443–470, 2005.
28. T. Prenzler and J. Ransley (eds.), *Police Reform: Building Integrity* (Sydney: Hawkins Press, 2002), Chapter 1, 25 ways to fight corruption.
29. Police reform: Ah, democracy, *Economist*, 10 November 2012. http://www.economist.com/news/britain/21565996-elected-watchdogs-are-flawedidea-boycotting-polls-worse-one-ah-democracy
30. Ndung'u Wainaina, *Kenya: Police Reforms Are Key to Rule of Law*, 20 October 2011. http://allafrica.com/stories/201110210753.html.
31. S. Walker, Institutionalizing police accountability reforms: The problem of making police reforms endure, *St. Louis University Public Law Review*, 32(1): 57, 2012.
32. G. Heyer, New public management: A strategy for democratic police reform in transitioning and developing countries, *Policing an International Journal of Police Strategies and Management*, 34 (3): 419–433, 2011.
33. A. S. Vitale, Police reform's next step, *The Indypendent*, 194. 25 February 2014. http://www.indypendent.org/2014/02/25/police-reform%E2%80%99s-next-step

34. R. Ritsert and M. Pekar, New public management reforms in German police services, *German Policy Study*, 5 (2): 17–47, 30, 2009.
35. B. Bowling, Transnational policing: The globalization thesis, a typology and research agenda, *Policing*, 3 (2): 149–160, 2009. (Globalisation results in homogenisation of police system and practice, in Western mode).
36. D. Bayley, *Changing the Guard: Developing Democratic Police Abroad* (New York, NY: Oxford University Press, 2006), p. 6.
37. F. Leishman, S. Cope and P. Starie, Reforming the police in Britain: New public management, policy networks and a tough old bill, *International Journal of Public Sector Management*, 8 (4): 26–37, 1995.
38. E. S. Fisher and S. M. Shortell, Accountable care organizations: Accountable for what, to whom, and how? *Journal of the American Medical Association*, 304 (15): 1715–1716, 20 October 2010.
39. J. B. L. Chan, Governing police practice: Limits of the new accountability, *British Journal of Sociology*, 50 (2): 251–270, 1999.
40. Police as a public institution is always accountable. The debate is over what, whom and how. M. Escotet Universities must be accountable, yes, but to whom? *Guardian (Professional)*, 10 December 2012. ('Universities, whether public or private, cannot be exempt from internal and external control and there has been a clear move towards implementing institutional assessment and accountability processes since the end of the twentieth century. But this process of accountability should not be influenced by the government in power or by political bias within universities.') http://www.guardian.co.uk/higher-education-network/blog/2012/dec/10/university-regulation-accountability-to-whom.
41. W. Skogan, Why reforms fail, *Policing and Society*, 18 (1): 23–34, 2008.
42. J. Donne, *From Devotions upon Emergent Occasions*, 1623. Mediation XVII (http://en.wikisource.org/wiki/Meditation_XVII; https://web.cs.dal.ca/~johnston/poetry/island.html).
43. A. Hill, The dialectics of police reform in Nigeria, *The Journal of Modern African Studies*, 46 (2): 215–234, June 2008. ('Based on developments in the Nigeria Police since 2005, this article suggests that reform can make a normative and organisational difference, but that in the absence of fundamental socio-political change, its effects tend to be superficial, localised and temporary. Reform's dynamic is better understood as a classic dialectic than a serial succession of movement.')
44. Ibid.
45. D. H. Bayley Democratizing the police abroad: What to do and how to do it. *Issues in International Crime* (U.S. Department of Justice: National Institute of Justice, 2001), NCJ 188472. www.ncjrs.gov/pdffiles1/nij/188742.pdf.
46. Ibid., Chapter 2: *Generic Lessons for Changing Police Organizations*, p. 17.
47. *Knowledge Management Symposium*. 20 May 2005. Hong Kong. http://www.psdas.gov.hk/content/doc/2004-2-22/Sym%20Handbook%20-2004-2-22.pdf.
48. 'HKP Reform Inquires' refers to major inquiries into HKP structure, process, policy or functions requiring changes. This is not a comprehensive list. Ad hoc and incidence-based inquiries, for example, charges of individual malfeasant, organisational cover up, operational problems or policy review, are not included. For the individual malfeasant, see Published under Section 48(2) of the Personal Data (Privacy) Ordinance (Cap. 486). Investigation Report: The Hong Kong Police Force leaked internal documents containing personal data via Foxy

(English translation) Report Number: R13–15218. Date issued: 24 October 2013. Office of the Privacy Commissioner for Personal Data, Hong Kong. For organisational cover up, see A summary of the report of the Commission of Inquiry into Inspector MacLennan's case (Hong Kong Government Printer, 1981). For operational problems inquiry, see Legislative Council Panel on Security. Security arrangements for the *Sixth Ministerial Conference of the World Trade Organisation* held in Hong Kong from 13 to 18 December 2005. LC Paper No. CB(2) 2362/05-06(01). 4 July 2006 and Legislative Council Panel on Security. Police Review of Policing Arrangements during Visits of Political Dignitaries to Hong Kong. LC Paper No. CB(2)921/11-12(07). 7 February 2012. For policy review, see LegCo Panel on Security. Subcommittee on Indebtedness of Police Officers. Minutes of meeting held on Tuesday, 16 November 1999 at 10:45 am in Conference Room A of the Legislative Council Building. LC Paper No. CB(2) 1050/99-00. http://www.pcpd.org.hk/english/publications/files/R13_15218_e.pdf

49. On 20 May 1858, Governor John Bowring appointed a Commission of Inquiry to investigate into Attorney General Anstey's charges, sent directly to the Secretary of Colony. See 'Warrant of Commission'. J. W. Norton-Kyshe, *The History of the Laws and Courts of Hongkong, Tracing Consular Jurisdiction in China and Japan and Including Parliamentary Debates, and the Rise, Progress and Successive Changes in the Various Public Institutions of the Colony from the Earliest Period to the Present Time,* Vol. 1 (London: T. F. Unwin, 1898), p. 508.
50. T. C. Anstey, Crime and government at Hong Kong, a letter to the *Times* (1859) RareBooksClub.com (4 July 2012).
51. D. R. Caldwell, A vindication of the character of the undersigned from the aspersions of Mr T. Chisholm Anstey, *Ex-Attorney General of Hongkong as Contained in His Charges, His Pamphlet, and His Letter to the Secretary of State for the Colonies to the Secretary of State for the Colonies* (Hongkong: Noronha's Office, 1860).
52. C. Munn, Colonialism in a Chinese atmosphere: The Caldwell affair and the perils of collaboration in early colonial Hong Kong, In: R. Bickers and C. Henriot (eds.), *New Frontiers: Imperialism's New Communities in East Asia, 1842–1953* (Manchester: Manchester Press, 2000), pp. 12–38.
53. Ibid., 25.
54. C. Munn, *Anglo-China: Chinese People and British Rule in Hong Kong, 1841–1880* (Hong Kong: Routledge, 16 December 2013), p. 332.
55. J. W. Norton-Kyshe, *History of the Laws and Courts of Hongkong,* Vol. 2 (London, 1898), p. 180. *Op cit.* 49, 180, supra.
56. Ibid., 178.
57. Ibid., 180.
58. Ibid., 200.
59. The Report of the Police Commission, CO 129/158, Paragraph 1, See Chapter 6: The Police Commission in Austin Kerrigan, Policing a Colony: The case if Hong Kong: 1844–1899. PhD dissertation. Cardiff Graduate Law School. University of Wales (January 2001).
60. Ibid., Austin Kerrigan, p. 203.
61. Ibid., 204.
62. J. W. Norton-Kyshe, *History of the Laws and Courts of Hongkong,* Vol. 2 (London, 1898), p. 189. *Op cit.* 49, 189, supra.
63. The Report of the Police Commission, CO 129/158, Paragraph 74.

64. Ibid.
65. Austin Kerrigan, op. cit., p. 207.
66. I. Ward, *Sui Geng: The Hong Kong Marine Police 1841–1950* (Hong Kong: Hong Kong University Press, 1991).
67. J. W. Norton-Kyshe, *History of the Laws and Courts of Hongkong*, Vol. 2 (London, 1898), p. 200. *Op cit*. 49, 200, supra.
68. Report of The Commission of Inquiry under Sir Alastair Blair-Kerr, Government Printer, Hong Kong, September 1973.
69. The best short history about corruption in Hong Kong is: de Speville, Bertrand, *Hong Kong, Policy Initiatives against Corruption* (Paris: Organisation for Economic Co-operation and Development, 1997) pp. 80. For a comprehensive study, see H. J. Lethbridge, *Hard Graft in Hong Kong: Scandal, Corruption, the ICAC* (Hong Kong: Hong Kong University Press, 1985).
70. Ibid., p. 12.
71. L. Lam, Forty years since its creation, how the ICAC cleaned up corruption in Hong Kong, *South China Morning Post*, 15 February 2014. http://www.scmp.com/news/hong-kong/article/1428093/forty-years-its-creation-how-icac-cleaned-corruption-hong-kong.
72. Those officers who are on the take are rewarded by 'good' postings, for example, CID or Vice, and 'golden beats' (money beats).
73. Sanctions ran from administrative transfer to undesirable sanction, for example, in the mild case being posed to the frontier (then a derogative term suggesting not being wise enough to be on the take), in the medium case being picked on by peers and reprimanded by seniors and in the worse case being disciplined and forced out of HKP, for some conjured-up reasons, for example, dereliction of duties, or no reason at all, that is, trump-up charges. The author was not on the take, and was posed to the frontier, at Sha Tau Kok in 1970.
74. See M. J. Macoun to Mr Crowson, 3 July 1973; FCO 40/451. Additional documents relating to the case can be found in FCO 40/456 and FCO 40/453. Reported in M. Hampton, British legal culture and colonial governance: The attack on corruption in Hong Kong, 1968–1974, *Britain and the World* 5.2: 223–239, 2012, note 24, p. 230.
75. From the Second Report of The Commission of Inquiry under Sir Alastair Blair-Kerr, Government Printer, Hong Kong, September 1973, p. 24, Section 99.
76. R. P. L. Lee, Incongruence of legal codes and folk norms, In: R. P. L. Lee (ed.), *Corruption and Its Control in Hong Kong* (Hong Kong, 1981), pp. 75–104.
77. E. Elliott, *The Avarice, Bureaucracy and Corruption of Hong Kong* (Hong Kong: Friends Commercial Printing Factory, 1971), pp. 12–14; J. Smart, *The Political Economy of Street Hawkers in Hong Kong* (Hong Kong, 1989), see the files in HKRS 301-1-1.
78. The best short history about corruption in Hong Kong is: de Speville, Bertrand, *Hong Kong, Policy Initiatives against Corruption* (Paris: Organisation for Economic Co-operation and Development, 1997), pp. 80.
79. Godber's downfall: The landmark case ICAC. http://www.icac.org.hk/new_icac/eng/cases/godber/html/case1.html.
80. For Hong Kong government effort to put corruption under control, see K. Hsin-Chi, Anti-corruption legislation in Hong Kong: A history, In: R. P. L. Lee and

T. Cheung (eds.), *Corruption and Its Control in Hong Kong: Situation Up to the Late Seventies*, (Hong Kong: Chinese University of Hong Kong, 1981).

81. Godber could be extradited for corruption from England, but not for living beyond means translated into legalese: *Possessing Financial Assets Disproportionate to an Official Emolument* (Section 10 of Prevention of Bribery Ordinance).
82. Pay out of SP Wan Chai was going for $60 to $100,000/month.
83. The ICAC began its work on 15 February 1974.
84. M. Hampton, British legal culture and colonial governance: The attack on corruption in Hong Kong, 1968–1974, *Britain and the World*, 5.2: 223–239, 232, 2012.
85. S. C. Y. Luk, Questions of ethics in public sector management: The case study of Hong Kong, *Public Personnel Management*, 41 (2): 361–378, 2012, n. 18 (referencing ICAC Godber case.)
86. R. Yep, The crusade against corruption in Hong Kong in the 1970s: Governor MacLehose as a zealous reformer or reluctant hero? *China Information*, 27 (2): 197–221, July 2013.
87. The best short history about corruption in Hong Kong is: de Speville, Bertrand, *Hong Kong, Policy Initiatives against Corruption* (Paris: Organisation for Economic Co-operation and Development, 1997).
88. See also Confession Statements and their admissibility in criminal proceedings (HKLRC Report). ('The central recommendation of the report is that a mechanism should be established to provide an accused person with an early opportunity to raise any complaint of ill treatment by the law enforcement agencies with an independent party'.) http://www.hkreform.gov.hk/en/publications/radmissibility.htm.
89. Minutes of meeting of the Panel on Security on 11 November 1996 (LC Paper No. CB(2) 1545/96-97). http://www.legco.gov.hk/yr96-97/english/panels/se/minutes/se 111196.htm.
90. LegCo Sitting (Hansard) 2 November 1995. http://www.legco.gov.hk/yr95-96/english/lc_sitg/hansard/han0211.htm
91. Coopers and Lybrand, *The Review of the Top Management Structure of the Royal Hong Kong Police: Final Report*. London: Coopers & Lybrand, 1993.
92. Emphasis on discipline with a 'can do spirit' and problem-oriented approach, lifetime commitment with a strong sense of loyalty and 'esprit de corps', strong rank consciousness and formalised internal communication and control system.
93. Ibid., 71.
94. Coopers and Lybrand, The proper title of the Cooper and Libra study was: 'Report on the Command Structure and Manning Level Review of the Royal Hong Kong Police Force'.
95. The LegCo Panel for Security, subcommittee on PMR has divided the PMR into the following classifications: Maintenance of law and order; prevention and detection of crime; enlistment of public support for the Force; reduction of traffic accidents; field of operations and others.
96. Hong Kong Legislative Council, Official record of proceedings, Wednesday, 29 March 1995. The council met at half-past 2 o'clock. Secretary for Security briefing on law and order in Hong Kong.
97. Hong Kong Legislative Council, Official record of proceedings, 30 November 1994. ('MR JAMES TO asked (in Cantonese): Mr President … (a) when the details of the Report will be disclosed, so that the public and Members of this

Council can have specific and accurate information for analysis and discussion and will thus be able to reflect their views to the Government; and (b) whether the Government is of the view that the appropriate time to release details of the Report is when it applies to the Finance Committee for funds to implement the measures recommended in the Report; if so, what the reasons are and whether the Report will be released in full then'?)

98. 'In May 1995, the Administration released 41 reports arising from a review of the manpower requirements of the Police Force. On account of the magnitude of subjects covered and the vast number of reports involved, the Security Panel decided on the formation of a subcommittee to examine the reports in more detail. The Subcommittee to study the reports of the *Police Management Review* was accordingly formed in May 1995'.
99. Parliamentary monitoring mechanism in Intelligence Agencies, RP03/95-96 Research and Library Services Division, Legislative Council Secretariat, October 1995.
100. 1994–1995 Hon James to Kun-sun (Chairman) Hon Mrs Selina Chow, Obe, JP Hon Zachary Wong Wai-yin 1995–1996 Hon James to Kun-sun (Chairman) Hon Mrs Selina Chow, Obe, JP Hon Andrew Cheng Kar-foo (until 29 April 1996) Hon Cheung Hon-chung Hon Ho Chun-yan Hon Bruce Liu Sing-lee terms of reference 4. The terms of reference of the subcommittee is 'to consider the reports of the *Police Management Review* and to make appropriate recommendations'. LegCo Panel on Security, Report of the Subcommittee on the *Police Management Review*. LegCo Paper No. CB(2) 120/96-97. Ref: CB2/PS/4/95. http://www.legco.gov.hk/yr96-97/english/panels/se/papers/se2810-3.htm
101. Finance Committee—Establishment Subcommittee (Papers) 9 July 96. Item for establishment subcommittee of finance committee. Head 122—Police: Royal Hong Kong Police Force. Subhead 001 salaries EC(96–97)32 on 9 July 1996. http://www.legco.gov.hk/yr95-96/english/fc/esc/papers/es090732.htm
102. Bokhary, Justice, *The LKF Disaster on January 1 1993: Interim Report,* Government Printer, 1993.
103. 20 killed in Hong Kong stampede, *Independence,* 1 January 1993. http://www.independent.co.uk/news/world/20-killed-in-hong-kong-stampede-1476034.html
104. Dr. G. Keith Still, 2.1. Crowded disasters, *Safer Crowd* (2000–2012). http://www.safercrowds.com/CrowdDisasters.html.
105. There were a total of 13 Commissions of Inquiry appointed by the Chief Executive in Council (or formerly the Governor in Council) between 1966 and 2003, starting with the Commission of Inquiry into Kowloon Disturbances which was appointed under the Commissioners Powers Ordinance (1) or Commissions of Inquiry Ordinance (Chapter 86) (12). None of them deal with fatalities resulting from crowd stamped. Information note Commissions of Inquiry, *Legislative Council Secretariat,* 20 March 2003. (Ref.: IN19/02-03).
106. Immediately (2 days) after the LKF incident, Hong Kong Governor Paten appointed the Honorary Justice Bokhary to inquire into the accident. The preliminary report was ready by 18 January 1993, and the final report published on 23 February 1993. Bokhary, Justice, *The LKF Disaster on January 1 1993: Interim Report,* Government Printer, 1993.

107. Cheng, Long-ping, Johnny, A consideration of the contagion and emergent-norm theories: A case study of LKF. MA dissertation, Centre for the Study of Public Order, University of Leicester in association with School of Professional and Continuing Education, University of Hong Kong, 1994.
108. The police officers on duty that night, being defensive, held a totally different view of what happened. The HKP officers felt that the there was nothing unusual about the crowd, in size, constitution or behaviour. In fact, they were fairly well behaved, given their collective mentality and festive mood. See Chapter 5, ibid.
109. K. Bokhary, Inquiry of the LKF disaster: Final Report 1993 Hong Kong Government, Hong Kong Government Printer, 1993.
110. K. K. Wu, C. C. Lu and E. Y. Leung, Responding to the LKF disaster: A case study from Hong Kong, *Community Psychologist*, 28 (5): 28–30, 1995; R. A. Cocks, The medical management of civil disasters in Hong Kong, *Hong Kong Journal of Emergency Medicine*, 3: 179–184, 2000; W. M. Fung, K. Y. Lai and A. Y. Loke, Nurses' perception of disaster: Implications for disaster nursing curriculum, *Journal of Clinical Nursing*, 18 (22): 3165–3171, 2009. ('Only 123 out of the 164 respondents (75%) gave a description of disaster in the open-ended question. Sixty-one per cent of them described unfortunate events with large numbers of victims as disasters. The "LKF tragedy—stampede caused by overcrowdedness" (90.9%) and the severe acute respiratory syndrome outbreak (89.6%) were commonly referred to as disasters in Hong Kong. Fires in tall buildings (61.6%), infectious disease outbreaks (61%) and stampedes caused by overcrowding (48.8%) were rated as the events most likely to happen in Hong Kong'.) http://www.ncbi.nlm.nih.gov/pubmed/19619209.
111. R. S. C. Lee and R. L. Hughes, Exploring trampling and crushing in a crowd, *Journal of Transportation Engineering*, 131 (8): 575–583, 2005; http://dx.doi.org/10.1061/(ASCE)0733-947X(2005)131:8(575); R. S. C. Lee and R. L. Hughes, Minimisation of the risk of trampling in a crowd, *Mathematics and Computers in Simulation*, 74 (1): 29m–37m, 2007.
112. HKP internal study of LKF included a model replication by SP Chin, then a CIP with BSU (Briefing and Support Unit), HKP. 'Retiring OC BSU looks back on his secondary duty', ('After serving as BSU's Second-in-Command, SP Chin was appointed OC in 1994, and has been leading the unit to take part in Force-wide Counter Terrorism Exercises. During his time in BSU, SP Chin also led its members in a number of extremely complex tasks, including providing scale models for the following incidents: "Shek Kong Camp Fire (1992)"; "LKF Tragedy (1993)"; 'Garley Building Fire (1996)", "Mei Foo Sun Chuen Fire (1997)", "Hong Kong Sanatorium and Hospital Vascular System Failure (1998)", "Hei Ling Chau Riot (2000)", "Tsui Chuk Garden Explosion (2002)", "Tuen Mun Highway Bus Accident (2003)", "Homantin Service Reservoir Police Opened Fire (2009)", and "Rizal Park and Coach Hostage Incident in Manila (2010)" '. Those models provided great assistance to end users and drew rare praise by police officers, judges, coroners, lawyers and jury members. *OffBeat*, 961, 2012.
113. O. W. M. Fung and A. Y. Loke, Disaster preparedness of families with young children in Hong Kong, *Scandinavian Journal of Public Health*, 38: 880–888, 2010.
114. Ibid., p. 884, Table II.
115. After the LKF incident, the Division of Clinical Psychology (DCP) of The Hong Kong Psychological Society set up a Critical Incident Team (CIT) in February

1993 to provide post-disaster psychological services in Hong Kong. http://www.dcp.hkps.org.hk/cit.php.

116. For a blogger's rendition of the tragic event and take away, see Marc Perton, Take a cup of kindness for LKF. (31 December 2006). ('Suddenly, what had started as a peaceful New Year's Eve celebration turned into a panicked mob, with all 20,000 souls rushing to get off of the street. When the melee ended, 21 people were dead and more than 100 were injured.... LKF became synonymous with death'.). http://www.perton.com/2006/12/31/take-a-cup-of-kindness-for-lan-kwai-fong-2/.
117. The HK government proposed to organise a New Year party up the peak to divert people and traffic from Central and LKF. An anxious Legco member immediately asked:
    a. *'of the estimated number of participants in the celebration programme on that night;*
    b. *whether it is expected that the activities there will help ease the overcrowding at LKF as experienced on similar occasions in the past;*
    c. *(c)what measures will be taken by the police and other departments concerned for crowd control including contingency measures to cope with emergency cases, if any, at the two locations on that night'?* The Secretary for Security was equally quick in providing reassurance: 'Mr President, yes, I can confirm that. The lesson learnt from the tragedy that occurred last year have been taken into account, not just in the event planned for this New Year, but in events that have taken place earlier this year. Loudhailers are used extensively, and specifically in Victoria Park there is a one-way pedestrian flow arrangement that has been introduced, and for that matter it will also be introduced at LKF to ensure that there is no buildup of crowds. And therefore no situation will arise that might result in an emergency'. Official proceeding records, Hong Kong Legislative Council—15 December 1993.
118. M. Ingham, *Hong Kong a Cultural History* (Oxford and New York: Oxford University Press, 2007), p. 146.
119. Installation of closed-circuit television systems at LKF. Item I of LC Paper No. CB(2)1444/01-02(01) Security Bureau. March 2002.
120. Traffic and crowd management during Halloween: LKF and Halloween crowd control set for LKF, Law and order Hong Kong Government, 27 October 2002. http://www.police.gov.hk/pprb/peb/english/102907_e.html; 27 October 2003 respectively. http://archive.news.gov.hk/isd/ebulletin/en/category/lawandorder/031027/html/031027en08002.htm Crowd management and traffic arrangements during Halloween in LKF, *Business News Asia*, 27 October 2011 ('Police will implement crowd control measures and special traffic arrangements in LKF from 29 October to 1 November to facilitate the public to celebrate the Halloween'.). http://asiarelease.asia/crowd-management-and-traffic-arrangements-during-halloween-in-lan-kwai-fong/.
121. Since then, mass gatherings have grown in frequencies, size, complexity, sophistication and audacities, making HKP crowd management and control duties more onerous and difficult. Chapter 8: Hong Kong Police Force, Hong Kong Government, 2008, 8.8 (d), p. 117, *Crowd Management, Policing Public Order Events and Major Events.* http://www.jsscs.gov.hk/reports/en/scds_gs_08/gs_ch8.pdf.
122. S. Leese, LKF: From sweaty taverns to decadent discos, *Cable News Network*, 6 September 2010. (LKF was ushered into existence in 1983 with the opening of the

California Bar, and later Disco Disco. LKF was famous for everything that goes jet-set life style, where drinks, drugs and sex were dispensed within abundance, all within the yards of Central Police Station and Victoria Prison. It was demolished on 2 September 2010 to make way for real-estate development.) See also S'porean undergraduate gang-raped in Hong Kong, asiaone.com 8 July 2010. http://www.asiaone.com/News/The%2BNew%2BPaper/Story/A1Story20100706-225546.html. http://www.cnngo.com/hong-kong/drink/lan-kwai-fong-used-to-be-more-fun-262656.

123. Hong Kong people's view towards privacy is mixed, attitudinally, cognitively, emotionally and behaviourally. For example, according to a survey, a majority is mindful of their privacy rights, but chose not to take steps to protect their entitlement, accepted on rare occasions. See 'Social Attitude Towards Privacy' in Graham Greenleaf, Comparative study of different approaches to new privacy challenges: Country study—Hong Kong (European Commission. Directorate—General justice, freedom and security, 29 May 2010), pp. 3–4. (Public awareness is high, but activism is low. Elite knowledge and activism is high, but achievement is insignificant.)
124. P. Tsang, Legco CCTV cameras raise privacy concerns, *South China Moring Post*, 15 April 2011. http://topics.scmp.com/news/hk-news-watch/article/Legco-CCTV-cameras-raise-privacy-concerns.
125. Audit Commission: Vision, mission, values. http://www.aud.gov.hk/eng/aboutus/about_vision.htm.
126. Audit Commission: About us: Regularity audit. http://www.aud.gov.hk/eng/aboutus/about_regm.htm.
127. Audit Commission: About us: Value for money audit. http://www.aud.gov.hk/eng/aboutus/about_valm.htm.
128. http://www.aud.gov.hk/pdf_e/e44ch06_summary.pdf.
129. Ibid., para. 1, p. 1.
130. Ibid., para. 2.
131. Ibid., para. 4, 5, 6, pp. 1–2.
132. Ibid., para. 9, p. 2.
133. Ibid., para. 2, p. 1.
134. Ibid., para. 3.
135. Ibid., para. 8, p. 2.
136. Ibid., para. 10, pp. 2–3.
137. Ibid., Delay in completion of the station improvement project—Insufficient internal communication, para. 2, p. 1.
138. Ibid., Management of pilot schemes, para. 3.
139. Ibid., Usage of identified spare spaces, para. 4.
140. Ibid.
141. Ibid., Additional spare space in the Tsing Yi Police Station, para. 5, p. 2.
142. Ibid., Surplus accommodation, para. 6.
143. Ibid., Remodeled report rooms.
144. Ibid., Need for reception area and deployment of staff to reception are, para. 7.
145. Ibid.
146. Ibid., Carpet problem in the back of house area, para. 8.
147. Ibid., Information kiosks in report rooms, p. 2.
148. Ibid., Hardware not in use, para. 9.
149. Ibid., Usage of information kiosks, para. 10.

150. Ibid., Alternative use of information kiosks, para. 11.
151. Ibid., Information kiosks not functioning properly, para. 12.
152. Ibid., Usage of resource centres, para. 13, p. 3.
153. Ibid., Resource centres in close proximity, para. 14.
154. Ibid., Late involvement of stakeholders, para. 15.
155. Ibid., Efficient use of resources, para, 17, p. 4.
156. Ibid., Congested accommodation in merged police stations, para. 16.

Policing in Colonial Hong Kong

6

Introduction

Before diving into an investigation on HKP reform, it is best to describe what colonial policing was like, in characteristics and from experience. This chapter comprises five sections: Section I, 'Policing with Colonial Characteristics', provides a list of defining characteristics of colonial policing; a macro picture. It examines (colonial) policing in Hong Kong in snap shots: historically, locally, culturally and politically. Section II 'Historical Developments of the HKP' provides an official view of how HKP developed over time. This shows how the HKP sees its own development. 'Colonial Policing: Continuity and Change' (Section III) discusses what it was like to police Hong Kong in a different era in the 1880s and 1920s, with three case studies of police careers. This creates 'up close and personal' illustrations of how HKP and policing in Hong Kong have changed over time. Section IV, 'Police Reformers', discusses selected HKP senior officers who contributed to HKP reform or left a mark. It makes the point that police reform is as much about personality as it is about leadership. Section V is a brief 'Conclusion'. All told, this chapter allows readers to see HKP reform in a different light, that is, as an enrichment project—dialogue with many, and not a monologue of one.

I: Policing with Colonial Characteristics

First, Hong Kong population, then as now, is predominantly Chinese. In April of 1843, there were about 19,000 people (12,561 people in March 1842) of which not more than 500 were foreigners. In 1961, there were 33,140 British and Commonwealth subjects in Hong Kong, excluding the armed forces. There were 16,607 other non-Chinese residents (2103 Americans, 323 French, 1863 Portuguese, 652 Japanese, 422 Filipinos, 386 Dutch, 329 Indonesian and 300 German). Hong Kong was also an international city, acting as a gateway to China before 1997. Hong Kong policing is Chinese policing with a distinctive British flavour, and international orientation.

Second, until very recently, people of Hong Kong were rootless and restless.[1] There were very few permanent residents of Hong Kong. Migrants, Chinese and Europeans came to Hong Kong to make quick money. Most of them have no intention of remaining. In time, everyone wanted to return to their respective homeland, to live, to retire or just to die. Hong Kong is a transient community. For example, in the 1840s, most migrants to Hong Kong were young and single. There were few families, and males outnumbered females by 6–7 to 1. In 1948, on the eve of the communist takeover, 2 million people entered the Colony.[2] Since 1844 and until the 1950s, Hong Kong adopted an open-door policy to refugees from other places, such as China and Vietnam; many entered illegally. Hong Kong had a difficult time in setting the boundary and imposing control on people entering and leaving; try, for example, branding and exile. In the early days of the Colony, Chinese from Kowloon could make the trip across the harbour with ease. In the later years, Mainlanders from China could cross into Hong Kong with little hindrance, notwithstanding police effort. This means that Hong Kong's economy and society has always been intimately related to China's fortunes, and most certainly impacted by whoever enters across the border in mass and individually for economic or criminal reasons:

> The ingress of over 700,000 refugees from mainland China since 1949 has had a marked effect on the labour situation in the Colony, the chief characteristic of which is an excess of unskilled labour. Previously the ebb and flow of the working population was closely aligned to the economic opportunities in Hong Kong and China. The refugees, however, have shown no desire to return to the mainland, even though Hong Kong is unable to offer to all the prospect of earning a reasonable living.[3]

It also means that, save for the European elites, there were few cohesive communities. Loose-knitted groups had little incentive and capacity to self-police.[4] It is no surprise that Hong Kong has been called a 'Borrowed Time, Borrowed Place' kind of town.[5] Hong Kong policing is more about keeping order and making peace more so than law enforcement and social control within a transient population. Self-help was the norm.

Third, Hong Kong's political economy and social conditions are much affected by the mainland. Since the 1950s, Hong Kong shares a lengthy, porous and restricted border with China. However, the border does not and cannot stop all contacts between the mainland and Hong Kong, for example, illegal immigrants travelling to the South and families visiting the North. Hong Kong policing, colonial and now SAR, is and has been very much affected by what happens across the border; witness the Opium War in the 1840s, Taiping rebellion in the 1850s–1970s, political struggle (cultural revolution) in the 1960s and economic development in the 1990s. Hong Kong policing is cross-border policing.[6]

Fourth, Hong Kong is a barren rock. It is often said that Hong Kong's claim to success is Chinese entrepreneurial skills and industry spirit, with the

British rule of law having played an important role. As observed by Endacott: 'The success of Hong Kong as an important commercial centre has been its stability.... British law courts have had the confidence of the population'.[7] The Hong Kong Police, by necessity, has to play an important role in maintaining order, stability and prosperity, for Hong Kong to survive and prosper.

Fifth, Hong Kong was a Crown Colony; administered by a governor appointed by the Crown and assisted by an executive council and a legislative council. On this count, Pottinger, when asked by Lord Aberdeen on political administration in Hong Kong, made clear that there would be 'no popular form of government'.[8] Hong Kong policing was colonial policing, an instrument of control,[9] albeit with a Chinese touch.

Sixth, as a Crown Colony, Hong Kong was administered in line with British foreign policy and strategic interests. Lord Stanley, Secretary of State for War and Colonies (1841–1945), wrote a letter to Pottinger in June 1843 to make clear that Hong Kong was to serve as a diplomatic, commercial and military post.[10] Hong Kong policing is about keeping order within, for example, Chinese gangs, and security without, for example, pirates in and around the Colony.[11]

Seventh, Hong Kong was administered in line with Chinese local customs and needs. In this regard, Hong Kong colonial administration reflected British philosophy, political values and administrative convenience.[12] Lord Aberdeen made clear to Pottinger that in terms of legal administration and police regulations, it was best to 'satisfy the claims of the British' as well as 'conciliate the respect and fall in the manners of the Chinese subjects of Her Majesty.' The HKP made every attempt to meet the local needs and follow indigenous customs, without compromising British values or interests. Viewed in this light, colonial policing sought mutual accommodation and flexible negotiation, rather than unilateral imposition and forceful domination.

II: Historical Developments of the HKP

Conventional wisdom had it that the HKP, building on the past, reformed and transformed itself in the run up to 1997, in multi-farious ways, from vision and mission to organisation, to operations, to culture and style. This is what the HKP said of the 'Historical Developments of the HKP' in hindsight:

> The early police in Hong Kong were established in 1844. The early 20th century saw the HKP building its policing capabilities, with the Criminal Investigation Department established in the 1920s and the first Emergency Unit formed in 1930, to deal with serious crimes and minor disturbances. After World War II, the HKP reorganized itself by recruiting ex-servicemen

> abroad and at home. The Police Tactical Unit was formed after riots in 1956, and given the responsibility of maintaining internal security, thus providing the HKP with a permanent reserve for emergencies. The 1970s marked the beginning of the formative years of present-day policing. The HKP Complaints Office and the Independent Commission Against Corruption (ICAC) were formed in 1973 and 1974 respectively following a series of serious corruption cases. Police Public Relations Bureau (PPRB) implemented the Police Community Officer Scheme in 1974 to improve relations with the public.
>
> Management reforms gained momentum in the 1980s and 1990s. The arrival of Mr. Christopher Patten, the last governor, in Hong Kong in 1992 brought the UK 'citizens' charter' concept of administrative responsiveness and quality service delivery to Hong Kong. Within the HKP, Service Quality Wing was established in 1994, taking over HKP inspections and instituting numerous service quality initiatives.[13]

The all-too-brief historical account of HKP development informed the readers about various kinds of ad hoc and piecemeal advancements through the years, for example, the establishment of Crime Investigation Department (CID) in the 1920s and EU in the 1930s, or the formation of ICAC and PPRB in the 1970s. The CID made HKP more effective in fighting crime. The EU made HKP speedier in attending to emergencies. The ICAC made HKP more accountable to the law and PPRB brought the HKP closer to the public. The systematic and comprehensive management reform in HKP started in the 1980s and 1990s, with the objectives of providing more responsive services to the public ('Citizens' Charter' (1992)) and achieving quality policing in the HKP ('Service Quality Wing' (1994)).

The above presentation from HKP College accurately describes various milestones in the development of HKP. However, this slim account, while informative for the purpose of presaging the need and effort in leadership in the last decade (1990–2010), is not adequate in providing the discerning public with an appreciation of the import and significance of such and other events in HKP development history. For this, the public has to consult 'Police History' parts of HKP website.

If the public were to consult HKP—'Police History', it would be informed that there are three main inflection points to HKP development history: 'The Modern Era 1945–67', 'Creating a Legend 1967–94' and 'Changes to the Policing Model and the Return of Sovereignty 1994–99'.

The Modern Era 1945–67[14] informs that 'In 1945, the force had to be built anew' and the Commissioner Duncan Maclntosh (1946–1953) was the one we looked towards for leadership and answers. He did not fail. He rebuilt the debilitated and dispirited HKP from the ground up. Under his watch, he established a new HKP HQ in Arsenal Yard, trained up a new force in thousands and built a border defence system with interlocking police points known as MacIntosh Cathedrals, all the while fighting criminals and gangs on the street, stopping illegal immigrants at the border, controlling civil unrests in the Colony, responding to natural disasters in storm and fire and fighting off provocations from China. The era ended with the bestowing of the honour of Royal Hong Kong Police.

In all, 'Commissioner MacIntosh laid strong foundations for a force meant to last. His redoubtable, forceful personality had transformed the disjointed, shattered police into an effective and stable force. This had happened just in time for them to cope with a calamity, both natural and manmade.'

Creating a Legend 1967–94.[15] This era is marked by three broad themes, in police reform, all in one way or another to improve the standing of the HKP in the eyes of the public, that is, a clean police force with high integrity. First, under the strong leadership of the Commissioner Charles Sutcliffe (1969–1974), the HKP was able to defange all the powerful Staff Sergeants, particularly the CID, who for all intent and purpose controls the front-line police operations by way of discipline of subordinates, cooptation of seniors and bribing of all. Second, the establishment of the ICAC was precipitated by the Chief Superintendent Godber corruption probe. Third, the continuation of HKP outreach to the public, particularly the young, with Junior Police Call.

Changes to the Policing Model and the Return of Sovereignty 1994–99.[16] This era is marked by radical political change in the community, that is, the return of Hong Kong to China in 1997. The occasion allows the HKP to rethink its mission, restructure its organization and rewire its operations. 'As the nature of Hong Kong society changed, the police force also changed with it, moving away from a para-military policing model to become a service orientated modern force, determined to engage the public in crime prevention, and remaining open and accountable for its actions. This change did not happen overnight; cultures take time to adjust. The professionalism of the serving officers, coupled with continued recruitment of motivated officers with higher academic standards, and introduction of information technology, enabled the Force to move forward and meet the rising expectations of the Hong Kong public'.

To summarise, the three periods of police show that the HKP has successfully modernised (1950s), cleaned (1960s–1970s) and professionalised (1990s) itself in the face of trying circumstances and overwhelming odds, and it 'is committed to seeking continuous improvement to meet the challenges of an ever-changing future'.[17]

The above 'Police History' of HKP, while more substantive than that of the HKP College version, still falls far short than what is needed to understand the dynamics and impact of change sufficient to plot the trend and assess the impact of change.

III: Colonial Policing: Continuity and Change

> A good march through the Settlement streets also served to remind Shanghai's residents where power lay.[18]
>
> **Robert A. Bickers (2003)**

The study of policing in Hong Kong has always been conducted from afar, outside in and a top-down perspective. There is a need to look at policing in Hong Kong from a personal perspective, bottom up.[19] The following pages will look at the career and experience of three police officers from different eras: Inspector Quincey (1870–1890), CIP Reynolds (1910–1932) and Chief Inspector Andrew (1912–1938); read together, they tell us how HKP and policing have changed, over time, before and after the Second World War.

In terms of analysis, the following questions will be raised, as appropriate: How was the HKP organised? Who joined the HKP? What were the requirements and process? How was HKP trained? What was the role and function of the HKP? How was policing conducted in Hong Kong, in process and style? What was the working relationship between HKP colleagues and with the public? How were HKP officers supervised and held accountable? What were some of the problems and issues with policing in Hong Kong? What was the organisational culture of HKP? How have the above aspects and dimensions of HKP changed over time?

Inspector Quincey (1870–1890)[20]

Inspector Quincey was the first Chinese HKP Inspector in Hong Kong. Quincey was born in Quinsa (Kunshan) County, Jiangsu Province, China, in about 1850–1851. Quincey was an orphan. He was adopted by Major Charles Gordon (DOB: 1833) of the Royal Engineer Corps who came to China in 1860. Quincey returned to England with his father in 1864. There he acquired a British education.

Quincey joined the HKP in October 1870.[21] In 1870, under the young and energetic leadership of Captain Superintendent Walter Meredith Deane,[22] HKP changed its recruitment focus from European to British officers. This moved the HKP entries from diversity to uniformity in background. From the 3 years of experimentation with International Recruitment Program, Deane learned that 'The excessive diversity in races and creeds among the officers, and the lack of universality in their background and training had made managing the Force incredibly, and unreasonably, difficult'.

Quincey joined HKP in a personal and backdoor way by passing the rudimental recruiting process in place. His father Major Gordon was on good relationship with Governor Kennedy (1872–1877). Quincey first worked as a batman (attendant to military officers) to Kennedy and next, he was inducted into the HKP as a police sergeant. Eight years later, on 21 August 1880, Quincey was promoted by Governor Hennessey as an Inspector third class with a salary of $840 in 1887. He was made Inspector second class in 1888 with a salary of $920, and later increased to $1091. A Chief Inspector was making $1440 at the time in 1879.

On 22 April 1882, Quincey petitioned for naturalisation as a British citizen and was granted on 24 March 1883.

At the time (1882), the 'HKP boasted 117 Europeans, 172 Indians and 197 Chinese, and 183 men from Water Police, majority of them Chinese: 1 Chief Superintendent ($3,840), 1 Adjutant (Army secondment), 1 Chief Inspector ($1,440), 12 Inspectors (4 First Class ($1,200), 3 Second Class ($960); 4 Third Class ($720), 1 unclassified—that being Quincey ($540, plus $60 for good conduct and $108 for special service, totaling $708), 11 Sergeants ($540) and 88 Constables ($480) [Essentially, Quincey was under the pay grade of an European sergeant. An Indian sergeant received $270, and his Chinese counterpart $300]'.[23]

The appointment as Inspector was not well received by his peers. It was reported by Hong Kong Daily Press: 'Sergeant Quincey has been transformed by His Excellency the Governor into an Inspector, and that considerable dissatisfaction prevails among the members of the Police force at the appointment, more particularly since he was, though nominally a sergeant, acted as an attendant at Government House.'

Quincey's peers had reasons to complain. Quincey was a Chinese. He was being promoted too fast. He did not earn his rank by merit at work and seniority in place. Quincey built his career on account of his father's relationship with the governors. Still in all, Quincey was the right person at the right time. He was then the only Chinese Inspector in the 666 men strong HKP.[24] The HKP needed Chinese officers to communicate with and fight crime in the Chinese community. Not long after, Quincey was promoted again in 1884 to Detective Inspector in charge of the whole Chinese detective contingent. Quincey was also responsible for liaison with the Chinese police authority. In such capacities, Quincey was allowed to travel between Hong Kong and China, to investigate cases and make arrests. In 1881, Quincey arrested 13 men based on Chinese requests. But Governor Hennessy wanted to have nothing to do with it since there was no legal arrangement between China and Hong Kong.

A cursory inspection of the ***China Mail*** of the time showed that Quincey was very productive and very successful as a police officer. The Editor in Chief of ***China Mail*** and its publisher George Murray Bain lauded Quincey as an overachiever and rising star. Bain was one of his followers and made sure Hong Kong people felt the same. The following are some of the news items from *The China Daily* about Quincey's exploits:

16 November 1883: Arrested and prosecuted a person in possession of a huge amount of smuggled opium.

9 December 1884: On 8 December 1884, at 8.30 p.m., Inspector Quincey and Sergeant Butlkin and a 'lukong' (Chinese officer) stopped and searched a suspected person who tried to elude the officers. He was found with 1 pound of gunpowder, kerosene-saturated paper and a box of matches. He was also armed with a dagger, eight skeleton keys and two pawn tickets. He was charged with illegal possessions.

17 July 1886: Inspector Quincey charged three Chinese dealers for the possession of light scales and measures. One was fined $10 and the other was fined two $15 each.

21 August 1886: Inspector Quincey was not able to track down a criminal Beltran who escaped to Canton.

2 March 1887: Inspector Quincey arrested two dealers and Sergeant Mann in the Pak Kop Piu lottery and were fined $100 each at the Police Court on 1 March 1887. One paid immediately. The other would not be far behind.

7 March 1887: Inspector Quincey arrested two Chinese servants of Messrs. Blackhead & Co. for stealing various items worth $17. They were sentenced to 3 months of hard labour.

7 September 1887: Inspector Quincey arrested three men who were suspected of burglaries attack on Messrs. Blackhead & Co.'s house at Tsim Sha Tsui. They were remanded for further investigation in Police Court.

12 September 1887: Inspector Quincey charged six men with public gambling. The first defendant was fined $50 or 6 weeks' imprisonment. The others were sentenced to a fine of $5 or 14 days of imprisonment.

18 September 1890 (Hong Kong Telegraph): Detective Quincey and Haddon raided a gambling den and arrested the keeper. He was sentenced to 4 months' imprisonment with hard labour.

24 October 1890: Inspector Quincey and others arrested two gambling club managers in Stanley Street. They were bailed at $250 for each prisoner.

19 November 1890 (Hong Kong Telegraph): Detective Inspector Quincey and Sergeant Mclver arrested an embezzler from Macau to be appeared in Police Court tomorrow.

16 June 1891: Detective Inspector Quincey and Sergeant Hadden arrested a man wanted by China on 15 June, 1891.

16 November 1894: Inspector Quincey charged an eating place in Bonham Strand for selling intoxicating liquors without licence. The case was dismissed, as there were no legal sales within the meaning of an act.
3 May 1895: Inspector Quincey saved a drowning Chinaman at Yaumati and gave artificial respiration.
22 April 1887 (The Brisbane Courier): Inspector Quincey was charged with accidental killing of a Chinese fruit hawker while chasing a thief. The manslaughter charge was later withdrawn. See also: 13 **March 1887 (unknown):** Inspector Quincey shot and killed a Chinese bystander with his service revolver, when he was not able to overtake. He was the first Chinese to be armed, shot and killed on duty with a service revolver. He was also the first Chinese police officer to be charged with manslaughter.

In 1878 Pope-Hennessy ordered firearm training for selected Chinese officers. By September of 1878, 30–40 Chinese constables were armed with rifles when they were on their night duties. That protocol was revoked in 1883 with Hennessy leaving, but was again approved in the 1920s.

In 1855, a Bubonic plague (Third Plague Pandemic) broke out in Yunnan Province. In 1894, it spread to Canton. In June of 1894, the death toll stood at 60,000. Quincey raised the first alarm on 26 April 1894 at a Hong Kong Sanitary Board meeting. 12 days later, Hong Kong was diagnosed with the first case of plague, with 20 more suspected cases at Tung Wah Hospital. On 8 May 1894, Hong Kong was proclaimed to be an infected port.

On 1 March 1895, for his plague-related services, Inspector Quincey was awarded a Plague Medal from Governor Robinson, as did Chief Inspector John Mathieson, and Inspectors George Hennessy, George Kemp, Alexander Mackie, J.W. Hanson, A. Mann and the acting Inspector William Bake. Quincey's medal citation read: 'Inspector Quincey was employed on actual plague work for a few days only, his state of health not permitting, but he rendered valuable services as an interpreter in obtaining information on all matter connected with the movement of the Chinese and other otherwise'.

As the first Chinese Inspector of HKP, Quincey's various achievements captured the attention of the media and imagination of the public, naturally. But for that, he also paid a high personal price. He was hated by his European peers, challenged by British subordinates and belittled by the Chinese officers. The European peers resented him for not having earned his keeps. Their attitude was that Chinese are not suitable for being a police constable, much less being an Inspector. The British subordinates challenged his authority. They refused to salute and obey the Chinese as a senior officer. The Chinese officers belittled him because he was a turncoat—a foreign bloke ('wei jiang lo'). Quincey could not be trusted, as a snitch for the British colonial administration.

The final chapter of Quincey's career with HKP was a tragic, anti-climatic one. He was summarily fired from the HKP for engaging in corruption. In the late 1880s, Captain Superintendent Deane was shot during a police raid. He retired a few years later in 1892. Major General (ret.) Alexander Gordon took over. He was taken ill and died after taking a medical leave. Mr Francis May, a veteran Cadet officer who was the private secretary to the 10th Colonial Governor George William Des Voeux, was appointed as Captain Superintendent on 10 February 1893.[25]

May was obsessed with law enforcement. In June 1897, May and his assistant CIP Alexander Macie conducted a series of gambling raids. The raids grabbed books which documented the largest Chinese gambling syndicate in Hong Kong in Sheung Wan. In the books, May found the payoff records to 14 Europeans (one CIP—acting deputy SP, six IP, one acting IP, four sergeants and two acting sergeants; 38 Indians, 76 Chinese police officers).

This led to one of the largest internal corruption investigation and shake up that the HKP has experienced in history. The HKP internal inquiry was conducted by Captain Superintendent May and Crown Solicitor Lardner Dennys at the Victoria Gaol. It was finished in August 1898. The inquiry was reported in HKP Annual Report of 1897:

> One European Inspector was convicted of receiving bribes and sentenced to 6 months' imprisonment with hard labor. Three Inspectors and one Sergeant were dismissed. Two Inspectors and two Sergeant (one was Acting Inspector when the list was discovered) have been called upon to resign. Two Sergeants and one Acting Sergeant were not re-engaged on the expiration of their terms of 5 years' service. One Acting Sergeant resigned. The Inspector who was Acting as Deputy Superintendent, had already retired from the Force when the list was discovered.

The corruption scandal rocked the Hong Kong community. The European community was particularly disturbed for three reasons. The scandal reflected poorly on the British (police) community. They were on the payroll of the Chinese and otherwise conspired with them to violate the law. At the time, Chinese corruption was expected; European corruption, while not accepted, was tolerated, within a tight-knit community of like-minded expatriates. But collusion between Chinese and European was out of bounds. The Europeans lost more than face; it lost its purported innocence and high moral ground. Second, the European officers were considered as being treated too harshly, being disproportionate to their liability. Third, the corruption involved Chinese gambling, one of their favourite pastime. The ill effect of gambling did not affect European communities.

The sentiment of the European community was best expressed by Dr. James Cantile (1851–1926) who was the Dean of Hong Kong College of Medicine for Chinese (1888–1897) and founding chairman of British Medical Association, Hong Kong Branch: 'At the present moment there is considerable scandal in connection with the acceptance of bribes by European police, and men of great experience are being got rid of because they took "tips"; surely a well-understood purloin of the police in all counties'.

Analysis

As to recruitment process: There was not much discussion about the formal recruiting standard or process, other than a reference to Deane's effort to make recruitment more English, and not too diversified. But there was clear evidence that Inspector Quincey got into HKP through a personal relationship, since he was adopted by Major Charles Gordon, a person with high social standing and who was well connected. Otherwise, Quincey was well qualified—proficient in Chinese and English, with good education from the United Kingdom.

As to peer relationship: Inside the HKP, relationship within and between ranks was soured by racial tension, with the British always in the higher rank, with no exception. British and Chinese officers just did not get along. British did not trust the Chinese. The Chinese did not trust the British. The British and Chinese were not working as a team. Beyond that, there was a lot of internal bickering over ranks and jostling for position. One got the distinct impression that it was who you know and not what you know that counts in the HKP.

As to police role and functions: Inspector Quincey attracted considerable media attention because those Europeans wanted to hear that the HKP officers were doing their job, in suppressing crime, catching criminals or quashing vice establishments. Mostly, the media played up the role of the police as a crime fighter. But fighting crime and suppressing vice was not all what policing is all about. Through newspaper accounts, we learned that HKP also has other civil duties from saving life, to secure sanitary conditions and attending to the sick.

We were told that policing was a dangerous job. The Chinese police were armed for night duties, and the use of guns while on duty was all in a day's work.

As to public relationship: Inspector Quincey had a good public image. He had a public following, thanks to the Editor in Chief of a major newspaper, who was his admirer. For the European community, Quincey was a rising star, and a picture-perfect HKP officer. But his fortune waned fast, with the discovery of his corruption with the Chinese.

As to police service ratio: Inspector Quincey worked for the HKP between 1870 and 1890, as an Inspector of Police. For most of the time, Hong Kong population hobbled between 1866 (115,098), 1881 (160,402) and 1891 (221,441) with 2113 Europeans and Americans in 1866 and 2500 British in 1891, policed by 117 Europeans, 172 Indians and 197 Chinese in 1882. The Europeans were well policed by European officers, being 2500 (1891)/117 (1882) or 21.37 to one European officer. This is much more than 160,402 (1881)/172 (1882) of 814.2 to one Chinese officer. Even if we take into account Indians, the ratio of Chinese to Asian officers is still high: 160,402 (1881)/369 (1882), that is, 434.7 to one Asian officer. This is to observe that Europeans were much better served by European officers, and Chinese were hardly served at all, being 38 times less. This is to say for most of the time that Chinese need to be prepared to seek self-help if and when needed. This is particularly the case for those Chinese living away from Victoria where the HKP HQ gathered.

As to police accountability: HKP officers were not above the law. They were held strictly accountable in corruption charges. At the time and until 1974, HKP was a corrupted organisation, with both Europeans and Chinese colluding. This also provides more evidence that in the policing of Hong Kong, collaboration between colonisers and the colonised was the rule, and not the exception.

As to police administration: It did not appear that HKP was well organised and rule bound. If anything, judging from Quincey's recruitment and promotion, HKP was ran by status power based on rank, not the rule or system. There was also little effort to train the police systematically and comprehensively.

CIP Reynolds (1910–1932)

In January 1910, Mr Reynolds, a British police officer, volunteered as an HKP officer. He provides a historical account of what it was like to do policing in Hong Kong in those days. When Reynolds first joined (1910), the HKP was a small department: 'about one thousand Chinese and Indians and about 125 Europeans; on the detective staff there would be about twenty-five Europeans and fifty Chinese'.[26] From his personal account we learned the following details:

First, the recruitment of Reynolds was haphazardly performed. At the time of his application, 14 people signed up, in response to an open advertisement. He was one of the two who was selected after an interview with a police agent from HKP. The whole process took less than a month. He applied in the first week of January 1910 and was shipped out by end of February.

According to him, his selection is a luck of the draw: 'probably all the names were put into a hat and we were the lucky (or unlucky) ones'.[27]

Second, there was no formal reception and reporting for duty. Reynolds arrived on a weekend. He just reported to the duty Inspector at Central Charge room. The next thing he knew was in the single's quarters, a large room at Central with 12 others sharing the space.[28]

Third, there was no formal training for new recruits, since there was no Police Training School. Reynolds had to learn the ropes of being a police officer in Hong Kong through personal and inconsistent instructing, mentoring and shadowing by senior officers. The final certification for his duties came from the Superintendent. The instructions were about facts of life, the custom of the Chinese, getting around and police duties, than what policing entails and requires in terms of role and responsibility, power and authority, procedures and skills:

> There was no Police Training School and instruction in Police duties was given by the Chief Inspector and the Barrack Sergeant; you were shown round the sections by older hands, from whom you probably learned more of the facts of life and police duties, than from the instructors and books; you also learned to know more of the highways and byways and the customs of the Chinese. After a month or so you were questioned by a Superintendent and if found satisfactory was posted to a district.[29]

Third, policing at that time suffered from a gross lack of resources and equipment. For example, the HKP's procedures had them show up to a fire by foot or on a rickshaw. Steam fire engines had to be drawn to the scene by colleagues. Thus, 'as can be well imagined, lack of transport and other modern facilities which go to make an efficient police force made police work of these days a foot slogging and laborious job'.[30] For example, inspection at New Territories needed to be conducted by foot:

> Inspector N. Lamont when in charge of the New Territories, accompanied by his bull terrier, would walk from Tai Po over the hills to Castle Peak and back by way of Ping Shan, Au Tau, Lok Ma Chau, Cheung Shui and back to Tai Po sounding the alarm at each station.[31]

Fourth, during Reynolds' service, the HKP was severely understaffed due to lack of finances: 'the Colony's finances were not over flush, and I would say that the cost of the present Police Headquarters was more than the entire police force of those days'.[32] Reynolds was asked to be the Acting Chief Inspector (one of the two CIP), without being paid.[33]

Fifth, Reynolds was basically a CID person, having retired as a CID-acting CIP. He made three observations of crime and its control in Hong Kong at the time. (1) The Hong Kong people were a law-obeying lot. 'During 1910 to 1925 the force really got under way. The Police Training School had started, finger prints and photography and other departments of the Criminal

Investigation Department were improved and strengthened, though in 1932 there was still only one man with a few Chinese assistants in charge of finger prints and photography'.[34]

To compare 1910 versus the 1950s, Reynolds did not think that the two periods were comparable, if only because things changed drastically after the war, that is, more resources, more expertise, more of a scientific approach taken, and in general, a more professional conduct: 'I would like to add here that after fairly wide experience I do not think there is to be found anywhere in the World, a more law abiding man than the average Chinese',[35] More importantly, crime detection and control could not have been done without a dedicated and professional CID staff: 'In speaking of the detective staff, the good work done by the Chinese staff must not be forgotten, without which indeed, success would have been impossible; there is only one person... and that is another Chinese'.[36]

The most difficult problem in fighting crime was the location of and communication with witnesses:

> The bringing in of witnesses and evidence was one of the biggest bugbears, as without immediate contact with the witnesses and without transport to bring them in, days often elapsed before they were forthcoming and the Chinese border was always open for wanted persons to get over and when this happened, it was a case of Good bye.[37]

However, the HKP had been making progress in reforming itself since the 1910s when Reynolds first joined, ever so slowly, but noticeably:

> During 1910 to 1925 the force really got under way. The Police Training School had started, finger prints and photography and other departments of the Criminal Investigation Department were improved and strengthened, though in 1932 there was still only one man with a few Chinese assistants in charge of finger prints and photography.[38]

Finally, the conditions of service were not very good. Officers had to live in single quarters. Married quarters were rare. There was little transportation available to the officers and the family. This meant that police officers were subject to and afflicted with many diseases:

> Police of the early part of the century had also a deal of sickness to contend with, small-pox and plague was still rife, malaria was quite common and police and their families suffered accordingly. I would like here to pay tribute to police wives, more especially to those of the past, some of whom were in out stations where transport, electricity, gas, etc. was nil—even living in Hong Kong and Kowloon was far from pleasant during the summer months...[39]

Analysis

CIP Reynolds' account offers another picture of HKP, 40 years later than Inspector Quincey's time. The obvious story line one can derive is that there was much continuity in the organisation, role and style, with sparse changes in the method and measures. The HKP was still very much disorganised in terms of recruitment, training and the overall administration: this was evidenced by the rudimentary recruiting process, ad hoc training and certification regiment. The small size of the HKP, centralised area of operations (Hong Kong Island), and an exclusive core command group, allowed for personal leadership and discretionary management. As to its role and duties, the HKP was still very much a bush fire-fighting outfit, for example, fighting fire and social service agency, attending to small pox and plague. As to style, policing in both eras was very personal, labour intensive and entrepreneurial, 'police work of these days a foot slogging and laborious job' and the fastest way to go to a fire scene was by a rickshaw.

There is little question that policing then was a dangerous job, that is, Superintendent Deane was shot and Quincey had to fire and kill a bystander. It was also a demanding assignment, on and off the job, for example, there is little support in fighting crime or putting out fire or attending to health hazards, and living in 'out stations where transport, electricity, gas, etc. was nil' is tough, particularly with a family. There is also a sense that the HKP was trying to do better, with limited resources at its disposal. In 1870, Deane tried to perfect the recruitment system by setting up standards and between 1910 and 1925, more formalised training at PTS and the establishment of a more dedicated CID Department is on the match.

Ultimately, police work anywhere and any time is about working with people. Police cannot fight crime and resolve disputes without communicating and commingling with the locals. In the Quincey case, he was in charge of CID because of his Chinese background. In Reynolds' case, he gave all the credit to the Chinese CID: 'In speaking of the detective staff, the good work done by the Chinese staff must not be forgotten, without which indeed, success would have been impossible; there is only one person… and that is another Chinese'.[40] The real HKP story—Chinese on Chinese—began with Chinese CID, not British UB. That should be the focus of future research.

Chief Inspector Andrew (1912–1938)

Inspector Andrew served with the Force from 1912 to 1938 and was promoted to Chief Inspector before retirement. He loved his job and spoke fluent Cantonese. The HKP remembers him fondly:

> Due to turn a grand-old 107 in October, Ken was born in 1893 and joined the Force in 1913 as a Police Constable, retiring as Chief Inspector in 1938.

> He was awarded the King's Police Medal in 1928 and Colonial Police Medal in 1936.... He could also tell his police tales in fluent Cantonese, outlining his exploits as being one of only 153 British policemen in Hong Kong, having answered advertisements in British newspapers and signing up soon after he stepped off the ship in 1911. He survived many near-death incidents including shootouts and attacks with knives and broken bottles, and was in and out of hospital 34 times in his 27 years in Hong Kong with everything from dysentery to malaria.[41]

As lauded by HKP, Mr Andrew was an iconic and much-loved police officer from Hong Kong. After his retirement in 1938, he wrote two books, one on policing in Hong Kong generally, and the other about his service with the CID in Hong Kong.[42] Both books informed about policing in Hong Kong, from the eyes of a British police officer who served 25 years in Hong Kong in different capacities—UB, CID and Water Police. He spent most of his career in CID since he knew Cantonese, and showed a keen interest and uncommon knowledge about Chinese culture. Both the books are rather short. The ***Hong Kong Detective*** (1962) is 176 pages long and ***Diary of an Ex-Hong Kong Cop*** (1979) is only 124 pages, in sparsely printed pages. Here, I will report on the ***Diary of an Ex-Hong Kong Cop*** by quotations.

Hong Kong Detective comprises 21 untitled short chapters, and each of it tells a story of many of Inspector Andrew's encounters in and out of work as a CID police officer in Hong Kong in the first half of the book. As the title suggests, the book recounts how Inspector Andrew went about investigating crimes (prostitution), arresting criminals and abating nuisances (drunken soldiers). The cases are told in the first person, and with a rich context. This allows readers to experience what was going on as the cases unfold, vividly and realistically. In doing so, the author offers the opportunity, at places, to think about the larger policing issues involved, such as how to exercise discretion or come to terms with cultural anomaly. Close reading and thoughtful analysis of each case, and as a corpus, allows readers to understand what it was like to perform (colonial) policing in Hong Kong as a European officer at the time.

As reported in ***Diary of an Ex-Hong Kong Cop,*** the following were some of CIP Andrew's observations about and impression of policing in Hong Kong.[43]

On being a police officer: 'In spite of all the long hours, loss of sleep, discomfort, the risks and injuries I found the policeman's lot a happy one' (p. 17).

On police training: 'After a very perfunctory course in police duties lasting one month, I was put on patrol in the company of an experienced P.C. This job mainly compromised the chasing and arresting of unlicensed hawkers or of licensed hawkers causing obstruction' (p. 16).

On police role and functions: 'Owing to the prevalence of stray dogs… a scheme of rewards was formulated for the capture of such dogs, but for some reason police of all ranks seemed to be averse to capturing these dogs. Perhaps it lowered their dignity to be seen chasing dog or, worse still, having caught one, tying a piece of string to it and leading it to the police station' (p. 32).

On fighting crime: (Policing in Hong Kong was dangerous.) 'It happened while staking out the Wah Long Distillery when he was attacked by two men from a gang, one wielding a gun, the other a dagger made of razor blades. (Andrew) 'Man Yat was the leader of the gang whom we had caught in the commission of armed robbery and he tried to shoot me. But his gun didn't go off, it was a bit damp. So I shot him through the heart…My sergeant shot the man with the dagger and he died in hospital the next day. One of the robbers hid behind a wall in the courtyard. Every time he saw a policeman he would fire at us. He was a good aim and shot one of my men through the head. Meanwhile two of the robbers fled on the junk'. 'But the former Hong Kong Police detective Andrew was prepared for this and had a police launch stationed in the bay. He set off a light in the direction that they fled and his sergeant at sea caught up with the junk and the two men'. 'We caught all seven: dead, alive and wounded'.[44]

On prostitution: 'There were two streets of prostitutes in Wan Chai—one for Chinese and one for Japanese. The girls were good people and they never bothered anybody. They all had a document with a photograph and a stamp on it showing they were prostitutes. If a client contracted VD all he had to do was contact the police and they would send a doctor down to the brothel. If a girl was infected she'd be in the hospital for six weeks. They never gave us any trouble'.[45]

On nuisance abeyance: 'That is to say, what instructions were we police officers given as to the right way and of avoiding the wrong way. Our instructions were that a rabid dog was to be killed by shooting it through the heart and that the brain must remain undamaged.… Qualified police officers armed with shotguns, patrolled the streets at night and were empowered to shoot on sight any dog not wearing a muzzle' (p. 36).

On police attitude towards work: 'Many of the European police seemed to know the knack of staying away from trouble. There was little doubt that the more work you did, the greater the risk of doing something wrong and of having to face the consequences' (p. 31).

On policing and 'guanxi': 'A police officer is always coming up against persons who claim friendship with people in high places, accompanied by the usual threat: 'You'll be hearing more about this' (p. 32).

On language ability: 'All the underworld knew that I could speak their language so they used to supply information to me at all hours of the day—and the early morning—in person on the street, on the telephone or anywhere else . . . My life was made very busy'.[46]

A European officer communication problem: 'The average European policeman found is very difficult to interview informers or take statements without using an interpreter' (p. 18).

On police uniform not functional: 'The uniform of the Chinese policemen looked like something from a music-hall sketch. The hat was made of bamboo, shaped like a pudding bowl. The tunic was more like a smock, and he wore white socks up to the knees and tied with blue tape. In pursuit of a criminal the poor fellow stood little chance of catching up without the aid of his whistle' (p. 25).

On European versus local culture: 'I also wonder why certain British-made motor cars were not popular, and found that the Chinese did not like the design of the front grille because they said it looked like a dead man's rib' (p. 26).

Analysis

Judging from the above, it is evident that policing in the early days of Hong Kong was more of order maintenance, hawker clearance and service delivery, for example, wild dog control, than crime fighting. This shows that for most of the time, colonial policing was not doing the business of the British Crown, but minding the affairs of the Chinese public; it was more about transforming the informal Chinese dispute resolution into a formal British legal adjudication. It also shows that on many occasions, colonial policing was not about dominating over people, but providing services to the community. This put 'colonial policing' on its head; for most of the time, community service, not order maintenance, defined 'colonial policing' (though this is not to deny that coercive and dominating aspects of 'colonial policing' were always present and keenly felt by the public).

Andrew observed that policing in Hong Kong at that time was not too professional. The police learned by doing and through on the job experiences. This portrayal of the British colonial police officer is a far cry from those of a superior trained, tightly organised and highly disciplined para-military force bent on controlling the indigenous people in every move and at every turn. The British colonial officer, as personified by Inspector Andrews, was more personable and even effable than officious, when conducting hawker duties or prostitution watch ('The girls were good people'). The one-person quest to save the world, which defines the ideal of policemen past and present in Hong Kong or the United Kingdom, was very much evident. This more so than any other factors—colour of the skin or mandate of the British Empire—defined the style of colonial policing in Hong Kong.

In terms of style of policing, colonial policing was quintessentially Chinese, that is, informal and contingent on relationships ('guanxi'). At its core, this is what community policing is all about. Community policing is build upon social networking and not based on rule of law, still less on principle of justice. In ingratiating themselves with the Chinese leaders, the British colonial officers were able to co-opt and rely upon the locals to do most of the policing (social control) work in the Chinese communities. This is despite the fact that the European and Chinese populations were separated by a wide cultural gap and many of the British officers did not speak the language.

As expected, an expatriate officer (like Andrew) who could speak fluent Chinese was in much demand, by the British administration and with the Chinese people, as with Caldwell of old (the 1840s). Both Caldwell and Andrew acted as an interface between the British command and local staff, Colonial police and the Chinese public. Interesting enough, beyond communication role and facilitating functions, bi-lingual officers, because of their rarity, attracted more attention from the Hong Kong public, and due to their increased efforts, earned more respect from the Chinese people. This allowed them to build bridges and establish trust with the Chinese community, making possible the gathering of intelligence, channelling grievance and resolving disputes. In this way, British colonial policing took on community-policing spirit, functions and process, which the colonial masters used to their utmost benefits in solving crime and anticipating 'trouble'.

Finally, colonial administration in Hong Kong, including policing, had to come to terms with cultural gaps, mistrust and misunderstanding. They surfaced in the most innocuous ways: British car grilles were commented to look like 'dead man's rib'; the Chinese police tunic was considered not functional in chasing after criminals by the British (Andrew). More telling on cultural exchange gone wild is the serendipitous revelation that the Chinese disliked all things that were British because they offended their sensitivity and spirituality (here, British cars remind them of death) and the British thought that all Chinese things and activities were non-functional or irrational (tunics).

In the end, CIP Andrew helps us to understand policing in colonial Hong Kong in two distinctive ways:

First, in terms of ideas, he tells us that there was a material and substantial difference between 'colonial policing' of Hong Kong and 'policing' in colonial Hong Kong. The study of 'colonial' policing in Hong Kong is the study of how the British sought to impose her will in controlling the Chinese. The study of 'policing' in colonial Hong Kong is a study of how the British police officers negotiated order and made peace, in furtherance of colonial objectives, with the Chinese.

Second, in terms of methods, Andrew achieved what other culturalists and anthropologists could only dream of in their continued struggle to decipher and unrelenting quest to understand what colonial policing was all about. In writing a book about a British police officer working in a Chinese beat day in and day out for a life time, Andrew was able to transform a theoretically sterile (and sterilising) cultural discourse and politically viral (and virulence) civilisation clashes, better suited for archived books and headlines, into touching human encounters and poignant personal moments. In doing so, Andrew reminded readers that life as lived was not quite that same as what people think it was (imagination) or should have been (ideology). To a police officer, in Hong Kong or otherwise, then as well as now, every day, people on the street were never idealists or pragmatists, friends or foes, colonisers or colonised. They were just people with different life experiences and personal ambitions, confined in a small social space, doing what they do best. As Professor Otwin Marenin puts it, 'The transformation of state intent into police action is problematic... The question, whose interests do the police protect is a meaningful one that cannot be answered by deduction from prior models of social formations'.[47]

As a British police officer working in the Colony Hong Kong, CIP Andrew was forced to come to terms with the reality he found, that is, Chinese people under the British rule. Once that was acknowledged, Andrew then had to go on living a life as he knew it, not as a British colonial officer (wearing conspicuously on the sleeve), but as a police officer, who happened to be a British colonial officer (hidden deep under the collar).

IV: Police Reformers

There are differences in opinion as to who contributed the most and in what way to the reforms and changes to the Force, from a high profile to the lesser known,[48] and from the grandiose to the mundane.[49] However, one thing is clear: the reform of and changes to HKP are not only attributable to the foresight of the best but are dependent on the fortitude of the rest.[50] Extant police reform research, in Hong Kong or otherwise, has a tendency to focus on the prominent and sensational (if only because those data are easy to be had) without paying sufficient attention to the obscured and real due to lack of awareness and interest. As a reminder and to proffer a different perspective, it serves to recall what the Chief Superintendent Tam Kwok-wing who served with HKP for 35 years, had to say about his small role with a real impact in changing HKP: 'I have been doing what I like to do and there are no regrets. It has been a perfect life. However, as a police officer, I think I have only barely passed! But I am satisfied with my career and what I have achieved. I know I have done what I was supposed to do'.[51]

An officer like the Chief Superintendent Tam, and many like him are the real unsung heroes of HKP reform, to whom this chapter is dedicated.

Commissioner Charles Sutcliffe (1969–1974) will always be remembered for cleaning up HKP corruption:

> In 1969, Mr. Sutcliffe was appointed Commissioner and set out to break the back of corruption. He changed the rank structure, raised pay scales, reformed recruit training and embarked on an ambitious course of building development to cater for the increasing populations in the New Territories. [52]

In doing so, Commissioner Sutcliffe was able to break the backbone of the almighty CID Staff Sergeant's network of control over the Chinese rank and file, effectively making them the de facto police chiefs of much of the HKP establishment.[53] That was when HKP developed the systemic capacity to police the Chinese people, beyond the CID. As the veteran HKP investigative reporter Kelvin Sinclair wrote about his legacy upon Sutcliffe demise:

> It was Sutcliffe who ordered a fiercely resisted restructuring of the force, which crippled the power of the mighty station sergeants who—until that time—had virtually run the police and organised the collection and distribution of the vast flood of dirty money.[54]

Commissioner Tang King Shing's (鄧竟成, 16 January 2007–2011, January 2011) performance was considered by many to be lackluster at best,[55] and controversial at least.[56] Still in some quarters, he too was the man of the hour for changing people's perception about the HKP, from a headstrong, macho and authoritarian agency to a principle-minded, reflective and responsive organisation. In this, Commissioner Tang was the first and only HKP Commissioner of Police who has apologised for HKP wrongdoings, from indiscretions to lack of performance, three times.[57]

This earned him the unflattering nickname of: 'Sorry Sir'[58] and with it scorns of the frontline officers for being weak and lacking leadership. However, to some, Tang not only did the right thing but also displayed visionary leadership. He demonstrated exceptional courage and visionary leadership under fire, a contrarian in the midst of the blind, when such qualities were much needed, and were yet in short supply. The apology from the top not only sent a clear message that HKP is a professional agency, transparent and accountable, worthy of public trust. In so doing Commissioner Tang allowed future staff to follow his example.[59]

Such and other one-upmanship arguments as to who was the best Commissioner of Police, cannot be definitively settled in one way or another, if only because reform to the HKP was a continuous process, conducted with an incremental approach and multiple objectives reflecting different conditions[60] and needs of the time.[61] Moreover, there are personality issues to be reckoned with in this type of evaluation. In essence, policing is operationally driven, context specific and people oriented. Over the course of history, there are many HKP memorable reformers and rainmakers.[62]

In 1867, HKP appointed Walter Meredith Deane (田尼) (1867–1892) as its first Cadet Captain Superintendent. Deane was the longest-serving police chief, and the youngest. He was also the only one to leave the Force for health reasons, after being shot in a police raid. Deane did not disappoint: neither the fact that he had no police experience nor his barebones colonial service credentials detracted from his uncommon drive in shaping HKP to his image. Deane was able to leave his mark as one of the most achieved leaders of HKP. His signature contribution was to make HKP a clean, competent, effective and racially integrated Force.

> Walter Meredith Deane destroyed the widespread myth that white people could not speak Cantonese, by learning it. It was not done to ask villains to learn English, he argued. Officers really should learn Chinese. Deane set up a police language school in 1869, but attendance was voluntary and most officers did not bother to turn up. He asked the governor for advice. The community to be served was almost entirely Chinese, and the force was largely Indian—but the government set up a Europeans-only commission. Six months' worth of discussions followed. Some commission members argued the only way to improve the force should be to turn the clock back, and make it 100 per cent white-skinned...[63]

Another tireless reformer was Commissioner Roy Henry. He is remembered for modernising HKP in the 1980s, long before Commissioner Hui Ki-on launched his own in the 1990s.

Commissioner Roy Henry of Sarawak Police (1964) and later Jiji Police (1967) joined the HKP in 1973 as Senior Assistant Commissioner of Police, Operations, and were promoted as Commissioner in 1979.[64] While in post, he improved standards, increased salaries and benefits and retained a zero-tolerance policy for corruption. 'He also dealt with government planners to provide a new generation of police stations, to increase and modernise the police fleet of vehicles and vessels and to ensure that Asia's finest were equipped and trained to the highest international standards. ...In looking at the modern police force, many of the foundations that make it so efficient were laid in the six years'. Roy Henry was the Commissioner.[65]

As a tribute to Commissioner Henry's life-time achievement in reforming HKP, and earning him a CBE, the then Deputy Commissioner (Management) Tsang Yam Pui had this to say at his funeral:

> He quickly set about redressing the Force's problems and restoring the public's faith in the police. Roy established a close and regular working relationship with the ICAC, launched a series of territory-wide 'Community against crime' campaigns, and spoke with as many junior police officers as he could. Roy

> set in motion the re-organisation of the Force through regionalisation and the devolution of command from Police Headquarters. His aim was to give commanders at ground level greater autonomy, which he strongly believed would increase efficiency and strengthen management. By April 1984 this restructuring was completed, and the Force's current structure of Regions, Districts and Divisions came into being. Roy was also very keen to improve police relations with the public. He embarked upon a policy of Community Policing to bring the Force closer to the people it served. To supplement this, he re-organised and strengthened the Complaints Against Police Office, and made it easier for the general public to complain about police malpractice. The welfare of serving police officers was something very close to Roy Henry's heart. As a result of a review conducted between 1979 and 1983, he was able to persuade the Government to grant a huge increase in the funds allocated to the Force. At the same time he successfully argued for the introduction of a salaries review mechanism. As a result, new married quarters were built for junior police officers and new police stations providing better working conditions and facilities for frontline officers came into being.[66]

Consider yet another game-changing Commissioner, Lee Ming-kuai (DOB: 1950). As of this writing, Lee is the only Chinese Commissioner to have graced the office (10 December 2003–16 January 2007) with a formal university education from Hong Kong. Lee joined the HKP in December 1972 and was promoted to the Assistant Commission rank in 1995, Senior Assistant Commission in 1998 and Deputy Commission in 2001.

In his career, Lee handled two major public order-policing events, the handover ceremony in July 1997 and 6th Ministerial Conference of the World Trade Organisation in December 2006.[67] The first event courted him with much local complaints, undeservingly, and the second earned him acclaim worldwide, rightly so. He was a hands-on operational-type leader. While in service, he was well liked by peers and subordinates due to his accessibility and openness.

Coming to the contribution to HKP as a change agent, Commissioner Lee was recognised for what he did not do, more so than what he did do out of office. Lee's retirement plan was to relax, enjoy life and do public service without being paid. This was unlike other retired Commissioners before him who went on to second careers in private enterprise,[68] independent consultancy[69] and/or government agencies. For example, when asked whether he would like to be appointed as the Secretary for Security after HKP, he diplomatically declined, self-effacingly: 'I lack political intelligence' (無政治智慧).[70]

Since retirement, Lee has kept to his promise in donating his services to educational institutions, for example, a lecturer on criminology and leadership[71] at the Chinese University of Hong Kong, non-profit organisations, for example, acting as the Executive Director of the Hong Kong Institute for Public Administration[72] and charitable activities. In the words of Commissioner Lee:

> I work on a voluntary basis and I am the Executive Director of the Hong Kong Institute for Public Administration. I share my experience by providing training to Mainland officials on public administration, media skills and crisis management. I also work as a co-ordinator for government departments and universities, overseeing seven or eight programmes a year. So life is certainly not quiet or dull these days.[73]

Ex-Commissioner Lee's words and deeds, lent support to his pledge to continue to cultivate himself, to promote HKP and to improve Hong Kong as a life course project. This recalled the legacy of President Jimmy Carter: 'Jimmy Carter is much more highly regarded today than when he lost his bid for reelection in 1980. He has produced an exemplary post-presidency, and today there is an increased appreciation for the enormity of the task he took on in 1977...'[74]

For his exemplary refusal to enter politics and stay clear of commercialism, the Commissioner set himself up as a much-needed role model of how ex-public officials should behave after retirement. This earned him applauds from all around and from many quarters. A Chinese University lecturer in a 'Salutation to Lee Ming-Kuai' had this to say:

> Lee Ming-Kuai retired last week. He promised to do volunteer work hereafter and not earn a living at private enterprise. As I think about a few of our past Commissioners, belatedly, I am much impressed, and allow me to salute him, my senior at CUHK. HKP is a unique organization. It requires a lot of public trust. If not, how can it enforce the law? If our citizens or law enforcement officers observed that their former wise and brave leaders, finally has to yield to the temptation of money and make friends with the rich and famous, lowering oneself to serve the rich, where is the pride and dignity of the HKP? The purpose of pension is to cultivate sense of dignity with comfortable pay, in hope that retired civil servants not have to worry about their retirement years. In this way they do not need to kiss up the financially rich and politically powerful to carve out a future, by catering to them, even to the point of engaging in money for power exchange. If we were to look at recently retired senior civil servants, the speed they flock to work for the commercial world to make money, we wonder why we should have been paying them or these high pension from the our taxes.[75]

V: Conclusion

This chapter reports on HKP reform and development in various ways as informed by several grounded and personal perspectives. The ultimate objective is for the readers to look at HKP reform and change in a different light, from a different angle, with a different purpose. The suggestion here is that HKP reform has many narratives, each adding more to an understanding of the reform process. The HKP official historical development account (Section

II), in process and essence, is very different from the personal account offered by the individual officers who worked to bring changes about, one day at a time, from the frontline, and below the surface (Section III). To the institutional (Section II) and personal views (Section III) on HKP changes, one needs to add that of the reformers' legacies: Who are these people? What did they try to accomplish? How did they go about influencing people and changing institutions to make things happen? What have they left behind? They too have stories to tell, in their own way and for their own reason.

The institutional narratives, personal accounts and reformer stories, how do they fit? Why should anybody care? What does it matter? The narratives fit because they have to. They were part of history in the making. Each seemingly disjoined narrative added something to the 'melting pot' of new ideas—a new narrative in the making. The struggle between and within narratives is expected, and the dominance of some facts over another is natural. Our job is to read all these narratives, account and stories to come up with our own.

As to the question of caring, it is simply necessary. Everybody is his/her own narrator, seeking to tell 'the' story about HKP reform, definitively. To the extent that one wishes to 'construct' his or her own narrative, one needs to 'fit' all what this chapter has to offer.

Endnotes

1. See Chapter 4, supra, p. 165.
2. Annual Report 1948, p. 9.
3. Commission of Labor in David Faure, *Society: A Documentary History of Hong Kong* (Hong Kong: Hong Kong University Press, 1997).
4. G.B. Endacott, *Government and People in Hong Kong* (Hong Kong: Hong Kong University Press, 1964), p. 4; R. J. Chaskin, *Building Community Capacity* (New York: Aldine De Gruyter, 2001), p. 7.
5. R. Hughes, *Borrowed Place Borrowed Time* (London: Deutsch, 1968).
6. S. H. Lo, The *Politics of Cross-Border Crime in Greater China: Case Studies of Mainland China, Hong Kong, and Macao* (Armonk, New York: M.E. Sharpe, 2009).
7. See R. Hughes, op. cit., note 5.
8. Lord Aberdeen to Sir Henry Pottinger, 4 June 1983, No. 3, CO 129/3. Cited in R. Hughes, *Borrowed Place Borrowed Time* (Andre Deutach, 1968), *Id.*, p. 20, note 1.
9. Ibid.
10. Lord Stanley to Sir Henry Pottinger, 3 June 1983, No. 3, CO 129/3. Cited in G.B. Endacott, *Government and People in Hong Kong* (Hong Kong: Hong Kong University Press, 1964), p. 20, note 1.
11. I. Ward, S. Geng, *The Hong Kong Marine Police: 1841–1950* (Hong Kong: Hong Kong University Press, 1991), pp. 6–8. (Piracy in and around the Colony has been a fact of life since at least the tenth century.)

12. Sir K. Roberts-Wray, *Commonwealth and Colonial Law* (London: Stevens & Sons, 1966).
13. Challenge in police leadership development. HKP College, July 2011. http://www.police.gov.hk/info/doc/Challenge_in_police_leadership_development.pdf
14. HKP Web. http://www.police.gov.hk/ppp_en/01_about_us/ph_03.html
15. http://www.police.gov.hk/ppp_en/01_about_us/ph_04.html
16. HKP Web. http://www.police.gov.hk/ppp_en/01_about_us/ph_05.html
17. HKP Web. http://www.police.gov.hk/ppp_en/01_about_us/ph_05.html
18. R. A. Bickers, *Empire Made Me: An Englishman Adrift in Shanghai* (New York: Colombia University Press, 2003), p. 69.
19. There are many personal reflections and stories to be had, see C. Knowles and D. Harper, *Hong Kong: Migrant Lives, Landscapes, and Journeys* (University of Chicago Press, 15 December 2009), On patrol (pp. 216–226). The chapter is about Bill who joined the HKP as an Inspector in 1977, on patrol at the border arresting illegal immigrants.
20. This section is based on Rudi Butt, Inspecteur Quincey and his master Dramatis son, *Hong Kong First* (16/12/2012). http://hongkongsfirst.blogspot.hk/2012/12/inspecteur-quincey-and-his-master.html
21. Depending on what historical sources one believes, Quincey could not have more than 6 years of British education.
22. Captain Superintendent Walter Meredith Deane (DOB: 1840) has an elite education, namely BA, 1862, MA, 1866, Trinity College at Cambridge. He was recruited to join HKP as a Cadet Officer. He spoke fluent Cantonese and knew his way around. He has no working experience other than being a Cadet in Hong Kong for 5 years, when he was first appointed to the head of HKP at 27 years of age.
23. R. Butt, Inspecteur Quincey and his master Dramatis son, *Hong Kong First* (16/12/2012).
24. In 1887, another Inspector named John Lee was found in a 1997 record. He might also be a Chinese—judging by the last name and work station. He was in charge of Women and Girls Protection Ordinance of 7 April 1891. He retired in 1902.
25. May arrived HK on 27 February 1883. He was appointed as the acting assistant audit general and acting assistant colonial secretary on 19 January 1897 and then the private secretary on 20 April 1889. He was the son of George Chuhester May, Lord Chief Justice of Ireland.
26. N. A. Reynolds, Looking backward. *HKMP*, 9(1): 5–9, Spring, 1959, p. 8.
27. Ibid., p. 5.
28. Ibid., p. 6.
29. Ibid.
30. Ibid., p. 7
31. Ibid.
32. Ibid.
33. Ibid., p. 8.
34. Ibid.
35. Ibid., p. 9.
36. Ibid., p. 8.
37. Ibid., p. 5.
38. Ibid., p. 8.

39. Ibid., p. 9.
40. Ibid., p. 8.
41. Centenarian Ken dies. *Police Beat*, 5 April to 18 April, Issue 676, 2000. http://www.police.gov.hk/offbeat/676/013_e.htm
42. K. Andrew, *Hong Kong Detective* (London: John Long, 1962).
43. K. W. Andrew, *Diary of an Ex-Hong Kong Cop* (Hong Kong: United Writers Publication, 1979).
44. Hong Kong's oldest surviving cop, *Police Beat*, Issue 8 October to 21 October 1997.
45. Hong Kong's oldest surviving cop, *Police Beat*, Issue 8 October to 21 October 1997.
46. Hong Kong's oldest surviving cop, *Police Beat*, Issue 8 October to 21 October 1997.
47. O. Marenin, Policing African states: Toward a critique, *Comparative Politics*, 14(4): 379–396, 1982.
48. There are also lesser known police reformers, especially on the frontline administration and operational staff. 麥文本 is a graduate of the Chinese University of Hong Kong serving between 1972 and 2012. http://www.alumni.cuhk.edu.hk/magazine/200203/html/p04-05.htm. For his contribution to HKP, see 星火飛騰 第1集 麥文本《警察故事三十年》(Published on 6 December 2013: 前助理警務處長, 曾指揮淘大花園封鎖及華航飛機斷翼事故。30年警察生涯見盡大場面, 秉持信仰真理, 令他悟出獨特的警界生存之道)。星火飛騰 is a religious-bearing testimonial TV programme. At 7.06/20.26麥文本distinguished himself by refusing to form a cliché and being an equalitarian. At 8.16/20.26, he refused to worship 'guandi' but insisted on using evidence-based policing to improve police work. Forming cliché and worshipping 'guandi' are entrenched HKP culture and practice. https://www.youtube.com/watch?v = PSe7OnSt7qM
49. Hong Kong Island regional commander Eric Leung Chi-bun retired after 34 years in the Force. His signature achievement was in making HKP more politically aware and socially connected: 'As an officer, we must always be politically neutral, but we should not be politically ignorant …Knowing what is happening in society and understanding the cause and effect of every incident is the key to an effective and fruitful negotiation with the public. It is so important when handling public processions and demonstrations'. In terms of operational style, this is a far cry from early years when Leung joined, where orders were given to constables and laws were imposed on citizens. Eric's words of wisdom, *OffBeat* Issue 705, 20 June to 3 July 2001. http://www.police.gov.hk/offbeat/705/index_e.htm; Chief Inspector Peter Ip Pau-fuk of the Criminal Intelligence Bureau's Research Unit retired after 35 years. His contributions include acting as the Police Adventure Club chairman for 24 years and researching into triad activities in Hong Kong, becoming a leader in both. Undefeated Peter retreat—Triad buster moves on, *OffBeat* Issue 676, 5 April to 18 April 2000. http://www.police.gov.hk/offbeat/676/02_index_e.htm
50. The Chief Superintendent of Police Patrick Lai Pak-hay retired about 30 years as the head of Traffic Branch Headquarter. The Shark's swansong, *PoliceBeat*, Issue 663, 8 September to 21 September 1999. http://www.police.gov.hk/offbeat/663/023_e.htm; Keith Braithwaite retired after 33 years of service as New Territories south regional commander, arresting drug lords and disposing bombs. KB's convictions, *PoliceBeat*, Issue 680, 7 June to 20 June 2000. http://www.police.gov.hk/offbeat/680/022_e.htm

51. Retirement pass for nonchalant CSP, *PoliceBeat*, Issue 686, 30 August 30 to 12 September 2000. http://www.police.gov.hk/offbeat/686/01_index_e.htm
52. Obituary. http://www.police.gov.hk/offbeat/809/eng/n16.htm Chapter 7: Hong Kong. J. S. T. Quah, *In Curbing Corruption in Asian Countries: An Impossible Dream? An Impossible Dream* (Emerald Group Publishing, 21 July 2011).
53. B. De Speville, Hong Kong: *Policy Initiatives against Corruption*, Vol. 769 (OECD Publishing, 1 January 1997) Commissioner Charles Sutcliffe is credited by ICAC head, the author, for 'determined leadership' in fighting HKP corruption in 1971–1973, p. 66. Police history: Creating a legend 1967–1994. http://www.police.gov.hk/ppp_en/01_about_us/ph_04.html 'To give him his due, much of the initiative for a cleaner police force came from its new Commissioner, Charles Sutcliffe … He dispensed with and disbanded the formidable "tigers" behind the rackets, the staff sergeants who—with all the force of a mafia—has controlled corruption within the ranks'. (p. 198), P. Moss, *No Babylon: A Hong Kong Scrapbook* (Universe, 1 January 2006).
54. K. Sinclair, Police chief who tore the mask of corruption from the force, *South China Morning Post,* 27 September 2005. https://groups.google.com/forum/#!topic/alt.true-crime/OPJ5fWW0LKE
55. Tang King-shing's four-year roller coaster ride comes to an end, *South China Morning Post*, 29 March 2012. http://www.scmp.com/article/734984/tang-king-shings-four-year-roller-coaster-ride-comes-end
56. 黃碩滔 (Wong Shik Tao), "焦點人物：笑罵由人　鄧竟成" (Focus Person: Laugh or Belittle Up To You—Tang King Sing) 大學線 (University Beat Magazine) 85 期 2008 年 5 月 香港中文大學新聞及傳播學院出版 (Hong Kong: School of Journalism and Communication—Chinese University of Hong Kong). http://www.com.cuhk.edu.hk/ubeat_past/080585/tang.html
57. 三公開道歉被冠 Sorry Sir' Singtao.com [04-04-2010]. http://news.singtao.ca/toronto/2010-04-04/headline1270368048d2408817.html
58. Police used civilian vehicles to set up a roadblock to stop illegal car races at the middle of the night, ending in accidents. Commissioner Tang said: 'According to initial investigations and the information we have gathered so far, we believe there has been some error in judgment in our operation. I apologize to the citizens affected, including the drivers involved in the traffic accident and the car owners'. D. Lee and N. Lau, Top cop's sorry saga: Hong Kong's top cop has made an unprecedented apology in the wake of the human blockade saga, *Standard*, 15 July 2009. http://www.thestandard.com.hk/archive_news_detail.asp?pp_cat=30&art_id=84861&sid=24568698&con_type=1&archive_d_str=20090715
59. E. Freidson, *Professionalism Reborn: Theory, Prophecy and Policy* (New York: John Wiley & Sons, 25 April 2013). (Professionalism is about professionals being able and allow to organise and control their own work, in process and outcome, i.e., being self-accountable.)
60. Given the position of political precariousness, Hong Kong found itself after the Second World War, under the leadership of the director of special branch (DSB) Peter Erwin, the deputy commissioner of police, and later DSB John Prendergast, the HKP expanded and professionalised the special branch within CID, packing it with seasoned counter-insurgency and intelligence officers transferred from Palestine, Cyprus, Suez Canal zone and Kenya. At the time, the SB was

in charge of all sensitive investigation, including corruption. I. C. Smith and N. West, *Historical Dictionary of Chinese Intelligence* ((Plymouth, UK: Scarecrow Press, 4 May 2012), p. 225. Scourged in secrecy and deception, this is one of the least-studied areas of HKP. See also, N. West, *Historical Dictionary of British Intelligence* (Plymouth, UK: Scarecrow Press, 2014), p. 482 for a background of DSB John Prendergast.

61. The item for establishment sub-committee of finance committee: Head 122—Hong Kong police force. EC(2013–2014)18, 12 January 2014. (Problem: The commissioner of police needs dedicated staffing support at the directorate level to tie in with the upgrading of the Tseung Kwan O Police Division [TKODIV] to a police district in 2015 and to meet the increasing policing needs arising from the massive development and the population growth in Tseung Kwan O [TKO].). http://www.legco.gov.hk/yr13-14/english/fc/esc/papers/e13-18e.pdf
62. This is an emerging rich and fruitful research field. D. K. Das and O. Marenin, *Trends in Policing: Interviews with Police Leaders Across the Globe* (Boca Raton, FL: CRC Press, 2009).
63. N. Vittachi, From farce to force to be reckoned with, *South China Morning Post*, 10 October 1998. *Saturday Review; The History Man*; p. 7. ('The next big break-through in police diversity happened in 1949, when the force opened its doors to two "minority" groups—dogs and women. Over the next 40 years, the character of the force changed from very British to quite Chinese'.)
64. In 1977, the deputy commissioner Henry, then at the age of 50, was tipped to be transferred to Rhodesia in transition, to fight terrorism. The man from Hong Kong, *Rhodesia Heralds*, 23 November 1977. http://rhodesianheritage.blogspot.com/2013/05/the-man-from-hong-kong.html
65. K. Sinclair, A fortunate life for a career cop: Kevin Sinclair looks at the life of Roy Henry, the former commissioner of the Royal Hong Kong Police who transformed law enforcement in the territory, *South China Morning Post*, 12 May 1998. http://www.scmp.com/article/240402/fortunate-life-career-cop
66. *OffBeat* (The electronic newspaper of Hong Kong Police).
67. H. Jing (黃靜), Lee Ming-Kwai's hair is all white (李明逵昨猶青絲今似雪) Wen Hui Bao 23 February 2025. http://paper.wenweipo.com/2005/02/23/RW0502230001.htm
68. The first eve Chinese HKP Commissioner Li Kwan Ha (1989–1994) joined Li Ka-shing's Cheung Kong (Holdings) and Hutchison Whampoa to advise the firms on security matters. In 1990, Li intervened in the kidnapping incident of Li-Ka-shing's son Victor Li Tzar-kuoi and Walter Kwok by Cheung Chi Keung. http://www.absoluteastronomy.com/topics/Li_Kwan_Ha Tsang Yam-pui served as the HKP Commissioner from January 2001 to December 2003. After retirement and in May of 2004, Tsang joined NWS Holdings (part of New World Development) as an executive director. His brother Donald Tsang was appointed as the chief executive of Hong Kong a year later (21 June 2005–30 June 2012). There was a wide spread question of whether it is appropriate for Tsang Yam-pui moving from a position of public trust (police commissioner) to a high executive of a real-estate firm, giving the appearance of influence peddling, if it is not even suggestive of corruption. E. Luk, Tsang family included in wider investigation, *Standard*, 31 May 2012. http://www.thestandard.com.hk/news_print.asp?art_id=122974&sid=

69. David Hodson, the Assistant Commissioner (retired), has been working with various private agencies as a consultant, the latest being a senior advisor to Steve Vickers Associates. http://stevevickersassociates.com/about/advisory-board/david-hodson/
70. Support Lee Ming Kuai as the chief executive. (支持李明逵做特首). http://bufishking.mysinablog.com/index.php?op=ViewArticle&articleId=246187
71. Talk with the ex-commissioner of police (Mr Lee Ming Kwai), 24 April, 2014. CUHK Business School. http://alumni.bschool.cuhk.edu.hk/en-gb/events/upcomingevents.aspx?udt_428_param_detail=9884
72. *The 35th Lecture of UM Distinguished Lecture Series*—'Leadership' by Mr Lee Ming-kwai—Executive director of the Hong Kong Institute for Public Administration at 2:15 p.m. on 13 November 2013.
73. The right ingredients: A recipe for a healthy and productive life, *Civil Service Newsletter*. http://www.csb.gov.hk/hkgcsb/csn/csn78/78e/pensioners_corner_1.html
74. American President: Legacy and impact, Miller Center, University of Virginia. http://millercenter.org/president/carter/essays/biography/9
75. Senior lecturer Choy, Chi-keung Ivan, Department of Government and Public Administration, Chinese University of Hong Kong. http://blogcity.me/BLOG/reply_blog_express.asp?f=QHA0SPQOHY120817&id=147017; See also Lee Ming Kuai do non-profit work without pay (李明逵自扣人工做善事). 5 December 2007. http://www.kui.name/event/2007-12-05/%E6%9D%8E%E6%98%8E%E9%80%B5%E8%87%AA%E6%89%A3%E4%BA%BA%E5%B7%A5%E5%81%9A%E5%96%84%E4%BA%8B_n84851.htm

Formation of Hong Kong Police in the 1840s

7

Introduction

This chapter describes the formation of HKP in the 1840s; this will be compared with HKP reform in the 1950s. This chapter has three sections. Section I is on 'Crimes in Hong Kong', which discusses crime and disorder problems in Hong Kong before and after British took possession in 1844. Section II is a discussion of 'Crime Control Measures' being deployed to fight crime, addressing the issue of why such discriminatory and harsh measures—'brute suppression and divisive seclusion'—were necessary. Section III 'Policing in Hong Kong' is about how Chief Magistrate Captain William Caine, Hong Kong's first police chief, fights crime and maintains order. Section IV 'The Legal Framework' describes and discusses the provisions, merits and impact of various police laws, from Police Force Ordinance to Gambling Ordinance to Native Chinese Peace Officer Ordinance, and others ('The legal framework') on policing and Chinese community. Coming to the last two sections, 'V. The Police Laws and role of HKP' and 'VI. Police Leadership and Policing in Hong Kong', the chapter turns to discussing the role of HKP in enforcing law (V) and the impact of police leadership in policing Hong Kong (VI). The chapter concludes (VII) with two major observations, namely, the following: first, from its inception, HKP as a colonial force functioned less as a legal agent than a moral and culture one. Second, in its formative years, the HKP was led by powerful men, strong individuals and colourful personalities, as in the case of Cain, May and Deane. This allows us to conclude that personal leadership, not rules or system, drives and defines policing in Hong Kong.

I: Crimes in Hong Kong

When the British first landed in Hong Kong in 1841, they discovered crime and disorder everywhere: piracy, robbery, theft, drugs, prostitution, assault, murder, and corruption, real or imagined. Fear of crime was in the air, and moral panic everywhere. There were just too few Europeans and too many criminals, criminally inclined. Chinese gangs roaming on the street, drunken soldiers creating disturbance in public, disgruntled workers struggling for survival, triad societies and anti-foreign nationalists conspiring behind closed doors all undermined the order of the day. In fact, crime was so bad in the colony that the 'History of the Laws and Courts in Hong Kong' reported the following:

> 'The state of crime during 1843 showed no improvement over the previous years. The number of nightly burglaries and gang robberies had alarmingly increased, and the credation of a body of Justices of the Peace, none of them of the slightest use and exceeding in number one-third of the whole constabulary Forces, was considered an absurdity... Crime was so rampant at this period that a correspondent of the local paper ...advised the residents, who had not yet been robbed "but who should soon be ...to nail their boxes to the floor, lock them and sleep with a good pair of loaded pistols under their pillows, for as soon as the moon got into her first or last quarter during the quarters, the robberies began...The town up this period was not lit at night, and it was dangerous to move out at all without running the risk of being attacked'.[1]

At this time, few were spared from the mayhem of crime and disorder, not even high officials, such as the Governor or the Chief and Assistant Magistrates.[2] While, there were no criminal statistics being kept at this point, there was a report made about the conditions of Victoria jail between 9 August 1841 and September 1843. The report documented two groups of prisoners by names. In the first group, there were a total of 482 prisoners listed, including 430 Chinese, 28 Lasears, nine Portuguese, five Seapoys, one American and the rest were Europeans. The second group, with 184 names, was mostly of European sailors, with a few court-martial soldiers. Given this breakdown, we can draw two conclusions: First, there were a lot of crimes perpetrated by Chinese and Europeans. Second, there appeared to be proportionately more Europeans in jail than the Chinese.[3]

II: Crime Control Measures

For the first 4 years, 1841–1844, Hong Kong had little institutionalised[4] or organised[5] social control. Formalised legal, bureaucratic and professional social control did not exist.[6]

Crime-fighting methods in Hong Kong during the earlier period (1841–1860) were one of brute suppression and divisive exclusion, through registration, curfew, surveillance, transport and lashing, and all were performed mostly on the Chinese. There were a number of reasons why the British colonial government adopted such measures. First, Chinese were deemed uncivilised and brutal people. They did not understand reason nor follow law. They only reacted to stern punishment because they understood force. Second, the British had no way of separating the law-abiding versus law-offending Chinese. In the eyes of the British, all Chinese looked alike and behaved the same; every Chinese was a potential threat, and a legitimate target of control. Third, the British had little cultural understanding of Chinese ways and means. They were not able to conduct discriminate regulation, for example, meaningful classification and registration scheme, and pursue discretionary policing, for example, through investigation and during interrogation. Fourth, British officials could not speak Chinese, and found the Chinese community inaccessible and indigenous people incomprehensible. Fifth, the British police officers in HKP were small in number and not well trained. They did not have the resources or capability to conduct community policing. Sixth, the police were overwhelmed by the violent nature and quantity of crimes they have to deal with. In the ultimate analysis, for the Europeans in Hong Kong, fear of crime ruled the day, moral panic displaced reason and racial animus stood for judgement.

III: Policing in Hong Kong

Policing of Hong Kong started with the appointment of Chief Magistrate Captain William Caine[7] on 30 April 1841. Caine was in charge of police, courts and prisons. As such, he was the person responsible for maintaining law, order and justice in Hong Kong.[8]

In this way, Caine's role, function and power were not unlike that of a Chinese magistrate—one 'person' having 'total responsibility' and 'absolute power' over the law and order, safety and security, welfare and happiness of the people.

In Imperial China, the local magistrate, as with the heavenly Emperor, personally assumed the role of the parent in taking care of the well-being of his charges. There was very little supervision and accountability; officials were guided and sanctioned by heavenly mandate. There was no institutional check and balance, such as legislative versus executive versus judicial separation of power. There was an integration of all three in search of what is right and wrong, more generally ought versus ought not. With the Chinese an 'ought not' ('bu gai') is something that should not have happened, not just violation of law or defeat of justice. The magistrate, in delivering 'what ought to be' is not assuming the role of a judge or adjudicator, per se, but functioning as a moral person passing judgement on the normative order of things. As such, one cannot separate the magistrate's role as a judge and the character of his personhood. They are one and the same. At the time, Caine certainly felt that way. The same can be said of Superman—with great power comes great responsibility. Escape is not an option.

There are a number of things of note here in terms of criminal justice administration with the Chinese community in Hong Kong: First, the local

Chinese community was very much left to its own devices, undisturbed, in justice administration. Second, systematic control and occasional punishment of Chinese in the colony was borrowed from traditional[9] China, for example, registration, shaming, lashing and deportation. Third, criminal justice administration is personal, not institutional. Chinese were judged by whom they were, not what they did. Fourth, substantive justice was preferred over procedural justice. Moral principle was more important than legal rules.

As a parent, Caine loved and cared for the British people, much like any responsible military commander would, and would stop at nothing to support the people, in holding them harmless from crime. As a military officer, he had zero tolerance for deviance, crime and disorder. As a disciplinary, he believed in using harsh punishment to exact retribution from the criminals and to deter people from committing crime. The Magistrates' Warrants of 1841 and 1842 permitted Caine 'to inflict on Chinese offenders sentences of imprisonment with or without hard labor of up to three months (increased to six months in May 1842), fines of up to $400, and corporal punishment of up to one hundred lashes'.[10]

As a professional soldier serving her Majesty the Queen in a foreign land, Caine was loyal, disciplined and hard working. He had but one goal in mind: to secure Hong Kong as a Crown Colony. He never took time off. He even patrolled the street himself. In time, Caine came to personify law and order in Hong Kong. He was the face of justice in Hong Kong. To the Hong Kong people, he was more famous than the Governor, and deservingly so.

On reflection and in defence of his harsh treatment of criminals, this is what Caine had to say:

> '[I]f it were ever my misfortune to be similarly situated, I should most probably adhere to the same determined and stringent measures which I consider to have protected the lives and property of the British public here...nine-tenths of our Chinese subjects, and about one half of our low European inhabitants have been in a most depraved condition...[draconian punishment was necessary]...as long as the people remain in their present state of immorality and total absence of principle'.[11]

To the Chinese, it is called '亂世用重典'—'applying stern punishment in chaotic time'.[12]

But one person, however resourceful and diligent, could not keep crimes in check and criminals at bay. Caine's law, order and security duties were divided in the following ways:

1. Elders and village representatives taking care of the Chinese inhabitants.
2. Justice of Peace helping with securing peace and order in the European community, mainly Victoria.

3. Marine Magistrate and water police in charge of the harbour and pirates.
4. Hong Kong Police in charge of public security in and around Victoria.
5. Private security and guards provide for safety and security for firms and private residents. 'During these first months of settlement, there was no organized public police force and the only kind of policing was provided by the occupants of the individual premises'.[13]

IV: Formation of Hong Kong Police Force: The Legal Framework

Introduction

In May 1844, John Francis Davis took over from Pottinger (26 June 1843–8 May 1844) as the Governor of Hong Kong. Governor Davis was the first Hong Kong governor at the time who knew intimately about China—he was completely familiar with the place, people and language. As intimated from above, at the time, Hong Kong experienced a general sense of social disorder,[14] moral panic, social malaise and racial discrimination. Correspondingly, police corruption, abuse of power and indiscretions rule the day. This called for a more disciplined, efficient and effective policing regime, and more systematic penal and justice administration.[15] It did not help that Governor (Davis)[16] was at odds with the Chief Justice[17] and in contest with the expatriate merchants and residents, over taxes, security and justice administration, with the local Chinese residents caught in the middle.[18] As Governor Davis put it to Lord Stanley in November 1844: 'it was much easier to govern the twenty thousand China inhabitants of this, than the few hundreds of English'.[19]

Governor Davis was very much responsible for establishing a legal framework for the HKP to prosper and function.

The Legal Framework

Police Force Ordinance (1844)

On 1 May 1844, 'An Ordinance for the establishment and regulation of a Police Force in the Colony of Hong Kong' (PFO) was passed to create the very first formal colonial constabulary in Hong Kong.

The Preamble (Section 1) to the PFO called for 'establishing an effective system of police within the Colony of Hong Kong' and the appointment by the Governor a 'Chief Magistrate of Police' residing in Victoria. The Chief Magistrate is to provide 'general direction' and overall 'superintendence' of the HKP by and through the Superintendent of Police, Marine Magistrate and Assistant Magistrate.

The Preamble spelled out the basic organisational structure of the HKP to be built: (1) *Vision and mission*: There should be an 'effective system' of police; (2) *ranking structure*: That there is a hierarchy of authority, that is, the Chief Magistrate is in command (policy) over the Assistant Magistrate (administration), Superintendent of Police and Marine Magistrate (execution); (3) *jurisdictional boundary*: There is a division of responsibility—land versus sea-bound policing, that is, Superintendent of Police versus Marine Magistrate; however, for all intents and purposes, land policing is restricted to places Europeans converge and gather, for example, commercial (Victoria) or residential (Peak) and (4) *residency*: Chief Magistrate is to live in Victoria, the main area of operations at the time.

Section 2 provides for the appointment, standards, role and functions of the HKP officers: (1) *Appointing authority*: The Governor is empowered to and responsible for appointing police constables to perform police duties. (2) *Establishment*: The Governor is empowered to and responsible for appointing 'sufficient number' of police constables. (3) *Standards:* Police constables so appointed must be 'fit and able men'.

Section 3 empowers the Chief Magistrate to make 'rules and regulations' governing the administration and operations of the HKP. These include but are not limited to the following rules and regulations:

1. *Roles and functions*: Constables are appointed to keep peace, arrest criminals and apprehend disorderly people.
2. *Police powers*: Sworn police constables have all 'such powers, authorities, privileges, and advantages' under common law, English stature and colonial ordinances.
3. *Administrative orders*: Police constables should obey all lawful orders given by superiors, from the Chief Magistrate to the Superintendent of Police to the Marine Magistrate.
4. *Accountability*: The Chief Magistrate is responsible for the efficient, effective and proper operation of the HKP.
5. *Discipline:* The Chief Magistrate has the power to suspend and dismiss the staff for a cause: remiss, neglect or abuse in the performance of duties.

Section 4 provides for terms of service. It makes clear that serving with HKP is not an at-will contract. Constables appointed cannot 'be at liberty to resign' without (1) giving 2 months notice; and (2) being approved by the Chief Magistrate.

Section 5 provides for cessation of police authority and return of police equipment when on an office vacation.

Sections 6 through 8 provide for disciplinary and accountability measures, that is, penalty against disobedience of lawful order (Section 6), penalty of possession of police uniform, guns and ammunitions (Section 7) and accountability proceedings (Section 8). Specifically:

Section 6 provides for a penalty of $200 or less, in cases of neglect of duties or disobedience of orders.

Section 7 provides a penalty of $200 or less in cases when a non-appointed person has accessed to and in possession of police uniform, guns and ammunitions for the purpose of using them to impersonate a HKP constable.

Section 8 empowers the Governor to appoint the Chief Magistrate, Assistant Magistrate, Superintendent of Police and Marine Magistrate to conduct an inquiry into a complaint about police neglect of duty and abuse of power.

Section 9 provides that any challenge of rights and powers of the Chief Magistrate Superintendent of Police and others in performance of duties can be satisfied by reputation alone.

Section 10 provides for the establishment of a 'Police Reward Fund' for the payment of 'rewards, bounties, and pensions'.

Section 11 sets forth arrest, detention and bail process. It provides that people who are arrested for minor crimes (misdemeanour and petty felony) shall be placed in the custody of a Sergeant who can then set bail for the appearance before JP.

Section 12 requires the Chief Magistrate to establish a police detail to attend to the magistrates' business and duties, including executing 'all lawful warrants, orders, and command of such Justices' in civil and criminal cases.

Section 13 sets forth the chain of command from the Chief Justice to the Police Superintendent to the other inferior ranks.

Section 14 provides HKP officers with immunity from prosecution and liability 'for any act done in obedience of the warrant'.

Section 15 exempts HKP officers and staff from jury duties.

Section 16 prohibits the keeper of liquor house from knowing 'harbor or entertain' any member of the police force while on duty.

Section 17 provides for penalties against assaulting of police or obstruction of justice.

The above PFO provided many of the general principles—constituting authority, role and function and accountability, to build the first HKP. The PFO is characterised by its lack of specificity and sense of overall direction, beyond fighting crime and keeping order. It was intended to be an aspirational, empowering and guiding document rather than an instructional or legal one. The HKP force was small enough and the operational area was limited enough for the HKP supervisors to be in touch with the police. The PFO, being the first, also contemplates changes over time. Finally, the PFO indicates that Hong Kong was gingerly experimenting with building up a

HKP. It did not want to be tied down and was unable to respond quickly to evolving situations or flexibly to novel cases.

Thus observed, the PFO leaves much room for creative experimentation and personal improvisation, in the hands of experienced police leaders, for example, May, seasoned colonial officials, for example, Caine or learned Hong Kong governors, for example, Davis, to make Hong Kong a success under a set of very difficult and uncertain circumstances. One must also remember that when the PFO was drafted and for a long time after, say before 1910, the Hong Kong expatriates lived in a small, knitted and intimate community, where people knew each other as neighbours, than strangers. The rule of the 'honorable man' prevailed over the rule of impersonal law. It is best to call policing at this time and under PFO 'entrepreneur policing'. Entrepreneurs do not like rules, they have learned to improvise and solve problems, with all the resources or no resource at all.

The first PFO is also revealing for what it did not provide. The PFO did not provide for a 'Colonial' police force. This should give a pause to those who argue that from day one, the colonists came prepared to set up a paramilitary force to control Hong Kong. The fact of the matter is, the colonists were neither prepared nor unprepared to rule Hong Kong, a Chinese habitat, miles from home, and the sight unseen. They did what they could, adjusting to well-established local conditions and reacting to a fast-evolving circumstance.

Native Chinese Peace Officer Ordinance (1844)

This was the first 'Chinese to Chinese' policing law. Policing in Hong Kong during her early days would not be complete without discussing how indigenous and migrate Chinese were controlled. No. 13 of 1844: 'An Ordinance for the appointment and regulation of Native Chinese Peace Officers (Paouchong and Paoukea) with the Colony of Hong Kong' (31st May 1844) set forth the basic idea of indirect rule. The Ordinance was promulgated in order 'to adopt and preserve such Chinese institutions as tend to the preservation of peace, and good order'. Thus understood, British colonial officials and HKP leadership expected the Chinese police to regulate themselves in keeping order and maintaining peace, by dispensing control more proactively (confronting disputes) than reactively (confronting crime), more informal (restorative) than formal (punitive) kind of social control. The Ordinance is seven sections long. It was more of a declarative, affirmative and validating document than an instructive and organising act.

The Governor was authorised under the Ordinance (Preamble) to appoint native Chinese Peace Officers in 'towns, villages, and hamlets' of the Colony of Hong Kong. The Peace Officers were supposed to be elected by inhabitants and recommended for appointment at the discretion of the Governor. These were the first elected officers in Hong Kong history. There was grass-root democracy in Hong Kong, under colonial rule.

In terms of authorities, privileges and immunities, the Peace Officers are like HKP officers in every way, except perhaps that they had no power to punish the offenders (Section 3). But the Chinese Peace officers, being indigenous, had other more pervasive and effective sanctioning power: that of moral and customary powers to shame, and relationship power to demand respect.

In terms of discipline and accountability, the peace officers adhered to the Chinese tradition: 'Peace officers… have the same authority…as any constable of the Police Force… shall be subject to be punished for neglect of duty, in like manner as hath been customary within the dominions of the Emperor of China…' (Section 3).

The Chief Magistrate of Police was responsible for enacting rules and regulation at the sufferance of the Governor in Council. The Peace Officers were under the Chief Magistrate's control and need to obey his order (Section 4). But in practice, the Chief Magistrate left the Chinese to do what they knew best. This is what 'indirect rule' is all about.

The Peace Officers were subject to monetary fines for neglect of duty and misconduct, at the hand of the Magistrate of Police (No. 10 of 1844). If the offense was serious, Peace Officers are subject to dismissal 'with marks of ignominy as are customary in China' (Section 7). Likewise, the Peace Officers could receive honours and awards for good conduct (Section 6).

The language and passage of Ordinance No. 13 of 1844 clearly shows that the British colonial administration was aware of and sensitive to Chinese ways and means, down to using shame and honour to discipline and control the would-be Peace Officers.[20]

Still the Ordinance, notwithstanding the good intention of Governor Davis, was not well received because the European public opinion of the time was squarely against a separate justice administration by and for the Chinese due to cultural ignorance and racial bias, though not without its reason, that is, lack of communication between British and Chinese in any meaningful way, due to language and cultural barriers. Thus, the European public was against placing powers of administration of justice in the hands of the Chinese who were considered not trustworthy and corrupted:

> We have been, are, and always will be, the consistent opponents of giving the administration of law into Chinese hands, and we do it on the strong belief we have, that from the Emperor on the throne to the beggar on the dung-hill, there is not a Chinese who is not prepared to lie and support his lie with an oath; and further, that with the little existing power of public opinion, there is not one

> who is not prepared to be bribed; for which reasons we are strongly opposed to the administration of justice by Chinese to Chinese in a British Colony.[21]

In the end, it is fair to observe that there were many British laws on Chinese but very little justice for Chinese people, and separate administration notwithstanding.[22]

Justice of Peace Ordinance (1844)

Ordinance No. 10 of 1844: 'An Ordinance to regulate summary Proceedings before Justices of the Peace, and to protect Justices in the Execution of their Office' (10th April 1844) details the powers of Justice of Peace in the execution of his office. Section IV, authorised the Justice of Peace to order the appearance of offenders to face criminal proceedings with the issuance of warrants of arrests. Under Section IV, Justice of Peace is authorised to issue warrants: 'IV. It shall and may be lawful for any Justice of the Peace, when any Information shall be exhibited before him, and in the opinion of such Justice it shall be fit and proper to do, to grant a warrant under his Hand, directed to some Constable, Peace Officer, or other proper person ...to take any offender against whom such Information shall be laid, and to bring him before such Justice or Justices of the Peace, as the Case may require, at a Time and Place to be named in such Warrant'.

Gaming Ordinance (1844)

Ordinance 14 of 1844 'An Ordinance for suppression of Public Gaming in the Colony of Hong Kong' (10th June 1844) outlawed gaming in the public, a favourite pass time of Hong Kong people at the time. The said Gaming Ordinance empowered the HKP to act against gambling with warrant from Justice of Peace. Section 4 in the Ordinance provided in pertinent part:

> And be it further enacted that it shall be lawful for any Justice of the Peace or constable of the Police duly authorized by warrant of any Justice of the Peace, to enter and if necessary to break into any house ...place either on land or water, within which such Justice of the Peace shall be credibly informed on oath, or have reasonable grounds of his own knowledge to suspect and believe that public gambling or playing is, or has been commonly carried on...

The provision further empowered the police to arrest all persons and seize all monies attending a gambling event.

This Ordinance reveals several things about the HKP at the time, which has a grave impact and far greater consequences on the relationship between police and Chinese society in the long term.

In terms of police role, the Ordinance required the HKP to act as a moral agent in the guise of a law enforcer, that is, extending and promoting of British Victorian values on an 'uncivilized' and 'immoral' crowd. At the time, and even now, gambling law enforcement was at odds with the ingrained habits of the Chinese,[23] socially and customarily. Personal indulgence among ethnic Chinese had been elevated to the level of addiction, sickness and moral flaws, requiring intervention, treatment and above all punishment.[24] Here, the British were not sensitive or unable to discriminate between gambling as a personal habit, social pastime, sickness or moral flaw. For control purposes, those were one and the same. As a result, it was the punishment that defines the crime, not the criminal conduct that controlled the reaction. Making punishment fit the crime was a classical and administrative approach to crime and punishment. It privileged the authority—reaction to crime, over and above the criminal's just desserts and treatment. In context, how Chinese (gambler) thought and felt about crime (choice vs. habits vs. addiction) had little bearing on the need for control. Or, simply, the British colonists cared little (indifference) and knew less (ignorance) about the Chinese in pursing administrative rule in Hong Kong. That was the pitfall of colonial policing.

More troublesomely, the way the Ordinance was drafted and applied was discriminatory along culture and class line. It was thus acceptable to play poker in a club house or bet on horses in the race track, but not playing mahjong in home or 字 花[25] in public. Boisterous bar card game is social while loud mahjong at home is nuisance.[26]

The race and class-based Gambling Ordinance and stern enforcement drew a loud and sharp rebuke from the local press. In an 1887 editorial, the ***China Mail*** has this to say about the colony's gambling policy:

> 'It is monstrous folly to regard a crime in a Chinaman an act which is not looked upon even with disfavor when practiced by others; for if the wrenched little Chinamen play with cash are to be stigmatized as gambling so also must be called the conduct of man in this colony who sits down to play for quarter dollar points after dinner or joins a 'pool' in a billiard room. If whist and billiards are innocent enjoyment then also is the Chinaman's cash game innocent enjoyment'.[27]

In terms of enforcement process, the Ordinance required a warrant from JP based on reasonable suspicion before any search of gambling place and seizure of gambling proceeds. This was not required with the Chinese judicial process, since magistrates and runners have unlimited access to enter illegal establishments and seize illegal goods, as warranted.[28]

In terms of HKP and the relationship with the underlying society (indigenous residents and transient population), this gambling law and strict enforcement policy was not understood, much less accepted by the Chinese. The HKP breached the faith of the public, who evaluated the HKP on moral grounds. In the eyes of the people, the HKP was not acting as a 'father and mother official' (*fu wu guan*) in a paternalistic, compassionate and sensible way. They were not looking out for the welfare of their charge as sons and daughters and in accordance with 'Qing-Li-Fa'. As a result, the Chinese people looked elsewhere for resources and support in meeting their expectations, security and well-being. They turned to communal groups, and ethnic associations; failing that seek out triads, as hire guns.

In terms of police operations, the HKP, having little Chinese knowledge and access, was not able to keep gambling under control. This invited abuse (shake down by police) and corruption (bribing by public). In time, syndication of corruption blossomed,[29] with little semblance of control, virtually an open secret.[30]

Distillation of Spirits Ordinance (1844)

No. 8 of 1844: 'An Ordinance for prohibiting the Distillation of Spirits within the Colony of Hong Kong' (20th March 1844). The Ordinance prohibited the distillation of spirits except under licence (Section 1), and only for professional or medical use, such as apothecary, chemist or druggist, and only limited to 8 gallons (Section 3).

Police authorities were given extensive search and seizure powers to stamp out illegal spirit making, on land or sea. A pertinent part of Section 4 of the Ordinance reads:

> IV: It shall and may be lawful for any Justice of the Peace, Officer of Customs, or other Person duly and lawfully authorized, having reasonable Grounds to believe and suspect that any private and concealed Still, or other Utensil or Vessel for the Distillation of Spirits, is set up or kept in any House or Place within the Colony or its Dependencies, to enter into such House or Place in the Daytime, and accompanies by a Peace Officer, to search for and seize any such Still, Utensil, or Vessel...

The making of spirits and alcohol was strictly regulated by law and inspected by officials. The Chief Magistrate of Police was authorised to take applications for licences to make sure that Public House licences did not fall into wrong hands, that is, criminals or a person of ill repute:

> III. And for the better preventing the granting Licences to unfit or improper Persons, be it further enacted, That every Person desirous of obtaining a License for keeping a Public House under the Provisions of this Ordinance or of obtaining the Renewal of a Licence before granted, shall, Ten Days before the Day of which his Application is to be taken into consideration deliver to the Chief Magistrate of Police a Notice in Writing of his Intention to apply for such Licence , and that in every such Notice there shall be contained a full description of the House proposed to be licensed, with a Statement of the Applicant's Trade or Calling and Situation in Life and whether married or unmarried, together with the Names, Residence, and Additions of his proposed sureties, and that every Person giving such Notice shall in like Manner deliver by three or more known respectable Housekeepers, residing within the said Colony...

The reason for prohibition of distillation of spirits was to stop illegal making and selling of alcoholic drinks, which was found to be a health hazard. For example, in a letter to the editor on 28 September 1843, a sailor described his misadventure and harmfulness of illegal wine selling and drinking in Hong Kong, particularly by sailors:

> I am a sailor on one of the receiving ships in the harbour. My captain keeps me working all week and I can only go ashore on Sunday. When I arrive on land, I find the pubs are all closed by government order. Some Chinese entrepreneurs stakeout the closed pubs and way-lay people like me. They secretly sell us grog at high prices. We either buy from them or go without. They take us up the hills at the back of the town to grottoes beside mountain streams where we drink the villainous stuff to the detriment of our health…Alternatively we can board one of the lorchas in harbour where we can buy another similarly noxious wine at even higher price and drink unconcerned for the attentions of the land or water police. This is hard for us sailors but if the matter was well represented to the nobs, they might care for us better without affecting the morals of the town. Yours Ben Brace[31]

However, the Ordinance did not go unchallenged. The Editor of the Friend of China, openly challenged the law as unreasonable:

> Editor—I don't understand this second law. Rum from Manila is landed at 30 cents a gallon. Spirits have to be expensive before people distil their own. Is the import of *sam shoo* from Kowloon to be prohibited? The Chief Magistrate recently disallowed a shopkeeper from making ginger beer because it was 'conducive to drunkenness'.[32]

Registry and Census of the Inhabitants Ordinance (1844)[33]

'An Ordinance to repeal Ordinance No. 16 of 1844, and to establish a Registry and Census of the Inhabitants of the Island of Hong Kong' (13th November 1844).

The Preamble of the Ordinance makes clear that the Ordinance was promulgated to keep track of the mobility of a transient population as it tried to prevent undesirables from coming to Hong Kong, such as 'abandoned characters' and persons without any ostensible means of subsistence.

In operations, the Ordinance called for registering all residents and sojourns in Hong Kong. Starting from 1st January 1845, all people living or travelling through Hong Kong were required to register at the 'Census and Registration Office' at Victoria, except for those who worked for the British government, including the East India Company, and professionals, clerks, shop keepers, householders, tenants and persons of independent means ($500 per annum) (Section 2). If the Registrar General and delegates found that any registered person was a vagabond or bad character or without visible means of subsistence, the Registrar General had the authority to prohibit the person from residing in Hong Kong, except for a resident (Section 3). Registered persons were given a ticket (Section 3) to be refreshed annually (Section 4). People who hired, hid or offered residence to a nonregistered person would be penalised (Sections 7 and 8). Businesses or households were also required to report the number, sex, country and occupation of each person in the premises or household (Section 11), as did boats and Chinese vessels visiting Hong Kong (Sections 13 and 14).[34]

The 'Registry and Census of the Inhabitants Ordinance' recalls an age-old household registration system, installed for social control, class maintenance, military conscription and taxation management purposes in Imperial China.[35] The household registration system survived the years until today, where it is enforced in the People's Republic of China.[36]

Preservation of Good Order and Cleanliness Ordinance (1844)[37]

On 20th March 1844, 'An Ordnance for the Preservation of good order and cleanliness within the Colony of Hong Kong' (No. 5 of 1844) was passed. The Preamble makes clear that the Ordinance is 'to provide for the preservation of good order and cleanliness within the Colony of Hong Kong'.[38] The Ordinance was amended on 26 December 1845.

The Ordinance later to be called Summary Offense Ordinances (1933),[39] regulated vice activities, offensive weapons, unlawful assembly, disorderly conduct, public nuisances, sanitary conditions, health threats, building maintenance, environmental protection and employee conducts, among others. In sum, anything and everything that disturbed the peace and well-being of a 'well ordered' community, in the British–European image.

The Ordinance starts with prohibiting any person from throwing or causes to be throwing filth, rubbish or offensive matters into the public, drainage[40] or around the house and neighbourhood.[41] It also prohibits causing a nuisance to others and obstruction in public roads.[42] It prohibits erecting unsafe buildings and spreading inflammatory materials in and around the premises. It prohibits trashing into the sea[43] and failing to raise the sunken boat from the sea. It prohibits driving on footpath and driving in a furious manner, not giving the right-of-ways to horses, cars or people. It prohibits barking and dangerous dogs,[44] and annoying and disturbing noises. It prohibits displaying and selling obnoxious and adulterated good/drinks, and cautioned against damaging and defacing government property.

In terms of criminalisation of immoral, offensive and dangerous conducts, the Ordinance prescripts against:

1. Houses of prostitution
2. Gambling shop
3. Offensive weapons

4. Unlawful assembly
5. Not reporting unlawful assembly, riotous conducts, insult of female and drunk in public; using profane and indecent languages; challenges to fight and offensive gestures likely to cause breach of peace[45]
6. Begging[46]
7. Indecent exposure
8. Bathing on the street
9. Not being 'able to give a satisfactory account of himself and his way of living'[47]
10. One 'who being abroad at night-time shall not give a satisfactory reason for so being'
11. Pretend to tell fortunes or exercise magic arts, or impose on credulity and superstition with a view to gain
12. Defraud people with counterfeit
13. Play noisy and obstructive games in public through fare
14. Resist and obstruct Justice of Peace and police in the exercise of duties
15. Domestic servants and employees leaving employers without adequate notice and timely replacement
16. Employee absent from duties without leave so as to injure or endanger the employer's property[48]
17. Employee willfully disobeys lawful and reasonable orders
18. Guards or watchmen sleeping on duty
19. Cruelty to and multination of animals without necessity

In violation of the above, and upon conviction, the offender was ordered by the Justice of Peace president to make good his transgression, or risk-enhanced punishment (Section 2). The Superintendent of Police and other officers were authorised by the Chief Magistrate to abate any observed nuisance, for example, requires the fixing up of any damages done (Section 3).

V: The Police Laws and Role of HKP

For the study of policing of Hong Kong in the 1840s, the above set of police laws is instructive.

First, for a long time, there was no definitive knowledge of what the role and functions of the HKP were. With the material above, there is a better idea. While Ordinance No. 5 of 1844 does not tell us what HKP actually did, it informs of what the colonialists had in mind: Hong Kong (European and Chinese) residents should behave like a British gentleman.[49] In China–Hong Kong traditionally, (not) doing what ought to be done or 不該 (*bugai*) is in context of time, place, people, circumstances or situation, as with deviating from the norm, high (Victorian) or low (customary).

The substantive provisions 'good order and cleanliness', individual or collectively, were codes for good citizenship and cultural correctness. Viewed in this light, HKP was acting at all times as cultural, not legal, agents. Recall Professor Henry Higgins in *My Fair Lady*. There, Professor Higgins was not only teaching English. He was teaching manners. In effect, he was trying to transform Eliza Doolittle into a lady, through the teaching of English; the HKP, in effect, was asked to operate as Professor Higgins did. The best example on using police to teach correct manners was when the General Commander of Armed Forces, Major General D'Aguilar could not go to sleep at night as a result of bamboo beating by night watchmen. To resolve his frustrations, an order in the council was issued pursuant to Section 1 of No. 5 of 1844 to stop such kinds of nuisance, once and for all.[50]

Second, the Ordinance did not regulate conduct; it controlled-lifestyle decisions and punished status. As such, it was not what a person did but who the person was that attracted police attention. Thus, not being 'able to give a satisfactory account of himself and his way of living' really punished people (mostly Chinese) for being in the wrong place (Peak) at the wrong time (walking out at night).[51] Provisions against playing noisy and obstructive games in public through fare really regulated (Chinese) collies who worked on the street and engaged in gambling in between jobs,[52] or more commonly still, hawkers trying to ply for trade in loud voices: 'Some colorful customs—irritating and a nuisance to people in the 1880s—are now rare...Street cries are an example. Tradesmen—knife—sharpeners, seasonable lychee-sellers—seldom call out business now in residential areas, as in 1880s and still in 1970s'.[53] Since Chinese need to venture out at night, somehow; collies need to take a break, somehow, and hawkers need to make a living, somehow, and the Ordinance promises to make their life difficult, with HKP as their enemy (contempt) or friend (bribe).

Third, the Ordinance showed that HKP at that time had many duties, and was relative to a different audience, for example, Chinese versus Europeans, and situations, for example, curfew versus storms. They were jack-of-all-trades and a troop for all seasons, and reasons. By design, the HKP was the only 'executive' agency in town, responsible for and capable of carrying out the policies of the Governor, a benevolent dictatorship. In this regard, the HKP was more like a general police agent than a specific one, at the disposal of the Hong Kong chief executive, with the advice of the Legislative Council and consultation of the Chinese community notwithstanding.

Fourth, in the 1840s and 1850s, policing in Hong Kong came close to the historical and original conception of police. Police, as an urban agency, existed to promote the overall order, safety, security and welfare of Hong Kong. However, the HKP could not be conceptualised with the original idea of police for a number of reasons. First, the original conception of role, functions, responsibilities and powers of police had little relevancy when transported to Hong Kong. Colonial officials thus needed to rethink and adjust mindsets about police role and relationship in Hong Kong, especially in the earlier years and before it took a definite shape. Second, the role and relationship of HKP evolved as it matured and mutated over time, growing with Hong Kong. This included mission creep and identity re-orientation. The best description of HKP at this time is that the HKP was an instrumentality of the state to protect Western values and British interests, in the name of transcendental values, high morality and universal rights.

Finally, the debate over whether HKP was a colonial force should be resolved in favour of a civil mandate by the provisions in and application of this Ordinance. In many instances, HKP officers were found deployed as sanitary agents, to keep the street and drains clean, as a public service:

> Capt Haly, as part of his police duty, has cleansed all the drains in the upper bazaar. The part of Queen's Road in our vicinity (beneath the upper bazaar) is now fragrant.... His procedure of holding back a head of water then letting it rush through the drains morning and evening has carried all the filth to the sea. We are sorry he is returning to India with his regiment.[54]
>
> Mrs Milne and Vesey are contracted to government to fix the drains but week after week nothing is done and now the hot weather is almost upon us. They should not turn over the soil now and expose us to the noxious disease-causing fumes in the decomposing granite subsoil. We prefer instead to rely on the Police Superintendent sluicing the drains daily.... The latest plan we hear is to form a 6′ diameter brick arched tunnel under Queen's Road with branches joining at every junction to carry off the sewage. With our surfeit of labourers they should complete this in 3–4 months but the work should only be done in winter...That part of the island that has a sandy soil overlying hard rock is free of disease. This is characteristic of land between Captain Burd's house and Dr Anderson's dispensary.[55]

VI: Police Leadership and Policing in Hong Kong

Soon after the PFO was promulgated, Mr Charles May was hired from London and appointed as Captain Superintendent of Police in Hong Kong on 3 September 1844. Inspector May is the first trained policeman in Hong Kong. He came to Hong Kong after serving 9 years with the London Metropolitan Police (LMP) (7 November 1835 and 7 October 1844). After arrival, May was instructed by Governor Davis by and through Chief Magistrate Caine to develop a plan for policing in Hong Kong.[56]

Before Superintendent May took office, Chief Magistrate William Caine was the law and order authority. Caine is a stern and industrious military officer. He took his law and order duties seriously, if not personally. At that time, the political status of Hong Kong had yet to be finalised. The Hong

Kong government did not have a coherent governing philosophy and administrative policy. By and large, it abided by a live and let live, see how it goes through mentality. By analogy, Caine could be described as someone similar to the new sheriff in the Wild, West of frontier America.[57] Caine was given a free hand to keep the criminals at bay. Lacking resources, Caine treated Hong Kong as a penal colony and enforced the law as if it was a military justice code, with public flocking, branding and deportation liberally administered. Still, disorder and violence remained unabated.

Thus, when Mr May came into the office, he had his job cut out for him, that is, trying to steer HKP into a civilian police force, with little guidance and still less resources.

First, the population of Hong Kong increased exponentially. The growth rate was beyond what the meagre police capacity and resource could handle.

Second, the people who came to Hong Kong—soldiers, sailors, labourers and artisans—were not the cream of the crop. They were more likely to be people with a shoddy past or criminal background.

Third, the people who came to Hong Kong were young, male, single, ambitious and aggressive, with outcasts and desperados in the mix. Most, if not all, lived for the moment, caring little about what the future might bring. They otherwise had little bonding to the society.[58] They were primed for crime, given the right opportunity.

Fourth, there were a lot of opportunities. There were also a lot of seduction and temptation, and overall bad influences. Overall and for most of the time, there were more motivated offenders and fertile opportunities than the availability of capable guardianship and existence of a secured environment.

Fifth, people could come and go as they like, over from China, across from Kowloon or travel by sea everywhere. This made prevention and detection of offenders very difficult.

Sixth, May was not given many financial or human resources to work with.

Seventh, May had difficulty of recruiting and training the right kind of people to join and stay as police officers. The Chinese were reluctant to join the police, due to cultural aversion, political rejection and legal liability. The morality (corruption, vice), integrity (honesty), loyalty (nationalism, anti-foreignism), competence (uneducated, cannot be trained) and dependency (lazy, bad habits) of the Chinese could not be trusted.

Eighth, May could not get enough qualified and dependable expatriates to join the police.

Ninth, the European and Indian police contingent did not understand Hong Kong culture or speak Chinese language, without which they could not communicate with local people and investigate crimes.

Finally, it was impossible to police Hong Kong beyond Victoria or the Peak.

Mr Charles May was the first-ever Captain Superintendent for the HKP.

He was appointed as the Superintendent of Police with Mr Thomas Smithers and Mr Hugh McGregor on 18th March 1845, with this government notification:

> In consequence of the arrival from England of Mr. May, the Superintendent of Police, all burglaries, robberies, assaults, nuisances, and other matters connected with duties of the Police, instead of being reported to the Chief Magistrate as heretofore should in future be at once brought to the notice of the Superintendent of Police, at the Central Police Station near the old Market Place.[59](76)

He was also the first to have trained and worked as a British police force before coming to Hong Kong. His mission was to organise the HKP in the image of LMP. As observed by Robert A. Bickers:

> The SMP (Shanghai Metropolitan Police) was founded on the model of the Hong Kong Police Force, itself based on London's Metropolitan Police. Over the years it looked directly to the Met for ideas about structure and practice, but also stiffened itself with a Royal Irish Constabulary backbone…Its Sheikh element meant that it liaised with the British Indian army experts and recruiters, and recruited senior personnel from colonial police and military forces in Malaya…[60]

No sooner had Superintendent May been appointed was he faced with three problems: how to shape the HKP's development, operation and identity, frequent riots and pervasive corruption.

First, there was the issue of how HKP is to be funded, to support the establishment, development and operation of HKP. England took a minimalist approach in colonial governance. She wanted colonies to pay for their own police. Hong Kong business people were reluctant to pay disproportionately for policing the Chinese communities. The Chinese felt no obligation to pay for a colonial police to lord over them. In 1845, the first Rating Ordinance, Ordinance (No. 2 of 1845) was enacted to pay for HKP out of property assessment, for example, 13% at Victoria and Hill district at 8.75%. Since then, it has been called Police Rate or in Chinese Chai Heung (差餉) literally means 'Police Pay'. In time 差餉 was raised to cover many of the municipal expenditures, such as the expense of public lighting, water supply, the fire brigade and so on.

Second, indigenous Chinese, especially at the bottom, had negative experiences and low opinions of the Chinese police, resulting in civil disobedience and riots. For example, on 25 March 1846, local Chinese expressed displeasure with the Chinese police stationed at West end of Victoria and stated a serious riot requiring the deployment of a large contingent of HKP led by the Superintendent coming to the rescue.[61]

Third, the HKP had a problem of corruption since its inception. In April 1845, a complaint of police officers taking bribe ('contribution') was lodged with the Chief Magistrate, who in turn investigated into the case to no avail.[62]

VII: Conclusion

This chapter describes and discusses HKP reform in the 1840s. Particularly, it provides an historical overview on how the early colonialists tried to establish law and order in Hong Kong, which to them must have been a herculean task.

'The Police Laws and Role of HKP' points to the fact that, under colonial rule, the role of HKP was very much a moral qua cultural agent, more so than a law enforcer or order maintainer per se. This is so because the various laws were drafted in such a way as to penalise Chinese age-old personal habits, for example, gambling, economic activities, for example, hawking and yelling, and traditional custom, for example, night watch and gonging.

The 'Police Leadership and Policing in Hong Kong' allows comparison and contrast of two very different police personalities and with it, exposure to two distinctively different styles of policing in Hong Kong. First came Caine, a no-nonsense military officer turned police chief who believed in stern military discipline and harsh punishment as a way to reform the Chinese and deter crime. Then came May, an experienced police Bobby from LMP coming East, who was committed to establishing an effective police force system and efficient patrolling process to prevent crime, catch criminals and protect victims.

Beyond personality and style, both Caine and May suffered from a gross lack of resources—material, financial and human, in keeping criminals/privacy at bay and Hong Kong (European) safe, in the face of ruthless desperados, listless migrants and illusive pirates.

Finally, given the historical circumstances, these two early police leaders were confronted with the limited resources they had to work with, and it is best to call their shared policing style as 'entrepreneurial policing', which is characterised by a high degree of improvisation, flexibility and pragmatism.

'Entrepreneurial policing' requires taking charge of people who can see risk and seize opportunities. It needs leaders who have a strong character, independent mind and innovative spirit to inspire the crowd and discipline their body. Thus, we can expect police chiefs of the time to have strong personality in order to take charge and run the show.

We can also be fairly sure that these people dislike rules and hate the system. They rather reply on their personality traits and leadership skills to get things done, in driving deadbeat people and building new programmes.

As it was, this trend of entrepreneurial policing would change with the 'HKP Reform in 1950s'. Before looking into 'HKP Reform in 1950s', it is necessary to be familiarised with the 'Hong Kong Police Reform in 1950s: Context and Framework'. The next chapter turns to this discussion.

Endnotes

1. HLCHK, 29.
2. Ibid.
3. Ibid., p. 89.
4. As used here, institution of social control means the consistency and persistency of form and functions of control by way of internalisation of norms or maintenance of disciplinary structure, in the family or at workplace. Being new to the governance of Chinese people, with an uncertain prospect, the colonialists were hard pressed to come up with any institutions of control, such as police, court, jail and still less institutionalisation of social control. L. G. Zucker, The role of institutionalization in cultural persistence, L. G. Zucker, *American Sociological Review*, 42(5): 726 n–743 n, 1977.
5. 'Organizing is the function of management which follows planning. It is a function in which the synchronization and combination of human, physical and financial resources takes place.' See 'Organizing Function of Management' MSG (n/d). http://www.managementstudyguide.com/organizing_function.htm
6. For analysis of social control in Hong Kong, police and policing are an important agency and activity. There is a need to clearly distinguish between policing of subjects (British nationals [U.K.] and naturalised [H.K.]), and Hong Kong inhabitants (Chinese national turned British subjects). For example, to the British colonisers and Chinese migrant workers, there were no institutions and institutionalised social control, formal (e.g., police) or informal (e.g., family). But to the local Hong Kong residents—villagers (before British), there were both institutions (e.g., family, clan) and institutionalised (village head, magistrate) social control. At the current juncture, the author is only interested in exploring social control, including policing, from the British perspective.
7. '8: William Caine'. In: G.W. Endacott, *A Biographical Sketch-Book of Early Hong Kong* (Hong Kong: Hong Kong University Press, 2005), pp. 60–66. Captain William Caine (1798–?) was the Colonial Secretary of Hong Kong from 1854 to 1859. He was the acting Governor of Hong Kong between May and September 1859. Caine was also the Chief Magistrate, who was the head of pre-Hong Kong Police Force from 1841 to 1844. Later, Caine became the Colonial Secretary and Auditor General Captain Cain was born in England in 1798 and served in the British Army's 26th (Cameroonian) Regiment of Foot during the Peninsular War against Napoleon in Spain. His regiment was later transferred to Hong Kong and he began his long association with the colony.
8. M. S. Gaylord and H. Traver, Colonial policing and the demise of British Rule in Hong Kong, *International Journal of Sociology of Law*, 23(1): 23–42, 1995. (This section discusses the origin and development of Hong Kong, particularly how it transformed itself from a colonial [discriminatory–coercive] force into a more democratic [indigenous–service oriented] organisation, as 1997 approached.)

9. The term traditional, not Imperial, is used here to make clear that in China of the ancient times, laws follow morals, of the secular and customary kind. This is because morality in China, unlike those of the West, is weaved from daily intercourse below (being secular in solving problems of human intercourse) than conjured up above as a secluded and prolonged exercise of speculative thought (being philosophical in dealing with logical issues).
10. C. Munn, Scratching with a Rattan: William Caine and the Hong Kong magistracy, 1841–1844, *Hong Kong Law Journal*, 25: 224, 1995.
11. J. W. Norton-Kyshe, *The History of the Laws and Courts of Hongkong, Tracing Consular Jurisdiction in China and Japan and Including Parliamentary Debates, and the Rise, Progress and Successive Changes in the Various Public Institutions of the Colony from the Earliest Period to the Present Time,* 2 Vols. (T. Fischer Unwin, 1898), p. 92.
12. Heavy punishment was used during the early Ming dynasty to deal with lawlessness in the realm by Emperor Ming Taizu Zhu Yuanzhang (朱元璋). http://zhidao.baidu.com/question/43650126.html?loc_ans=149491992
13. S. E. Hamilton, *Watching over Hong Kong: Private Policing 1841–1941* (Hong Kong: Hong Kong University Press, 2004), p. 16.
14. Governor Davis was appointed on 16 July 1844.
15. P. Lim, *Forgotten Souls: A Social History of the Hong Kong Cemetery* (Hong Kong: Hong Kong University Press, 2011). For social conditions of the time, see Chapter 16: 'Hong Kong Society in This Period'. For government policy and practice, see Chapter 18: 'Government Measures and Their Effect on Society'. (The HKP officers lived a shabby life, suffering from lack of amenities at work, few marriage opportunities, no family ties and low social and economic status. They were asked to control huge illegal enterprises. There was tremendous pressure to perform and a lot of opportunities for abuse or corruption. E.g., in Wan Chai Squeezing Club), p. 378.
16. J. F. Davis, *The Chinese: A General Description of the Empire of China and Its Inhabitants* (London: Charles Knight, 1836); J. F. Davis, *Sketches of China; Partly during an Inland Journey of Four Months between Peking, Nanking, and Canton; with Notices and Observations Relative to the Present War,* Vols. 1 and 2 (London: Charles Knight & Co., Ludgate Street, 1841). In 2 volumes; and Sir J. F. Davis, *A Vocabulary, Containing Chinese Words and Phrases Peculiar to Canton and Macao, and to the Trade of Those Places* (Honorable Company's Press, by P. P. Thoms, 1824).
17. J. W. Norton-Kyshe, pp. 155–166.
18. R. Buckley, *Hong Kong: The Road to 1997* (New York: Cambridge University Press, 12 June 1997), pp. 4–5.
19. Ibid., p. 5.
20. See also Ordinance No. 3 of 1953. On 2 December 1853, the legislature passed Ordinance No. 3 of 1953 titled: An Ordinance to extend the duties of Chinese Tepos appointed under Ordinance No. 13 of 1844; to determine their emoluments; and to provide for the amiable settlement of civil suits among the Chinese population of Hong Kong. For eventual failure of this Ordinance, see B. Hsu, *The Common Law in Chinese Context* (Hong Kong: Hong Kong University Press, 1992), p. 12.
21. J. W. Norton-Kyshe, op. cit., note 49, p. 339.

22. C. Mum, The criminal trial under early colonial rule, In: Tak-Wing Ngo (ed.), *Hong Kong's History: State and Society under Colonial Rule* (New York: Routledge, 11 September 2002), pp. 43–73, p. 66.
23. J. M. Loo, N. Raylu and T. P. Oei, Gambling among the Chinese: A comprehensive review, *Clinical Psychology Review,* 28: 152–1166, 2008. ('Social gambling is widespread among Chinese communities as it is a preferred form of entertainment.... Cultural differences exist in patterns of gambling when compared with Western samples; however, evidence is inconsistent...' (Abstract).
24. T. P. Oei and N. Raylu, Gambling and problem gambling among Chinese. 2007. This is a report submitted to the Research and Community Engagement Division, Queensland Office of Gaming Regulation, Queensland Treasury for the fulfillment of a research grant no.: 2002001746 awarded to Professor T. P. Oei. http://www.olgr.qld.gov.au/__data/assets/pdf_file/0006/249945/gamblingAndProblemGamblingAmongChinese.pdf
25. http://zh.wikipedia.org/wiki/%E5%AD%97%E8%8A%B1
26. Gambler and informers, In: G. Bickley (ed.), *A Magistrate's Court in Nineteenth Century Hong Kong* (Hong Kong: Proverse, 2005), pp. 331–337.
27. G. Bickley (ed.), *A Magistrate's Court in 19th Century Hong Kong* (Hong Kong: Proverse, 2005), p. 331.
28. China has an integrated and holistic legal system, substantively and procedurally, criminal and civil. What matters is whether things being done conform to moral principles espoused by the sage scholars, with Confucius in the lead. The actions of all people—officials versus public, sage versus base, are judged by one uniform standard, that is, whether it is morally correct and appropriate in context ('ying gai'—'what should be the case'). What is right versus wrong is self-evident to people and eminent in nature. Chinese philosophy affects people's reaction to deviance. Nothing should stand in the way of doing justice, which amounts to seeking the truth and punishing the deviant. General response to social disorder turns on the corrigibility of the offender. The corrigible people should be re-integrated and for those who are incorrigible, they should be punished, and exterminated. The ultimate purpose of punishment are two: transformation through education and suppression by incapacitation (capital punishment, exile). Punishment ranges from persuasion, prevention, cooptation and suppression. B. E. McKnight and H. Kuklick, *Law and Order in Sung China* (New York: Cambridge University Press, 30 October 1992), Chapter 1, especially 'Basic Belief' (pp. 6–9) and 'Responses to Deviance' (pp. 11–15). In order to reform, offenders need to tell everything. In order to excommunicate, offenders are expected to fest up. In order to do justice, officials need to know the truth, most of the time by way of confession.
29. In August 1886, there was a major police scandal involving illegal gambling. Fifty-three Chinese policemen ('lukongs') were on the take from the owner of a gambling establishment. G. Bickley (ed.), *Magistrate's Court in Nineteenth Century Hong Kong* (Hong Kong: Proverse, 2005), p. 336.
30. With colonialism, structural corruption is obtained when the demand for cultural goods (here gambling) does not match with the supply of legal activities.
31. Friend of China 28.9.43 edition.
32. Friend of China 30.3.44 edition.
33. http://www.hklii.hk/eng/hk/legis/HKHistLaws/1890/72.html

34. Friend of China 5.3.44 supplement: The government has published a set of rules to suppress vagabonds by the regulation of small boats in the harbour.
35. F. L. Wang, *Organizing through Division and Exclusion: China's Hukou System* (Stanford, CA: Stanford University Press, 2005).
36. W. Huen, Household registration system in the Qing dynasty: Precursor to the PRC's Hukou system, *China Report*, 32(4): 395–418, 1996.
37. This was followed up by Ordinance No. 8 of 1866 that was passed:[37] 'An Ordinance to make further Provision for the Maintenance of Order and Cleanliness with the Colony of Hong Kong' (16 August 1866). The Ordinance Section 8 provides that no person in Victoria should keep or give away any poultries that are considered as a health hazard, such as a pig: Section 8 in a pertinent part provided against 'The keeping of pigs, or other animals likely to be injurious to the public health, within the city of Victoria without special license from the Registrar General is strictly prohibited…' The Ordinance further prohibits the keeping and selling of adulterated food, liquor and provisions.
38. Friend of China 23.3.44 edition. 'Editorial—for over two weeks there have been no robberies. The Chief Magistrate may be congratulated but we think it is D'Aguilar who deserves the credit. He has augmented the police force. The boat regulations have likely also helped. The Superintendent has since been busy clearing the drains daily. We hope he continues to have enough help to do this, as it is too late now to do all the things we should have done to avoid another feverish summer. A survey is to be made of Happy Valley. Hopefully the stagnant malarial water there will soon be drained'.
39. Chapter 228. The Summary Offences Ordinances. (1st January 1933). To amend and consolidate the law relating to summary offences.
40. 'The abattoir has been sited on the hillside above the town and the offal and blood, and so on, trickles down a stream on its way to the sea. This stream passes beneath the market place. Some of the muck gets stuck *en route* and creates a really foul smell as it rots until a rain shower washes it away. The proper place for slaughtering cattle is at the seashore. We cannot use natural watercourses as sewers without first training and lining them. The local people have different ideas. For example, in Magistracy Street the residents empty their commodes each morning in the centre of the road'. Friend of China 3.8.43 edition Letter to the Editor from '*Snooks*'.
41. A Letter to the Editor concerning land allocations by 'Good Faith' in Friend of China 5.3.44 edition complained of: 'The drains up there in the Upper Bazaar are a bit smelly, and amongst the genuine traders are a few 'houses of disrepute'…'
42. 'Editorial—Last Saturday night our Chinese residents chin-chinned the moon (the full moon—*sheung yuet*—8th moon 15th day). They erected poles from their houses, many 20–40 feet long, and placed lanterns on them, together with grotesque figures of men and dragons. They let-off firecrackers from morning to night along the entire length of Queen's Road. The noise of the crackers was bad but the smell was worse. They should be allowed to enjoy their festivals but not let-off crackers on the public highway'. Friend of China 12.10.43 supplement.
43. 'The bodies of seamen dying on Her Majesty's vessels in the harbour are lowered into boats and rowed a short way off and dumped. Does this accord with naval regulations? Is there no service for the dead'? Friend of China 3.8.43 edition: Letter to the Editor from '*Snooks*'.

44. 'Letter to the Editor: Several garden houses have unchained dogs that rush upon anyone venturing through the fence to approach the house. Last Friday I went to collect a debt from a house on Queen's Road and, on entering the garden, a dog rushed at me and savaged my right hand. I have kept a record of doctor's fees for treatment and I will try to get it back from the responsible person. Meantime victims should report to the magistrate. This nuisance should not be permitted to continue'. Friend of China 2.11.43 edition.
45. 'We are pleased to see the Chief Magistrate has commenced his long threatened attack on delinquents. These people mostly lurk on the hill at the back of the lower bazaar (known to the British as Tai Ping Shan, the Cantonese name for the Peak) and the preponderance of burglars either live there or have confederates there… A few attempts to set fire to the housing have recently been discovered and doused. We must make sure these delinquents cannot come back…Perhaps we should adopt the Chinese method of graduated personal responsibility. The Dutch have done this in Batavia with their Chinese. It has not been done in Singapore and robberies are also frequent there'. Friend of China 19.10.43 edition.
46. Hong Kong Crime Report: 'The beggars have also largely disappeared. We are not surprised. Several bands of them passed our doors in the custody of the police last week and were taken down to the harbour and embarked on boats for their native land (Kowloon)'. Friend of China 26.10.43 supplement.
47. These provisions were used to get rid of undesirable and unsightly people from the street, and those who were unwelcomed were out of Hong Kong. The law was set up in such a way that the police were authorised to accost and arrest anyone they like to secure order and reduce fear. For example, in 1868 alone, 427 persons were convicted as 'suspicious persons' when the main serious criminal charges were not possible due to lack of evidence or witnesses. C. Munn, *Anglo-China: Chinese People and British Rule in Hong Kong, 1841–1880* (New York Routledge, 16 December 2013), p. 347.
48. Employer (foreign) and employee (Chinese) relationship was a real problem. There was no love lost between the two, and still less trust. Friend of China 12.3.44 edition has this to report: 'Many residents have employed watchmen to protect their property but it is suspected that some of these employees are in league with robbers'. On 2 March 1844, Rev Charles Gutzlaff was appointed as the Chinese assistant to the Chief Magistrate. He was warmly welcomed and positively endorsed by an editor at Friend of China 2.3.44 edition. 'Editor—Mr Gutzlaff's appointment is very satisfying and will be highly conducive to the impartial administration of justice. It would be difficult to find a more competent person for this job'. Since then (15th March 1844), Rev Gutzlaff has offered to investigate into the character and issue certificate on an honest watchman.
49. There were very few ladies at the time.
50. J. W. Norton-Kyshe, p. 57.
51. The light and pass rules: Unenlightened law? In: G. Bickley, *A Magistrate's Court in 19th Century Hong Kong: Court in Time* (Hong Kong: Hong Kong University Press, 2005), pp. 99–116.
52. C. M. Fung, *Reluctant Heroes: Rickshaw Pullers in Hong Kong and Canton, 1874–1954* (Hong Kong: Hong Kong University Press, 1 November 2005), p. 31.
53. Ibid., p. 346.
54. Friend of China 2.3.44 edition.

55. Friend of China 30.3.44 edition.
56. David to Stanley, 21 May 1845. CO 129/12, p. 97. See also G. Sinclair, *At the End of the Line: Colonial Policing and the Imperial Endgame, 1945–1980* (Manchester: Manchester University Press, 2006), p. 175.
57. W. MacLeod Raine, *Famous Sheriffs and Western Outlaws: Incredible True Stories of Wild West Showdowns and Frontier Justice* (New York: Skyhorse Publishing Inc., 1 February 2012).
58. T. Hirschi, *Causes of Delinquency* (Berkeley, CA: University of California Press, 1969).
59. J. W. Norton-Kyshe, p. 65.
60. R. A. Bickers, *Empire Made Me: An Englishman Adrift in Shanghai* (New York: Colombia University Press, 2003), p. 65.
61. Ibid., p. 79.
62. Ibid., p. 80.

HKP Reform in the 1950s: Context and Framework[1]

8

> In 1945, following the end of the Second World War, Hong Kong started along the final stretch of road in its history as a British Crown Colony. At that time, nobody could predict with any degree of certainty the way ahead...
>
> **Brian Hook (1997)**[2]

> The fundamental political problem of the British Colony of Hong Kong is its relationship with China and not the advancement to self-government and independence as in the case of most British colonies.
>
> **Hong Kong Governor Grantham (1948–1958)**[3]

Introduction

In its long, winding and storied history, the HKP has gone through four distinctive reform periods[4] worthy of note,[5] namely, the 'formation period' (1845),[6] the 'reorganisation period' (1872),[7] the 'modernisation period' (1950s)[8] and finally the 'decolonisation period' (1990s).[9]

In each of the above reform periods, the HKP saw the need to change—to adjust its vision and mission, organisation and process, administration and operation, and ultimately ethos and identity, to fit the time. Through the years, the HKP has transformed itself from a colonial policing force in 1844 with a coercive policing style to a post-colonial civil policing with a service orientation in the 1990s informed by professional practices. From its inception (1844) to now (2014), the HKP has assumed the role of defending the government regime, with corresponding formidable militaristic internal security capacity, unchanged.[10]

The first two reform periods (1844, 1870) helped in building the foundation for later reforms to follow. In the process, they generated much policy debate from the top (within the Hong Kong colonial administration) and criticism from the bottom (mostly with the commercial establishments and expatriate residents).[11]

The last two reforms (1950s, 1990s) were for self-renewal as compelled by history and in search of destiny. In the 1950s, the HKP had to rebuild its organisation and expand its operations after WWII to confront new challenges and reformed visions. In the 1990s, the HKP had to realign its vision and mission in anticipation of 1997.[12] All of the above reforms, in one way or the other, were an adaptation to changed conditions of Hong Kong.[13] In the 1950s, the Chinese were coming to help reconstruct Hong Kong, in their image. In the 1990s, the British were departing, keen on leaving a legacy.

This chapter and the next chapter are discussions of reforms to the HKP, focussing on the modernisation period (1950s), for reasons to be discussed later. This chapter mainly aims to provide a 'context and framework' for the next chapter to expand and expound upon.

Invariably, depending on the research purpose, analytical framework and evaluative benchmark, there are bound to be disagreements as to when, how and how long a reform period should be labelled, such as whether it is a rebuilding or reconstruction process.[14] Rebuilding calls for revisiting the old. Reconstruction entails engaging the new. Issues with periodisation aside, there is no denying that post-WWII Hong Kong reforms of all kinds—political,[15] social[16] and economic[17]—and types—education,[18] welfare[19] and prison[20]—is a transformational process: 'The combined effects of reconstruction and expansion helped shape the beginning of a transformation of the education system, from the uncertain imitations of foreign models to a more self-sufficient, home-bred and home-grown arrangements'.[21]

After WWII, the Hong Kong society changed fundamentally and radically. Similarly, criminal justice agencies at the time, the HKP and Prison Department, changed into different organisations from what they were a decade ago, in appearance, outlook, role and ethos. WWII offered a unique opportunity for HKP-bound researchers to conduct cutting-edge research into Hong Kong post-war recovery, and with it, the rehabilitation of police. There is few, if any, HKP research in this era.

These two final chapters investigate into HKP reform and development in the 1950s to the 1960s, as compared with the HKP reform in the 1840s and after the 1990s. At heart, this is a case study[22] of new beginnings for the HKP. According to John Kotter, an organisation change guru, transformational change is 'to make fundamental changes in how business is conducted in order to help cope with a new, more challenging market environment'.[23] By 'new beginning', this chapter observes that the HKP was able to 're-engineer' and 'transform' itself, alternatively, in vision and mission, organisation and process, theory and practice, and culture and identity. This research finds that after the reform of the 1950s, the new HKP bore little resemblance to the old HKP before WWII.

'Police reform in the 1950s' is the main focus of this research. This chapter provides the necessary context to inform the research into HKP reform. It is organised as follows. Section I: 'Research Data' describes the data consulted and the analysis framework adopted. Section II: 'Contexts of Reform' discusses a number of contexts that help in understanding the HKP reform of the 1950s, such as social, political, cultural and law and order contexts.

Section III: 'Direction of Reform' illuminates as to where the HKP is heading with the reform, gathered from official pronouncements, for example, commissioner of police or governor of Hong Kong, or private opinions, for example, experts. After being informed of the 'context and direction' of the reform, the study proceeds to discussions of 'process and methods of reform' in 'Decolonisation' (Section IV) and 'Localisation' (Section V).

Chapter 9 will pick up and conclude on 'process and methods of reform' with investigation into 'localisation', 'legalisation', 'modernisation', 'communalisation' and 'organisation' on the way to provide an overall 'conclusion' to this book.

I: Research Data

To observe the change in the HKP, particularly at the policy and legal levels, the LegCo archives on governor—executive policy speeches and legislative debates on bills are used. For police law and ordinances,[24] two databases are used: Historical Laws of Hong Kong Online[25] and Hong Kong Legal Information.[26] For the 1950 reform process and outcome, the *Hong Kong Police Magazine* (HKPM) (香港警察雜誌) (1951–1962) data is used as the primary data source.[27] For contextual information, relevant data on HKP reforms library—books, journals, government reports and media accounts—research materials are used, such as Hong Kong Journals Online (HKU).[28]

The HKPM was launched in September 1951 by the then acting HKP commission Maxwell. It was a first-of-a-kind effort to promote communication within and without the HKP. In its inaugural editorial, Commissioner Maxwell made it clear that the magazine had internal as well as external audiences. It was meant to be a communication tool between colleagues (vertically and horizontally) and with the public (inside and outside of Hong Kong). It was designed to inform colleagues of what was going on in and around the HKP. It also served personal enrichment purposes. The ultimate goal was to build up a corporate identity that the HKP and Hong Kong people could be proud of.[29] Besides the aforementioned communication and information sharing functions, HKPM also serves vital lifelong education and self-promotion functions.

Thus, the first issue of HKPM covered a range of subjects, from a pair of Chinese police inspectors sharing their training experiences in the United Kingdom,[30] to a specialist discussing the intricacies of ballistics and firearms,[31] to officers discussing what was going on in the HKP,[32] to hobbyists within the HKP enlightening readers on the fine art of Chinese porcelain.[33]

Each of the HKPM contains standard features, including an editorial, around the police news items, sports news, gossip columns from divisions, and professional and personal interest articles. When HKPM was first published, it had 36 pages. A year later, it grew to 44 pages. There was never a lapse of publication, except during the riots when the pages were substantially reduced. In 1956, a Chinese version was introduced, with contributions mainly by Chinese rank and files.

In terms of data collection, the HKPM was read through and through two times. The first time was to familiarise its content, looking for tell-tale signs of police reform—direction, plan, measures and impact. In the process, thematic structures of the reform process were developed, for example, how has post-WWII geopolitical concerns (e.g., aversion to Communist China) or socioeconomic conditions (e.g., influx of migrants) in Hong Kong came to impact upon policing in Hong Kong. The second time was to select data—evidence to support my observation that the HKP has made marked changes in 'decolonisation', 'localisation', 'legalisation', 'modernisation', 'communalisation' and 'organisation'.

II: Contexts of Reform

A. Social Context

In 1950, Hong Kong, coming out of WWII, was exposed to a huge population explosion with hordes of immigrants—particularly refugees from war-torn China.[34] The refugees were a motley crowd with great energy, fortitude, resourcefulness and entrepreneurship.[35] Many of them were apolitical and pragmatic.[36] More than a few were nationalistic and patriotic towards China of old. They were keen on seeking survival and security, in amassing fame and fortune in Hong Kong, in whatever way they could.[37] To them, Hong Kong is a home away from home. They were living in a borrowed place on borrowed time, with a 'lifeboat' mentality.

While all the immigrants coming to Hong Kong in the 1950s were looking for a new lease of life, not all of them were ready to give up their past lives. Many were unable to make it in Hong Kong. These people turned to criminal groups for protection and support.[38] Triads flourished, as mutual aid organisations, and in rare instances, as political instigators.[39]

The influx of this huge refugee crowd in a short period of time created insurmountable social and economic problems, for example, housing and welfare, law and order, for example, crime and gangs, and political and security problems, for example, social protests and political riots, for Hong Kong. As the then Attorney General D. T. E. Roberts put it:

> We wish we could allow them to come, but we cannot afford to receive large numbers of immigrants in our overcrowded city and to add to the heavy

> burdens already placed upon our housing, educational, medical and social welfare facilities. Nevertheless, the government will give further consideration to the position of those persons who have been here for a considerable period, and who have settled down to make an honest living in Hong Kong.[40]

With the infusion of new blood, Hong Kong proceeded to remake itself in uncharted territory with no map on hand, compass to guide or destiny in sight. That did not stop, and to some extent actually helped, the wholesale transformation of Hong Kong's political economy, from a regional entreport to a global manufacturing centre. The end result was a Hong Kong fully capable and deserving of its name as one of Four Asian Tigers (亞洲四小龍) along with Singapore, South Korea and Taiwan.

B. Political Context

Internationally, the post-WWII political development in Hong Kong (British stance on decolonisation and democratisation) reflected post-global trend (emerging nationalism[41] and self-determination[42]), international pressure (America insistence, U.N. conventions) and British home politics (election of Labour government, contraction of British empire[43]).

Domestically, constitutional reform in Hong Kong was affected by the attitude of the Hong Kong Government towards China, alternating between distrust towards Chiang's KMT and fear of Mao's PRC. The uncertainty over China's civil war and ambivalence towards Mao's intent resulted in Governors Young and Grantham taking radically different approaches to the political–constitutional development of Hong Kong.

Governor Young, a seasoned colonial caretaker, wanted the Hong Kong people to have a say over their city–state within the British Commonwealth, starting with the development of a sense of identity, though stop short of nationalism.[44] The way forward was for the Hong Kong people to play 'a fuller and more responsible share in the management of their own affairs' on the one hand and 'the fullest account being taken of the views and wishes of the inhabitants' on the other. This was to be achieved through the establishment of an elected Municipal Council and broader representation of Chinese in the Legislative Council.[45] With this in mind, Governor Young proposed setting up a Municipal Council consisting of 10 appointed members and 20 elected members, with equal Chinese and expatriate representation.[46] According to Young, Hong Kong needed to develop an active sense of citizenship and to become capable of openly expressing and giving practical effect to the general desire of its inhabitants if it were to remain under British rule and to resist absorption by China.[47]

The Young Plan did not materialise, as it faced opposition from the Colonial Office, Foreign Office and Hong Kong Government.

However, Governor Grantham, an old Hong Kong hand (1922–1937), was more cautious, and measured with political reform. Given the political threat across the border from China and security risks at home from refugees, it was not prudent to open up the political process to Chinese elites and grassroots. Rather, Grantham preferred a 'benevolent autocracy' model of governance, leading off with localisation of administration at the bottom and British control at the top. Still, political liberation came to Hong Kong, starting with the introduction of Urban Council elections (May 1952).[48]

C. Cultural Context

Global–regional politics aside and national–British agenda notwithstanding, domestically, Hong Kong was a divided city. Historically, there was no love lost between the British and the Chinese. Political, social, cultural, language and legal barriers divided the two people. Survival brought them together, and cultural competition set them apart. They lived in two different worlds. The British looked down on the Chinese. The Chinese hated the British. Try as they might have, neither trusted the other.

At the end of the day, Hong Kong was still very much a Chinese place with people having a strong ethnic identity, cultural superiority and national pride.[49] Such deep-seated and volatile sentiments manifested themselves, opportunistically from time to time, as social unrests[50] from anti-foreign resistances[51] to patriotic rebellions to labour strikes. This prompted the colonial administrators to adopt a cautious stance in ruling Hong Kong after WWII—liberalisation without democratisation, localisation in lieu of democratisation, administrative responsiveness over political accountability and finally performance legitimacy in lieu of constitutional legitimacy. Ultimately, Hong Kong was much more a dependent territory, resembling a Commonwealth city-state, more so than a Crown colony.

It serves to mention at this juncture that the political reform viewed from above and social development as experienced down under were two different but inter-dependent processes or projects. Depending on one's vantage point (where to look), perspective (how to look) and frame (what to look for) of reference,[52] the vista was completely different, generating disputes and inviting debate, as to the nature and extent of political–social development in Hong Kong.[53]

D. Law and Order Context

On the law, order and security front, communists, nationalists and Triads roamed the streets of Hong Kong, with a menacing People's Republic of China just across the border, which had otherwise made it known that she had no interest in taking back Hong Kong.

> The situation in Hong Kong had become unstable as a result of the Chinese Communist victories over the Nationalist forces under Generalissimo Chiang Kai-Shek, and by the approach of the former to the borders of the New Territories. There was also a danger of internal unrest in Hong Kong and Kowloon, initiated by Communist agents who had infiltrated over the border with the stream of refugees... The arrival of the Chinese Communist Forces on the frontier of the New Territories on 24th October made little visible difference to life in Hong Kong. There were no alarms, for the Chinese showed no inclination to cross, but there were continual raids by Communist and Nationalist aircraft along the frontier and at Sham Chun station.[54]

The Hong Kong Government and its leadership at the time were taken aback, and were overwhelmed by the political and security problems, international (Hong Kong indefensible)[55] and domestic (Chinese nationals—KMT vs. PRC agitations).[56] A Hong Kong Secretariat official said in his resignation note: 'I saw a City stone-walled bound/A little one that can't be found./It wasn't there again today./I wish that it would go away'.[57] More than a few observers considered the Hong Kong Government's indecisiveness as a mark of muddled thinking.[58]

E. Wei Ji (Danger and Opportunity)[59]

The military administration in Hong Kong ended on 30 April 1946 and the colony was returned to civil administration on 1 May 1946.

After WWII, the HKP, as with the rest of Hong Kong, had to rebuild herself[60] from scratch, due to a total loss of facilities, records, staff, leadership, experience, capacity and above all else institutional memory.[61] Many of the European officers returned home for health-related reasons to be replaced by a new stock of officers, and more than a few with military and counter-insurgency experience from overseas, for example, Palestine. The bulk of HKP Chinese officers rejoined the Force, after having served with the Japanese as wartime police officers. Many new recruits came from the refugee ranks, with good education and background, from Shanghai.

> In 1945, the force had to be built anew. The 200 expatriate officers who emerged from Stanley Internment Camp were in poor physical health. When the camp gates opened, many went back to their former stations, determined to ensure a peaceable transition to British rule. Later, most were repatriated for medical leave; many left Hong Kong. Back from China where they had spent the occupation years, many Chinese constables and sergeants reported for duty. ....From this nucleus, a new force had to be forged.... Duncan Maclntosh appointed Commissioner in 1946. The police force he took over was decimated, its equipment lost or looted, its stations largely destroyed. Strength was down to under 2000. Maclntosh, who had been a policeman in Ireland and Malaya, came to Hong Kong from Singapore, where he had been Commissioner and had spent

> the war in internment. He was a truly formidable individual, unbending, determined and utterly professional.[62]

The two Chinese characters for crisis are 'wei ji' (danger and opportunity). The post-war rebuilding of the HKP reflected this kind of Chinese mentality and Hong Kong spirit, that is, with danger came opportunity and without danger there would be no taking chances. The changed and changing Hong Kong social and economic conditions of the time—growing population, illegal immigration, transforming economy, menacing China—all took their toll on an HKP struggling to find its stabilising anchor and create a legacy. Still, the complete destruction of the old made possible for the rebuilding of a new, more modern, professional and progressive HKP, in line with international best practices:

> The Japanese occupation of Hong Kong meant for the Police Force, as much as for the territory itself, a definitive line drawn across the page of history; 'a fresh start' in almost every sense. Such a complete break is comparatively rare in any organization and brings with it both advantages and disadvantages. The disadvantages in terms of loss of continuity for personnel and systems are fairly obvious, although from the policing point of view the situation was made much worse by the fact that almost all the pre-war records had been lost. But the advantages were considerable. Starting almost 'from scratch' presented an opportunity to stand back and take a long, hard look at the Force and its manpower, systems and organization. Rebuilding could then be properly planned with due allowance for the changed state of the world—and China—after years of war. Fortunately this is broadly what happened, although nothing is ever perfect.[63]

F. United Kingdom Thinking: China Factor

Seven thousand miles away in the White Hall, England, drained of political will, financial resource and military capacity, adopted a decolonisation policy for most of her overseas possessions and dependent territories. However, Hong Kong was made an exception for economic, political and security reasons,[64] with anticommunism dogma and Cold War mentality playing their destined role.[65]

While traditionally Hong Kong was by and large self-financed, England was still responsible for Hong Kong's defence (£7 million in 1957), infrastructure construction, for example, airport (£3 million), economic development and social maintenance.[66] In the meantime, the Hong Kong Government was busy with the rehabilitation of the old social foundation and the building of a new economic base.[67] There were also real internal threats of social unrest in Hong Kong and external military conflict with China.

While the cost of keeping Hong Kong was considerable, the British government decided to maintain Hong Kong to check the growing threat of Communist regionally and the increasing influence of China, across the border. As the governor of Hong Kong (1948–1958), Alexander Grantham, observed: 'The fundamental political problem of the British Colony of Hong Kong is its relationship with China and not the advancement to self-government and independence as in the case of most British colonies'.[68] Furthermore:

> The Colonial Office argued these costs were worth meeting because Hong Kong provided Britain with 'prestige and influence' in Asia: Hong Kong provided a demonstration in the Far East of what can be done by the West and by private enterprise, not only in economic affairs but in good government, justice, individual freedom, and protection for refugees.[69]

The containment of China at the time was not without its anxiety and attending costs. This was not lost on the British.[70] As the U.S. Consulate observed at the time:

> There always was that feeling of uncertainty. The British were very cautious; they went out of their way not to antagonize the PRC but were at the same time quite firm about their rights in Hong Kong. They tried to make sure that no aspect of the Chinese civil war would take place in Hong Kong. They were not entirely successful. The KMT organized thousands and thousands refugees who would demonstrate whenever called upon. The communists organized the labor units who would periodically take to the streets for demonstrations. The British would squelch all demonstrations as quickly as possible.[71]

Ultimately, British government kept Hong Kong because it was profitable[72]; Hong Kong imported more goods and services from the United Kingdom than it exported to the United Kingdom.[73] The United Kingdom also kept Hong Kong because of regional security needs, that is, as a bulkhead against a revolutionised China. To the West, the Communist must be closely monitored and effectively contained:

> The areas in which freedom nourishes will continue to shrink unless the supporters of democracy match Communist fanaticism with clear and common understanding that the freedom of men is at stake; meet Communist-regimented unity with the voluntary unity of common purpose, even though this may mean a sacrifice of some measure of nationalistic pretensions; and, above all, annul Communist appeals to the hungry, the poor, the oppressed, with practical measures untiringly prosecuted for the elimination of social and economic evils that set men against men.[74]

The importance of Hong Kong to the United Kingdom, militarily and economically, after WWII is best summed up in the following speech by secretary of state for the colonies Lennox-Boyd in 1958:

> We have to ensure good government in fortress Colonies vital to the defense of the free world ... I have in mind Hong Kong Singapore, Aden, Kenya, Cyprus, Malta and Gibraltar ... Hong Kong ... made an astonishing recovery after the war ... She has bought since the war 300 million worth of goods from the U.K., nearly three times as much as she sold us.[75]

For the above political, security and economic reasons, the White Hall pursued a policy of decolonisation without granting independence, freedom without democracy and security without restrains to Hong Kong people.[76]

> Ernest Bevin and Arthur Creech: Recommendation to the Cabinet: While we should be prepared to discuss the future of Hong Kong with a friendly [and democratic] and stable Government of a unified China, the condition under which such discussions could undertaken do not exist at present and are unlikely to exist in the foreseeable future. Until conditions change, we intend to remain in Hong Kong and should so inform other Commonwealth Governments and the United States, while refraining in public from pronouncements, which exacerbated our relationship with China.[77]

Under this set of circumstances, the HKP was allowed to develop freely and was compelled by prevailing circumstances to improvise in meeting Hong Kong's rapid economic development needs, that is, providing for a good business environment in maintaining stability, order and security and attending to emerging social challenges, for example, illegal immigrants,[78] labour unrests, street hawkers, social welfare and services for the poor and more generally enforcing law and fighting crime.[79]

G. Refugee Problem

On the social front, the biggest challenge to the HKP was population control, that is, the influx of people to Hong Kong. From 1945 to 1960, the population of Hong Kong increased from 700,000 to 3,000,000 (1945 (770,000), 1950 (2,200,000), 1960 (3,000,000)),[80] which constituted political and economic refugees from China.[81]

The problem of and difficulty with controlling the 'refugee flood' can be gauged by looking at the post-WWII prison population, immediately after the civil administration took over the British Military Administration in 1947:

> 16,160 persons were admitted to prison to serve sentence, 11,982 of which were for periods of under 3 months, 9216 of them being for under 1 month. A total of 7967 persons were committed for short and completely ineffective terms of

> imprisonment for 'Obstruction' and 'Hawking without a licence', this being a big factor in causing the overcrowding of the prisons and frustrating all efforts made to classify and improve the real criminals therein. Many of these persons were well able to pay their fines but preferred to come to prison.[82]

In essence, right after the war, Hong Kong prisons were turned into relief agencies as a last resort for refugees who were economically and socially ill adjusted, that is, those who were deprived or depraved, due to force of circumstances. As Samuel Wallace observed of the nature and function of total institutions, of one kind or other:

> In part total institutions are created because we feel some individuals in our society need to be given, forcibly if necessary, a new identity; for example, those whom we think world harm others...(and) ...those we feel are incapable of taking care of themselves.[83]

The unexpected and unplanned influx created different kinds of problems for the HKP: controlling the border, maintaining public order and providing security. In practical terms, the HKP had to render services, abate nuisances, handle emergencies, fight crime, suppress vice and remove hawkers.

Colonial Hong Kong, from the time of its inception, prided itself on 'non-interventionism.'[84] Except for essential services, for example, police, medical and emergency, Hong Kong relied on the private sector and marketplace to direct and support herself, through thick and thin. This means the Hong Kong Government did not have the desire to or capacity in thinking ahead and acting proactively. This also means that the Hong Kong Government and the HKP were adept in reacting to crisis[85] and adjusting to evolving circumstances.

H. WWII Impact

Before proceeding, the impact and fall-out of the war effort on the governance of and policing in Hong Kong must be discussed. The focus on the impact of WWII on Hong Kong governance and policing suggests two kinds of inquiry:

First, how did the collaborative effort and established relationship in the defence of Hong Kong against a common enemy between the British government and the Chinese people, such as Chinese patriots—nationalists versus communists, Triad gang members and guerrilla,[86] survive the war and come to affect post-war security policy and policing?

Second, how did the Japanese occupation of Hong Kong affect the thinking of the people of Hong Kong about the British Empire and their role and relationship thereto?[87]

Particularly, how did the reversal of roles, with the Hong Kong Chinese police officers working under the Japanese military government in controlling British POWs, affect their relative mindset about colonial relationship?

The WWII Japanese invasion of Hong Kong was the watershed of Hong Kong's colonial (policing) history. It spelled the death of the belief of the British being an invincible and unquestionable imperial power as it gave birth to an empowered and emboldened Hong Kong identity. This happened in three ways. Externally, since WWII, Hong Kong was being recognised as a colony only in name.[88] Internally, Hong Kong was beginning to develop an identity of its own, separate and distinct from British and Chinese ones. Third, WWII was a traumatic and life-changing event. It forced people to take sides, for or against the British versus the Japanese. In doing so, it set boundaries and inculcated identity. For the British and Chinese who fought the war and suffered together, they were now forever bonded to each other, not by the colour of their skin but by the mutuality of their plight, under wartime conditions. A Hong Kong community under equalitarian conditions was thus obtained.

All of the above helped Hong Kong to develop on its own terms, increasingly as an (relatively) independent political, economic and social entity to be reckoned with.

III: Direction of Reform

Introduction

In the main, the general direction for HKP reform came from two quarters and four sets of inputs.

The first was a 1947 HKP commissioner's report by Pennefather-Evans,[89] guiding future police reform from 1947 to 1957 (Section A). The second was a 1957 Governor Grantham HKP review summarising the achievements and prospecting the future of policing in Hong Kong during his tenure as governor (1946–1957) (Section B). Taking the 1947 Commissioner Pennefather-Evans report (looking forward) and the 1957 Governor Grantham HKP review (looking back) together, the direction and achievements of the HKP reform can be reconstructed.

Beyond the two formal pronouncements, this section looks at four inputs: the colonial agenda (Section C), legislative agenda (Section D), HKP operational agenda (E) and Western expert opinion (F) for their individual contribution and collective wisdom of where the HKP should be heading.

A. 1947 HKP Commissioner Report

The direction of 1950 HKP reform was anticipated by and provided for, in part, by a 1947 HKP commissioner report[90]:

> In 1947 a former commissioner of the pre-war Hong Kong Police responded to the crisis in local policing by composing the Pennefather-Evans[91] Report, an

analysis and set of recommendations for problems in the existing force. The chief weakness the report identified was the failure of the Hong Kong Police to inspire identification among the public it governed. Among the strategies for police reform, the report advised an increase in local hires, an expansion in operational duties, ad an enhanced of professional training.[92]

After about 3 months on the job, before WWII descended on Hong Kong, the Commissioner of Police Pennefather-Evans had made the following observations of the HKP:

> (a) The excellence material of the Force, particularly of the European contingent. (b) The corruption prevalent in the Force. (c) The lackadaisical baring of the Indian Contingent. (d) The unintelligent manner in which the 'means' has so often been mistaken for the 'end'. Systems of checking intended to ensure that men carry out their duties satisfactorily have become the main object in place of the duties themselves. (f) The inertness of the Force. There is little pride in it. There is no Officers' Mess, no police colors, no symbols of the 'soul' of the Force and nothing to distinguish it from being just another 'department of Government' (p. 169).[93]

As to the concrete reform, Evans made the following controversial, far-sighted propositions:

1. Do away with organising the HKP along racial lines, that is, Chinese versus Indian versus British officers. In essence, do away discriminatory policy in terms of recruitment, training, assignment, promotion and retention. More generally, having a unified police force based on qualification, not entitlement, with uniform terms and conditions of service based on merits, not preference.
2. Police should have authority corresponding to responsibilities in role and function. Police power should be commensurate with ranks, not race or sex.
3. Since Hong Kong is a Chinese society, policing should be conducted by Chinese, with a few national contingents in specialised fields.

As for the Water Police, Pennefather-Evans offered the following ideas:

1. Organisationally, 'Water Police should be made a specialized branch of the Police and that men join, be educated and promoted inside that branch'.
2. Water Police should enjoy the same terms and conditions of service, such as pay and benefits, as the Land Police.
3. Administratively, Water Police should be divided into two parts, that is, Sea-Going Personnel and Shore Establishments.

4. Commanders of units should be of superintendent rank.
5. Water Police should have their own CID and not those from the land division, Kowloon.
6. Water Police should have their own marine and nautical school.
7. Water Police should have their own air support units and land-based stations, for example, Cheung Chau.[94]

The Pennefather-Evans report was well received, and it was timely for its purpose. Still, it did not please everyone, especially the old guards. Most the recommendations were adopted; some took longer than others, for example, localisation of the HKP and equal prospects for promotion and advancement. As a whole, it can fairly be said that Pennefather-Evans report was instrumental in shaping HKP development in the second half of the nineteenth century, with Water Police as a case study, until 1992 when the next cycle of HKP reform started.[95]

B. 1957 Annual Police Review[96]

In 1957, the first governor of Hong Kong, Sir Alexander Grantham, retired. On the occasion of Governor Grantham's final Annual Police Review 1957, he reflected on the challenges and achievements of the HKP.[97]

First, the HKP burden is increasing. As Hong Kong grew after WWII, so did the burden on the HKP. Looking into the future, the burden on the HKP was not likely to be reduced.

Second, the HKP is expanding. The HKP had been growing and expanding with the 'growth in the size of the Colony'.

Third, the HKP needs more human, material and modern resources. The growth and expansions of the HKP meant more officers, quarters, stations and equipment. This also meant that old equipment is replaced with new and up-to-date version.

Fourth, the HKP is building a unified Auxiliary Police. The HKP had fully integrated with the Police Reserve and the Special Constabulary, formerly auxiliary bodies, into one with the HKP, that is, the Auxiliary Police. The newly integrated Auxiliary Police was needed 'so that in times of emergency the Colony will have one quickly mobilised Force instead of three separate forces'.

Fifth, the HKP is effective in keeping law and order. The HKP had been effective in maintaining 'the general state of law and order' in the colony in 1957.

Sixth, the HKP needs to control and eradicate secret societies. Secret societies were an evil for Hong Kong society and a major problem for the HKP. Reducing crime required first eradicating secret societies. This was job one for the HKP.

Seventh, the HKP takes on internal security role. The October 1956 riot highlighted the need for the HKP to play a more organised, mobile and adaptive internal security role in facing future challenges.

Eighth, the HKP requires up-to-date training. In order to deliver good service and to meet expectations of people in keeping Hong Kong safe and its economy vibrant, the HKP needed to be better and timely trained in all areas.[98]

C. Colonial Agenda

On 17 July 1950, a secretary of state for the colonies' memorandum on localisation of Hong Kong civil services was forwarded to the cabinet. Specifically, it called for the employment of native-born administrators in the higher grades of colonial civil servants. In it, the situation of Hong Kong on this subject was mentioned:

> In Hong Kong there are 395 higher civil service posts, of which 51 are at present held by local officers, mostly in the educational, medical, nursing and other professional services. There is one local-born member of the Administrative Service. In correspondence concerning a Bill to authorise the appointment of a Public Service Commission the Governor expressed the opinion that for some years to come the majority of Hong Kong vacancies in the higher posts would have to be filled from the United Kingdom; he emphasised in particular the difficulty of finding good local material for the Administrative Service and the Police.[99]

The policy direction for Hong Kong was clear: localisation for the HKP, but not necessarily at the expense of expatriate posting, certainly not at the very top, that is, commissioners of police.

D. Legislative Agenda

Economy and Reform

In a LegCo discussion[100] of the Appropriation for 1949–1950 Bill, LegCo member Hon. D.F. Landle raised the issue about the efficiency and cost-effectiveness of public service with respect to justifying huge outlay, for example, every department had its own messengers, presumably for inter-departmental communication. The suggestion was to centralise. The same observation was applied to the HKP:

> If Government offices were more centralised perhaps some of these would not be necessary. … And another instance is that under the Secretariat for Chinese Affairs I notice that a Private Force is run in the form of a District Watch Force which costs some $190,000. This seems to me a relic of the past, and greater economy might be achieved if the functions of this Force were taken over by the Police.[101]

Human Rights and Reform

On 8 September 1948, the colonial secretary moved the council to endorse the Draft International Declaration of Human Rights annexed to the Order of Business.[102] This is the first time that the issue of human rights had been brought to the forefront for considering by dint of a UN mandate.

The draft was first considered at the third session of the Human Rights Commission under the Commission of the Economic and Social Council of the United Nations[103] in the Spring of 1948. In proposing the motion to adopt the draft, the colonial secretary made it clear that it would be difficult, if not impossible, to achieve the lofty human rights goals set forth under the draft declaration, due to local conditions, over education. For example, Section 23 calls for universal free education for children. Hong Kong was far behind in reaching such a goal, in terms of capacity or resource:

> This right is one we cannot fulfill now or next year, or I venture to say, in ten years. We must as practical men face that fact: but it does not prevent us from acknowledging that elementary education should be free and universal and from so ordering our affairs that some day, though not in ours, it will be so.[104]

But the colonial secretary was quick to point out that it was Hong Kong's obligation to try, even if it failed in the beginning: 'By adhering to this draft Declaration, civilised man promises, in the words of proclamation in the preamble, to 'strive by teaching and education to promote respect for these rights and freedoms'.[105] Mindful of the circumstances in Hong Kong, the colonial secretary pointed out that the draft declaration did contain escape clause under exceptional circumstances: 'no man may use any of these rights at the expense of his neighbour's freedom, or of public order or of the general welfare' (Sections 27 and 28).

The draft declaration was adopted after Hon. Sir Man-Kam Lo called for its acceptance, not as an attainable realistic goal, but as a worthwhile cause to strive for.

The adoption of the motion was telling of the mindset of British-dominant Legislative Council at the time:

First, Hong Kong was no longer functioning as a colony. It was to be developed as a world-class city, with human rights guaranteed by UN conventions and declarations. This was not unlike the 1990s when Governor Patton was trying to protect Hong Kong with UN treaties and international conventions.

Second, the British government accepted the fact that Hong Kong would never be like the United States and the United Kingdom with more advanced system of law, rights and justice. But it was its duty to introduce Hong Kong to those fine traditions, which set it apart from China.

Third, Chinese LegCo members accepted the fact that the Chinese were under British rule, and thus had to follow British human rights traditions, even if the Chinese did not have the tradition, or otherwise felt it was inappropriate.

E. Operational Agenda[106]

The publication of the HKPM in 1951 turned a new leaf for the HKP. The HKPM has an ambitious agenda. Besides acting as an unofficial history of sorts for the HKP, the HKPM sought to facilitate communication between the ranks (past and present), make the HKP more transparent to the public and allow officers to reach out to the world. In sum, it sought to promote the HKP morale within and advance public relationship without. A prideful acting commissioner of police, A. C. Maxwell, had this to say about the purposes of the HKPM on the occasion of its launch:

The object of this magazine then, is to give us of the Hong Kong Police a means of expression, an interpretation of the Force to the Force and to the public, a medium for the spread of special knowledge and a page on which some record of the Force may be written.[107]

Nine years later, on the event of his retirement, CP Maxwell bid farewell to the force and had this to say about the HKPM:

The intervening years have seen a lot of changes in the Force. We have expanded rapidly and the problems of this expansion are still with us but are slowly being overcome. The magazine has grown with the Force. It has benefited morale and has contributed towards good relations with the Public. In this alone it has justified its existence.[108]

The HKP was growing and changing fast; the HKPM bore witness to such changes, within and without the organisation.

A close inspection of the content of the inauguration issue of the HKPM revealed where the HKP was heading:

First, the HKP was growing, along with Hong Kong. This is to say that HKP reform and changes were very much driven by the society it was an integral part of.

Second, the HKP was remaking itself into a modern police force. It is to observe that while the force of changes came from outside, the change management was predominately an internal affair. To this end, the HKP sent officers overseas for training as well as career development.[109]

Third, the HKP transformed itself from a colonial police force to a civil policing agency. This is to observe that the HKP shed its colonial armour and colours long before 1997. This started with training its frontline inspectorate officers in the United Kingdom, the birthplace of modern policing, which excelled in policing by consent.

F. Expert Opinion

The HKP reform agenda was a larger and broader post-WWII Hong Kong reconstruction–re-engineering plan.[110] The objective was to rebuild the HKP, consonant with Hong Kong's social, economic and political development,[111] in the image of the West, beginning in earnest shortly after WWII.[112] With the treatment of youth offenders, this meant having professional social workers, dealing with them instead of family or police: 'In countries where the practice of probation for youthful offenders is better established, and where there are more social agencies to help in the management of delinquents, the handling of juveniles has become less and less a matter for the police'.[113]

Juveniles needed help from the society more than punishment, and still less retribution when they violated the law. In developing an enlightened and effective juvenile policy, the society needs to forgo its knee-jerk retributive instinct and punitive reaction. It needs to dig deep to find the true causes of youth offending as it thinks long and hard about the impact of punishment on the development of youth and the future of society. In sum, Hong Kong needed a thorough understanding of the youth and the station he finds himself in before taking action.

If Hong Kong had cultivated such an understanding, it would have found that youth offended less so because they were evil or vicious but more so because they were immature, and thus temperamental, less developed and easily influenced.[114] The families, peers, community and society they found themselves with had much to do with what they did and how they behaved. If that should be the case, the society should change its ways in dealing with juveniles, instead of the other way around.

For example, 'we have those who have to commit crime because they are suffering from a deprival (a lack of food or clothes, which may cause a normal person to steal or to become a prostitute or to embezzle funds and so on). When there are a lot of crimes of this nature, we know that it is time to overhaul the law, or to look into the social life of the offenders'.[115] For example, it is known that in the United Kingdom, 'Gypsy people are a law unto themselves, for instance—and in Hong Kong the boat people and the rickshaw pullers have many behaviours, acceptable to themselves, which vary widely from those approved by the law'.[116] In such cases, police should treat juveniles differently when their family teaches them how to conduct themselves in a normal manner.

At the end of the day:

> If justice is retributive you know that the culture is primitive or unorganized and the level of moral understanding is low. If justice is deterrent you can be sure that the stability of the society is uncertain—for otherwise, how could we defend a system of justice that treated A severely so that 13 would behave himself. The only justification would be that the law was being broken and it

was necessary to be firm to uphold government. When the accent in the courts is upon reformation, you can be certain that there are well organized bodies in the community who have humanity at heart and the community itself has a high degree of social organization. And when the courts think in terms of 'treatment' rather than reformation, it is obvious that we have a most sophisticated and enlightened system of government.[117]

In this regard, the message was, in rebuilding Hong Kong, she had much to learn, again from the more progressive Western society!

Discussion

The above reconstruction of 'directions of reform' from a variety of sources creates the ability to see where the HKP has been (1957 Annual Hong Kong Police Review) and where it is heading (1947 HKP commissioner report). It also provides a sample of more important aspirational goals (Draft International Declaration of Human Rights) and operational objectives (civilisation, modernisation) to be achieved, otherwise deemed to be politically possible (decolonisation, localisation) and economically viable (expenditure bearing on reform) and socially acceptable (security over reform).[118]

What can be gleaned from this reconstruction of 'directions of reform' exercise?

First, except perhaps for the fact that there was a dire need for re-establishing the Hong Kong Government and reconstructing the HKP out of the ashes of WWII ruins, remnants and remembrance, there was little consensus on the direction, priority and speed of change.

Second, HKP reform was not a typical case of planned change process in organisation development, to wit: 'Organization Development is an effort planned, organization-wide and managed from the top, to increase organization effectiveness and health through planned interventions in the organization's "processes", using behavioural-science knowledge'.[119] The process of planned organisation involves the following considerations, steps and processes:

- *Planned.* OD takes a long-range approach to improving organizational performance and efficiency. It avoids the (usual) 'quick-fix'.
- *Organisation-wide.* OD focuses on the total system.
- *Managed from the top.* To be effective, OD must have the support of top-management. They have to model it, not just espouse it. The OD process also needs the buy-in and ownership of workers throughout the organisation.
- *Increase organisation effectiveness and health.* OD is tied to the bottom-line. Its goal is to improve the organisation, to make it more efficient and more competitive by aligning the organisation's systems with its people.

- *Planned interventions.* After proper preparation, OD uses activities called interventions to make systemwide, permanent changes in the organisation.
- *Using behavioral-science knowledge.* OD is a discipline that combines research and experience to understanding people, business systems, and their interactions.[120]

What happened is that the HKP leadership of the time was pressed into action by the need to create a new organisation out of clean cloth, and having to respond to fast-developing social, economic and political situations in Hong Kong, with little time to react, and still less to reflect. Under the circumstances, the lack of research capacity and empirical data did not help in making informed and enlightened policy decisions.[121] In 1938, Sir Geoffrey Northcote was the first to point out the problem with lack of basic policy tools, that is, data, in running good government:

In many respects the statistical information at the disposal of this Government is deficient or unscientifically arranged; there is a serious lack of machinery for the co-ordination of such statistics as exist, and in nearly every case these are crude. In such circumstances it might with some truth be alleged that figures are given to us to conceal the facts. The first-rate importance of well-digested and well-correlated statistics to a Colony, which is so largely dependent upon commerce and has, for example, such grave population problems as Hong Kong, is indisputable.[122]

That being the case, it is fair to observe that the 1950 HKP reform was less of scientific, systematic engineering than that of 'muddling through' process,[123] as befitting the chaos and disorganisation of the time.

Third, that being the case, one can expect that the reform direction was not driven by rigorous policy analysis, but by ad hoc decision making that was driven by events and circumstances, involved in political negotiations between interested parties and stakeholders, and was based on value predispositions and vested interests. In such a policy environment, neither the deliberative policy-making process nor the rational decision-making model held sway.[124] Pragmatism, not principle, prevailed; personality cults and political clout were the order of the day. Here, Elizabeth Sinn aptly points out: 'Individual Governors, with different backgrounds, personalities, attitudes, and styles, profoundly affected the course of events and the development of institutions in Hong Kong'.[125]

In sum, what was missing at the time was a policy framework to structure policy decision making: As Leo Goodstadt observed in another context:

> A major obstacle to assessing the impact of the data deficit on government decisions is that throughout the period under review Hong Kong had a

government in which internal policies were not written down as a coherent guide to decision-making, and forward planning and strategic management were not much in evidence. This was administration with minimal policies and few statistics, which was in line with the official commitment to non-interventionism. In their approach to policy-making, however, senior Hong Kong officials took a more pragmatic view of Laissez-faire than is generally recognised.[126]

IV: Process and Measures of Reform

This section will discuss the 1950s HKP reform, in measures and processes. The focus here is on how the HKP transformed itself from improvisational–entrepreneur policing, to structured and organised policing, by way of modernisation. The distinctive features characterising the modernisation reform of this period were 'decolonisation', 'localisation', 'legalisation', 'modernisation', 'communalisation' and 'organisation'.

A: Decolonisation

Decolonisation without Being Decolonised

Hong Kong was returned to China on 1 July 1997. This officially terminated the colonial stage of Hong Kong history. However, in terms of decolonisation analysis, the critical stage was 1945. This was the time when the British government seriously contemplated returning Hong Kong to China for moral and diplomatic reasons.[127] In this regard, it was George Kitson, Head of China Department at the Foreign Office, who argued forcefully and compellingly for the return of Hong Kong to China in late 1945. His reasoning was a simple one; it is the right thing to do. In support, Kitson rendered the famed, and much quoted, 'Isle of Wight analogy'. The analogy made clear that on the issue of returning Hong Kong, at the end of the day, it was not what the United Kingdom had done for Hong Kong (i.e., offering security and prosperity for millions) that mattered. It was how China felt about foreigners occupying her land and lording over her citizens that held sway. In essence, on the matter of sovereignty, it was always the case of principle over expedience, nationalism over utilitarianism:

> The Chinese feelings towards Hong Kong can perhaps be most easily described by using the Isle of Wight analogy. Supposing the Chinese had taken the island against our will 100 years ago and covered it with pagodas, etc., and developed it by means which they had invented and we had not learned to use, doing all this for their own purpose, although talking a great deal about the material advantages to the United Kingdom, and all the time emphasizing the value of this heaven of good government, a protection against insecurity, in the Isle

> of Wight. Even if they have created a heaven on earth in that small island we should have only one feeling about it. We should want it back.[128]

Given the above sentiment, and not being able to divest Hong Kong through decolonisation due to geopolitical reasons,[129] Hong Kong was allowed to be decolonised in effect, though not in form. Hong Kong was no longer a Crown colony, but a dependent territory,[130] enjoying a high degree of freedom and autonomy.[131]

Informed of this historical context, the HKP started to informally decolonise after WWII, incrementally but purposively, in the form of management philosophy (localisation),[132] administrative policies (bureaucratisation), operational practices (communalisation) and organisational culture (professionalism); so much so that by 1997, it had operated very much autonomously, without any conspicuous vintages of a colonial force, except perhaps (ironically) earning the prefix of 'Royal' to Hong Kong Police for a job well done.

Decolonisation and Differentiate Policing

Particularly, after WWII, the HKP adopted a hybrid policing strategy with civil policing in Hong Kong and Kowloon and para-military policing at the border.[133] 'Dual track' administration still survived in the New Territories and the outer Islands, except in the New Towns (Tsuen Wan, Shatin), but in a much diluted and mutated form.[134] James Hayes, long-time district officer from New Territories turned Hong Kong historian had this to say about New Territories administration:

> It was not until the early postwar years that the Hong Kong Government institutionalized local leadership by establishing a formal system of Village Representatives in 1948, and then by setting up 27 Rural Committees in the traditional sub-districts or heung (xiang) by degrees in the 1950s. In taking these steps, they had been anticipated by the measures adopted for local management by the Japanese during their wartime occupation of Hong Kong.[135]

As to policing, most certainly village self-help was on the way out, ever so slowly:

> Bands of armed villagers from the Tin Shui Wai region first mobilised themselves to defend the clan from bandits who hid in remote hills...An ancestral hall in Ping Shan village once served as a community court, and punishment was often meted out within its sturdy stone walls before police arrived. But the Ping Shan vigilantes—who obtained a licence during World War II—no longer deal out their own punishment to those caught stealing or breaking in. ... And in the 1950s, after the Communist Party took over on the mainland, large

> numbers of illegal immigrants flocked to Hong Kong...The numbers of police could not handle the situation, so villagers formed their own 100-strong self-defence team, with police consent. But police are warning villagers frightened by recent killings and robberies that forming new vigilante teams could add to the cycle of violence.[136]

In emergency–internal security situations, the HKP has acquired formidable public order policing (PTU) and highly mobile emergency response capacities (EU). On a moment's notice, the HKP could jointly operate with British forces through an integrated command and control structure, supposed by seamless communication and coordination capabilities.

More significantly for decolonisation analysis, during emergencies and internal security operations, the HKP was in command and control, with British forces standing by. As to the overall policing policy in emergencies, the HKP and British armed forces were required to defer to civilian leadership. They all had to take into consideration the sentiment and support of the local population before using force and conducting militarised operations.[137] This public order policing and internal security operational protocol had been institutionalised, and still retained today, for example, during the planning of the Sixth Ministerial Conference of the World Trade Organization (2005), the Legislative Council members were much concerned with the need to strike a balance between security and freedom:

> Facilitating demonstrations: 12. While acknowledging the importance of upholding law and order, some Members stressed the need to strike a reasonable balance between enforcing security measures on one hand, and respecting the freedom of expression of demonstrators on the other. They urged the Police not to resort to high-handed action lightly and to adopt a tolerant attitude as far as possible when dealing with demonstrations during MC6. The Administration re-affirmed its high regard for freedom of expression and assured Members that the Police had always tried to facilitate lawful and peaceful demonstrations, yet without losing sight of the need to maintain law and order.[138]

Through the 'decolonising years' (1945–1997), the HKP had in effect transformed itself into a professional local law enforcement agency, in the service of the community, and assumed a highly disciplined expansive military role, in securing Hong Kong internal security[139] and British national interest.[140] Recalling the 1967 riot:

> The left wing paid a heavy price for instigating the riots which briefly brought the Hong Kong society to a standstill...The general strike and food strike caused huge inconvenience to the public and the image of the left wing was particularly undermined by the bomb attack.

But to a few die-hard anti-colonialism observers, the HKP is still the 'Royal Hong Kong Police' of yester years. As a rejoinder and closer to the facts, the title 'Royal' was worn with pride by the HKP, before 1997. It was embraced as a badge of honor, as a validation of the public trust in the HKP's professionalism. It was not taken as a scarlet letter, reminding people of a subservient past. It signified and symbolised that the HKP had gone through the rite of passage as a professional force, and was now capable of managing itself, without British countenance, still less approval. The HKP had come of age, on its own terms, at its own pace and in line with its own vision.

The impact of decolonisation on Hong Kong, with the drastic transformation of personal attitude and racial animus on both British and Chinese parts, is best summed up by a Canadian police officer (RCMP) turned intelligence agent, who served in Hong Kong for 13 years (since 1967) only to return in 1987:[141]

> Even the description of Hong Kong as a British Crown Colony ...was amended to British Dependent Territory in 1983 ...On returning to Hong Kong in 1986, it did not take long to notice the differences in the manner in which the Chinese were treated by the foreign expatriates...from the manner in which they were treated during my first tour in the late 1960's and early 1970's. In my mind, it was positive change. They were now looked upon with more respect by the British and others and in fact the Chinese were commanding more respect. During my first tour, it was very rare to find a Chinese officer in the Royal Hong Kong Police who had attained the Gazetted rank of Superintendent. By the time I departed Hong Kong in 1991, Li, Kwan-ha had been appointed as the first commissioner of the Force.[142]

Decolonisation Model

The study of colonial rule and colonial policing is about purpose, method and effect of colonialism on the indigenous people.[143] In the study of HKP reform in 1950s, it is about ascertaining the ideology—philosophy of governance and policy—practice of regulations, in the midst of decolonisation, viewed over time. Here, there is a distinctive shift in governing philosophy, from coercive to consensus, and on policy, from penal to remedial.

Table 8.1 Colonial Development in Governance Philosophy and Penal Policy

	Coercive	Consensus
Penal	Colonial: 1840s—Captain William Caine[144]	Late colonial: 1950s—Governor Young[145]
Remedial	Early colonial: 1880s—Governor Hennessy[146] (1877–1882)[147]	Decolonisation: 1990s—Governor Pattern[148]

Decolonisation and Penal Policy

The best example of the change in colonial governance after WWII comes from the Hong Kong Government philosophy towards penal administration and juvenile justice. This is so because in the study of the colonial government and governance, how it deployed coercive resources is the best evidence of its inherent nature and adopted style of control.[149] After all, it was Weber who stated: 'Monopoly over the legitimate use of force is as essential a characteristic of the state as compulsory jurisdiction and continuous organization in a given territorial area'.[150]

After WWII, there was a move to abolish capital punishment in Hong Kong and do away with corporal punishment for juveniles. But both proposals were met with strong oppositions, from conservatives, Chinese in particular, within and without the government.

With the corporal punishment abortionists, which included the acting superintendent of prison, the Rt. Rev. Bishop of Victoria, the Hon. Director of Medical Services and Dr. Adam, they argued that corporal punishment was cruel and inhuman, besides having 'no good effect and frequently does harm'. For the supporters, which included the Hon. Secretary for Chinese Affairs, the Commissioner of Police, the Director of Education, the Rev. Father Ryan and the Chairman, immediate abolition was opposed on the grounds that 'the time is not yet ripe for the abolition of corporal punishment in this Colony because of conditions which are peculiar to Hong Kong and because of present lack of other sanctions for the maintenance of law and order'.[151]

The conservatives won the debate. Capital and corporal punishment stayed. Still, the policy debate had its impact on penal administration, for example, in 1950, there were only 405 juveniles receiving corporal punishment, as compared to 4367 in 1949. Most of the 405 were for non-criminal offenses, such as hawking.

The liberalisation of penal policy here discussed has been taken as evidence of change of hearts in colonial mentality. This is to observe that, in order for colonialists to effectively control indigenous people of a different cultural orientation, it had to first obtain obedience coercively and check deviance punitively, until a habit of obedience was obtained; only then did surveillance set in. Any move away from being coercive and punitive suggested that either colonialists had given up control, that is, decolonisation, or colonised people no longer needed control, that is, 'habit of obedience'. In this way, it can be said that decolonisation implied liberalisation of penal policy.

In achieving decolonisation, the liberalisation of penal policy was a double-edged sword. To the extent liberal policy spared many Chinese from coercive punishments, it ameliorated the impact of discriminatory and harsh colonial rules. However, the promotion of liberal penal policy is just moving from one expression of colonialism to another, that is, from 'coercive' penal policy to 'liberal' jurisprudential thought, both of which were 'made in U.K.'

In real terms, Chinese objections to 'coercive' penal policy were philosophical ones. It had little to do with harshness of punishment per se. Harsh punishment was objectionable because of the way it was deployed, and not its nature, to obtain obedience to British rule and culture. 'Coercive' penal policy was also deemed objectionable because it was applied in a discriminatory way. In both instances, 'coercive' penal policy was found wanting in coming to terms with Chinese culture, in its conception (why punish) and application (what to punish).

In equating decolonisation with liberalisation, the colonialists failed to achieve decolonisation because the imposition of 'liberal' penal policy by the British was considered as objectionable the application of 'conservative' penal policy to the Chinese. In both cases, they failed to respect traditional Chinese culture as the basis of deciding who, what and how to punish.

The ultimate issue in decolonisation is to what extent, how and why was the HKP decolonised? Depending on whom you ask, there is likely to be two answers to this question. First, it was decolonised to make policing more social service oriented ('Decolonisation and Social Service'). Or second, it was decolonised to making policing more Confucius like ('Confucianisation of Policing').

Decolonisation and Social Service[152]

In 1935 and just before WWII, European and Chinese HKP officers started a Boys' and Girls' Club Association (BGCA) for the poor and deprived kids of Hong Kong, with the support of the Magistrate of Juvenile Court. By 1941, there were 595 girls and 648 boys in 21 clubs. The project was abandoned in WWII after a propitious start. The aim of the club was set forth in 1940 as follows[153]:

> The object of the club is to provide a centre where adolescent children may meet together, and by engaging in a variety of activities, grow up into fit, happy men and good intelligent citizens. This work is urgently needed in Hong Kong where a very large percentage of the children have little or no education or opportunity for comradeship and recreation other than that provided by the life of the streets. It is a disturbing fact that through poverty many thousands of children are driven to work, for which they are not sufficiently developed and even to beg and to steal. If one considers the lives of children of poor families in Hong Kong one does not find evidence of juvenile crime in the least surprising. Their home life is a bed space shared with several others, their recreation hanging about the streets. Many have to earn their living and even to support their parents at an age, when, in other countries, they would not be beginning their education. It is impossible therefore to exaggerate the opportunities for clubs in Hong Kong. The clubs have to fill almost the whole leisure

> of the children they cater for and provide education from the beginning, and indeed start their moral education from scratch. It is, nevertheless, remarkable how much can be achieved in a short time and at very little expense.

After WWII, there were frantic efforts to rebuild, including constructing infrastructure,[154] training leaders,[155] launching programmes[156] and providing services.[157] It was a phenomenal success. By 1960, there were 203 clubs catering for 11,105 children. From this humble beginning, the BGCA developed into one of the major social service institution for youth development today.[158]

The establishment of the BGCA before and after WWII was telling of the Hong Kong Government's support for more social services in Hong Kong. This marked a change in government policy, from a detached colonial rule to a more involved paternalistic administration.

In a similar manner, the HKP is observed to be changing in the same direction, from a predominantly law enforcement, crime-fighting and order maintenance agency to a more social-service- and community-oriented one. The era of social-service- and community-oriented policing in Hong Kong has just begun. This shift in the roles and functions of the HKP runs counter to the traditional image of the HKP as a hard-nosed and hardcore colonial policing agency, devoted to and obsessed with security and order alone.

Decolonisation and Confucianisation of Policing

In the study of colonial policing, much is known about what the Hong Kong colonial officials and police thought about policing philosophy, policy and strategy. However, little, if anything, is known about how the Chinese police officers felt and think about colonial policing. In sum, more is understood about the more formal aspects of colonial policing than the realities of street policing. It is thus important to hear from the Chinese officers about their experience with policing in Hong Kong, specifically to ascertain the role and relationship between the police and the public.

In the reform of the HKP, the feeling, thinking and action of the members of the HKP matters. If the British colonial authority was interested in decolonising the HKP, they needed to get feedback from the rank and file about: What is it that works? What is it that does not work?

In 1959, the HKP launched a 'Hong Kong Police Gold Medal Essay Competition 1959' open to all Force members. The winner of the essay, Detective Police Constable 4726 Mui Wah Fuk (CID PHQ), discussed his understanding of the role of policemen and what the relationship between policemen and citizens should be.[159]

Peng started the essay by asking a simple, but important, question in policing and society: 'What is the relationship between policemen and citizens?' To answer this question, Peng first asked the question: why did Hong Kong society need the police?

Here, Peng observed that if people were all perfect, there would be no need for police. Thus, police are needed to make sure that people do the right thing. How, then, could police make sure that people always do the right thing?

Peng observed that the police could make people do the right thing by guiding them with morality and deterring them with law. 'In view of this, governments, being instructed by the people, have no alternative but to use policemen to lead people along the right track and if necessity requires it, to deal with them according to the law'.[160] In essence, police should act both as a moral as well as a legal agent of the state.[161] The first is to inspire and the latter is to awe.

Between these two roles, the moral role is by far the more important, for the HKP. This is because people will try every way they can to avoid the law. The law itself is never perfect, and it is too complex and overly technical. Guilty people will be able to escape punishment by exploiting the technicalities allowed by law. Thus, the best way to make people do the right things is not by making them fear the law but by making people follow their moral at heart. According to Shavelle, law and morality both contribute to good behaviour, but do so with different means:

> It is evident that both law and morality serve to channel our behavior. Law accomplishes this primarily through the threat of sanctions if we disobey legal rules. Morality too involves incentives: bad acts may result in guilt and disapprobation, and good acts may result in virtuous feelings and praise.[162]

To Peng, morality was also more effective than the law in settling conflicts and resolving disputes. Once people internalise a moral compass, they will feel shame and be self-regulating. A moral person will avoid the law at all costs, as a manifestation of 'duty calls'. Alternatively, having the police enforce the law or getting judges to settle disputes would destroy personal relationships and generate animosity between people. Breaking relationship and alienating people would promise more, not less, disobedience, out of resistance or perhaps even defiance.

Turning to relationship between the public and the police, Peng believed that the public has a duty to respect and assist the police in the performance of duties. The failure of the public to cooperate with the HKP made policing much more difficult. For example, riots (1954) in earlier years in Hong Kong would have been easily subdued if the public had been more cooperative and helpful, such as reporting on rioters and not violating curfew.

What does it mean by saying that police officers should be moral agents? This meant that police should set a personal example, to inspire and guide people to develop a sense of moral approbation.

> Being a policeman, one's fundamental duty is to cultivate a feeling of morality among citizens. During the course of his duty, the policemen must show his

concern and must guide citizens, encouraging them to express their feeling of morality in their daily lives and their speech, as well as in their movements, so that they will, from deep within their own consciences, feel that doing something the wrong way is a shameful thing.[163]

More controversially, Peng believed that policemen should be educators and philosophers, not just law enforcers and crime fighters. They should guide people to stay clear of material goods in search of personal happiness.

It will cause them to believe that wealth can never bring forth real happiness and satisfaction during their lifetimes. The noble character will be respected and revered by others and to obtain this respect should be the highest aim of a person's life.[164]

Peng's essay was a timely and important essay. It was timely because the HKP was undergoing radical changes. The essay provided new ideas for the reformers and enriched the decolonisation process. Moreover, as a work, it is telling on the process and direction of the reform–decolonisation process, in the mind of rank and file.

In terms of process, the essay competition serves decolonization in a number of ways:

First, the Hong Kong Police Gold Medal Essay Competition (1959) was designed as a high-profile consultation exercise. Its purpose was to show the staff and public that the HKP was changing its mode of operation, from an insulated and secretive organisation, to a transparent and open one.

Second, the Hong Kong Police Gold Medal Essay Competition (1959) solicited and welcomed submissions from all ranks, with a DPC winning the top prize. This was unheard of before in the old colonial days. In old Hong Kong, policing officers were to be seen not heard from, that is, the police serves with an 'obedient servant mentality'—spoken to but not interacting with. Within the HKP, PCs were order takers, not opinion leaders. This showed that the HKP was trying to reverse the trend, by showing interest in the suggestions of its officers, even at the lowest ranks. The message included the following: (1) The HKP wants the best ideas, wherever they can be found. Ideas are judged by their merits, not rank; a scientific process. (2) The HKP wants ideas from its staff, a first principle in participating management; a democratisation move. (3) The HKP wants to engage its staff in the plan-changed process, to foster identification and promote buy-in. (4) The HKP wants Chinese people to play an active part in the building of a new HKP; a localisation process.

As to the content of the essay, it highlighted the following:

First, the essay 'Policemen and Citizens' was based entirely on traditional Chinese jurisprudential thoughts and social control practices, that is, promote Confucianisation of the law (morality before law, law promotes law);

cultivate individual morality and personhood; pursue dispute resolution to repair and foster relationship; avoid litigation at all costs; and have officials act as *junzhi*.

The whole foundation of Chinese (Confucian) ethical order was based upon the ideal of self-cultivation. It was believed that 'self-cultivation alone could solve all political problems and usher in the perfect society'.[165] More specifically, 'wishing to govern well in their states, they would first regulate their families. Wishing to regulate their families, they would first cultivate their persons. Wishing to cultivate their persons, they would first rectify their minds…'.[166]

The police officer, as a standard bearer of the ethical order, was expected to possess a strong ethical conviction and refined moral sensitivity, in thought as well as in action. Confucius said, 'To subdue one's self and return to propriety, is perfect virtue'. This included sacrificing himself to promote virtue: 'The determined scholars and the man of virtue will not seek to live at the expense of injuring their virtue. They will even sacrifice their lives to preserve their virtue completely'.[167]

Lastly, to strive for virtue was a relentless pursuit and enduring affair. Confucius said: 'The superior man does not, even for the space of a single meal, act contrary to virtue'.[168]

For Confucian researchers, it is far-fetched to equate police officers in the twentieth-century Hong Kong to sage scholars (*junzhi*). Still, there was nothing to stop Peng to pursue Confucius ideals (i.e., self-cultivation) to become better than he really was. Such is the power of ideas and attractiveness of ideals.

As to the utility of law and punishment in bringing about a well-ordered society, Confucius has this to say:

> Govern the people with regulations and organize them with penal law (*xing*), and they will avoid punishments but will be without shame. Govern them with virtue and organize them through the *li*, and the people will have a sense of shame and moreover will become transformed themselves.[169]

Parenthetically, Confucius observed that the rule of law, instead of settling conflicts generates more disputes and antagonism, as people are invited to and rewarded by unremitting challenges about the meaning and application of law, in every possible way. This corresponds to what Peng observed to be the technicality and complexity of the law.

In the end, the ultimate objective of any ruler is to resolve disputes by negotiation and prevent wrongdoing by cultivating a virtuous man, thereby doing away with contentious litigation altogether: 'In hearing litigation, I am not different from any other man. But if you insist on a difference, it is, perhaps, that I try to get the parties not to resort to litigation in the first place'.[170]

Second, the essay 'Policemen and Citizens' provides a new script on policing, away from the decolonisation narrative. Whereas decolonisation called for democratisation, legalisation, localisation, professionalisation and modernisation, 'Policemen and Citizens' called for Confucianisation of policing, a change in paradigm, vision and mission of policing. Simply put, Peng called for the transformation of Hong Kong society, people and culture from a British legalistic and punitive orientation to Chinese moralistic and educational approach.

B: Localisation

Localisation of the HKP has most often been described as replacing British police officers with Chinese ones, in senior ranks,[171] and staffing of all rank and file with local officers.

Localisation has been defined as a conscious process to adapt what is foreign to local conditions, culture and context:

> Localization... is the process of adapting a product or service to a particular language, culture, and desired local 'look-and-feel'. Ideally, a product or service is developed so that localization is relatively easy to achieve—for example, by creating technical illustrations for manuals in which the text can easily be changed to another language and allowing some expansion room for this purpose.[172]

As applied, localisation means different things to different people and in different contexts. In transplantation of law, this means customisation of foreign law to fit into domestic soil.[173] In justice administration, this means conducting legal transactions in Chinese. In litigation, this means retaining of local lawyers, as strategists or as lead counsel. In technology, this means adopting local protocol.[174] In scholarship, this means conducting research with indigenous theory and grounded data.[175] In education, this means adopting teaching materials with local content and local context. In research, this means informed by indigenous theory as support by local data. In public service, this means providing services with local staff, conforming to local expectations.[176]

Historically, the localisation of the HKP moved in different directions and took up a variety of forms, from appointing a well-groomed cadet officer as commissioner of police to hiring Chinese as Water Police to having Chinese Police Reserve units.

Over the years, in order to improve and perfect colonial governance of Chinese, the HKP sought to 'localise' their 'colonial' policing practices through strategies of 'disengagement', 'delegation', 'collaboration', 'customisation' and 'assimilation'.

Disengagement

The strategy of 'disengagement' in colonial policing spoke of a 'targeted deployment' of police resources, and in some instances exercising 'selective law enforcement' as warranted by local circumstances and grounded situation, for example, having direct British patrol versus supervised Chinese watchmen, depending on tactical needs. In the 1840s, this meant having British and Indian officers patrolling in Victoria and Chinese working under close supervision of British at sea.[177] For the rest in rural Hong Kong, the outer islands (Cheung Chau) and Chinese communities (New Territories), the British would only intervene if and when they were needed. There self-help policing was the rule.

In this way, it can be said that the colonial government had 'localised' their policing operations through selective (non)presence or, selective policing. HKP officers were not being deployed on the frontlines, but were being held in reserve. Operationally, 'disengagement' as 'localised' policing manifested itself as graduated and guarded British participation in Chinese communal affairs or social activities, depending on exigencies, for example, emergency or crisis, such as riots or typhoon. The prime example of this type of elective presence was the policing of the Kowloon Walled City:

> This was the last of government enforcement, the Chinese wanted rights to the city but didn't have them, and the British just ignored it and focused on Hong Kong. It to all intents and purposes became an independent nation, an enclave of China. In this absence of governance the criminal underworld thrived. In just a few years the Chinese Triads, a very menacing group of criminals the equivalent to the American Mafia, had a stranglehold on the city, making it rife with crime and drugs. The only time the Hong Kong government had any jurisdiction there was to solve a murder and of course many attempted police raids on the many brothels, gambling parlors and opium dens operated by the Triads in the city.[178]

Delegation

'Delegation' is the assignment of duties and responsibilities to others. In the context of policing in Hong Kong, delegation was when the HKP affirmative assigned 'colonial' policing duties to other social control agents, for example, private guards or communal institutions, for example, District Watch Force (更練所). In theoretical terms, this meant the British devising policies (steering) with Chinese administering them (rowing). In the context of Hong Kong policing, this was the practice of 'indirect rule' or 'rule by proxy'.

The District Watch Force Ordinance (29 April 1949) provides in pertinent parts:

1. 'The functions of the District Watch Force shall be
    a. To assist the Secretary for Chinese Affairs in the execution of the duties of his office;

b. To perform such duties as it may be required to perform in assisting to—
   i. Preserve the public peace;
   ii. Prevent and detect crimes and offences'.

The district watchmen were under the direct head watchman but subject to the 'supreme direction and administration' of the Secretary of Chinese Affairs, who 'may from time to time make orders to be known as "District Watch Force Orders" as he may think expedient, not inconsistent with this Ordinance, and District Watch Force Regulations, for the better control, management and regulation of the District Watch Force' (Section 4).

When performing his duties, '[a] district watchman shall, in relation to such duties as he may be required to perform, have all the powers and privileges of a constable of the police force' (Section 5).

The District Watch Force came into being in 1887 to supplement the HKP in areas and with people the British had little control over due to the small size of the Force, inaccessibility to culture and lack of trust from the Chinese community. Over time, the District Watch Force took over much of the duties and responsibilities of the HKP, by delegation, and in fact were more effective and productive, especially in settling disputes and fighting crime, besides other duties as assigned:

> The District Watch Force performed such tasks as acting as census enumerators, providing guides for census officials, tracing runaway girls for the Po Leung Kuk, intercepting young girls brought into the colony for prostitution, and engaging in detective work in the Chinese quarters. The public also accepted members of the police as arbiters in disputes. Since the official police force was at first small and corrupt, the District Watch Force played a key role in maintaining social order.[179]

Collaboration

Collaboration is about parties with common goals working together for mutual benefits.[180] Collaborative policing requires integration of organisation and/or coordination of functions, such that policing is conducted jointly, from planning, decision making to operations. Whereas 'disengagement' and 'delegation' envisions that the HKP took a hands-off approach to crime prevention and order maintenance, collaborative policing contemplates the active involvement of both British and Chinese in the conduct of policing, such as community-oriented policing wherein the community worked with the police to set priorities and facilitate implementations.[181] In the West, collaborative policing has most often been associated with community policing, and in the policing literature referred to as 'co-production of law and order'.[182]

Historically and in colonial Hong Kong, collaborative governance and policing was achieved mostly with the co-opting of the political–moral–social support, enlisting the personal–physical–financial help, and relying (leveraging) on the private resource network of the Chinese elites in the running of Hong Kong.[183] The idea of collaborative political rule was a derivative of collaborative commercial ventures—the comprador system, first in Canton and then in Hong Kong:

> The comprador system was soon imported to Hong Kong when British firms flocked to open their business there. It lasted until the Second World War; longer than at any other Chinese coastal city. During the growth of early colonial society in Hong Kong, by the 1850s the Chinese community was beginning to develop leaders and most of them were successful compradors, merchants and contractors. Typical of this emerging Chinese middle class were Cantonese compradors like Wei Yuk (Wei Yu), Robert Ho Tung (He Dong), and Law Pak Sheung (Luo Bochang). They formed the core of leadership in the local Chinese community...Wei succeeded his father Wei Kwong who came from Choy Mei village near Macau as the comprador of the Chartered Mercantile Bank of India, London, and China in Hong Kong in 1879. In 1896, he was appointed an unofficial member of the Hong Kong Legislative Council, being the fourth Chinese to this post (the first was Ng Choy [Wu Tingfang]). Wei held a lot of appointments in public and private organizations and represented Chinese interests in the government.[184]

The 'collaboration with Chinese elites' strategy did not work well in the earlier years because no such elites could be found. Most of the people coming to Hong Kong were then economic migrants—small shopkeepers, labourers and coolies. More than a few were sojourns living in the margins of society, such as destitute, pirates and criminals. Overall, these people had little social standing, economic power and political clout to act for and on behalf of the British. This social reality led British colonists to adopt a farsighted and pragmatic approach in grooming future Chinese leadership through education in British schools, as potential collaborators.

Beyond cultivating elites, the British also relied upon traditional Chinese institutions to facilitate colonial rule, such as Kai-Fang for urban community, ethnic associations for various migrant groups (*tongxian hui*) and guild associations for different working groups.[185]

The most controversial aspect about collaboration as a strategy of colonial rule perhaps was the idea of collaborating with local community leaders and influential individuals who had less-than-sterling reputations, or even criminal backgrounds and associations. The understanding of collaborative policing holds much promise but has rarely been explored.[186] The observation here is that, more often than not, in order for the British colonial rule to work efficiently and effectively, it needed to collaborate with people and groups of all kinds, elites and popular, mainstream and marginalised, legal as well as illegal. In as much as colonial rule, in real terms, it was about control and power, not legitimacy or morality; it mattered little to the colonialists whom, what and how they are collaborating, provided it was beneficial to do so.[187] Below is a discussion of the potential utility of Triad rule is Malaysia under colonial rule:

> There is a traditional practice in seeking triad assistance in the settlement of disputes and for private protection rather than the assistance of the police as Macau citizens have little confidence in the law enforcement agencies under Portuguese administration. Most people have difficulties in understanding the law because most legislation is written in Portuguese, and legal channels for disputes settlement are often time consuming, expensive, ineffective and involve a complex chain of procedures. Furthermore, legal channels are unavailable to illegitimate business such as local sharking and bookmaking. Thus, triads provide real services and settle dispute among different gambling rooms and different chip roller teams in a more effective and efficient manner than the state.[188]

Given the origin of the Triad as a nationalistic organisation and a mutual aid group, with instinctive appeal and induced fear in the indigenous people, it would have been foolhardy for the colonial administrators not to take into account the Triad societies' political and social influences, particularly in uncertain times, as in after WWII.[189] Reluctantly, they did. For example, a 1993 study found that in District Board election in 1983, 10% of the candidates had connection to Triad societies. In 1984, Triads helped to come up with a 'vote planning' scheme in Tai Po.[190]

In 1850, Assistant Superintendent Caldwell was openly using his connections with the secret societies to obtain intelligence and effectual control with the underworld,[191] with fellow British colonial officials cheering him on.[192]

A modern form of collaborative policing requires the HKP to reach out to the community (District Crime Fighting Committee) and NGOs to develop crime-fighting programmes. One such project is that of 'Guardian Angel' programme:

> The PCRO's work in collaboration with social workers and through support offered by local authorities and businesses to create a so-called 'Household, Chain and Community structure' network. Guardian Angel's goal is to foster partnerships between the police and local community stakeholders to enhance local police understanding of community needs, and, to provide support and care to vulnerable families. This has been undertaken in a number of ways, including the provision of information and training on 'household security' to help residents combat property crime, and, offering support facilities to vulnerable families. This community policing initiative has proved particularly challenging in relation to the organisation of a provider network and,

by extension promoting trust and cooperation with the 'customer'. However, as set within the range of current community policing initiatives, the overall outcomes have witnessed a positive trend in relation to crime prevention and detection, and, winning the trust and confidence of the public (Lam, 2013).[193]

Customisation

Customisation is a make-to-fit process. In colonial policing, it is following local custom than following general law of the land,[194] or, as applied seeking particular than universal justice.

In Hong Kong, it meant tailoring British policing theory and practice to fit with local culture and social conditions, for example, having colonial police commanders functioning as *fuwu guan* ('parental officials') or decentralised police decision making to the local level. Alternatively, it involved appropriating British policing values and style by the indigenous Chinese, for example, promoting rule of law and natural justice in a disciplinary proceeding.

The issue of whether British common law or Chinese law and custom should have applied to Chinese nationals and Hong Kong indigenous residents has been a major point of contention in the negotiation over the Treaty of Nanking (29 August 1842).

In October 1984, Governor Alexander Grantham appointed a committee chaired by George Strickland to make recommendations on the application of Chinese law and custom in Hong Kong.[195]

On 2 February 1841, after the formal possession of Hong Kong on 26 January 1841, Captain Elliot, the Chief Superintendent of Trade and Her Majesty's Plenipotentiary in China, issued the following proclamation of rule over Hong Kong:

> The island of Hong Kong having been ceded to the British crown under the seal of the Imperial Minister and High Commissioner Keshen, I has become necessary to provide for the Government thereof...And I do hereby declare and proclaim, that, pending Her Majesty's further pleasure, the native of the island of Hong Kong, and all natives of China thereto resorting, shall be governed according to the laws and customs of China, every description of torture excepted.

On 30 April 1841, Captain Elliot was appointed by the first Chief Magistrate of Hong Kong to be in charge of the execution and adjudication police laws. The warrant 'authorise and require (Cain) to exercise authority, according to the laws, customs, and usages of China, as nearly as may be (every description of torture excepted) for the preservation of peace, and the protection of life and property, over the native inhabitants in the said harbours thereof'.

It is apparent from the above two proclamation and warrant that the British wanted to establish a four-tier criminal justice system based on the offenders' ethnic and residence background:

First, if a Chinese committed a crime in Hong Kong, they would be subject to Chinese jurisdiction and law. This arrangement was justified on two grounds. From the Chinese perspective, the Chinese Government had absolute jurisdictional claim over her own nationals, either for protection or punishment. Once a Chinese, always a Chinese. Chinese nationality cannot be divested, for protection or prosecution purpose. From the British point of view, since they asked for extraterritorial judicial treatment for British nations on Chinese soil,[196] it was only fair that the same principle be applied to Chinese national committing an offense on British–Hong Kong soil.

Second, if Hong Kong (local) inhabitants committed a less serious crime (defined as under $400, under 100 lashes, or a non-capital crime), they would be subject to Hong Kong jurisdiction, but Chinese law, custom and usages, excepting torture. This was based on the tried-and-tested colonial practice of indirect rule.[197] In effectuating colonial rule, to the extent that it did not challenge British interest or values, it was best (more efficient and effective) to respect and follow indigenous customs and local usages, here Chinese law, such that local people were less inclined to obstruct, resist and rebel against the colonisers.[198]

Assimilation

Assimilation is to immerse in and transform oneself into another's culture. This means remaking oneself into other's image, for example, by way of overseas education or cross-cultural marriages.[199] All migrants have gone through a process of assimilation in the form of socialisation and acculturation, before being relatively integrated in the adopted country, calling it home.

In the context of colonialism, while the British argued for preservation of indigenous culture on the way to self-government as the end goal of colonialism, the French preferred the transformation of local culture, with total integration of others into one large Franco family of nations.[200] 'Until the close of nineteenth century, French colonial theory was based on the idea of assimilation, which gave France the responsibility of "civilising" its colonies by absorbing them administratively and culturally'.[201] The French argued for assimilation into French culture on grounds of universality of human rights and malleability of human kind through mutual association and cross-cultural education—a civilising project.

For much of its chequered political and cultural history, Hong Kong lived two worlds—one Chinese and the other British. There were 'six degrees of separation' between the two, but separation no less. The Hong Kong official colonial policy was one of segregation, not integration, right up to WWII (and to some beyond); from living (housing), playing (socialising), procreating (marriage) and ordering (policing). There were few attempts to assimilate with the British or the Chinese. Both knew, defined and described each other in racial terms. To the British, Chinese were uncivilised. To the Chinese, British were foreign devils. This led to a Hong Kong-assimilated expatriate official to reflect on the post-WWII British versus Chinese relationship in the following way: 'In general, and on each side, the two people did not really want a closer acquaintance, I soon gathered that there were deep seated, long standings feelings that make each vastly prefer the social company' of their own kind.

Take cross-cultural marriage for example. In Hong Kong, notwithstanding the fact that it was developed as an international port with a mixed population, inter-racial marriages were rare, and were frowned upon before 1950s. This resulted as much from racial segregation colonial policy since 1842 to just after WWII as from the lack of availability of eligible females. For the first 50 plus years (1844–1900), Hong Kong was inhabited by males with no family. Married females came much later. As to local females, they usually stayed at home. If they ventured out, they were not supposed to mix with foreigners. The only eligible females were professional ones, of the Suzie Wong type—bargirls and prostitutes. These marriages between police and street ladies had their collective impact on policing in Hong Kong. These professional girls, hardly the mainstream, initiated many of the HKP officers into Hong Kong.

Localisation Efforts before WWII

A cursory reading of Hong Kong history informs that racial discrimination and segregation was institutionalised before WWII, and still lingered in subdued and subtle forms afterwards.[202] In 1858, Governor Browning made the following frank admission about race relations in Hong Kong: 'We rule them in ignorance, and they submit in blindness'.[203] Specifically,

> At the present movement the separation of the native population from the European is nearly absolute. Social intercourse between the races is wholly unknown. A few Chinese speak a strange 'jargon' ...to convey their ideas to foreigners. ...(not) ... a single merchant or Tradesman in Hongkong who speaks or understands the native dialect, who has seen a Chinaman at his Table, or admitted him to the slightest confidential intimacy. The influence of the European settler upon the native mind many be said to be nil.[204]

With policing, there appeared to be little attempt to reduce racial discrimination and/or ameliorate its impact on Chinese community. However, on close inspection, through time, the Hong Kong colonial government with the HKP in the lead achieved localisation through a number of initiatives, programmes and practices, as intimated above, to promote effectiveness of governance. The following reviews some of HKP's efforts to localise its organisation, operation and ethos:

First, *in terms of localisation of personnel*, since 1844 and before the rise of trusted Chinese elites, the Hong Kong Government always had at its disposal learned Chinese hands (sinologists) to make or advise on Chinese policy and to communicate with the Chinese community, in an informed, reflective, sophisticated and articulated way. For example, the early governors all had

had long experience with Asia and came to know China while in public service (colonial office) or private enterprise (East India Company). Governor John Francis Davis (8 May 1844 to 21 March 1848) was a learned sinologist[205] and an administrator at East India Company and superintendent of trade in China. Indeed, because of his expertise in China and knowledge of Chinese customs, culture and dispositions, his policies were not well liked by European residents and expatriate traders. Hong Kong colonialists, at least in high places, were hardly ignorant about China and Hong Kong. Dr. Ernest John Eitel, a German missionary who was a sinologist and historians,[206] served as Inspector of Schools and later Chinese Secretary to Governor John Pope Hennessy.

Second, *in terms of customisation of British law and policy,* starting with Captain Elliot proclamation of 2 February 1841: 'the native of the island of Hong Kong, and all natives of China thereto resorting, shall be governed according to the laws and customs of China, every description of torture excepted'. Successive governors were concerned with the impact and implications of British law on Chinese customs, lest they impinged on the autonomy of the Chinese community and otherwise compromised the welfare of the Chinese people. For example, in 1844, Governor David set up the *ti-pao* system[207] to settle disputes within the Chinese community. Later the Secretariat of Chinese Affairs was established (1913) to promote the welfare and protect the interests of Chinese, mostly in the rural areas. I.D. Lightbody described his experience as an administrative officer working at Assistant Chinese Secretary (ACS):

> But the ACS does far more than just settle family quarrels. There are three or four Administrative Officers in the Department and it deals with an enormous variety of work ranking from the operation of Chinese temples to liaison with the Kaifang movement (local residents' associations which do a great deal of welfare work in their own districts). It advises on effect of particular schemes on Chinese opinion, and it is kept very busy nowadays ensuring that the many development schemes afoot in Hong Kong are not forced through without due regard for any old village in the areas of development.[208]

Third, *in terms of British and Chinese officers integration*, the Water Police (later Marine Police) showcased the first fully integrated HKP work force with British and Chinese police officers working, living and socialising together under one roof and for extended period of time, as a family, since 1844:

> Considering the vast social and cultural differences between Europeans and Chinese in the early days they have got on together remarkably well starting with a wary co-operation which has matured over the years into mutual trust and respect...Hard conditions and close proximity over extended periods must produce either conflict or rapport; that it was the latter that developed...[209]

The reasons why they were working (and socialising) are less important as the fact that they *were*, even in early Hong Kong. The Marine Police mixed British–Chinese work force offers valuable lessons about the true nature, organisation and function of Colonial HKP at sea.

This observation that the Marine Police worked as a team, survived as confidants and lived as a family is best documented by one HKP informant:[210]

> The shift system for the Marine police is basically twenty-four hours on duty followed by forty-eight hour off duty. During their duty time, they remain onboard the police launch, including eating, working, sleeping. The causal contact between them changes the crew into a family. However, as the inspectorate officers and station sergeants work on board the launch too, the discipline aspect has still to be maintained. But the gap between the Inspector and the Junior Police Officers is much narrower in comparison with the Land Police. They love as a family and work in a group so that a subculture is formed to protect themselves from outsiders.[211]

Working at sea meant that Marine Police officers had little opportunity to 'shine' individually, for example, making arrests. They also suffered from damnation for personal mistakes, which might have spelled the end of their career.

Since all Marine Police officers were in the same boat, literally and figuratively, they learned to help each other out any way they could, for example, consulting with each other before making decisions and covering up for each other should there be mistakes and problems. They worked together as a team and had incentives to avoid mistakes, at least collectively to cover up their discovery.

The Marine Police also needed to work and stick together against outsiders, internal (Land Police), external (public) and above (superior). The Land Police looked down upon the Marine Police as not doing real police work. After all, Marine Police officers were merely sailors, inspectors and service workers. They were not competent in catching criminals and lacked knowledge in police procedures.

In truth, the Land Police were envious of the Marine Police work conditions and pay. To them, the Marine Police had less pressure, more leave time and extra pay, for example, O/T. As a result, the Land Police adopted a critical, non-cooperative and at times confrontational attitude towards the Marine Police colleagues.[212] For example:

> Normally, according to police procedures, maritime arrest cases have to be handed over to land police for further investigation. Marine Police Inspectors or Sergeants will usually accompany their subordinates to go to land station for processing. This is often necessary to prevent lack of co-operation with the Marine Police by the Land Police as a result of minor technical or procedural mistakes, as the junior ranking land police have to respect the senior ranking marine police officers.[213]

With the Marine Police, the most important lesson for this research project on HKP reform is perhaps the realisation that Hong Kong was not entirely and certainly not always under a colonial police in organisation (paramilitary, foreign rule), function (security control and law enforcement) and style (coercive and repressive), awaiting liberalisation and localisation.

At the minimum, the evidence suggests that British colonial masters were known to be ready and willing to compromise colonial policing principle—racial segregation, to bring about colonising outcome, that is, law, order and security. Moreover, once individual racial prejudice was replaced with mutual understanding, trust and respect, the complete breakdown of colonialism was not far behind. It took the HKP land formations 100 years to start localising in major ways (1950s). It took the Marine Police no more than 50 years to come to achieve perfect integration as 'family' (1900).

Fourth, *in terms of assimilation*, Caldwell was the first Assistant Superintendent to become a Whitefaced Chinese, the first of its kind in the 1850s.[214] He was able to completely immerse in the Chinese culture. Caldwell spoke fluent Chinese, married a Chinese and commingled with Chinese people, including undesirables, with ease.[215] This made him functionally a Chinese to the British, and an adopted son to the Chinese.[216] In 1857, Caldwell was investigated for corruption and abuse of office.

> The inquiry concluded that Mr. Caldwell's long and intimate connexion with the pirate, Ma-chow Wong, was of such a character as to render him unfit to be continued in public service, and the Council recommended his dismissal therefrom.

There is little doubt that Caldwell was a corrupt official, but so were others of the time. What got him into trouble is that he breached the silent, but deadly, racial segregation code by marrying a local Chinese, openly.[217]

Fifth, *in terms of acculturation* of colonial officers, perhaps the most ambitious and successful localisation–assimilation programme was that of Cadet Program,[218] which turned out governors, Secretary of Chinese Affairs, police commissioners and district officers. These British handpicked, trained cadet officers—versatile in Chinese language and culture—formed the backbone of the Hong Kong Government administration until 1997, with a sense of mission (paternal administration) and identity ('fuwun guan') to match. These groups of British trained 'colonial' officers, individually and collectively, did much to customise colonial policy to fit local circumstances, by cutting out objectionable features here and shouldering unintended impact there, thereby changing objectionable colonial policy to successful colonial practice. The leadership these cadets provided, the vision they promoted, the policy they made and the programme they developed changed the tone and pretext of Hong Kong governance from an alien and repressive colonial regime to a home-grown and progressive modern state. The police reform of 1950s was built upon that progressive mentality, doing what the people want than what the Colonial office desires.

At the end of the day, it is right to ask: is it the policy or the people that make for objectionable colonial rule? The same question can be asked of the HKP. Before the 1950s, the HKP suffered from wrongheaded[219] colonial policy of imposition, segregation and discrimination. After the 1950s, the HKP underwent a right-hearted reformulation–localisation of colonial policy, with the British meeting the Chinese as people not agents and subjects of regime.

V: Conclusion

This chapter describes the context of and proposes a framework to investigate into 'Hong Kong Police Reform in 1950s' (Chapter 9). To further explore localisation, a separate discussion of legality, modernisation and communisation of the HKP after WWII is presented in Chapter 9.

Endnotes

1. For a competent, if all too brief, account of the makeover of Hong Kong after WWII, see Chapter 6: 'A New Hong Kong', In: J. M. Caroll, *A Concise History of Hong Kong* (Latham, MD: Rowman & Littlefield, 2007), pp. 140–160.
2. B. Hook, From Repossession to Retrocession: British Policy toward Hong Kong 1945–1997, In: pp. 1–31, P.-k. Li (ed.), *Political Order and Power Transition in Hong Kong* (Hong Kong: Chinese University Press, 1997), p. 1. For British policy towards Hong Kong, see pp. 4–9.
3. Public Record Office, London CAB 129/35 CP(49) 120.
4 O. Marenin, *Policing Change, Changing Police: International Perspectives* (New York: Garland Publication, 2006). For political governance which implicates on policing, Vagg has divided Hong Kong into three periods, namely, colonial rule, administrative state and democratic participation. See J. Vagg, *The Legitimacy of Policing in Hong Kong*, pp. 107–135, 125. Under this scheme, I surmise Vagg would collapse the first two periods (1840s, 1870s) into colonial and 1950s as administrative, and 1990s as democratic participation. Ibid.
5. This study does not include crisis-driven reform, for example, 1967 civil disturbances. For 1967, riot and related social and political reform, see G. K.-w. Cheung, *Hong Kong's Watershed: The 1967 Riots* (Hong Kong: Hong Kong University Press, 2009). In the MacLeHose years (19 November 1971–20 May 1982), Hong Kong society underwent fundamental changes in social policies: In housing, education, workers' rights and medical services. Governor MacLeHose has taken a much more proactive and interventionalist approach to colonial administration.
6. The 'Formation Period' was very first HKP reform period. It was launched by Captain Superintendent Charles May after he was appointed (3 September 1844) and took up office on 28 February 1845.

7. N. Vittachi, From farce to force to be reckoned with, *SCMP*, 10 October 1998, p. 7.
8. Chapter 8: 'Meeting the Challenges of Modernity'. p. 139. S. Tsang, *Governing Hong Kong: Administrative Officers from the 19th Century to the Handover to China, 1862–1997* (London and New York: I.B. Tauris, 15 December 2007). During the first decades after WWII, Hong Kong experienced dramatic changes in population, politics, economy, housing and education. As such, education policy cannot be understood in isolation, but in historical and social context. Admiral Cecil Harcourt, the Military Governor, was quick to add his terms: Re-energising and re-forming the community with 'the 1946' outlook, which helped to breach the gap between rich and poor, British and Chinese, looking forward to a new beginning or constituting the old.
9. There is an issue of whether the reversion of sovereignty necessarily means decolonisation, calling for radical policy change. It has been observed in some quarters that China's policy towards Hong Kong enshrined in the Basic Law—'one country two systems' for 50 years actually made possible, if not encouraged, the continuation of colonial rule by default. See 梁文道去殖的缺席 (1) 去殖的缺席 (2) ('Absence of Decolonization') 週五 2007-06-22 and 2007-06-8. (The reversion of ruler is not about a change of colonial system of governance but a change of rule. China has no interest in HK political development. Hong Kong has little desire to ask for democratic change. The return of sovereignty has been completed, and the decolonisation process has yet to take place, e.g., there is no universal suffrage in Hong Kong). http://www.inmediahk.net/node/225772 and http://www.inmediahk.net/node/226667, respectively. For English translation of 去殖的缺席 (2) (The Absence of De-Colonization in Hong Kong—Part 2. By Leung Man-tao (梁文道). 28 June 2007, see http://www.zonaeuropa.com/20070708_1.htm
10. To observe that HKP has an 'unchanged' regime defence role with militaristic capacity is not to say that the 'role' and 'capacity' of HKP are not adjustable, or has not been adjusted, to social and political change in Hong Kong. Theoretically speaking, the regime defence role of HKP shifted from active pacification of rebels (1925 Hong Kong—Canton Seamen Strikes) to passive monitoring of dissidents (1950s Nationalists and Communists). The HKP militaristic capacity shifted from replying to U.K. armed force (acting as police in 1840s) to the HKP replacing the armed force (after 1997). See Chung, Hung-fung, Harry (鍾雄峰), An analysis of policing the border: A shift of responsibility, MPA Dissertation, HKU, 1994.
11. G. R. Sayer and D. M. E. Evans, *Hong Kong 1862–1919: Years of Discretion* (Hong Kong: Hong Kong University Press, 1985).
12. S. K. Lau, *Decolonization without Independence: The Unfinished Political Reforms* (Hong Kong: The Hong Kong Institute of Asia-Pacific Studies, 1987).
13. G. E. Caiden, Innovation in administration, *Hong Kong Journal of Public Administration*, 4 (1): 15–30, 1882.
14. For example, see Part Two: 'Reconstruction, Expansion, and Transformation, 1945–1964', In: A. Sweeting, *Education in Hong Kong, 1941 to 2001: Visions and Revisions* (Hong Kong: Hong Kong University Press, 2004), p. 137.
15. L. Butenhoff, *Social Movements and Political Reform in Hong Kong* (Westport, CT: Greenwood Publishing Group, 1999).
16. A. Smart, *The Shek Kip Mei Myth: Squatters, Fires and Colonial Rule in Hong Kong, 1950–1963* (Hong Kong: Hong Kong University Press, 2006).

17. L. F. Goodstadt, *Uneasy Partners: The Conflict between Public Interest and Private Profit in Hong Kong* (Hong Kong: Hong Kong University Press, 2005).
18. A. Sweeting, *Education in Hong Kong, 1941 to 2001: Visions and Revisions* (Hong Kong: Hong Kong University Press, 2004), p. 137.
19. D. T. L. Shek (ed.), *Advances in Social Welfare in Hong Kong* (Hong Kong: Chinese University of Hong Kong, 2002).
20. S. Chan, Colonial penalty: A case study of Hong Kong's penal policy and programmes under British administration (1945–1997). Ph.D. Thesis. Department of Social Science (Criminology), University of Hull, 2012. https://hydra.hull.ac.uk/resources/hull:7167; M. Adorjan and W. H. Chui, *Responding to Youth Crime in Hong Kong: Penal Elitism, Legitimacy and Citizenship* (Abingdon, Oxon: Routledge, 2014).
21. A. Sweeting, *Education in Hong Kong, 1941 to 2001: Visions and Revisions* (Hong Kong: Hong Kong University Press, 2004), p. 137.
22. R. K. Yin, *Case Study Research: Design and Method* Fourth Edition (Thousand Oak, CA: Sage, 2009). ('A case study is an empirical inquiry that investigates a contemporary phenomenon in depth and within the real life context, especially when the boundaries between phenomenon and context are not clearly evident.' p. 16).
23. See J. P. Kotter, Leading changes: Why transformation effort fails, *Harvard Business Review on Change* (Cambridge, MA: Harvard Business Press, 1998), p. 2.
24. By police law and ordinances, I mean laws and ordinances that informs on police organisation, constitution, role, functions, powers and accountability.
25. http://www.hklii.hk/eng/hk/legis/HKHistLaws/
26. http://www.hklii.hk/eng/
27. Hong Kong Police Magazine (HKPM) (香港警察雜誌) (1951–1968). http://ebook.lib.hku.hk/HK/HKGS/21019060.pdf (1951). http://ebook.lib.hku.hk/HK/HKGS/21019061.pdf (1956). http://ebook.lib.hku.hk/HK/HKGS/21019062.pdf (1959). http://ebook.lib.hku.hk/HK/HKGS/21019063.pdf (1960). Source: University of Hong Kong Library (香港大學圖書館)
28. http://hkjo.lib.hku.hk/exhibits/show/hkjo/home
29. *HKPM* 10 (4): 1, Winter, 1960.
30. Impressions of Police Course in England, *HKPM* 1 (1): 5–9, September 1951.
31. Ibid., Ballistics and the Police, pp. 16–20.
32. Ibid., Chatter from the Stations, p. 24.
33. Ibid., Chinese Porcelain for the Beginner, p. 20.
34. Hong Kong population was growing before the war. Population in Hong Kong: 1891 (Total: 221,000); 1901 (283,274); 1911 (456,444); 1921 (660,645); 1931 (850,821). L. Butenhoff, *Social Movements and Political Reform in Hong Kong* (Westport, CT: Greenwood Publishing Group, 1999), p. 17.
35. These refugees included industrious Cantonese and business savvy Shanghaies, non-organised labourers, enterprising businessmen and capital-rich industrialists. Lest one jumps to conclusion that Hong Kong's success is attributable to this or that group, Cantonese versus Shanghaies, it must not be forgotten that Hong Kong earns its keep because of its ethnic diversity and international convergence. For entrenched ethnic diversity in Hong Kong, see G. Evans and M. Tam, *Hong Kong: Anthropological Essays on a Chinese Metropolis* (New York and London: Routledge, 31 October 2013). For emerging cosmopolitanism, see C. A. Breckenridge, S. Pollock, H. K. Bhabha and D. Chakrabarty, *Cosmopolitanism*

(Durham, NC: Duke University Press, 2002), esp. 'Hong Kong and Shanghai', pp. 209–229.
36. M. Sing, *Hong Kong's Tortuous Democratization: A Comparative Analysis* (New York, NY: Psychology Press, 2004). (A study of Chinese refugees in who came to Hong Kong between 1949 and 1952 did so for economic reasons. They wanted to avoid real or potential political persecution or otherwise loss of civil liberties. In 1977, a survey showed that 57.3% regarded the duty of government to be providing for stability, and only 10.5% wanted the government to establish democracy or equality.), p. 46.
37. A. S. Ku. Immigration policies, discourses, and the politics of local belonging in Hong Kong (1950–1980), *Modern China*, 30 (3): 326–360, 333, 2004.
38. K. Bolton and C. Hutton, *Triad Societies: Triad Societies in Hong Kong* (London and New York: Taylor & Francis, 2000). IV: A Hundred Years of Triad Societies in Hong Kong, pp. 59–92. (Upon the demise of KMT, the first wave of refugees arriving in Hong Kong was from the North and Central provinces, and with them came the Green and Red Pang, criminal groups. The Green Pang started organising themselves and reached out to the new immigrants, offering them support and assistance in a foreign land, including how to avoid deportation and providing protection from local criminal elements (pp. 76–78).
39. KMT Lt. General Kot Siu Wong, a Triad leader, enlisted help from Hong Kong residents and Chinese migrants to facilitate the return of KMT rule. K. Bolton and C. Hutton, *Triad Societies: Triad Societies in Hong Kong* (London and New York: Taylor & Francis, 2000). IV: 'A Hundred Years of Triad Societies in Hong Kong.' pp. 59–92, 80–81. (Triad membership grew exponentially between 1951 and 1954, claiming 300,000 members (p. 83).
40. *Hansard*, 1967: 262.
41. Jawaharlal Nehru, *Speech on the Granting of Indian Independence*, 14 August 1947.
42. Universal Declaration of Human Rights, 1948.
43. N. J. White, *Decolonization: The British Experience Since 1945*. (London and New York: Longman, 2014). (The British empire shrank from 7 hundred millions before WWII to 5 millions after WWII (mainly in Hong Kong.)
44. Hong Kong needed 'to develop an active sense of citizenship and to become capable of openly expressing and giving piratical effect to the general desire of its inhabitants [if it were] to remain under British rule and to resist absorption by China'.
45. W.-B. Zhang, *Hong Kong: The Pearl Made of British Mastery and Chinese Docile-Diligence* (Hauppauge, NY: Nova Science Publishers, 2006), p. 60.
46. The Hong Kong Planning Unit at the Colonial Office was responsible for drafting plan to rehabilitate Hong Kong and restoration of civil government, after military rule by the Japanese during the war and British immediately after the war.
47. Young to Creek Jones, No. 255, Secret, 7 February 1947. F) 371/63387.
48. Dr. Y. C. Wong, *Public Policy on Local Administration: Past, Present and Future*. No. 38 (10/96) CPPS, Lingnam University (1998), p. 8.
49. P. Kua, *Scouting in Hong Kong, 1910–2010* (Hong Kong: Scout Association of HK, 2011), Chapter Two: 'Reconstruction and Researching Out: 1945–1964', pp. 225–283. The history of scouting in Hong Kong allows us to see the

development of HKP from another prism (p. 16), for example, the development of Chinese identity of youth under colonial rule, which allows us to gauge the mentality, policy and implementation of British colonialism, at different times and in civil society. 'Hong Kong Scouting could finally lay claim to being a mass movement with a broadly-based membership which was representative of the postwar colonial community' (p. 226). At the same time, there was a revival of nationalistic scouting, reminiscent of the 1935–1940s era.

50. J. F. Tsai, *Hong Kong in Chinese History: Community and Social Unrest in the British Colony, 1842–1913* (New York: Columbia University Press, 1993).
51. E. Sinn, The strike and riot of 1884—A Hong Kong perspective, *Journal of the Hong Kong Branch of the Royal Asiatic Society*, 22: 65–98, 1982.
52. C. Loh, *Underground Front: The Chinese Communist Party in Hong Kong* (Hong Kong: Hong Kong University Press, 2010). (Zhou Enlai on Hong Kong police: 'China's Hong Kong policy was part of the overall strategic plan for the East–Wear struggle.' p. 80).
53. D. Akers-Jones, *Feeling the Stones: Reminiscences by David Akers-Jones* (Hong Kong: Hong Kong University Press, 2004).
54. 1st Battalion. The Argyll and Sutherland Highlanders. Hong Kong 1949–1950. http://www.argylls1945to1971.co.uk/
55. Wm. R. Louis, Hong Kong: The critical phase, 1945–1949, *American Historical Review*, 102 (4): 1056, 1997.
56. In 1947, the HKP evicted residents from Kowloon Walled City, under Chinese rule, and created an international incident, with the Chinese burning down the British Consulate in January 1948. Ibid., p. 1071.
57. HK Secretariat, FO371/69577.
58. R. Buckley, *Hong Kong: The Road to 1997* (Cambridge University Press, 12 June 1997).
59. J. Hayes, *The Great Difference: Hong Kong's New Territories and Its People 1898–2004* (Hong Kong: Hong Kong University Press, 2012); A. Grantham, *Via Ports: From Hong Kong to Hong Kong* (Hong Kong: Hong Kong University Press, 2012).
60. Hong Kong officially abolished opium trade in Hong Kong in August 1945, and a Narcotics Bureau was established to suppress and eradicate drugs. M. S. Gaylord, D. Gittings and H. Traver (eds.), *Introduction to Crime, Law and Justice in Hong Kong* (Hong Kong: Hong Kong University Press, 2009), p. 84.
61. Police History: The Modern Era 1945–67. HKP. http://www.police.gov.hk/ppp_en/01_about_us/ph_03.html
62. Ibid.
63. I. Ward, *Sui Geng: The Hong Kong Marine Police 1841–1950*, (Hong Kong: Hong Kong University Press, 1991), p. 169.
64. J. T. F. Tang, From empire defence to imperial retreat: Britain's postwar China policy and the decolonization of Hong Kong, *Modern Asian Studies*, 28 (2): 317–337, 1994.
65. Lord Milverton, Colonial problem, *Hong Kong Sunday Herald*, 15 December 1949, p. 12.
66. D. Clayton, British foreign economic policy towards China 1949–60, *Electronic Journal of International History—Section 6*, 2000, para 10. http://sas-space.sas.ac.uk/3393/1/Journal_of_International_History_2000_n6_Clayton.pdf

67. Hong Kong population grew from less than 600,000 in 1945 to over 2 million in 1950, with many of them requiring education, medical and welfare support. Meantime, HKG suffered from a shortage of financial resources. In the first post-war budget, HKG faced a shortfall of HK$115,425,965.
68. A. Grantham, *Via Ports: From Hong Kong to Hong Kong* (Hong Kong: Hong Kong University Press, 1965).
69. D. Clayton, British foreign economic policy towards China 1949–60, *Electronic Journal of International History—Section* 6, 2000, para 10.
70. Section on 'Invasion Scare' in D. Bray, *Hong Kong Metamorphosis* (Hong Kong: Hong Kong University Press, 2001), p. 39. In 1950, with the onset of the Korean war, British intelligence estimated there were five Chinese army divisions, with two on reserve amassed at the border, ready to attack. The British military was poised for action, at moment of notice. The author, a cadet officer, had to be on standby, to assist Colonial Secret if and when there was an invasion from the North. All these were kept secret from the public.
71. Charles T. Cross, USIS, Hong Kong (1951–1954), Consul General Hong Kong (1974–1977). In Hong Kong—Association for Diplomatic Studies and Training. Reader. http://www.adst.org/Readers/Hong%20Kong.pdf
72. 'Then came WWII; the West lost its extra-territorial privileges in the Chinese treaty ports. …Then came the Korean war and the UN embargo. That barred Hong Kong from exporting goods that were made on the mainland; they had to be manufactured in Hong Kong itself. So it lost some connection with the PRC; but at the same time, it became a major exporter of its own wares to the rest of the world. Manufacturing increased sharply as Hong Kong discovered that its goods were in high demand, and that was really the birth of Hong Kong's economic boom.' Ibid.
73. Ibid., 51 B. U.K. Trade with China and Hong Kong.
74. Hong Kong Legislative Council. 30 March 1949. 95.
75. Alan Lennox-Boyd, 9 October 1958.
76. S. K. Lau, *Decolonization without Independence: The Unfinished Political Reforms of the Hong Kong Government* (Hong Kong: The Hong Kong Institute of Asia-Pacific Studies, The Chinese University of Hong Kong, 1987).
77. S. R. Ashton, G. Bennett, and K. Hamilton, *Britain and China 1945–1950: Documents on British Policy Overseas*, Series I, Volume 8 (London and New York: Routledge, 2013). CAB. 128/16: CM(49)2, p. 330.
78. Immigrants Control Bill (1949) and the Expulsion of Undesirables Ordinance (1949).
79. 何仲詩 (Ho Chong See), 風雲背後： 香港監獄私人檔案 (Behind the Wind and Cloud: Private Files of Hong Kong Prison (香港 (HK): 藍天圖書 2008).
80. By the end of 1946, the Hong Kong population was restored to the prewar number of 1,600,000; by 1950, it increased to 2,360,000. By the end of 1956, it was estimated to be over 2.5 million, approximately one-third of which were refugees. A Problem of People, A reprint of Chapter I of the Hong Kong Annual Report, 1956 (Hong Kong, 1957); Meeting of 27 February 1957, *Hong Kong Hansard: Reports of the Meetings of the Legislative Council of Hong Kong, Session 1957* (Hong Kong, 1957).
81. M. Houf, Protect Our Borders: Immigration and Identity in Post-War Hong Kong, *World History Connected*, 8 (2), June 2011. http://worldhistoryconnected.press.illinois.edu/8.2/index.html

82. Commissioner of Prisons, Annual Departmental Reports 1947–48.
83. S. Wallace, *Total Institution* (New Brunswick, NJ: Transaction Publishers, 1971).
84. L. F. Goodstadt, *Uneasy Partners: The Conflict between Public Interest and Private Profit in Hong Kong* (Hong Kong: Hong Kong University Press, 2005), p. 10.
85. A. Smart, *The Shek Kip Mei Myth: Squatters, Fires and Colonial Rule in Hong Kong, 1950–1963* (Hong Kong: Hong Kong University Press, 2006).
86. C. Sui-jeung, 陳瑞璋 *East River Column: Hong Kong Guerrillas in the Second World War and After* (Hong Kong: Hong Kong University Press, 2009).
87. S. Tsang, *A Modern History of Hong Kong* (London and New York: I.B. Tauris, 2007). See Chapter 9, *Japanese Invasion and Occupation*, esp. p. 119 (Japanese invasion and occupation destroy the myth of British invincibility.)
88. The status of 'British Dependent Territory' was created by the BNA 1981.
89. 'Interim Report on Hong Kong Police' October 1943 was briefly referenced in P. Snow, *The Fall of Hong Kong: Britain, China and the Japanese Occupation* (New Haven, CT: Yale University Press, 2004), p. 201.
90. Ibid.
91. Pennefather-Evans joined the police in 1914, aged 20, as a Police Probationer of the Federated Malay States. During WWII, he became a POW in Hong Kong for three years. It was during the internment that Pennefather-Evans compiled the Commissioner Report for HKP reform after the war.
92. A. Burton, *After the Imperial Turn: Thinking with and Through the Nation* (Durham, NC: Duke University Press, 29 May 2003), p. 297.
93. Enclosure to Governor Sir Mark Young to Secretary Lord Moyne, confidential letter, 1 December 1941 (extracts) (source: CO129/588) Preliminary Report on the Hong Kong Police Force. See S. Tsang, *Government and Politics: A Documentary History of Hong Kong* (Hong Kong: Hong Kong University Press, 1993).
94. I. Ward, *Sui Geng: The Hong Kong Marine Police 1841–1950* (Hong Kong: Hong Kong University Press, 1991). See '14. The Reconstruction of the Fleet 1946–1948', pp. 167–177, esp. pp. 169–173.
95. Karen Fang, 'Britain's Finest: The Royal Hong Kong Police', In: p. 293, A. Burton (ed.), *After the Imperial Turn: Thinking with and through the Nation* (Durham, NC: Duke University Press, 2003), p. 297.
96. S. J. Chan, *Democracy Shelved: Great Britain, China, and Attempts at Constitutional Reform in Hong Kong 1945–1952* (Hong Kong: Oxford University Press, 1988), pp. xvi–xvii.
97. The Police Review 1957 Address of H.E. the Governor, Sir Alexander Grantham (1947–1957).
98. *HKPM* 7 (4): 32–33, March 1957.
99. Colonial Reports Hong Kong 1946.
100. *Hong Kong Legislative Council.* 30 March 1949. 82–118. ('An Ordinance to apply a sum not exceeding one hundred and seventy-nine million five hundred and eighty-six thousand nine hundred and seventy dollars to the Public Service of the Financial year ending 31 March 1950.') http://www.legco.gov.hk/1949/h490330.pdf
101. Ibid., p. 92.
102. Hong Kong Legislative Council, 8 September 1948. 251–261, 'Motion', 251–254 ('Hon. Sir Man-Kam Lo: —Sir, for at least two reasons, to-day's sitting is an

unique and will become a historic occasion in the annals of this Council. First I think I am right in saying that this is the first occasion on which an International Declaration has ever been referred to this Council, and if I may do so, I would like to congratulate Government on taking this step'.)

103. Membership: Australia, Belgium, Byelo-Russia, Chile, China, Egypt, France, India, Lebanon, Panama, the Philippines, Ukraine, the United Kingdom, the United States of America, the U.S.S.R., Uruguay, Yugoslavia.
104. Hong Kong Legislative Council. 30 March 1949. 82–118. The Council is much concerned about the plight of juvenile after WWII. Chau Tsun-Nin 'I see from the Annual Report that there are in the Colony an estimated 100,000 children between the ages of five and twelve, who are still receiving no education. This is almost half of the estimated 225,000 children in this age group in the Colony (p. 95)'.
105. Hong Kong Legislative Council. 8th September 1948. 252–261, 252.
106. D. Akers-Jones, *Feeling the Stones: Reminiscences by David Akers-Jones* (Hong Kong: Hong Kong University Press, 2004). http://books.google.com/books?id=PnQAsA0oIPoC&lr=&source= gbs_navlinks_s A. Grantham, *Via Ports: From Hong Kong to Hong Kong* (Hong Kong: Hong Kong University Press, 2012). http://books.google.com/books?id=LNNhhpkKJ10C&lr=&source=gbs_navlinks_s
107. *HKPM*, September 1951.
108. CP Maxwell, Farewell, *HKPM*, Spring, 1959.
109. Impressions of police course in England, *HKPM*, September 1951, 5.
110. 'Restructuring, reengineering, transformation, renewal, and reorientation are words that describe the same general phenomenon—A change in how business is conducted'. See Liběna Tetřevová, Concept of Corporate Restructuring and Reengineering. Institute of Economics, Faculty of Economics and Administration, University of Pardubic. https://dspace.upce.cz/bitstream/10195/32208/1/CL655.pdf
111. Chapter 6: 'A New Hong Kong'. J. M. Carroll, *A Concise History of Hong Kong* (Latham, Maryland: Rowman & Littlefield, 2007).
112. D.A.E. Peterson, Principal Probation Officer, The Policeman and Juvenile, *HKPM* 2 (2): 5, March 1952.
113. Ibid.
114. E. S. Scott and L. Steinberg, Adolescent Development and the Regulation of Youth Crime, *Juvenile Justice*, 18 (2): Fall 2008. http://futureofchildren.org/publications/journals/journal_details/index.xml?journalid = 31
115. D.A.E. Peterson, Principal Probation Officer, The Policeman and Juvenile, *HKPM* 2 (2): 5, March 1952.
116. Ibid.
117. D.A.E. Peterson, Principal Probation Officer, *The Policeman and Juvenile*, *HKPM* 2 (2): 5, March 1952.
118. G. Ure, *Governors, Politics and the Colonial Office: Public Policy in Hong Kong, 1918–58* (Hong Kong: Hong Kong University Press, 2012). (The Hong Kong government had limited policymaking capabilities, pre and post war.)
119. Richard Beckhard, *Organization Development: Strategies and Models* (Reading, MA: Addison-Wesley, 1969), p. 9.
120. R. H. Rouda and M. E. Kusy, Jr., *Organization Development: The Management of Change* (1995). http://alumnus.caltech.edu/~rouda/T3_OD.html

121. Leo F. Goodstadt, Government without Statistics: Policy-Making in Hong Kong 1925–85, With Special Reference to Economic and Financial Management. HKIMR Working Paper No. 6/2006. http://www.hkimr.org/uploads/publication/210/ub_full_0_2_128_wp200606_text.pdf
122. Ibid., p. 4.
123. C. E. Lindblom, The science of 'muddling through', *Public Administration Review*, 19: 79–88, 1959.
124. This is not to suggest that there was a total absence of policy making framework without constitutional, legal or administrative control over process or outcome. As a British Crown colony, Hong Kong Government was led by an all powerful appointed governor. The governor was empowered by Letter Patent, constrained by Royal Instructions and guided with Colonial Regulations. In practice, all these documents told the governor what not to do rather than what should be done. Senior civil servants, appointed by the Crown, assisted the governor. He also reported to Secretary of State on major issues affecting colonial administration, for example, revenue and expenditure, appointment and dismissal of senior officials. Governor's policy decision making is informed by Executive Council. Law established by Legislative Council runs the government. In both instances, British could and did intervene, through legislation of British Parliament or Privy Council or invalidation of Secretary of State. The traditional approach of colonial governance was by relying on the 'man of the spot' due to lack of expertise, information, and knowledge of Hong Kong in Britain. G. Ure, *Governors, Politics and the Colonial Office: Public Policy in Hong Kong, 1918–58* (Hong Kong: Hong Kong University Press, 2012), pp. 2–3. At the end the day, it is fair to say that Hong Kong government enjoyed a high degree of autonomy in the running of Hong Kong. The best that can be said of the autonomy of Hong Kong government is that it enjoyed relatively free 'political' autonomy, but near unchecked 'administrative' autonomy. Ibid., p. 4. For a description of literature on colonial government policy making, see Ibid., pp. 8–9.
125. E. Sinn, *Power and Charity: A Chinese Merchant Elite in Colonial Hong Kong* (Hong Kong: Hong Kong University Press, 2003), p. 2.
126. Leo F. Goodstadt, Government without Statistics: Policy-Making in Hong Kong 1925–85, With Special Reference to Economic and Financial Management. HKIMR Working Paper No. 6/2006. Ibid., p. 2.
127. W. R. Louis, Hong Kong: The critical phase, 1945–1949, *The American Historical Review*, 102 (4): 1052–1084, 1053, 1997.
128. G. Kitson, Memo, *The Future of Hong Kong*, 28 February 1946, FO 371/53632.
129. Mao was not interested in taking back Hong Kong at the time.
130. G. Drower, *Britains Dependent Territories: A Fistful of Islands* (Aldershot: Dartmouth Publishing Company Ltd. 1992).
131. Hawksley, Charles Michael, Administrative colonialism: District administration and colonial 'middle management' in Kelantan 1909–1919 and the Eastern Highlands of Papua New Guinea 1947–1957, Doctor of Philosophy thesis, Faculty of Arts, University of Wollongong, 2001. http://ro.uow.edu.au/theses/1732
132. See Hong Kong Police/Military Agenda (p. 98) to Georgina Sinclair, 'Hong Kong Headaches: Policing the 1967 disturbances', In: R. Bickers and R. Yep (eds.), *May Days in Hong Kong: Riot and Emergency in 1967* (Hong Kong: Hong Kong University Press, 2009), pp. 89–103.

133. Ibid., p. 90.
134. J. W. Hayes and E. Sinn, *Colonial Administration in British Hong Kong and Chinese Customary Law* (Hong Kong: Centre of Asian Studies, University of Hong Kong, 2001). For a digitised version, see https://archive.org/stream/colonialadminist00jame/colonialadminist00jame_djvu.txt
135. Ibid., p. 69.
136. B. W. Wai-yuk, Village vigilantes' 300-year patrol, *SCMP*, 18 August 1996. http://www.scmp.com/article/170956/village-vigilantes-300-year-patrol
137. Ibid., p. 98.
138. Panel on Commerce and Industry Meeting on 17 January 2006. Background Brief on Hong Kong's Hosting of the Sixth Ministerial Conference of the World Trade Organization. LC Paper No. CB(1)682/05-06. http://www.legco.gov.hk/yr05-06/english/panels/ci/papers/ci0117cb1-682-e.pdf
139. 10 Impact of the 1967 riots, G. K. W. Cheung, *Hong Kong's Watershed: The 1967 Riots* (Hong Kong: Hong Kong University Press, 1 October 2009), pp. 131–143.
140. R. Bickers and R. Yep, *May Days in Hong Kong: Riot and Emergency in 1967* (Hong Kong: Hong Kong University Press, 2009), p. 100.
141. L. N. Giles, *Wearing Red, Tracking Reds: What a Ride!: Policing and Counter-Espionage from Canada to Hong Kong* (Victoria, British Columbia, Canada: Trafford Publishing, 8 April 2011), specifically see '37: Hong Kong Liaison', pp. 249–314.
142. Ibid., 257–258.
143. M. E. Page and P. M. Sonnenburg, Police and policing, *Colonialism: An International, Social, Cultural, and Political Encyclopedia. A-M. Vol. 1* (Santa Barbara, CA: ABC-CLIO, 2003), p. 475.
144. See section on 'The lash and the noose: The deterrent approach to punishment, 1841–1877' F. Dikötter, A paradise for rascals: Colonialism, punishment and the prison in Hong Kong (1841–1898), *Crime, History and Society*, 8 (1): 2004, Varia. http://chs.revues.org/515
145. During his short tenure, Governor Young's signature achievements were in proposing increasing Chinese representation in Legislative Council, doing away with racial segregation at the Peak and promising opportunities and promotion for Chinese in government. It was Governor Young who, during the budget debate for 1946–1947, stated that 'The policy of Government is to ensure that every opportunity shall be given to locally recruited persons not only to enter but to rise in the service of the public up to the highest posts and to fulfil the highest responsibilities of which they are capable or can be assisted to become capable'. Colonial Reports Hong Kong 1947, p. 6. For penal policy in Hong Kong, see House of Lords' Debate on Corporal Punishment in Hong Kong, Hansard, 1 August 1951, vol. 173. cc. 166–70.
146. Governor John Pope Hennessy is noted for his policy stances on 'native race craze', 'grand-in-aid' schools, 'separate cells in prison and long-term convict labour for unreformed prisoners. For his penal policy, see section on "Stone and shot": The redemptive virtue of prison labour, 1877–1898'. F. Dikötter, 'A paradise for rascals: Colonialism, punishment and the prison in Hong Kong (1841–1898), *Crime, History and Society*, 8 (1): 2004; Varia. http://chs.revues.org/515. 'Soon after arriving on the island, he tackled the question of corporal punishment and ordered an investigation into the administration of the

prison. Contrary to his predecessors, he emphasised the need for reformation in the treatment of criminals'. The Prison Commission he appointed however disagreed.

147. In the House of Commons on 26 July 1860, Hennessy urged a shift in colonial policies and rule in India: 'the military administration of India would be conducted with greater skill, with more economy, and, as a natural result of a higher educational standard, with a greater regard for the feelings and interests of the Native population. Indeed, recent events furnished us with the most conclusive evidence that many of the British officers, entrusted with grave authority in India, had, from an ignorance of popular customs and a disregard of national habits and traditions, given great cause of complaint and encouragement to disaffection. As long as we send out officers to India who seem inclined to treat the Natives as slaves, who seem unable or unwilling to appreciate the noble qualities, of that unfortunate people, and who add the grossest military outrages and insults to the civil misgovernment and financial burdens we have imposed upon them, so long will our rule in India be a blot upon civilization'. House of Commons debate, 26 July 1860, Hansards, Vol. 160, cc. 231–59, 235.
148. On political philosophy, see C. Patten, *East and West: The Last Governor of Hong Kong on Power Freedom and the Future* (London: McClelland & Stewart, 1998). The pattern was called 'whore of the East' for introducing electoral reform in the Legislative Council (p. 69). On penal policy, see Samson Chan, Colonial penality: A case study of Hong Kong's penal policy and programmes under British administration (1945–1997). Ph.D. Dissertation, Department of Social Studies (Criminology), University of Hull (2012). ('The political reform in Hong Kong during Governor Patten's time in late 1990s had witnessed the increased participation and influence of the legislators in penal policy legislation. In the legislative process for the Post-release Supervision Scheme, the initial proposal by the Correctional Services Department and the Government carried a much stronger disciplinary welfare principle with the involvement of a policeman in the supervision team.') p. 310. https://hydra.hull.ac.uk/assets/hull:7167a/content
149. M. Alagappa, *Coercion and Governance: The Declining Political Role of the Military in Asia* (Stanford, CA: Stanford University Press, 2001). Chapter One: 'Investigating and Explain Change: An Analytical Framework', pp. 29–69.
150. M. Weber, *The Theory of Social and Economic Organization*. Translated by A.M. Henderson and Talcott Parsons; edited with introduction by Talcott Parsons (New York: Oxford University Press, 1947).
151. Samson Chan, supra, Note 148, p. 209.
152. R.H.W., Boys' and Girls' Club of Hong Kong 香港小童群益會 *HKPM* X (4): 18–22, Winter, 1960.
153. Report of the Boys' and Girls' Club Association for 1940/41.
154. In 1956/7, the Hong Government provided the land and Rotary Club donated the fund to build the first BGCA training centre at Jaffe Road and Lockhart Road. Ibid., p. 22.
155. In 1948, two leadership courses were organised. One leader was send to the United Kingdom for observation and training by the British Council. In 1949, specialised training in child psychology, first aid, leadership and games were provided for the Club Leaders. Ibid., p. 20.

156. In 1951, 'two Boy Scout troops and two Cub packs were formed and steps were taken to commence a Girl Guide Company'. Ibid., p. 20.
157. Chinese Medical Association and doctors offered free medical services for the clubs. Ibid., p. 20.
158. In 2013, there were 45,860 Integrated Children and Youth Service Centers, serving 18,652 children. About Us—Vision and Mission. BGCA, 2013. http://www.bgca.org.hk/files/bgca/PDF/1213/p6-p18.pdf
159. Peng, Policemen and citizens. *HKPM* 1X(3): 3–6, Winter, 1959. (In the Hong Kong Police Gold Medal Essay Competition 1959, the first prize of a gold medal and $100 was awarded to Detective Police Constable 4726 Mui Wah Fuk (CID PHQJ, who wrote under the pen name of 'Peng').
160. Ibid., p. 3.
161. S. Shavell, Law versus morality as regulators of conduct, *American Law and Economics Review*, 4 (2): 227–257, 2002.
162. Ibid., Abstract.
163. Ibid., p. 4.
164. Ibid., p. 4.
165. See Wm. T. De Bary, W.t. Chan and B. Watson, *Sources of Chinese Tradition* Vol. I (New York: Columbia University, 1960), p. 28. (Sources of Chinese Tradition), p. 114.
166. Ibid., p. 115.
167. *The Analects*, Book XV, Chapter 7.
168. *The Analects*, Book IV, Chapter 5:3.
169. *The Analects*, 2:3.
170. *The Analects*, 12:11.
171. P. Tsang, HK police force nears 'localisation' goal with exit of expat officer, *SCMP* 12 October 2009. ('At the most senior level, the proportion of overseas officers in directorate ranks has shrunk from 55 per cent in the 1980s to little more than 3 per cent last year. Natural attrition and language obstacles for new recruits are set to trim the number further, with the last overseas officer in the police force—the largest department—set to retire in 2027'.). http://www.scmp.com/article/695108/hk-police-force-nears-localisation-goal-exitexpat-officer
172. http://searchcio.techtarget.com/definition/localization
173. Legal Transplant and Legal Culture. The World Bank. http://web.worldbank.org/WBSITE/EXTERNAL/TOPICS/EXTLAWJUSTINST/0, contentMDK:20759640 ~menu PK:2035153~pagePK:210058~piPK:210062~theSitePK:1974062,00.html
174. http://www.w3.org/2003/p3p-ws/pp/uld.html
175. https://www.gala-global.org/education-training-programs
176. 'The person who is closest to a problem, by impact or with resource, is the person to solve the problem', In: Kam C. Wong, State Police Power as a Social Resource Theory (2000). a/k/a Expectation Theory of Social Control (2014). Discussed in K. C. Wong, *Chinese Policing: History and Reform* (Bern, Switzerland: Peter Lang, 2007), Chapter 8.
177. The Hong Kong Water Police was the first localised and integrated HKP, portending things to come. It also debunks the myths that Chinese officers were all corrupt, disloyal and could not be trusted. 'See Old Hong Kong, water people and police 1952' for 'staged' photos of Europeans working with Chinese marine police officers. https://www.youtube.com/watch?v = OI_CsgA_pTw @1.30

178. 102. Kowloon Walled City Most Odd—Facts of Interest. http://mostodd.wordpress.com/2011/05/02/kowloon-walled-city/
179. C. K. Chan, *Social Security Policy in Hong Kong: From British Colony to China's Special Administrative Region* (Latham, MD: Rowman & Littlefield, 2011), p. 67.
180. The rationale, idea, and practice of collaborative–indirect rule is best explained by Nantang Ben Jua, Indirect Rule In Colonial And Post-Colonial Cameroon, The Centre for Social Anthropology and Computing, University of Kent. http://lucy.kent.ac.uk/csac/lucy/Chilver/Paideuma/paideuma-Indirec-2.html
181. A. M. Hiatt, Holder and Donovan join New York police commissioner to discuss collaboration, *Washington Post*, 16 January 2014. http://www.washingtonpost.com/politics/holder-and-donovan-join-new-york-policecommissioner-to-discuss-collaboration/2014/01/16/9e072906-7ea4-11e3-95c6-0a7aa80874bc_story.html
182. B. C. Renauer, D. E. Duffee and J. D. Scott, Measuring police-community co-production: Trade-offs in two observational approaches, *Policing: An International Journal of Police Strategies & Management*, 26 (1): 9–28, 2003.
183. L. Pomerantz-Zhang, *Wu Tingfang (1842–1922): Reform and Modernization in Modern Chinese* (Hong Kong: Hong Kong University Press, 1 August 1992). Chapter 2: 'Hong Kong Barrister 1877–1882', pp. 41–71.
184. P. T. Lee, Business networks and patterns of Cantonese compradors and merchants in nineteenth century Hong Kong, *Journal of the Hong Kong Branch of the Royal Asiatic Society*, 31: 1–39, 9, 1991. shttp://hkjo.lib.hku.hk/archive/files/c606bc91afb7cfc0c8aebafd36b8dac2.pdf
185. Between 1885 and 1900, a total of 1,830,572 Chinese emigrants embarked at the port of Hong Kong.
186. 9. The Place of Secret Societies in the Problem of Colonial Administration, In: K. Bolton and C. Hutton (eds.), *Triad Societies: Western Accounts of the History, Sociology and Linguistics of Chinese Secret Societies, Vol. 5* (London and New York: Taylor & Francis, 2000), p. iv.
187. The framework for the student of colonial rule inter-penetration black societies is that of PCN (political–criminal nexus). PCN studies the relationship between political elites and criminal understood, for mutual benefits. Political elites get money and control. Underworld gets license and tolerance. The result is order and stability, at the expense of legality and morality. It is commonly recognised that in the 1950s, Hong Kong was by and large stable and secured, in spite of onslaught of migrants, tension between political factions, discontent with labours, and growth in criminal elements of all kind. At that point, the PCN was justified, some say inevitable, because it was good for economic development. But there was a high cost for such stability, as there were pervasive corruption and institutionalised collusion between HKP and Triads, for example, in the supply of illegitimate services and need for illegal protection. R. Godson, *Menace to Society: Political-Criminal Collaboration around the World* (New Brunswick, NJ: Transaction Publishers, 2003).
188. M. C. Howard, *Transnationalism and Society: An Introduction* (Jefferson, NC: McFarland, 28 February 2011), p. 180.
189. K. Chin and R. Godson, Organized crime and the political-criminal nexus in China, *Trends in Organized Crime*, 9: 5–44, 2006.

190. T. Wing Lo, 8. Minimizing crime and corruption in Hong Kong, In: R. Godson, *Menace to Society: Political-Criminal Collaboration around the World* (New Brunswick, NJ: Transaction Publishers, 2003), p. 231.
191. T. C. Anstey, *Crime and Government at Hong Kong, a Letter to the 'Times'* (1859); Thomas Chisholm Anstey, Henry Pelham Fiennes Pelham Clinton (Duke of Newcastle), Case of Hong Kong. Correspondence between T. C. Anstey, late Attorney-General of Hong Kong, and the Duke of Newcastle, Secretary of State for the Colonies. 3–29 July 1859 (London: Effingham Wilson, Royal Exchange, 1859).
192. D. R. Caldwell and T. C. Anstey, *A Vindication of the Character of the Undersigned from the Aspersions of Mr. T. Chisholm Anstey, Ex-Attorney General of Hongkong as Contained in His Charges, His Pamphlet, and His Letter to the Secretary of State for the Colonies* (Wellington Street, Hong Kong: Noronha's office, 1860). http://books.google.com/books?id=jwsTAAAAYAAJ&printsec=frontcover&dq=A+Vindication+of+the+Character+of+the+Undersigned+from+the+Aspersions+of+Mr.+T.+Chisholm+Anstey,+Exattorney+General+of+Hongkong+as+Contained+in+His+Charges,+His+Pamphlet,+and+His+Letter+to+the+Secretary+of+State+for+the+Colonies+%28Noronha%27s+office,+1860%29&hl=en&sa=X&ei=9uF7VMugAu_msATw54HYBA&ved=0CB0Q6AEwAA#v=onepage&q&f=false
193. Community Policing in Hong Kong; 'Engaging' the Lantau Island Community (CAPPLEX, 2014). http://capplex.com/news/2014/4/7/community-policing-in-hong-kong-engaging-the-lantau-island-community
194. Ihekwoaba D. Onwudiwe, Chapter 4: 'Community Policing: The Case of Informal Policing in Nigeria', pp. 103–125, In: D. Wisler and I. D. Onwudiwe (eds.), *Community Policing: International Patterns and Comparative Perspectives* (CRC Press, 8 June 2009). (Decentralised police allows for customisation of police service to meet with local needs, instead of centralisation law enforcement.)
195. B. F. C. Hsu, *The Common Law in Chinese Context* (Hong Kong: Hong Kong University Press, 1 January 1992), p. 17.
196. M. W. Ma, Foreign jurisdiction in China, *The American Journal of International Law*, 18 (4): 676–695, 1924.
197. A dominant narrative portrays British colonial presence as one of 'indirect rule' by a political neutral state pursuing a *lazier-fare* policy. T. W. Ngo (ed.), *Hong Kong's History: State and Society under Colonial Rule* (London and New York: Taylor & Francis, 1999), p. 3. Indeed, with this account, British rule over Hong Kong would not be possible without the active collaboration of Hong Kong's elite and tacit approval of the populace, p. 5. Viewed in this light, Hong Kong is less a British colony as it is a market place for all sorts of people to pursue their own interests, of which seeking adventure and making money are common denominators. Then as now, different actors, chasing their own dreams, make Hong Kong what it is.
198. The Christians were appalled and abhorred at how indigenous natives such as the aboriginals were treated at the hands of the settlers, that is, taking their land and enslaving them. They objected to British colonialists meddling with the lifestyle of the indigenous people, for example, sailors corrupting the local with alcohol and sex. They were critical of hypocritical liberal elites denying autonomy and destroying culture of the people overseas, in order to liberate and

enlighten them. Report of the Parliamentary Select Committee on Aboriginal Tribes (British settlements) (1837).

199. V. Lee, *Being Eurasian: Memories across Racial Divides* (Hong Kong: Hong Kong University Press, 1 August 2004), p. 14.
200. There are other ways of handling multi-cultural relationship, such as American's 'melting pot' theory.
201. R. F. Betts, *Assimilation and Association in French Colonial Theory, 1890–1914* (Lincoln, NE: University of Nebraska Press, 2005). 'Origins and Growth of French Doctrine of Assimilation', pp. 10–33.
202. L. F. Goodstadt, *Uneasy Partners: The Conflict between Public Interest and Private Profit in Hong Kong* (Hong Kong: Hong Kong University Press, 1 January 2005). Chapter 1: 'The Colonial Culture and Its Siege Mentality', pp. 19–31. (From the earliest days, British administrators (AO) enjoyed unsurpassed privileges in Hong Kong, in terms of service, including salary, pension, housing, education, and medical. In 1950s, there were 42 of them running a city of 2.5 million Chinese.)
203. C. Munn, *Anglo-China: Chinese People and British Rule in Hong Kong, 1841–1880* (New York: Psychology Press, 2001), p. 2.
204. Ibid.
205. J. F. Davis, *Chinese Novels, Translated from the Originals, etc.* (London: John Murray 1822); J. F. Davis, *The Chinese: A General Description of the Empire of China and Its Inhabitants* (London: Charles Knight, 1836); and J. F. Davis, *Sketches of China; Partly during an Inland Journey of Four Months between Peking, Nanking, and Canton; With Notices and Observations Relative to the Present War.* (Charles Knight & Co., Ludgate Street. London. 1841). In two volumes.
206. E. J. Eitel, *Europe in China: The History of Hongkong from the Beginning to the Year 1882* (London: Luzac & Co., 1895); E. J. Eitel, *A Chinese Dictionary in the Cantonese dialect, Vols. 1 & 2* (London: Trübner and Co., 57 & 59, Ludgate Hill. Hong Kong: Lane, Crawford & Co., 1897).
207. A. R. Sweeten, T-PAO as bottom level bureaucrates: Evidence from local criminal cases from south China: 1860–1877, *Modern History Research Center Journal*, 7: 627–658, 2002.
208. I. D. Lightbody, An administrative officer in Hong Kong, pp. 82–84, In: Anthony Kirk-Greene (ed.), *On Crown Service: A History of HM Colonial and Overseas Civil Services, 1837–1997* (London: I.B. Tauris, 12 June 1999).
209. I. Ward, *Sui Geng: The Hong Kong Marine Police 1841–1950* (HKU, 1991), pp. xvi–xvii.
210. Lau, Yat-hung. (劉日雄) An assessment of the historical origins and role of the marine police in contemporary Hong Kong. M.Soc.Sc. (Criminology) Thesis. HKU (1988). Lau, Yat-hung (劉日雄), SSP retired (2012), B.S. Cuhk (1982). I used informant because in his research into Marine Police, he was more interested describing the HKP as he knew it, not by any independent research.
211. Ibid., p. 39.
212. Ibid., p. 40.
213. Ibid.
214. C. Munn, *Anglo-China: Chinese People and British Rule in Hong Kong, 1841–1880* (New York and London: Routledge, 16 December 2013). Finding an Equilibrium, pp. 255–373.

215. S. Heaver, Flagrant harbour: The sordid affair that cemented Hong Kong's reputation for vice and corruption, *SCMP Magazine*. http://www.scmp.com/magazines/post-magazine/article/1431060/flagrant-harbour-sordid-affair-cemented-hong-kongs
216. Daniel Richard Caldwell was born in 1816 on an East India Company island. His father was a common solider in a local militia. In 1834, Daniel Caldwell worked on opium-smuggling ships in South China Coast and mixed freely with pirates. There he learned to speak Chinese fluently as a native. Caldwell then served as an interpreter in the First Opium War. In 1842, he worked for HKG as court interpreter and head of detective. There he made a name for himself for helping the Royal Navy and ran down pirates as well as catching crimes on land, through informants. In 1855, he left HKG to work with Ma-Chow Wong, who had a god daughter ('qi nui') whom Caldwell treated as a mistress or concubine. In 1851, Caldwell married Chan—approved by the Anglican Church. With Caldwell's access to the government and Royal Naval, Wong was able to control the pirates with the help of the RN. C. Munn, *Anglo-China: Chinese People and British Rule in Hong Kong, 1841–1880* (Routledge, 16 December 2013). Finding an Equilibrium, pp. 255–373, 307.
217. Ibid., pp. 322–323.
218. S. Tsang, *Governing Hong Kong: Administrative Officers from the Nineteenth Century to the Handover to China, 1862–1997* (London; New York: I.B. Tauris; New York: In the United States of America distributed by Palgrave Macmillan, 2007).
219. Whether a right-hearted colonial policy could have saved the day for the British is still up for debate. But without being right headed, the British did not have a chance.

HKP Reform: The 1950s 9

The complete break with old Hong Kong caused by the war is a unique opportunity to start afresh.[1]

HKP Police Commissioner John Penneather-Evans (1947)

Introduction

This final chapter investigates HKP reform and development in the 1950s–1960s, as compared with HKP reform in the 1840s and after the 1990s.

This chapter makes three claims:

First, HKP modernisation reform began in the 1950s. It was substantially completed by the 1960s. There were two objectives to the reform, that is, making HKP less colonial, a liberation process, and making it more modern, a professionalisation exercise.

Second, of all the HKP reforms, past and present, the 1950 HKP reform counts as one of the most ambitious and transformative. It created HKP in its modern form, with a brand new structure, functional process and progressive ethos to match. It gave birth to HKP as we know it today, as a legalised, modernised and communalised force, all be it in an embryotic state. The 1950s reform also laid the foundation and provided the platform for future police reform in HK, such as 1997 reform.

Third, the much-hyped 1997 HKP reform[2] is neither new nor innovative, in conception, process or outcome. It is built upon an old (though not worn) reform platform, with much continuity amidst gradual changes, from the past (1950).

This chapter follows on the heel of Chapter 7, which provided us with 'Contexts and Framework' to illuminate and analyse the HKP reform. This chapter is organised as follows: Section I is on 'Localisation' of HKP. It is followed by 'Legalisation' (Section II), 'Modernisation' (Section III), 'Communalisation' (Section IV) and 'Organisation' (Section V). Section VI 'HKP Voices' informs us of what some HKP officers think about HKP reform and policing in HK. Section VII is a 'Conclusion', which compares and contrasts police reform efforts between the 1840s and 1950s, from a frontline perspective as a fitting ending to this book.

I: Localisation

Localisation

The most conspicuous and consequential change to HKP in the 1950 reform period is that of localisation. It happened organisationally, for example, more Chinese officers, as inspectors and constables, operationally, for example, more collaboration with locals and culturally, for example, more acceptance of interracial marriages. The espoused purpose of localisation is to make HKP more representative of and attuned to HK demographics, conditions and concerns. It tries to be responsive to Chinese sense and sensitivity,[3] without formally decolonising or legally democratising the HKP. This is a tall order. But the HKP has been successful.

The observation here is that, after WWII, HK colonial administration sought decolonisation without democratisation, with the shelving of the Young plan for constitutional reform. Instead, the HK government launched a robust localisation campaign.

For the HKP, a street-level bureaucracy in the service of the people, localisation measures are perhaps more important than a democratisation process. Localisation improves police performance. Democratisation attracts political dissention and invites social disorder. Chinese traditional attitude and HK people's pragmatic mindset prefers performing than talking. This is certainly true with HK people who are aversive to politics. If HK people are giving a real choice, they would prefer 'finding eat' (making money) over 'blowing water' (discussing issues), every time.

From its inception and until the 1950s, HKP has been a predominately British colonial force, in constitution, organisation, ethos and style. It is organised in a very British way and operated with a colonial policing style. All aspects of 'Chineseness' were missing. The Chinese police played a subsidiary, for example, translator, perfunctory, for example, watchman and marginalised role, and only as an afterthought. Chinese were distrusted and never taken seriously as a respected member of the HKP. This is not surprising. Historically, HK-Chinese were treated as Chinese subjects to be controlled, not HK citizens to be served and respected.

There are exceptions. At various times, due to practical necessity, for example, liaison with the community, or progressive sentiments, for example, 'native race craze', there had been repeated calls for localisation of HKP.[4] For example, during his tenure, Governor John Hennessy (22 April 1877–30 March 1883), has pushed for more egalitarian treatment of HK people, compatible with the then prevailing social and economic influences.

In 1844, the year HKP was formed, under the stewardship of Superintendent May, there were 78 European (48.7%), 34 Indians (21%) and 48 Chinese (30%) officers. In 1865, there were 610 police officers, made up

Table 9.1 Nationalities of Police Officers in the Nineteenth and Early Twentieth Centuries

Nationality	1867	1881	1908	1927	1946
European	89	103	131	246	377
Indian	377	194	410	753	325
Guangdong Chinese	132	351	501	600	1630
Shandong Chinese	—	—	—	216	305

Source: M. S. Gaylord, D. Gittings and H. Traver, *Introduction to Crime, Law and Justice in Hong Kong* (Hong Kong: Hong Kong University Press, 2009), Chapter 4, pp. 57–76.

Table 9.2 Annual Salaries of Rank and Files by Nationality, 1855–1915

Year (Currency)	European	Indian	Chinese
1855 (pounds sterling)	47.10	20	13.15
1885 (HKD)	480	150	108
1915	100 pounds sterling	150 HKD	150 HKD

Source: See Prisons Department Annual Report of 1938.

of 76 Europeans (13%), 368 Indians (60.3%) and 65 Chinese (11%).[5] In 1898, the HKP was made up of 630 policemen, with 112 Europeans (17.7%), 292 Chinese (46%) and 226 Indians (35.9%). In 1909, there were 1050 officers, of which 128 were Europeans (12.2%), 511 Chinese (48.7%) and 411 Indians (39.1%).[6] In 1939, HKP boasted 306 Europeans (14%), 774 Indians (35%), 884 Cantonese (38%) and 296 northern Chinese (13%).

By 1950, HKP was predominately a local force. There were 3084 Chinese officers (83%), which included 2861 Cantonese (77%) and 507 northern Chinese (13%). There were only 266 Europeans (7%), 107 Indians (3%) and 31 Portuguese (<1%).[7]

In terms of command and control, in 1999, there were 37% (176/473) Chinese superintendents and 27% Chinese commissioners (6/22). By 2000, it was 67% (253/380) and 77% (17/22), respectively.[8]

HKP did not have a Chinese Commissioner of Police until 1989, with Li Kwan Ha (Tables 9.1 and 9.2).

Colonial Policy of Localisation

Post-war HKP is not the only government agency to be localised. In fact, localisation is the standing policy for HK government after WWII, including all the disciplinary services. For example, at the HK Prisons Department before the war, prison officers were all Europeans recruited from the military, while prison warders were entirely filled by Pakistanis and Sikhs. Chinese were not allowed due to loyalty and security concerns. In 1938, there were more than 230 Pakistani and Sikh staff.[9]

Prison-staffing policy changed after the war. Chinese were hired to replace foreign staff who were retiring and resigning. However, the localisation effort was not successful in recruiting locals. Prison officers were paid too low and their social status was not high. Chinese were aversive to joining as prison officers. In 1948, with the increase in salary and later improvement in training, the quantity and quality of warders improved substantially:

> The situation improved since 1947 when the Salary Commission increased the salary of the local prison staff to be in line with that of the police. Arising from this financial improvement, better quality local Chinese were attracted to join as Warders. Proper trainings were arranged for the newly recruited Warders since 1950. A month long training covering foot-drill, weapon training, Prison Rules and duties of a Warder.[10]

Localisation after WWII

WWII is the watershed in HK colonial history. It precipitated the transformation of HK from a colonial enclave to a global city. HK was not returned to China (KMT or PRC), as envisioned. It did get a makeover of HK constitutional order, as promised. However, HK did not start a long and arduous journey to return HK to the HK–Chinese, beginning with removing all conspicuous signs of racial discrimination, for example, with the removal of segregation law ('An Ordinance to repeal the Peak District (Residence) Ordinance, 1918' and 'An Ordinance to repeal the Cheung Chau (Residence) Ordinance, 1919' in 1946[11]) and adopting an explicit localisation policy by the HK government.[12]

The decolonisation at HKP took a number of forms:

First: *The installation of first de facto Chinese police chiefs*

HKP has a de facto Chinese police force beginning in the 1950s under the charge of the four Heads of CID.

In the 1950s–1960s, Detective Sergeants[13] had a lot of powers. Their power came from three sources: First, formal powers as Detective Sergeants. Second, personal powers as go-between to British senior officials and Chinese junior police officers, sometimes even Inspectors. Third, informal powers because they could get things done, that is, 'problem solving' with Chinese characteristics, known as 搞惦.[14]

The CID Heads kept the British boss happy by maintaining discipline within, for example, getting rid of trouble makers, and fighting crime without, for example, solving high-profile cases and posing high clearance rates. They also catered to the British boss's every fancy and whim, over and beyond the call of duties, for example, servicing their personal vehicles. In those days, expatriate commanders, Sub-Division Inspector (SDI) and Division Superintendent (DS) lived like a king.

The CID Heads kept the rank and file happy by helping with their promotion, for example, influencing paddling, and protecting them from their misadventures, for example, bribing off complainants. (Acting as a police welfare officer, Chinese style in the image of a Godfather.)

The CID Heads kept the community happy by delivering what they wanted, that is, pursuing street justice and providing Chinese order, sometimes for a price (tea money). (Doing true Chinese-style community policing [CP].) They kept the shopkeepers, businessmen and Taipans happy by doing their bidding, for example, keeping an undesirable off their back and providing them with face. (Doing effective HKP—public relationship, Chinese style.) In that, CID Heads were treated like a 'Godfather'.[15]

The Heads of CID were able to do all these and more with their organisational power, police knowledge, language skills, work experience, social network, underworld contacts, problem-solving skills and above all else being resourceful and entrepreneurial, as a 'cop merchant'.[16] One blog account described the CID status, role and power as follows:

> There were three or four staff sergeants at any one time, and they were in charge of all the rank-and-file officers in their areas. Unlike today's division by districts, they were responsible for huge geographic areas—Hong Kong Island, Kowloon—Yau Ma Tei had its own sergeant—and New Territories. A sergeant major lorded over them. Notionally, the staff sergeant ranked below an inspector, but even senior inspectors had to show them respect. This is because these powerful sergeants knew the pulse of the street, and effectively controlled gang activities and the territories each was allowed to operate—all the while taking a large chunk of commissions.[17]

In doing so, the Heads of CID became the de facto police chiefs running the HKP police operations, by and for the Chinese. The CID Heads were able to command and control most junior officers and some senior ones at will, in line with unspoken but well-recognised police code of conduct. They did so through bribe, promotion, appointment, assignment, posting and discipline; above all doing favours for others.[18] On one hand, the CID Heads offered police officers protection from bureaucratic blunder and professional indiscretion. On the other, the CID Heads provided them with welfare support when in need.

Once the CID Sergeants were in place, they were able to fight crime and maintain order by collaborating with Triads, a new form of CP.[19] Triads as a community group has an incentive to work with the HKP in keeping their community secure against internal strife, for example, gang fights and external interference, for example, police raids, and overall stability and order for Triad business. Working with the HKP would help them to secure their business model. Triads as new 'deputised' policing agents in town, turned colonial policing and later CP on their heads. Instead of the colonial master controlling the Chinese, the Chinese were controlling the colonial master. Instead of having community-fighting crime in collaboration with the HKP, the HKP was collaborating with criminal elements in keeping the community in order.

It is not unfair to observe that in the 1950s–1960s, there were two HKP forces, one in the front (British) and the other behind closed doors (Chinese), down to having its own unofficial office, administrative structure and case-processing system. For example, this author lived in Shamshuipo (SSP) as a child in the 1950s. In an upscale commercial–residential building (J/O Taipo Road and Nam Cheong Street), there was a CID unofficial office on the third floor. Detectives came and went 24/7. The office was used as a duty room for investigation and interrogation. CID came to work on their cases, worked on the suspects or just chilled out. The office has a set of report books, which recorded all the criminal cases CID officers have worked on. These include cases that were not reported to the main police station, for a variety of reasons, for example, cases with little leads or witnesses, more generally unsolved, and unsolvable cases. This way, the CID could manage their case-load, such that only those cases with a realistic hope of clearing found their way to the main police station.

The era of authentic HK–Chinese policing has begun, with the appointment of Detective Sergeants, acting effectively as police chiefs of their tufts.[20] According to a version of an 'unofficial' historical account about the power of CID Sergeants, which comports with HKP insiders' knowledge:

There were four Heads of CID in HK in the 1950s–1970s, being Hon Sum (韓森), Lui Lok (呂樂), Nan Kong (顏雄) and Ngan Hung (藍剛).

Lui Lok (呂樂) was promoted to Chief of Head CID—NT in 1958. He joined HKP in 1940 as a police constable. He earned his rank through hard work, distinguished performance and professional achievements and above all else not rocking the corruption boat. In one way, Lui was dedicated to fighting crime. In another way, he was not different from any black society people, doing whatever needed to get what he wanted. He would bribe the boss above and collect bribes from below. He used his power to obtain money from people in his jurisdiction to provide for a protective umbrella (保護傘). 'Lui Lok maintained complicated relationship above and below. He has a lot of brothers eating off his plate and depended on him for survival. He could not ignore them. He wanted them to live a good life'.

The other Head of CID is Nan Gang (藍剛). He was well respected within the HKP and the four Triad families '四大家族' (新義安、潮州幫、14K、和勝和). He need not do anything, the Triad families would help him with solving the crimes and deliver to him the culprits, including confession.

'When a new Commissioner of Police is appointed. They need to first visit with these four heads of CID, as a matter of courtesy, otherwise Hong Kong law and order would deteriorate and HKP could do nothing to be maintained a safe society'.[21]

Second: *The grooming of Chinese Inspectorate officers*

Increasingly, Chinese Inspectorate-grade officers were given important command posts, and were excelling at them. For example, at the 5th Annual Police Review held at Happy Valley on Wednesday, 28 November 1951, Inspector Tsui Po Ying won an award as the first Chinese Inspector in charge of a difficult division, that of Shau Ki Wan in 1948 for 3 years. Another high-flyer was Sub-Inspector Fong Yik Fai[22] who was given an award for playing a leadership role as a senior Chinese officer at PTS in the training of 2000 police recruits from 1945 to 1948. Since 1948, until he departed for 6 months training at Hendon Police College, U.K., he was responsible for the building of the Railroad Police.[23]

Grooming of locals officers was not without its attending security risks. Senior HKP—Chinese officers working for the Chinese government—PRC or KMT, was a distinct possibility and a real concern for HKP senior management at the time. As such, Chinese officers were less trusted. The worse security breach within Chinese senior ranks happened in 1961. In 1961 (6 October 1961), Assistant Superintendent Tsang Siu-Fo (曾昭科),[24] Deputy Commandant PTS and then the highest-ranking Chinese officers, were arrested for being a Communist China spy, and later deported after 58 days of interrogation by British M16 agents (21 December 1961).[25]

Third: *Chinese police officers placed in high-profile international leadership position*

One way to promote localisation of staff is by way of showcasing Chinese officers who were elected by peers to lead police international professional organisations. This has two effects. First, it establishes a role model for other Chinese officers. Second, it changes the image of HKP as a British-dominated police agency.

One such case was with the formation of HK Section (5 July 1958) to the International Police Association (IPA). IPA was established in Great Britain in 1950, to promote international exchanges between officers from different countries and across cultures. The motto of IPA is 'SERVO PER AMIKECO', an Esperanto term which means 'SERVICE THROUGH FRIENDSHIP'.[26] Besides professional association and social exchanges, IPA also consulted with international bodies—United Nations Educational, Scientific and Cultural Organization (UNESCO) and entertained heads of state.

At that time, HK was the only Chinese city police force to have joined IPA. Others were Great Britain, Holland, Belgium, France, Norway, Switzerland, Italy, Sweden, Turkey, Chile, Germany, Federal Republic, Eire, Spain, Austria, Canada and Finland. The President of the IPA (HK) organisation was Li Fuk-ki[27] and Vice President D.R. Harris. The Honorary President was the Commissioner of Police Heath. For IPA-HK, Chinese and European officers joined under the IPA—British section.

Inspector Li got the idea of setting up the IPA-HK section when he was under training at Police College—Ryton—on—Dunsmore in the United Kingdom in 1956.[28] SIP (Detective) Li retired from HKP and is now a security consultant.

The establishment of IPA-HK section is significant in understanding HKP development as an institution. IPA-HK was the first-time HKP that allowed a Chinese officer to represent itself, internationally, as the head of a professional organisation, with full endorsement of the HKP Commissioner of Police. From an institutionalisation point of view, it sent a clear message, and in the most conspicuous way; HKP was coming of age as a professional and international organisation. As such, HKP made clear that as an organisation, it embraces an international norm, sending the message that as a policing agency with global reach and international presence, it preferred professionalism over colonialism. In this regard, HKP preferred not to be known as a colonial police organisation. Witness the fact that HKP was not joining as IPA—U.K. but on its own terms, zips—HK. Chinese officers were not subservient, and were much less discriminated by the British; witness the fact that the IPA (HK) was headed by a Chinese official with a British deputy on the side. In one masterstroke, HKP has been decolonised, at least symbolically, to its members and with the world community.

Fourth: *The standardisation of promotion process*

The promotion process of local police officers has improved much after the 1950s. By and large, the process is based on merit, with detailed uniform criteria, standard professional examination, objective assessment, multiple evaluators and time-in-grade requirements. All officers are treated the same, in principle, with structured paper tests and final interview boards. For example, since 1961, in order to advance from probationary inspector to Inspector of Police, the candidate must have

1. Successfully complete 3 years of service in grade
2. Completed Standard I Professional Examination upon completion of initial training at Police Training School
3. Passed Standard II Professional Examination
4. Passed the first colloquial Cantonese Examination (overseas officers only)
5. Recommended by the regional/branch commander based on overall performance reports
6. Accepted by the Commissioner

However, the HKP promotion system is not flawless.

In 1982, a Chinese HKP senior officer, Tsui Yiu-Kwong conducted an empirical study of the fairness of HKP promotion system, with internal recruitment to promotion data. The data and analysis tentatively showed that HKP promotion process is discriminatory against Chinese. Specifically, controlling for maturity, education, experience and performances, Tsui found that expatriate police officers were promoted faster and disproportionately against Chinese officers.[29] The findings could not be satisfactorily explained, on merits alone.

For the study, the study examined a sample (33%) of Chinese versus expatriate officers inducted between 1961 and 1974.[30] The study shows:

First, 'if age were used as an indicator of maturity and as maturity is likely to affect an officer's promotion ... locals are older and therefore more mature' (p. 51). However, the author considered the marginal difference in maturity between Chinese and expatriates is too small to be deemed significant as a discriminator.

Second, 'If education were used as an indicator for knowledge and intelligence, which are important qualities for promotion it would seem that expatriates are more knowledgeable and intelligent as they generally received more education than local...' (p. 51). Again, the author discounted this slight difference in education favouring the expatriates on account of the fact that HK education system is not comparable with the expatriate systems.

Third, 'Previous working experience, especially that in discipline services, would be expected to enhance work performance and subsequent promotion, however, the previous working experience of the two groups of officers was similar at entry' (p. 52). Tsui failed to find actual difference in the training performance between locals and expatriates (p. 52).

Fourth, 'The time taken to achieve confirmation to Inspector and advancement to Senior inspector was roughly the same for locals and expatriates. There is, therefore no significant difference in this aspect of their work performance' (p. 53).

Fifth, the author concludes that the findings could only be explained by differences in terms of services between expatriates and Chinese, specifically promotion within the expatriate stream is sped up based on political necessity of keeping more expatriate officers on top as a 'right balance':

> Instead, the promotion system in the officer cadre of the Royal Hong Kong Police Force is based on the principle of 'right balance'. By this it is meant that the Force maintains an appropriate ratio of expatriates to locals at various levels within the officer cadre (p. 56).

This research was and is the only empirical research bearing upon promotion discrimination in the HKP, singling out the British administration for constructive criticism. One can certainly challenge the methods, for example, how various dependent variables, such as performance, is defined and measured, or the validity of the findings, that is, the author attributing non-significance to differences in age of entry (Chinese ahead) or comparability between educational attainments (expatriate ahead), between expatriates and Chinese. Notwithstanding these and other methodological and interpretation flaws, there is no denial that the expatriate officers were promoted faster and more often than Chinese officers. This made for a HKP top command structure with disproportionate expatriate presence.

For our purpose, the sole question that needs to be asked is why the disparity in promotion in favour of the expatriate officers, in the first place. Is this a blatant case of discrimination to keep a 'right balance' or a justifiable case of 'right merit'? Or, are there any other explanations?

Whichever the interpretation, the differential promotion prospect is likely to be accepted or rejected based on one's personal experience on account of his ethnic identity. For the losers (Chinese), they would object to the disproportionate representation of White officers at the top, whatever the reasons. For the winners (expatriates), they would approve the promotion system as being fair, notwithstanding disproportionate representation. The truth possibly lies somewhere in between.

From my investigation into HKP reform, it is clear that there was structural discrimination in favour of the expatriate officers in the 1950s, for example, nearly all sought-after posts, for example, operational commander (DDI, SDI and DS) at key police stations (Yamati, Mongkok) and high-profile positions, for example, Editorial Board of HKPM, were held by expatriates.

Before we jump to the conclusion about racial discrimination, let us consider four plausible explanations for such noted racial disparity at key places:

First, the locals were less experienced. The localisation process has just started and yet to take roots. The locals were less seasoned and not yet prepared to take up key/high command. For example, in the later issues of HKPM, I found more Chinese in command and HKPM provides more space for Chinese officers' reporting.

Second, the locals 'naturally' do not mix well with the expatriates, for example, they do not hang out with the expatriates in the officers mess or at the bar downtown after work and into the late hours. They have a home and family to return to. In essence, it is observed that there are personal, social and cultural distances between the expatriates and Chinese. Thus, Chinese were not professionally connected and socially bonded with the expatriates, sufficient for them to know each other. Validation of this observation can be found by comparing Marine officers versus police tactical unit (PTU) officers versus uniform branch (UB) officers, with Marine officers most bonded and UB officers less bonded. The thesis being, professional bonding is a function of police assignments, and promotion is contingent on bonding.

Third, since promotion decision makers (gatekeepers) need information to make sound decision, and they are not limited to information on the file before them, it is likely that they will fall back on their personal knowledge of candidates, expatriates or Chinese, to make a decision. Since most of the gatekeepers at the time (1950) were expatriate officers, the personal information is likely to be from their social interaction with the candidate, that is, mess night or bar talks. This gives the expatriate officers a distinct advantage over the Chinese.

Fourth, after WWII, many high-ranking officers were hired overseas to replenish the stock. These overseas senior appointments limited promotion opportunity from below to high places, such as a Gazetted officer, even if the promotion prospect for Chinese and expatriates was the same.

The above discussion is not to deny that there is a lot of racial animus, institutionalised (legacy), imported (African officers) or personal (bigotry—both Chinese and expatriate) within HKP, at the time. But such an assumption, while valid to a point, cannot be generalised across the board. In essence, subtle personal favouritism (Chinese as well as expatriate) did exist, institutional racism, perhaps did not exist as much.

Quite apart from personal favouritism and institutional racism, this research finds that HKP promotion system was getting better at regularising promotion on meritorious grounds. More pointedly, even if there was an 'unspoken' rule in favour of the expatriates, it is tempered by the newly adopted HKP promotion SOP: all candidates must compete on meritorious grounds, before the final decision was made. When all things were considered, race factor was given extra consideration, but not in the manner (arbitrary) or to the extent (dominating) people believed it existed, after WWII. In essence, there are ample evidence showing social familiarity turning into professional bias, for example, Chinese did not speak Queen's English. Invidious discrimination, for example, Chinese should not be promoted, no matter what, rarely happened.

Still in all, for expatriates and Chinese alike, the 1950s rule-bounded promotion system was much fairer than the old one, where promotion was based on personal bias of the superiors. The introduction of a more stringent and exacting promotion system is in line with other HKP developments, that is, legalisation.

Legalisation of HKP is needed because HK is fast moving to be an international city with a global community at its base. This calls for transparency, consistency, predictability and formality in negotiating differences between multinationals. The same applies to HKP, with an international work force—Chinese (Hakka, Shandong, Shanghainese and Cantonese), Indian, Sikh and expatriate (British, Africans), with different cliques ('horse stable') organised around senior officers as a mentor or protector ('tai lo') or factions based on ethnic affinity or philosophical bent. The most important point is, once HKP decided to localise, the expatriates want more assurance that they will not be discriminated against, in reverse by the Chinese.

> Back in August 2001, the Overseas Inspectors' Association (OIA) has already persuaded management to bring greater objectivity and wide dimensions into

> the promotion process. OIA also addressed that members continue to express grave concerns that over the apparent biases. Many feel that the time is right for the management to undertake a thorough reform of the promotion system.[31]

This is most evident with the all-pervasive disciplinary code.[32] The concern with reverse discrimination by Chinese officials is real and personally felt by 'Bob', an expatriate chief inspector of police (CIP) after 1997:

> [O]f course promotion is still done on merit and through the promotion boards ...a dead man's shoes as one goes the next one goes up and it is done on merit and not necessarily on seniority ...the only thing now is that unless you are a Chinese national or of Chinese origin you cannot become a commissioner or deputy commissioner—the top three posts you cannot hold .... [however] I am sure it does help if you do know the Chairman of the Board or something like that who is familiar with your work. The Chairman of this Board is a gentleman that I have known for a number of years [gives a Western sounding name] voted through the ranks and I have worked with him ...it must be an advantage.[33]

The fact that the promotion process is getting more objective and fairer goes to show that the HKP is interested in providing an equal opportunity for its officers, with the objective of integrating the expatriate and Chinese officers under one roof, ever so slowly, for progressive as well as self-serving reasons.[34]

Fifth: *The open embrace of mixed marriages*

The best way to bridge the gap between East and West is through mixed marriages. Before the war, colonial policy disallowed inter-racial marriage; a professional death sentence. Socially, mixed marriage is a taboo, and very much looked down upon.

Although there was no law against miscegenation, inter-racial marriages were rare and with people engaging in paying a heavy price, personally, professionally and socially, for example, Europeans who violated the colonial etiquette jeopardised their career and risk ostracism. Vicky Lee reported:

> Kenneth Andrew, who came to Hong Kong in 1912 to join the Royal Hong Kong Police, recalls the first document he has to sign was a promise not to marry a Chinese female. Governor Henry May (1912–1919) boasted that under his administration no European police officers or prison officers were married to Chinese or Eurasians.[35]

In 1947, HKP Police Commissioner John Pennefather-Evans has an occasion to comment on mixed marriages of Europeans and Chinese and was very much against them based on two reasons, one moral and the other practical. Morally, Europeans should not marry Chinese women because they have 'low standards of morality' typical of lower-class Chinese women.

Practically, it was considered 'difficult to have mixed marriage partners living in European quarters without causing dissatisfaction'.[36]

To demonstrate HKP conviction in and commitment to breaking down the racial gap, it publicised marriages between expatriate officers and local maids, just like any other marriages. For example, in 1951 HKPM, there were five police marriage announcements; two of these were mixed marriages:

> On 2nd May 1951, Sub-Inspector A. B. Harteam was married to Miss Chan Po Lin, at the Registry, Supreme Court.
> On 14th May 1951, at St. John's Cathedral, Sub-Inspector J. H. Eees was married to Miss J. B. E. Halkon.
> On 19th May 1951, at St. John's Cathedral, Sub-Inspector M. Todd married Miss E. A. McNaughton.
> On 24th May 1951, at the Supreme Court Registry, Sub-Inspector David Lam married Miss Lo Chun Chu.
> On 15th June 1951, Sub-Inspector A. J. Deveraux married Miss Lily Chin Ping Lain.
> On 20th July 1951, Sub-Inspector G. P. Tebb was married to Miss Cheung Wai Lin at the Supreme Court Registry.[37]

Again, in December of 1951, HKPM reported another five pairs of police weddings, of which one was a mixed marriage.[38]

Sixth: *Promoting cross-cultural awareness*

One of the many ways to localise is to increase language competency and cultural awareness, thus bridging the gap between the European colonialists and HK–Chinese subjects. It has been observed that Europeans know of their Chinese subjects by their amah from poor families and wife as bar girls,[39] and Chinese know of their colonial masters by their pompous ceremony and drunken mannerism.[40] 'Cultural assimilation in a true sense is impossible and meaningless if education is not spread'. [41] This is taken to heart by HKP reformers with the publication of HKPM, such that effective cross-cultural exchanges in knowledge and sentimentality can be achieved by exposing the Europeans to Chinese culture—custom and festivities,[42] arts and crafts and vice versa.

To this end, HKP has published multiple articles on Chinese and European culture, such as 'Collecting Chinese Porcelain for the Beginner' in the first issue of HKPM.[43] The author painstakingly but masterfully explained the history, categories, and assessment of porcelains, with dos and don'ts and pictures to match. It ended with a light-hearted reminder: 'For the humble beginner sheer beauty should be his objective; the significance of antiquity, technique, and history will have to be left to scholars and archaeologists, but a successful collector does require to exercise keen discernment and immense patience'.[44] The same can be said of cross-cultural appreciation and assimilation, of all things Chinese.

Beyond seeking Chinese knowledge in high places, British colonists see the need to bridge the gap through language training, first with the cultivation of Chinese elites and then with preparing of English administrators.[45]

Reflection

There is little question that the British colonialists were trying to 'reach out' to the Chinese or 'customise' their policy to fit with the HK conditions. Contemporary scholars can debate on the intent (discrimination vs. penetration), impact (subjugation vs. empowerment) and merit (benevolence vs. dictatorial) of such efforts, but few could argue that there were many efforts to close the cultural gaps between the two races since the 1950s. This observation, and others to follow, allows us to assert with confidence that in the decolonisation of HK, localisation is not an afterthought. The follies of those who argue against the existence of localisation in all its multifaceted manifestations, from strategic collaboration to cultural assimilation, suffer from too much ideological blinder and too little sociological imagination.[46] Such denials ignore the utility of localisation in ameliorating the discriminatory impact of the colonial rule, for both the ruler and the ruled.

II: Legalisation

As used here, 'legalisation' means the empowerment and regulation of HKP by law for operational, accountability[47] and legitimacy reasons.[48] When British colonial officials first arrived in HK, they promised HK residents the rule of law. In 1848, Chief Justice John Hulme, told the Chinese:

> As inhabitants of a British Colony, one of the greatest privileges you enjoy is the right to a due and even-handed administration of the English laws, and I am satisfied that the more you become acquainted with these Laws, the more you will learn to love and respect them.[49] The promise was not kept, until late in the game, and well into the 20th Century.[50]

In spite of a sincere motive and honourable intent, the sanctity of British rule of law never materialised in HK, for many reasons.

The Chinese have very little understanding of and identification with the British legal system. Otherwise, Chinese have limited access to the legal process, structurally and economically. From the British perspective, the Chinese did not appreciate, respect, honour or otherwise were not deterred by the majesty of British law. The cultural superiority of British and social inferiority of the Chinese was taken for granted. As a result, the rule of law, characterised by independency of the judiciary and accountability of police, applied to the Chinese in name only, if at all.[51] Some argued that the discriminatory law and abusive legal process only applied to the indigenous Chinese, structurally poor and displaced marginal (migrants, sojourns), who lived and worked within foreign communities (European hongs, Victory Peak), for the protection of the Europeans. Otherwise, indirect rule and collaborative administration helped in ameliorating much of the adverse impact of such legal practices, for example, District Watch Force and self-help social control in NT.[52]

It is the argument in this chapter that 'rule of law can provide an effective instrument of legitimacy for strong executive governments'.[53] Thus observed, post-WWII ushers in a new chapter for HKP with the promulgation of police laws (such as Police Force Ordinance) that are more detailed and specific, thereby making HKP more accountable to the rule of law.

The legalisation of HKP after WWII serves to kill three birds in one stone: First, the HKP is living up to the ideal of British colonial administration; with law and justice as the moral foundation of its rule. Second, HKP is acting more responsively and responsibly to the stricture of the law in protecting and serving the people, even handedly. Third, rapid HK economical and social development after the war requires a predictable rule of the law regime, in settling disputes and enforcing expectations.[54]

The HKP formally turns a new page with the introduction of the Police Force Bill, on 28 July 1948: 'An Ordinance to amend and consolidate the law relating to the Police Force'. The bill promised to do away with the old Police Force Ordinance, 1932, before WWII, and replaced it with 'a new Ordinance which has been drafted in the light of experience gained not only in this Colony but in other Colonies'. This means an ordinance better suited to 'changed conditions' in HK and was in line with 'best practice' of other colonies abroad (most of them independent by now).[55] For HK, it recognises the importance of the role of HKP in facing up to the myriads of social and criminal challenges after WWII, from influx of refugees to prevalence of Triads, as it rebuilds step by step, from building—refurbishing police stations to crafting jurisdictions to streamlining recruitment and training. The most pressing challenge is how to realise the objectives of 'decolonisation', for example, democratisation in politics, localisation in staffing and liberalisation in policy, with an ever-watchful eye towards providing for internal security[56] and heightened sensitivity towards external threat across the border from China. As observed by David Anderson and David Killingray, such law, order, security and stability issues are foremost in the minds of retreating colonialists, now serving as progressive reformers:

> But whatever the social or political circumstances of particular territories, the colonial police forces played a major and increasing role in the attempts to maintain the authority of the colonial state and in upholding law and order during the process of disengaging and transferring power to the new rulers.[57]

As intimated, the challenges with the transfer of power and recalibration of control are many, pressing and uncharted in HK. These included the taming/containment of incipient nationalism, defusing of communal conflicts, strengthening of political surveillance, changing of policing philosophy and militarisation of police.

In the context of HK, the biggest difficulties are with an orderly transfer of power without losing control, threatening order and disturbing stability. The British Colonial Office and HK government took a number of legislative steps to achieve local administrative autonomy without lessening of political control. They found it with absorption of politics with administration, for example, consultation with elites, localisation of policing, for example, Chinese controlling CID, and legitimacy through performance, for example, keeping criminals at bay.

If we were to look at other colonies undergoing decolonisation, we will find the following prominent issues that need to be addressed:[58]

1. If police should change, what should they be changed into?
2. How fast and far should the process of change take place?
3. Which part of colonial policing should change and why certain aspects of it should stay?
4. In what way should the police change: in terms of philosophy, mission, organisation, role, function, style and culture?
5. Should the police change their leadership?
6. Should the police change their organisational structure?
7. Should the police change their composition?
8. Should the police be expanded?[59]
9. Should the police be militarised?
10. Should policing be localised?
11. Should policing be civilianised?
12. Should police be communalised?
13. How should the police be held accountable?
14. Should police morph into the British mode and style, in leadership, organisation and style?
15. What is the role of Home office versus HK government in the transitional period?

Such and other reform issues can be addressed with the development of policing laws in HK. As used here, policing laws means laws that define, organise, empower and regulate HKP, such as Police Force Ordinance, and policing in HK, such as District Watch Ordinance. The research focusses on how such laws have changed over time from 1844 to 1950. The comparative study of the legal regime tells us how efforts to reform and transform HKP and policing in HK took shape. The observation and proposition is that 1950 is the beginning of a new phase in HKP reform and a different type of policing in HK. As for periodisation, I have limited the research to laws of HK in the 1850s (beginning with 1844, the year the HKP was established by law) and the 1950s (beginning with 1946, the year civil government returned after WWII). Here, we see a growing maturation and sophistication in how HKP is organised and regulated. The year 1840s is the beginning of HK rule, and the 1950s witnessed the total and comprehensive rebuilding of HK society, and with it the HKP. We also observed a change of mindset towards governance, in general, and policing in particular.

The resource used for this research includes Historical Laws of Hong Kong Online (1 May 2012) which covers 1890, 1901, 1912, 1923, 1937, 1950, 1964[60] and associated Hong Kong Legislative Council archived materials bearing on the legislative process of relevant laws.

HKP started to re-organise itself with the promulgation of an all new Police Force Ordinance (Cap. 232) on 20 August 1948 (41 of 1948, amended 50 of 1949 and 20 of 1950) (hereinafter PFO). While building upon the skeleton of the old, it is not a revision or extension, but a totally new formulation.

This PFO is distinguishable from the past versions in the following ways:

First, it is a comprehensive and stand-alone police law. The PFO is organised into seven parts (60 articles) namely: 'Preliminary' (Part I); 'Constitution of Police Force' (Part II); 'Disciple and Duties' (Part III); 'Welfare Fund' (Part IV); 'Unclaimed Property and Interstate Estates' (Part V); 'Procedure' (Part VI) and 'Miscellaneous Provisions' (Part VII); provides for the structure, organisation and operations of the HKP. Some of the most important provisions are the following:

Coverage of PFO: Article 2 makes clear that the PFO applies to all persons who work for the HKP, without exceptions, from the Commissioner to the Police Cadet to the Inspector to the clerical staff. However, PFO, HKP regulations and Civil Service Regulations provide for a different treatment of different rank and staff, for example, police constables can be fired summarily by the Commissioner but Inspectors are entitled to due process hearing. As it worked out, PFO disciplinary proceeding is disposed in favour of commander informal dispositions, avoiding the disciplinary code all together, for example, extra duty watch on Marine launch. That is to observe that PFO has the effect of personalising discipline, instead of formalising it, especially with minor transgression.

Command and control: Article 4 details the chain of command at the top level. The Commission of Police is charged with the 'supreme direction and administration' of the HKP only to be subjected to 'orders and control of the Governor'. This makes clear that the HKP is an executive arm of HK government, reporting only to the Governor, with the Commissioner holding the position at his pleasure. In practice, the Governor has to consult the Foreign Secretary and Colonial Office before acting. Throughout the years, there is only one Commissioner of Police, Edward Tyler (19 December 1966–21 July 1967), who was suspected of having been replayed because of his refusal to take order from the acting Governor Michael Gass to suppress the riots on 21 July 1967, against his better professional judgement in the field.[61]

Limitations of power: Article 6 provides that police should exercise powers and perform duties according to colonial law, police regulations and supervisors' orders.

This Article and Oath of Office (Schedule) makes clear that HKP officers are legal agents serving the interest of the HK colonial government. It also makes sure that prospective police officers do not operate outside the law, which only protects the interests of the colonial rule, and not in serving the Chinese people's interests, rights and welfare. In the past, this kind of provision has proven difficult for Chinese officers to follow. For much of the time, the Chinese harboured an attitude of nationalism and anti-foreignism. This is especially the case for economic migrants from China or indigenous residents living in NT, who find British rule alien, abusive, distasteful, and above all else contrary to local custom or Chinese culture. After the war, things change for the better because many migrants from China are political refugees seeking the protection from the British government. For them, they are more willing to go along in order to get along, building a new life in a foreign land. Still, there are many cases of obeying the police code in the breach.

Sociologically speaking, the promulgation of more comprehensive and stringent police laws has the effect of making HKP and policing in HK more colonial than Chinese. This is so because colonial law in the book reflects and reinforces British philosophy, values and interests, while policing on the street gives expression to Chinese tradition, culture and custom. The legalisation of HKP, while intending on restricting the unlimited and unguided HKP abuse of power against Chinese rights, also has the unintended effect of limiting the judicious, paternalistic and benevolent exercise of police discretion in accommodation of Chinese ways and means. The former is disciplining the Chinese (police), 'making Chinese more like British' kind of colonisation process. The latter is empowering the Chinese (police), 'making British more like Chinese' kind of decolonisation project. More problematically, legalisation of policing, if successful, centralises police decision making in the hands of the British colonial officials in search of legal justice, at the expense of decentralising police decision making in the hands of the Chinese police and public in actualising street justice. This is a reversal of fortune for the decolonisation of policing in HK.

No unionisation: Article 7 makes it 'unlawful for a police officer to be a member of any trade union'. Given a long history of industrial strikes and civil unrests in HK in the years by, HKP is fearful of any industrial action on the part of the HKP. In addressing concerns of police workers, HKP has conducted active consultation and sought systematic feedback through the chain of command or staff associations. It otherwise tries to prevent industrial actions by increasing salary and benefits, such as housing for family and education for kids, after the war.

Article 9 specifies the 'duties of the police force'. These include

1. Preserving the peace[62]
2. Prevention and detection of crime[63]
3. Protecting life and property[64]
4. Apprehending people[65]
5. Public order policing[66]
6. Traffic control and obstruction clearance[67]
7. Keeping public order[68]
8. Assisting in carrying out any revenue, excise, sanitary, conservancy, quarantine, immigration and alien registration waters[69]
9. Preservation order and enforcing law in colonial waters[70]
10. Executing legal papers, for example, summons, and process, for example, commitments[71]
11. Conducting prosecution[72]
12. Safeguarding lost and found property[73]
13. Dealing with stray animals[74]
14. Protecting life and property in fire[75]
15. Protecting public property[76]
16. Attending courts[77]
17. Escorting prisoners[78]
18. Executing other legal duties[79]

Article 9 defines the role and functions of the HKP in specific terms. It makes clear that, as envisioned, HKP after the war is less a law-and-order, crime-fighting agency, than a protection and service organisation, from protecting life at fires 9 (o) to impounding stray animals 9 (m) to directing traffic 9 (f) to processing lost and found 9 (l). This makes HKP a social service agency par excellence than a prototypical colonial policing agency, more in tune with the development of civil society than fortifying the imperial empire.

Ultimately, the charge of the HKP is in maintaining order and keeping peace as enabled and restricted by law—HKP is to perform 'such other duties as may by law be imposed on a police officer' 9 (r) and do so by 'lawful measures' (9). For example, the specific delineation of police duties allows citizens and police officers[80] alike to hold the HKP to account, challenging its (non) exercise of duties as required.

Part II 'Constitution of Police Force' of the PFO set forth the details of how the HKP is to be established.

Article 10 provides that the overall constitution of the HKP is to be decided upon by the Governor and Legislative Council. But the 'payment and maintenance' of the same is to be charged to the general revenue by the Legislative Council (Article 11).

In terms of appointment, promotion and termination, the process is different between Gazetted police officers[81] as provided in Article 12—appointed, interdicted, suspended or dismissed in accordance with Regulations for His Majesty's Colonial Service and General Orders of HK government, Inspectors provided in Article 13(1)—appointed and promoted by the Commissioner, dismissed in accordance with Article 14(2).

The HKP legalisation reform movement has its intended effect, belatedly. One of the ways to ascertain the impact of legalisation of HKP is to document the utilisation of law to settle police disputes, from abuse of power to illegal performance of duties. This can be achieved by analysing HK court cases in the 1950s and 1960s. A search of electronic Hong Kong Legal Information Institute, with 'All Case Law Databases' (from 1947 to the present) with the key word 'police' uncovered 18,260 cases, of which only two cases[82] preceded 1960. Police-related case started to grow after the 1960s. For the current research, I will be looking at three cases before 1970, to inform us how people of HK use law to vindicate their claims against the HKP.

Shum Hung vs. Tam Fun (1961) HKCA 1; CACC338/1961 (11 November 1961)[83]

A Magistrate, Mr Sanguinetti,[84] decided the first successful legal complaint against an HKP officer acting in the line of duty by a Chinese hawker on 30 June 1961.

The case was denied on appeal, and reversed, by the Supreme Court of Hong Kong on 11 November 1961. The case involved the arrest of a street hawker by a Police Corporal with 15 years of service, in KLN.

The Police Corporal, Shum Hung, was convicted by a Magistrate, Mr Sanguinetti, on two counts of 'causing willful and malicious damage to property and using abusive language in a public place' towards a female hawker, Tam Fun. Shum was ordered by the court to pay $15 fine and $1 as compensation for the first charge. Otherwise, the Corporal was discharged without a criminal record upon posting a bond of $250 for 3 months, against personal recognisance. Shum appealed on facts and findings of his conviction.

The facts of the case are rather simple and straightforward. But the process, findings and decision making in the case is very instructive on the issue of accessibility of the law to the street people. One of the major lessons offered is that the majesty of colonial law in the book rarely catches up with the administration of street justice by the HKP.

On 23 June 1961, hawker Tam Fun, pleaded guilty to hawking without a licence. She was discharged with a caution. At the hearing, Tam complained of police misconduct during her arrest. The Magistrate asked whether she wanted to file a formal complaint, solicitously. Tam welcomed the invitation. Upon listening to the complaint and satisfied that it is 'bona fides', the Magistrate issued summonses to the police officer for a hearing on 30 June 1961.

At the hearing, it was learned that hawker Tam Fun was hawking at No.72 Fa Yuen Street outside Victoria Theatre, KLN at mid-day, 22 June 1961. The Police Corporal Shum Hung was on hawker clearance duty. According to Tam Fun, during the arrest, Corporal Shum Hung kicked over one of her kerosene tins and broke two eating bowls. He then further picked up two drinking-water tins and poured it on the ground. When she tried to reason with him, he swore at her. There was no corroborating witness, and she told the court: 'In a place like Hong Kong, it is very difficult to get witnesses. Even if one hears or sees one does not come forward to be a witness'.

The Corporal Shum Hung denied the charges. Instead, he claimed that the complainant refused to leave and was arrested. His testimony was corroborated by that of P.C.1485. Two hawkers at the scene were also called as witnesses. One testified to Corporal Shum Hung shouting to them. They observed that the complainant yelled back and was arrested. He did not see the 'appellant kick over the complainant's tins, hear him abuse her, or assault or attempt to assault her'. The second witness gave a similar testimony. Several police officers testified to not hearing any complaint filed by the complainant.

The Magistrate believed the uncorroborated evidence of the female complainant and found it against Corporal Shum Hung.

The grounds for appeal were two: (1) The Magistrate took over the prosecution and became a party to the case. This raises issues of objectivity of the hearing officer and conflict of interest; (2) The Magistrate's conduct at trial, that is, aggressive interrogation of defence witnesses, showed that he was biased. According to the defence counsel, Mr Bodilly, 'the Magistrate had allowed his sympathy to run away with him and that he was determined to convict the appellant'.

The Senior Puisne Judge for Corporal Shum Hung set aside the convictions with the return of fine and compensation:

> On a consideration of the whole record I am impelled to the conclusion that in his anxiety to ensure that justice was done to this illiterate female hawker, unrepresented by counsel, he unconsciously identified himself with her case and that that fact clouded his judgment in a proper assessment of the evidence given before him and of the very considerable weight of that evidence, much of which was based upon the testimony of two independent witnesses, which negatived the truth of the complainant's testimony or at least, ought to have

> raised a very real doubt as to whether her allegation had been proved with that certainty required to substantiate a conviction in a criminal charge.[85]

Analysis

This case—in process and disposition—tells many stories.

The first story is about the working relationship between street people (hawkers, taxi drivers, hookers and homeless people) and the police. Police manage the street, while street people live (homeless), work (pimp) and play (juveniles) on it. Since street people need to survive on the street, they have to do go along with the street cop, in order to get along. People on the street have to learn when to shut up (being discrete about what they observe and know) and put out (paying cops, with information or money). Thus, it is most unlikely for street people to complain about or bear witness against the street cops. In order to survive the street, the street people learn not to cross the street cop. This has few things to do with the sanctity of the colonial law, that is, being discriminatory against locals, or the culture of the Chinese people, for example, being deferential to the authority. In as much as most of the people in HK at the time are in one way or another street people, from homeless poor, to listless refugees, to street workers and to godown labourers, they are at the mercy of the street police, who is their protector and squeezer. In post-war HK, the relationship between the street people and police is best understood by street identity, relationship and culture, than colonial narrative and repertoire. Revisiting the facts of the case, it is highly unlikely that hawker Tam Fun, as a streetwise person, unless being desperate, would yell at a Police Corporal (a supervising authority) on the street in front of fellow officers, and expect to get away with it. In essence, Tam was not arrested for hawking per se but for not reenacting the role of a compliant street worker, knowing her place on the street. She was also punished for 'reasoning' with or 'yelling at' the officer which is one step beyond the lack of compliance into defiance of authority.

This is a teaching moment for all. Tam has to be taught a lesson of respect to the authority, a venerable Chinese custom and habit. Other hawkers have to learn to obey and respect police authority, that is, pack up and leave before the police arrive, and never talk back to the police. Police constables around also need to learn how disrespect to the HKP is properly dealt with forcefully, and resolutely.

The second story is about accessibility to the law. The common refrain about inaccessibility of (British) colonial law to the (Chinese) people is that it is opaque (language, culture) and discriminatory (racial, financial). The antidote is to make law more transparent, objective and free. The case shows that British language and legal cultural barriers and racial and financial obstacles aside, the British legal system is inaccessible to the Chinese for a different reason. Chinese prefer to resolve disputes differently in style and mode. In terms of process, Chinese prefer negotiation, mediation and reconciliation, over litigation, trial and confrontation. In terms of outcome, Chinese prefer substantive justice over procedural justice, moral justice over legal justice, particularise justice over universal justice and personal justice than impersonal justice. In this case, substantive justice requires that an abusive police officer be punished. Police Corporal should not be able to avoid punishment because the Magistrate has erred pursued justice for the hawker in seeking the truth. Moral justice means that the police officer should be condemned, less so for being abusive, and more so because he is not acting the role of a 'fu wu guan' in being solicitous to the welfare of the hawker. The same moral compass should apply to the appellate Senior Puisne Judge who appears to care more about the nicety of the law, than the perversity of the police, in person and conduct. Particularised justice means that the plight and harm of the crime victim more so than the overall legality of the adjudicative process or the universal integrity of judicial norm should be made the focus of justice quest. Finally, personal justice means that all those who seek justice must identify and empathise with the victim to the point of hating the criminal, as did the Magistrate. The reason being, in Chinese thinking, the more one hates crimes, the more one loves justice. The difference between British versus Chinese over justice is not best expressed than a first female Magistrate in HK Marjorie Chiu in 1992:[86]

> Righteousness to the Chinese is somewhat different from Justice in the Western sense. It includes a sense of morality, apart from adherence to the letter of the law. The concept is personified by the legendary Pau Kung (包公), who for centuries has served as a model of wisdom and righteousness for the Chinese, similar to King Solomon in the West.

The third story is about the relationship between decolonisation of policing by law and re-colonisation by the judge through justice. This story line requires us to look at judicial philosophy, as personified by Magistrate, Mr Sanguinetti.[87] From what we can gather from the news account[88] and personal interview,[89] Mr Sanguinetti is an honourable, compassionate and principle-minded jurist, who strongly believes in the power of (British) law in creating a more just (HK) society. This is the reason why Mr Sanguinetti reached out and invited the hawker—Tam to file a complaint against the HKP Corporal, against all odds, in a colonial judicial system known for protecting the police and consolidating colonial rule in dispensing with British justice. This qualified him as a good British judge and an effective HK reformer, vindicating my earlier assertion that not all colonial officials are equally oppressive and abusing (Chapter 3: 'Assessing Colonial Policing'). Indeed, there are many Mr Sanguinetti-like HKP officers who can be trusted to do right by the Chinese, as in this case.

However, if we were to reflect on this and other cases, where colonial judicial officials come to the rescue of colonized locals, humbly or lowly, we soon realise that the willingness and zealousness of the Magistrate Sanguinetti to do justice is not without condition and agenda, the chief of which are a chivalrous attitude and paternalistic mentality, institutional and personal. These self-centred sentiments and others regarding disposition, if unchecked, promise to subvert, or at least contaminate, the lofty ideal of the helper, consciously and unconsciously.

In the eyes of Magistrate Sanguinetti, the hawker needs help because she is not able to do so as a powerless Chinese under colonial rule. Magistrate Sanguinetti is willing and obligated to help because he is a British national, colonial judge, dispensing universal justice, according to British jurisprudential principles. In the ultimate analysis, it is the British, not Chinese, law and justice principles that inform upon who is deserving of legal help, that is, powerless Chinese in the hands of the oppressive British colonial HKP, and who, what and how is legal help to be provided, that is, a British 'blind' judge, delivering 'universal' justice, in an 'independent' process and 'even-handed' way.

Once people in HK—the hawker in this case, accept British law and justice, they accept *ipso facto* the legitimacy and merit of British (colonial) rule as superior than Chinese (indigenous) rule. British colonial government in HK has now domesticated another willing alien 'subject' on account of social contract of the West, in the guise of benevolence returned or 'reciprocity of kindness' (*bao en* 报恩) from the East.[90]

The colonisation process has completed, and will move on to other domestication projects; call this a battle of 'hearts and mind', one person at a time.

Before we move on, a caveat is in order, lest we fall into the same kind of unreflective mental trap, with blinders to our mind,[91] (essentialism as overdrawn criticism) that all 'colonial' agencies, process and practice are *ipso facto*, inevitably and equally, repressive and abusive of locals, thereby making colonialism objectionable, without exception, and affording no redemption. Colonial law is subject to individual colonial officer discretionary application as fitting with the individualised treatment of colonised subjects and local conditions.

Re Yeung Lam (1968) HKCFI 40; HCMP135/1968 (18 September 1968) [92]

The greatest impact of PFO is perhaps in making the HKP a legal organisation, that is, a police agency that is empowered by and limited with law. Failing that, its policies, procedures, decisions and actions are subject to challenge. In this regard, the biggest beneficiary of PFO is not the external clients, that is, the public, but the internal ones, that is, the police officers.

With PFO in place and over time, entrenched traditional norm, for example, loyalty, and incestuous para-military ethos, for example, discipline, will be tested against the law. If successful, HKP will be governed by legal rule, that is, legalism, and civil culture, that is, professionalism. For example, before PFO, no HKP members dare to or can afford to challenge the HKP leadership, high or low. Beginning with 1960, if not earlier, first with the management cadres and then the frontline officers, HKP increasingly looks towards the PFO to secure its interests and vent its dissatisfaction.

Coming 20 years after PFO, the court case below, titled 'IN THE MATTER of An Application by YEUNG LAM for leave to apply for An Order of Certiorari and An Order of Mandamus etc.' best exemplified the emerging trend of a police officer testing the limits of HKP discipline with law. Once PFO legal challenges starts, it cannot be stopped.

In this case, Staff Sergeant Yeung Law (SS Yeung) petitioned the court for an Order of Mandamus calling into question the justification and legality of the Commissioner's decision to demote him from SS to PC.

SS Yeung joined the HKP in 1946. He was promoted to Sergeant in 1954 and further to SS in 1965. He served with Traffic Office, KLN from May 1966 to January 1968 before being transferred to the Central Police Station, Hong Kong Island on 20th of January 1968.

On the 11th of April 1968, SS Yeung was interviewed by the SOP, Personnel Department. SS Yeung was told that there was a corruption racket at Traffic Office, KLN while he served. Since then, many officers have been dismissed (PC) or reduced in ranks (Sergeant). SS Yeung was faulted for not being forthcoming with corruption information at Traffic Office, KLN at the time. As a result, the Commissioner of Police was considering reducing him to the rank of PC for not reporting corruption. He was asked to resign, or be treated to a reduction in rank from SS to PC as an alternative. SS Yeung was promised an audience with the Commissioner of Police over his resign–demotion treatment. However, on 16 April 1968, SS Yeung was asked by the Superintendent in charge of personnel whether he wanted to resign or be demoted. He chose to stay in the HKP as a PC. On the same day, he was issued with a Memo dated 16 April 1968 signed by the Deputy Commissioner of Police Mr Wright-Nooth per Commissioner of Police informing him that he was demoted effectively from 18 April 1968 based on Section 14(4) of the Police Force Ordinance. Since then and on 10 May 1968, Deputy Commissioner of Police Mr Wright-Nooth has issued another Memo signed by him reverting SS Yeung's rank, in lieu of the Police Commissioner's Memo on 16 April 1968.

SS Yeung retained Mr Mayne as his solicitor who accepted that the Commissioner of Police has absolute power to revert in rank all junior police officers under 14(4) of the Police Force Ordinance. However, the Commissioner of Police decision to revert must be compatible with natural justice. Particularly, SS Yeung challenged the order of the Commissioner dated the 10th May 1968 on two grounds: first, the order-reverting rank of SS Yeung was ultra vires; second, the order was based on a judicial or quasi-judicial inquiry into complaints on SS Yeung's wrong doing, thus its conduct and process must comport with the rule of law and natural justice.

The court—three Justices—agreed in principle that it is against natural justice for the Commissioner of Police to summarily revert the rank of SS Yeung from SS to PC, after 22 years of meritorious service to the HKP, without giving him a hearing. Still, Section 14(4) of PFO provides that an N.C.O. 'may be reverted in rank by the Commissioner' unconditionally, and the court conceded. As to the denial of natural justice claim, the Justices were of the opinion that natural justice principles did not apply to Section 14(4), since it is an administrative and not a judicial act.

In support of its decision, the court reasoned:

> It is to be observed that Section 14(4) provides that an N.C.O. 'may be reverted in rank by the Commissioner'. Section 31—the punishment section—provides for 'reduction in rank or class'. In various other sections, both in the Ordinance and in the Police (Discipline) Regulations, the expressions 'reversion' and 'reduction' in rank are indiscriminately used. Mr. Mayne addressed an interesting argument to this Court that the expression 'revert in rank' used in Section 14(4) only enabled the Commissioner to revert the Applicant to the rank he had held immediately preceding his substantive appointment as a staff-sergeant, and not to reduce him in rank to that of a police constable. In view of the conclusion I have reached that Section 14(4) is a purely administrative power conferred upon the Commissioner of Police, and that whatever misuse or abuse of that power there may, or may not, have been made, this Court has no jurisdiction to interfere, either by way of certiorari or mandamus, it becomes unnecessary, and perhaps undesirable, to consider and determine Mr. Mayne's argument as to the proper meaning to be attributed to the words 'revert in rank'.

Analysis

In the annals of HKP and in a Chinese society, this case is an anomaly at the time for one reason: in the HKP, subordinates never dared to challenge the superiors, particularly those at the very top, and Gazetted officers. This case changed it all.

HKP officers rarely if ever challenged their superiors for cultural, organisational and personal reasons.

First, *culturally*, Chinese society and HK culture taught the young one to be obedient to the authority and deferential to the boss. A disobedient person violates all cultural rules and hierarchy boundary. It makes you a poorly disciplined (by parents), socialised (by others) and adjusted (by self) person. It reflects poorly on your family and self.

Challenging the authority and being disrespectful to the boss is frowned upon, even if the authority and boss are wrong. But the authority–boss has a right to do so because of their elevated position. In essence, they have earned their keep to make a mistake, or more likely do whatever they like, and still be right.

Second, *organisationally*, HKP was a very well trained and disciplined force, with a strong tradition and in-grained culture of doing things in the HKP way. Recruits were trained at PTS and socialised by peers not to question the authority. 'Yes sir, no sir, no excuse sir' was the mantra, attitude and routine. Obedience and respect was also rewarded. Asking a question and talking back was punished. The obedience to order and respect for senior culture while having its genesis with Chinese culture, are reinforced by a British-run para-military colonial police force that demanded complete and absolute obedience and loyalty. The Chinese promoted it on moral grounds; obedience, loyalty and respect of authority are good unto themselves. The British justified it on functional grounds; obedience, loyalty and respect make control of colonial subjects easier. This is especially the case with British not trusting Chinese integrity and loyalty. It was accepted by the British that Chinese were resentful and defiant of colonial rule. Well running of the HKP organisation and effective ordering of Chinese society required a disciplined police force.

Third, *personally*, in Chinese society and HK culture of the time, people are taught to face up to adversity in life in a stoic manner. Accepting reality—obstacles, setbacks—as presented—tolerance in the short term, working around it in the medium term and over and above it in the long term—is drummed into the head of many young people and workers, as the way to survive and thrive.

Moreover, obedience and respect in the HKP, while intrinsic to the Chinese culture and fundamental to British rule, was also endearing to the HKP Chinese force members, for two reasons. It validated their self-worth, as senior members of an organisation. They have learned to obey, loyal and respectful, as young recruits and now they expected the same from the younger generation, as a 'reciprocate' duty. The justification being: 'I have earned my keep. Now it is your turn'. This mentality still survives in today's HKP. For example:

Historically, HKP has a highly effective system of breaking young police officers into the HKP making them well-adjusted members of the HKP community. This breaking-in process entailed introducing the new officers to the ins and outs of policing—skills, attitude and relationship, such that now they could become an insider.

'Elder learned brother "(大師兄)"',[93] is usually an experienced member of the HKP. They are well-regarded seniors for their years of service and insights into how things are being done, past, present, situation, local and more importantly, here and now. His personal relationship with the young officers resembles that of the elder brother towards younger ones. If they are older in age, the relationship is one of father and son. His role is one of a mentor, advisor and friend. The functional relationship is that of 'master vs. apprentice'.[94] Of late (2001), there were discussions in some quarters inside HKP whether senior 大師兄 still deserves respect and demands obedience:[95]

> Ten odd years ago, I got out of PTS. The original TPC was on leave, another PC46XXX took me to walk the beat during night shift. After we took the midnight snack, signed in duty roster, we closed the gate. After a while, we have tea at the police station. No sooner, he said he was still hungry and asked me to buy food at 7-11. He said: '4XXXXX師兄 wanted to eat chicken'. I said: 'OK. You want to eat. You buy it yourself'. After this, the fucker told everybody that I was new and acted like VIP. Have no idea of big and small, etc. After that I was being treated badly by his friends and colleagues. After a long, long time, after and all his buddies went to camp before I can have a new life. I never forget this.[96]

The blog entry tells us a lot about 大師兄 system, and in turn its current status and historical evolution. 大師兄 was once a functional and powerful system to train the young officers, and now, it is falling into disuse because time has changed.

In the 2000s, HKP and with a newer generation of officers, that is, the post-1980s kids, police learned more from a book than from the street, that formal training counted more than informal socialising, technical know-how was treated as more useful than implicit knowledge. It also tells us that obedience and respect is slowly, but surely, disappearing, to be replaced by following of rule and responding to law.

This discussion on Chinese cultural attitude towards obedience to authority and seniority and HKP traditional discipline on the respect for ranks immediately raises the issue of legal rights of officers versus cultural norms of China and organisational tradition of HKP. Legal rights empower as they liberate the HKP officers from the straight jacket of Chinese culture and HKP tradition. This is exactly what SS Yeung did, suing in court to protect his own well-being at the expense of viability of Chinese culture and sustainability of HKP discipline structure. We need not judge the merits of the policy debate, but we need to understand the impact of legislation on culture and tradition. Coming to the impact on police administration, legalisation of HKP spelled the demise of personalised command (effective telling) and control (instinctive obedient), since the 1840s, and ushered in the institutionalised rule-bound management (rational reasoning) style of administration after the 1950s. The change in command and control to the management and administrative style of organising—leading the HKP is not of its own making. In the end, HKP changed its style of management because HK society has changed from an inward-looking society to an outward-looking one. (See Chapter 8: 'Context and Framework'). If that is true, HKP ways of doing things—here legalisation, is not running up against old Chinese culture, but it is in fact trying to catch up with HK emerging culture, a step behind.

Wong Ching Yuen vs. the Queen (1900) HKCA 13; CACC278/1972 (Judgement Date Unknown)[97]

This is an appeal against conviction on a charge of robbery. On 2 February 1972, a student was robbed of his watch at J/O Tin Kwong Road and Sheung Shing Street at 4.00 p.m. Two police officers came along and upon complaint arrested the defendant for robbery (now appellant). The appellant claimed that he was first arrested at KLN City smoking heroine. One of the officers offered him $600 to rob and admit guilt, after.

The Puisne Judge P.F.X. Leonard found the case of paid for robbery, if true, to be incredulous. Still, he sided with the Magistrate because he could not make out what happened in the lower court due to lack of clear statements of facts and findings. 'I have, however, had to read the entire record in detail to discover what that story was. The learned magistrate's statement of findings was terse to the point of being useless to me.'

Analysis

The case is telling in a number of ways, about police, law and justice administration in HK.

First to observe is that, at the time—the 1950s–1970s, HKP officers, particularly CID, was known to have created crime in order to get credit for arresting criminals. While the Judge P.F.X. Leonard found it hard to believe, it actually happened, as a way to manage police case load and enhance performance. For example, HKP–CID Sergeants have been known to pay criminals arrested for robbery to confess to other robberies to clean up the cold cases. The common inducement is 'Now that you have committed one robbery, admitting to others would not make you less a criminal. If you admit to more, the CID promises you a light sentence, and your family will get monthly payment from us'.

Second, there was a tendency for the frontline Magistrates[98] to turn a blind eye to police malpractices so as not to disrupt the justice process[99] in handling increased criminality after the war.[100] Otherwise, the Magistrates considered the Chinese lower class not deserving of British justice.

III: Modernisation

The Age of Enlightenment in the eighteenth century gave rise to the Idea of Progress, becoming an ideology by the end of the nineteenth century associating itself with industrialisation and colonialism.[101]

Idea of Progress is the idea of doing away with old thinking and doing, replacing them with something new, that is, modernisation. Modernisation is the process of using technology and science to improve the efficient and effective social organisation.

The sociologist Robert Nisbet offers five 'crucial premises' of Idea of Progress:

1. Value of the past,
2. Nobility of Western civilisation,
3. Worth of economic/technological growth,
4. Faith in reason and scientific/scholarly knowledge obtained through reason,
5. Intrinsic importance and worth of life on earth.[102]

In the 1950s, for the first time, HKP sought modernisation through science and technology, for example, crime scene investigation (CSI). It also includes other new and progressive ways of doing things, for example, integrating females into HKP and changing the treatment of juveniles. Modernisation ushered in a new era of policing in HK.

A: Modernisation through science

In September 1951, the inaugurate issue of HKPM leads with an article on 'Ballistics and the Police'.[103] The article begins with the following observation as an introduction:

> A new departure in crime detection in Hong Kong introduced during the past few months has aroused considerable interest amongst members of the Police Force and the general public. This has to do with the Identification of Firearms, or 'Ballistics', which is described as the science of firearms and their projectiles.[104]

The article then proceeds to explain in detail the science of ballistics and how and why it might be of use in helping with investigation and solving crime problems. The article ends appropriately with this invitation: 'It is hoped that this article will enable those interested to follow the intricacies of this kind of work, and also gain some understanding of a complex problem from new angles every day'.

The reason and purpose of publishing such a piece is made abundantly clear with an added separate note: 'Take notes on the spot; a note is worth a cartload of recollection' (R. Emerson). In essence, experiential lessons remembered and rote learning should be replaced by scientific knowledge on paper. HKP is coming of age and a learning organisation with instructions of science and technology leading the way.

The scientific investigation of crime, involved more than ballistics. The next article in the series is one on forensic science, namely: 'The Police Laboratory'.[105] The article informed the readers on the nature, functions, organisation and utility of a police laboratory, in historical and comparative terms.[106] For example, at the end of the article, the author, a servicing HKP officer informed his readers the importance of knowing about police laboratory:

> It is only by knowing the kind of results a Police Laboratory can submit that a police officer would be able to know intelligently what kind of material, how much of it, in what manner he should remove it, pack, and handle it for sending to a Police Laboratory for examination. In serious cases, an expert from a Police Laboratory can always be requested to visit the scene of the crime to give suggestions and assist in any way possible in obtaining evidence and clues. Thus a Police Laboratory, or sometimes it may be called, a Forensic Science Laboratory, is a valuable asset to modern law enforcement and public tranquility, and when properly used, provides yet another important tool to modern police work in the interest of peace and justice for the members of the community.[107]

B: Modernisation through CSI

With the 1950s HKP reform, modernisation means using knowledge, resourcefulness, discipline and CSI to solve crime. This is clearly demonstrated with the successful solving of a murder case in 1952. The case was prominently published in HKPM to show how 'modern' investigation is conducted and can achieve. The Commissioner of Police introduced the case, thus: 'This was an outstanding case in which the Police effort reached a level unexcelled in my thirty years Police experience'.[108] Scientific criminal investigation is also going to be a trend of the future.

The facts of the case are complicated. The investigation is complex and tedious. A farmer discovered a Chinese female lying in a ditch dead at Fung Shu Au near Ta Shek Wu Village, on Route 2, NT, at 20.15 h on 23rd December 1952. There was no eyewitness. The HKP CID was able to solve the case through systematic and scientific investigation process. Preliminary investigation showed that:

1. The decease was not a local.
2. She was killed and transported there.
3. The murderer was suspected to be a military person or Indian.

The HKP mounted one of the largest manhunt at the time in search of the murder culprits. All available resources were deployed. No effort was spared.

> To carry out the enquiries, all available inspectorate officers were moved into the New Territories to check on the movements of military and civilian personnel stationed at the Army camps in the vicinity. This alone entailed the checking of ten to fifteen thousand persons. Chinese detectives were set to checking all villages and cycle shops in an effort to establish a history of the deceased and a complete laboratory staff was moved to Shek Kong where they set up Headquarters. The Military authorities were requested to co-operate

> and they mustered all transport and log books, all personnel and kits and made all their civilian personnel available for questioning.[109]

The HKP was able to crack the case and successfully prosecuted the three soldiers for murder after a lot of hard work and careful analysis, with the help of CSI.

First, the CID was able to identify the deceased and soldiers involved through tracking down key witnesses (taxi cyclist who picked up the deceased,[110] cycle shop who rented cycles to soldiers[111]). Then the police surgeon was able to ascertain the time of death (by estimating the lag time between coma and death)[112] and instrumentality of murder with forensic science and a pair of handcuffs used by the military.[113] CID then reconstructs the crime scene and process, to pinpoint the time of death (having soldiers riding a bike to the crime scene to ascertain the bike time).[114] Then the CID interrogated the suspected soldiers on their whereabouts at the time of murder, to find out conflicts and discrepancies (three suspects gave different stories of their travel at night/time of murder).[115]

This sort of methodical and scientific investigation could not have happened as little as 30 years ago, as recounted by a retired CIP detective, Mr Reynolds who served between 1910 and 1932:

> I have often been asked since my return, what I think of the Police of to-day compared with those of my day. Making comparisons are generally in my opinion a waste of time and mean nothing...When you have a highly efficient police force as of today, supplied with all the latest scientific and medical aides and experts on various subjects to help and who deal in hundreds, what comparison can be made with the police force of thirty years ago or more who only dealt in tens and where every dollar spent on improvements was queried.... The bringing in of witnesses and evidence was one of the biggest bugbears, as without immediate contact with the witnesses and without transport to bring them in, days often elapsed before they were forthcoming...

C: Modernisation with communication technology

Communication is important for policing.[116] Without communication devices and electronic linkages by phone, fax and in a teleprinter, police work suffers; from lack of information to make a decision to the inability to call for support when needed.[117]

> Police Boxes, which were introduced thirty years ago, were then claimed to be the solution to many Police communication problems. However, the advancement in two-way speaking radio has provided even better means of communication and has ensured that regular contact can be maintained with the rural policeman and the mobile patrol, as this is not always possible by telephone.... It is hard to realise in this modern age, that our present means

> of communication in the form of radio networks, teleprinters and—more recently—television, which are now taken for granted, have been developed only in recent years. One wonders how a police force could have functioned effectively without them. One also wonders what would have been the reaction twenty years ago to the idea to directing traffic, on important occasions, by the use of radio from helicopters.[118]

Communication technology also has transformational impact. Overall, it allows for better management and deployment of police resources, for example, just-in-time policing (JIT). Administratively, communication technology helps with keeping track of people/events, in providing for command and control, facilitation and coordination. Operationally, communication makes possible the integration of diverse functions and availability of resources, in the service of a common goal. Finally, organisationally, communication allows joining of disparate parts of an organisation into a whole.

Then (the 1950s) as of now (the 2010s), advancement in communication technology prominently figured in the modernisation of HKP. Beyond the need for Special Police operations in HK at the time, such as crisis management in fire and typhoon, the improvement to communication is driven by advances in communication technology worldwide. A Communication Branch in HKP was long overdue in achieving strategic control at the border, JIT response to citizens, 999 calls or as required by emergencies.

In 1952, HKP formally established its Communication Branch, allowing it to communicate interactively, in real time, with police stations, Marine launches and mobile units in the field.[119] This is a far cry from earlier days when stations have to work independently. Beat officers could only be reported and checked by Lock Box. Marine launches communicated with Morse code.

As described in a 1952 HKPM article on the history of 'Community Branch' establishment:

> Before 1946, HKP has no communication network between police stations, nor 999 call system, nor radio for patrol cars. There were Morse code between Marine boat and Tsim Sha Tsui Police Station…In 1946, two S.C.R. 610 radio sets were obtained and field tests were carried out. These tests proved successful and, subsequently, in 1948 all stations including those in the New Territories and on the Border were equipped with radio. Radio was also fitted to four patrol cars and a 999 emergency call system was instituted. The harbour and cruising launches were also equipped with radio and were able to maintain contact with Radio Control and their Marine Headquarters. … At this time, the Communications Branch was known as the Radio Section and was a part of the Traffic Division. The control room was situated in an upper room at Central Police Station … the Radio Section became known as the Police Communications Branch …facilitate the rapid distribution of crime information, a teleprinter network was installed with a transmitter at control and receivers at all the Hong Kong and Kowloon Stations. A receiver was also

installed at Tai Po Police Station in the New Territories, making the total of twenty two receivers in all...to bring Divisional Stations into a Command radio network and this was achieved with the aid of the S.C.R. 528.10 channel push button sets...However, in 1952 these sets were replaced by more modern radio sets obtained from the Amalgamated Wireless (Australasia) Company. These were installed in all Stations, with additional sets fitted to the Divisional Land Rover cars and Marine Harbour launches...a new Police Headquarters was under construction and in 1954, the Communications Branch moved once again, this time to Police Headquarters which will be our permanent home... 999 room ... has five emergency telephone lines and also direct lines to the Fire Brigade and to the Hong Kong Telephone Company. On the wall are alarms for the principal banks and for various Government buildings.[120]

D: Modernisation through methodical traffic accident investigation (TAI)

TAI is an important step to reconstruct what, how and why an accident happened. It answers the question of who is at fault, if any, to posit liability and support prosecution. Such an investigation requires many skills, one of which is the precise reconstruction scene of accident, through measurement.

In December 1951, the HKPM published an article: 'The Constable with a Tape Measure' instructing HKP traffic officers on how a traffic accident scene should be processed, through precise measurement and detailed documentation to be used later in judicial proceedings or insurance claims process. For this purpose, the two parts of the article were written up as an instruction manual and investigative guideline.

E: Modernisation through professional training

Modernisation requires keeping up with best practices in the field, worldwide. Overseas training helps to improve performance by exposing the officers to the latest development in the field.

In 1950, HKP Inspectors were trained alongside with U.K. police officers and other colonial officers around the world, in all aspects of policing, from CID (Scotland Yard) to UB (Metropolitan Police Training School). On 25 September 1950, Sub-Inspectors Hung Hung Heung and Fong Yik Fai were sent to the United Kingdom for 6 months of 'Colonial Officers Course' with participants from all over the world, including '2 Superintendents from Cyprus, 2 Superintendents from Trinidad, 2 Inspectors from Barbados, 2 Inspectors from Tripolitania, 2 Superintendents from Malaya, 5 Inspectors from Kenya, 1 Inspector from Grenada, 1 Superintendent from Mauritius, and 1 Sergeant Major from British Honduras'.

The pair of Inspectors were housed in the Metropolitan Police Training School with 300 recruits undergoing a 14-week basic training course. 'The recruits had no connection with Colonial class in training, but good relationship was established in daily and social life, i.e. at dancing parties, concerts, boxing matches, etc.' (p. 5). The course was a general policing training course covering CID, 'beat duties, traffic accidents, protection of children and young persons, prevention of cruelty to animals and the use of pocket-books' with visits to police districts, Army, Parliament, Old Bailey and police.

What is the impact of such kinds of overseas training on the HKP police officers? The pair finished the course with this observation:

> It not only increased one's knowledge in police work, but also broadened one's outlook in many other ways. ...Equally praiseworthy are the policemen in London who are extremely polite and helpful to the public, and always appear to be 'steady and sure' under all circumstances.... The women police are a remarkable feature of the Police Forces in United Kingdom. Their smartness and ability compare favourably with the male police officers. (p.7)

The pair was particularly impressed with CP. They were attached to Metropolitan Police District for 3 days and saw what it is like to be a police officer in the United Kingdom:

> I saw information requested by the public, such as 'Where could I get some ice in the City?' 'What is the time of the flood tide today?', 'My baby has no milk and refuses to stop crying. I cannot find any milk in the City, could the Police help?' and 'What is the result of the football match yesterday?' etc. All these questions were appropriately answered. This shows the confidence the public have in the police, and that the police are really public servants.

This attests to the fact that the Colonial Office that organised the training is not interested in making HKP more colonial, that is, militant and imperialistic, per se. Rather, it is to make HKP more professional along British civil policing line.[121] In fact, except for a brief visit to 'School of Chemical Warfare at Salisbury for instruction in the use of Tear Smoke', the whole course was meant to impress upon the young Chinese officers what best practices in modern and professional policing are all about.

To be complete, HKP officers were also sent to other specialised 'militant' training courses with SB, bomb squads, and army command schools. We do not know the relative distribution of training resources and availability of opportunities in various overseas assignments. Still, the suggestion that U.K. Colonial Office or HKP was only interested in turning out colonial police officers of the menacing kind rather than service types should be questioned, if not put to rest.

The same kind of observation can be made about institutionalisation of colonial–military policing in HK, by dint of para-military formation, PTU training and internal security deployments. This crude institutionalisation thesis based on conventional wisdom (myths), personal bias and incomplete research, underestimated the impact and over-determined the influence of some salient HKP features over others, for example, civil policing functions versus public order policing role.

Why is PTU training being singled out and elevated as an evidence of institutionalised colonial policing, while overseas LMP orientation being underplayed as a compelling evidence of institutionalisation of civil policing? The simple fact is that HKP has a lot of traditions (Officers Mess Night vs. CID Guandi worship) and practices (public order exercise vs. anti-smuggling campaigns), and still more experiences (28 February 1918 Happy Valley Racecourse fire, 25 December 1953 Shek Kip Mei fire) and memories (1937 Great Hong Kong Typhoon, 1962 Typhoon Wanda). By accentuating the militaristic over social aspects of HKP role, capacity and duties, the proponents of such a thesis have failed to recognise that HKP has many traditions to spare and still more diverse experiences to share. Such traditions and experiences, individually and in their totality, mean many things to many people; a truly kaleidoscope experience. They cannot be bottled up in a small jar, called colonial policing, without mislabelling its content.

F: Modernisation through university education

In 1950, the HKP sought HKU help in developing courses for HKP officers.

University education is not the same as PTS training; the first opens minds and the later imparts skills. University education also allows the police to look at policing from a different and many perspectives, as informed by multiple academic disciplines. Successful university education will change how HKP sees the world.

> An extramural studies course was held at the Hong Kong University in December, 1959. The course, under the heading of social and psychological background of crime, was of two weeks duration and twenty four police officers, both Gazetted Officers and Inspectors, and three Probation Officers attended.[122]

The course lectures included: The conflict between Chinese attitude and British law; problems of youth and psychological aspects of crime–crowd behaviour.

G: Modernisation by way of new thinking on juvenile crime

The change in thinking over juvenile crime and punishment in HK speaks to two concerns, that is, change of HKP role as an enforcer of law ('bogey man' syndrome) to a helper of children, and reform of juveniles through social services, instead of punishment.

Two articles in the HKPM addressed the above two issues. The issue of police role visa via the juvenile was addressed by Inspector J. D. Adams of West Riding of Yorkshire Constabulary article on 'Police and Youth' in 1956.[123] The issue of rehabilitation for youth was dealt with by Miss Dorothy

Lee, Assistant Director (Youth Welfare) Social Welfare Department, on 'Youth Welfare in Hong Kong' in 1959.[124]

Differences of focus aside, both 'street-level' bureaucrats sought to change the image and role of HKP from one of law enforcement to one of social service. As Inspector J. D. Adams proposed, with British policing in mind:

> The role of policeman has gradually changed from that of the 'bogey man' to that of the 'children's friend', functions which may roughly be described on the one hand as repression and on the other as persuasion. These two roles are diametrically opposed. Both have their strength and their weakness and it is as well to pay some little attention to these at the outset.[125]...The power to deal with children and young persons who are deemed to be in need of care or protection offers to the police a practical means of saving children from cruelty and from drifting into a life of misery or dishonesty.[126]

As to why the all-mighty police officer should be the one to save the child from a lifetime of misery, Inspector J. D. Adams advanced three reasons:

First, the police have the obligation and power to help the children to develop in the right direction. 'The power to deal with children and young persons who are deemed to be in need of care or protection offers to the police a practical means of saving children from cruelty and from drifting into a life of misery or dishonesty'.[127] In essence, with greater power (capacity) comes greater responsibility.[128]

Second, police have the power to make a difference, particularly when the children look upon the police as a role model, or superhero. In this way, police pass on positive and negative lessons, influencing the children for life, in many ways. In treating the children in a rough and tumble manner, the children will do the same to others, besides pushing them into a life of crime and delinquency, through labelling and rebellion. On the other hand, if children are treated in a fair, understanding and humane way, they will grow up to be model citizens.

> Young people are naturally hero-worshippers and the policeman, armed with the full panoply of the law, is often regarded as something of a hero by the local children. 'Unwittingly (but not unconsciously) the child evaluates the adult and is impressed either favorably or unfavorably. The success of a plan of discipline—depends upon the adult personality.' So it is important, when dealing with youth, that the police should always conduct themselves in the best traditions of the service.[129]

Third, the police works on the street and with the children. He knows the conditions of the home and history of the children, besides the circumstances and situation of the child's offending. In some instances, he might know even more than the parents. The police also have made available to him the legal power and social resources to help the child to go straight. The police are the best persons to intervene because he has more information to analyse, he has more experience to judge, he has more resources to deploy, he has more legal power to act and he is more available to sanction or monitor the child's conduct. In essence, the police are the ideal persons to steer the child from misconduct to upright personhood, and do so in the most efficient and effective manner:

> It is the police officer who, in the first place, sees the home conditions and the background of the youthful offender and who is in a position to assess fairly accurately the probable cause of his behaviour. Much useful work can be done by the individual police officer in helping to reclaim youths who have made mistakes.[130]

Inspector J. D. Adams's article is a sobering piece of advice. It earned him the Queen's Police Gold Medal Essay Competition (1955). It is also in line with what the HKP was thinking in seeking to reformulate the vision and mission of HKP.

To date and for all too long, HK has taken a stern law and order approach to policing, with little tolerance for deviance, adult or children, notwithstanding mitigating circumstances or compassionate consideration. For example, on 29 March 1882, a 14-year-old Chinese boy was arrested and convicted for pickpocketing. The Magistrate sentenced him to 1 year of imprisonment with hard labour, 12 strokes with rattan and the last week in solitary confinement.[131] In sentencing him, the Supreme Court Judge, Honorary F. Snowden justified the sentence as follows:

> [H]e had already been found guilty of picking pockets, and that it was quite clear that he was under the control of a set of men, who sent him to commit the crimes, and then obstructed any attempts that were made to arrest him…he was not over sixteen years of age else his punishment would have been heavier; but as it was, a severe sentence would have to be imposed in order to teach him to reform his ways.[132]

The above is instructive on the philosophy, policy and application of punishment at the time in the following ways:

First, this is a minor offence, that is, pickpocket.

Second, the offender is a fairly young person, that is, 14 years old.

Third, this is case with extenuating circumstances, namely, the young offender was pressed into criminality and later obstruction of justice because as the court opined 'he was under the control of a set of men'. In essence, the young offender acted under duress and otherwise not being able to resist control of others (the circumstances of which have not been fully disclosed).

Fourth, we were told that in another case 'the punishments given to the children took account of their age and circumstances, their offence, the values of what they had stolen…and their means'.[133]

Fifth, the young offender was not spared for severe punishment 'in order to teach him to reform his ways'.

The above attitude towards Chinese offenders, including children, resulted as much from the ignorance of Chinese culture as it is from indulgence in the British way. Ignorance bleeds contempt, of all Chinese conducts. Indulgence elevates the sense of righteousness, of all British ideas. When righteous meets ignorance, the heavy arm of the law falls heavily and blindly. Classical jurisprudence stands ready to spare any residual doubt on legitimacy of punishment, that is, if you do the crime, you do the time, and provides an antidote to sporadic guilt on the nature, extent and degree of punishment, that is, harsh punishment deters. Neither arbitrariness nor cruelty of punishment deserves a second look. Such is the certainty and certitude of colonial thinking on crime and punishment; basically a re-enactment of British sense of orderliness—if the skin is not white, he is damned, and if the person is yellow, he can do nothing right. Chinese must be punished for not being British (like). This is colonial criminological thinking at its best:

> The dichotomy of European and Other have seen non-European peoples relegated to inferior status—their culture and laws subservient to the universal claims of western civilisation. …The racialized construction of offenders not only defines the offender in terms of race, it also constructs the *apparent* non-racialized vision of the normal, respectable and responsible citizen…When we see criminology as a racialized discourse, as a system of meanings that produce knowledge and practice about crime and race, we can begin to understand how the discipline controls both the mode of representation and their meaning. The discourse controls the process through which we understand crime and deviance (e.g., the legitimation of statistical representations of, for example, juvenile crime and its causes) and the symbolic meanings we attach to those representations (for example, black youth as crime-prone). In the case of racialized criminality we see simultaneously the offender as racial and the racialized individual as criminal. As Fanon once remarked, 'not only must the black man be black; he must be black in relation to the white man' …[134]

In 1959, Miss Dorothy Lee, Assistant Director (Youth Welfare) Social Welfare Department, published an article in HKPM appealing to the HKP to adopt a new way of thinking and dealing with Chinese juveniles, as victims of society than instigators of crime. The article made the case that youth crimes in HK, from hawkering to gang fights, were not a serious crime problem, but a pressing social issue. The purpose is to change the police officers' perception of and reaction to youth offenders of all kinds, that is, treating youth offenders as victims more so than villains. Given the children's life circumstance and attending social conditions they were found in, the police should reach out to them, to help them with assistance from other government agencies (Social Welfare) or NGO, such as Boy and Girls Club. The approach to be taken is one of task force, a collaborative approach, proactively seeking to prevent the crime than react to situations of crime. There is also a bit of pre-emptive problem-solving policing there. This requires the police to reach out and work with communities, not as a legal agent, but as a social reformer.

> We have often heard of complaints about many children who roam the streets begging, fighting and gambling. These street children are unloved, and so they become good haters; they are hungry and badly clothed and so they steal; they are starved of the normal experiences of a child and so they seek self-glorification in gangs and self importance in contempt for authority. They can only be helped by discovering what their needs are and meeting those needs with love, friendship, under-standing and good example.[135]... Some of us who were here soon after the Liberation may recall the young toughs who roamed the streets of the central district and posed quite a problem for the Police. However, some of them were collected to form the first post war club in this district. Through the club, these lads learnt something of give and take, of what is good and what is not so good. Gradually these children were able to influence some of the other street gangs and today several of them are earning a respectable living in restaurants, as office boys, shop fokis, etc. Some return to the club regularly to give a helping hand, to give to the younger ones some of the things they have learnt in the club.[136]

Director Lee's paper came as the HK government tried to adopt legislation to reform the juvenile justice system. For example, in 1959, the Attorney General moved for the first reading of Industrial and Reformatory Schools (Amendment) Bill (1959).[137] The existing Industrial and Reformatory Schools Ordinance (Chapter 225), reflecting British practice, is to imprison young people only as a last resort, and only over 14 years of age.[138] The normal practice is to place the youthful offender under the supervision of the Probation Officer or parents. The bill allows the court to sentence the offender to be detained for a minimum period of 2 years but not longer than 5 years or until such time as he reaches the age of 18, whichever is the earliest. The Director of Social Welfare may take the offender back before the court, which will be empowered, after inquiry, to send him to a training centre or even to prison.

In time, the HKP would be playing a critical role in the diversion of troubled youth from the formal criminal justice system, thereby giving them a second chance. Under the Police Superintendent's Discretion scheme (1 January 1963),[139] the HKP has the discretion of prosecuting a juvenile or placing him under supervision of the HKP:[140]

a. 'When a juvenile under the age of 18 has committed an offence, and there is sufficient evidence to charge him/her with the offence, Police may take prosecution action like a normal case and take the juvenile offender to the Juvenile Court'.

b. 'Another way to deal with the case is for a Police Officer of the rank of Superintendent or above to exercise discretion to issue a caution to the juvenile offender, instead of taking him/her to the Juvenile Court. The juvenile offender to whom the caution was administered must be put under Police's supervision for a period of two years or until he/she reaches the age of 18, whichever is earlier'.[141]

The eligibility of Police Superintendent's Discretion scheme has changed over time, for example, only apply to kids 4–14 years in 1963 but extended to 16 in 1967 and 17 in 1978, and topping off at 18 in 1993.

The HK 'child saver' movement above championed by Director Lee and Inspector Adams tells a larger story of political, social and economic transformation of HK, with HKP very much in the play.[142]

Drawing upon science of all kinds—political (legitimacy), social (Darwinism) and medical (pathology), Lee and Adams move us beyond colonial criminological tenets to a post-colonial corrections narrative, calling for helping juveniles (rehabilitation and re-integration) than condemning them (punishing and labelling).

As to the importance of science in penal measures, HKP pointed to the professor of criminology in Mainz University, A. Mergen, who promoted positive criminology and with it evidence-based policing in understanding crime and punishment.[143] In his article, 'Values in Penal Theory and Scientific Criminology', published in International Criminal Police Review, Number 103, December 1956 and abstracted in HKPM, he made the following pronouncements, which captured the HKP thinking of the time:

> The present crisis in positive criminal law is due to trickery of a methodological order. There has been a mixing of these axiological systems, which, from the point of view of the theory of knowledge, are incompatible. All penal theories are useless, if they are not based on an exact knowledge of realities, as Hans Gross has already pointed out. This requirement cannot be fulfilled unless the method of investigation is suited to the biosocial object, and this object, of course, is the offender, who is in a socialsphere, which is essential to him, but which he does not accept without conflict and to which he should adapt himself. Because, of this, the delinquent is situated, not in the axiological sphere of the normative and abstract rules of law, but on the ontological plane (which is accessible to the natural sciences) of socio-biological interdependence, which cannot be violated and which necessarily provokes the reaction of self-defence.[144]

In one small step, and with the help of science, the likes of Professor Mergen, Director Lee and Inspector Adams, have decolonised the juvenile justice system, in a huge way.

The decolonisation of juvenile justice administration is achieved in three ways. (1) It has straightly delimited the scope and severely limited the reach of the British rule, exercised through the instrumentality (police) or intermediaries of the state (NGO—reform school), that is, for social control purpose, a juvenile is no longer a jural but a social subject. (2) It has weakened the nature and changed the style of British power, that is, a juvenile is to be saved (rehabilitated), not wasted (punished). (3) It has returned the 'problem' child rightfully to the Chinese civil society, allowing it to determine the nature and remedy to address the child's 'problem',[145] with the help of Western science and British philosophy.

In this way, the HK social control agents—parental, social and legal—departing from Chinese cultural norms, influenced by British philosophy and guided by Western science, are being challenged to develop a different, hybrid approach, to tending (the heart), mending (the soul) and disciplining (the body) of the juvenile; commonly referred to in Chinese jurisprudence as the 'qing–li–fa' approach.[146]

This hybrid approach would likely involve considering such juvenile delinquencies as a failure to take individual responsibility (Confucius duty to others) and acting out of personal impulsivity (Hobbes—individual right), both of which require inculcation of the right attitude (Confucius—self-cultivation) and administering tough love discipline (Bentham—moral calculus), failing that a heavy dosage of familialism understanding and communal tolerance is required to save the child for another day. At all times, the family, community, society and government needs to take responsibility in creating a more moral and just world.

The change in scope and style of British rule and power is going to have an impact on the political control of British government, and future of colonial rule in HK.

From henceforth, juveniles are the ward of the Chinese civil society, to be studied by a social scientist, helped by the social agency, rehabilitated with help from medical profession and supervised by socialised police. While all of them work for or report to the colonial authority, they are otherwise independent professionals, moved not by colonial rules but scientific principles in trying to 'save' and not 'punish' the child. While it is true that 'child saving' movement has a net-widening tendency for juveniles, which just means more Chinese watching over Chinese, at the expense of the British rule.

For the Chinese, decolonisation by way of 'child movement' emboldens the young, who are full of 'zest' (a liberating exercise), and weakens the old, who are fond of the 'best' (a disciplining routine).[147] It registered an intergenerational, cross-cultural struggle between the East and West, on a dear-to-heart project, how to bring up our next generation. The struggle renews itself, even today.[148]

Eighth: *Modernisation through integration of Woman Police Constable/Officer (WPC or WPO)*

In the 1950s, females rarely work outside the home, except perhaps as labour hands and in sweat shops. In 1961, only 5.2% females worked in the production line, 3% as clerical workers and 8% were in administration. Those who worked outside home were pressed to do so for economic reasons.[149]

Formation

On 1 December 1949, the first Woman Police Sub-Inspector, Ms. Kimmy Koh (高建美)[150] (1949–1961) was appointed.[151] She was born in Borneo. Koh came to HK from Singapore to seek medical treatment (malaria) in 1947. She then joined HKP as a Sub-Inspector because 'Being active and outgoing, I wanted something challenging and so joined the Force instead of working as a civilian'.[152] In her 12 years of service, Koh served at Police Headquarters, Kowloon Regional Crime Headquarters and the Police Training School. Her major duties were clerical, for example, taking statements or acting as an interpreter, with occasional assignments to vice duties—prostitution, gambling and drugs, commonly referred to ask for 'moral duties'. During the time, Koh recommended the hiring of more WPCs in order to support frontline male HKP work, such as tending to lost and found children or in station administration.

Two years later in May 1951, the first training class of 10 WPCs was inducted. WPC then were numbers from 5001 to 5010. Of the 10, most of them served a short sting. The rest passed away, got married or resigned. 林靄思 (#5010— 'Sister Ten') served the longest. She was the first authorised gun-carrying female officer, for investigation (a murder case) needs.[154] Since then, she

Figure 9.1 First generation woman inspector. (Classic Kimmy looks back, *PoliceBeat*, Issue 699, 21 March to 3 April 2001. Kimmy Kok (left).)

Figure 9.2 Passing out parade of women police constable–1950s. (Kimmy control: Sub-Inspector Koh leads another batch of recruits passing out in the 50s. *OffBeat,* Issue 699, 21 March to 3 April 2001. http://www.police.gov.hk/offbeat/699/021_e.htm)

moved on to investigate many drugs and fraud cases. She also served in the Witness Protection Unit (WPU).[155]

Kimmy control: Sub-Inspector Koh leads another batch of recruits passing out in the 1950s.[156]

In 1956, Sub-Inspector Margaret Clarke, with 10 years of police experience in the United Kingdom joined HKP to help assess and improve the WPC programme:

> In January 1956, I arrived in Hong Kong to join the Women Police. Basically my task was to utilise my experience of 10 years as a woman officer in the UK, to help re-evaluate conditions of service, recruitment and training, and to co-ordinate the employment, supervision and welfare of women police.[157]

Leadership

By December of 1960, a short 10 years after the WPC was first inducted, the WPC corps are fully established as an integral part of HKP.[158] The final organisational touch was with the appointment of Mrs M. E. Lovell, as the Assistant SOP, December, 1960.[159] Mrs M. E. Lovell began her police service with St. Helens Borough Police Force in June 1949 as a beat officer, and later a detective, before she was seconded to Cyrus British Police Unit as a woman police inspector in May of 1957. She achieved Woman Assistant SOP in November of 1957.[160]

Training

There were 10 WPC recruits in the first training class in August 1951. The training lasted for 3 months. They were trained alongside male recruits at the PTS, fully integrated. They have to be familiar with the drill and musketeer, such as formation drill and firearm nomenclature, together with police routines, such as criminal law court procedure, general orders, police regulations, miscellaneous ordinances and statement taking.

In addition, WPC needs to be knowledgeable about a variety of social service resources and functions in the community, for example, the work of the Probation Officer or the work of the Hong Kong Society for the Protection of Children. They also need to know how to take care of women and children in need, such as community relief and social hygiene, women and girls' welfare and emergency childbirth.

To complement their classroom lectures, the WPCs visited with 'Lai Chi Kok Prison, Stanley Training Centre, The Home of the Good Shepherd (young prostitutes) and the Hong Kong Society for the Protection of Children nursery at Shaukiwan (where mothers are advised about feeding, and given food for undernourished infants)'.[161]

Role and Treatment

The first batch of 10 officers was all assigned to work in plainclothes in various police formations in KLN or Hong Kong Island. They undertook charge room duties, guarding and fingerprinting of women prisoners and assisting in the inquiries of women and juveniles.[162]

Female officers were first recruited as a necessary complement to an all-male HKP, in carrying out its role and mission, that is, administer (Report Room, clerical duties), protect (female and juvenile) and serve (social service). At first (the 1950s and 1960s), they were hired to do what the male officers could not do, for example, searching females, or unwilling to do, for example, traffic duties, or not good at doing, for example, consoling kids and mediating conflicts. Female qualities and maternal instincts define their police duties and confine their policing career. For example, without a side arm, they were less likely to be assigned CID duties and without PTU training, they were limited to office-support functions. Without CID and PTU training and experience, they were less likely to be promoted to a high command and control or important operational posts.

Later (the 1970s and 1980s), female police officers were fully integrated into HKP, including public order policing. They excelled at crowd control because crowds seemingly react to female officers in a less aggressive way. For example, in 1962, all 274 of the women police officers were deployed to handle illegal immigrants at the border. Finally, women police gained the same status with males in pay in 1970. They were allowed to shoot arms in 1973. They were allowed to join PTU in 1997. From then on, women police are treated equally in every respect.

Retirees' observations:[163]

HKP retirees are some of the best sources of grounded information for policing in the 1950s. The following are some of the more lasting impressions and penetrating insights into the WPC the retirees served with from recruitment, to training, to assignment and to role:

1. On stereotype: Before 1947, HKP has been an all-male profession. There were a few female staffers to do female jobs, for example, search female prisoners. In earlier times, HKP officers were called, fondly, as 「男子漢」 (Man of Man). They look down on women police officers (WPOs) as marginal, that is, 'non-regular, appendage' (「非正規的、附屬的」). They think that WPOs are not made for police work. They should be deployed as support staff and not during an emergency.[164]
2. On recruitment: In the 1950s, WPO was managed differently than with males, that is, separate command. The recruitment standards however were basically the same. Then HK did not accept women joining police, that is, 'good girls do not work as police 「好女唔當差」' much more so than males. 「好仔唔當差」 ('good boys do not work as police'). Thus, very few applied. In the 1960s, whenever there were recruitment activities at police stations, there would only be 40–50 applicants with four to five selected. This is because most girls have only primary education and do not know how to dictate 「讀默」, part of the qualification process.[165]
3. On training: During the 1950s and 1960s, WPOs were trained alongside with males because of its small number. This raised a number of problems, for example, WPO has to adjust to the male in marching, stepwise. WPO also picked up bad language and habits from male officers. At that time, WPOs were not armed, but have to be trained and certified. They only have to shoot three times.[166]
4. On assignment: After passing out of PTS, many WPOs signed up for Marine duties. But they soon quit because of the long hours and social isolation. A fair number applied to be traffic officers and was assigned to directing traffic. WPO-directing traffic has different hours then, 8–10 a.m., 2–4 p.m. and 6–8 p.m. No night shift.[167]
5. Terms and conditions of service: In the 1950s and 1960s, WPO entered HKU with a different set of terms and conditions. First, WPO was paid less than male officers. Before 1970, male officers were paid $220 and a WPO was paid $180, $40 short. Second, WPOs were entitled to a lump sum $3000 marriage dowry (嫁妝費), if she

married a civilian. Third, WPOs have no pension, because policing was not considered a career for them.

6. Role and function: WPOs were 'all-purpose officials' (「通天老倌」). WPO was an independent force. They served at the will of the male commander. As such, they were often discriminated, as well as protected. They would not be assigned dangerous duties. But they also would not be promoted. However, they were considered indispensable still, for police operations and administration. According to official documents, WPOs were supplemental staff. They were not intended to be frontline officers, only support staff. These included court duties, escorting prisoners, conducting searches, taking statements, logistic coordination, community education, public relations and crowd control. WPOs were 'all-purpose officers' helping HKP to complete its mission, for example, they would be assigned to take care of women functions. WPOs take statements in sex crime cases. WPOs attend to abandoned babies when found—pick up, get a birth certificate and work with social work organisations.

   WPOs were not assigned night duties. If they were so assigned, they did not go on patrol unless in the company of male officers. WPOs started to do patrol with the issuance of two-way beat radio in the 1970s.[168]

Frontline Observations

Every effort was made to properly orientate and integrate female officers into operational roles and duties. The following were two reports from the field, reported in HKPM:

From Central Police Station in 1952:

> For the first time in our history, we welcome two very smart, and attractive young Police-women. Their first assignment, a rather formidable one, is to learn the 'ins and outs' of the Charge Room, and in doing so, they have quite unconsciously caused quite a stir here, from the Sub-Divisional Inspector down.[169]

From Eastern Police Station 1952:

> We welcome our two young women police constables Nos. 5022 Chan Kwai Hing and 5023 Wu Chun; they do look a smart and capable pair of constables. The first day W.P.C. 5022 Chan Kwai Hang did patrol on No. 5 beat on Hennessy Road, we had a slight accident: it appears that a young blood driving his sleek roadster, ran into an 'inert object' and on being questioned, said that his attention was 'distracted' by the appearance of the Woman P.C. on the beat.[170]

From Academic Studies

There are very few academic studies on women policing in HK. For a long time, the only research output available were graduate papers from HKU.[171]

The earliest one is by Lai-sheung Ho, a HKP WPO, who investigated into the treatment of WPO in the HKP.[172] The latest to enter the field is A.H. Chan and Lawrence Ho's 'Women police officers in Hong Kong: Femininity and policing in a gendered organization' on gendered relationship with the HKP.[173]

Since Lai-sheung Ho's work is closest in time to this research (the 1950s) and it offered up personal views of HKP officers, it helps us to understand the impact of integrating female police with male police, in 1988; 40 years from the first appointment of women officers.

Ho was interested in finding out whether there was direct (formal or informal barriers in law, policy or programme) and indirect discrimination (disproportionate the impact of law policy or programme) of WPO in terms of recruitment, deployment, attitude and roles.[174] The study was based on four data sources: (1) Interview with HKP informants—10 females (including the author) and four male police officers. The interviews were conducted to ascertain HKP officers' personal experience with and opinion of treatment of WPO. (2) The author's personal experience as a WPO commander. (3) Official HKP documents on recruitment, deployment and promotion (1987–1988) of WPOs.[175]

The author found discrimination in the following ways:

First, Ho found the recruitment standards and training requirements to be discriminating, for example, the age of recruitment for WPC was 19–25 years old and for male police constable (MPC) it is 17.5–30 years old. Females must be single and males could be both. Both needed to be trained at PTS for 32 weeks away from home. This created hardship for female recruits who have to tend to a family (p. 37).

Second, in 1987, Ho found under representation of WPO in every rank: Gazetted 11 (2.6%), Inspector 284 (12.6%) and JPO 2004 (8.4%), for an overall of 2299 (8.8%) (p. 39).

Third, in terms of 'Objective selection criteria', the WPO range is smaller and lower. This resulted in selection out of a number of otherwise interested or eligible candidates (p. 39).

Fourth, in terms of 'Selection interview', WPOs were successful in 9/83 or 0.9% cases (with 611 applicants). This according to Ho was too low. But there was no comparable data, other than to argue that the decision was possibly based on male subjective criteria.

Fifth, in terms of deployment, Ho found that at the Inspector and Gazetted rank level, WPO deployment to UB versus CID was nearly the same: WPO: 1638 (78.4%) versus 507 (23.6%) and WPO: 205 (78%) versus 58 (22%) (Table 9.3). However, when it comes to JPO, WPOs were assigned to more UB duties: Male Police Officer (MPO): 14,887 (69.8%) versus 6744 (31.2%) and WPO: 1700 (84.8%) versus 304 (15.2%) (Table 9.4).[176]

Sixth, it was common knowledge within HKP that certain police departments and functions were off-limit to WPO: traffic, dog, firearm and scene of crime units. So much so that WPOs were advised not to apply to those

Table 9.3 HKP–WPC Establishment: 1949–1963

Year	W/SSP	SP/ ASP	CIP	IP/SIP	Station Sgt	Sgt	Clp	WPC
1949	—	—	—	—	—		—	—
1950	—	—	—	1	—		—	—
1951	—	—	—	1	—		—	10
1952	—	—	—	1	—		—	26
1953	—	—	—	2	—		6	48
1954	—	—	—	2	—		6	48
1955	—	—	—	3	—		6	48
1956	—	—	—	3	—		6	48
1957	—	—	—	4	—		10	63
1958	—	1	—	4	—		12	90
1959	—	1	—	4	—		16	123
1960	—	1	—	8	—		18	138
1961	—	1	—	8	—		22	160
1962	—	1	—	11 + (1)	—		31	242
1963	—	1	—	13 + (1)	—		34	284
1964	—	1	—	13 + (1)	—	#13	#34	285
1965	—	1	—	17 + (1)	—	16	39	354
1966	—	1	—	18 + (3)	—	16	39	353
1967	—	1	—	18 + (3)	—	16	39	353
1968	—	2	—	18 + (2)	—	16	39	353 + 20*
1969	—	2	—	18 + (2)	—	17	39	357
1970	—	2	—	18 + 5* + (2)	—	17	39	360 + 110*
1971	—	2	—	20 + 5*	—	56	—	380 + 160*
1972	1	2	4	23	—	92	—	569
1973	—	2	4	26	—	83	—	573
1974	—	3	3	45	—	52	—	637

Note: As of 1 April each year:

- Excluding 45 Sgts and 11 Cpls telephone posts which from 1964 onwards were shown separate though technologically, they maintained contact with WPC.
- Supplemental posts.

Table 9.4 Women Police Leaders—First in Rank: 1949–1995

The first Woman Sub-Inspector of Police Kimmy Koh 1 December 1949
The first Woman Senior Inspector of Police J Panter 21 June 1963
The first Chinese Woman Senior Inspector of Police Lui Che Ying, Lee O'lin 1 April 1967
The first Woman Assistant SOP Margaret Mary Patrick 1 April 1958
The first Woman SOP Marjorie Elsie Lovell 8 December 1963
The first Chinese Woman SOP Lui Che Ying 1 August 1971
The first Woman Senior SOP Marjorie Elsie Lovell 23 June 1971
The first Chinese Woman Senior SOP Wong Leung Kam Shan Felicia 1 October 1981
The first Woman Chief SOP A H Calderwood 14 May 1977
The first Chinese Woman Chief SOP Wong Leung Kam Shan Felicia 10 June 1987
The first Chinese Woman Assistant Commissioner of Police Wong Leung Kam Shan Felicia 21 January 1995

Source: Police then and now: Woman officers in important jobs. *OffBeat*, Issue 770 (March 3, 2004 to March 16, 2004). http://www.police.gov.hk/offbeat/770/eng/index.htm

departments. It was also understood that the 'mark of affinity' would attract only MPO and WPO officers to those departments, and WPO would not be discriminated by Sgt supervisors, on assignment or promotion.[177]

Seventh, when asked, three of the MPOs thought that WPOs would have a better chance of serving as CID due to their specific capacity to investigate specialised crime, for example, domestic sexual abuse. But to the author, this too was a form of discrimination.[178]

Eighth, when asked, 10 female informants confirmed that WPOs were always asked to do back-office administration work, such as routine police station duties.[179] In one case, a WPO was assigned a Special Duty Squad and ended up doing administrative work most of the time: 'Even I am now working in the Special Duty Squad, I find myself staying in the station over 90% of the time with the remaining 10% is the time for going out for dinner and tea. They just called me administrative WPC'.[180]

Ninth, as to why the WPOs were assigned indoor duties and in desk job, it is because the supervisor thought that street duties were not safe. The author, a WPO PSU commander explained that the decision to exclude WPO for outdoor duties was a spontaneous one. This is because street duties were more interested. In this regard, commanders like to play it safe, that is, they did not want to explain to the superior when WPO got into trouble or sustained injury while on the beat.

Tenth, as to beat patrol, the supervisor would like to keep WPC off the beat, as much as possible. If need be, WPCs would be kept close and closely monitored, so as to avoid less risky and less busy beats.[181] Some of the WPCs were afflicted. WPCs wanted beat duties but they were also afraid of getting hurt. WPOs were risk adverse.[182]

Eleventh, as to beat assignment, it is a common practice to put a WPO on beat with two other MPOs to keep the female safe.[183]

Twelfth, as to routine duties,[184] WPOs were always assigned to female-related jobs: escort female prisoners, court duties, interviewing women and juveniles and petty crime. WPOs were also asked to handle 'traditional women duties', that is, juvenile, sex crimes and vice duties.[185]

Thirteenth, WPOs got fewer promotions because of lack of command, control and supervision skills, with little male officers' experience.[186]

Issues

One thing is for sure, when first introduced, WPOs have to earn their keeps as a separate but equal member of the HKP, professionally (competency) and personally (sociability), once they have worn out their welcome as a novelty. There were issues of sexual stereotype and favouritism, office romance and politics, family jealousy and infidelity, professional competence and liabilities, would be sure to come, and go, in time.[187]

The biggest issue is perhaps objections from MPO about WPO joining HKP, as Susan Martin observed from other parts of the world:

> The incursion of women into traditionally 'male' occupations has been opposed, resisted, and undermined wherever it has occurred. In few other occupations, however, has their entry been more vigorously fought on legal, organizational, informal, and interpersonal levels than in policing.[188]

HKP MPO objected to WPO working mostly because of strong male versus female cultural role in traditional Chinese society. There are three objections, namely: the role of male versus female; nature of femininity versus masculinity and nature of police versus other work.

First: *Role of male versus female*. In traditional Chinese society, the male masters outside the family (男主外) as a bread winner (economic pillar) and the female lords over the inside of the home (女主内), as a care taker. It is considered appropriate for females to stay at home and take care of the husband, kids and household, making it a perfect home. For females to go out to work is a violation of entrenched social role and neglect of traditional family duties.

Second: *Nature of femininity versus masculinity.* Males should act like a male, that is, being masculine. Females should behave like a female, that is, being feminine. Police is a muscular job, that is, strenuous, risky and corrupting work. Female has no place in HKP, lest it makes the female less feminine and undesirable for males and an inappropriate role model for female and children.

Third: *Nature of police work.* Policing work is physically demanding, emotionally stressful, morally corrupting and personally dangerous. Policing is a high pressure and distressing vocation.

In the end, the three objections boiled down to one: Females are not acting like female, in a male-dominated world that is HK, and HKP at that. According to Carole Jones, male domination of sexual politics is dominating in HK, perpetuated by the economic and professional elites:

> In this way, Chinese culture ... became a fixed, static, and monolithic set of values emphasizing an unchanging hierarchical and patriarchal order. This imperial assimilation of Chinese culture has had long-term effects, especially for women ... In courts of law, this [imperial] interpretation was supplied by 'China experts,' usually missionaries ... Their view of Chinese women was filtered through their own patriarchal world-view, aided and abetted by their male informants from the Chinese community, typically elite Chinese men. Women then were doubly colonized, first by their colonial masters and secondly by male interpretations of their role in society.[189]

The male-disparaging views of the female in the HKP still survive today, though much attenuated. For example, some MPOs think that WPCs were assigned more enjoyable administrative work indoor. MPOs think that WPOs could not be trusted to do real police work in catching criminals and making arrests. Otherwise, WPOs did not work very hard and just kissed up to the MPO boss, to get ahead.[190]

The following WPO in a HKP web forum summed up the debate over MPO versus WPO relationship, on both sides:

> Lastly, do not under estimate WPO! You might not realize with your work at PSU (Patrol Sub Unit), WPO can handle their work completely by themselves, such as working on I.O. An officer's job and capacity is not only measured by criminal arrests. It is not easy to be successful in handling administrative work. Do not be a small minded male? Have a broader perspective![191]

From the above brief response to an MPO's remark about the unprofessionalism of WPO working as administration PC and other conversations in the web blog, we can gather that:

First, MPOs are not too happy with WPO in monopolising indoor administrative duties, away from inclement weather and high work pressure.

Second, MPOs think that office–administrative work is not really police work.

Third, MPOs think that WPOs cannot do real work like going on patrol and catching criminals.

Fourth, WPOs have a lot of power because they are in control of duties, leave and assignments.

Fifth, WPOs have a lot of privileges because they kissed up to the boss.

The other issue is with sexual infidelity at work. This is a sensitive and explosive subject matter in Chinese society, especially between HKP colleagues.

'Disloyal to the other half' is a discussion topic on Police Forum Web about marital infidelity between HKP officers.[192] The topic attracted 62 comments, between 07-06-2001 at 16:05 h and 08-01-2001 at 22:11 h. The facts of the case, according to one entry, are as follows:

> Rumor had it that a married WPC in Hung X (Hum) was dating another PC. It is sad that the husband was being kept in the dark. As it turned out, the husband is also a police colleague. The PC colleague was just playing (not serious) with the WPC. One night he was embracing the WPC on a Night Club in my presence. The WPC was calling the husband and telling him she missed him. She lied about drinking at a bar. Sometimes we go together to karaoke with the WPC. The PC (lover) told me that it is just like going to Club, with a girl, hugging and kissing, with no need to pay. The WPC would lie to the husband that she was with other WPC drinking. Although I do not know the WPC's husband, I wish the WPC has been more careful with her conduct. Paper cannot be wrapped up fire.

All the postings disapprove such a relationship, albeit for different reasons and degree. Responses range from visceral condemnation, for example, betrayal of colleagues is unacceptable, to subdued resignation, for example, people are only human, to frank acceptance, each to his/her own.

There are many proposals to deal with the issues, from keeping quiet to counseling the parties.

The topic of discussion offers us a unique opportunity to investigate into the moral bearing of HKP. It squarely raises the issue of whether HKP officers should be held to (a higher) moral standard, on or off work.[193] Collaterally, how does the moral character and unethical conduct of HKP officers affect work performance, internally and externally? While sexual indiscretion and martial infidelity is not specifically mentioned in HKP disciplinary code, in a traditional Chinese society, they certainly have the effect of 'bringing the public service (HKP) into disrepute', sufficient to warrant heightened scrutiny.

The other avenue of investigation is to inquire into how HKP officers relate to and deal with moral breach by fellow officers. This has the potential of telling us how much HKP officers would cover up for each other. Furthermore, how does HKP compare with general public or foreign police officers?

The overall observation is that there is little official sanction and peer concern with extra-marital affairs involving fellow police officers, though all consider such indiscretion to be very immoral and grossly unacceptable. There is also clear evidence that officers are reluctant to get involved in fellow officers 'private' affairs, due to privacy and professional reasons.

Self-Promotion of HKP

In order to showcase the acceptance of WPO, as a planned change project at HKP, the HKP spared no effort to publicise the achievements of the WPO. For example, we read in HKPM the following entry: 'RIFLE SHOOTING WOMEN'S POLICE TEAM WIN. 22 RIFLE COMPETITION'.[194] 'The bi-annual Competition for the Women's Inter-Service .22 Rifle Challenge Cup was held 'at the Royal Hong Kong Defence'. This showed that WPOs were not recruited as flowerpots, for looks and beauty. This is a statement of full integration of WPO into HKP. It also made the statement, what MPO could do, the WPO were not far behind, and indeed in some instances, excel. This is also a statement about WPO capacity.

In an HKPM entry, the female Sub-Inspector Patrick from the United Kingdom also told us that HKP treated WPC better in every way, from training to job opportunity, than in the United Kingdom. As a result, WPC in HK performed and adjusted much better than those in the United Kingdom, though the United Kingdom WPO programme was started much earlier than in HK, in 1914. This led Sub-Inspector Patrick to ask rhetorically of the U.K. Parliament: 'I wonder what their impression would be if they paid a visit to police stations, police cells, court cells and magistrates' courts in Hong Kong? How would it compare with their previous visits to the stations, cells and courts of England at the beginning of this century'?[195] The expected answer would be, the U.K. Parliament should come and learn from HKP, a reversal of colonial relationship.

H: Modernisation and problem-oriented policing (POP)

In 1986, Professor Goldstein of Wisconsin Law School, first proposed to solve recurring community problems at their roots. The concept and practice of POP was born. Since then, POP has been the preferred policing strategy in the United States, and around the world. However, it appears that HKP has anticipated POP by decades.

In the 1950s, HKP has embraced POP principles to deal with juvenile crime, from the United Kingdom.[196] The premise was, it is not useful to punish the juvenile to deter for reform unless we can figure out the root causes of juvenile delinquency, that is, personality defects or environmental influence, through scientific investigation.

POP was also used to deal with 'Squatter Fire in Hong Kong'.[197]

In March 1956, CIP Roberts wrote about 'Squatter Fire in Hong Kong' as a chronic problem that HK government and HKP needed to solve.

The problem CIP Roberts was concerned about was with squatter fires, which Roberts found to be frequent, ferocious, deadly and impactful. He found that where there were squatters and congested living, there were fires, and repeatedly.

CIP started the POP with investigation of the problem, the first step of SARA (scanning, analysis, response and assessment) in POP framework. In Shek Kip Mei Squatter area alone, there were growing fire incidents: 1953 (14 fires), 1954 (24) and 1955 (43), with a huge attending loss, damages and injuries. He found that squatter fires have serious consequences and they were entirely avoidable.

Then came to the analysis part of SARA, to find the cause and response. CIP Roberts discovered that in Christmas 1953, fire burned down Shek Kip Mei Squatter area in Shamshuipo with 7500 squatters destroyed and 60,000 people homeless.[198] In July 1954, Tai Hang Tung fire destroyed over 2000 squatters with 25,000 persons homeless. The fires were avoidable if residents would be more careful. For example, in Shek Kip Mei, the fire was caused by falling of a kerosene lamp onto rubber and in Tai Hang Tung, it was kerosene stove exploding.[199]

After SARA step-two analysis, CIP Roberts now made recommendations for 'response' (SARA step three). He recommended multiple ways to reduce squatter fires: (1) Resettle fire victims in new settlements that are safer. (2) Mount a publicity campaign to raise fire consciousness with the people. (3) Promote fire prevention education. (4) Move factories further away from squatters to reduce accidental fire. (5) Remove incentives from criminal elements to set fire to obtain resettlement privileges.[200]

In a still larger context, according to Roberts, the root cause of the problem is a lack of effective social-housing policy, and not a robust police–crisis management capacity or criminal prosecution strategy.[201]

The only steps left in the SARA process were implied, more so than expressed.

Roberts concluded with this recommendation: 'In the meantime every effort is being made to eliminate the problem which the squatter areas create, by the removal of the squatter areas themselves'.[202]

I: Modernisation of police station facilities

In September of 1952, HKPM reported the opening of 'The New Kowloon City Police Station'.[203] The new police station was one of the best-designed and built police stations, commissioned after WWII. It was clear that the above news item served the purpose of reminding the police and public that HKP had been completely over-hauled, starting with the buildings and facilities. The news article was accompanied with five photos: Kowloon City Police

Station and Married Quarter; the charging room; Constables' Recreation Room and Constables Canteen. All these photos told a story and sent a message, about HKP reform direction, process and achievements.

A photo is worth a thousand words. What does this set of an old (1951) HKP photo display tells us now, or tried to convey, then? Here, historical context is important. Comparison is necessary. Intent is relevant.

There were many messages being sent by this set of photos.

First, this set of photos, shows us about HKP officers at work (Report Room) and at play (quarters, recreation room and canteen). Three of the four photos are about police welfare, and with JPO.[204] The photos made clear that at work, HKP might be a para-military organisation, and after work, officers enjoyed a relaxed civilian life, just liked other civilians in the community. HKP identity was not only wrapped up with policing, and was much less a colonial–para-military policing. For that matter, HKP officers working in uniform and under discipline were no more intimidating and worthy of note than fire and ambulance officers working in uniform.

Second, this set of photos, selectively and proudly presented, evidenced a period of fast growth and expansion with HKP. The expansion was matched with modernising of services to the public, witnessing the efficient design of the Report Room and improvement in the quality of life for the staff. Witness also the top of the line facilities, for living and playing, from a living quarter, to the creation room, to the staff canteen.[205] Compared with the civilian world, the living quarters and recreation facility was unsurpassed, most certainly a cut above what the average middle-class HK people could afford or expect.

Third, more significantly, the photos were there to showcase a progressive managing spirit. The Report Room was functionally designed and did not look like a traditional Chinese Yemen (ornate and majestic) or an old Colonial Office (imperial and imposing). Perhaps more symbolically, gone were the days when police report bench was higher than people coming to do business with the HKP, and the people have to look up to officers to plea for help.

IV: Communalisation

The ultimate objective of decolonisation is self-determination; a government that is for the people, of the people and by the people. Communalisation of policing is HKP's way of decolonising without being officially decolonised, that is, getting close to the people—listening to the people, knowing what the people want and be responsive and accountable; what is called community-oriented policing in modern times.

A: Communalisation through community visits

After the war, HKP has taken steps to ingratiate itself with the leadership of the community. This included visiting with the community at Kai

Fong Associations from time to time. Traditionally, as a rule, Chinese officials and the community did not visit each other, socially or officially. In colonial HK and before the war, police and public interaction and exchange were rare.

After the war, the British commanders were instructed to mix with Chinese leadership to make them feel important, that is, giving face. For example, in SSP Division, the divisional senior officers often made a point to go for tea with the local communities:

> During the Quarter under review, a tea-party was held in the Station to which representatives of all the local Kai Fong Associations were invited; the object being to promote a better relationship between the guests and the hosts. We learnt many of the more obscure functions of the Kai Fongs and the Kai Fong representatives went away happy in the knowledge that the Division was in the safe hands of sober tea-drinking policemen! In truth, the subsequent relationship between the two has been greatly improved.[206]

The two photos ('The Divisional Tea-Party for the Local Kai Fong Association') taken at the police station accompanying the story are revealing. There were six people at the head table, four Europeans and two Chinese, sitting side by side drinking tea. The head of table sandwiched between the Europeans was an older Chinese gentleman. The Chinese lady sitting by the side cannot be discerned. Both of them wore traditional, upscale Chinese clothes. The officers were wearing uniform. The rest of the audience in the room, nine Chinese (dignitaries) and all older gentlemen, were in their best behaviour, dressed in ties and shirts, except for two who were obscured, with back to the camera.

In as much as Chinese at the time did not speak much, if any English, and Europeans have little facility with languages, one can only guess at how the parties communicated with each other, and more importantly how such meeting could possibly contribute to a better community relationship.

Still, the HKP community must gather for a show of good relationship, diplomatically; a kind of meet and greet type of gesture.[207] The HKP needed to show respect to the elder community leaders. The Chinese community members must show deference to the government officials. In doing so, the parties enacted their respective role as community seniors and police officials, lest the Chinese betrayed their own cultural admonitions and the British failed in their professional duties.

B: Communalisation through part taking in community events

In conjunction with tea party–courtesy visits, Sham Shui Po police leadership have other community responsibilities. When called upon, the police needed to provide extraordinary amount of police officers to tend to major ceremonies, such as shop opening (here a restaurant), when dignitaries appeared (usually starlets) and crowds gathered.

In order to understand community and police relationship in HK at the time, we need to understand how Western (British) versus Eastern (HK) looked upon HKP deployment of officers to cover private events in public places. To the outsider—Westerners, the police were there for a functional reason, doing their job to keep order, control crowd and direct traffic. To the Chinese, however, police deployment at such events, served additional purposes. Police turned out to a private event, such as shop opening, or public affairs, for example, seasonal opera show, was a way to show how much HKP cared about the importance of the local elites and community gathering. The reasoning goes, what is important to the owner/community is double important to the police. From the public point of view, the more police presence at the shop opening, the more social status the owner enjoyed.[208] The more police presence, the more influential the owner appears to have over the police, the more people around pay tribute and show deference. Ultimately, the business titans, community leaders and social elites would like to say to others: 'Do you know who I am'? In HK, then as now, bragging right is important.[209] That is why Chinese leaders have more titles and associations on their business cards than the current-day CV of successful professionals. In the Chinese world, it is all about *mianzi* (face) and *guanxi* (relationship). How important you are, who you know and what you know[210] are status symbols, and signs of importance and influence. With status, one can be a power broker, trading with *renqing* (favour) and *bao* (reciprocity),[211] that is, what you can do for others and demand in return. In essence, social capital is more important than financial capital. As a currency exchange process, financial capital might be more useful, generally, but social capital is more influential, within a particular set of relations.[212]

In essence, community–police relationship at the time (the 1950s) turned on one's ability to manage relationship, giving face, asking for 'favour' and returning 'favour'.[213]

Another strategy for the HKP police to build relationship, this time with the younger crowd, is to entertain them with HK's favourite past time—soccer. This allowed the HKP to reduce the insurmountable official distance between the police and people, in years past, by playing up to what the young people like in sports. In order to impress upon the public that the police were not all about enforcing law and arresting people, from time to time, they showed their lighter side, in dressing themselves up to arouse the crowd. For example, in a soccer game, the Sham Shui Po soccer team making up of Europeans as well as Chinese put on imperial Chinese warrior clothes to entertain the crowd. There was no evidence that this tactic worked; still, it impressed upon the public that the police cared enough, and that they let down their guard to entertain all, for a day. [214]

C: Communalisation through incentive and recognition

Another HKP communalisation device was to recognise citizens for helping with HKP in fighting crime, or generally as a good citizen.[215] 'On 6th

February 1952, at Central Police Station, the Commissioner of Police, Mr. D. W. Macintosh, presented awards to seven members of the public, who had personally effected the arrests of individuals committing serious crime'.[216]

D: Communalisation through image management

For all too long, police in general and HKP in particular has a bad image with the community. So much so when people think about the HKP, people think about corruption and abuse of power.

This is how Tam Pui Lin (DOB: 1946), a hawker at Yau Ma Tei, remembered the HKP, being corrupt and abusive, in the 1950s:

> The citizens did not have a strong legal awareness in the early post-war period. It was common to see peddlers fight with each other and police receive bribes. Peddlers had to socialize with one another in order to survive. Tam Pui Lin reminisced that the police often sent agents to collect bribes from her parents when they were running their stall at Yung Shu Tau Market. The amount of bribes depended on the size of the stall. The average would be $30 per stall per week. Bribes would be collected several times a week. Each payment was $5 or $10. This phenomenon of police bribery was generally known as 'Escape the Big Rat' among the peddlers. In 1950s, the Tams were always in financial difficulties. All their earning could barely afford their living. One day an agent came to collect bribe as usual. As Tam's parents were not able to pay the protection money, their goods were confiscated. At that time Tam was only 5 to 6 years old. She came forward and desperately fought back. Finally she was arrested. She recalled that, as a child, she was simple-minded and straightforward. Family's interest was on top of anything else so she had no ideas of the outcome. Since her parents were unable to pay for her bail, she was held in custody in Kowloon City overnight and released the next day. Since she was too young, she was looked after by the police. The constable who arrested her was scolded by his senior for catching a child. Afterwards Tam's parents stood trial at South Kowloon Magistracy. It was a common practice to detain hawkers who were unable to pay protection money. Many male hawkers were even whipped by rattan stick coated with liquid medicine. Bribe was no longer required after the Tams' stall moved to Reclamation Street Market in 1956.[217]

Another restaurant owner in Yau Ma Tei, then a delivery boy at the time, Yeung Hon Yuen,[218] recalled that the HKP officers were lazy, drunk and irresponsible:

> Yuen Gor delivered takeaways to the policemen in the district. In those days, it was the policemen's habit to order food at street-side stalls for delivery to a designated place. It was an unwritten rule that the policemen shall eat free. Yuen Gor delivered the takeaways to the Yau Ma Tei Police Station on a bicycle. He would see policemen watching television in the arrest room (the lounge). On one occasion, he noticed more than 100 bottles of white liquor in the police station. Sometimes, the stall workers would be discontent with the

picky and wasteful policemen, but they dared not utter a word. Instead, they played tricks on them by cooking their food with a mixture of drainage and corn starch. It was common for the Yau Ma Tei police to shun work and eat at bakeries in the evening. The takeaways were delivered to various 'dodgers' hangouts'. They included the Leung Kin Kee Pastry at 12-14 Battery Street, Ma Po Shan on Temple Street, and Lucky Bakery at 529-531 Canton Road.[219]

In the 1950s and 1960s, the HKP spared no effort in rehabilitating the image of HKP to make it softer, that is, more compassionate, and more professional, for example, more competent. Below is a demonstration of how HKP goes about promoting a better image with the public, that is, HKP is there to help, when needed.

In five photos spread over two pages in HKPM, the HKP tried to tell the story of a transformed HKP. The story line: a kid was lost and found, helped by caring police officers, male and female, old and young, expatriate and Chinese. At each step, police behaved not as tough and tumble law enforcement agents, but as kind and concerned citizens in uniform.[220] The photo shots were as telling as they were moving.

Photo#1: 'Boy, Am I glad you came along'! (Caption) Showed a police officer squatting down and tending to a lost kid (girl) on the street, not more than 5 years old. The kid has a worrisome facial expression, as anxious as she was fearful. 'I want to be with my mother' was written all over her body.

Photo#2: 'I wonder where this is, it looks like a police station so it must be alright'! (Caption) Showed the little girl was holding the male policeman's hand approaching a police station, with another police standing on guard. The child seemed to have calmed down.

Photo#3: 'What's Going on, I am lost, that's all'! (Caption) Showed a puzzled and dazzled girl with the back to a European duty officer standing up and bending over, reached over the desk to touch her. The police who found her was on the side, watching over her, as he tried to make an entry into the daily log book.

Photo#4: (Below left) 'Well, now, this isn't too bad, not bad at all. I like this'! (Caption) Showed a WPC attending to her at the canteen, over a drink and with a pair of warm eyes. The girl reciprocated, looking at the WPC, calm and composed.

Photo#5: (Below right) 'Who wants to go to the Social Welfare? I want to go back to the police station'! (Caption) Showed the girl crying, with two WPCs looking on, helpless.

The photos captured a new image and identity of HKP, that is, HKP is a community service agency, trying to help citizens in need at every turn. All the HKP officers—from patrol officer, to European

> Inspector, to WPC, were all trying to do the best to make the girl feel at home. At the end, the public should get the message that HKP is a service agency, not a colonial master.[221]

E: Communalisation through integration of the civilian as Auxiliary Police

The best way to communalise is to engage the citizens in protecting themselves and the community they live, work and play. The idea that police are drawn from the citizens and citizens also act as police, comports with British democratic ideal, and was enthusiastically embraced by Sir Robert Peel as one of the nine fundamental principles of policing in 1829:

> (7) To maintain at all times a relationship with the public that gives reality to the historic tradition that the police are the public and that the public are the police, the police being only members of the public who are paid to give full-time attention to duties which are incumbent on every citizen in the interests of community welfare and existence.[222]

There is no better way to have citizens doing police work, as Auxiliary Police officers after work.

In March 1956, issues about the necessity, suitability and capacity of citizens' police were raised and discussed[223] with reference to the Regular Police[224] and the Special Police,[225] (emergency police), in an HKPM article: 'THE HONG KONG POLICE AUXILIARIES TAKE OVER' (March 1956).

The Regular Police observed that both the HK public and regular HKP officers have great reservations about the competence and capacity of private citizens in handling—'take over' police tasks, when called upon to do so. This is especially the case in emergency situations, when the pressure is high, stress is great and margin of error is small.

From the perspective of the public, they were not getting what they paid for, with weekend amateur police.

The HKP has a bigger concern. The amateur Auxiliary Police could not be made to perform alongside professional Regular Police, especially in emergencies and crisis situations. This was so for three reasons. First, citizen police were amateur volunteers, doing part-time police work. They were less experienced, dependable and reliable to do the fill range of police duties, 24/7. Second, citizen police were too socially, ethnically, culturally, educationally and professionally diverse, to work together as a uniform whole. Third, the idea has never been tried before:

> Policemen have always been skeptical of the amateur and in Hong Kong we were no exception….We would blush with embarrassment if it were pointed out that to take men of several nationalities from every walk of life and to weld them into an organised body which can be called up almost at the drop of a

> hat to understudy us in just about every phase of the whole complicated police machine—is quite something. That it is possibly unique in Police history, has never occurred to us.

The HKP officers have a reason to be concerned. HKP has a negative experience with other forms of citizens police, from Special Police to Police Reserve. Special Police were ill prepared to do real police work, in readiness and temperament for example, attending the sick, walking a beat or staffing a police post. They just wanted to play cops and robbers.[226] The Police Reserve was only good at emergencies, for example, typhoon,[227] and crowd control duties, such as race-course and football duties.

It turned out that the public and HKP concerns were ill founded. The HK Auxiliary officers have proven them wrong by offering to run a police command and did well:

> Where, I ask you, is there any Force in the World that can produce an Auxiliary organisation capable of organising themselves at a few hours notice to produce 1,500 men to take over the watch and ward of almost an entire Force?[228] This was in reaction to the Hong Kong Police for Auxiliary Police to 'take' over a Hong Kong Police police station for one day.[229]

Viewed in a historical context, the relationship between the HKP and HKAP has not been a smooth one. As intimated above, HKAP officers have always been considered as less prepared, less professional, less competent and less reliable. Thus, they were always considered not to be able to do the full range of police work efficiently and effectively. As a result, they were not trusted to perform like a HKP officer. Case in point: In 1999, before the LegCo, the Deputy Commissioner—Operations (DCP–OPT) has this to say about HKAP officers:

> Dir of Ops said that training provided for Auxiliary Police officers was only a part of the package of training for the regular Police officers. Hence, Auxiliary Police officers could not perform all types of duties undertaken by the regular Police Force, for example, duties in the Police Tactical Unit or related to crime investigation. In addition, the duty pattern of Auxiliary Police officers was irregular where most of them resumed duty during weekends and public holidays. Whereas the regular Police officers provided round-the-clock service throughout the year. Thus, most of the responsibilities of regular Police Force could not be assumed by Auxiliary Police officers.[230]

Like the WPO, the HKAP officers were considered by the HKP as second-class 'reserve' officers. They were called upon only when needed, for example, crowd control or guard and escort duties. Although the people on the street hardly notice the difference, the HKAP has never been treated as a fully functional police unit, by the HKP, bearing shortage or crisis. This was not lost in the HKAP. Indeed, in 1980, HKAP officers were treated very much the same as Regular Police officers,[231] when there was a great demand for their service.

As to the role and functions, an exchange in the LegCo in 1990 over the training, capacity and performance on HKAP officers 'in crisis' gives us some clue as to the distinction in role and capacity between HKP and HKAP: Mr Tien: Sir, would the Secretary please inform this Council whether in time of crisis the performance of the Auxiliary Police on beat patrol will measure up to that of our Regular Police?

Secretary for Security: Sir, yes. The Auxiliary Police go through essentially the same training as their regular counterparts, and they operate on the street and indeed in other duties in very much the same way as the Regular Police. I do not believe that there is a problem of difference of standard.[232]

Still, HKAP officers were not treated on par in every respect operationally with the regular HKP officers. On 29 June 1999, a discussion paper on 'Legislative Council Panel on Security Review of the Hong Kong Auxiliary Police Force (HKAPF)[233]' (paper) (re) defined the post-1997 role of HKAPF as follows:

> In their redefined role, Auxiliary Police officers mainly serve as a trained manpower reserve to support the regular Police Force in crowd management operations during major public events and festivals. In addition, their main functions in an internal security situation include key points protection, manning the command and control centres, Police station defence and consular premises protection.[234]

The paper made clear that the redefined-limited role of HKAP was not a result of or required by the Enhanced Productivity Programme. In essence, according to HKP leadership, this was not a cost-saving measure at all. The role and functions of HKAPF needed to be refined in 'light of changing circumstances' of the day, namely, 'the regular Police Force is now up to establishment and has sufficient manpower to perform frontline operational duties'.

The tense relationship between HKP and HKAP came to the forefront when the HKP–CP disallowed Hong Kong Auxiliary Police Association activities in official buildings.[235]

This abrupt change of HKP versus HKAP relationship was not considered as important as the HKP–HKAP reform programme.[236] Except in the LegCo archives, the HKAP downsizing was rarely reported in the news and discussed in the public.

Even within LegCo, the matter of HKAP did not take on much urgency or importance, as compared to its impact and implication. The lackluster performance of the LegCo members most probably has something to do with public interest and members' competence.

The public have little interest in such low-visibility HKP administrative issue. To the more inquisitive public, the issue was whether HK should have 'real' HKP versus 'part time HKAP' on beat duty. For many people, more professional police in the street-fighting crime should be preferred.

In the end, it is argued here that the decision to redefine and marginalise the role and functions of the HKAP is not a well-researched and reasoned one:

First, since the 1970s, HKP has been moving towards CP. CP calls for enlisting citizens' help and getting the community involved to fight crime, maintain order and provide service. Given this reform vision and mission, it makes little sense to reduce the establishment, capacity and presence of the citizen police, in favour of professional ones. The issue here is who can do CP better? The answer is a clear one. Having community members walking the beat is the best way to realise the goals and objectives of CP, on the cheap. (1) Being from the community, the HKAPF is more aware of and sensitive to public concerns. (2) Being from the community, the HKAPF knows more about the community, in culture as well as with intelligence. (3) Being from the community, the HKAP will be better able to relate, communicate with and liaison between the people as a fellow citizen. (4) Being from the community, the HKAP brings instant legitimacy—credibility, authority and empathy—to the task. (5) Being from the community, the HKAP will be able to draw upon the resources in the community to solve local problems. (6) Being from the community, the HKAP would be better able to reduce mistrust and improve communication between HKSAR and the community, and resolve disputes between the community and HKP.

Second, in implementing CP and improving police–public relationship, actions speak louder than words. In removing the HKAPF from the beats, and reducing their number on duty, in favour of HKP officers, the HKP is sending a number of wrong messages, detrimental to CP:

1. The HKP does not trust the community to police themselves.[237] The development of an effective community-based crime-fighting capacity, that is, District/Area Security Group, was first proposed by the LegCo in 1974,[238] but never materialised.
2. The HKP has little confidence in HKAPF officers to work independently, suggesting that they are less competent, reliable or trained: 'Mr CHAN Kwok-keung asked why Auxiliary Police officers would be required to perform operational duties in conjunction with regular Police officers having regard to the fact that the former received proper training and performed operational duties independently before the review. Mr CHAN questioned whether, in other words, training previously provided for Auxiliary Police officers was considered insufficient'.[239]

3. The HKP is more interested in promoting professional and technocratic policing by regular HKP officers than in promoting CP with HKAPF officers.
4. The HKP is more interested in cost cutting than be committed to HKAP professional development and capacity enhancement. On 29 June 1999, DPC–OPT briefed LegCo Panel on Security after cutting of staff at HKAP, in a circumlocutory way:

> As outlined in the paper, the total savings generated was almost $170 million when the establishment of HKAPF was reduced to 4500 through natural wastage. Dir of Ops stressed that the Force fully appreciated the dedicated service provided by the Auxiliary Police officers in the past. The review was to tie in with the value for money principle[240] adopted in the Force. The review of HKAPF commenced as early as in 1992.[241]

This has prompted LegCo Member Howard to ask whether training for HKAP is adequate and cost-effective.

1. The HKP showed little interest in treating HKAP as equal partners, as CP envisions and requires order to be successful. As it turns out, the community is not driving the HKP, as it should be. Instead, the HKP is dictating to the community. HKP is only interested in using the community (HKAP) to advance its own agenda, that is, either as a public relation ploy or crowd control resource.[242]
2. The HKP has expanded little effort and committed limited resources in developing the capacity and enhancing the performance of the HKAPF. Every effort was to keep HKAPF in a limited and circumscribed role as a reserve crisis management and emergency security detail.
3. 'Miss CHAN Yuen-han (LegCo member) was of the view that the Force management failed to address members' concerns expressed at the last meeting, in particular the specific plan put in place to ensure the capability of Auxiliary Police officers to perform operational duties in case of emergencies and the reasons for introducing the drastic changes[243] within such a short period of time'.[244]
4. The decision-making process over 'Review of the Hong Kong Auxiliary Police Force (HKAPF) demonstrated HKP's management's ignorance of and insensitivity to HKAP's aspirations, desire, right and capacity to serve the community,[245] and expectation of the public.[246] It most certainly poorly reflected upon HKP's decision making process and ability, thereby bringing the HKP into disrepute'.
5. 'Mr Howard YOUNG asked whether the Force management had examined the respective cost effectiveness of the training provided

for regular and Auxiliary Police officers in drawing up the recommendations. ... Miss CHAN Yuen-han wondered if the manpower situation in the regular Police Force was the decisive factor for the engagement of Auxiliary Police officers....

6. The way HKP treats HKAP is unfair/disrespectful, and serve to rupture the relationship to and alienate the loyalty of HKPF members.
7. 'Mr CHEUNG Man-kwong said that the trust between the Force management and HKPF had been destroyed to some extent as a result of the implementation of the recommendations arising from the review. Thus, the request from HKPF for independent body as an arbitrator over the implementation of the recommendations was understandable'.[247]
8. The HKP review of HKAP in process and outcome, has openly denigrated HKAP leadership and subtly undermined HKAP frontline morale.
9. 'Mr CHAN Kwok-keung pointed out that the proposed integrated deployment of Auxiliary Police officers with their regular counterparts was an area of concern of the Auxiliary Police officers. He learnt that many Auxiliary Police officers had hard feelings that they were a burden on the regular Police officers under the new arrangement for performing beat duties. Dir of Ops stressed that the Force management had no intention to cause any hard feelings by introducing the proposed integration'.[248]

V: Organisation

HKP was not well organised before the war. After WWII, HKP had to be rebuilt organisationally. This was a huge challenge. The Japanese had destroyed most of the police records. The HKP had lost most of its police managers. Millions of people were coming across the borders. HK economy was expanding fast and radically transforming. The HKP was pressed into action, in building police stations, training people and designing systems, all at lightning speed.

The HKP reformers were confronted with two basic tasks, namely, how HKP should be organised, for example, centralised versus decentralised, and how it should be operated, that is, command and control.

The HKP decided upon centralised administration, that is, bureaucratisation, and decentralised operation, that is, localisation. That is to say uniform and standardised administration in hiring, firing, training, auditing and accounting, and diversifying and customising operational command and control.

Bureaucratisation[249]

Standardise Administration

In 1959, a decade into HKP reform and reorganisation, the HKPM saw fit to publish an article titled 'Organization' by J. B. Fleetwood, deputy chief constable, Admiralty Constabulary, United Kingdom.[250] The article, first of its kind in HKPM, described in detail the best practice of police organisation, its basic principles and operational importance.[251]

Fleetwood began by citing W. L. Melville Lee's observation in his classical work on policing:[252] 'The rough and the criminal do not fear the prowess of the individual policeman, they fear the organisation behind him'.[253] The republication of Chief Fleetwood was telling about the mindset of HKP leadership on police reform.

First, HKP reform was very much an organisational reform.

Second, organisationally, HKP was moving towards a bureaucratic model (Weber),[254] and general practices around the world at the time.[255]

> Police forces are fundamental proponents of rational/legal states. Overall, their legitimacy is based on the principle of 'rule of laws, not of men'. That is, formal rules define their authority and govern their conduct. They are a Weberian bureaucracy—or have evolved over the years to become one. The police are hierarchically organized; they are chosen on the basis of examinations and other specified qualifications; they are paid fixed salaries; in theory employment is a career, with promotion according to achievement or seniority; their conduct is subject to strict and systematic discipline and control. (Citation omitted).[256]

Third, Webertian bureaucratic model of policing is preferred for HKP because of its legal–legitimation functions, and not military potentiality.

Fourth, HKP reform was adopting best practices of policing from around the Western world, as found in British Constabulary.

In the end, Chief Fleetwood's article registered a change of mood at HKP HQ, namely, making a break with the past, HKP leadership realised that the success or failure of policing did not rest on the loyalty and heroism of individuals, in the days past, but efficiency and effectiveness of the police officers in organisational ways.

From the HKP reformers' perspective, a rational–legitimacy model (RLM) of policing which Weber offered, served important functions of the time, real or imagined.

First, RLM, with starched Khaki, precision drill and sharp salutes to match, allowed colonial police administrators to be in control, up top, speaking the familiar language of order, discipline and leadership, drummed into each member at PTS. British senior colonial police officers could be in control without cultural understanding. JPO would obey orders without personal identification with the colonial master. Even today, the prideful tradition of HKP is still one of, first obey, and then debate.

Second, RLM allowed colonial leadership to claim, much like in 1829 when the LMP Force was set up such that, strict discipline and unforgiving rules, achieved perfect control of police and public. Performance accountability is to displace political accountability.

Diversified and Customised Operations

Policing in general and colonial policing in particular conjures up images of a monolithic force with uniform practice. This is distortive and misleading. Understanding HKP reform requires contextualisation and particularisation. There is a dire need to first discover and then demonstrate how HKP police in different times, places and people, in terms of philosophy, role, administration and operation. In more concrete terms, there is a need to investigate into policing practices in various policing units, for example, UB versus CID versus SB, formation, for example, Marine versus land, regions, Hong Kong Island versus KLN versus NT and sub-divisions, for example, Mongkok versus Wanxhai. Such a comparative study should allow us to see that HKP is hardly uniform.

Command and Control

HKP was and is a top-down organisation.[257] As a colonial force, policy and directives for HKP emulated from the top, from the White Hall to the Foreign Secretary to the Colonial Office to the Governor of HK[258] to the HKP. Commissioner of Police serves at the pleasure of the Governor, as head of the executive branch.

Until the latest round of reform in the 1990s, HKP leadership, management and operational style was very personalised and decentralised,[259] with strict centralised administration and policy formulation at HKP HQ, but a wide latitude of operational control with the local commanders, such as Regional Commander (RC), DS and SDI. These commanders were trusted to manage their command as they deemed fit, within the confinement of police general order (PGO).

Research on Command and Control: Policy Formulation and Implementation

In 1981, the then Inspector W.I. Nicholas wrote a research paper on HKP policy formulation and implementation process on hawker control[260] in Hong Kong Island by comparing and contrasting 'Police Policy Process' at five policing units: HKP HQ,[261] Central Division,[262] Waichai Division,[263] Eastern Division[264] and Western Division.[265] What he found, as an insider,[266] is instructive on how HKP made and executed hawker policy in 1981. The most salient findings are HKP HQ proposes frontline commanders—DS, SDI disposes.

First, HKP HQ set the overall all-police hawker policy by working with other public bodies, such as the Urban Council (Hawker Select Committee), the Executive Council and the Hawker Policy Working Group (Attorney General, HKP, ICAC and Urban Council). The working group establish the overall general policy on how bests to deal with the hawker problems in HK, with HKP 'seeking to determine a proper division of responsibility for hawker control…'[267] within the respective legal and policy bound of various agencies. For example, HKP statutory responsible with respect to hawker control was derived from Section 10 of Police Force Ordinance, such as Section 10(f) controlling traffic upon public thoroughfares and removing obstacles therefrom; 10(h) assisting in carrying out any …sanitary …laws.[268] In terms of policy, the Urban Council has determined in 1979 the responsibility of HKP for controlling hawkers as follows: 'The control of hawkers and enforcement of hawker legislation depends on the police and General Duties Team, The task of the Police is to keep main thoroughfares clear of obstruction…'[269]

Second, within the HKP HQ, hawker policy was established by the CP in the HKP—Support Wing,[270] in providing 'supreme direction and administration' of the HKP.[271] In 1977, the CP has issued the following policy statement to the Director of Urban Council, namely: '(a) The Force should not dissipate its effort on hawker control but concentrate on more important constabulary duties; (b) The areas of conflict between the public and Police must be reduced; and (c) As hawker control is primarily concerned with public health rather than law and order, it should be regarded as a non-constabulary duty'.[272] This broad non-policy, hawker policy statement basically removes HKP as the main hawker law enforcement regime, making it an Urban Council problem. In 1980, the CP in a visit to Support Wing, asked for a reassessment of hawker control policy, specifically 'manpower commitment by law enforcement agencies to be quantified' and 'action against hawkers by enforcement agencies be evaluated'.[273] This CP policy statement asked for a renewed effort to 're-assess' hawker policy, and not how to enforce it.

It was in this ambivalent hawker policy environment at HKP HQ that hawker policy implementation process should be examined.

Third, in terms of hawker policy enforcement, it was generally agreed within HKP that the local commanders, particularly at the division level, have much influence and control, to wit: 'the degree of cooperation from the police seems to depend largely on the initiative of the local divisional superintendent' and 'local action and policy seemed to depend whether the divisional superintendent has a bee in his bonnet about the subject or vice versa (sic)'.[274]

Fourth, with the non-committal (1980) and non-directive (1977) CP hawker policy, the divisional commanders were left to their own accord, resulting in a variety of enforcement policy, strategies, input, output and outcome, across divisions (KLN vs. Hong Kong Island divisions) and within a division (Central vs. Water Front). For example:

a. Policy across divisions: There was no written hawker policy in all four Hong Kong Island divisions (Central, Wanchai, Eastern and Western) and four of six KLN divisions have one (except the airport and MTR).[275]
b. Policy within divisions: Within Central Division, since there was no divisional hawker policy or directives, it was up to the SDIs to instruct the sub-unit commanders as to what is the appropriate level of enforcement, and under what circumstances and to what end, against what results. In the case of Central Sub-Division, the SDI has written an operation memo of sorts: 'Action by beat PCs against hawkers is to be confined to keeping hawkers off prohibited streets. Police action is to be dependent the severity of the case and in preferential order of formal warnings, summons, and lastly arrest…'[276] Further comparing SDI—Central hawker enforcement instruction to SDI—Waterfront (WF) Instruction#8, we found that SDI/WF Instruction#8 incorporates by reference to Hong Kong Island District Commander Circulation Letter No. 6, in regard to nuisance squad duties.[277]
c. Sub-division policy across divisions: If we were to compare hawker polices between Wanchai Sub-Division (within Wancahi Division)[278] versus Causeway Bay Sub-Division (within Eastern Division),[279] we will find that in Wanchai, it has no standing policy. Hawker enforcement was the responsibility of Prisoners Escort Team, if and when available, as supplemented by Auxiliary Police duties. 'Enforcement is generally taken on a reactive basis' and is dependent on the nature, consistency and publicity of the complaints, per divisional complaint policy.[280] With Causeway Bay Sub-Division, there was no written policy. The standing policy of SDI was 'to contain hawkers inside Mercury Street and under Tsing Fung St. Flyover. An absolute prohibition on King's Road exists, and frequent operations in Electric Road…'
d. There were substantial differences in resource input and productivity out in hawker control effort between sub-divisions.

Anecdotal Evidence of Divisional Control

YMT Police Station reported the following item in HKPM (1952/2:37):

> An innovation at Yaumati (in fact in the Force as a whole) has been devised, built and installed at Yaumati Police Station. This is Mr. I. G. MacPherson's duty scheme which shows, by a series of coloured lights, the positions of all men on duty. Of this we say no more at the time of writing…the scheme is still in the experimental stage. We are, however, sure of its success in helping to obtain the maximum beat efficiency in our district.

The message here is that local commanders were given much authority to experiment with ideas of management and operations, provided they do not conflict with HKP HQ general policy and specific instructions, for example, uniform haircut, training and assignments. The standard refrain for operational commanders was: 'Do not disturb the boss'. Alternatively, the boss cannot be bordered with. This provides the frontline officers with a wide latitude, and a tint of caution.

In effect, DS and SDI ruled their post and officers like fiefdom. It was an open secret in the 1950s that divisional commanders recruit the officers they liked and disciplined, and eventually transferred, staff they did not like. This is called the 'horse stable' system of management. In terms of career development, it was whose harbour you moored your boat, not how you steered your boat that matters when it comes to promotion and assignments.

The following item in the HKPM hinted at the existence of such a personal 'recruitment' system at work at Eastern Division, in a light-mannered way. To contextualise the item, one must remember: 'Immediate post war reforms abolished the recruitment of British and Commonwealth personnel into subordinate ranks, joining instead as Probationary Sub-Inspectors. ... The end of the British Mandate in Palestine in 1948 occasioned an influx of officers over the next two years, along with further arrivals from a now independent Malaysia'.[281] Much like the Chinese immigrants and other sojourns coming to HK through the years, these newly arrived overseas cops need to find an ethnic identity and cultural anchor, before coming to terms with HK and surviving the HKP. They found it with former colleagues within the Colonial Police Service system or Palestine Police Force:

> Our D.S. 'Bill' Segrue came from Palestine in 1948 and after a spell in Special Branch took over Western before coming to this Division in 1950. He strongly denies the rumour that Eastern will employ a publicity agent, having found that results supply their own advertisement. Rex Davies, the Chief Inspector, is also from the Special Branch and came here to replace Geordie Harris now home on leave.[282]

As it is and at all times, policing is not a one-size-fits-all business.

Police operations in focus and methods are more differentiated than uniform.

In the 1950s and 1960s, what HKP officers did and how they did it, differed substantially between and across (sub) divisions.

There was a common saying within HKP then that 'Hong Kong police are *jingcha,* Kowloon police are *charen,* New Territories police are *dagenglao* 「香港警察,九龍差人, 新界打更佬」'. Both the police and the public perceived HK versus KLN versus NT police differently in organisation, role, administration, ethos and conduct.[283] As folklore has it: *jingcha* are colonial police agents and organised and operated along Western line. *Charen* are central penal officials behaving in imperial Chinese ways. Finally, *dagenglao* are local communal security agents, who functioned according to local norms. With this folksy remembrance: HK police were more polite and business like, projecting a professional image. KLN police were more rough and tumble, displaying a persona of rough cops. NT police were more down to earth, acting as unsophisticated but caring neighbours.

History and folklore aside, HKP organisation culture and personal conduct, then as now, are very much determined by policing environment of the time, from geographic characteristics, for example, contiguous with China with a porous border, to population demographics, for example, Shanghai business elites versus Canton working poor, to business conditions, for example, HK Central with teams of white collar workers, and industrial setting, for example, Tsuen Wan saturated with industrial workers. A blogger on policing wrote:

> There is a common saying in HKP; 'Hong Kong are police officers. Kowloon are *yamen* officials. New Territories are night watchman (security guards)'. ... Police image, ethos and appearance are not the same in different district. In Hong Kong Island, since there are a concentration of major and important government administrative units, judicial offices, bank and financial organizations, international enterprises headquarters, other top businesses, senior executives' residences and HKP HQ, the police officers need to conduct themselves in a most careful manner. From outward appearances or service manner, they should leave an impression of being civilized and warm. That is why they are called police. In Kowloon, it is packed with dense shops and residential areas. Also there are many recreational sites, with a mix-bags of criminals, the environment are very complicated. Comparatively, there are more criminal activities. Thus when the police officers carried out their duties, they are lacking in politeness but with more authority. That is why people call police '*yamen officials*'. Such an image (of police) has been accepted by the public with no negative connotation. As to New Territories region, since it is located in the rural area with fewer people, besides routine policing, the police have no extra-operational duties. They behave like security guards. Thus, they are called 'watchman.' Judging from the above, police ethos and image to a certain extent is influenced by the environment.[284]

These customary labels of police have real-life consequences, internally and externally. First, it comes to define and reinforce HKP self-image, public persona and organisational culture. Second, over time, it becomes a self-fulfilling prophecy, making reification as real. Third, it comes to shape police role. Fourth, it influences police versus public and public versus police expectation and relationship, and how police treat the public and public relate to police. Fifth, it affects staff deployment, for example, the best police are assigned to Hong Kong Island, and career development, for example, less advancement with Marine police.

All Policing Are Local

All policing are local and different, if only because places and people are different, in history, culture and conditions. Take Aberdeen as an example. Historically, Aberdeen was the centre of HK in the 1840s. In 1841, HK was named after the 4th Earl of Aberdeen, George Hamilton-Gordon, British Secretary of State for War and the Colonies. In the Ming Dynasty, Arberdeen was called 'Small Hong Kong'. Aberdeen was then a key fishing village and vibrant market place, with a huge Tanka and Hoklo boat community. In 1964, a British officer who was stationed in Aberdeen had this to say about the town:

> This then is Aberdeen, Fishing centre, industrial town in embryo, farming community, high class residential district—it is all these things and yet the place manages to preserve for itself a unique character. With the buzz of factories in the background and the noise of the mechanized fleet, there remains a feeling of rural tranquility and friendliness of the local people which one never seems to get on the other side of the Island.[285]

Aberdeen is a long way from Central Victoria that cannot be any more different. From the earliest of time, Central Victoria was a commercial centre in an urban setting and with modern facilities. Most of the people working there were expatriates, and attended by the poor Chinese.

The diversity of police work and operation in and around HK can be had by reading 'Chatters from Stations' in the HKPM.

Policing for All Seasons and Reasons

In 1964, when post-WWII HKP reform has well settled in, a European officer reported on police work in and around Eastern Division: 'Eastern Division: Reflection of a Duty Officer'.[286] What we learned from him is that police work is not all alike in all districts and divisions. In the case of Eastern, it is all about settling disputes between American soldiers versus British sailors versus bar girls. A regular night would start with Americans and British getting drunk and getting into fights: 'Eastern has its share of U.S. and Royal Naval Shore Patrols and Military Police operating in the Division and keen rivalry exists to prove the efficiency of the various forces'. Thus, it is best for the duty officer (DO) to handle such rowdy behaviour as he deemed fit, extra-legally and not to arrest every offender in sight, by the book. Zero-tolerance policing would create too much work for everyone. As a way to settle interpersonal disputes ending in fistfights, the benefits hardly justify the costs. In such and other circumstances, the DO has to learn how to use discretion to reduce ferocious fights into amicable settlement, or turn a police station into a temporary pacification centre or detoxification tank, until people calm down or sober up.

If the problem with Eastern is in settling scores between drunken sailors and prideful soldiers, or servicemen wanting a reprieve from Shore Patrol and Redcaps at night, the problem with Wong Tai Sin is one of population growing out of control. In the face of continuous influx of workers, constant expansion of the industry and building of housing estates, the community has to find ways to adjust to the growing pain of crime and order. Wong Tai Sin Division has to keep expanding and readjusting its jurisdictional boundary:

> As most readers will be aware, Wong Tai Sin has been in existence as a separate Division since January of this year. Since then, the furious rate at which new buildings and resettlement estates have been built has posed the problem of continuously having to readjust to a growing population. The sheer size of the division has been, up to the present time, an aggravation in the sense that transport and communications have been rendered that much more difficult. From the station to Yau Tong Bay, where a large resettlement estate is at present being built, is slightly over four miles. Transport is often tied up because of prior claims, and the net result is that the man on the beat may be forced to leave the area for an hour or more if he makes an arrest. He becomes bogged down by the problem of transporting the defendant to the station, and returning from the station, when his time could much more profitably be spent on the beat. However, the opening of the new sub-divisional station at Kwun Tong will improve the situation.[287]

Two town centres, two police outfits, one to do less, the other has to do more, it is a tale of two cities, and the difference is between night and day. We now turn to more differences in policing style across different jurisdictions in HK.

Policing in KLN City

KLN City Division covers 'Everything east of the Kowloon-Canton Railway is ours, and … all land bounded by Tolo Harbour, Tolo Channel and Mirs Bay in Sai Kung District'. The main drag of KLN City is the Kai Tak Airport.[288] It was basically a very undeveloped port, with a small industrial development at Hung Hum Sub-Station:

> Hung Hom our sub-station takes in all our industrial area, from Army Depots to zephyrs from the uncovered nullahs, although regarding the latter we think Kowloon City has a nose start. Green Island Cement Works is a bit dusty—but Watson's Mineral Water Factory is pretty handy.[289]

KLN City Division also contained the 'Kowloon Walled City' a/k/a 'city of anarchy'[290] where HKP has only a symbolic presence, but no real control.[291]

Historically, the KLN-Walled City was a military outpost established in the Song Dynasty (960–1279). In 1842, HK was ceded to Britain after the Opium war.[292] In 1898, the Second Convention of Peking extended British rule to include KLN and NT except for the KLN-Walled City.[293]

In 1987, the Chinese-Walled City housed 330,000 people, 8800 families and 1000 businesses in a little more than 2.8 hectares. That amounted to 1.2 million people/hectare (Manhattan is 27,000 people/hectare). It is common knowledge that the KLN-Walled City was a lawless place, being infested with all kinds of illegal activities, from prostitution, to drugs, to gambling. Fugitives also called this their home. The KLN-Walled City was out of reach of China and refused to be policed by HK authorities.[294]

Through the years, policing inside the Walled City by HKP has been minimal, inconsistent and perfunctory.[295] There was a void in government and lapse of control locally known as 'zone of three non-control' (「三不管」).[296] The Triad seized control and roamed at will:

> After a particularly grisly murder in 1959, the British decided it was time to start convicting the walled city's criminals in local courts. The Chinese made no objection. However, at this point, the Triads were already in domination. Prostitution, drug use and even Japanese sex tourism were rampant. The police were forced to step up their game—between 1973 and 1974, they confiscated 1,800 kg of drugs and made 2,500 arrests in 3,500 raids. This marked the beginning of a change of control. By 1983 it was reported by the police commander of the Kowloon City District that the crime levels were roughly the same as other parts of Kowloon, although the area's reputation for unsavory acts and debauchery had already been propelled to an almost mythical level.[297]

In light of the above, and given the lack of interest in reporting in any of the HKPM, it is fair to observe as far as HKP is concerned, KLN Walled City is a well known and accepted crime 'hot sport' by the public (indulgence) and with the HKP (toleration). On hindsight, now that it is completely demolished, KLN-Walled City[298] is best considered as a case of out of sight, out of mind or policing by neglect.[299] According to an old-time resident, a barber who has lived in the KLN Walled City for 30 plus years, that is, since the 1940s.

Ten or 20 years ago there were a lot of illegal activities conducted openly. It is now getting less.

> I have lived here for 30 years. People called me Lui Pak (Uncle Lui). I worked here as a barber. Many criminals came here to evade arrest[300] because it is very difficult for police to find them here, due to the disorganized streets.[301] There was no policing in here until 1976.[302] Still local residents do not consider the crime and order here to be bad. That is because outside criminals are easily discovered by the residents.[303] Crimes like thefts and robberies are usually committed by outsiders.[304] People are still selling dog meat openly and doing

drugs in here in the dark alleys.[305] Now there are much less selling of drugs and fewer opium dens.[306] As to gambling stalls and brothels, they are no longer everywhere, and not confined to the Kowloon Walled City.[307] Although it is said that Kowloon Walled City is 'three non-control', it is really not that terrible, as though everyone is in fear of being killed or hurt.[308] Yes, people here would size you up as you enter. So is everywhere....This place is filled with rubbish. I thus volunteer to remove them.[309] The place is full of fat rats and dripping waters. Kids pee and shit everywhere.[310]

How then was KLN Walled City policed? A HKP British police inspector who has patrolled inside the Walled City in the 1970s has this to report:

I was a British police inspector in Hong Kong (joined in 1975) and the Kowloon Walled City was one of my first beats. The police did go in at that time on drug raids and for criminal activities (no health and hygiene inspectors etc. though) but regular police patrols were a sergeant and 5 constables in a group rather than single constable. Boundary Street was actually the border between the colony and China when Kowloon was ceded and before the New Territories was leased. It didn't have anything to do with the walled city but there may have been a local name for a street bordering the walled city. If you are still active here and interested I have loads of memories of the place.[311]

Policing in SSP

In 1952, SSP Division 'stretches from Prince Edward Road on the south and reaches to beyond the San Miguel Brewery on the Castle Peak Road. Industries? Certainly, any industry you could wish, from the lowly hawker to engineering, wolfram mining, pearl button making and myriads of others'.

There were two main roads running through from KLN to NT. Away from the main thoroughfare, the streets were jam packed with people, making a living or just finding a place to stay.

The division was policed by 200 PCs under an Inspector. It has its fair share of crime from murder to robberies, breaking and entering and petty larcenies. The CID and UB officers worked very well together. The hawkers and street sleepers were the greatest problems for patrol officers, and the squatters were health and fire hazards requiring constant attention.[312]

Local residents were poor. Most of them were illegal immigrants from China. They came to HK to escape the civil war, avoid communism or otherwise seek survival. The living conditions, on the street or up the hillside, were dirty, unhealthy and dangerous from fire. They worked from hands to mouth, barely surviving.

The dwellings in the villages are mostly of wood and in the main streets several have two storeys. These main streets are busy from dawn until well after

> midnight and there is little one cannot find—shops, restaurants, mahjong schools, workshops of every description, wood and ivory carving, sewing, spinning and weaving, metal works, dyeing and even rattan work which is exported to the U.S.A.[313]

The living conditions were poor. The hillside make-shift housing was not numbered. The whole place appeared totally disorganised, with many crimes and much disorder. Looks are deceptive. The people living together in the squatters helped each other, whenever and however they could. They tended to each other's affairs and helped each other when needed. The people living there organised themselves to form firefighting teams and night watchers, a communal government of its own. It is a heart-warming story of 'with adversity comes true friendship', 'a friend in need, is a friend indeed'.[314]

> The mail is handled by the Village Fire Services. If one is about the villages at night, as we unfortunate policemen have to be, these worthies can be seen at work. They are more likely to be heard before they are seen as their approach is heralded by the noise of a drum, which the first of the party usually carries. The party consist of three men and the drum is beaten every third or fourth pace. The second man carries nothing, and the third man carries a long bamboo pole. Why the drum is beaten is a mystery, but it might be to warn would be felons that they are approaching. No uniform is provided but each member wears a bright red steel helmet with the name of the village painted on in white characters. These fire-watching parties patrol the villages from evening until dawn, ready to combat and give warning of that most deadly enemy of the villages—fire. In a brief period, thousands of unfortunate persons could be homeless. With thousands of wooden huts one on top of the other and the nearest water about half a mile away, there is no wonder that these villages are a constant headache to the Fire Brigade! Outside the villages the policeman patrols his beat and sees what is going on. Inside the villages, however, there are no beat constables. The population consists of hardworking but mostly poor people living under most trying conditions. The very nature of these conditions enables the criminal to carry out his dirty work without too much undue disturbance. He can hide himself or his loot very easily. When organised and decent living conditions are available, there will be considerably less crime than there is no.[315]

The social bonding that developed out of adversity in SSP squatters living together and later suffered baptism by fire when their households were burnt overnight, was transferred and blossomed into the legendary SSP resettlement housing community spirit, which lasted until today.[316] What SSP community spirit showed is that community self-help does work, without help from the HKP.

Policing in YMT Division

The following correspondence from YMT Division serves to illustrate how policing was conducted in a 'typical' police division in HK—Kowloon: (1952/1)

> This being the first article about Yaumati Division to appear in the first edition of the first Hong Kong Police Magazine, we feel that for the sake of posterity a description of Yaumati Division in the year 1951 A.D. should be given. There are four Police Stations, a prison which is modern and politely referred to as a place of detention, and a population of about 700,000 persons.
>
> There is a Divisional Superintendent, a Chief Inspector, some Inspectors at all stages of experience and some 370 R. & F. to look after this area. If you want to travel from the Hong Kong Island to Kowloon the comfortable way you will arrive at Yaumati. If you want to travel from Kowloon to the Hong Kong Island the comfortable way you must pass through Yaumati and leave Kowloon from the shore of Yaumati! This is our source of worry—for far too many important people with that all-seeing eye travel through Yaumati. Of the remainder who pass that way many have cared to stop, for Yaumati has its attractions: a reasonably large residential area, a larger Chinese working class area, fairly good shops and more than its fair share of the bright lights. Hence we have every type of person from the respectable European and Chinese citizens to slick racketeers; from the hard working shopkeepers and coolie class through every grade to the armed robber, petty thief, pimp and prostitute. This is our lot: interesting, worrying at times, amusing and always hard work. Interesting and amusing, such as when the boat people in the Yaumati Typhoon Shelter decided that there was a band of lepers looking for fresh human hearts to eat in order to cure their disease.

From the above report, we learned that YMT was commanded by a DS, a CIP, and a number of Inspectors. In terms of police strength, the police (R & F) to population ratio was 370:700,000 or 52.9/100,000. But this police–population ratio has little meaning in YMT, in as much as it has a sizable sea-bound population coming ashore and many commuters and transient visitors, coming and going, all hours of the day. YMT was a sleepless community.

One gathers from the tone and texture of the write up, that the police strength hardly matches the diversity, complexity, magnitude and intensity of happenings in the district. In terms of the nature of police work, we can expect a lot of traffic control, order maintenance (from nuisance complaints to dispute resolutions to hawker obstructions), criminal investigation (Triads, extortion, drugs and fights) and vice raids ('red light' district).

We were told by police officers serving in the YMT district that they suffered from three chronic police problems: hawker, suicide and vice.

Unlike HKP—Central, the land use pattern was mixed—from residential to commercial. The people to be served were also of a mixed bag, from foreign tourists to transient visitors to local residents. The undesirables also came in all colours and shapes: gang members, habituate criminals, opportunistic offenders and juvenile delinquents. The police would be expected to handle a whole host of issues and different kinds of people in need.

For a seasoned—salted and tested—HKP officer, policing in YMT was little different from policing anywhere, except perhaps an awareness that civil disturbances might happen anytime; thus, the military and police must be prepared for it. Thus, YMT was built like a fortress. To some, that was clear evidence of 'colonial policing' at work, and to others, this is an over-statement. To the OIC (officer in charge), this was just being prepared for any and all contingencies.

From a resident's point of view, YMT was different, than any other place. Li Ping-sum, a long-time resident of YMT, described the area of the YMT as follows:

> Dundas Street as the north boundary and Austin Road as the south. He found Yau Ma Tei Police Station both the geographical centre and power centre of Yaumatei. Geographically, it was located in the mid way between Austin Street and Dundas street. Outside the police station there was a pier called 'the Royal Bridge', serving as the docking location for marine police vessels. The area outside Prosperous Garden used to be the harbor front and the typhoon shelter. Li believed that in the mind of the local residents Yung Shue Tau was the centre of Yau Ma Tei. It was the place where people met, took rest and gathered. Middle-aged men love to play chess and read newspaper there, and talked with each other freely in public. Tin Hau Temple used to be frequented by many worshippers particularly on Tin Hau Festival on the 23rd of the third lunar month. It was attended by many fishing folk. Li's mother and sister-in-law usually stayed at home taking care of housework and rarely hang around on the street or go to Yung Shue Tau. His mother loved Cantonese opera but would go home soon after the performance was over. He believed that neighbourhood relations in multi-storey buildings in the district were not close, because the environment was not open like public housing.[317]

For the police as with the people who worked and lived in YMT, it was not a place (major traffic thoroughfare to HK) or a set of activities (shopping, recreation and vice) that defined it. YMT is a home.

In understanding what HKP does in YMT, we need to see YMT in its eyes and in the ever-changing context of people's routine activities.[318] From Li Ping-sum's perspective, YMT is not a police district—with traffic problem here, robbery cases there and called-for services everywhere, known only to the HKP by its vital sign: daily crime rate and police per hundred thousand people.

To Li, YMT is broken down as a place to worship (Tin Hau Temple) and a corner to hang out (Yung Shue Tau).[319] Li's perception and experience of the place was as much affected by the people coming and going (fishing people, tourists and worshippers) as by the building structure and landscape ever changing. If we learn anything in policing, specifically community or expectation policing, it is that in policing, people in the environment matter.

The most telling part of the above-cited HKPM report was the closing statement. As HKP officers, in dealing with people's problems, both 'Europeans and Chinese', respond the same way, that is, hoping for the best and preparing for the worse, staying out of trouble as best as they can: 'Amusing, and it shows that there is a lot in common between Europeans and Chinese'.

Policing in NT Division

As intimated above, policing in NT was much different from policing in other divisions, in terms of the problems it faced and methods used.

First, geographically, NT covered a much larger area than KLN or HK, combined. Thus, policing in NT differed from sub-division to sub-division, for example, Tsuen Wan, an emerging industrial town versus Ping Shan, a historical border area. Let us compare Ping Shan and Shatin.

In Ping Shan, policing took up border security missions, for the most part in lieu of (peace time) and at times complimentary to (border incident) the military. Thus, Ping Shan Station and other border posts were organised in such a way as to provide the first line of defence of HK against military incursion, cross-border crime and illegal immigrants. This was achieved by strategically built interlinked police posts, segmented by routine police security patrol. The OIC of Ping Shan, the nerve centre, was in total command and control:

> Travelling on we reach Ping Shan where S.I. E. C. Sharp and his wife reign supreme. This is a station which creates the impression of a modern fortification rather than a police station. A flat roof prevails with a 'lookout' post in each corner, gun emplacements have also been erected for emergencies. Ping Shan is also the Headquarters of Criminal Investigation Department for the N.T. West ...Attached to Ping Shan are the three police posts, namely Lau Fau Shan (S.I. Lo Kwok Tung) Sap Pat Heung (N.C.O. in charge) and Nam Sang Wai (N.C.O. in charge) which further provide for the policing of this large area....Apart from Chuk Yuen Police Post also in Lok Ma Chau District is Ma Cho Lung and Pak Hok Chau posts...to house the personnel who operate the post. They are each equipped with search-lights and maintain constant radio communications with their parent station, and are in fact the eyes and ears of the British frontier. Border patrols are in operation twenty-four hours of the day for the strict supervision of immigration to the Colony.[320]

HKP role, functions and style changed at the border is the message here.

Second, for the most part, NT at that time, was sparsely populated. The distance between police stations and population centres was big. In fact, in many areas, there was no police presence. If available, police response time was long, 'The "splitting" of the N.T. enables a senior officer to be at any spot in the district in a matter of minutes'.

HKP jurisdiction is structured by geography, is the lesson drawn.

Third, except for town centres, Shatin or Yuen Long, NT policing was rural policing. It was patrolled by a specially formed Village Penetration patrol:

> In 1947/1948, the New Territories' Superintendent of Police founded the Village Police Patrols, informally known as 'pangolin' and in short as 'VPP'. The Superintendent of Police invited Cheung Koon Fu to join the VPP, considering that Cheung is an indigenous Hakka person of the New Territories. Cheung led a four-person unit, patrolling villages, liaising with villagers and helping villagers apply to the government for the construction of bridges and roads. The VPP was a special unit in the police force, which worked four days a week and took rest on the other three. The team members prepared their own equipment rather than signing out firearms from the police station. … Village matters were still under indigenous inhabitants' control. The rural disputes that VPP dealt with mostly involved only the indigenous inhabitants. …The most common quarrels had to do with cattle going out of the boundary or with private arguments between villagers. Sometimes the VPP needed to intervene and mediate villagers' fight. In those cases, Cheung Koon Fu would contact the village headman. Since he had the headmen's respect, the disputes would come to a peaceful end most of the time. New Territories residents rarely had disputes over borders on their land, because the Lands Department clearly defined the fields and houses in all villages.[321]

The observation here is that urban policing is not the same as rural policing, in organisation, operations and style. In rural policing, community members are more connected, intergraded, and personally bonded. Mechanical solidarity is usually obtained. They possess social capital and collective efficacy.[322] A prima facie for true community-driven crime control can be made.[323]

Fourth, since the earliest days, policing in NT has been done with self-help, for example, mutual surveillance, communal discipline and watch and ward system. In some instances, villages were expected to fend off the bandits. 'The villages in the New Territories had their own self-defence forces formed of young people with good character. The VPP supplied firearms to the self-defence forces; this built a sense of mutual goodwill'.[324]

Policing the Border[325]

Policing the frontier and at the border with China is different than any other divisions and functions, throughout HKP. In organisation, operation and style, policing in the frontier resembles more like a military operation, than regular civil policing. Indeed, during the 1950s and up through the 1990s, policing the frontier is conducted in conjunction with the British military, under civilian

(HKP) command and control. Command and control of joint police and military operations reverted to the British under exceptional military situation, for example, incursion by Chinese or armed insurgency by bandits.[326]

The land border between HK and China—the length of Shum Chun River—runs 16 miles from Mirs Bay in the East to Deep Bay in the West. Police and military presence is required to defend against military incursion or illegal immigrants. During 1948–1949, in order to secure the border against influx of refugees and in light of repeated cross-border raids following the Shum Chun River, a Frontier Defense System was established. The Frontier defence for HK was severely challenged during the 1948–1949 period when there was a large influx of refugees from Mainland China due to civil war. Then, the Commissioner of Police, Sir Duncan William MacIntosh, caused seven inter-locking Police Observation Posts to be built across the border known as 'MacIntosh's Cathedrals' as HK first line of defence.

Policing the Peak[327]

Anticipating what I said about context and in particular of policing, Jackson began his descriptive account of policing in the Peak with the following note:

> The police are so much a part of the life of any community that it is impossible to write about them without mentioning to some extent the district in which they work. This is particularly true of the Peak, and so I trust readers will excuse my referring to the history of the area as well as the station, but this helps to make the story more interesting and complete.[328]

What follows was a tortuous but riveting account of how the Peak Police Station developed and policing the Peak evolved, over time. The Peak Station is an old and storied police station. Policing in the Peak changed with the development of transportation facilities and attending social ecology.

The Peak (Victoria Peak) is the tallest hill in Hong Kong Island (1811 feet). For much of the time before WWII, it was isolated from the rest of the island, geographically, commercially and socially. It was then primarily used as a summer retreat for the wealthy people, especially during the summer. In 1859, Sir Hercules Robinson built a path to Victoria Peak. A signal station was set up in 1860. The sixth Governor of HK, Sir Richard MacDonnell had a summer residence built on the Peak circa 1868. Many well-to-do expatriates followed. The first police station #6 was built at Victoria Gap in 1869. In 1888, the Peak Tram opened, making accessibility much easier but was still prohibitive to most due to high cost (30 cents ride). Still, British access was privileged while Chinese seating was restricted. For example, during the peak office hours—8–10 a.m., the tram is reserved for first-class people, or people with status. In the late 1890s, Europeans flocked to the Peak, to avoid commingling with the Chinese on account of unbearable cultural habits and unhygienic living conditions.[329] The last straw was with the 1894 deadly Third Pandemic of Bubonic plague which spread from China to HK, causing thousands of deaths in a few months.

In 1904, the Peak was zoned British by the Peak District Reservation Ordinance, except with the permission of Governor in council. The Peak at the time was referred to by the British as 'Little England'.[330]

All this changed after WWII.

Policing in the Peak was more about rendering services and providing for emergency relief, than fighting crime and pacifying criminals. This is so for much of the time before 1960 because the Peak was not part of HK, in accessibility, temperature and culture. By the same token, police and policing were not much affected by what was going on in and around the town (Victoria), and totally disconnected from KLN, and NT. Whatever that was of concern downtown HK, rural KLN or undeveloped NT has little to do with people in the Peak. That being the case, what went on in the Peak, stayed in the Peak, unknown to others, was unknowable except for those who lived there. It was an exclusive enclave, in but no of HK.

This final policing the Peak story informed us, clearly, that there was British style–civilian policing in HK, very early on. The existence of British civilian policing in the Peelian mode under a colonial-policing Royal Irish Constabulary (RIC) framework raises interesting research questions: How could RIC kind of colonial policing co-exist with British type of civil policing? In as much as RIC-type colonial police officers were recruited, trained, socialised and organised for the colonial policing mission, role and functions, how could and did they perform as a British civil police agent? When HKP officers have to perform both police roles—colonial and civil, at a moment or over time, how might such role expectations and personal experience affect them?

The larger lessons we can draw are, colonial policing or civil policing notwithstanding, policing the rich and powerful is not the same as policing the poor and powerless, that being the case, how might the status of Chinese—economical, social and political impact on the conduct of colonial policing? For example, would wealthy and/or influential Chinese be treated the same or differently by HKP? If we find that the wealthy and influential Chinese were treated by HKP compatible with their station in the English way, do we still claim discrimination? What if wealthy and influential Chinese were treated by HKP in Chinese ways, commensurate with its wealthy and influential status, but different from British citizens, what then?

VI: HKP Voices

What HKP frontline officers feel, think and (re) act about colonial policing is best captured by their 'voices' reported in HKPM in the form of 'essays', 'letters', 'opinions' and 'reports', with formalism and light heartedness in the mix. Interpreted in context, each of them tells us a bit more about 'what is going on inside' HKP—Just in Time. Considered cumulatively and in totality, they provide us with a distinctive cognitive understanding and emotive resonance of 'what policing is all about' in HK, in a point of time.

A few words on methods of analysis:

First to notice is that the reports and comments in HKPM reacting to HKP programs or practices is telling of HKP positions from inside, for example, promoting reform, versus revealing of officers' (readers) concerns, for example, feedback on changes.

Second, as to how to read relevant HKPM items as official promotion or informal feedback, the idea is one of reading behind and between the lines, asking as in here, beyond the levity what is the true intent and real meaning of the message. In cases of policy promotion by HKP, this means reinforcing formal instructions with informal stories and educational essays. This allows officers to have the autonomy and flexibility of choices. In cases of a critique by subordinates, this means affording deniability for the speaker and saving of face by the listener, for example, after work, bar talk or mess night bantering.

Third, in reading behind the lines to ascertain the real meaning and true message, there is a need to take a 'peeling of onion' approach, that is, there is more than one layer of meaning to a set of comments.

On Police Reform Measures

In summer of 1951, a local newspaper reported on an innovative police patrol by bicycle being experimented within Eastern Divisions. The new bicycle patrol programme was introduced to extend traditional police foot patrol coverage: 'Police are now utilising bicycles in the City and Eastern Divisions to speed up patrolling. They made their appearance in Eastern Division a few weeks ago and on the flat stretches of the mid-levels area a few days ago. An officer said that the men on the beat are now able to cover a much greater area more effectively'.[331]

This positive, complimentary and promotional news report, meant to showcase HKP reform activities, provided an opportunity for HKP officers to air their deep-seated feelings—resentment to the ongoing reform in a light hearted, if sarcastic, way. The message seems to be, police reform is much to do about nothing:

> One Divisional Superintendent, in a rural area, is said to have remarked how much the personnel in his Division deprecate this craze for newfangled ideas, and that he sees no reason at all to alter the present arrangement which he has of borrowing a pony and trap for use in cases of extreme emergency. It is rumoured that he is most concerned because there is talk of those modern automobiles

> and crystal sets being issued to Stations, in fact he does not know what is likely to happen next in 'Sleepy Valley'. This same Divisional Superintendent is said to have recently remarked in public, that he prefers to stick to the 'horse and buggy' mode of transportation (the anatomy of most of his personnel seems most suited to this), but he is prepared to do all he can to instill some 'devil' into the Division, by agreeing to the suggestion of his go-ahead D.I. that he should train his dog Pluto to perform second-night patrols, complete with brandy flask at neck. He contends that the development of this idea will ensure coverage of the mountain areas as well as mid-levels. (At the moment the dog is being taught Cantonese in order that he can ring in reports each half hour).[332]

Coming to the messages of the HKPM reaction piece:

First, it tells us that, more often than not, police reform and innovative measures during the time were not uniformly imposed from HKP HQ but separately developed by divisions. This is so because at the time (the 1950s), the individual police division was a self-contained administrative and operational unit, with the DS as the titular head of the police family.[333] As such, the DS's personality and philosophy dictated what all was going on within his charge, subject to veto by HKP HQ, a veto that was rarely if ever rendered, especially when DS actions were well accepted by locals and not unduly resented by subordinates. DS at the time would most certainly get the nod upstair if he had a track record as a performer and achiever. In those days, reputation matters. With HKP at the time, the evaluation of any policing policy or measures was based on performance, that is, how well did a policy work in practice and how well did the operation/division function/suffer, with or without the policy. In most cases, the litmus test for a policy or decision was a no-trouble' (麻煩 *ma fang*) for senior officers test.

Second, the DS was meant to be the voice of reason, against unreasonable reform. In this regard, the DS made clear that reform measures must be based on local needs or customised to fit street conditions. Transplantation of policing practice from one place to another is not likely to work, at least in the short term. In this case, bike patrol might work well in Central–mid-level, but has little use in rural areas where they were sparsely populated and too little activities were going on in between towns (Yueng Long) and villages (Pak Hueng). Time might be better spent commingling with the villagers and befriending them. As a community-policing tool, bike patrol was not the way to go.

Third, the DS made clear that he was against constant changes in a traditional setting, such as rural NT. This is particularly the case when reform measures and programmes were imposed from above, in rapid succession without a detailed consultation and timely notice. 'It is rumoured that he is most concerned because there is talk of those modern automobiles and crystal sets being issued to Stations, in fact he does not know what is likely to happen next in "Sleepy Valley"'.[334] Notice that HKP HQ was not only pushing for 'modern automobiles', but it was also talking about 'crystal sets' which looked pretty and fragile, not suited to police work, which is rough and tough.[335] Even with good measures and ample notice, it nevertheless takes time to adjust and adapt to change meaningfully.

Fourth, the DS made clear that his staff were resisting changes. The notion here is that if it is not broken, do not fix it. 'This same Divisional Superintendent is said to have recently remarked in public, that he prefers to stick to the "horse and buggy" mode of transportation (the anatomy of most of his personnel seems most suited to this)'. Sarcastically, he suggested a number of ill-conceived but fancy reform measures such as: (1) He is prepared to do all he can to instill some 'devil' into the division, that is, motivating the division with intimidating and scary talk; (2) 'train his dog Pluto to perform second-night patrols, complete with brandy flask at neck', that is, getting dogs on patrol with nothing better to do in a rural area and mountainous side at night and get drunk and (3) finally, teach a dog to speak Cantonese so that it is able to report often, that is, it is hard to teach dogs a new trick, here expatriate officers speak to Cantonese, and at the same time, to provide for meaningless reports, repeatedly.[336]

This 'commentary' on HKP reform said it all. There were a lot of problems with the ongoing HKP reform, the chief among which is that it was ill conceived, from not being functional, for example, bike patrol in an open field, to not being applicable, for example, urban measures to a rural setting, to a potential for abuse, for example, sleeping at night while on mountain patrol, to resistance of expatriate officers, for example, having to learn Chinese to report to Chinese.

On Police–Public Relationship

A Magistrate in the HK Magistracy, told a shoe-shine urchin on trial for assaulting a policeman, that he should regard the police as his friends.[337]

Sub-Inspector R. Apedaile found the opinion of the Magistrate's invitation incredulous, and decided to write a retort, telling his peers and the public how he felt about police role and relations with the public. The central message of the piece was that, in HK at least, policemen enforce the law, and they are not friend of the public. First, the police have little interest in developing a friendship with the public, much less a criminal. Second, the police job is in enforcing the law without fear or favour, and not to befriend the people. Third, structurally, a criminal violates the law and police enforce the law. There is not a middle ground. The criminal is not going to like the police.

> Policemen are my friends, you say,
> From your lofty magisterial ledge;
> A lot depends, I'd say, from what side of the hedge
> You gaze. From where I stand, they Don't resemble friends so much
> As vultures with an eager clutch.

To swoop on every mouse they see
And add one more to their inventory
Of victims. I'm not allowed to shine'
My shoes, but I'm obstructing all society;
I'm not allowed to gamble in a very minor key
But I'm outside the law. The law is fine
For those inside it, or those to whom it lends
An air of honesty; but I; Policemen; Friends!!!

The Inspector of Police started by observing that what one sees and understands of a situation very much depends on one's perspective and station in life ('from what side of the hedge'), and is thus relative. In this case, there are three perspectives: the judge from a 'lofty' position, the shoe-shine child from an outsider perspective ('urchin') and finally the policemen from a law enforcer perspective.

From the judge's 'lofty' position, the judge does not see and could not understand the plight of the shoe-shine boy on the street and the challenges of the police doing his job. The shoe shine has to make a living, the more money the merrier. The police have to arrest people, the more people the better. The police are vultures and the shoe-shine, the prey (inventory to fulfill a quota, to get promotion).

From the shoe-shine urchin stand, from the bottom of the society, and trying to make ends meet, he can do no right. He is always at the mercy of the police. If he is not arrested for shoe shining, he would be taken in for obstruction.

The Inspector saves his more critical comment till the last: 'The law is fine For those inside it, or those to whom it lends, An air of honesty'. By this, the Inspector meant to say that the laws of HK favour the rich and powerful, and punish the poor and powerless. The people who made (judge) and enforced the law (police) should not think that they can ever pretend to be the friend of the (Chinese) poor people.

The relationship between the police (British coloniser) and the shoe-shine (Chinese colonised) is always an antagonistic one, notwithstanding any attempt to dress it up as a 'friendly one'. The British colonial police should not put on an air of fairness and compassion, when suppressing the poor Chinese is the end goal, and inevitable result.

British colonists should not be hypocritical, or otherwise delude themselves, and fool others. History will be the final and 'honest' judge.

On Police Self-Image

The A.S.P. awakes at dawn
Permits himself a mighty yawn
Blinks owl-like at the windowpane
Then settles down to sleep again

But soon his servant's hateful rap
Abruptly ends his final nap
So throwing the bedclothes o'er his head
He take a leap right out of bed;
A hasty shave; a rousing splosh
A spot of grease on his moustache
And he's prepared for come what may
Those guardians of our law and peace
From work are seldom known to cease
They ferret cut with well trained eyes
The opium dens and other Dives
And never turn the Nelson's eye
At things that happen in Wanchai.
Should any criminal dare to stray
From off the straight and narrow way
He soon discovers to his cost
That everything he 'gained' is lost
While he is hauled before the Beak
And fined two dollars or a week.
They never get the slightest chance
To dine at 'Gripps' or seek romance
But spend their spare time, to a man
In catching gamblers at 'fan tan'.
These much respected men in blue
Are unlike blokes like me and you
Who having left the office din
Occasionally imbibe a gin
For when they take a proffered drink
They pour the liquid down the sink.
The A.S.P., in fact my lad,
Like Gunga Din,[338] is not too bad.[339]

One of the many ways to understanding the nature, role and function of policing in HK is ask the British colonial officers how they feel about themselves as a police officer at the height of their occupation, here the 1900s. The opportunity is made available with the discovery of a poem titled 'POLICE' at the Stanley Camp @1942. We do not know who the author is or why he wrote. The author wrote in the first-person term as a police officer in HK (Wanchai). It is likely that he wrote the piece while under internment at the Stanley Camp in 1942.[340]

The poem is valuable because the author tells us what it was like to be a police officer before WWII in HK. As an Assistant Superintendent of Police (ASP), he must have served over 20–30 years. This put his reflective work to about 1910–1920. We can also surmise that the author served as an ASP in Wanchai, a place known for its wild drink and loose women.

The poem begins with the ASP being hauled out of bed to go on duty, suggesting he was working 24/7 non-stop, and fighting crimes in HK, large and small, everywhere. This is what he said: 'They (police) never get the slightest chance. To dine at "Gripps" or seek romance'. All they ever know was to provide law and order for the people, an endless task ('From work are seldom known to cease').

And he's prepared for come what may
Those guardians of our law and peace
From work are seldom known to cease
They ferret cut with well trained eyes
The opium dens and other Dives
And never turn the Nelson's eye.[341]

The interesting part of this passage is that:

1. ASP considered himself as a crime fighter and law enforcer.
2. That people needed ASP to keep the place safe and sound ('guardians of our law and peace') because he was trained and prepared for everything ('come what may').
3. Coming at the end of his duty call, he seemed to express a slight regret of spending so much time and youth with the job. But it was too late to turn back 'And never turn the Nelson's eye'.[342]
4. Finally, there is no one word about ASP functioning in a non-law enforcement rule, for example, suppressing the people.

The conclusion, if one cares to draw, after a careful reading of the poem is that in early (1900) HK, police role was not only into political control but also to fight crime and disorder, with the latter being more important. That is also very apparent from the work of another HKP detective of the time (1920–1930s).[343] This does not mean that the HKP officers have no political control role to play, especially of the surveillance kind, but just that for the most part, HKP was doing what other police agencies are doing all over the world: fighting crime, keeping order and rendering service, to the best of their ability.

VII: Conclusion

Introduction

The single most important contribution of this book is in deconstructing the institutional image of HKP in the colonial era ('Policing with Hong Kong Characteristics') (Part I) and reconstructing the practice of policing in HK during the modernisation period ('HKP Reform in the 1950s') (Part II).

In Part I, we find that colonial policing with HK characteristics is more about mutual negotiation and collaboration, than British coercing and Chinese complying. It takes two to tangle, is the take-away lesson here.

In Part II, we find that HKP reinvented itself after WWII, with localisation, legalisation, modernisation, communalisation and organisation. HKP was being decolonised through the localisation of staffing, customisation of operation and indigenisation of investigation, not withstanding misleading name shakes, that is, Crown Colony (the 1840s), Royal Hong Kong Police (the 1960s) and British-dependent territory (the 1980s).

In retrospect, HKP has gone through four noteworthy reform periods: formation (the 1840s), reorganisation (1870), modernisation (the 1950s) and decolonisation (the 1990s). HKP reform in the 1950s is the watershed. It parted company with colonial policing and jointed modernised policing of the future.

As demonstrated and discussed in the text (Chapter 9), the 1950 reform to HKP is a class by itself, due to historical (WWII), social (influx of migrants, change to economy) and political reasons (U.K. decolonisation, emergency of PRC), and HKP has taken on itself to localise (staff, culture), legalise (detailed rule, strict process), modernise (POP, evidence-based policing and scientific-informed policing) and communalise (reach out to Kai Fong, transformed civil image), in drastic and substantial ways, for example, regularising recruiting/training/promotion standard and process with resources and facilities to match, centralisation of administration and decentralisation of control, grooming of Chinese Inspectorate officers for high command, enabling Chinese policing Chinese through CID and establishing frontier defence. All of the above are to be achieved through a formalized-legalised system and process. Coming out of the 1950s HKP reform, the HKP has been systematically and comprehensively transformed into a legal, bureaucratic and professional force, with a law enforcement and common service mission, and a heavy footprint in internal security capacity and readiness. If we were to compare the run up to 1997 police reform, we would not find very different from that of the 1950 reform. For example, 1997 reform moved along the same line and adopted the same methods, in substance and process: localisation, legalisation, communalisation and modernisation.

HKP reform past (the 1950s) and present (the 1990s) raised an issue, rarely discussed, that is, for whom the bell tolls with HKP reforms? Particularly, to what end and for what purpose was HKP reform conducted? The 'Child-saving' movement in HK discussed in this chapter provided some answers.[344]

Reflecting on 'saving child' movement, we find that it is a decolonisation process and modernisation movement to nowhere, for the British as well as the Chinese, elite and grassroots. After WWII, British wanted to leave. But the Chinese did not know where to go.

In the mind of the traditional Chinese, the 'child-saving' movement was a recipe for disaster, not a plan for remedial change. The 'scientific' driven 'child-saving' movement while fulfilling British-liberating political objective (decolonisation) in HK and liberal agenda (Labor Party) at home, ill served the traditional Chinese idea of indigenous rule, that is, family centred, parental control and paternal care and concern, and the ideal of parenting, that is, Confucius order with self-cultivation at its core. Chinese parents believe in setting high expectations and dishing out strict discipline, by the family.[345]

> According to Wolf (who conducted observational study of Taiwanese families in 1950s and 1960s)...(with Chinese families)... Emphasis was not placed on developing warm emotional relationships with children; instead, part of a father's role was as a disciplinarian who should 'not encourage or tolerate emotional indulgence'.[346]

For most local Chinese who were not Westernised, decolonisation in the British way is jumping from the frying pan into the fire. To them, it appeared that while the British flag was slowly coming down, the Chinese way of doing things was not rising fast enough.

Still, to many and for the moment, 'saving child' was an improvement over the past, when the British treated children unjustly, abusively, arbitrarily and capriciously, in inexplicable and offensive ways.

Finally, with the introduction of scientific policing of juveniles, and Chinese elites, this time, Westernised professionals and scientists finally have a say over the future of their children.[347]

Intellectual Challenge

Both of these projects—debunking colonial policing myths and reconstructing HKP reform, challenge us to reevaluate what policing in HK is all about, in form and substance, professional identity and operational style. The reevaluation is to be conducted in the context of a murky and evolving colonial past anchored in a multifaceted and emerging Chinese political economy, without pre-disposition, blind assumptions and hidden agenda. Then and only then can we begin to discern the many colours and shades of a rich, vibrant and dynamic 'colonial' HKP, working among the Chinese people.

Following the above admonition, this book finds that before the 1900s, HKP policing styles differed substantially between British Victoria versus Chinese KLN. After WWII, HKP officers kept order in the exclusive enclave at the Peak as they enforced the law in the busy streets for the poor at Shek Kip Mei and conducted 'neglect policing' in no man's land of KLN-Walled

City.[348] At all times, UB officers provided hot tea and a warm cell for U.S. Marines in vice-infested Wanchai while Marine police officers sailed the high sea in search of victims in peaceful Cheung Chau.

One of the hopes of this book is for moving the study of Hong Kong Police away from tired and old diatribes that HKP, then and now, is colonial policing par excellence, that is, militaristic, coercive and oppressive, and nothing else. Alternatively, all that is disagreeable about colonial rule came from the British, and is not reflective of HK culture, for example, being authoritarian and punitive.

Finally, I am not suggesting here that HKP's colonial past has no role to play in defining and shaping of the present HKP, as a legacy project. It has. What I am suggesting is that understanding HKP's colonial past should start with asking what does colonial policing mean to different people and in a different context. That is to say, policing in HK must be HK policing, in more ways than one, starting with the use of HK language which carries with it history and culture, connotations and denotations.[349] For example, police jargons used by HKP served to give meaning, fair or foul, as it provides validation, good or bad, of what police officers do and do not, and they are all culturally bound.[350] It is also important to consider colonial policing as an evolving, mutating and contested idea and practice. That is to say we should begin the study of HKP with questions to investigate rather than an opinion to assert, and worse, an ideology to promote.

Analytical Framework Proposed: Methodological Individualism

Human-to-Human Interface

With our intellectual quest set in motion, we need to deconstruct colonial HKP at its roots to reconstruct it from inception (1840) to reconstruction of colonial policing in HK after WWII. To do so, we need to look at colonial policing as a living human interface process, with one human being (not a colonial master) interacting with another (not colonialised subjects), on equal terms as resourceful humans, seeking survival and living dreams. Such interactions happen within a social structure (bounded rationality), with certain professed values and vested interests (colonialism) that inform life choices and instruct actions.

With such a humanistic and interactive approach, we can now investigate into how human beings, colonisers and colonised, each with different personalities and propensities, come together to negotiate the meaning of colonial policing. In doing so, human beings give vent to their individuality, identity and culture, in an epic struggle between the push and pull of structuralism and symbolic interactionism.

Colonialism as Negotiation: It Takes Two to Tango

Envisioning colonialism as a negotiation of meaning between people and not titles, asks us to reconstruct how colonists come to terms with colonised, in their habitat, and vice versa. If this be the intellectual quest, the first step is to investigate how the 'colonialists' in their multiple and multiplex roles interact with the 'colonised' in their different and differentiating capacities, over the give-and-take colonial policing process that of necessity involves both involvement and disengagement. If we had done so, we would most likely find that colonialists must first acknowledge and then deal with the colonised as people, who have to live a cultural mismatch problem created by the colonialists. This requires a political settlement, intimating cultural conversion, on the part of both colonialists and colonised, working together collaboratively and making concessions willingly.

In order to investigate into how policing in or ordering of HK is negotiated, it is best to look at how HKP officers—British or Chinese engage the HK people on the streets of HK. The simple question is: How to do 'negotiated' colonial policing in HK, at a micro-personal level? In doing so, we can return the human agency in the study of colonial policing, which is sorely missing.[351]

Such a cross-cultural project can start with CIP Anthony Annieson, a HKP officer retired, from Edinburgh. CIP Anthony Annieson grew up in an adopted Edinburgh family. He started working as a whaler after WWII (1945), one of the youngest, for 3 years, before joining the Royal Navy (date unknown). He worked first on HMS Glasgow for 3 years, a flagship for Americans and West Indies. Then he worked as a submariner before joining the HKP in 1958 until 1976.[352]

Anthony Annieson loves HK and her people.

> The great majority of the Hong Kong Chinese are, in my opinion, the most hard, working, likeable, intelligent, shrewd, entrepreneurial, innovative, boisterous, fun-loving, family-loving, good-food-loving, gambling people in the world. They should be declared a 'major human asset of planet earth' by the world community.[353]

Cross-Cultural Negotiating: Case of CIP Annieson

Anthony Annieson does not approve of the opium trade, in making British rich, unabashedly, and China poor, beyond imagination. His reading of HK history is one of disgust and resignation: Dutch introduced opium to China. The rich Chinese traders were corrupted by the West and in the company of 'foreign devils' and 'barbarians' to indulge in drugs. The opium habits soon 'spread widely through the lower and porter classes to the great joy of the European trader, especially the East India company…In 1840 it was revealed in British Parliament that one sixth, 16.7 per cent, of all the public revenues of Britain and India together, came from opium profits and tea tax'![354]

A love for HK and the Chinese people and a resentment of the Opium war and disapproval of British colonial policy made him an ideal person to reconstruct colonial policing in HK, at ground zero. Reading Annieson informs that there is more to colonial policing than meets the eyes; a figment of imagination at White Hall and recruitment posters all over London. Colonial policing is the bastard child born to a labour of love and hate relationship, dependency and resentment, consummated in the back allies of HK, in gestation over 150 years. HKP was born of mutual hate, resentment and distrust, before WWII. It matured through joint efforts and a common aspiration, ending in mutual respect and admiration, after the war. Anthony Annieson tells the story of a hate first and later love relationship that defies every imagination and label. To Annieson, HKP and policing in HK is a class and experience unto itself; 'miracle of Hong Kong Police' awaits edification, and coronation.

Chief Inspector Anthony Annieson (1956–1978)

The most conspicuous symbol of British rule in HK is the smartly turned out police officers who matched in perfect formation to the tune of 'God Save the Queen'. The HKP officers projected authority and promised security.[355] They were everything the Chinese people were not, but everything foreign investors needed. In this way, HKP, then as now, stands for 'stability and prosperity'. The importance of HKP to the British colonial was conspicuously on display everyday, with pompous ceremony on the Queen's birthday to the head turning #1 licence plate of the Commission of the Police.[356]

Beyond appearance, the HKP was more than just a symbol of British rule. Like police everywhere, HKP lived to solve people's problem large and small, from helping school kids across the busy road to hunting down a buffalo in a crowed street. The HKP might match to 'Good Save the Queen' once a year but it must learn to whistle to the Chinese tune every minute of the day in order to ingratiate itself to the HK people.[357] That is the reality of colonial policing in HK; Crown servant working un-relentlessly for the HK people, solving their problems and keeping their faith. Failing that, strikes, protests and riots await.

Who made for a good Hong Kong Police in those days? In those days, HKP sought after resourceful people with strong character and high motivation,[358] more so than a 'well-educated idiot'.[359] Professionalisation of police has yet to come. But the HKP was trying hard to catch up, more importantly and own up.

The HKP officers were very well trained in law[360] and disciplined in the use of force.[361] They were trained to deal with riots, and conducted themselves in the most restrained and civilised manner.[362]

Expatriate officers led the HKP almost exclusively. Local officers, where allowed, were few and far between.[363] Thus, it was not surprising to find a lot of racial animus within the police ranks. Local officers did not like the foreign officers. The foreign officers looked down on local officers.[364] Signs of icebreaking were appearing.

HKP was organised along colonial police line, labouring under a para-military model. Police were organised into functional specialties from criminal investigation to patrol to traffic.[365] Police operated in shifts and worked out of a fortress such as buildings, which was meant to protect the coloniser from the locals, in a by-gone era.[366] HK people were beginning to appreciate 'their' police more, for all the stuff they did, for example, providing for security, witnessing the 1956 riot, and did not do, for example, abdicate their responsibility and accountability.

Beat police officers were augmented by EUs mobile patrol. EU mobile patrol was one of the most desirable assignments. It was always challenging and exciting, and at times rewarding and fulfilling. There was a lot to learn and see.[367] It is certainly better than to struggle to deal with non-stop workload in an understaffed[368] Mongkok town centre[369] or having nothing to do in the Aberdeen seaport.[370] Policing in HK was one big contradiction: violent and restive, glamorous and mundane.

HKP has a lot of discretion[371] and attracted as many complaints filed against them.[372] It was clear that if one were to be a HKP officer, he could not survive for long without the exercise of discretion or be able to avoid complaints. It was also clear that many foreign officers were quite sensitive to Chinese concerns with police corruption and abuse.

Finally, one of the greatest difficulties of policing in HK was how to deal with conflicting expectations, for example, British desired rule-bound order versus Chinese wanted spontaneous order. British loved the rule of law versus Chinese fancy personal give-and-take relationship.[373]

HKP officers were held responsible for (non)actions and indiscretions on and off duty, such as conduct unbecoming of an officer. For example, the author used his Bombay horn too close to the cyclist, causing him to fall by the roadside. The Superintendent asked for an explanation and ordered the horn to be removed (p. 109).

Themes and Contributions

In the end, this book makes four kinds of contributions, methodologically, substantively, theoretically and culturally.

First, *substantively*, it observes that colonial policing is less about imposing British colonial rule and more about negotiating Chinese social order. It is less about British colonialists running amok and at wimp, but more about British and Chinese, as people and culture, working together, calculatingly and judiciously. Both parties conspired together at times and connived between the self and another, all within the confines of historical circumstances, social conditions and personal situations, to make and remake HK over time, in one's image, to one's interests, for one's agenda and with one's resources. In this way, this book offers a reflective treatment of HKP in search of a revisionist account of how policing in colonial HK was conducted. In doing so, this author parts company with other more conventional and critical commentators, who proclaimed that policing in HK was a well-rehearsed narrative of British lording over Chinese, with every means and at every turn. In placing 'policing' before 'colonial', instead of the other around, the book is making clear that 'policing' has 'high'(political) versus 'low' (social) tendencies, with the latter as a default mode and the former always in the background (surveillance), and jumping into action at a moment's notice (public order policing). In the study of 'colonial policing' from the people's perspective, it is the latter 'low-social' policing that is more important than 'high-political' policing, now at the centre stage.

Conceding problems with colonial policing, we need to make note that policing 'high' or 'low' can be done well or poorly in colonial as in decolonised HK. Depending on one's philosophical take on legitimacy–process based versus performance oriented, a well-organised and effective 'colonial' HKP might be better than a poorly managed and inefficient 'decolonised' HKP. That is why in HK of late, there are talks of returning to 'colonial' policing of the ancient times being better for HK than 'democratic' policing, currently.

In the study of police and society relationship in HK, scientific and apolitical study of HKP history and reform awaits; which is the chief aim of this study. Looking ahead and moving in that direction, the first step is to debunk the myth that colonial policing is all bad (immoral, dysfunctional) and decolonised policing is all good (moral, effective). The book implores us to look at colonial policing in a different way and light; being less quick to condemn ideologically, and be more attuned to how policing in colonial HK has been conducted, theoretically, and empirically. The ultimate question to be addressed is: Did HKP address the concerns and meet the expectations of the HK people, however conceived and achieved?

Second, *methodologically*, HKP and policing in HK needs to be investigated from 'inside out and bottom up' (IO–BU) building upon, or at least supplemented with, HKP frontline officers' voices on their 'thinking' and more importantly 'with their feelings'. This approach is preferred because thus far, the studies of colonial policing have been exclusively dependent on official data, from colonial records, to official reports, to commissioned studies and to routine surveys.

In advancing the IO–BU approach, this book makes two observations.

1. Questionnaire survey and field observation cannot get to the bottom of what policing is about. Policing can only be fully understood by leading the life of the people who 'live' policing, as a job, career and/or life project. Those people who 'live' policing include those who share space and life with the police, as relatives, associates and partners. In one way or another, all these people are outsiders turned insiders for the moment when engaging the police, in the family or on the job. The reminder here is that it takes one to know one. The other reminder is: implicit knowledge on policing matters, in deciphering police personality, ascertaining the motive and breaking down conduct.
2. Police 'feeling' (disposition, emotion) is more important than police 'thinking' (cognition, logic) in understanding policing. In fact, all police thinking is pre-determined and wrapped up in police feelings, imperceptible and indivisible.

The voices of the HKP officers are seldom, if ever, documented, either as oral history (reflective), with canteen chat (spontaneous) or pillow talk (intimate). There is a dire need in listening to what the HKP officers of all ranks and kinds have to say about the HKP and its work routines, on their own terms and in their own voices. This can be achieved by analysing their graduate thesis for their informed opinion (thinking) and their web-blog exchanges for their impromptu utterances (feelings). This allows us to (re) construct HKP culture and personality, one person at a time, inside out, from the soul, not the head; existential, not essence.

Third, *theoretically*, this book offers up two frameworks in analysing 'dual track' versus 'self-help' policing as manifestations of state (police) and society relationship, based on conquest (dual track) versus consent (self-help) theory of governance.[374] Conquest thesis argues that state formation is born out of invasion and subjugation. After conquest, the pacification of the conquered requires mutual accommodation for the benefit of all, that is, the conqueror offers up protection and the conquered pays tributes, with the former acting as the final arbiter of disputes.[375]

The book offers a 'more or less governmental control' framework to explicate and explain how 'dual-track' policing might work in practice in colonial HK. In doing so, it removes 'dual-track' policing from its sterile colonial policing anchor, placing it in a larger and more dynamic (re)distribution of state police versus people-policing context. In doing so, it allows us to see that distribution of policing role and functions, powers and authorities, duties and responsibilities, is made dependent on relationship, domain and circumstances of control. It asserts that power to rule is a fungible commodity and always in flux, to be negotiated and adjusted between the state—government versus society—people, continuously. This makes the relationship between state policing versus people's policing less total or absolute. In essence, make the study of (colonial) policing sociological than political, empirical than doctrinal. In context, it makes a comparative study of pre- and post-1997 HK policing arrangements possible.

Turn to exploring and explicating consent policing as 'self-help' policing with the help of 'State Police Power as a Social Resource Theory (SRT)'. SRT invites us to look at crime and policing not from the state's monopolistic perspective but from the people's pluralistic viewpoints, thus achieving 'consent' in policing (a/k/a Peel: 'people are the police, police are the people'). In doing so, it allows us to see how the colonial (British) HKP failed to meet up to the cultural and personal expectations of the (HK) people, and why they seek out alternative resources in solving their own problems. Again, as with the 'more or less governmental control' analytical framework, the SRT does not look at 'crime' to be dealt with by 'police', invariably, but as 'problems' to be solved by the people with 'resources' (including the police as a resource), flexibly. This has the effect of making the study of (colonial) policing, theoretically informed and empirically driven. In this way, we can share with a world audience what is unique about HKP and policing in HK in theoretical terms, reversing the trend of importing theory and exporting findings, to formulating theory and comparing findings of our own.

Finally, *culturally*, this book observes, 'colonial policing' is 'people policing'. People policing makes the claim that in policing, people matter, as police and with the policed. In real terms, colonial policing is Chinese policing ('Chinese policing') Chinese ('policing Chinese').

Since policing in HK, then as now, is Chinese policing Chinese, there is a dire need to study how Chinese history and culture comes to affect and define policing in HK (Chapter 5). This study offers up some initial findings. During the early colonial period (1841–1900), HKP policy was to conduct 'dual-track justice', with Chinese being policed by 'District Watch Force' (1877). In 1950, Chinese rank and files expressed their disaffection with the HKP, based on a traditional Chinese cultural referent. In 1999, a survey shows that Chinese people do not take rule of law seriously. Finally, there is increasing evidence to suggest that Chinese culture and values matter in the study of HKP or policing in HK, post-1997. In the case of HKP, there is a distinct difference between HK–Chinese versus Chinese–HK officers in value orientation and issue disposition. With policing in HK, we observe a difference in how local Chinese residents react to public order events than Westernised elites. Looking ahead, how Chinese culture and orientation affect HKP needs to be further explored and explained, lest we think HKP is through and through Westernised. In this, I join Professor Robe Low,[376] in calling for writing a history of HK (HKP) from below, particularly one that gives vent to HK people's aspirations and culture. Thus far, the Chineseness of HK has been effectively suppressed by British colonialists for ease of rule and conveniently ignored or dismissed by Chinese professional reformers in their rush to be globalised or Westernised local elites in returning HK to its golden era, that of British rule of law.

Future Research

Looking ahead, the most pressing research is to investigate what policing with HK–Chinese characteristics means in theory and practice; the central focus of this book. This book tells us that colonial policing in HK is unique because Chinese attitude towards deviance and control differs from the West, in substantive and substantial terms, sufficient to change the shape and contour of colonial rule in multiple, discernible but yet-to-be-defined ways.

For all too long, HKP and policing in HK has been operating, seemingly, without being mindful of and affected by HK cultural content and social context. Before 1997, HKP served as a colonial force, in promoting British value and securing her interests. After 1997, HKP serves as a professional force, disregarding local sentiments and unaware of HK culture. In neither case is the HK identity and culture an important or even a consideration in HKP policing philosophy, policy and practice. If that should be the case, how might it be said that HKP is serving the best interest of HK? More generally, is HKP a 'Hong Kong' force of order and service?

The answer rests with unpacking the relationship between HK culture and policing in HK. That said, and having observed that colonial policing adapts and adjusts to local conditions as a result of necessity ('policing Chinese') and due to convenience ('Chinese policing'), the issue is no longer whether HK–Chinese culture affects (colonial) policing in HK, but it is how, how much and how it is manifested. Posing the question this way, this study finds that colonial policing in HK is in effect Chinese policing in more ways than one; in some cases explicit, in other cases implicit, at some time apparent and at other times hidden, with some issues obvious, and with other issues subtle.

Looking at colonial policing as 'policing Chinese' raises two kinds of research issues. First, how do British colonial officials adjust to Chinese culture in enforcing law, maintaining order or providing services? Second, how do Chinese react to British policing in ideology, methods and style?

Looking at HK policing as Chinese policing ('dual track'), we observed two kinds of operations.

First, Chinese policing under British colonial rule investigates how Chinese conduct policing under the stricture of colonial law or impact of British culture? This research moves in two directions. First, how did Chinese officers conduct policing under British law and culture? Second, how did

Chinese public (private security, District Watch Force and self-help policing) do policing under British law?

The latter, British—colonial policing by and through the Chinese agent, direct (HKP Chinese officers) or indirect (District Watch Force), investigates how British colonial policing law, policy and practice is mediated by the Chinese agent and culture.

To begin investigating Chinese policing Chinese, as a general practice and not a limited exception to the rule, we can start with examining the golden era of HK–Chinese policing, the four Heads of CID regime between 1950 and 1974, as compared to the lesser varieties, as in the case of the District Watch Force.

Endnotes

1. HKP Police Commissioner John Penneather-Evans, 'Interim Report on The Hong Kong Police' (1947) is most instructive on the 1950 reform agenda: (1) HKP should seize the golden opportunity to start anew because of a massive defection of Europeans from HKP during the first 2 weeks of Japanese invasion on 7 December 1941. (2) In terms of constitution, first and foremost, HKP should employ more Asians in responsible positions. (3) HKP should hire 'a more educated type of Chinese'. (4) HKP should do away with $50 bonds against good behaviour for Asian recruits. (5) HKP should hire 'a few Eurasian lads of good standing'. (6) HKP should provide the recruits with better training, more acceptable living and working conditions. (7) The inspector rank should not be monopolised by Europeans. (8) The Europeans should learn Cantonese. (9) 'Every effort should be made to enlarge the outlook and contacts of European members of the Force'. (10) Europeans should have single quarters while Asians do not mind communal living. (11) It was desirable for non-Cantonese to deal with Cantonese crowds. (12) The Commissioner was very much against mixed marriages between European policemen and Asian women. This is because Asian women have 'low standards of morality' typical of lower-class Chinese women. (13) It was 'difficult to have mixed marriage partners living in European quarters without causing dissatisfaction'. (14) Hong Kong would turn out to be substantially different than its former self, after the war. P. Snow, *The Fall of Hong Kong: Britain, China and the Japanese Occupation* (New Haven, Connecticut: Yale University Press, 2004).
2. P. Tam, From enforcement to service delivery: A study of strategic change in the Hong Kong Police Force, MPA dissertation, Hong Kong University Press, 2012. As an HKP officer, Tam observed the successful transformation of HKP from a law enforcement agency to one of service organisation with the arrival of New Public Management against the backdrop of 1997. The author did not place HKP reform in a historical context. He used limited contemporary sources, such as Lo and Cheuk on community policing to make his case. C. Wing-Hung Lo Albert Chun-Yin Cheuk, Community policing in Hong Kong: Development, performance and constraints, *Policing: An International Journal of Police Strategies and Management*, 27(1): 97–127, 2004.

3. A. Bartz, Sense and sensitivity. *Psychology Today* 5 July 2011. http://www.psychologytoday.com/blog/sense-and-sensitivity.
4. K. Lowe and E. McLaughlin, Sir John Pope Hennessy and the Native race craze: Colonial government in Hong Kong, 1877–1882, *The Journal of Imperial and Commonwealth History*, 20(2): 223–247, 1992; P. S.S. Yu, 法訟趣聞: 雪廠街九號的故事 (Tales from No. 9 Ice House Street) (Hong Kong: Hong Kong University Press, 1 June 2002), p. 1 (Attorney General invited him to be the first criminal prosecutor in 1951).
5. A. Wright and Captain F. W. Lyons, Acting Captain-Superintendent of Police, Hong Kong, Police, prisons, and fire brigade, In: A. Wright (ed.), *Twentieth Century Impressions of Hongkong, Shanghai, and Other Treaty Ports of China: Their History, People, Commerce, Industries, and Resources*. Vol. 1 (London: Lloyds Greater Britain Publishing Company, 1908), pp. 267–269. https://archive.org/details/twentiethcentury00wriguoft.
6. C. Y. Y. Chu, *Foreign Communities in Hong Kong, 1840s–1950s* (New York: Palgrave Macmillan, 2005), p. 162.
7. M. S. Gaylord, D. Gittings and H. Traver, *Introduction to Crime, Law and Justice in Hong Kong* (Hong Kong: Hong Kong University Press, 2009), Chapter 4, pp. 57–76.
8. Ibid.
9. See Prisons Department Annual Report of 1938.
10. S. Chan, Colonial penality : A case study of Hong Kong's penal policy and programmes under British administration (1945–1997). PhD dissertation. Department of Social Sciences (Criminology), The University of Hull, p. 56.
11. Hong Kong Legislative Council. Friday, 19th July 1946.
12. J. M. Carroll, *A Concise History of Hong Kong* (Latham, MD: Rowman & Littlefield Publishers, 7 Jun. 2007), p. 134.
13. For an historical account of how a Chinese CID got into power in HKP in the 1950s and ended in trouble with the ICAC in 1974, see A Police Detective Sergeant and the mystery of his wealth (n/d). http://www.icac.org.hk/new_icac/eng/cases/detective/DETECTIVE%20SERGEANT_Eng.pdf. For a fictional but realistic account of the risk of Chinese CID sergeants within the HKP in the 1950s, see *Lee Rock* (Chinese: 五億探長雷洛傳: 雷老虎) (1991). *Lee Rock* (1991) is a Hong Kong movie about how a real-life HKP CID Sergeant Lui Lok was able to beat out his competitors at Yau Ma Ti and became the most powerful chief of all Chinese CIDs in the Colony; a position that was more powerful than the Commissioner of Police of the time because he controlled all operational functions of police through corruption and bribery. He institutionalised corruption operations in HKP, setting rules and procedures for collecting and distributing bribes.
14. C. C. Fung, Solving problems with whatever means necessary. The four skill characteristics of Hong Kong accounting for his success are: 'being opportunist', 'being brainy', 'being aggressive' and being 'committed'. See F. C. Cheong, *To Bash the Hong Kong People Again* (Hong Kong: Sub-Cultural Publishing, 1998).
15. The opening scene had people from all walks of life converge on one of Godfather's wedding party, asking for favour. He then went about making deals

people could not refuse, by favours, mixing with intimidations. 'Godfather' (1972).

16. A 'cop merchant' is one who treats policing like a business, trading favours to advance one's interest.
17. http://www.bigwhiteguy.com/archive/2006/05/case_closed/
18. I Corrupt All Cops (2009) (The movie tells the story of Gale (Eason Chan), a cop that has risen to a high rank, not because of his police work, but willingness to do favors for his superiors Lak (Tony Leung Ka-Fai) and Gold (Wong Jing), most notably taking care of their mistresses.)
19. T. Wing Lo, 8. Minimizing crime and corruption in Hong Kong, In: R. Godson, *Menace to Society: Political–Criminal Collaboration around the World* (New Brunswick, NJ: Transaction Publishers, 2003), pp. 231.
20. '四大總華探長的沒落' (The demise of four Heads of CID). http://www.discuss.com.hk/viewthread.php?tid=21070537
21. Ibid.
22. Fong first enlisted with HKP on 20.9.1938 in the newly created rank of 'Chinese Sub Inspector', as the first batch of ten Chinese sub-inspector trainer. He received his first commendation from HE governor in 1947 (circumstances unknown). He was OC Administrator at PTS in 1948, and commandant 1965. He was awarded CPM on 8.6.1950, Coronation Medal in 1953, Queens Police Medal 1967. Fong earned a number of first with HKP: 1.1.1954 First Chinese chief inspector; 1.12.1954 First Chinese assistant superintendent; 1.12.1957 First Chinese superintendent; 1.1.1966 First Chinese senior superintendent; 1.4.1968 First Chinese chief superintendent. http://gwulo.com/node/19235, http://gwulo.com/node/14819
23 Annual police review 1952, *Hong Kong Police Magazine*, 2(1): 22, March 1952.
24. Tsang was born in Guangzhou, China, May 1925. He studied economics in Japan. He joined the HKP in 1947 as an inspector. He was sent to London Scotland Yard for training. Thereafter he served in many police functions: Traffic, CID and Special Branch. In 1960, he was sent to study public administration in Cambridge University, and was promoted to assistant superintendent, serving as deputy commandant PTS. 前香港警务处助理警司曾昭科为中共从事间谍活动一案(Former Assistant Superintendent of Police Tsang Siu-fo engaged in spying case) 2013-07-16. http://www.xfjs.org/read.php?tid=103764
25. 港督随身保镖曾昭科, (Body guard of HK Governor) 屋檐下过客 (Guest under the Roof) Feb. 25, 2012. http://www.360doc.com/content/12/0225/14/449862_189521837.shtml
26. *Hong Kong Police Magazine* X (4): 37, Winter, 1960.
27. Li was embraced as a role model because he could be trusted. Li Fuk Ki was not just another RHKP officer. He fought alongside the British in WWII in Burma and with Rhodesian African rifles. He was leading the Far East investigation and security services. J. P. Zabolski, *The Man from Waukegan* (Lulu.com, 1 February 2005), p. 15. Li Fuk Ki 852-2388-8577, 852-2384-8862 lifk@hkabc.net
28. CP opens IPA HK Section Clubhouse. *OffBeat* Issue 905, 2009. http://www.police.gov.hk/offbeat/905/eng/n19.htm
29. Tsui Yiu-kowong (徐耀光), The promotion system in the officer cadre of the Royal Hong Kong Police Force, Master of Social Science, Public Administration,

University of Hong Kong, 1982. http://hub.hku.hk/bitstream/10722/29416/1/FullText.pdf?accept = 1

30. Target population: 26.8.1961 and 16.9.1973 (1308). Sample size: 437 (p. 33). The independent variables were: (a) age (p. 39); (b) education (p. 39); (c) previous working experience (p. 42) and training performance (p. 43). The outcome variable was: promotion performance (p. 35); (d) work experience (p. 44).
31. Wong, Chung-chun, Dick (王忠巡.), An analysis of the CIP, SP and SSP promotion system of the Hong Kong Police Force, MPA dissertation (Hong Kong University Press, 2005), p. 29.
32. Police (discipline) regulations (1964).
33. P. Leonard, Old colonial or new cosmopolitan? Changing white identities in the Hong Kong police, *Social Politics*, 17 (4): 508–538, 526, 2010.
34. Wong, Chung-chun, Dick (王忠巡.), An analysis of the CIP, SP and SSP promotion system of the Hong Kong Police Force, MPA dissertation (Hong Kong University Press, 2005).
35. Great Britain Public Record Office CO 129/392, 14/12/12, 58. V. Lee, *Being Eurasian: Memories across Racial Divides* (Hong Kong: Hong Kong University Press, 2004), p. 16.
36. P. Snow, *The Fall of Hong Kong: Britain, China and the Japanese Occupation* (New Haven, CT: Yale University Press, 2004), pp. 201–202.
37. Ladies Page, *Hong Kong Police Magazine*, 1(1): 34, September 1951.
38. Ladies Page, *Hong Kong Police Magazine*, 1(2): 23, December 1951.
39. M. Chan, Women in Hong Kong fiction written in English: The mixed liaison, *Renditions*, 29 & 30, 257–274, 1988. http://www.cuhk.edu.hk/rct/pdf/e_outputs/b2930/v29%2630P257.pdf
40. W. B. Zhang, *Hong Kong: The Pearl Made of British Mastery and Chinese Docile-Diligence* (Hauppauge, NY: Nova Publishers, 2006).
41. Ibid., p. 172.
42. H. C. Ching, 'The dragon boat festival, *Hong Kong Police Magazine,* 1(1): 35, September, 1951; The Chung Yeung festival, *Hong Kong Police Magazine*, 1(2): 23, December, 1951.
43. Learning Chinese characters, *Hong Kong Police Magazine,* 9: 19–20, Spring, 1959; P. W. Kam-on, Collecting Chinese porcelain for the beginner, *Hong Kong Police Magazine,* 1(1): 20–24, September, 1951.
44. Ibid., p. 23.
45. D. Bray, *Hong Kong Metamorphosis* (Hong Kong: Hong Kong University Press, 2001).
46. M. C. Wright, *The Sociological Imagination* (Oxford, UK: Oxford University Press, 1959).
47. World Justice Project (WJP)—Rule of Law Index (Hong Kong in ranked second in 2012–2013, fourth 2013–2024.). http://www.police.gov.hk/info/doc/WJP%202014%20-%20Order%20&%20Security-E.pdf
48. S. Austin, et al. (eds.), *The Limits of Law* (Stanford, CA: Stanford University Press, 2005).
49. K. Jayasuriya (ed.), *Law, Capitalism and Power in Asia: The Rule of Law and Legal Institutions* (London and New York: Routledge, 19 June 2006), p. 47.
50. Ibid. C. Jones, Politics Postponed: Law as a Substitute for Politics in Hong Kong and China, pp. 45–69.

51. Chapter 4: *Law and Justice*, S. Tsang, *A Modern History of Hong Kong* (London and New York: I.B. Tauris, 15 August 2007), pp. 45–55.
52. The reach of colonial state, In: T.W. Ngo (ed.), *Hong Kong's History: State and Society under Colonial Rule* (New York and London: Routledge, 11 September 2002), pp. 3–5.
53. K. Jayasuriya (ed.), *Law, Capitalism and Power in Asia: The Rule of Law and Legal Institutions* (London and New York: Routledge, 19 June 2006), p. 46.
54. R. Wacks (ed.), *The New Legal Order in Hong Kong* (Hong Kong University Press, 1 November 1999), p. 46. (Professor Benny Tai placed the legalisation of Hong Kong in the 1970s, while I argue that the process began with the promulgation of an all new Police Force Ordinance in 1950. While I credit the HKP with taking the leadership in legalisation, the uptake of the rule of law movement has to wait till the formation of ICAP in the 1970s).
55. D. Anderson and D. Killingray, *Policing and Decolonisation: Politics, Nationalism, and the Police, 1917–1965* (Manchester, UK: Manchester University Press, 1992).
56. A. Mills, Police reform in post-colonial states, Geneva Centre for the Democratic Control of Armed Forces (DCAF), Working Paper Series No. 36, 2002.
57. Op. Cit. note 55, p. 2.
58. Policing and the policed in the Postcolonial State Session 1 (1.33.22), 29 April 2010; Session 6 (2.03.43), 30 April 2010. Organized by Colonial and Postcolonial Policing Group (COPP), International Centre for Comparative Criminological Research, The Open University and School of Advance Studies, Institute of Commonwealth Studies, University of London Speakers will include Professor David Anderson (University of Oxford), Dr. Graham Ellison (Queen's University, Belfast) and Professor Alice Hills (University of Leeds). For conference brief, see http://icommlibrary.blogspot.com/2010/04/policing-and-policed-conference-and.html, https://www.youtube.com/watch?v = 1-gHCly0wR4 (Session 1); https://www.youtube.com/watch?v = Jth8z45h0HU (Session 2).
59. Ibid., p. 3. In India, the police grew from 190,000 (1938) to 300,000 (1943). With the Gold Coast, police grew from 2,5000 (1945) to 5360 (1956). With the Nigeria police, it grew from 5000 to10,5000 between 1945 and 1956.
60. http://www.hklii.hk/eng/hk/legis/HKHistLaws/
61. C. Loh, *Underground Front: The Chinese Communist Party in Hong Kong* (Hong Kong: Hong Kong University Press, 2010), p. 112.
62. 9 (a) Preserving the public peace.
63. 9 (b) Preventing and detecting crimes and offences.
64. 9 (c) Preventing injury to life and property.
65. 9 (d) Apprehending all persons for whom it is lawful to apprehend and for whose apprehension sufficient grounds exist.
66. 9 (e) Regulating processions and assemblies in public places or places of public resort.
67. 9 (f) Controlling traffic upon public thoroughfares and removing obstructions therefrom.
68. 9 (g) Preserving order in public places and places for public amusements, for which purpose any police officer on duty shall have free admission to all such places and meetings and assemblies while they are open to any of the public.
69. 9 (h) Assisting in carrying out any revenue, excise, sanitary, conservancy, quarantine, immigration and alien registration laws.

70. 9 (i) Assisting in preserving order in the waters of the Colony and in enforcing port and maritime regulations therein.
71. 9 (j) Executing summonses, subpoenas, warrants, commitments and other processes issued by the courts.
72. 9 (k) Exhibiting information and conducting prosecution.
73. 9 (l) Protecting unclaimed and lost property and finding the owners thereof.
74. 9 (m) Taking charge of and impounding stray animals.
75. 9 (n) Assisting in the protection of life and property at fires.
76. 9 (o) Protecting public property from loss or injury.
77. 9 (p) Attending the criminal courts and, if specifically ordered, the civil courts and keeping order therein.
78. 9 (q) Escorting and guarding prisoners.
79. 9 (r) Executing such other duties may be by law imposed on a police officer.
80. Willim Henry Cowie vs. Attorney General [1948] HKCFI 13; [1946–1972] HKC 520; HCA336/1947 (2 September 1948).
81. From Commissioner to police cadet (Article 3).
82. Robert Sandeman Lamb vs. A. D. Monkhouse [1900] HKCFI 35; HCA77/1947 (judgment date unknown); Willim Henry Cowie vs. Attorney General [1948] HKCFI 13; [1946–1972] HKC 520; HCA336/1947 (2 September 1948).
83. http://www.hklii.hk/cgi-bin/sinodisp/eng/hk/cases/hkca/1961/1.html?stem=&synonyms=&query=police
84. For personal background and contribution to Hong Kong, see HK's Rumpole was tireless in the search for justice, *South China Morning Post*, 8 November 2009 ('Before arriving in Hong Kong in 1958, Sanguinetti spent two years in Kenya with Britain's Colonial Legal Service. He was assistant attorney general of Gibraltar from 1952. Arriving in Hong Kong aged 35, he soon became a magistrate'. He retired from the bar in 1994, and died in 2008. Sanguinetti is a social activist and rebel. He represented Elsie Tu for $1 in her appearance before the inquiry in 1966 Star Ferry riot. 'Sanguinetti came to believe that the harsher the punishment, the less chance it had of being either a deterrent, or useful for rehabilitation. His philosophy was a direct challenge to the prevailing colonial justice system, in which corporal punishment was common. He relentlessly pursued its abolition'). http://www.skyscrapercity.com/showthread.php?t = 117521&page = 22 For judicial philosophy, see Does punishment work? An interview with Judge Albert Sanguinetti. By Margret Chen (29 April 2008) (Judge Albert Sanguinetti, http://www.icubed.us/node/1522
85. Ibid., para. 10.
86. M. Chiu, *Justice without Fear or Favor: Reflections of a Chinese Magistrate in Colonial Hong Kong* (Hong Kong: Ming Bao, 1999), p. 1.
87. For personal background and contribution to Hong Kong, see HK's 'Rumpole' was tireless in the search for justice, *South China Morning Post*, 8 November 2009. http://www.skyscrapercity.com/showpost.php?p=46723179&postcount=431
88. Does Punishment Work? An interview with Judge Albert Sanguinetti. By Margret Chen (29 April 2008). http://www.icubed.us/node/1522
89. See Op. cit., Note 84, supra.
90. S. H. Tan, In attributing legitimacy, British 'social contract' (SC) theory and Chinese '报恩' (*bao en* [BE]) principles work differently. First to observe is that SC and BE are built upon a completely different philosophical foundation and

assumption. SC is built on a dog-eat-dog world. BE is built on a harmonious universe. SC assumes that human beings are born brutish, selfish, but are rational. BE assumes that human beings are born good, at least pure of heart, and moved by emotion. For SC, individuals enter society through negotiation and exchange, that is, trading freedom for security. For BE, individuals are born in a society in the image of a well-integrated universe, wherein people's roles are defined: (1) ruler to subject, (2) father to son, (3) elder brother to younger brother, (4) husband to wife and (5) friend to friend. Under SC theory, an individual is bonded to the collective by way of agreement. Under BE principles, an individual is born with status and duties (ascriptive role and assigned responsibilities.) Under SC, the individual attributes legitimacy to the government because of a rational consent to the government. Under BE, the individual accepts governance, at birth, and continues until there is a breach of faith, that is, Emperor or rulers acting beyond an ascriptive role (despotic ruler) and assigned responsibilities (neglectful officials) in providing for the people materially and ethically ('Tian Ming'). Acceptance is based on BE of a ruler treating subjects like parents. Thus, Confucius acceptance of the ruler is based on benevolence extended and obedience returned, or 'performance legitimacy'. S.-H. Tan, *Confucian Democracy: A Deweyan Reconstruction* (New York: State University of New York Press, 2003).

91. B. Knaus, 5 mental traps relationships can't escape, *Psychology Today*, 30 April 2014. http://www.psychologytoday.com/blog/science-and-sensibility/201404/5-mental-traps-relationships-cant-escape
92. http://www.hklii.hk/cgi-bin/sinodisp/eng/hk/cases/hkcfi/1968/40.html?stem=&synonyms=&query=%22Commissioner%20of%20Police%22
93. In China 'elder learned brothers' (師兄) are those who enter tutorage of a trade, profession, or organisation before you. This means that they are more senior and can teach you about the trade or skills, that is, mentoring. You as a 'junior learning brothers' 師兄 have the duty to respect and learn from them. http://www.baike.com/wiki/%E5%B8%88%E5%85%84
94. Now, we called this force training the officer system.
95. There were to be a total of three topics on 大師兄 web discussion in a series, namely: Talk about colleagues who are 大師兄 (2001-09-04 at 12:07), 大師兄 system (2001-09-06 at 19:26) and II (2001-09-09 at 19:17). The above topic on 大師兄 started at 2001-09-04 at 12:07 and finished at 2001-09-05 22:08 with 11 entries. The series on 大師兄 tells us a traditional peer-to-peer mentoring system that is responsible for the transmission of vocational skills and inculcation of institutional culture on the next generation of HKP officers, in informal and personal ways, from what to do with situations and cases to how to deal with people (seniors, colleagues, public and offenders) and relationship. In doing so, it reveals the working relationship among police officers, old and new, senior and junior, mentor and mentee. The clear observation is that the nature, role and relationships of 大師兄 system have changed, drastically.
96. Blogger: family man. On 001-09-5 at 20:47.
97. http://www.hklii.hk/cgi-bin/sinodisp/eng/hk/cases/hkca/1900/13.html?stem=&synonyms=&query=police
98. M. Chui, op. cit, note 6. Op. cit.
99. H. L. Packer, *The Limits of the Criminal Sanction* (Stanford, CA: Stanford University Press, 1968).

100. In 1949, Magistrates (Amendment) Bill (1949) was introduced to improve the efficiency and effectiveness of the judicial process to catch up to the rise in minor court cases in the colony after the war and in transition to civil administration. The bill calls for adding more magistrates (permanent and special, clause 3); allowing for a letter plea of guilt in minor offences (clause 8) and allowing for a review by magistrates (clause 39). 'Although this measure was originally passed as an emergency measure, its utility since the return of Civil Government has been demonstrated by the fact that increased Powers were resorted to by magistrates in a vast numbers of cases, all of which would otherwise have had to be tried by an already over-burdened Supreme Court or been inadequately punished. It is perhaps significant that despite the trial of these more important cases by magistrates there have been very few successful appeals against sentence since the restoration of Civil Government'. *Proceedings*, Hong Kong Legislative Council, 9th February 1949. http://www.legco.gov.hk/1949/h490209.pdf For an insider view of the magistrate's court and process, see G. Bickley (ed.), *A Magistrate's Court in Nineteenth Century Hong Kong* (Hong Kong: Proverse, 2005).
101. T. Shanin, The idea of progress, In: M. Rahnema and B. Victoria (eds.), *The Post-Development Reader*, (London: Zed Books, 1997), pp. 65–71.
102. R. Nisbet, *History of the Idea of Progress* (New York: Basic Books, 1980).
103. F. A. Ewins, Ballistics and the police, *Hong Kong Police Magazine*, 1(1): 16–20, September 1951, Part II, *Hong Kong Police Magazine*, 1(2): 32–34, March 1952.
104. Ibid., p. 16.
105. Sub-Inspector Cheng Loon Hooi, The police laboratory, *Hong Kong Police Magazine*, 1(2): 21–22, September 1951.
106. Ibid., p. 21.
107. Ibid., p. 22.
108. Extract from the minute by Mr J. M. Macintosh, the then Commissioner of Police.
109. The route 2 murder, *Hong Kong Police Magazine*, 9 (1): 10–15, 10, Spring, 1959.
110. Ibid., p. 11.
111. Ibid.
112. Ibid., p 10.
113. Ibid., p. 14.
114. Ibid., p. 15.
115. Ibid., p. 13.
116. D. W. Stephens, J. Hill and S. Greenberg, *Strategic Communication Practices: A Toolkit for Police Executives* (NIJ, COP, 2011). http://cops.usdoj.gov/Publications/e081129395_Strategic-Comm-Practices-Toolkit_rev.pdf
117. P. K. Manning, Information technologies and the police, *15 Crime and Justice*, 349: 356, 1992.
118. *Hong Kong Police Magazine*, 4(1): 3, March, 1956.
119. HKP Archive, Communications branch, *Hong Kong Police Magazine*, 4(3): 4–6, Autumn, 1956.
120. *Hong Kong Magazine Police*, 6(3): 17, Autumn, 1956.
121. Sub-Inspector H. H. Cheung, My impressions of the six months police course in England, *Hong Kong Police Magazine*, 2(2): 5–8, March 1952.
122. University courses in 1950, sponsored by the Hong Kong University Press, *Hong Kong Police Magazine*, 11(3): 42, Autumn, 1959. The Prison Department

followed HKP footstep in 1968. In 1968, the new Staff Training School for the Prisons Department was completed. The first course for newly recruited prison staff started in the same year with 171 men and four women recruits. The basic training for the staff was extended to 6 months and apart from courses run by the department, the Extra Mural Department of the University of Hong Kong was involved in the training in social science subjects such as: 'The Evaluation of Law and Punishment'; 'The Objects and Ethics of Punishment'; 'Delinquency and Human Nature'; 'Theories of Deviant Behaviour'; 'Chinese Attitudes to Law'; 'Social Aspects of Crime'; 'Drugs and Crime'; 'Psychiatric Aspects of Crime'; 'Group Counselling' and 'The Effects of Various Treatments in Law'.

123. Inspector J. D. Adams, Police and youth, *Hong Kong Police Magazine,* 6(3): 16–21, Autumn, 1956. (This was the winning essay in the Queen's Police Gold Medal Essay Competition held in 1955. It is reproduced by kind permission of the author and the Committee of the Queen's Police Gold Medal Competition).
124. Miss D. Lee Youth welfare in Hongkong, *Hong Kong Police Magazine,* 9 (4): 21–15, Spring, 1959.
125. *Hong Kong Police Magazine,* 6(3): 16–21, 16R, Autumn, 1956.
126. Ibid.
127. Ibid.
128. N. A. Vincent, *Neuroscience and Legal Responsibility* (Oxford University Press, 7 March 2013), pp. 309.
129. *Hong Kong Police Magazine,* 6(3): 16–21, 20R, Autumn, 1956.
130. *Hong Kong Police Magazine,* 6(3): 16–21, 19L, Autumn, 1956.
131. Due to the prison condition of the time, that is, no separate facility for children, children and young persons were placed in solitary confinement for their own good! G. Bickley, *A Magistrate's Court in 19th Century Hong Kong* (Hong Kong: Proverse, 2005), p. 319.
132. G. Bickley, *A Magistrate's Court in 19th Century Hong Kong* (Hong Kong: Proverse, 2005), p. 320.
133. Ibid., p. 319.
134. C. Cunneen, Postcolonial perspectives for criminology (January 2011). *University of New South Wales Faculty of Law Research Series 2011.* Working Paper 6. http://law.bepress.com/unswwps-flrps11/art6, http://law.bepress.com/cgi/viewcontent.cgi?article=1275&context=unswwps-flrps11
135. Miss D. Lee, Youth welfare in Hong Kong, *Hong Kong Police Magazine,* 9 (4): 15–21, Spring, 1959. Lee was the assistant director (Youth Welfare) of the Social Welfare Department.
136. Ibid., p. 22.
137. 'An Ordinance to amend the Industrial and Reformatory Schools Ordinance, Chapter 225'.
138. The idea of separate correctional facility for young people first materialised with 'West Point Reformatory' (1863). The reformatory handled minor indiscretions of juveniles (6–12 years old) recommended by the police magistrate. On 12 February 1966, Steard spoke out for a government reformatory, for 'children in out streets and on the Praya, who are growing up in ignorance and bidding fair to surpass their predecessors in the practice of violence and

theft...' G. Bickley, *A Magistrate's Court in 19th Century Hong Kong* (Hong Kong: Proverse, 2005), p. 365.
139. W. S. Chan (陳華勝), An assessment of the police superintendent's discretion scheme. Thesis (M.P.A.)—University of Hong Kong, 1998. http://sunzi.lib.hku.hk/hkuto/record/B31965581.
140. The police superintendent's discretion took after the U.K. Liverpool Police Juvenile Liaison Scheme (1949).
141. 2. What is police superintendent's discretion? HKP Web. http://www.police.gov.hk/ppp_en/13_faqs/faq_cri.html
142. T. Platt, The rise of the child-saving movement: A study in social policy and correctional, *Annals of the American Academy of Political Science*, 389(1): 21–38, 1969. http://www.umass.edu/legal/Benavides/Fall2005/397G/Readings%20Legal%20397%20G/3%20Anthony%20Platt.pdf
143. To make the point clear, *Hong Kong Police Magazine* 7(2): 7, Summer, 1957.
144. Ibid. ('Values in Penal Theory and Scientific Criminology'. Extract from an article by A. Mergen, Professor of criminology in Mainz University, published in International Criminal Police Review, Number 103, December 1956).
145. 'Problem' child focusses on the child, as a deviant, requiring treatment by experts. Child's 'problem' focusses on the difficulties confronted by the child, requiring attention of the family and community. For example, Mencius's mother moved three times to provide Mencius the best educational environment to succeed. This is the legendary story of 孟母三遷 (mèng mǔ sān qiān; literal translation: 'Mencius's mother, three moves').
146. K. C. Wong, Chinese jurisprudence and Hong Kong law, *China Report*, 45(3): 213–239, 2009.
147. Permissive Western vs. demanding Eastern: Which style of parenting is best for children? *Wall Street Journal*. http://online.wsj.com/community/groups/general-forum/topics/western-parents-too-indulgent
148. P. T. K. Lin and E. C. Lin, *In the Eye of the China Storm: A Life between East and West* (Montréal, Canada: McGill-Queen's Press—MQUP, 4 August 2011).
149. D. W. Clayton, Labour-intensive industrialization in Hong Kong, 1950–70: A note on sources and methods, *Asia Pacific Business Review*, 12(3): 375–388, 2006.
150. https://www.facebook.com/permalink.php?story_fbid=666915996667684&id=648757011816916
151. Police History: Women—An equal force. HKP Web. http://www.police.gov.hk/ppp_en/01_about_us/ph_06.html By 1954, the strength of women police had arisen to that of 53:2 cub-inspectors, 10 sergeants and 41 constables. The first Pakistan Woman Police joined in 1952. Lawrence K. K. Ho and Y. K. Chu, *Policing Hong Kong, 1842–1969: Insider's Stories* (Hong Kong: City University of Hong Kong, 2012), p. 21 Calderwood, Annie Hannah. *In Service of the Community* (服務社會). (Hong Kong: Liang Yu Printing Factory, 1974).
152. 「我生性好動，富挑戰性的警務工作正好符合我的性格，因此我當時放棄另一份文職而選擇了加入警隊。」 '第一代女督察' ('First generation Woman Inspector') or Classic Kimmy looks back, *PoliceBeat*, Issue 699, 21 March to 3 April 2001. http://www.police.gov.hk/offbeat/699/021_c.htm
153. Ibid.

154. '專題報道：香港第一個陀槍師姐' A Special Report: First WPC allowed to carry a gun, *Apple*, 3 October 2006. http://hk.apple.nextmedia.com/news/art/20061003/6368042
155. Hong Kong's policewomen (30/3/2013). http://casualtvb.blogspot.com/2013/03/hong-kongs-policewomen.html
156. *OffBeat*, Issue 699, 21 March to 3 April 2001. http://www.police.gov.hk/offbeat/699/021_e.htm
157. Recalling Kimmy, *PoliceBeat*, Issue 702, 9 May to 22 May 2001.
158. Ho, Lai-sheung, Cora 何麗嫦, Women in the Royal Hong Kong Police Force: Equal or unequal partners? Master thesis. (Hong Kong University Press, 1988); Cheung, Wing-kan, Simon, 張永勤, The changing role of women police officers in the Royal Hong Kong Police during the past ten years, MPA dissertation. (Hong Kong University Press, 1997).
159. New women assistant superintendent of police, *Hong Kong Police Magazine*, 10(4): 3, Winter, 1960.
160. Ibid.
161. *Hong Kong Police Magazine*, 7(3): 6, Autumn 1957.
162. A. H. Chan and L. Ho, Women police officers in Hong Kong: Femininity and policing in a gendered organization, *The Journal of Comparative Asian Development*, 12(3): 489–515, 2013.
163. 香港警務處退役同僚協會專欄 《警聲》 第825期. http://www.police.gov.hk/offbeat/825/chi/h14.htm 五六十年代的香港女警結婚有嫁妝 《警聲》 第826期, http://www.police.gov.hk/offbeat/826/chi/h14.htm
164. http://www.police.gov.hk/offbeat/825/chi/h14.htm
165. Ibid.
166. Ibid.
167. Ibid.
168. http://www.police.gov.hk/offbeat/826/chi/h14.htm
169. *Hong Kong Police Magazine*, 2(3): 42, September 1952, Central.
170. *Hong Kong Police Magazine*, 2(3): 44, September 1952, Eastern.
171. Lai-sheung Ho (何麗嫦.), Women in the Royal Hong Kong Police Force: Equal or unequal partners? Dissertation. Master of social science (criminology) University of Hong Kong, 1988.
172. Ibid.
173. Op. cit., N162, supra.
174. Ibid., pp. 7–8.
175. Ibid., p. 8.
176. Ibid., p. 42.
177. Ibid., p. 43.
178. Ibid., p. 44.
179. Ibid. p. 45.
180. Ibid., p. 45. 'Police Station duties'.
181. Ibid., p. 46.
182. Ibid., p. 46. 'Allocation of beats'.
183. Ibid., p. 47. 'Pairing up with male colleagues'.
184. Ibid., p. 47. 'Allocation to incidence'.
185. Ibid., p. 48.
186. Ibid., p. 48.

187. T. Prenzler and G. Sinclair, The status of women police officers: An international review, *International Journal of Law, Crime and Justice,* 41: 115–131, 2013. http://oro.open.ac.uk/36665/1/Status%20of%20women%20police%20an%20international%20review.pdf
188. Ibid., p. 116.
189. C. Jones, Women and the law in colonial Hong Kong, In: B. K. P. Leung and T. Y. C. Wong (eds.), *25 Years of Social and Economic Development in Hong Kong,* Centre of Asian Studies Occasional Papers and Monographs, no. 111. (Hong Kong: Hong Kong University Press, 1994), pp. 111–132, 118–119.
190. Topic 'Please report on mouthy (多口), bad mouthing colleagues'. The Police Forum web blog discussion was started by WAT HKI on 05-01-2001 at 11.39. It ended on 13-07-2001 at 20:14. There were a total of 70 entries. There were 41 separate commentators.
191. 27-05-2001 at 01:28. Little Sister.
192. A research conducted by Hong Kong Caritas on extra-marital relationship shows that from 1997 to 2001, there were 96 news reports on extra-marital infidelity disputes leading to 35 deaths or 65 injuries. From October 2002 to 2005, 335 people sought help from Caritas, with 118 violence cases and 54 suicide cases. Z. Y. Guo, Extra-marital relationships and family crisis (婚外情與家庭危機) fcsc.caritas.org.hk/DOC/article/03marriage.doc. People seeking help with Hong Kong extra-marital infidelity doubled, 70% involved female, Hong Kong people easy to fall in love with colleagues ('香港婚外情求助倍增女性占70% 港人易恋上同事') *Xinhua News* 5 January 2013. According to data released by Caritas on extra-marital infidelity counseling service, there were 693 cases of infidelity last year (12/2011 to 11/2012), compared with 336 cases in 2011. 70% were female. 20% were married between 4 and 9 years. 40% involved co-workers or friends. Reasons include boring marriage (30%), lack of communication (28%) and having fun (18%). http://news.xinhuanet.com/gangao/2013-01/05/c_124186152.htm. According to Caritas extra-marital relationship counseling centre, the reasons for extra-marital relationship that differ between male and female were as follows: For male, they are: (1) prove charm at 40; (2) not satisfied with sex; (3) sudden urge at work; (4) boredom; (5) escape from home or work pressure; (6) universal lover and (7) disgusted with the partner. For female: (1) revenge; (2) boring life and (3) no attention from the husband. Caritas. http://ema.caritas.org.hk/couple/reason01.html
193. 2. The Force is committed to ethics and integrity in the Hong Kong Police Force where *Ethics and Integrity in the Hong Kong Police Force* (HKP: Hong Kong Police College, August, 2009).
194. *Hong Kong Police Magazine,* 6(1): 25, March, 1956.
195. Inspector Patrick, Women police, *Hong Kong Police Magazine,* 7(3): 4, Autumn, 1957.
196. D. A. E. Peterson (principal probation officer), The policeman and the juvenile, *Hong Kong Police Magazine,* 2(2): 10–13, March, 1952.
197. Hong Kong squatter village fire 1953. https://www.youtube.com/watch?v=evIwMJRVoHQ
198. 'However on Christmas night 1953 the biggest fire in Hong Kong's history occurred in the Shek Kip Mei Squatter area in Shumshuipo. About 7,500 huts were destroyed and nearly 60,000 people were rendered homeless.... the Tai

Hang Tung fire in July 1954, which destroyed over 2,000 huts and rendered 25,000 persons homeless', CIP Roberts, Squatter fire in Hong Kong, *Hong Kong Police Magazine*, 6(1): 13–15, 14 March 1956.

199. Ibid., p. 14.
200. Ibid., p. 15.
201. A. Smart, *The Shek Kip Mei Myth: Squatters, Fires and Colonial Rule in Hong Kong, 1950–1963* (Hong Kong: Hong Kong University Press, 2006). Chapter 6: *Shek Kip Mei*, pp. 95–117.
202. CIP Roberts, Squatter fire in Hong Kong, *Hong Kong Police Magazine*, 6(1): 13–15, 14 March 1956.
203. The New Kowloon City Police Station, *Hong Kong Police Magazine*, 2(3): 19–20, September, 1952.
204. The same with the report from Central: 'The New Aberdeen Street Quarters for Bank and File were opened in April by Lady Grantham. The fine white edifice rising as it does from Paddy's Market and looking down onto the Harbour is without a doubt a proud start to the solution of our accommodation troubles. Less magnificent buildings, the wooden huts to be precise, have been erected at Upper Level for Single Constables and should accommodate 100 men'. Chatter from the state—Left column, *Hong Kong Police Magazine*, 1(1): 25, 1951.
205. This recalls the station improvement and amalgamation projects. HK Audit Commission, 2005. http://www.aud.gov.hk/eng/pubpr_arpt/aud_HonPol.htm
206. *Hong Kong Police Magazine*, 10 (4): 56, Winter, 1960.
207. This kind of meet and greet type of HKP—community relationship should be separate from and distinguished with frequent meetings between local business people and well-connected residents with Chinese police officers at the sergeant level, for social exchange, for example, shop-opening banquets or official business, for example, intelligence sharing. Our family-watch business, one of the oldest and a household name by now, started in Shum Shui Po in 1952. We lived on 59 Tai Po Road opposite many watch shops my father had established through the years, until the 1960s. My father was a self-made man. He was respected and loved by the community for his business acumen and industriousness, integrity and honesty, generosity and gregariousness. I recalled my father having a lot of influential friends inside the Shum Shui Po Police Station. The police, UB and CID, all knew him well. One ring to Shum Shui Po Police Station and the police would be all over the place. He was on first-name basis with them. The police purchased watches from him at a deep discount and watch repairing was for free. Sometimes, the courtesy was extended to friends and associations of the police. When asked, my father would say: 'They worked hard day and night. They protected us. We repair watches for them'. My father drank a lot. CID officers came over to wine and dine on many occasions. All got drunk. When my father wanted something done with the government, he would call up the CIDs. When troublemakers appeared demanding for tea money in New Years, my father would call the CID, and the problem would be solved. There was no need for station visit and report entry. Strange enough. I never met an expatriate officer, nor inspectorate and above-grade police officer, dropping by. I guess they were too busy doing official community-policing work. My father never missed them.

208. My father has his fair share of shop opening with the biggest movie stars in attendance, cutting the ribbons. Reporters would come. People would gather. Cars would be parked and double parked. No one could get through, for about an hour, usually at noon.
209. In Washington, DC or New York City, NY, the bragging right is when and where you reserve a table by the window. Or what kind of public events you were invited to. T. Alexander Smith and L. O'Connel, *Black Anxiety, White Guilt, and the Politics of Status Frustration* (Westport, CT: Greenwood Publishing Group, 1 January 1997), p. 38.
210. W. Y. Jiang, Mianzi (face) and Guanxi (relationship) in Chinese culture and their implications for business management, *American Review of China Studies*, 7.1: 15–29, 2006.
211. A. Chan, The Chinese concepts of *Guanxi*, *Mianzi*, *Renqing* and *Bao*: Their interrelationships and implications for International Business, 2006. http://arrow.uws.edu.au:8080/vital/access/manager/Repository/uws:7413
212. K.-P. Huang and K. Y. Wang, How Guanxi relates to social capital? A psychological perspective, *Journal of Social Sciences*, 7 (2): 120–126, 2010, 2011.
213. The author's family business is a household name in Hong Kong, in the watch business. The author's father was an influential member of the community. He opened the first watch shop in Shum Shui Po. The author thus saw at first hand how relationship—face management worked. G.-M. Chen and R. Ma, *Chinese Conflict Management and Resolution* (Westport, CT: Greenwood Publishing Group, 2002). (The Chinese look for five things in cultivating a meaningful and durable relationship, namely: harmony, *Guanxi* (relationship), *Mianzi* (face), seniority and authority. p. 4)
214. Photos: The Shamshuipo Divisional Soccer Team in full array and The two teams—Kowloon City and Shamshuipo—Photographed prior to the commencement of the game, *Hong Kong Police Magazine*, 10 (4): 57, Winter, 1960 and *Hong Kong Police Magazine*, 10 (4): 62, Winter, 1960, respectively.
215. Presentation of letters of appreciation to members of the public on 17th March 1959, *Hong Kong Police Magazine*, 9 (4): 30, Spring, 1959.
216. Presentation of awards to members of the public, *Hong Kong Police Magazine*, 2(1): 14, March, 1952.
217. Hong Kong Memory. http://www.hkmemory.hk/collections/oral_history/All_Items_OH/oha_60/records/index.html#p48801
218. Owner of Lai Heung Yuen Café, Hong Kong Memory. http://www.hkmemory.hk/collections/oral_history/All_Items_OH/oha_74/highlight/index.html#p56936
219. Ibid.
220. *Hong Kong Police Magazine*, 10(4): Winter, 1960.
221. Story in pictures. Wandering child found. A story heard many times but each with its own differences and heart-touching reality, *Hong Kong Police Magazine*, 10(2): 12–13, Summer, 1959.
222. Sir Rober Peel's principles of law enforcement. http://www.impsec.org/~jhardin/gunstuff/writings/Peels_Principles_Of_Law_Enforcement.pdf
223. *Hong Kong Police Magazine*, 6(1): 9, March, 1956.
224. Ibid. 'LET'S Face It by Regular', p. 9.
225. Ibid. 'On Taking—Over' by Special, p. 11.

226. Ibid. 'Let's Face It by Regular', p. 10.
227. 'However on Christmas night 1953 the biggest fire in Hong Kong's history occurred in the Shek Kip Mei Squatter area in Shumshuipo. About 7,500 huts were destroyed arid nearly 60,000 people were rendered homeless.... the Tai Hang Tung fire in July 1954, which destroyed over 2,000 huts and rendered 25,000 persons homeless,' CIP Roberts, Squatter fire in Hong Kong, *Hong Kong Police Magazine*, 6(1): 13–15, 14 March 1956.
228. Ibid., p. 10.
229. Ibid.
230. Paper on Legislative Council Panel on Security Review of the Hong Kong Auxiliary Police Force (HKAPF) (Security Bureau, June 1999). http://www.legco.gov.hk/yr98-99/english/panels/se/papers/se1006_5.htm
231. Royal Hong Kong Auxiliary Police Force (Amendment) Bill 1980 'The Auxiliary Police Force came into existence in 1959 on the amalgamation of the two former reserve bodies known as the Police Reserve and the Special Constabulary. Its role was to provide a nucleus of trained personnel who would be available to supplement the regular police in times of emergency. ...However as a result of the deteriorating crime situation in 1972 it was decided that elements of the auxiliary police should be called out to supplement the uniform branch of the regular police in a normal constabulary role'. Hong Kong Legislative Council, Official Report of Proceedings, Wednesday, 25 June 1980, 902–903.
232. Hong Kong Legislative Council, Official Report of Proceedings, Wednesday, 5 December 1990, p. 26.
233. 'A Committee consisting of regular Police officers and officers from the HKAPF including its Deputy Commandant was set up in November 1998 to conduct a comprehensive review of the HKAPF. The results were announced in mid-March 1999. Copies of the review report were sent to Members for information in April 1999. ...The Committee has made a total of 33 recommendations covering the role, establishment, organization structure, recruitment and training of the HKAPF'. Paper on Legislative Council Panel on Security Review of the Hong Kong Auxiliary Police Force (HKAPF) (Security Bureau, June 1999).http://www.legco.gov.hk/yr98-99/english/panels/se/papers/se1006_5.htm
234. Paper on Legislative Council Panel on Security Review of the Hong Kong Auxiliary Police Force (HKAPF) (Security Bureau, June 1999). http://www.legco.gov.hk/yr98-99/english/panels/se/papers/se29061a.htm
235. On 28 April 2003, Hong Kong Auxiliary Police Association (HKAPA) wrote to the chairman of the Legislative Council (LegCo) Panel on Security to discuss and resolve issues on the status and rights of HKAPA. The HKAPA is registered under section 5A of the Societies Ordinance (Cap. 151). Unlike the Police Force Ordinance (Cap. 232), Hong Kong Auxiliary Police Force Ordinance (Cap. 233) does not preclude the formation of staff association or trade union. According to section 8 of the Police Force Ordinance (Cap. 232), police officers are not allowed to join the trade union or take part in industrial actions. At issue is the fact that the HKP management failed to acknowledge HKAPA as a proper consultative body and would not allow HKAPA to use any of the government building or official time to promote its activities. HKP objected to HKAPA's representative, advocacy and consultative role and activities on two grounds. First, HKAPA

registered under the Society Ordinance (Cap. 151) and are permitted to function under the Hong Kong Auxiliary Police Force Ordinance (Cap. 233) as a private association. For example, HKAPA included retired auxiliary officers as its members. Second, HKAP was officially represented by HKP Internal Review and Management Committee (IRMC). IRMC is a standing committee established in September 2000 with HKP force wide membership. It was charged with facilitating communication and addressing issues of concern to auxiliary police officers. Legislative Council Panel on Security, Status of the Hong Kong Auxiliary Police Association in representing Auxiliary Police officers, Paper No. CB(2)2247/02-03(04). Discussed 5 June 2003.

236. This author has been consulted by the HKAP senior management on the issue in 1999–2000. At the time, there was a siege mentality prevailing in HKAP HQ with frustration and resentment in the mix. At the time, I was perplexed by what I considered as 'dime wise pound foolish' cost-cutting measures, by the HKP.
237. At a public lecture at HKP HQ, with 500 officers attending, a Commissioner of Police openly challenged the wisdom and feasibility of community policing, as applied to Hong Kong. 'State Police as a Social Resource Theory'. Professional Development Seminar, Police College, Hong Kong Police. 16 October 2009.
238. In order to facilitate crime fighting better, Mr Cheong-Leen, called for the establishment of district or area security groups (地區安全隊) (ASG) in all CDO offices. ASG would be community organised but is selective, voluntary, uniformed and trained with limited power. It would be the responsibility of the HKP, with the co-operation of the CDOs and the Fight Violent Crime Area Committees. ASGs were second-class auxiliaries—less trained, less well-turned out, less well paid, less armed and less powerful in law. Hong Kong Legislative Council, Official Report of Proceedings, Wednesday, 30th January 1974.
239. LegCo Panel on Security. Minutes of special meeting held on Tuesday, 29 June 1999. LC Paper No. CB(2) 2783/98-99. http://www.legco.gov.hk/yr98-99/english/panels/se/minutes/se290699.htm
240. This is to suggest, indirectly, that the training up of HKAPF to serve regular policing role is not the best value for money.
241. Op. cit, N239, supra.
242. Ibid.
243. Redefine and limit the role and functions to crowd control and guard duties, not general policing duties.
244. Op. cit, N239, supra.
245. Ibid. 'The Chairman requested the Force to consider addressing some of the concerns of the Auxiliary Police officers which did not involve a matter of principle before the trial period ended such as abolishing the symbol on their uniform which differentiated an Auxiliary Police officer from a regular Police officer. Mr CHEUNG Man-kwong echoed the Chairman's view'.
246. Ibid. 'Mr Howard YOUNG said that the revised role of Auxiliary Police officers, whom were mainly responsible for crowd control, was quite different from the perception of the general public on HKAPF. He enquired whether the Force had critically examined the respective roles of HKAPF in drawing up the recommendations'.
247. Ibid.
248. Op.cit, N239, supra.

249. HKPM Summer, 1959, p. 28.
250. 'Reproduced by kind permission of the Author and the Editor of the Police College Magazine'. Ibid.
251. 'The importance of organisation in police work'.
252. 'A History of Police'.
253. W. L. M. Lee, *A History of Police in England* (London: Methuen, 1901).
254. W. R. Miller, Chapter 16: *Weber's Rational-Legal Model of Legitimation and the Police in London and New York City, 1930–1870*, In: Wilbur R. MillerVarisol Lopez Menendez, Mr Fanon Howell, Professor David Chalcraft, Mr Hector (eds.), *Max Weber Matters: Interweaving Past and Present* (Farnham, Surrey, UK: Ashgate Publishing, Ltd., 28 December 2012), pp. 257–271.
255. D. Bordua and A. Reiss, 'Command Control and Charisma', Working Papers, #10, The Center for Research on Social Organization Department of Sociology, University of Michigan, June 1965.
256. Ibid., p. 258.
257. H. E. Egerton, The system of British colonial administration of the crown colonies in the seventeenth and eighteenth centuries compared with the system prevailing in the nineteenth century: A lecture delivered before the [Royal Historical] Society on 9 April, 1918, 1919.
258. This is not to say that various policy centres always agree on the policy line. In fact they do not.
259. Retrospect, *Hong Kong Police Magazine*, 3 (2): 10, June 1952.
260. W. I. Nicholson, *Use of Discretion and the Law: Formal and Informal Perspectives in the Royal Hong Kong Police*, Master of social science (Hong Kong University Press, 1981).
261. Ibid., p. 30.
262. Ibid., p. 33.
263. Ibid., p. 36.
264. Ibid., p. 39.
265. Ibid., p. 41.
266. Ibid., p. 4.
267. Ibid., p. 27.
268. Ibid., p. 22.
269. Ibid., p. 27.
270. Ibid., p. 30.
271. Ibid.
272. Ibid., p. 31.
273. Ibid., p. 30.
274. Ibid., p. 31.
275. Ibid.
276. Ibid., p. 31.
277. Ibid., p. 33 (SDI–Central), p. 34 (SDI–WF).
278. Ibid. 36.
279. Ibid., p. 40.
280. Ibid., p. 36.
281. Looking back—A need for marines, *OffBeat*, Issue 688, 27 September to 10 October 2000. http://www.police.gov.hk/offbeat/688/024_e.htm
282. *Hong Kong Police Magazine*, 1(1): 24, September, 1951.

283. 香港警察拾趣. http://bbs.tiexue.net/post_4116775_1.html
284. Ibid.
285. F. R. D. Aberdeen, *Hong Kong Police Magazine,* 15(4): 14, Winter, 1964.
286. *Hong Kong Police Magazine,* 15(4): 22–23, Winter, 1964.
287. Wong Tai Sin Divisional Newsletter, *Hong Kong Police Magazine*, 15(4): 14, Winter, 1964.
288. For development of Kai Tak Airport since inception, see http://hongwrong.com/kai-tak-airport-photos/
289. Chatter from the station: Kowloon City Division, *Hong Kong Police Magazine.* 1(2): 31, December, 1951.
290. Kowloon Walled City: Remembering Hong Kong's Chaotic City of Darkness. http://gizmodo.com/5995070/kowloon-walled-city-remembering-the-chaotic-city-of-darkness; For an oral history, see RHKTV http://www.youtube.com/watch?v=YbrqjNWOuko
291. City of Imagination: Kowloon Walled City—20 years later (Photographer: Greg Girard, City of Darkness: Life in Kowloon Walled City) *Wall Street Journal* (21-11-1991). http://on.aol.com/video/walk-police-in-kowloon-walled-city-518196214.
292. E. Sinn, Kowloon Walled City: Its origin and early history, *Journal of the Hong Kong Branch of the Royal Asiatic Society*, 27: 30–31, 2009.
293. The convention between the United Kingdom and China, respecting an extension of Hong Kong Territory (Second Convention of Peking) (1898).
294. HKP started routine patrol in 1975. RHKTV: Kowlooned Wall City (2 December 1975): 鏗鏘集: 城寨。 編導: 麥繼光, 蕭景路　監製: 潘朝秀 播出日期: 1975年12月2日. https://www.youtube.com/watch?v = YbrqjNWOuko
295. The author was posed to Walled City as a relief IC while attached to Kowloon City Police Station in 1970.
296. Kowloon Walled City is considered without the control of Chinese, British and Hong Kong authorities. 「三不管」的九龍城寨. http://news.stheadline.com/figure/?id = 132
297. Kowloon Walled City: A special retrospective 20 years after its demolition, *Time Out Hong Kong,* 18 April 2014. http://www.timeout.com.hk/big-smog/features/65777/kowloon-walled-city-a-special-retrospective-20-years-after-its-demolition.html
298. 'Photography—Rare shots from inside the old Kowloon Walled City, Date: 05.07.2012. http://hongwrong.com/kowloon-walled-city/
299. Policing by neglect is when the police ceded control of an area, allowing other forms of social control to claim the territory, such as China town in New York.
300. Because of a deal between China and Great Britain at the time, British police had no power within the Kowloon City walls. My dad recalls thieves robbing people on the outskirts of the city and then immediately running into the Kowloon City center in order to evade capture. The British police were simply not allowed into Kowloon Walled City, *My Father Lived in Kowloon Walled City* Doobybrain.com 1 May 2008. http://www.doobybrain.com/2008/05/01/my-father-lived-in-kowloon-walled-city/
301. 鏗鏘集：城寨 (1975) @ 2.47. https://www.youtube.com/watch?v=x29vVQiV4_o
302. Ibid., p. 2.57.
303. Ibid., p. 3.06.

304. Ibid., p. 3.14.
305. Ibid., p. 3.38.
306. Ibid., p. 3.43.
307. Ibid., p. 4.23.
308. Ibid., p. 4.34.
309. Ibid., p. 5.21.
310. Ibid., p. 6.00.
311. Comment: Mark, 13 June 2012. 10.05 a.m. My father lived in Kowloon Walled City, Doobybrain.com 1 May 2008. http://www.doobybrain.com/2008/05/01/my-father-lived-in-kowloon-walled-city/There's also a good recent article in *The Mail Online* at: http://www.dailymail.co.uk/news/article-2139914/A-rare-insight-Kowloon-Walled-City.html
312. Chatter from stations: SSP, *Hong Kong Police Magazine*, 1(1): 31, September, 1951.
313. Chatter from stations: SSP, *Hong Kong Police Magazine*, 2(1): 40, March, 1952.
314. 患難見真情. http://chengyu.xpcha.com/506g518jsn6.html
315. Ibid.
316. Shek Kip Mei—Those were the days (1): Built in 1954, Shek Kip Mei Estate was Hong Kong's first resettlement estate with a long history of more than 50 years. With the redevelopment of the estate in 2006, all but one 'H' shaped resettlement blocks had to be demolished. Those who had lived in Shek Kip Mei Estate before shared the fond memories when neighbours helped and cared for each other. Those days would remain the most precious memory deep in their hearts. https://www.youtube.com/watch?v=8gOwc22YyG8
317. Li Ping Sum, Retired journalist. DOB 1944. 67 years old. Upper Secondary. The two centres of Yau Ma Tei: Yau Ma Tei Police Station and Yung Shue Tau. (14/12/2012) Hong Kong Memory. http://www.hkmemory.hk/collections/oral_history/All_Items_OH/oha_34/records/index.html#p57148
318. See Felson, Routine Activities Theory.
319. Yue Shue Tau has not changed much, except now, it is visited more by bargain hunters, tourists, foreign and Chinese, who want to spend an evening in Temple Street.
320. For problems with refugee policing, see History—Newly restored Old Hong Kong Newsreels: Part 1, Refugees (Entitled: Refugee Turned Back, 1962). http://hongwrong.com/category/video/
321. Hong Kong Memories: Cheung Koon Fu: Retired policeman. https://www.hkmemory.hk/collections/oral_history/All_Items_OH/oha_112/records/index.html#p73022
322. R. J. Sampson, J. D. Morenoff and F. Earls, Beyond social capital: Spatial dynamics of collective efficacy for children, *American Sociological Review*, 64: 633–660, 1999.
323. A community-oriented policing (COP) is to have police working with the community to define, prioritise and solve a problem. A community-driven crime control (CDCC) is having the community solving their problems with procurement of resources, with the police being one of the resources made available. Kam C. Wong, 'State Police as a Social Resource Theory' (2000), a/k/a CDCC, alternatively 'Expectation theory'. K. C. Wong, *Policing in China: History and Reform* (New York: Peter Lang, 2009).
324. 'Hong Kong Memories: Cheung Koon Fu: Retired policeman'. *Op. cit.*

325. Tse, Ching-kan, Curry (謝正勤), The fortified line: Police observation posts in the frontier closed area at the border of Hong Kong and Shenzhen. Dissertation. Master of science in conservation at the University of Hong Kong.
326. In 1970, the author was involved with a border incident at Sha Tau Kok, as OIC Sha Yau Kok Police Post, when a number of British soldiers drove into China for a visit. Both the PRC militia and PLA were mobilised, as did the British military. The incident lasted for 12 h.
327. P. Jackson, Hong Kong Police Stations: The Peak Police Station, *Hong Kong Police Magazine*, 10(4): 29–32, Winter, 1960.
328. Ibid., p. 29.
329. L. W. C. Lai, Discriminatory zoning in colonial Hong Kong: A review of the post-war literature and some further evidence for an economic theory of discrimination, *Property Management*, 29(1): 50–86, 2011.
330. C. Courtauld and M. Holdsworth, *The Hong Kong Story* (Hong Kong Publishing, Oxford University Press, 1997).
331. The police patrols, *Hong Kong Police Magazine*, 2(2): 10–11, Summer, 1951.
332. Ibid.
333. Since the last publication of the *Police Magazine,* we have lost our Divisional Superintendent Mr Wright-Nooth. We were very reluctant to lose him since we have been a very happy division under his direction. Chatter around stations, *YMT Hong Kong Police Magazine*, 1(1): 35, Spring 1951.
334. The police patrols, *Hong Kong Police Magazine,* 2(2): 10–11, Summer, 1951.
335. This recalls the debate over: 'Station improvement and amalgamation projects'. Hong Kong Audit Commission (2005), The auditor found that the carpet used to beautify the Report Room and back areas was not suitable for heavy use and needed to be replaced. http://www.aud.gov.hk/pdf_e/e44ch06_summary.pdf
336. The police patrols, *Hong Kong Police Magazine,* 2(2): 10–11, Summer, 1951.
337. Sub-Inspector R. Apedaile, Policemen are my friends, *Hong Kong Police Magazine,* 7(3): 23, Autumn, 1957.
338. *Gunga_Din* is a movie in 1939. http://en.wikipedia.org/wiki/Gunga_Din_%28film%29
339. The above poem was originally published in a magazine at Stanley Camp, in 1942.
340. G. C. Emerson, *Hong Kong Internment, 1942–1945 Life in the Japanese Civilian Camp at Stanley* (Hong Kong: Hong Kong University Press, 2008).
341. *Hong Kong Police Magazine,* 6(1): 23, March, 1956.
342. *Hong Kong Police Magazine,* 6(1): 23, March, 1956.
343. K. W. Andrew, *Hong Kong Detective* (London: Adventurers Club, c.1962).
344. T. Platt, The rise of the child saving movement: A study in social policy and correctional reform. *Annals of the American Academy of Political and Social Science*, 381: 21–38, 1969.
345. A. Chau, *Battle Hymn of the Tiger Mother* (New York: Penguin Books; Reprint edition (December 27, 2011)).
346. C. Ruth and V. Tseng, Parenting of Asians, In: M. Bornstein (ed.), *Handbook of Parenting,* 2nd edition, Vol. 4. (Mahwah, New Jersey: Lawrence Erlbaum Associates, Inc., 2002), pp. 59–93, 63.
347. The struggle for dominance between Western science and Chinese culture as a mediator of Hong Kong decolonisation and HKP reform needs to be studied,

lest we fall into the traps of borrowing Western science to trump Chinese culture, thinking it is a liberating give-and-take process, and not a dominating zero sum gain experience.

348. J. Liederbach and L. F. Travis III. Wilson Redux: Another look at varieties of police behavior, *Police Quarterly*, 11: 447, 2008.
349. Y. King-cheung, Hong Kong police jargon and some sociolinguistic correlates. MA dissertation. (Hong Kong University Press, 1981).
350. Ibid., p. 17. My supposition here is that whatever the law said or British boss asks of them, HKP officers must find their work 'culturally' meaningful before they can do it well. This does not mean that they need to understand the law or agree with the boss, but whatever they do, they need to translate them in cultural terms, such that they know what they are doing. This includes going rogue when there is a disjuncture between legality and cultural correctness. I would go as far as an argument, and much of police corruption at the time resulted from mismatch between British law and Chinese culture. As simple as it is, if the Chinese culture encouraged *Guanxi* and approved of gambling, why should it be street care if the residents provided it with a few dollars to look the other way?
351. G. M. Hodgson, 10: Reconstitutive downward causation: Social structure and the development of individual agency, In: E. Fullbrook (ed.), *Intersubjectivity in Economics: Agents and Structures* (London and New York: Routledge, 2 September 2003), pp. 159–168.
352. A. Annieson, *The One-Eyed Dragon. The Inside Story of a Hong Kong Policeman* (Scotland: Lochar Publishing, 1989).
353. Ibid., p. 10.
354. Ibid., p. 14.
355. '*Police as security agent*'.
356. '*Hong Kong Police is the government*'.
357. '*Police role and functions*'.
358. '*Police recruitment*'.
359. '*Police training*'.
360. '*Police instructor*'.
361. '*Police use of force*'.
362. '*Police use of force*'.
363. '*Police organization/administration*'.
364. '*Police foreign officers vs. local rank and file*'.
365. '*Organization of police work*'.
366. '*Policing Mongkok—town center*'.
367. '*Mobile patrol*'.
368. '*Understaffing*'.
369. '*Organization of police work*'.
370. *Policing Aberdeen—sea port.*
371. '*Police discretion*'.
372. *Complaint against police*'.
373. *Conflicting expectations.*
374. W. Mcelroy, Defining state and society, *The Freeman*, 1 April 1998. http://www.fee.org/the_freeman/detail/defining-state-and-society#axzz2Z14HtqAp
375. Oppenheimer 'discovered the origin of the state in those who wished to satisfy the economic impulse through the political means. He posited six stages

through which a conquering group typically passes in order to become a state. At first, a warlike group raids and plunders a vulnerable group. Second, the victimized group ceases to actively resist. In response, the raiders now merely plunder the surplus, leaving their victims alive and with enough food to ensure the production of future wealth to plunder. Eventually, the two groups come to acknowledge mutual interests, such as protecting the crops from a third group. Third, the victims offer tribute to the raiders, eliminating the need for violence. Fourth, the two groups merge territorially. Fifth, the warlike group assumes the right to arbitrate disputes'. Read more: http://www.fee.org/the_freeman/detail/defining-state-and-society#ixzz2Z1Dy3DGF

376. K. Lowe, Hong Kong's missing history, *History Today,* 41 (12): 1991. http://www.historytoday.com/kate-lowe/hong-kongs-missing-history

Index

D

E

P

For Product Safety Concerns and Information please contact our EU representative GPSR@taylorandfrancis.com
Taylor & Francis Verlag GmbH, Kaufingerstraße 24, 80331 München, Germany

www.ingramcontent.com/pod-product-compliance
Ingram Content Group UK Ltd.
Pitfield, Milton Keynes, MK11 3LW, UK
UKHW020025200926
475702UK00014B/2059
9780367866952